NextText

Moving Across and Beyond the Disciplines

NextText
Moving Across and Beyond the Disciplines

Anne Kress
Sante Fe Community College

Suellyn Winkle
Sante Fe Community College

Bedford/St. Martin's   Boston ◆ New York

For Bedford/St. Martin's

Developmental Editor: Genevieve Hamilton Day
Production Editor: Kendra LeFleur
Production Supervisor: Dennis Conroy
Senior Marketing Manager: Karita dos Santos
Editorial Assistant: Melissa Cook
Production Assistant: Katherine Caruana
Copyeditor: Hilly van Loon
Text Design: Tom Carling, Carling Design Inc.
Cover Design: Billy Boardman
Composition: Pine Tree Composition, Inc.
Printing and Binding: R. R. Donnelly & Sons Company

President: Joan E. Feinberg
Editorial Director: Denise B. Wydra
Editor in Chief: Karen S. Henry
Director of Marketing: Karen Melton Soeltz
Director of Editing, Design, and Production: Marcia Cohen
Managing Editor: Elizabeth M. Schaaf

Library of Congress Control Number: 2007922529

Manufactured in the United States of America.

2   1   0   9   8   7
f   e   d   c   b   a

For information, write: Bedford/St. Martin's, 75 Arlington Street, Boston, MA 02116 (617-399-4000)

ISBN-10: 0-312-40106-X
ISBN-13: 978-0-312-40106-1

Acknowledgments

Chapter 1
Opening Image: © Neville Elder/CORBIS.
Steven D. Levitt and Stephen J. Dubner, "What the Bagelman Saw," pp. 46–51 from *Freakonomics.* Copyright © 2005 by Steven D. Levitt and Stephen J. Dubner. Reprinted by permission of HarperCollins Publishers.

Acknowledgments and copyrights are continued at the back of the book on pages 601–05, which constitute an extension of the copyright page. It is a violation of the law to reproduce these selections by any means whatsoever without the written permission of the copyright holder.

Preface
for Instructors

We began thinking of this book when we identified a need for a new type of composition reader. Our community college's English department conducted a survey of the various colleges within the giant university up the road. (Sixty percent of our college track students transfer to this particular university.) While in our hearts we hoped that all of our students would go on to become English majors, we knew that this was likely not to be the case. Rather, our students would go on to major in political science and physics, education and engineering, business and biotechnology, art and anthropology. So, we asked the chairs of each university department: What type of writing do you ask students to do?

The chairs took the time to provide comments about the types of writing students were expected to do in their disciplines and stressed the importance of working with sources, of conducting field research and collaborative projects. They noted that few students understood how to integrate multiple perspectives and voices – whether from their peers or authorities – into coherent and interesting writing. They emphasized how difficult it was to transition them into the critical thinking and disciplinary conventions required of reading and writing in their fields.

We couldn't agree more. These skills and abilities are what we teach and want to teach. We recognize that composition courses – our bread and butter – are essentially service courses. Our job is to provide students with the thinking, writing, and research skills that they will need to succeed in college – and in the real world beyond. As students move into their majors, they need to take with them the ability to read, engage, and write about multisourced texts as well as become fluent in a host of new discourse communities – social networking websites, blogs, wikis – that are rapidly changing.

Once we identified the need for this type of reader, we started to draft this book. Our reader would engage writing in the disciplines in a new way by helping students move from their comfort zone to the more demanding requirements of academic reading and writing. This reader would push them to think critically about the context of a text and how it influences audience and content. Its assignments would ask them to push their writing out of the confines of the classroom and into the world of research, which is rarely an individual enterprise.

We wrote *NextText* out of a central belief: Writers are shaped by the texts they read. If our goal as instructors is to create writers prepared for a new world of multiple literacies and emerging fields of study – for a complicated and multilayered realm of communication and community – then we need different types of readings. So, most importantly, the selections in this reader would encourage students to understand and interact with multiple voices, genres, and disciplines. And, ideally, these readings will speak to and about each other to create a framework for students who wish to become observant, critical, and (dare we say it?) smart writers, willing to be aware of how they are shaped by the texts they read.

We are longtime composition instructors ourselves. And we realize that the way we have taught composition has changed over time. We wanted to make visible in *NextText* what our teaching experience tells us – that in order to engage students in the reading and writing process fully, we need to hit them where they live: in the intersection between academic life and "real" life. We need to go beyond the isolation of the traditional college English classroom, and we need to prepare our students for an academic life where even the ways we perceive academic disciplines are changing.

In short, we wanted to create a reader that ventured across the disciplines and traveled in and out of the academy. We wanted to create a reader that took into account how new technologies were influencing not only our teaching practice but our own reading, writing, and research practices as well. Here is what *NextText* offers you:

Carefully Selected Readings that Build on and Speak to Each Other
The selections in each *NextText* chapter can stand on their own, but they also create a cumulative whole that is greater than the sum of its parts. They address a common central topic, but they bring a diversity of voices to this topic. They also represent a broad range of genres of writing. Each chapter contains selections that model the range of possibilities, from informal journalism to researched academic writing.

Readings that Capture Emerging and Essential Genres *NextText* recognizes that writing is taking place in more modalities – blogs, websites, ads, online 'zines, and others – than ever before. Forms of writing that used to be marginal, such as graphic novels, have moved into the mainstream, and ads that used to be static sales pitches have become multimedia campaigns. In addition to the traditional forms of writing, students must be able to navigate, analyze, and create in these emerging forms.

Topics that Reflect the Interdisiplinarity of Academic Study and Research Writing Across the Curriculum is not new, but few WAC readers recognize that the curriculum is a living entity that, too, has evolved. The line between disciplines has blurred, so each chapter in *Next-Text* looks at a specific topic from the vantage point of two academic fields.

- Chapter 1, Putting a Price on Integrity
  [Education + Ethics]

- Chapter 2, The Changing Landscape of Family
  [Sociology + Public Policy]

- Chapter 3, Defining Identity in a Virtual World
  [Psychology + Technology]

- Chapter 4, Branding a Way of Life
  [Business + Marketing]

- Chapter 5, Making and Remaking History
  [History + Media]

- Chapter 6, Mapping the Human Genome
  [Biology + Art]

This approach encourages students to think critically and creatively about the central topic, which is rarely as black and white as it might seem.

Headnotes that Identify the Context of Each Piece   We strongly believe that context influences text. The headnote for each selection identifies the original publication source and its audience. This information is essential for students to think analytically about the piece that follows. We want readers to be thinking not just "what," but also "why" and "how." Knowing more about the author and the context provides students with an initial frame for the piece so they know which store it came from in the giant marketplace of ideas.

Thinking and Writing Prompts that Encourage Thoughtful Analysis and Connections Between Selections   We wanted the prompts in *NextText* to do more than we had seen in other readers. Students should start to recognize rhetorical choices and how these choices are driven by audience and publication context. After all, they need to make the same types of choices as maturing writers in their fields. We also wanted the writing prompts at the end of each selection to follow a natural progression from most familiar (reflective writing) to least familiar (active research and synthesis of ideas). Each set of prompts also includes an item that explicitly requires students to think about two chapter pieces and how they speak to the topic. Many also ask students to work with their peers and present their findings rather than writing them up in isolation.

A Closer Look at Genre　Each chapter includes a Focus on Genre portfolio that presents a set of selections that model a specific genre. Each genre is introduced and annotated to provide students with a framework for engaging with the other examples in the portfolio. Some of these are emerging genres (for example, blogs, graphic novels), others are multimedia (art, websites). All of these genres represent types of writing that will likely follow the students outside of academia into their daily lives. Thus, they need to become critical consumers of these genres in order to understand how and why they work.

An Emphasis on Reading Deeply　Reading as a writer is a messy enterprise when done right. Students must get in there and muck about to figure out how and why a piece works. Each chapter in *NextText* ends with a Reading Deeply essay — most are research papers taken from academic journals in fields such as sociology, psychology, history, and religion — that models scholarly reading, showing students how to *read deeply* — to drill down below the surface of the text. The annotations map key references, allusions, sourcing conventions, and terminology in the feature essay, providing a visual snapshot on every page of how the selection works so students can *see* how taking the time to investigate these references helps them understand the writer's point of view and the wider context that informed readers require for analysis of any work.

We hope that you will enjoy the variety of texts we have chosen. We have tried to choose topics students are familiar with and interested in, both in and out of the academy, and we hope to engage them in examining these topics from a variety of perspectives and levels of discourse. In short, we hope to teach students to become active and savvy consumers of information and to help them develop the multiple literacies they will need in the twenty-first century. *NextText* is a good way to start.

Acknowledgments

We would like to thank our ever-hopeful and tenacious editor Genevieve Hamilton Day for the long hours, enthusiasm, and kindness she brought to this project. Bedford/St. Martin's president Joan Feinberg has also been a gracious presence throughout our work, from her interest and decision to sign us to write the book on day one to her support on days both sunny and rainy as the book went through the long development process. Karen Henry has been a mainstay throughout this project, lending her expertise every step of the way. We would also like to thank Karen Melton Soeltz and Karita dos Santos for their support. Our production editor, Kendra LeFleur, was remarkably efficient and timely, and Melissa Cook, editorial assistant, has been a great help on matters big and small.

A special thanks goes to Linda Finnigan, our permissions editor, for her hard work clearing rights to the visual and verbal texts in the book. Billy Boardman came up with the wonderful and evocative cover design. Finally, we are very grateful to Dominic F. Delli Carpini for developing the instructor support material for *NextText*.

Our deep appreciation also goes out to all of our reviewers for the thoughtful comments and suggestions that helped shape *NextText* into the book it is today. Susan Bailor, Front Range Community College, Larimer Campus; Gary Bennett, Santa Ana College; Dominic F. Delli Carpini, York College; Christine Farris, Indiana University; Sybylle Gruber, Northern Arizona University; Amy Hawkins, Columbia College; Paul Heilker, Virginia Tech; Gary Hoffman, Orange Coast College; Shari Horner, Shippensburg University; Emily Isaacs, Montclair State College; Ronald Janssen, Hofstra University; Megan Knight, University of Iowa; Lindsay Lewan, Arapahoe Community College; Kimberly Manner, Modesto Junior College; Mark McBeth, John Jay College; Gerri McNenny, Chapman University; Nancy Morrow, University of California, Davis; Whitney A. Myers, University of New Mexico; Geraldine Roberta McNenny, Chapman University; Beverly Neiderman, Kent State University; Lisa Nelson, University of Southern Maine; Pamela Ralston, Tacoma Community College; Georgia Rhoades; Appalachian State University; Rich Rice, Ball State University; Mahta Rosenfeld, Moorpark College; Mary Soliday, The City College of New York; Scott Stevens, Western Washington University; Donna Strickland, University of Missouri, Columbia; Deborah Coxwell-Teague, Florida State University; Susan Topping, Three Rivers Community College; Patricia Webb, Arizona State University; Ashley Taliaferro Williams, George Mason University; Bronwyn T. Williams, University of Louisville.

Throughout the years at Santa Fe Community College, we have been honored to teach students and to work alongside colleagues who have inspired us, making us better instructors and people. We are grateful to be part of this extraordinary community of learners.

And, of course, we both want to thank our patient, clever, funny, remarkable, and loving families who stuck with us through the years (years!) we have spent on this project. To Doug, Ned, Harper, and Penn — without you we would be much less and with you we are much, much more. You are the very best.

Contents

CONTENTS

CONTENTS

CONTENTS

NextText

Moving Across and Beyond the Disciplines

Introduction

We wrote *NextText* out of a central belief: Writers are shaped by the texts they read. This seems a simple statement, but as its writers, we (of course) think it is profound. Let's unwrap it.

First, to be an effective writer, one must be an effective reader, one who understands how a sentence makes meaning, how word choice builds tone and reveals bias, how an essay twists and turns, how an image becomes more than its component parts. Writers read with an eye toward dismantling a work, understanding its parts, and then putting it back together. For example, they ask questions like, Why do the sentences above use a repeating structure? How does this structure support the message about reading? These are questions readers need to ask because they reveal decisions writers have made. For example, repetition is commonly used to highlight a point or reveal a direction. In the first sentence of this paragraph, we repeat an embedded question structure (that is, "how," "how," "how"). We do this because we want you – always – to think about the "how" of writing (how it works), not just the "what" (the simple meaning).

Second, as readers, writers know that texts are written for specific audiences. Frequently, the intended audience shares a common vocabulary, subject knowledge, and point of view with the author. When the audience and the writer have this level of community, the writer can effectively use a form of shorthand because he or she can take certain things for granted. However, sometimes, an author writes in expectation of a novice or even a hostile reader; in these cases, nothing can be taken for granted. For example, a writer of an article in *Sports Illustrated* on the glories of college football does not have to justify football's place in a university; a writer of an essay on the same topic for the *Chronicle of Higher Education* could not expect the same uniformly welcoming audience.

Third, writing takes many different forms, and these define – in part – the writing that can be produced within them. Some forms have very specific purposes. For example, an abstract exists solely to provide an overview of a longer essay so that the reader knows whether or not to keep reading. Other forms are more flexible. An essay can hold a personal exploration, a tidy rhetorical argument, a substantial research study. Some forms are just now emerging as recognized genres: the website, the blog, the graphic novel.

Fourth, texts are not just black and white and two-dimensional. We are surrounded by texts. Some are verbal, some are visual, some are both. As readers, we interact with them in a fluid, dynamic manner. Imagine you are in the checkout line in the supermarket texting a friend about meeting to shop for jeans when you see a photo of an ever-shrinking celebrity on the cover of *People*. You buy carb-free energy bars to eat on your way to work because you won't have time to eat dinner before heading to the gym, where you'll watch *America's Next Top Model* while running on the treadmill and listening to Gwen Stefani. This flow of life can be read as a series of texts that speak to each other and inform you as a writer. Not a single one is in a textbook, but as a careful and clever reader, you could easily use them to provide the context for an essay on body image.

The Texts

Sometimes, as writers, we are most influenced by pieces that we initially find incredibly difficult and dense. Our arduous engagement with these texts produces sparks that ignite our own writing. But sometimes, the most difficult works just leave us confused and frustrated. They only obscure the issue rather than illuminate it. In these cases, we need another point of entry, one that may be more straightforward or that offers a familiar point of view. Then, we can use this reading to build a scaffold to the next, and so on.

In pulling together the readings for the book, we wanted to build this set of scaffolding for each topic. Thus, we offer a range of texts you might encounter both in and out of class. These texts are verbal and visual, formal and informal, serious and humorous, classic and of the moment. Taken together, they provide a map for thinking about the topic at hand. Some routes are short and direct, like articles from *People* or *USA Today*. Others are long and scenic, such as essays from *Atlantic Monthly* or *The Lancet*.

Also, as we suggested, the texts included are not limited to traditional written works. You might be asked to read an ad, a sculpture, a website, or a graphic novel. Because writing is a dynamic endeavor that both shapes and responds to the needs of readers, you are also asked to consider emerging texts, such as blogs.

The Topics

We recognize that – although it would fulfill both our dreams – few of you will continue on to become English majors. However, all of you will be writers, and the shape of your writing will be largely determined by your major and your work. So, we have selected topics that reflect current discussions within intersecting academic disciplines.

- Chapter 1: Putting a Price on Integrity
  [Education + Ethics]

- Chapter 2: The Changing Landscape of Family
  [Sociology + Public Policy]

- Chapter 3: Defining Identity in a Virtual World
  [Psychology + Technology]

- Chapter 4: Branding a Way of Life
  [Business + Marketing]

- Chapter 5: Making and Remaking History
  [History + Media]

- Chapter 6: Mapping the Human Genome
  [Biology + Art]

The readings clustered around these topics represent diverse voices within the ongoing dialogue that is included in academic, journalistic, entertainment, political, and personal writing. This diversity arises because these themes resonate inside and outside of academia. For example, the intersection of history and media can be expressed in a lecture by a National Endowment for the Humanities fellow or a film by Spike Lee. The impact of changes to the nuclear family affect public policy on marriage and spurred the creation of Babble.com, a website for Gen-Y parents. As a present and future writer, you need to know both what to write about and for whom you are writing. These clusters give you direction on both fronts. For example, in Chapter 1, Putting a Price on Integrity, you will find the topic of plagiarism engaged in both serious academic studies and popular journalism. You will see how the issues impacting integrity look through the eyes of an economist, an artist, a faculty member, and a student. Each of these topics will provide a lens to help sharpen your viewpoint and your ability to express it in writing. They offer a treasure trove of writing know-how: how the intended audience shapes vocabulary, style, and substance; how an author's point of view shades topics that might otherwise seem black and white; how to think differently about a topic to bring something new to the table. All of these "hows" are embedded in each chapter, but you must read deeply to find them.

Special Features

Every textbook worth its salt provides "apparatus" – the materials that help you get to the "why" and "how" of writing. *NextText* includes writing questions and prompts to spur your thinking about the texts and frame your writing. Some of these assignments move well beyond the standard essay and ask you to engage in active problem solving, in team-based projects, and in original research. That is, they push you to do the type of writing and project management you will be asked to do in your major and in the workplace.

In creating *NextText*, we also wanted to widen the definition of "apparatus" to include features not traditionally part of a composition reader. These features build on our experiences as classroom teachers and offer a robust support system for your growth as a writer.

CONTEXT: We think the original context of any text is incredibly important to understanding it. None of these works was written specifically for this book; all come from a good home elsewhere. You need to know what that home was and what kind of people lived there. It makes a difference if an article on hybrid cars came from *Consumer Reports* or the Toyota website. The readership of *Forbes* differs from that of *Nature*; a book published by a university press will have a different market than one published by a trade paperback imprint. As an informed reader, you need to know the context for the pieces you read, so we provide it and in the questions that follow each selection, we ask you to reflect on how this context shaped the text.

FOCUS ON GENRE: It is easier to understand a form or genre if you have more than one example. In researching any topic, you need a significant "n" (a denotation we've borrowed from the field of statistics) – a number of events, items, samples, and so on. So, in each chapter, we provide a portfolio of samples of one form of discourse. Each portfolio begins with an annotated example to identify essential elements of the form. The texts in the portfolios are drawn from modes of discourse you are likely to encounter in your day-to-day life: websites, memoirs, graphic novels, blogs, and art. Our goal is to increase your sophistication in reading these modes and thereby increase your ability to write effectively with and about them.

READING DEEPLY: We think effective reading is a key to effective writing. But reading as a writer is a skill, not a native ability. We model this skill in each chapter in the Reading Deeply feature, which annotates a researched essay to explicate the choices made by the writer. By mapping key references, allusions, sourcing conventions, and terminology in the featured essay, we enable you to see how these references help define the writer's point of view and the wider context that informed readers require for analysis of any work. The Reading Deeply essays also represent the wide variety of forms that researched writing can take, from academic essays to popular magazine pieces. These essays model the types of writing you will encounter in your academic career, and they frequently represent the conventions and vocabulary associated with specific fields of study (for example, business, psychology, science, and art). As such, the Reading Deeply essays underscore how important understanding the audience and the context is to writing – and reading – effectively.

An Invitation

We hope that you will find these sets of readings engaging, not unfamiliar, and perhaps eye opening, or even fun. We hope to provoke some spirited class discussion. We hope that you will begin to see the texts that surround you every day, both in and out of school, as contributing to an important conversation of which you as a student and as a citizen are an integral part.

We hope that you will experience this book as an opportunity to read and write as a process of inquiry – that you will experience thinking, reading, and writing as opportunities to inquire into your world and your experience, both academically and in everyday life – that you will realize we all are always engaged in the process of creating meaning for ourselves (and not just accepting someone else's vision). Take off from these layers of ideas, images, and forms and build the scaffolding you need to see something anew. Use them as entryways into other classes you take, as you read and write, not just in English classes, but throughout your college career.

As we said at the beginning, we believe writers are shaped by the texts they read. Each time we read and write we are contributing to the cultural and academic conversation of our time. Join in. Be smart. Look around yourself at your world. Read. Think. Observe. Write your world. You are writing your life.

Putting a Price on Integrity

IN THE OPENING IMAGE FOR THIS CHAPTER, A YOUNG WOMAN IS buying a Louis Vuitton Murakami Cherry Blossom bag. Or is she? This Louis Vuitton bag is being sold out of a pressed steel street-vendor booth. One would think that a bag retailing for about $1,500 would be displayed better, but here the bags – a surprising mix of LV styles for almost every season and some Burberry bags thrown in for good measure – are crammed into all the space not used for the glittering "gold" chains. Even at this distance, the handles of the bag look stiff and bent, as does the bag itself. Upon closer inspection, this bag doesn't look as much like an LV as it did at first. It is a fake: It captures the general look and feel of the original but has lost something in translation. Of course, rather than paying $1,500, the young woman will likely pay around $25. In this transaction, everyone is in on the deception. The vendor knows the bag is not an original; at this price, the purchaser knows it, too; her friends likely know she cannot afford a ridiculously expensive purse and will assume it is counterfeit. So, what could be the ethical dilemma in saving $1,475 . . . on a purse?

Sales of counterfeit goods of all types, from batteries to bags, account for 7 percent of the global

economy – over $500 million annually – so arguments about intellectual property and artistic integrity do not seem to hold much sway in the marketplace. Suppose we add a twist to this scenario: This young woman now posts the bag on eBay for $500 as an authentic, rare but used LV Murakami Cherry Blossom bag . . . and you buy it. What if she now profits from this deception?

In a university classroom, a similar act of deception would likely fall under the general heading "academic dishonesty." You are now a student in a college with a code of conduct or ethics that addresses academic dishonesty; you may even be attending a college with an explicit honor code. The assumption is that you will adhere to these rules

Neville Elder, Counterfeit Items on Canal Street, New York

and stay within these guidelines. Do you know what they are? What are your responsibilities as a participant in your academic community? Initially, these may seem like very straightforward questions. However, as you engage with this chapter, you will find that lines that once seemed clearly defined are slipping and may seem almost too easy to cross.

This chapter asks you to consider the topics of plagiarism and cheating from several different points of view. The works that follow suggest that both acts are more common and more complex than ever before. As we rely more on technology for producing works ranging from the average term paper to the extraordinary artistic collage, distinctions between the derivative and the creative are more difficult to draw. When is a Louis Vuitton bag not a Louis Vuitton bag? What makes something original? The definition of plagiarism relies on the definition of originality. And as originality becomes harder to identify so does plagiarism.

Still, several of the authors in this chapter suggest that there is always a warning when you are coming close to crossing an ethical line. Look again at the young woman in the picture. Does she look like a satisfied consumer? Perhaps she is hearing the small voice deep inside that lets her know when her core ethical beliefs are in danger, when she may be selling out her ideals for something less than worthy. A voice that whispers, "How much is that really worth?"

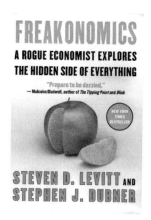

FREAKONOMICS
A ROGUE ECONOMIST EXPLORES
THE HIDDEN SIDE OF EVERYTHING

"Prepare to be dazzled."
—Malcolm Gladwell, author of *The Tipping Point* and *Blink*

STEVEN D. LEVITT AND
STEPHEN J. DUBNER

What the Bagelman Saw

By Steven D. Levitt and
Stephen J. Dubner

FROM: *Freakonomics: A Rogue Economist Explores the Hidden Side of Everything,* William Morrow, 2005

CONTEXT: This piece is an excerpt from *Freakonomics: A Rogue Economist Explores the Hidden Side of Everything*; it was also published on June 6, 2004, in the *New York Times Magazine*. Steven D. Levitt holds a doctorate in economics from MIT and is a professor of economics at the University of Chicago. Stephen J. Dubner is a journalist and nonfiction writer. *Freakonomics* grew out of a profile that Dubner wrote on Levitt for the *New York Times* and has itself grown into a website, a blog, and a *NYT Magazine* column. *Freakonomics* sets out several premises, chief among them that most of human behavior can be explained through the economic principle of incentives. As you read this piece about selling bagels on the honor system and what Levitt and Dubner found out about incentive, consider the last time you purchased something on the honor system. How did you behave?

DESPITE ALL THE ATTENTION PAID TO ROGUE COMPANIES like Enron, academics know very little about the practicalities of white-collar crime. The reason? There are no good data. A key fact of white-collar crime is that we hear about only the very slim fraction of people who are *caught* cheating. Most embezzlers lead quiet and theoretically happy lives; employees who steal company property are rarely detected.

With street crime, meanwhile, that is not the case. A mugging or a burglary or a murder is usually tallied whether or not the criminal is caught. A street crime has a victim, who typically reports the crime to the police, who generate data, which in turn generate thousands of academic papers by criminologists, sociologists, and economists. But white-collar crime presents no obvious victim. From whom, exactly, did the masters of Enron steal? And how can you measure something if you don't know to whom it happened, or with what frequency, or in what magnitude?

Paul Feldman's bagel business was different. It did present a victim. The victim was Paul Feldman.

When he started his business, he expected a 95 percent payment rate, based on the experience at his own office. But just as crime tends to be low on a street where a police car is parked, the 95 percent rate was artificially high: Feldman's presence had deterred theft. Not only that, but those bagel eaters knew the provider and had feelings (presumably good ones) about him. A broad swath of psychological and economic research has shown that people will pay different amounts for the same item depending on who is providing it. The economist Richard Thaler, in his 1985 "Beer on the Beach" study, showed that a thirsty sunbather would pay $2.65 for a beer delivered from a resort hotel but only $1.50 for the same beer if it came from a shabby grocery store.

In the real world, Feldman learned to settle for less than 95 percent. He came to consider a company "honest" if its payment rate was above 90 percent. He considered a rate between 80 and 90 percent "annoying but tolerable." If a company habitually paid below 80 percent, Feldman might post a hectoring note, like this one: 5

> The cost of bagels has gone up dramatically since the beginning of the year. Unfortunately, the number of bagels that disappear without being paid for has also gone up. Don't let that continue. I don't imagine that you would teach your children to cheat, so why do it yourselves?

In the beginning, Feldman left behind an open basket for the cash, but too often the money vanished. Then he tried a coffee can with a money slot in its plastic lid, which also proved too tempting. In the end, he resorted to making small plywood boxes with a slot cut into the top. The wooden box has worked well. Each year he drops off about seven thousand boxes and loses, on average, just one to theft. This is an intriguing statistic: the same people who routinely steal more than 10 percent of his bagels almost never stoop to stealing his money box — a tribute to the nuanced social calculus of theft. From Feldman's perspective, an office worker who eats a bagel without paying is committing a crime; the office worker probably doesn't think so. This distinction probably has less to do with the admittedly small amount of money involved (Feldman's bagels cost one dollar each, cream cheese included) than with the context of the "crime." The same office worker who fails to pay for his bagel might also help himself to a long slurp of soda while filling a glass in a self-serve restaurant, but he is very unlikely to leave the restaurant without paying.

So what do the bagel data have to say? In recent years, there have been two noteworthy trends in the overall payment rate. The first was a long, slow decline that began in 1992. By the summer of 2001, the overall rate had slipped to about 87 percent. But immediately after September 11 of that year, the rate spiked a full 2 percent and hasn't slipped much since. (If a 2 percent gain in payment doesn't sound like much, think of it this way: the nonpayment rate fell from 13 to 11 percent, which amounts to a 15 percent decline in theft.) Because many of Feldman's customers are affiliated with national security, there may have been a patriotic element to this 9/11 Effect. Or it may have represented a more general surge in empathy.

The data also show that smaller offices are more honest than big ones. An office with a few dozen employees generally outpays by 3 to 5 percent an office with a few hundred employees. This may seem counterintuitive. In a bigger office, a bigger crowd is bound to convene around the bagel table, providing more witnesses to make sure you drop your money in the box. But in the big-office/small-office comparison, bagel crime seems to mirror street crime. There is far less street crime per capita in rural areas than in cities, in large part because a rural criminal is more likely to be known (and therefore caught). Also, a smaller community tends to exert greater social incentives against crime, the main one being shame.

The bagel data also reflect how much personal mood seems to af- 10
fect honesty. Weather, for instance, is a major factor. Unseasonably pleasant weather inspires people to pay at a higher rate. Unseasonably cold weather, meanwhile, makes people cheat prolifically; so do heavy rain and wind. Worst are the holidays. The week of Christmas produces a 2 percent drop in payment rates — again, a 15 percent increase in theft, an effect on the same magnitude, in reverse, as that of 9/11. Thanksgiving is nearly as bad; the week of Valentine's Day is also lousy, as is the week straddling April 15. There are, however, a few good holidays: the weeks that include the Fourth of July, Labor Day, and Columbus Day. The difference in the two sets of holidays? The low-cheating holidays represent little more than an extra day off from work. The high-cheating holidays are fraught with miscellaneous anxieties and the high expectations of loved ones.

Feldman has also reached some of his own conclusions about honesty, based more on his experience than the data. He has come to believe that morale is a big factor — that an office is more honest when the employees like their boss and their work. He also believes that employees further up the corporate ladder cheat more than those down below. He got this idea after delivering for years to one company spread out over three floors — an executive floor on top and two lower floors with sales, service, and administrative employees. (Feldman wondered if perhaps the executives cheated out of an overdeveloped sense of entitlement. What he didn't consider is that perhaps cheating was how they got to *be* executives.)

If morality represents the way we would like the world to work and economics represents how it actually does work, then the story of Feldman's bagel business lies at the very intersection of morality and economics. Yes, a lot of people steal from him, but the vast majority, even though no one is watching over them, do not. This outcome may surprise some people — including Feldman's economist friends, who counseled him twenty years ago that his honor-system scheme would never work. But it would not have surprised Adam Smith. In fact, the theme of Smith's first book, *The Theory of Moral Sentiments*, was the innate honesty of mankind. "How selfish soever man may be supposed," Smith wrote, "there are evidently some principles in his nature, which interest him in the fortune of others, and render their happiness necessary to him, though he derives nothing from it, except the pleasure of seeing it."

There is a tale, "The Ring of Gyges," that Feldman sometimes tells his economist friends. It comes from Plato's *Republic*. A student named Glaucon offered the story in response to a lesson by Socrates — who, like Adam Smith, argued that people are generally good even without enforcement. Glaucon, like Feldman's economist friends, disagreed. He told of a shepherd named Gyges who stumbled upon a secret cavern with a corpse inside that wore a ring. When Gyges put on the ring, he found that it made him invisible. With no one able to monitor his behavior, Gyges proceeded to do woeful things — seduce the queen, murder the king, and so on. Glaucon's story posed a moral question: could any man resist the temptation of evil if he knew his acts could not be witnessed? Glaucon seemed to think the answer was no. But Paul Feldman sides with Socrates and Adam Smith — for he knows that the answer, at least 87 percent of the time, is yes.

READING

1. Levitt is a serious academic economist; Dubner is a journalist and nonfiction writer. This piece is aimed at a general audience. How would you imagine they work as a writing team to make highly intellectual ideas accessible and interesting to average readers?

2. Levitt and Dubner begin this piece by moving from a very abstract concept to a concrete example of this concept. What is the concept? What is their example? How do they draw you in?

3. Although this story concerns a bagel salesman, it still contains a good bit of data. What types of data do Levitt and Dubner use to support their conclusions? Is it easy or difficult to follow the quantitative aspect of this piece? Why?

4. Feldman draws his own conclusions about the honesty of the office workers. What are they? Do they seem to bear out observations you have had regarding honesty in other situations?

5. Levitt and Dubner end the essay with a story from Plato's *Republic*. What is the relevance of this story to that of the bagelman? Whom would you side with, Glaucon or Feldman? Why?

WRITING

1. Levitt and Dubner observe that "a smaller community tends to exert greater social incentives against crime, the main one being shame." Write a reflective essay or journal entry that discusses this observation. Are you more likely to be honest and to follow laws when you are being closely observed or when you are more anonymous?

2. The authors support their discussion of the topic with many figures, and it can become daunting if you are unfamiliar with working with data. Write a short summary of the essay that describes the main points without using the data. Think about summarizing the concepts for a younger audience.

3. In the latter part of the essay, Levitt and Dubner write that Feldman reached the conclusion that executives may have "cheated out of an overdeveloped sense of entitlement." But, they also note that Feldman did not question whether "cheating was how they got to be executives." This comment adds a touch of irony to the essay while maintaining a consistently serious tone that runs through the piece about executive-level employees. Write a critical analysis that discusses the portrayal of middle/lower-level office workers with that

of higher-level workers in this essay. Be certain to support your analysis with concrete examples.

4. The essay ends with a reference to "The Ring of Gyges" from Plato's *Republic*. Find the complete version of this story, read it, and then reread this essay. Survey at least ten other students with just one question: "Could you resist the temptation of evil if you knew your acts could not be witnessed?" Write an essay summarizing your findings and explain whether they support those of Feldman.

5. Levitt and Dubner write that, while the office workers seem to feel little hesitation about stealing bagels, almost none will steal the money left by those who pay for their bagels. They conclude that this is "a tribute to the nuanced social calculus of theft." Think about this conclusion in light of Jason M. Stephens's observations in "Justice or Just Us? What to Do about Cheating" (p. 40) that students seem to set up their own "pragmatic reasons" for cheating. Working with a group of your peers, write an essay in which you set up a scale of cheating, balancing the incentive to cheat with the social consequences of cheating. At what point is the incentive outweighed by the cost?

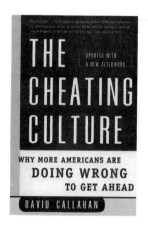

Everybody Does It

By David Callahan

FROM: *The Cheating Culture: Why More Americans Are Doing Wrong to Get Ahead,* Harvest Books, 2003

CONTEXT: This piece is an excerpt from a chapter titled "Everybody Does It" in David Callahan's book *The Cheating Culture*. He has written five other books and numerous articles. He received his Ph.D. in politics from Princeton University and was a fellow at the Century Foundation from 1994 to 1999, where he pursued research on public policy. In 1999, he cofounded Demos, a think tank in New York City. Callahan's website states that Demos "combines research and advocacy, working to strengthen democracy and expand economic opportunity within the United States." Callahan maintains a weblog at www.cheatingculture.com/cheatingblog.html. A former U.S. secretary of labor said of *The Cheating Culture*, "Here, finally, a lucid explanation for why America seems on its way to becoming a nation of cheaters. Cheating begets more cheating, from our boardrooms to our classrooms. With verve and insight, Callahan shows that too many Americans feel the dice are already loaded, so they might as well give them an extra roll when no one's looking." As you read this piece, reflect on the atmosphere regarding cheating at your school. Do you agree with Callahan that the "everybody does it" mentality is on the rise in our culture?

IN 1981, AFTER HE WAS SWORN IN AS PRESIDENT, RONALD Reagan pronounced: "Government is not the solution, government is the problem." Elsewhere, Reagan articulated another adage that summed up both his philosophy and the dawning ethos of the time: "What I want to see above all is that this remains a country where someone can always get rich."

Ronald Reagan's election stands as a historic turning point that helped crystallize and accelerate emerging trends in American society. Government activism was out. Making money was in. And over the next twenty years, the ideas and values associated with the free market would reign in U.S. society with more influence than at any time since the Gilded Age. "By the end of 2000," wrote one observer, "the market as the dominant cultural force had so infiltrated society that it is increasingly difficult to remember any other reality."[1]

This seismic change has altered the terms of American life. First, thanks to America's laissez-faire revolution, a focus on money and the bottom line has swept into areas that previously were insulated from market pressures. Partly this has been a good thing. Consumers have more choices and get better service these days, and we have an economy that nurtures innovation and entrepreneurialism. Yet there's been a cost. More people in more occupations are chasing money — or being chased by bean counters.

Second, income gaps among Americans have soared over the past quarter century. When profits and performance are the only measure of success, old-fashioned ideas about fairness go out the window. Lean-and-mean business strategies have conspired with trends like globalization and techological change to ensure huge income gains by well-educated professionals — while many less-skilled workers have been running in place or losing ground. Fewer people also control more of the nation's wealth. In fact, the top 1 percent of households have more wealth than the entire bottom 90 percent combined. Economic inequality has led to striking changes in our society.

- In America's new winner-take-all society there is infinitely more to gain, and to lose, when it comes to getting into the right college, getting the right job, becoming a "hot" reporter, showing good earnings on Wall Street, having a high batting average, or otherwise becoming a star achiever. [5]

- Higher inequality has led to more divisions between Americans and weakened the social fabric — undermining the notion that we're all "in it together" and bound by the same rules.

- Inequality is also reshaping our politics as wealthier Americans get more adept at turning money into influence — twisting rules to their benefit and escaping punishment when they break the rules.

- The dramatic upward movement of wealth to top earners has resulted in less wealth for everyone else. Anxiety about money is rife, even among solidly middle-class Americans.

A third consequence of the market's ascendancy is that government's ability to enforce norms of fair play, serving as a "referee" of competition, has been hobbled. Government watchdogs in many areas were disarmed in the '80s and '90s in the name of privatization and deregulation. Extreme laissez-faire thinking has held, foolishly, that the business world can police itself — that the "hidden hand" of market competition will enforce moral behavior and fair outcomes.

Finally the character of Americans has changed. Those values as- 10
sociated with the market hold sway in their most caricatured form: individualism and self-reliance have morphed into selfishness and self-absorption; competitiveness has become social Darwinism; desire for the good life has turned into materialism; aspiration has become envy. There is a growing gap between the life that many Americans want and the life they can afford — a problem that bedevils even those who would seem to have everything. Other values in our culture have been sidelined: belief in community, social responsibility, compassion for the less able or less fortunate. The decline of civic life, famously described by Robert Putnam, has both fueled these changes and been fueled by them. Everywhere the collective spirit needed for a vibrant civil society is struggling to survive in an era where shared goals are out of fashion.

Why have these transformations led to more cheating? There are four key reasons:

New Pressures   In today's competitive economy, where success and job security can't be taken for granted, it's increasingly tempting to leave your ethics at home every morning. Students are cheating more now that getting a good education is a matter of economic life and death. Lawyers are overbilling as they've been pushed to bring in more money for the firm and as it's gotten harder to make partner. Doctors are accepting bribes from drug-makers, as HMOs have squeezed their incomes. The list goes on. You can even see this problem among cabdrivers in some cities. As cabdrivers have gone from salaried workers with steady incomes to "free agents" who rent their taxis and have to hustle to make a living, they've been feeling new pressures to pick up and drop off as many fares as possible every day. And big surprise: They're speeding and running more red lights.

Bigger Rewards for Winning   As the prizes for the winners have increased, people have become more willing to do whatever it takes to be a winner. A CEO will inflate earnings reports to please Wall Street — and increase the value of his stock options by $50 million. An A student will cheat to get the A+ that she believes, correctly, could make the difference between Harvard and a lifetime of big opportunities — or NYU and fewer opportunities. A steady .295 hitter will take steroids to build the muscles needed to be a slugger — and make $12 million a year instead of a mere $3 million. A journalist will fabricate sources in his quest to write as many hit pieces as possible —

so that the day arrives sooner rather than later when he can command six-figure book deals and get lucrative lecture gigs. A partner at a top accounting firm will keep quiet and go along as a client cooks the books — in order to protect a mid-six-figure bonus pegged on bringing in and retaining clients, not angering them.

Twenty-five years ago, many of the huge rewards being dangled in front of professionals didn't exist in a society with less wealth and a stronger sense of fairness. But in the '80s and '90s we came to live in a society where lots of people were striking it rich left and right — and cutting corners made it easier to do so.

Temptation   Temptations to cheat have increased as safeguards 15 against wrongdoing have grown weaker over two decades of deregulation and attacks on government. Many of the recent instances of greed and investor betrayal on Wall Street, for example, could have been prevented by reforms intended to keep accountants honest — or to ensure the independence of stock analysts, or to stop corporate boards from being packed with cronies, or to keep companies from handing out so many stock options. Reformers tried to enact such measures for years, only to be blocked by powerful special interests and antigovernment zealots. At the same time, federal agencies like the SEC, the IRS, and the Justice Department have been starved of the resources needed to stop white-collar crime. Why not inflate earnings reports if the chances of being prosecuted are next to nil? Why not commit a fraud that nets you $70 million — when a year or two in a Club Fed prison camp is the worst possible punishment? Why not hide your income in an illegal offshore bank account when you know that the IRS is too overwhelmed to bother with you because it actually lost enforcement capacity during the '80 and '90s — even as the number of tax returns increased?

Professional watchdog groups have also been asleep on the job. Why worry about being disbarred for bilking your clients when state bar associations lack the resources or wherewithal to fully investigate much of the misconduct by lawyers reported to them? Why worry about being censured by your state's medical society for taking kickbacks to prescribe certain drugs when those groups are more interested in protecting the interests of doctors than of the general public? Why worry about being thrown out of baseball for using steroids when neither of the major leagues has mandatory drug testing?

Growing temptations to cheat have been all the more seductive given the trumpeted morality of the free market. If competition is good — if even greed is good — then maybe questionable cutthroat behavior is also good. In principle, few Americans embrace the idea that "might makes right." In practice, this idea now flourishes across our society, and much of the new cheating is among those with the highest incomes and social status. The Winning Class's clout inevitably has produced hubris and a sense that the rules governing what Leona Helmsley called "the little people" do not apply to them.

This hubris is only partly founded on the kind of delusions made possible by a culture that imputes moral superiority to those who achieve material success. It is also founded on reality. The Winning Class *can* get away with cheating, if not always then certainly often. And when they do get punished, they often find that it's a cinch to later repair their public image. Rehabilitation in the wake of what scholar David Simon memorably labeled "elite deviance" has become easier in recent decades as bottom-line commercialism has steered the media away from critical inquiry toward a new focus on infotainment, much of it celebrating the accomplishments of the rich and famous.[2]

In short, the Winning Class has every reason to imagine that they live in a moral community of their own making governed by different rules. They do.

Trickle-down Corruption   What happens when you're an ordinary middle-class person struggling to make ends meet even as you face relentless pressures to emulate the good life you see every day on TV and in magazines? What happens when you think the system is stacked against people like you and you stop believing that the rules are fair? You just might make up your own moral code. Maybe you'll cheat more often on your taxes, anxious to get a leg up financially and also sure that the tax codes wrongly favor the rich. Maybe you'll misuse your expense account at work to afford a few little luxuries that are out of reach on your salary — and you'll justify this on the grounds that the people running your company are taking home huge paychecks while you're making chump change. Maybe you'll lie to the auto insurance company about a claim or about having a teenage driver in the house, convinced that the insurer has jacked up your rates in order to increase their profits — then again, maybe you have nothing against insurance companies but the payments on that flashy new SUV you just had to have are killing you and you're desperate for any kind of relief.

In theory, there is limitless opportunity in America for anyone willing to work hard, and it seemed during the boom of the '90s that everyone could get rich. The reality is that a lot of families actually lost ground during the past two decades. Middle-class Americans are both insecure and cynical these days — a dangerous combination — and many feel besieged by material expectations that are impossible to attain. It shouldn't come as a surprise that more people are leveling the playing field however they see fit.

NOTES

[1] Zachary Karabell, *A Visionary Nation: Four Centuries of American Dreams and What Lies Ahead* (New York: HarperCollins, 2001), 122.

[2] David R. Simon, *Elite Deviance*, 6th ed. (Boston: Allyn & Bacon, 1999). Simon's work, in turn, draws heavily from C. Wright Mills, who described the phenomenon of "higher immorality" among American power elites. C. Wright Mills, *The Power Elite* (New York: Oxford University Press, 1999).

READING

1. Callahan situates his social criticism of cheating within American history, specifically the Ronald Reagan years. He says, "Government activism was out. Making money was in." In what way does this "seismic change" set up his argument concerning the increase in cheating in America?

2. The title of the chapter this excerpt appears in is "Everybody Does It." What does this common saying mean to you? Have you heard it lately? If so, in what context? Was the person discussing some aspect of cheating that Callahan touches on in this excerpt? What is your opinion of the rationale for this statement?

3. Callahan speaks of cheating in broad terms in many areas of American life today. He writes that "desire for the good life has turned into materialism; aspiration has become envy. There is a growing gap between the life that many Americans want and the life they can afford." Discuss some examples of this apparent gap in our culture today.

4. Callahan maintains that there are four ways *how* this materialism has "altered the terms of American life." He conveniently devotes a paragraph to each in the opening of this excerpt. Discuss each of these changes.

5. Callahan then analyzes *why* these changes have led to increased pressure to cheat. His organization again is very clear. The chapter proceeds with four key reasons. Reread the section on "Temptation" and discuss how the diction in this section makes his viewpoint clear. Consider using the terms "Winning Class" and "little people."

WRITING

1. In the section titled "New Pressures," Callahan says, "Students are cheating more now that getting a good education is a matter of economic life and death." Write a reflective piece or a journal entry in which you define academic integrity to yourself. What would you consider cheating to be in an academic setting? Do you believe that cheating is a commonplace event in your classes?

2. This excerpt from "Everybody Does It" uses many examples – everyone from cab drivers to CEOs. Write a narrative essay that tells the story of an experience you have had observing someone cheating.

3. Later in this piece Callahan asserts that another reason for in-creased cheating in our American culture is that "professional watchdog groups have also been asleep on the job." Write a re-searched essay exploring the work of a particular "watchdog group." Does Callahan's assertion hold true for this group?

4. This excerpt is the first chapter of Callahan's book. In broad strokes, he has outlined the direction the rest of the book will go. In order to place this excerpt in a larger context, get the book out of the library and read chapter five, "Temptation Nation." Then, write a summary of this new chapter, citing concrete examples of temptation that Callahan addresses.

5. With a group of your peers, decide on what aspect of American cul-ture you would like to investigate – business, sports, entertainment, schools – and research a specific example of cheating in that area. With your group, write a proposal describing the problem and what strategies your group would use to prevent cheating or dissuade the cheaters.

Rebekah Nathan

The Art of College Management: Cheating

By Rebekah Nathan

FROM: *My Freshman Year: What a Professor Learned by Becoming a Student,* **Cornell University Press, 2005**

CONTEXT: Rebekah Nathan is the pseudonym of Cathy A. Small, a professor of anthropology at Northern Arizona University, who undertook anthropological fieldwork by becoming a freshman at NAU; she lived in a dorm, completed coursework, and joined student organizations. In the summer of 2005 the *Chronicle of Higher Education* ran several pieces on the book before it was published, though her actual identity was never revealed. These pieces raised questions about the ethics of her work, which, she maintains, strictly adhered to anthropological standards of behavior and research. Traditionally, university press books such as Nathan's do not gain much attention outside the academy and have a very narrow market of readers. A book like Nathan's might be read by other anthropologists and possibly be assigned in a class before disappearing into the library stacks, but because of her interesting findings, the accessibility of the book's writing, and the intrigue about her identity, *My Freshman Year* attracted much attention. One unwelcome side effect of the attention was that Nathan's identity was uncovered – by the *New York Post*.

CHEATING. IF YOU BELIEVE THAT CHEATING IS SIMPLY A manifestation of individual morality, then the current data on student behavior lead to the conclusion that the majority of today's youth are amoral at best. The national literature is consistent and undeniable. College students cheat. At least half engage in serious cheating, more than two-thirds admit to cheating on a test, and more than three-quarters have cheated in some capacity.[1]

But looking at cheating as an individual character issue disregards the role of undergraduate culture. Although cheating has increased slightly, particularly in some key areas, it has figured prominently in all the years academics have measured it. In 1963 a national study determined that 81 percent of college students had engaged in some form of dishonest academic behavior; in 1993 the percentage was 83 percent. Cheating was an active part of classic college culture of the nineteenth and twentieth centuries and remains so in the twenty-first, as schools across the country report high levels of academic dishonesty.

In these excerpts from an on-line article, one can hear the contemporary tone regarding cheating. The article, "How to Master Test-Taking — Without Technically Cheating," makes clear that at least some forms of academic dishonesty in college culture are literally nothing to be ashamed of:

> Now this, understandably, is a bit of a thorny issue. Some parts will depend on your definition of cheating, other parts on whether you care if you cheat. And others still will depend on how great the lengths you'll go to in order not to get caught. But the key to the whole thing is understanding this: Practically every single class you'll take has already been taken by someone else. Think about what that potentially means. Besides, cheating is kind of like traveling in basketball or stealing signs in baseball — everybody does it.

The article goes on to advise, among other things, that students should locate others who have taken the course before and solicit copies of their old tests or their memories about test questions. "If none of this will fly," the author concludes, "good luck doing things the old-fashioned way. Your halo will arrive with your diploma, six to eight weeks after graduation."[2]

Cheating is a fascinating subject, because, from a student's as opposed to a teacher's vantage point, it has many subtleties and complexities. As the article suggests, cheating is like "stealing signs in baseball" — practically part of the game. It's really not that bad a thing, everyone knows you do it, and sometimes it is too much to your disadvantage not to do it.

Evidence from national studies suggests that an increasing number of students question whether certain behavior — such as getting questions from former students, as the article advises — qualify as cheating. Twenty-one percent of students nationally said they didn't consider copying from another student on a test or exam to be a serious cheating offense. Even more students questioned the seriousness of using crib notes (23 percent), helping someone else cheat on a test (28 percent), and plagiarism (31 percent).[3]

I did not collect data on the frequency of cheating or admitted cheating, but I did ask fellow students about the idea of cheating. Like students across the country, most who spoke with me were well aware that cheating is rampant in college life. In studies, as many as 90 percent of college students reported seeing another student cheat in the previous year; the national average was 80 percent.[4]

Most students I questioned, though, did not support the general idea of cheating when it was understood as consistently gaining unfair advantage over classmates by engaging in dishonest academic behavior. At the same time, just as in national samples, they had serious questions about what really constitutes cheating and what does not. Isn't it OK to work on homework together? We don't have to cite other people's ideas on tests, so why is it cheating if we don't cite in papers? Is it really cheating to sign in a friend on an attendance roster? Moreover, the students recognized many circumstances that might justify a particular instance of cheating as well as gradations in behavior that would cause one to question the label of academic dishonesty.

In a posted query, I asked "(When) is it OK to cheat?" At least one-third of respondents said that it is never acceptable to cheat, but in response to the students who answered "never" were challenges like these:

> "Oh come on. Don't you think that everyone has cheated at least once?" — damn, no one is a saint."
>
> "Excuse me, but there are worse things to do than cheat on homework."
>
> "Haven't any of you ever looked over just to see if the other person had the same answer as you. Yes, sometimes it's just reassurance."

Well over half of the students who responded thought that in some way or other, it really depends.[5]

On what, then, does cheating depend? In a policy-focused study at one North Carolina university, students offered reasons that they thought should be taken into consideration in disciplining students caught cheating. These were: (1) performance pressure, (2) personal problems that made it difficult or impossible to study, (3) unrealistic expectations from instructors, and (4) meaningless or irrelevant assignments.

Many of the answers I received at AnyU regarding situational justifications for cheating fell into similar categories, and then some.[6] By far the largest number of responses were related to items (3), which I will modify to read "unrealistic or *unfair* expectations from instructors *or the university*," and (4). Here are some samples of AnyU student responses to the posted question "(When) is it OK to cheat?"

> "If you don't give a shit about the class but are required to take it and the info they are making you learn you know you won't ever use again."
>
> "If it's on-line. On-line courses suck."
>
> "When the info on the test/paper/homework is totally irrelevant!"
>
> "When it's a liberal studies class that has no relevance to your major."
>
> "If you studied but the test doesn't test what the instructor promised. As long as you learned the info, what's wrong with it?"
>
> "When it pertains to absences. I cheat on absent slips. We pay to come to college — they shouldn't make us sign in for any class!"

These responses are consistent with research across the country, which shows that students increasingly find cheating more acceptable and justifiable. Donald McCabe and the Center for Academic Integrity have conducted national studies of academic honesty for more than forty years. One of the most disturbing recent shifts, McCabe contends, is "the ease with which many of these students are able to justify or rationalize their cheating. And often they find a convenient way to place the 'blame' on others — other students who cheat; faculty who do a poor job in the classroom; institutions that don't try very hard to address the issue of cheating; and a society that supplies few positive role models when it comes to personal integrity."[7]

Although it is tempting to pin the reason for increased cheating on the character failings of students, I rely on a helpful concept that anthropologists employ when trying to understand other cultures: cultural relativism. In this view, the observer is entreated to withhold judgment and attempt to understand behaviors and customs within the framework of that culture's structures, values, and goals. In this way we avoid attributing realities that disturb us to evil people. In utilizing cultural relativism, I recite a mantra to myself: assume that people are alike (and overall decent) in their basic character. When trying to understand a strange or objectionable behavior, assume that you would do the same thing in that culture or those circumstances. Then explore why someone like you might behave as others behave.

Such an inquiry is aided, of course, by participant-observation research, and, indeed, I gained some added insight into student mindsets by walking in the shoes of a student. In one of my smaller classes I remember thinking how silly it was that another older student encircled her quiz papers with her arms so that those on either side couldn't see. In an act of unspoken solidarity with my classmates, who had become at least friendly acquaintances, I consciously left my test papers open to view. No one, to my knowledge, ever used them, but neither did I have any pressing interest in preventing it.

Although I never thought of myself as actually cheating (like many students on national surveys), there were two other incidents that would certainly qualify as such by national measures when I collaborated with another student on a homework problem or assignment that probably should have been done individually.

My own brief encounters with academic integrity convince me of 20 the inadequacy of published characterizations, which typically emphasize the more dramatic and negative findings in national studies. Cheating must be interpreted in its lived contexts, and when it is, it can be said that most of the time, most students don't cheat. Seventeen percent of students are habitual test cheaters (defined as three or more self-reported incidents),[8] a statistic that offers a very different picture of the student body from reports highlighting the 83 percent of students who admit engaging in some dishonest act.

Moreover, some cheating seems impelled not by moral laxity but by competing cultural values, particularly those of classic college culture. While most students value honesty, they are reluctant to turn in another student for cheating (only 9 percent nationally say that they would) or turn down a classmate's request for help on the homework. The most frequent types of cheating include those that seem to value student mutual aid and reciprocity over scrupulousness: signing in a classmate for attendance; getting questions or answers from those who have taken a test; working on an assignment with others.[9]

Other examples of the most common forms of cheating involve buying time or cutting scholastic corners, such as making false excuses to gain extra time on tests or papers, adding phony bibliographic sources, and copying from a source into a paper without footnoting. While I can't condone many forms of academic dishonesty, selective cheating operates as one in a larger set of related behaviors that give students a measure of control over their lives and their time. In a sense, such practices must be understood as part of an overarching system that includes shaping schedules, taming professors, and limiting workload.

In the few instances when one can't handle a recalcitrant professor, or has overcommitted time to a paying job, or simply finds course demands to be "busywork" and unfair, then cheating offers an "out" — a way to save time and get the work done without sacrificing one's grade. Students nationwide cheat less as they move up in year, suggesting to me that as they become more skilled in manipulating the other elements of the system, their need to cheat dissipates.

In this light, increases in contemporary rates of cheating reflect not only students' personal ethics but also the shifting societal tides that churn the waters through which students navigate. Political forces, for instance, may determine tuition rates, which decide how many hours a student must work at a job, which affects the amount of time left for coursework, which in turn influences the extent to which cheating becomes a more attractive option.

Cheating, like other aspects of student culture, must be seen as entangled with other issues in the university environment and ultimately with the more telling questions, "What is the purpose of the university?" and "Who gets to go to college?" These larger forces affecting university life and hence the student experience must be figured into the equation not just of student cheating but of student culture.

NOTES

[1] McCabe, Donald L., and L. K. Trevino. 1996. "What We Know about Cheating in College: Longitudinal Trends and Recent Developments." *Change* 28, no. 1: 29–33.

[2] "How to Master Test-Taking — Without Technically Cheating." From an information website directed at college students, August 2002.

[3] McCabe, Donald L., 2000. Interview. "The New Research on Academic Integrity: The Success of 'Modified' Honor Codes." Asheville, N.C.: College Administration Publications. http://www.collegepubs.com/ref/SFX000515.shtml.

[4] North Carolina State University 2001. Academic Integrity at NC State University: Survey Results and Action Plan. Division of Undergraduate Affairs and Office of Student Conduct, October 16, 2000. http://www.ncsu.edu/undergrad_affairs/assessment/files/projects/acadint/academic_integrity_at_ncstate.pdf.

[5] Whitley, Bernard E., and Patricia Keith-Spiegel. 2002. *Academic Dishonesty: An Educator's Guide*. Mahwah, N.J.: Erlbaum Associates.

[6] I did not ask what should be taken into consideration in punishing students for cheating, and therefore elicited different answers. Students were asked when it was OK to cheat, and thus emphasized performance issues (such as "when you're failing") and money issues ("If I need extra funds, I write papers for money") but also the ease of cheating ("anytime you can't do the work yourself and know you won't get caught").

[7] McCabe, 2000. 5.

[8] Ibid.

[9] North Carolina State University 2001.

READING

1. Nathan opens her piece with a conditional ("if/then") statement: "If you believe that cheating is simply a manifestation of individual morality, then the current data on student behavior lead to the conclusion that the majority of today's youth are amoral at best." Does she support this conclusion in the text that follows? What evidence would you cite in support of your opinion?

2. Nathan does not conduct a comprehensive study on cheating, but she does speak personally with many student peers about it. What do these students say about cheating? How do they define it? When do they feel it is "OK to cheat"?

3. Rather than focus on character failure as a reason for cheating, Nathan introduces an anthropological concept: "cultural relativism." What is cultural relativism? How does it explain student cheating?

4. Nathan's piece moves back and forth, easily, from a fairly informal type of discourse to one that is much more academic. Find examples of both. How are they different? Would you feel comfortable enough with the latter to read the entire book? Why or why not?

5. Nathan has written a book that is largely for her academic peers, anthropology professors, but she is taking a very different approach to the topic of student cheating than might be expected from an academician. What strategies does she use to convince her audience that cheating might be more complex than they want to admit?

WRITING

1. Early in the excerpt, Nathan writes, "looking at cheating as an individual character issue disregards the role of undergraduate culture." Write a reflective essay or journal piece that defines the undergraduate culture at your college or university. What is there about this culture that might make it easy to cheat?

2. Nathan uses different types of data. She cites quantitative data collected by others and supplements it with qualitative data that she collected herself. Write a comparison and contrast essay that discusses the relative merits of both types of evidence. What types of audiences would be drawn to each? Given the topic and Nathan's goal (to identify why students cheat), which is more effective for her work?

3. Without justifying cheating, Nathan – as an anthropologist – attempts to put it in a cultural context: "selective cheating operates as one in a larger set of related behaviors that give students a measure of control over their lives and their time." Write an essay that identifies other such behaviors, providing examples from your own life as a student. Why is this sense of control so important?

4. The excerpt contains a list of six student responses to the question, "(When) is it OK to cheat?" Form a group of at least three other students and have each member collect the responses of six students at your college to the same question. Analyze the resulting data and write up your research results, identifying the common threads in the responses. Does your research support Nathan's conclusions?

5. Both Nathan and Jason M. Stephens, in "Justice or Just Us? What to Do about Cheating" (p. 40), are writing to an academic audience: faculty members. On one level, the two writers use the same types of source material – data from studies about cheating, interviews with students, personal reflection. But these pieces evolve in different directions; they do not have the same tone toward students nor do they draw the same conclusions about why students cheat. Write an essay that compares the two works and discuss which, in your opinion, would be more acceptable to a faculty audience.

Psssst . . . What's the Answer?

By J. D. Heyman et al.

FROM: *People*, January 24, 2005

CONTEXT: This article first appeared in *People*, a celebrity-oriented publication of Time Inc. Feature articles in the magazine are usually researched by a team of reporters, similar to the group that compiled this piece ("et al." is Latin for "and others" and, in this case, the other authors are Frank Swertlow, Michaele Ballard, Steve Barnes, Tom Duffy, Lisa Gray, Jodi Mailander Farrell, Sharon Harvey-Rosenberg, Denise Pang, and Alicia Shepherd). These reporters are assigned to research a topic, and just one or two in the team actually pull together the background research into an article. Such a collaborative approach permits a more widely sourced piece. In this case, the topic of cheating has been brought to the attention of *People* readers more accustomed to stories about stars because of the involvement of a Wal-Mart heiress. As you read the article, think about how the story of Elizabeth Paige Laurie serves as a contextual frame for the issue of cheating.

IF NOTHING ELSE, ELIZABETH PAIGE LAURIE LEARNED THIS at college: Wealth has its privileges. According to Elena Martinez, her freshman roommate at the University of Southern California, while other students studied, Laurie — an heiress to part of the $2.9 billion Wal-Mart fortune — hit Hollywood clubs, sat courtside at Lakers games, and hopped to the Caribbean in the family jet. "Paige would come home late, talking about all the celebrities she'd met," says Martinez, a student from rural Banning, California. "I saw her study maybe once or twice." Yet with a little help from her roomie, Laurie scored mostly A's and B's at USC and coasted to graduation with a communications degree in May 2004. According to Martinez, Laurie, twenty-three, paid her a total of about $20,000 to write her papers and help her prepare for tests, even after Martinez dropped out of school and moved back home. "I never got less than a B for her," Martinez, twenty-two, says. "What started as a favor became a lot more complicated."

But not that unusual. The USC scandal — which Laurie's family has not commented on and which is now under investigation by university authorities — is merely an egregious case of what some educators are calling an epidemic of cheating at colleges and high schools across the country. Pushed by pressures to succeed and armed with the latest technology, a growing number of today's students seem to feel less and less reluctant to borrow rather than create. Last January, students at Saratoga High School in California's Silicon Valley were caught using a high-tech device to steal a teacher's computer password and access tests and answers stored on a computer. In the fall of 2003, a female student at Salem High School in Salem, New Hampshire, was suspended for scanning report cards into a home computer system and changing the grades at a fee of $25 to $50 per report. In a 2002 campus survey of Texas A&M students, fully 80 percent admitted to cheating — a number that so shocked administrators they instituted a college-wide honor policy that flunks students for the first cheating offense and expels them for the second. "There's a lot more anxiety about getting ahead," says David Callahan, author of *The Cheating Culture*. "Here's the curious thing. Indicators of moral decline have stopped or been reversed on issues like drug use, teenage sexuality, and crime. Not on cheating."

Experts point to a constellation of contributing causes, from the premium placed on brand-name colleges to the example of Enron and the blurring of right and wrong when it comes to things like illegally downloading music from the Internet. "Young people have seen their parents cheat on income taxes, they've heard about coaches who lied on their résumés, they know major athletes who have taken drugs to perform better," says Gregory Cizek, a University of North Carolina at Chapel Hill assistant professor who has studied the phenomenon. "There certainly isn't the stigma there once was." Nor do students today necessarily share their parents' definitions of what belongs to whom. Got homework? Outsource it! "These kids don't think of information as property," says Marcia Hilsabeck, a high school teacher from Round Rock, Texas. "They download music for free. They don't see anything wrong with downloading ideas."

In fact, downloading from the Internet is the most common form 5 that cheating takes today. University of Texas authorities report that half its plagiarism cases involve students lifting information from a website without crediting the source. Any student can simply Google the words "term paper" and find millions of sites offering essays on any subject. In an effort to combat the problem, educators at about nine hundred colleges and 3,200 high schools have turned to services like TurnItIn.com, which scans students' papers against 6 billion pages of archived documents. Evidence of copying shows up in seconds. At the University of Maryland last year, a group of instructors mounted a "techno sting," posting false answers to a 30-question accounting exam on a website. Twelve students were caught in the snare, including several who admitted using web-connected cell phones to access the site during the exam itself.

Although teachers are undoubtedly becoming more proficient at detecting it — "We started looking for students with one arm on the desk and one under it [using their cell phones]," reports Justin, Texas, high school principal Jim Chadwell — banning technology in the classroom can create its own problems. Post 9/11, many parents insist their children carry cell phones so they can be easily reached. Last March, Coral Springs High School senior Ebony Jones, eighteen, was flunked on a Florida state test required for graduation after she was found with a cell phone in her hand during an exam bathroom break. She claims she was merely turning the device off and had committed no offense. "They automatically assume you're cheating," says Jones. "Kids should be allowed to have cell phones — what if something goes wrong?" Jones's family protested the decision, but school officials insisted the senior retake the exam.

Faced with a problem that many educators feel powerless to reverse, Anita Cava, co-director of the University of Miami's Ethics Program, believes ethics should be taught as early as kindergarten and suggests that a bit of high-maintenance, hands-on teaching, such as requiring outlines and drafts in advance of term papers, can also help. "These steps actually inspire students to get engaged in the work," Cava says.

Of course, students willing to cheat to compete can always opt out of such courses — or as alleged in the case of Paige Laurie, simply hire someone to sit in for them. Elena Martinez, her former roommate turned accuser, says for three and a half years she "was reading her books and doing pretty much everything else for her," including impersonating Laurie in phone conversations with her professors. In response to the allegation, Laurie's family has maintained her academic records are "private." (*People* was unable to reach them despite repeated attempts.) As for Martinez, who hopes one day to get a communications degree, she says her conscience eventually got the best of her. "It was wrong," she says of the alleged cheating. "I had to be true to myself and do the right thing."

READING

1. Heyman et al. begin the piece with the story of Wal-Mart heiress Elizabeth Paige Laurie, who reportedly paid over $20,000 to her roommate for doing her academic coursework. Given the figures involved, this is not a typical example of college cheating. Why use it? How does it serve to jump-start the article? Does the context of this piece play a role in the selection of this example?

2. The authors cite a 2002 campus survey of Texas A&M students in which 80 percent admitted to cheating. Did this figure strike you as too high, too low, or just right based on your experiences in high school and college? Would your opinion change based on the definition of "cheating" the students used?

3. The article seems to assume a common definition of "plagiarism" is shared by its readers. Do you feel this is a valid assumption? For example, one of the article's sources, a high school teacher, is quoted as saying, "These kids don't think of information as property," which suggests this concept is a foundation of plagiarism. But if information is indeed property, why can't it be bought and sold? What issues complicate a simple definition of plagiarism?

4. This article was written by ten *People* journalists, but it is not an especially long piece. Why do you think so many different writers were involved? What aspects of the article reveal that it might be a collaborative effort?

5. The authors cite several possible reasons for the increase in cheating. What are they? Is any one reason more convincing than another? Why?

WRITING

1. One of the sources for the article is quoted as saying of cheating, "There certainly isn't the stigma there once was." Write a reflective essay or journal piece discussing the degree to which cheating is still stigmatized. Do you feel differently about friends or acquaintances who cheat? Does the fear of being stigmatized stop you from cheating?

2. The authors of this article use a number of directly quoted sources to document the widespread impact of cheating. Write an essay discussing these sources. What is their authority on the subject? Why do you feel they were selected? Do they serve to convince you that

cheating is a nationwide and educational system-wide problem? What voices seem to be missing from this piece?

3. The article suggests that cheating is on the rise for several reasons. Identify these reasons and, working with a group, write a follow-up article that suggests strategies to address them. The article should offer concrete ideas that would help teachers prevent and combat cheating.

4. The story of Elizabeth Paige Laurie that begins and ends this article "had legs," in journalism parlance. Laurie eventually relinquished her USC diploma, and the University of Missouri removed her name from a new stadium which was financed by her family. Write a researched essay that examines another high profile cheating scandal and the personal fallout for those involved.

5. The authors write, "Any student can simply Google the words 'term paper' and find millions of sites offering essays on any subject." The Focus on Genre section in this chapter (p. 56) contains several such sites. Write a critical review of one term paper site based on the observations made in this *People* article. For example, does the site suggest that faculty are not doing enough to craft engaging assignments? Do students feel too much pressure to get ahead? Be certain to support your analysis with concrete examples.

Justice or Just Us? What to Do about Cheating

By Jason M. Stephens

FROM: **Carnegie Foundation for the Advancement of Teaching, www.carnegiefoundation.org/perspectives/perspectives2004.May.htm**

CONTEXT: This piece initially appeared on the website for the Carnegie Foundation for the Advancement of Teaching as a "Carnegie Perspective," a series of articles encouraging faculty and administrators in higher education to think differently about teaching and learning. Each Carnegie Perspectives piece is accompanied by an online discussion board to continue the conversation. Jason M. Stephens was a research assistant at the Carnegie Foundation, where he worked on the Project on Higher Education and the Development of Moral and Civic Responsibility. He is currently a faculty member at the University of Connecticut. As you read this piece, consider his plea for us "to look for ways to make deep and searching honesty both palpable and attractive." Can you think of any ways you could encourage this viewpoint on your campus?

EARLIER THIS YEAR, LOCAL PAPERS WERE FULL OF HORRIFIED reports of cheating in an affluent Silicon Valley high school. Stories like this are a regular occurrence. Last year cheating at the University of Virginia made headlines, and before that, it was the military academies.

Adults always seem shocked and surprised to learn of cheating, especially in high-achieving and high-socioeconomic settings. They shouldn't be so surprised. Research on cheating has shown over and over that most students do cheat, at least some of the time. Research in high schools shows that two thirds of students cheat on tests, and 90 percent cheat on homework. The figures are almost as high among college students. Furthermore, it is clear that rates of cheating have gone up over the past three decades.

Why? Do students fail to understand that cheating is wrong? Well, yes and no. In a recent study of high school students that I conducted, many students acknowledged that cheating is wrong but admitted they do it anyway, seemingly without much remorse. Jane, a tenth-grade honors student, is typical of these students:

> Like people have morals, they don't always go by them. . . . So I mean, even if you get that test and you're like, "Oh yeah, I cheated on this test," it doesn't lessen that grade. It says an A on the paper and you don't go, "Oh, but I cheated." You're just kind of like, "Hey, I got that A." So it doesn't really matter necessarily, if it has to do with your morals or anything, you just kind of do it.

Like Jane, other students in the study said that they cheat for 5 simple, pragmatic reasons — to get high grades and because they don't have time to do the work carefully. Especially for college-bound students, the pressure for grades is real. According to the Higher Education Research Institute's annual survey, 47 percent of incoming college freshmen in 2003 reported having earned an A average in high school. As Jane put it:

> It's not always necessary (to cheat). I guess if you already have straight A's, then why cheat? But yet, we still seem to do it. It's kind of like insurance, like you feel better, you feel safer, if you do it. . . . Then I will have that 95 instead of like the 90, because that's almost like a B or something.

But despite the pressure for consistently high grades, students don't generally cheat in all of their classes. And somewhat surprisingly, it is not the difficulty of the course that predicts in which classes they are more likely to cheat. Instead, I found that high school students cheat more when they see the teacher as less fair and caring and when their motivation in the course is more focused on grades and less on learning and understanding. At least in these classes, they can justify cheating. They don't claim it is morally acceptable, but they don't seem to feel that it really matters if they cheat under these circumstances.

In most studies of cheating, the researcher decides which behaviors constitute cheating, and students are only asked to report how often they engage in those behaviors. In my survey of high school students, I asked them to report both their level of engagement in a set of twelve "academic behaviors," as well as their beliefs concerning whether or not those behaviors were "cheating." Not surprisingly, the vast majority (85 percent or more) indicated that behaviors such as "copying from another student during a test" and "using banned crib notes or cheat sheets during a test" were cheating. However, only 18 percent believed that "working on an assignment with other students when the teacher asked for individual work" was cheating. Subsequent interviews with a small subsample of these students revealed that students regarded this forbidden collaboration as furthering their knowledge and understanding, and therefore saw it as an act of learning rather than a form of cheating. These findings suggest that students make a distinction between behaviors that are overtly dishonest (such as copying the work of another, which effectively serves to misrepresent one's state of knowledge) and behaviors that are not inherently dishonest (such as working with others, which can serve to enrich one's interpersonal skills and academic learning). Educators, too, should be cognizant of this distinction and be judicious in prohibiting collaboration.

With this pervasiveness of acceptance by students, is it acceptable to us as a society to tacitly accept cheating as a fact of life and not be so shocked when it comes to light? I don't think so. Cutting corners and compromising principles are habit-forming. They don't stop at graduation, as we have seen in recent scandals in business and journalism. And cheating or cutting corners in one's professional or personal life can cause real damage — both to oneself and to others. We need to care about it.

And I believe we can do something about it. The best ways to re- 10 duce cheating are all about good teaching. In fact, if efforts to deal with cheating don't emerge from efforts to educate, they won't work — at least not when vigilance is reduced. These suggestions are easier said than done, but I believe they point in the right direction, both for academic integrity and for learning more generally.

- Help students understand the value of what they're being asked to learn by creating learning experiences that connect with their interests and have real-world relevance.

- Consider whether some of the rules that are frequently broken are arbitrary or unnecessarily constraining. For example, is individual effort on homework always so important? Given the evidence that collaboration in doing homework supports learning, it doesn't seem so.

- As much as possible, connect assessment integrally with learning. Create assessments that are fair and meaningful representations of what students should have learned. Make sure assessments provide informative feedback and thus contribute to improved performance. When possible, individualize evaluations of students' progress and offer them privately. Avoid practices that invite social comparisons of performance.

- Give students images of people who don't cut corners: scientists who discover things they don't expect because they approach their work with an impeccable respect for truth and a genuinely open mind; business people who exemplify integrity even when it seems like it might cost them something. But don't preach. Take seriously the fact that, in some contexts, being consistently honest can be hard.

Finally, as educators, we must do our best to exemplify intellec- 15 tual integrity ourselves — in everything from how we treat students and each other to how we approach the subject matter, to how we approach mandatory high stakes testing to how we think and talk about politics. We need to look for ways to make deep and searching honesty both palpable and attractive.

READING

1. Stephens opens his essay with evidence suggesting that most students cheat, yet cheating scandals are still news. Why? What is it about cheating that makes it newsworthy?

2. Stephens includes comments from one student, Jane, in his piece. Why does he quote her directly rather than summarizing her remarks? What does he gain by having us hear her voice?

3. According to Stephens, researchers frequently define collaborative work on assignments as cheating, but students do not. What influences this difference in opinion? How does Stephens feel about the topic?

4. Initially, the essay seems to be about why students cheat; but toward the end of the piece Stephens turns to his main point: teaching. How does Stephens link the quality of teaching to the willingness of students to cheat? Consider his audience. Why would he delay introducing this connection until close to the end of the piece?

5. Stephens offers four concrete suggestions for improving teaching to deter cheating. What are they? Do you think they would work? Have you participated in classes in which one or more of these practices was implemented?

WRITING

1. According to research cited by Stephens, 90 percent of high school students have cheated on homework. Write a reflective essay or a journal entry about a past situation in which you cheated or witnessed cheating. Was the rationale behind this situation the "simple, pragmatic reasons" discussed by Jane, the sophomore honors student, or other more complex ones?

2. This essay was first published on the Carnegie Foundation for the Advancement of Teaching website, whose audience is mainly administrators and instructors. Write an analysis of the piece discussing how it characterizes students. Pay careful attention to the descriptive language used and the comments from Jane. Do you feel the portrait of students is fair?

3. Along with others in this chapter, Stephens identifies the increase in high-stakes testing as an integral variable in the rise in cheating. Write a researched essay that explains the perceived benefits and

costs of such tests. Your goal is not to argue for one side or the other, simply to summarize the positions of both groups.

4. Stephens observes that cheating studies may not fully represent the picture of what Is happening in classrooms because teachers and students do not share a common definition of what acts constitute cheating. Working with a group of classmates, create a catalog of activities that constitute cheating. Conduct an anonymous survey of at least ten fellow students about whether they have ever engaged in these activities. Conduct a parallel survey of at least ten faculty members, asking them if they feel their students have participated in these cheating activities. Write a collaborative essay in which you discuss your findings. Do the responses of the two groups match? If they do not, why do you think they differ?

5. Stephens notes that students do not cheat in all their classes: "High school students cheat more when they see the teacher as less fair and caring." Interestingly, Paul Feldman (in Steven D. Levitt and Stephen J. Dubner's "What the Bagelman Saw" (p. 13) came to a similar conclusion about bagel thieves: "An office is more honest when the employees like their boss and their work." Write an essay that discusses the relationship between satisfaction/morale and the desire to cheat. Draw examples from both the essays mentioned and your own experience.

God's Little Toys: Confessions of a Cut and Paste Artist

By William Gibson

FROM: *Wired*, July 2005

CONTEXT: William Gibson's essay appeared first in *Wired*, a monthly magazine that identifies itself as "the first word on how technology is changing our world." *Wired* claims its advertising reaches "2.1 million connected and successful individuals" (www.whatsnextnow.com/publ_frmset.html). Gibson is one of the deans of postmodern science fiction, sometimes called "cyberpunk." He is the author of books, including *Neuromancer* (1986), *Virtual Light* (1993), and most recently *Pattern Recognition* (2003); he maintains an active blog on his website (www.williamgibsonbooks.com). Gibson's early works favored a "cut and paste" or jump-cut style, as the title of this essay suggests. As you read it, think about how technology (whether scissors and glue or a computer) affects creativity and originality. ("God's Little Toys" reprinted courtesy of William Gibson. *Wired* © 2005 Condé Nast Publications, Inc.)

WHEN I WAS THIRTEEN, IN 1961, I SURREPTITIOUSLY purchased an anthology of Beat writing — sensing, correctly, that my mother wouldn't approve.

Immediately, and to my very great excitement, I discovered Allen Ginsberg, Jack Kerouac, and one William S. Burroughs — author of something called *Naked Lunch*, excerpted there in all its coruscating brilliance.

Burroughs was then as radical a literary man as the world had to offer, and in my opinion, he still holds the title. Nothing, in all my experience of literature since, has ever been quite as remarkable for me, and nothing has ever had as strong an effect on my sense of the sheer possibilities of writing.

Later, attempting to understand this impact, I discovered that Burroughs had incorporated snippets of other writers' texts into his work, an action I knew my teachers would have called plagiarism. Some of these borrowings had been lifted from American science fiction of the '40s and '50s, adding a secondary shock of recognition for me.

By then I knew that this "cut-up method," as Burroughs called it, 5 was central to whatever it was he thought he was doing, and that he quite literally believed it to be akin to magic. When he wrote about his process, the hairs on my neck stood up, so palpable was the excitement. Experiments with audiotape inspired him in a similar vein: "God's little toy," his friend Brion Gysin called their reel-to-reel machine.

Sampling Burroughs was interrogating the universe with scissors and a paste pot, and the least imitative of authors was no plagiarist at all.

Some twenty years later, when our paths finally crossed, I asked Burroughs whether he was writing on a computer yet. "What would I want a computer for?" he asked, with evident distaste. "I have a typewriter."

But I already knew that word processing was another of God's little toys, and that the scissors and paste pot were always there for me, on the desktop of my Apple IIc. Burroughs' methods, which had also worked for Picasso, Duchamp, and Godard, were built into the technology through which I now composed my own narratives. Everything I wrote, I believed instinctively, was to some extent collage. Meaning, ultimately, seemed a matter of adjacent data.

Thereafter, exploring possibilities of (so-called) cyberspace, I littered my narratives with references to one sort or another of collage: the AI in *Count Zero* that emulates Joseph Cornell, the assemblage environment constructed on the Bay Bridge in *Virtual Light*.

Meanwhile, in the early '70s in Jamaica, King Tubby and Lee 10 "Scratch" Perry, great visionaries, were deconstructing recorded music. Using astonishingly primitive predigital hardware, they created what they called versions. The recombinant nature of their means of production quickly spread to DJs in New York and London.

Our culture no longer bothers to use words like *appropriation* or *borrowing* to describe those very activities. Today's audience isn't listening at all — it's participating. Indeed, *audience* is as antique a term as *record*, the one archaically passive, the other archaically physical. The record, not the remix, is the anomaly today. The remix is the very nature of the digital.

Today, an endless, recombinant, and fundamentally social process generates countless hours of creative product (another antique term?). To say that this poses a threat to the record industry is simply comic. The record industry, though it may not know it yet, has gone the way of the record. Instead, the recombinant (the bootleg, the remix, the mash-up) has become the characteristic pivot at the turn of our two centuries.

We live at a peculiar juncture, one in which the record (an object) and the recombinant (a process) still, however briefly, coexist. But there seems little doubt as to the direction things are going. The recombinant is manifest in forms as diverse as Alan Moore's graphic novel *The League of Extraordinary Gentlemen*, machinima generated with game engines (*Quake, Doom, Halo*), the whole metastasized library of Dean Scream remixes, genre-warping fan fiction from the universes of *Star Trek* or *Buffy* or (more satisfying by far) both at once, the JarJar-less *Phantom Edit* (sound of an audience voting with its fingers), brand-hybrid athletic shoes, gleefully transgressive logo jumping, and products like Kubrick figures, those Japanese collectibles that slyly masquerade as soulless corporate units yet are rescued from anonymity by the application of a thoughtfully aggressive "custom" paint job.

We seldom legislate new technologies into being. They emerge, and we plunge with them into whatever vortices of change they generate. We legislate after the fact, in a perpetual game of catch-up, as best we can, while our new technologies redefine us — as surely and perhaps as terribly as we've been redefined by broadcast television.

"Who owns the words?" asked a disembodied but very persistent voice throughout much of Burroughs' work. Who does own them now? Who owns the music and the rest of our culture? We do. All of us.

Though not all of us know it — yet.

READING

1. Gibson opens his essay with the memory of his discovery of the Beat writers. You may be unfamiliar with these writers but still may be able to infer something about them from his comment, "my mother wouldn't approve." What information about the Beat writers and about the artists to follow is packed into this simple remark?

2. Gibson writes, "Burroughs had incorporated snippets of other writers' texts into his work, an action I knew my teachers would have called plagiarism." What definition of "plagiarism" is Gibson using here? Why does he not believe that Burroughs's actions constituted plagiarism?

3. In this essay, Gibson favors the remix over the record. How is he using these musical products as symbols to argue his case? Why might this argument appeal to the readers of *Wired*? Of Gibson's other works?

4. Gibson's thesis is encapsulated in his second to last paragraph. What is it? Why does he delay stating it until near the end of his piece? Is this approach effective?

5. The essay ends with an ominous single sentence. How do you read this sentence? Do you think the readers of Gibson's piece in its original context would feel themselves among those who "know it" or those who don't "know it – yet"? Why?

WRITING

1. Gibson writes of his "palpable" excitement at discovering the creative process used by William S. Burroughs. Write a reflective essay or journal entry in that you discuss a time when you felt a similar excitement of discovery. Did you feel inspired? If so, did you follow through on this inspiration?

2. In discussing our relationship with the ever-moving target of technology, Gibson observes, "our new technologies redefine us." Write a narrative piece that discusses how you have been "redefined" by a technological innovation.

3. In paragraph ten, Gibson introduces the term *recombinant*, which will play a critical role in his argument, but he does not explicitly define this term, which is most frequently used in science. Write an essay in which you define "recombinant" as it is used in Gibson's essay. Support your definition with examples from his piece and other contexts.

4. Gibson writes, "We live at a peculiar juncture, one in which the record (an object) and the recombinant (a process) still, however briefly, coexist." He provides several examples of this phenomenon. Identify another case in which the original and a recombinant coexist – for example, a song and a remix, a film and a parody, a television show and a fan fiction. Write a researched essay in which you compare the two, identifying the purpose served by the recombinant. Would you judge the recombinant as plagiarism?

5. Gibson's essay, though short, contains the names of many artists whose work he places far above plagiarism, though they might be accused of this crime by others. Like Gibson, Malcolm Gladwell, in "Something Borrowed" (p. 60), seems to believe that there are some aesthetic attributes of a "cut and paste" work that can put it above mere plagiarism. Write an essay that identifies these qualities, using the pieces by Gibson and Gladwell in support of your position. When is "borrowing" art and when is it simply plagiarism?

Rise of the Plagiosphere: How New Tools to Detect Plagiarism Could Induce Mass Writer's Block

By Ed Tenner

FROM: *Technology Review*, June 2005

CONTEXT: Edward Tenner is an independent scholar and an affiliate of the Center for Arts and Cultural Policy Studies at Princeton University. He is author of *Our Own Devices: Past and Future of Body Technology* (2003), and *Why Things Bite Back: Technology and the Revenge of Unintended Consequences* (1996). Tenner is also monthly columnist for *Technology Review*, in which this piece appeared. *Technology Review* is a publication of the Massachusetts Institute of Technology and the oldest technology magazine in the world. According to the magazine's website, "*Technology Review*'s mission is to promote the understanding of emerging technologies, and analyze their commercial, economic, social, and political impact on business and leaders. Our editorial is designed for today's business and technology leaders – CXOs, senior technologists, entrepreneurs, and venture capitalists, who are shaping markets and driving the global economy" (www.technologyreview.com). As you read this piece, think about the metaphors that Tenner uses throughout and how they frame the topic.

THE 1960s GAVE US, AMONG OTHER MIND-ALTERING IDEAS, A revolutionary new metaphor for our physical and chemical surroundings: the biosphere. But an even more momentous change is coming. Emerging technologies are causing a shift in our mental ecology, one that will turn our culture into the plagiosphere, a closing frontier of ideas.

The Apollo missions' photographs of Earth as a blue sphere helped win millions of people to the environmentalist view of the planet as a fragile and interdependent whole. The Russian geoscientist Vladimir Vernadsky had coined the word "biosphere" as early as 1926, and the Yale University biologist G. Evelyn Hutchinson had expanded on the theme of Earth as a system maintaining its own equilibrium. But as the German environmental scholar Wolfgang Sachs observed, our imaging systems also helped create a vision of the planet's surface as an object of rationalized control and management — a corporate and unromantic conclusion to humanity's voyages of discovery.

What NASA did to our conception of the planet, Web-based technologies are beginning to do to our understanding of our written thoughts. We look at our ideas with less wonder, and with a greater sense that others have already noted what we're seeing for the first time. The plagiosphere is arising from three movements: Web indexing, text matching, and paraphrase detection.

The first of these movements began with the invention of programs called Web crawlers, or spiders. Since the mid-1990s, they have been perusing the now billions of pages of Web content, indexing every significant word found, and making it possible for Web users to retrieve, free and in fractions of a second, pages with desired words and phrases.

The spiders' reach makes searching more efficient than most of 5 technology's wildest prophets imagined, but it can yield unwanted knowledge. The clever phrase a writer coins usually turns out to have been used for years, worldwide — used in good faith, because until recently the only way to investigate priority was in a few books of quotations. And in our accelerated age, even true uniqueness has been limited to fifteen minutes. Bons mots that once could have enjoyed a half-life of a season can decay overnight into clichés.

Still, the major search engines have their limits. Alone, they can check a phrase, perhaps a sentence, but not an extended document. And at least in their free versions, they generally do not produce results from proprietary databases like LexisNexis, Factiva, ProQuest, and other paid-subscription sites, or from free databases that dynamically generate pages only when a user submits a query. They also don't include most documents circulating as electronic manuscripts with no permanent Web address.

Enter text-comparison software. A small handful of entrepreneurs have developed programs that search the open Web and proprietary databases, as well as e-books, for suspicious matches. One of the most popular of these is Turnitin; inspired by journalism scandals such as the *New York Times*'s Jayson Blair case, its creators offer a version aimed at newspaper editors. Teachers can submit student papers electronically for comparison with these databases, including the retained texts of previously submitted papers. Those passages that bear resemblance to each other are noted with color highlighting in a double-pane view.

Two years ago I heard a speech by a New Jersey electronic librarian who had become an antiplagiarism specialist and consultant.

He observed that comparison programs were so thorough that they often flagged chance similarities between student papers and other documents. Consider, then, that Turnitin's spiders are adding 40 million pages from the public Web, plus 40,000 student papers, each day. Meanwhile Google plans to scan millions of library books — including many still under copyright — for its Print database. The number of co-incidental parallelisms between the various things that people write is bound to rise steadily.

A third technology will add yet more capacity to find similarities in writing. Artificial-intelligence researchers at MIT and other universities are developing techniques for identifying nonverbatim similarity between documents to make possible the detection of non-verbatim plagiarism. While the investigators may have in mind only cases of brazen paraphrase, a program of this kind can multiply the number of parallel passages severalfold.

Some universities are encouraging students to precheck their pa- 10
pers and drafts against the emerging plagiosphere. Perhaps publications will soon routinely screen submissions. The problem here is that while such rigorous and robust policing will no doubt reduce cheating, it may also give writers a sense of futility. The concept of the biosphere exposed our environmental fragility; the emergence of the plagiosphere perhaps represents our textual impasse. Copernicus may have deprived us of our centrality in the cosmos, and Darwin of our uniqueness in the biosphere, but at least they left us the illusion of the originality of our words. Soon that, too, will be gone.

READING

1. Tenner begins this essay by comparing his new metaphor for our "mental ecology," the "plagiosphere," with that for the physical ecology, the "biosphere." What links are we to draw between these two metaphors? How do the limits on our mental and physical ecologies differ? How are they similar?

2. Tenner writes, "We look at our ideas with less wonder, and with a greater sense that others have already noted what we're seeing for the first time." When was the last time you experienced "wonder" at an idea that you had? Did you ever learn that this thought was not original? If so, how did this make you feel?

3. As an example of plagiarism, Tenner cites the case of Jayson Blair at the *New York Times*. Look up this example on the Internet. How might the context of this piece influence Tenner's selection of this example? What were the consequences for Blair? For the *New York Times*?

4. Tenner discusses text-comparison software, such as that available from Turnitin.com. Have you ever used such software? Would you have concerns about submitting your papers to such a site, even if you thought they were original?

5. In his conclusion, Tenner refers to Copernicus and Darwin. Who are they? How do their discoveries relate to the "plagiosphere" and the death of originality? Why might these figures appeal to the anticipated audience for Tenner's article in *Technology Review*, where this article first appeared?

WRITING

1. Write a reflective essay or journal entry in which you discuss Tenner's metaphor of the plagiosphere. What does it mean to live in a world that is a "closing frontier of ideas" (which is itself a metaphor)?

2. Toward the end of his piece, Tenner observes, "The number of coincidental parallelisms between the various things that people write is bound to rise steadily." What is Tenner's attitude toward the antiplagiarism programs? Write an essay in which you support your point of view using evidence that illustrates Tenner's tone.

3. Tenner writes, "And in our accelerated age, even true uniqueness has been limited to fifteen minutes. Bons mots that once could have

enjoyed a half-life of a season can decay overnight into clichés." Write an essay in which you define a slang term that Is new to you using examples gathered solely from the Internet, paying special attention to blogs. How widespread is the use of this term or phrase that struck you as original and unique?

4. As plagiarism becomes more widespread, colleges and universities are increasingly using text-comparison software like that offered by Turnitin. Research the issues surrounding the use of such software and write a documented essay in which you argue for or against its use.

5. Though they are writing on essentially the same topic, Tenner's view of originality seems to differ markedly from William Gibson's in "God's Little Toys" (p. 46). Write an essay in which you compare Tenner's more restrictive world view to Gibson's more liberating one.

FOCUS ON GENRE

Websites

A Portfolio of Term Paper Websites

IN ONE OF OUR FAVORITE BAD/GOOD MOVIES, *GREASE II*, THE desperate-to-be-cool protagonist writes term papers for his classmates to make enough money to buy a beat-up motorcycle. Well, that was then, and this is now. Selling term papers is big business, and the ease of buying and downloading papers from the Internet has made it an even bigger business. As the authors of "Psssst . . . What's the Answer" observe, "Any student can simply Google the words 'term paper' and find millions of sites offering essays on any subject" (p. 36). On such sites, term papers are just another commodity: something to be sold. And, as the sites proliferate, they increasingly stress standard commercial selling points: price, turn-around time, and product quality. However, unlike a site selling clothes, books, or cosmetics, term paper websites must walk a thin line because purchasing this product might be perceived as unethical and could even end a college career.

We have annotated the website for one term paper vendor to demonstrate how it balances the need to sell the product with the need to make a student feel good about purchasing the paper. We do not recommend buying a term paper ever, but we definitely do not recommend Term Paper TERMINAL because it is a purely fictional site. Ironically, getting permission from the term paper sites to use their materials in this book was quite difficult, so we supplemented our portfolio with a site designed by a graphic artist in the manner of the dozens of sites out there. In this case, imitation may or may not be the sincerest form of flattery. Following this annotated site, you will find similar sites for your analysis and discussion.

Flight metaphor used throughout.

Image: oppressive to impressive ... plus, you look like you are doing all the work.

None of this is your fault; you're a victim of circumstance.

What does this mean?

Note the slam at competitors.

Your key concerns are clearly identified.

Sold like any product – it's got more than its competitors.

Note how they sell their staff as professional.

What is the definition of plagiarized here?

What happened to the "quality research help"?

Term Paper TERMINAL

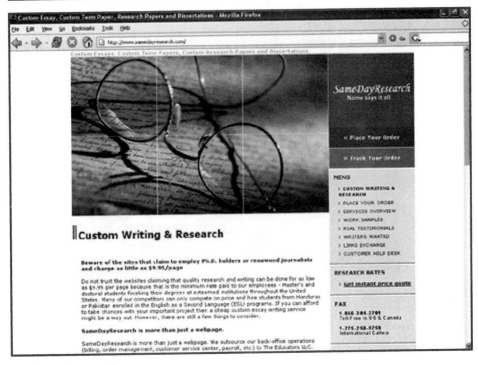

Same Day Research

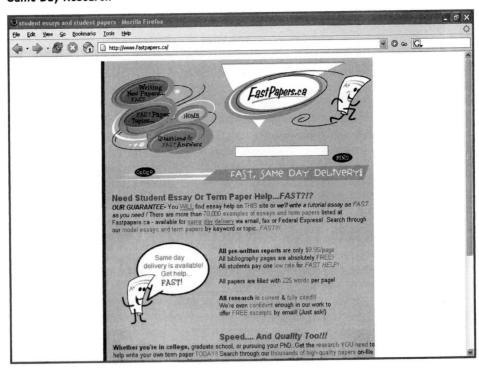

Fast Papers

RESPONDING

1. Each site contains a standard set of appeals: to emotion, to logic, to authority. Identify an example of each type of appeal. Which of the sites is most appealing to you? Why?

2. Although elements of each site clearly suggest that students will simply turn in the purchased paper, each also includes a disclaimer that insists the paper is to be used for research purposes only. What aspects of the sites hint that students may simply be purchasing papers for submission, not for research? What can you infer about the status of the disclaimer based upon its location, size, and color?

3. Some sites stress that they offer "non-plagiarized" papers. What does "non-plagiarized" mean in this context? If you were to submit one of these papers, would it be "non-plagiarized" according to your college's conduct code?

4. Marcia Hilsabeck, in "Psssst . . . What's the Answer?" is quoted as saying, "These kids don't think of information as property" (p. 36). At base, these websites are selling a product that, once purchased, becomes your property. If you were to purchase a paper from one of these sites and use it for research as suggested, would you feel any ethical dilemma about reselling this paper to another student? Why or why not? Do you think the owners of the site would approve of such a sale?

READING DEEPLY

Something Borrowed

By Malcolm Gladwell

FROM: *The New Yorker*, November 22, 2004

THE FOLLOWING ESSAY WAS WRITTEN BY MALCOLM GLADWELL FOR the prestigious magazine *The New Yorker*. According to its website, "Since 1925, *The New Yorker*'s mission has been to report and reflect on the world at large with wit, sophistication, and originality. Its distinctive coverage of culture and art, fiction and non, business and politics, science and technology, has earned *The New Yorker* a singular place in the national consciousness – and more National Magazine Awards than any other publication" (www.newyorker.com).

Gladwell has been a staff writer for *The New Yorker* since 1996. He is most famous, however, for his two influential books: *The Tipping Point: How Little Things Can Make a Big Difference* (2000) and *Blink: The Power of Thinking Without Thinking* (2005). In this essay, Gladwell traces the concept of plagiarism and his experience with being a plagiarized writer himself. He also explores the relationship between copying and creating and suggests that these two things are inextricably linked.

To help you read more deeply and critically, we have provided annotations and boldfaced some terms or passages that call attention to rhetorical choices Gladwell has made in his essay. With his trademark thoughtful and original thinking, he guides the reader toward a new view of plagiarism. ("Something Borrowed" © Malcolm Gladwell. Reprinted with permission. *The New Yorker* © 2004 Condé Nast Publications, Inc.)

Born in 1947 and raised in Dewsbury, UK, Lavery has written over 40 plays. *Frozen* (1998) was nominated for 4 Tony Awards, and *Playbill* reported in 2004 that the play may be made into a film. Her latest play is *A Wedding Story* (2000).

Gladwell stresses Lewis's background as a recognized expert so that we will understand the importance that her ideas have within the field of psychiatry. Her publications are featured in the *Journal of the American Academy of Psychiatry and the Law*.

ONE DAY THIS SPRING, A PSYCHIATRIST NAMED DOROTHY Lewis got a call from her friend Betty, who works in New York City. Betty had just seen a Broadway play called *Frozen*, written by the **British playwright Bryony Lavery.** "She said, 'Somehow it reminded me of you. You really ought to see it,'" Lewis recalled. Lewis asked Betty what the play was about, and Betty said that one of the characters was a psychiatrist who studied serial killers. "And I told her, 'I need to see that as much as I need to go to the moon.'"

Lewis has studied serial killers for the past twenty-five years. With her collaborator, the neurologist Jonathan Pincus, **she has published a great many research papers, showing that serial killers tend to suffer from predictable patterns of psychological, physical, and neurological dysfunction:** that they were almost all the victims of harrowing physical and sexual abuse as children, and that almost all of them have suffered some kind of brain injury or mental illness. In 1998, she published a memoir of her life and work entitled *Guilty by Reason of Insanity*. She was the last person to visit Ted Bundy before he went to the electric chair. Few people in the world have spent as much time thinking about serial killers as Dorothy Lewis, so when her friend Betty told her that she needed to see *Frozen* it struck her as **a busman's holiday**.

But the calls kept coming. *Frozen* was winning raves on Broadway, and it had been nominated for a Tony. Whenever someone who knew Dorothy Lewis saw it, they would tell her that she really ought

This phrase is very important in this context. *The American Heritage Dictionary* defines busman's holiday as "a vacation during which one engages in an activity that is similar to one's usual work." In this case, it is studying serial killers and then going to a play about them.

Notice how Gladwell helps us feel that we are there talking to Lewis. After introducing us to her through a story, he tells us how she went gladly and innocently to the play. By making her very real to us, we can sympathize with her reaction to the situation.

to see it, too. In June, she got a call from a woman at the theatre where *Frozen* was playing. "She said she'd heard that I work in this field, and that I see murderers, and she was wondering if I would do a talk-back after the show," Lewis said. **"I had done that once before, and it was a delight, so I said sure.** And I said, would you please send me the script, because I wanted to read the play."

The script came, and Lewis sat down to read it. Early in the play, something caught her eye, a phrase: "it was one of those days." One of the murderers Lewis had written about in her book had used that same expression. But she thought it was just a coincidence. "Then, there's a scene of a woman on an airplane, typing away to her friend. Her name is Agnetha Gottmundsdottir. I read that she's writing to her colleague, a neurologist called David Nabkus. And with that I realized that more was going on, and I realized as well why all these people had been telling me to see the play."

Lewis began underlining line after line. She had worked at New York University School of Medicine. The psychiatrist in *Frozen* worked at New York School of Medicine. Lewis and Pincus did a study of brain injuries among fifteen death-row inmates. Gottmundsdottir and Nabkus did a study of brain injuries among fifteen death-row inmates. Once, while Lewis was examining the serial killer Joseph Franklin, he sniffed her, in a grotesque, sexual way. Gottmundsdottir is sniffed by the play's serial killer, Ralph. Once, while Lewis was examining Ted Bundy, she kissed him on the cheek. Gottmundsdottir,

The similarities between her life and the play build until she realizes the playwright has used her ideas and her life in *Frozen*. Gladwell lets her speak directly to us about how she felt "robbed" and "violated." He is setting us up to feel sympathy for her, which will influence our attitude toward the apparent plagiarism.

in some productions of *Frozen,* kisses Ralph. "The whole thing was right there," Lewis went on. "I was sitting at home reading the play, and I realized that it was I. I felt robbed and violated in some peculiar way. It was as if someone had stolen — I don't believe in the soul, but, **if there was such a thing, it was as if someone had stolen my essence.**"

Lewis never did the talk-back. She hired a lawyer. And she came down from New Haven to see *Frozen*. "In my book," she said, "I talk about where I rush out of the house with my black carry-on, and I have two black pocketbooks, and the play opens with her" — Agnetha — "with one big black bag and a carry-on, rushing out to do a lecture." Lewis had written about biting her sister on the stomach as a child. Onstage, Agnetha fantasized out loud about attacking a stewardess on an airplane and "biting out her throat." After the play was over, the cast came onstage and took questions from the audience. "Somebody in the audience said, 'Where did Bryony Lavery get the idea for the psychiatrist?'" Lewis recounted. "And one of the cast members, the male lead, said, 'Oh, she said that she read it in an English medical magazine.'" **Lewis is a tiny woman, with enormous, childlike eyes, and they were wide open now with the memory.** "I wouldn't have cared if she did a play about a shrink who's interested in the frontal lobe and the limbic system. That's out there to do. I see things week after week on television, on *Law & Order* or *C.S.I.,* and I see that they are using material that Jonathan and I brought to light. And it's wonderful. That would have been acceptable. But

By describing Lewis so vividly, we can see her as the traumatized victim, "a tiny woman, with enormous, childlike eyes."

> This quotation again emphasizes that she felt "violated" – a very powerful word. Gladwell elects to have her voice her feelings directly, again underscoring the potentially harmful effects of plagiarism.

> Notice the shift in focus from Lewis to Gladwell, taking us to a new development in the story. Here we see not only how Gladwell's *New Yorker* profile influenced the playwright but that he too has been victimized.

she did more than that. **She took things about my own life, and that is the part that made me feel violated."**

At the request of her lawyer, Lewis sat down and made up a chart detailing what she felt were the questionable parts of Lavery's play. The chart was fifteen pages long. The first part was devoted to thematic similarities between *Frozen* and Lewis's book *Guilty by Reason of Insanity*. The other, more damning section listed twelve instances of almost verbatim similarities — totalling perhaps six hundred and seventy-five words — between passages from *Frozen* and passages from a 1997 magazine profile of Lewis. The profile was called *Damaged*. It appeared in the February 24, 1997, issue of *The New Yorker*. **It was written by me.**

Words belong to the person who wrote them. There are few simpler ethical notions than this one, particularly as society directs more and more energy and resources toward the creation of intellectual property. In the past thirty years, copyright laws have been strengthened. Courts have become more willing to grant intellectual-property protections. Fighting piracy has become an obsession with Hollywood and the recording industry, and, in the worlds of academia and publishing, plagiarism has gone from being bad literary manners to something much closer to a crime. When, two years ago, Doris Kearns Goodwin was found to have lifted passages from several other historians, she was asked to resign from the board of the Pulitzer Prize

> This is the first sentence that actually speaks directly about the concept of plagiarism and intellectual property. Gladwell is setting up his working definitions of the concepts at play in the essay and begins to ground them in sources outside the essay.

Gladwell begins to use "I" consistently in this section of the piece, personalizing the story. Now, it is no longer Dorothy Lewis's work that is in question; it is his own.

committee. And why not? If she had robbed a bank, she would have been fired the next day.

I'd worked on *Damaged* through the fall of 1996. I would visit Dorothy Lewis in her office at Bellevue Hospital, and watch the videotapes of her interviews with serial killers. At one point, I met up with her in Missouri. Lewis was testifying at the trial of Joseph Franklin, who claims responsibility for shooting, among others, the civil-rights leader Vernon Jordan and the pornographer Larry Flynt. In the trial, a videotape was shown of an interview that Franklin once gave to a television station. He was asked whether he felt any remorse. I wrote:

> "I can't say that I do," he said. He paused again, then added, "The only thing I'm sorry about is that it's not legal."
> "What's not legal?"
> Franklin answered as if he'd been asked the time of day: "Killing Jews."

That exchange, almost to the word, was reproduced in *Frozen*.

Lewis, the article continued, didn't feel that Franklin was fully responsible for his actions. She viewed him as a victim of neurological dysfunction and childhood physical abuse. **"The difference between a crime of evil and a crime of illness," I wrote, "is the difference between a sin and a symptom."** That line was in *Frozen*, too — not once but twice. I faxed Bryony Lavery a letter:

It is now so much more Gladwell's story than Lewis's that he is quoting himself. And he finds that his own writing is being used in the play without permission. Notice the quote he pulls as evidence of the violation. His fax to Lavery shows that initially, he sees her plagiarism as a crime.

65

> But now his tone begins to change significantly. He doesn't feel robbed after all. And because Lavery didn't even try to hide what she was borrowing, he thinks that perhaps she wasn't clever enough.

I am happy to be the source of inspiration for other writers, and had you asked for my permission to quote — even liberally — from my piece, I would have been delighted to oblige. But to lift material, without my approval, is theft.

Almost as soon as I'd sent the letter, though, I began to have second thoughts. **The truth was that, although I said I'd been robbed, I didn't feel that way.** Nor did I feel particularly angry. One of the first things I had said to a friend after hearing about the echoes of my article in *Frozen* was that this was the only way I was ever going to get to Broadway — and I was only half joking. On some level, I considered Lavery's borrowing to be a compliment. A savvier writer would have changed all those references to Lewis, and rewritten the quotes from me, so that their origin was no longer recognizable. But how would I have been better off if Lavery had disguised the source of her inspiration?

Dorothy Lewis, for her part, was understandably upset. She was considering a lawsuit. And, to increase her odds of success, she asked me to assign her the copyright to my article. I agreed, but then I changed my mind. Lewis had told me that she "wanted her life back." **Yet in order to get her life back, it appeared, she first had to acquire it from me.** That seemed a little strange.

Then I got a copy of the script for *Frozen*. I found it breathtaking. I realize that this isn't supposed to be a relevant consideration. And yet it was: instead of feeling that my words had been taken from me,

> The question of whose words belong to whom has gotten more complicated and ambiguous. We would think that he would be siding unilaterally with Lewis, but as we soon see, this is not the case. Although he, too, has been plagiarized he begins to think about the complexities involved.

Gladwell reads Lavery's play for the first time and finds it "breathtaking." This aesthetic concept will be quite important later in the essay: the notion that one can take the words of another in service of a "grander cause."

I felt that they had become part of some grander cause. In late September, the story broke. The *Times*, the *Observer* in England, and the Associated Press all ran stories about Lavery's alleged plagiarism, and the articles were picked up by newspapers around the world. Bryony Lavery had seen one of my articles, responded to what she read, and used it as she constructed a work of art. And now her reputation was in tatters. Something about that didn't seem right.

In 1992, the Beastie Boys released a song called "Pass the Mic," which begins with a six-second sample taken from the 1976 composition *Choir*, by the jazz flutist James Newton. The sample was an exercise in what is called multiphonics, where the flutist "overblows" into the instrument while simultaneously singing in a falsetto. In the case of *Choir*, Newton played a C on the flute, then sang C, D-flat, C — and the distortion of the overblown C, combined with his vocalizing, created a surprisingly complex and haunting sound. In "Pass the Mic," the Beastie Boys repeated the Newton sample more than forty times. The effect was riveting.

In the world of music, copyrighted works fall into two categories — the recorded performance and the composition underlying that performance. If you write a rap song, and want to sample the chorus from Billy Joel's "Piano Man," you first have to get permission from the record label to use the "Piano Man" recording, and then get permission from Billy Joel (or whoever owns his music) to use the

Notice the abrupt shift from the literary world to the world of music; there is no transition between the paragraph above and this one. The essay really falls into three distinct parts: Lewis's story, Gladwell's story, and now Gladwell's thinking process about "borrowing."

Gladwell's example shows the difficulty, legally, of defining originality and ownership. That the Beastie Boys won the case without obtaining Newton's permission underscores the complexity of the issue.

underlying composition. **In the case of "Pass the Mic," the Beastie Boys got the first kind of permission — the rights to use the recording of** *Choir* **— but not the second. Newton sued, and he lost** — and the reason he lost serves as a useful introduction to how to think about intellectual property.

At issue in the case wasn't the distinctiveness of Newton's performance. The Beastie Boys, everyone agreed, had properly licensed Newton's performance when they paid the copyright recording fee. And there was no question about whether they had copied the underlying music to the sample. At issue was simply whether the Beastie Boys were required to ask for that secondary permission: was the composition underneath those six seconds so distinctive and original that Newton could be said to own it? The court said that it wasn't.

The chief expert witness for the Beastie Boys in the *Choir* case was Lawrence Ferrara, who is a professor of music at New York University, and when I asked him to explain the court's ruling he walked over to the piano in the corner of his office and played those three notes: C, D-flat, C. "That's it!" he shouted. "There ain't nothing else! That's what was used. You know what this is? **It's no more than a mordent, a turn.** It's been done thousands upon thousands of times. No one can say they own that."

Ferrara then played the most famous four-note sequence in classical music, the opening of Beethoven's Fifth: G, G, G, E-flat. This was unmistakably Beethoven. But was it original? "That's a harder case,"

Gladwell's friend uses a vocabulary that suggests he is an expert on the subject. Mordent: "A series of two or more grace notes played before the principal note." *Virginia Tech Multimedia Music Dictionary*. www.music.vt.edu/musicdictionary/.

Ferrara said. "Actually, though, other composers wrote that. Beethoven himself wrote that in a piano sonata, and you can find figures like that in composers who predate Beethoven. It's one thing if you're talking about *da-da-da dummm, da-da-da dummm* — those notes, with those durations. But just the four pitches, G, G, G, E-flat? Nobody owns those."

Ferrara once served as an expert witness for Andrew Lloyd Webber, who was being sued by Ray Repp, a composer of Catholic folk music. Repp said that the opening few bars of Lloyd Webber's 1984 "Phantom Song," from *The Phantom of the Opera*, bore an overwhelming resemblance to his composition "Till You," written six years earlier, in 1978. As Ferrara told the story, he sat down at the piano again and played the beginning of both songs, one after the other; sure enough, they sounded strikingly similar. "Here's Lloyd Webber," he said, calling out each note as he played it. "Here's Repp. Same sequence. The only difference is that Andrew writes a perfect fourth and Repp writes a sixth."

But Ferrara wasn't quite finished. "I said, let me have everything Andrew Lloyd Webber wrote prior to 1978 — *Jesus Christ Superstar, Joseph, Evita*. He combed through every score, and in *Joseph and the Amazing Technicolor Dreamcoat* he found what he was looking for. "It's the song 'Benjamin Calypso.'" Ferrara started playing it. It was immediately familiar. "It's the first phrase of 'Phantom Song.' It's even using the same notes. But wait — it gets better. Here's 'Close Every

> Again Gladwell paints a portrait for us of the subject he is interviewing – the expert witness, professor of music at New York University. This description helps us to "be there" with Gladwell.

Door,' from a 1969 concert performance of *Joseph*." **Ferrara is a dapper, animated man, with a thin, well-manicured mustache, and thinking about the Lloyd Webber case was almost enough to make him jump up and down.** He began to play again. It was the second phrase of "Phantom." "The first half of 'Phantom' is in 'Benjamin Calypso.' The second half is in 'Close Every Door.' They are identical. On the button. In the case of the first theme, in fact, 'Benjamin Calypso' is closer to the first half of the theme at issue than the plaintiff's song. Lloyd Webber writes something in 1984, and he borrows from himself."

In the *Choir* case, the Beastie Boys' copying didn't amount to theft because it was too trivial. In the "Phantom" case, what Lloyd Webber was alleged to have copied didn't amount to theft because the material in question wasn't original to his accuser. Under copyright law, what matters is not that you copied someone else's work. What matters is *what* you copied, and *how much* you copied. Intellectual-property doctrine isn't a straightforward application of the ethical principle "Thou shalt not steal." At its core is the notion that there are certain situations where you *can* steal. The protections of copyright, for instance, are time-limited; once something passes into the public domain, anyone can copy it without restriction. Or suppose that you invented a cure for breast cancer in your basement lab. **Any patent you received would protect your intellectual property for twenty years, but after that anyone could take your invention.**

> Here the writer invites us to think with him about the ambiguity of owning an idea. Clearly, stealing intellectual property is not simple theft, as we were encouraged to think at the beginning of the essay. Patents, for example, have time limits.

To show us how embedded this idea is in our American culture, Gladwell quotes the Constitution as evidence of time limits to "Writings and Discoveries." His example also suggests that the issues surrounding plagiarism and the theft of intellectual property are long-standing.

You get an initial monopoly on your creation because we want to provide economic incentives for people to invent things like cancer drugs. But everyone gets to steal your breast-cancer cure — after a decent interval — because it is also in society's interest to let as many people as possible copy your invention; only then can others learn from it, and build on it, and come up with better and cheaper alternatives. This balance between the protecting and the limiting of intellectual property is, in fact, enshrined in **the Constitution: "Congress shall have the power to promote the Progress of Science and useful Arts, by securing for limited"** — note that specification, *limited* — **"Times to Authors and Inventors the exclusive Right to their respective Writings and Discoveries."**

So is it true that words belong to the person who wrote them, just as other kinds of property belong to their owners? Actually, no. As the **Stanford law professor Lawrence Lessig argues in his new book** *Free Culture*:

> In ordinary language, to call a copyright a "property" right is a bit misleading, for the property of copyright is an odd kind of property. . . . I understand what I am taking when I take the picnic table you put in your backyard. I am taking a thing, the picnic table, and after I take it, you don't have it. But what am I taking when I take the good idea you had to put a picnic table in the backyard — by, for example, going to Sears, buying a

A "Stanford law professor" is another credible source in his investigation of the many perspectives of plagiarism and the ownership of words.

table, and putting it in my backyard? What is the thing that I am taking then? The point is not just about the thingness of picnic tables versus ideas, though that is an important difference. The point instead is that in the ordinary case — indeed, in practically every case except for a narrow range of exceptions — ideas released to the world are free. I don't take anything from you when I copy the way you dress — though I might seem weird if I do it every day. . . . Instead, as Thomas Jefferson said (and this is especially true when I copy the way someone dresses), "He who receives an idea from me, receives instruction himself without lessening mine; as he who lights his taper at mine, receives light without darkening me."

Lessig argues that, when it comes to drawing this line between private interests and public interests in intellectual property, the courts and Congress have, in recent years, swung much too far in the direction of private interests. He writes, for instance, about the fight by some developing countries to get access to inexpensive versions of Western drugs through what is called "parallel importation" — buying drugs from another developing country that has been licensed to produce patented medicines. The move would save countless lives. But it has been opposed by the United States not on the ground that it would cut into the profits of Western pharmaceutical companies (they don't sell that many patented drugs in developing countries anyway) but on the ground that it violates the sanctity of intellectual property. "We as a culture have lost this sense of balance," Lessig writes. **"A certain property fundamentalism, having no connection to our tradition, now reigns in this culture."**

> Gladwell introduces a new concept, "property fundamental-ism," which has a negative connotation, according to Lessig. The sympathetic tone that opened the article has definitely shifted. Somehow this fundamentalism "reigns" like a king; this offers a contrast to the democratic concepts quoted from the Constitution, above.

Even what Lessig decries as intellectual-property extremism, however, acknowledges that intellectual property has its limits. The United States didn't say that developing countries could never get access to cheap versions of American drugs. It said only that they would have to wait until the patents on those drugs expired. The arguments that Lessig has with the hard-core proponents of intellectual property are almost all arguments about *where* and *when* the line should be drawn between the right to copy and the right to protection from copying, not *whether* a line should be drawn.

But plagiarism is different, and that's what's so strange about it. The ethical rules that govern when it's acceptable for one writer to copy another are even more extreme than the most extreme position of the intellectual-property crowd: when it comes to literature, we have somehow decided that copying is *never* acceptable. Not long ago, the **Harvard law professor Laurence Tribe was accused of lifting material from the historian Henry Abraham for his 1985 book,** ***God Save This Honorable Court.*** What did the charge amount to? In an exposé that appeared in the conservative publication *The Weekly Standard*, Joseph Bottum produced a number of examples of close paraphrasing, but his smoking gun was this one borrowed sentence: "Taft publicly pronounced Pitney to be a 'weak member' of the Court to whom he could not assign cases." That's it. Nineteen words.

Not long after I learned about *Frozen*, I went to see a friend of

> Now he cites an example of a strictly interpreted case of plagiarism, which further reinforces the idea that intellectual property has limits. Perhaps in our eagerness to protect what we believe to be ours, we have taken the concept of plagiarism too far.

Gladwell moves the discussion of plagiarism to a more local level. Even though his article appeared in *The New Yorker*, it is unlikely that most of his readers will have seen *Frozen*. However, most will be able to hum at least some of these songs, especially given the wide range of examples.

mine who works in the music industry. **We sat in his living room on the Upper East Side, facing each other in easy chairs, as he worked his way through a mountain of CDs.** He played "Angel," by the reggae singer Shaggy, and then "The Joker," by the Steve Miller Band, and told me to listen very carefully to the similarity in bass lines. He played Led Zeppelin's "Whole Lotta Love" and then Muddy Waters's "You Need Love," to show the extent to which Led Zeppelin had mined the blues for inspiration. He played "Twice My Age," by Shabba Ranks and Krystal, and then the saccharine seventies pop standard "Seasons in the Sun," until I could hear the echoes of the second song in the first. He played "Last Christmas," by Wham!, followed by Barry Manilow's "Can't Smile Without You" to explain why Manilow might have been startled when he first heard that song, and then "Joanna," by Kool and the Gang, because, in a different way, "Last Christmas" was an homage to Kool and the Gang as well. "That sound you hear in Nirvana," my friend said at one point, "that soft and then loud, kind of exploding thing, a lot of that was inspired by the Pixies. Yet Kurt Cobain" — Nirvana's lead singer and songwriter — "was such a genius that he managed to make it his own. And 'Smells Like Teen Spirit'?" — here he was referring to perhaps the best-known Nirvana song. "That's Boston's 'More Than a Feeling.'" He began to hum the riff of the Boston hit, and said, "The first time I heard 'Teen Spirit,' I said, 'That guitar lick is from "More Than a Feeling."' But it was different — it was urgent and brilliant and new."

He played another CD. It was Rod Stewart's "Do Ya Think I'm Sexy," a huge hit from the nineteen-seventies. The chorus has a distinctive, catchy hook — the kind of tune that millions of Americans probably hummed in the shower the year it came out. Then he put on "Taj Mahal," by the Brazilian artist Jorge Ben Jor, which was recorded several years before the Rod Stewart song. In his twenties, my friend was a d.j. at various downtown clubs, and at some point he'd become interested in world music. "I caught it back then," he said. A small, sly smile spread across his face. The opening bars of "Taj Mahal" were very South American, a world away from what we had just listened to. And then I heard it. It was so obvious and unambiguous that I laughed out loud; virtually note for note, it was the hook from "Do Ya Think I'm Sexy." It was possible that Rod Stewart had independently come up with that riff, because resemblance is not proof of influence. It was also possible that he'd been in Brazil, listened to some local music, and liked what he heard.

My friend had hundreds of these examples. We could have sat in his living room playing at musical genealogy for hours. Did the examples upset him? **Of course not, because he knew enough about music to know that these patterns of influence — cribbing, tweaking, transforming — were at the very heart of the creative process.** True, copying could go too far. There were times when one artist was simply replicating the work of another, and to let that pass inhibited true creativity. But it was equally dangerous to be

A new idea emerges in the pattern of his thought – borrowing is essential to the creative process.

> Gladwell's use of the term "policing" calls back to the earlier notion of "property fundamentalism" – again underscoring that a simplistic interpretation of plagiarism may be wrong and harmful.

overly vigilant in policing creative expression, because if Led Zeppelin hadn't been free to mine the blues for inspiration we wouldn't have got "Whole Lotta Love," and if Kurt Cobain couldn't listen to "More Than a Feeling" and pick out and transform the part he really liked we wouldn't have "Smells Like Teen Spirit" — and, in the evolution of rock, "Smells Like Teen Spirit" was a real step forward from "More Than a Feeling." A successful music executive has to understand the distinction between borrowing that is transformative and borrowing that is merely derivative, and that distinction, I realized, was what was missing from the discussion of Bryony Lavery's borrowings. Yes, she had copied my work. But no one was asking why she had copied it, or what she had copied, or whether her copying served some larger purpose.

Bryony Lavery came to see me in early October. It was a beautiful Saturday afternoon, and we met at my apartment. **She is in her fifties, with short tousled blond hair and pale-blue eyes, and was wearing jeans and a loose green shirt and clogs. There was something rugged and raw about her.** In the *Times* the previous day, the theatre critic Ben Brantley had not been kind to her new play, *Last Easter*. This was supposed to be her moment of triumph. *Frozen* had been nominated for a Tony. *Last Easter* had opened Off Broadway. And now? She sat down heavily at my kitchen table. "I've had the absolute gamut of emotions," she said, playing

> With the mention of Bryony Lavery we have come full circle. We move into the closing sections of the essay's structure. Again, Gladwell sets the stage. This time we see the portrait of the playwright whose play began this discussion: She is not a faceless thief; she is a real person.

Her description of her own method of writing seems to be the kind of "cribbing, tweaking, transforming" that he referred to earlier as "the heart of the creative process."

nervously with her hands as she spoke, as if she needed a cigarette. "I think when one's working, one works between absolute confidence and absolute doubt, and I got a huge dollop of each. I was terribly confident that I could write well after *Frozen*, and then this opened a chasm of doubt." She looked up at me. "I'm terribly sorry," she said.

Lavery began to explain: "What happens when I write is that I find that I'm somehow zoning on a number of things. **I find that I've cut things out of newspapers because the story or something in them is interesting to me, and seems to me to have a place on-stage. Then it starts coagulating. It's like the soup starts thickening.** And then a story, which is also a structure, starts emerging. I'd been reading thrillers like *The Silence of the Lambs*, about fiendishly clever serial killers. I'd also seen a documentary of the victims of the Yorkshire killers, Myra Hindley and Ian Brady, who were called the Moors Murderers. They spirited away several children. It seemed to me that killing somehow wasn't fiendishly clever. It was the opposite of clever. It was as banal and stupid and destructive as it could be. There are these interviews with the survivors, and what struck me was that they appeared to be frozen in time. And one of them said, 'If that man was out now, I'm a forgiving man but I couldn't forgive him. I'd kill him.' That's in *Frozen*. I was thinking about that. Then my mother went into hospital for a very simple operation, and the surgeon punctured her womb, and therefore her intestine, and she got peritonitis and died."

Again we are invited to sympathize with the person he is interviewing. What might otherwise be a philosophical meditation on plagiarism is made into a very personal affair.

When Lavery started talking about her mother, she stopped, and had to collect herself. "She was seventy-four, and what occurred to me is that I utterly forgave him. I thought it was an honest mistake. I'm very sorry it happened to my mother, but it's an honest mistake." Lavery's feelings confused her, though, because she could think of people in her own life whom she had held grudges against for years, for the most trivial of reasons. "In a lot of ways, 'Frozen' was an attempt to understand the nature of forgiveness," she said.

Lavery settled, in the end, on a play with three characters. The first is a serial killer named Ralph, who kidnaps and murders a young girl. The second is the murdered girl's mother, Nancy. The third is a psychiatrist from New York, Agnetha, who goes to England to examine Ralph. In the course of the play, the three lives slowly intersect — and the characters gradually change and become "unfrozen" as they come to terms with the idea of forgiveness. For the character of Ralph, Lavery says that she drew on a book about a serial killer titled *The Murder of Childhood*, by Ray Wyre and Tim Tate. For the character of Nancy, she drew on an article written in the *Guardian* by a woman named Marian Partington, whose sister had been murdered by the serial killers Frederick and Rosemary West. And, for the character of Agnetha, Lavery drew on a reprint of my article that she had read in a British publication. "I wanted a scientist who would understand," Lavery said — a scientist who could explain how it was possible to forgive a man who had killed your daughter, who could explain that a se-

> Lavery confesses that she thought she could use his words, copy from him—that his writing was called *news*, part of the public domain. As this section goes on, a gap opens between the factual domain and the creative one.

rial killing was not a crime of evil but a crime of illness. "I wanted it to be *accurate*," she added.

So why didn't she credit me and Lewis? How could she have been so meticulous about accuracy but not about attribution? Lavery didn't have an answer. **"I thought it was O.K. to use it," she said with an embarrassed shrug. "It never occurred to me to ask you. I thought it was *news*."**

She was aware of how hopelessly inadequate that sounded, and when she went on to say that my article had been in a big folder of source material that she had used in the writing of the play, and that the folder had got lost during the play's initial run, in Birmingham, she was aware of how inadequate that sounded, too.

But then Lavery began to talk about Marian Partington, her other important inspiration, and her story became more complicated. While she was writing *Frozen*, Lavery said, she wrote to Partington to inform her of how much she was relying on Partington's experiences. And when *Frozen* opened in London, she and Partington met and talked. In reading through articles on Lavery in the British press, I found this, from the *Guardian* two years ago, long before the accusations of plagiarism surfaced:

> Lavery is aware of the debt she owes to Partington's writing and is eager to acknowledge it.
>
> "I always mention it, because I am aware of the enormous debt that I owe to the generosity of Marian Partington's piece. . . . You have to be

> Again, he invites the reader to consider just how subtle these distinctions can be – and this time at his own expense.

hugely careful when writing something like this, because it touches on people's shattered lives and you wouldn't want them to come across it unawares."

Lavery wasn't indifferent to other people's intellectual property, then; she was just indifferent to my intellectual property. That's because, in her eyes, what she took from me was different. It was, as she put it, "news." She copied my description of Dorothy Lewis's collaborator, Jonathan Pincus, conducting a neurological examination. She copied the description of the disruptive neurological effects of prolonged periods of high stress. She copied my transcription of the television interview with Franklin. She reproduced a quote that I had taken from a study of abused children, and she copied a quotation from Lewis on the nature of evil. **She didn't copy my musings, or conclusions, or structure.** She lifted sentences like "It is the function of the cortex — and, in particular, those parts of the cortex beneath the forehead, known as the frontal lobes — to modify the impulses that surge up from within the brain, to provide judgment, to organize behavior and decision-making, to learn and adhere to rules of everyday life." It is difficult to have pride of authorship in a sentence like that. My guess is that it's a reworked version of something I read in a textbook. Lavery knew that failing to credit Partington would have been wrong. Borrowing the personal story of a woman whose sister was murdered by a serial killer matters because that story has real emotional value to its owner.

> It appears that he is not offended and does not feel "stolen" from because she didn't copy the parts of his writing that were originally his – his "musings, or conclusions, or structure" – what he created.

Another point in Lavery's favor seems to be that she did not use his work to write another piece like his—a profile. She wrote a play. This raises a thorny question. When is one work derivative of another? The Chilling Effects Clearinghouse cites the change in definition of "derivative" in the copyright statute: "Congress revised the federal copyright statute in 1976 to provide copyright owners with statutory protection for derivative works. A derivative work can take the form of any . . . work [that] may be recast, *transformed*, or adapted. A work consisting of editorial revisions, annotations, elaborations, or other modifications which, as a whole, represents an original work of authorship, is a 'derivative work.'" www.chillingeffects.org/derivative/faq.cgi.

As Lavery put it, it touches on someone's shattered life. Are boiler-plate descriptions of physiological functions in the same league?

It also matters *how* Lavery chose to use my words. Borrowing crosses the line when it is used for **a derivative work.** It's one thing if you're writing a history of the Kennedys, like Doris Kearns Goodwin, and borrow, without attribution, from another history of the Kennedys. But Lavery wasn't writing another profile of Dorothy Lewis. She was writing a play about something entirely new — about what would happen if a mother met the man who killed her daughter. And she used my descriptions of Lewis's work and the outline of Lewis's life as a building block in making that confrontation plausible. Isn't that the way creativity is supposed to work? **Old words in the service of a new idea aren't the problem. What inhibits creativity is new words in the service of an old idea.**

And this is the second problem with plagiarism. It is not merely extremist. It has also become disconnected from the broader question of what does and does not inhibit creativity. We accept the right of one writer to engage in a full-scale knockoff of another — think how many serial-killer novels have been cloned from *The Silence of the Lambs*. Yet, when Kathy Acker incorporated parts of a Harold Robbins sex scene verbatim in a satiric novel, she was denounced as a plagiarist (and threatened with a lawsuit). **When I worked at a newspaper, we were routinely dispatched to "match" a story from the *Times*: to do a new version of someone else's idea.** But had we "matched" any of the

He cites his experience as a newspaperman to make the distinction between copying an idea and copying words. It also suggests that news falls into the category of facts, which are noncreative and thus outside the bounds of plagiarism.

He returns to the point he made earlier—the importance of not hampering the creative process with hypervigilance.

Times's words — even the most banal of phrases — it could have been a firing offense. The ethics of plagiarism have turned into the narcissism of small differences: because journalism cannot own up to its heavily derivative nature, it must enforce originality on the level of the sentence.

Dorothy Lewis says that one of the things that hurt her most about *Frozen* was that Agnetha turns out to have had an affair with her collaborator, David Nabkus. Lewis feared that people would think she had had an affair with her collaborator, Jonathan Pincus. "That's slander," Lewis told me. "I'm recognizable in that. Enough people have called me and said, 'Dorothy, it's about you,' and if everything up to that point is true, then the affair becomes true in the mind. So that is another reason that I feel violated. If you are going to take the life of somebody, and make them absolutely identifiable, you don't create an affair, and you certainly don't have that as a climax of the play."

It is easy to understand how shocking it must have been for Lewis to sit in the audience and see her "character" admit to that indiscretion. **But the truth is that Lavery has every right to create an affair for Agnetha, because Agnetha is not Dorothy Lewis. She is a fictional character, drawn from Lewis's life but endowed with a completely imaginary set of circumstances and actions.** In real life, Lewis kissed Ted Bundy on the cheek, and in some versions of *Frozen* Agnetha kisses Ralph. But Lewis kissed Bundy only because he kissed her first, and there's a big difference between responding to a kiss from a killer and initiating one. When we first see Agnetha, she's rushing

> Gladwell distinguishes between a work of fiction and real life: Agnetha is not the real woman, Dorothy Lewis, but a fictional character, existing only within the literary world of *Frozen*.

> Gladwell is clearly sympathetic to Lewis's sense of betrayal, but makes the point that art by nature changes real life, and though sometimes "unsettling," it is a necessary part of the creative process.

out of the house and thinking murderous thoughts on the airplane. Dorothy Lewis also charges out of her house and thinks murderous thoughts. But the dramatic function of that scene is to make us think, in that moment, that Agnetha is crazy. And the one inescapable fact about Lewis is that she is not crazy: she has helped get people to rethink their notions of criminality because of her unshakable command of herself and her work. **Lewis is upset not just about how Lavery copied her life story, in other words, but about how Lavery *changed* her life story. She's not merely upset about plagiarism. She's upset about art — about the use of old words in the service of a new idea — and her feelings are perfectly understandable, because the alterations of art can be every bit as unsettling and hurtful as the thievery of plagiarism. It's just that art is not a breach of ethics.**

When I read the original reviews of *Frozen*, I noticed that time and again critics would use, without attribution, some version of the sentence "The difference between a crime of evil and a crime of illness is the difference between a sin and a symptom." That's my phrase, of course. I wrote it. Lavery borrowed it from me, and now the critics were borrowing it from her. The plagiarist was being plagiarized. In this case, there is no "art" defense: nothing new was being done with that line. And this was not "news." Yet do I really own "sins and symptoms"? There is a quote by Gandhi, it turns out, using the same two words, and I'm sure that if I were to plow through the body of English literature I would find the path littered with crimes of evil and crimes of illness. The central fact

His closing statements are forceful. Perhaps the self-righteous indignation he was feeling at the beginning of this piece was misplaced. Gladwell helps us to see, upon closer examination, that plagiarism is a much more complicated problem than we thought. He seems to be urging us to be more charitable and generous with the ownership of our words, to consider the "chains of influence" in the creative process.

about the "Phantom" case is that Ray Repp, if he was borrowing from Andrew Lloyd Webber, certainly didn't realize it, and Andrew Lloyd Webber didn't realize that he was borrowing from himself. Creative property, Lessig reminds us, has many lives — the newspaper arrives at our door, it becomes part of the archive of human knowledge, then it wraps fish. And, by the time ideas pass into their third and fourth lives, we lose track of where they came from, and we lose control of where they are going. **The final dishonesty of the plagiarism fundamentalists is to encourage us to pretend that these chains of influence and evolution do not exist, and that a writer's words have a virgin birth and an eternal life.** I suppose that I could get upset about what happened to my words. I could also simply acknowledge that I had a good, long ride with that line — and let it go.

"It's been absolutely bloody, really, because it attacks my own notion of my character," Lavery said, sitting at my kitchen table. **A bouquet of flowers she had brought were on the counter behind her.** "It feels absolutely terrible. I've had to go through the pain for being careless. I'd like to repair what happened, and I don't know how to do that. I just didn't think I was doing the wrong thing . . . and then the article comes out in the New York *Times* and every continent in the world." There was a long silence. **She was heartbroken.** But, more than that, she was confused, because she didn't understand how six hundred and seventy-five **rather ordinary words** could bring the walls tumbling down. "It's been horrible and bloody." She began to cry. "I'm still composting what happened. It will be for a purpose . . . whatever that purpose is."

So, in the end, we are empathizing with the playwright, who was the villain at the beginning of the piece. He notes that she had brought him flowers. She is heartbroken.

Gladwell stresses the "ordinary" value of these words, not the "grander" quality he cites earlier. So was this true plagiarism? Gladwell — via his language, structure, and method — models his own thought process, bringing readers to a more complicated understanding of "Something Borrowed."

MAKING CONNECTIONS ACROSS AND BEYOND THE DISCIPLINES

1. Several of the pieces in this chapter suggest that the traditional definition of "cheating" in our culture is shifting. William Gibson and Malcolm Gladwell, both professional writers, seem to condone the borrowing of ideas as part of the creative process. Write a compare-and-contrast essay of "Something Borrowed" and "God's Little Toys: Confessions of a Cut and Paste Artist" in which you focus on the new definition of cheating that these two writers suggest is emerging and how this definition might change our concept of "originality."

2. In "Psssst . . . What's the Answer?" J. D. Heyman et al. comment that "indicators of moral decline have stopped or been reversed on issues like drug use, teenage sexuality, and crime. Not on cheating." Jason M. Stephens in his piece for the Carnegie Foundation, "Justice or Just Us? What to Do about Cheating" asks, "Why? Do students fail to understand that cheating is wrong?" With a small collaborative group devise a survey that explores attitudes on cheating on your campus. What constitutes cheating and what does not? How many students on your campus admit that they sometimes cheat? What are their reasons? Use examples from the pieces in this chapter, as well as your own research, to create your survey. Present the results to your class, putting them within the context of the ideas expressed in this chapter. Discuss what constitutes academic integrity on your campus and how you might discourage cheating at the college.

3. Many thinkers today, including several in this chapter, focus on the role technology plays on students' willingness to cheat and plagiarize. This school of thought suggests that cheating is encouraged by the ease with which students can download information from the Internet, buy essays from term-paper sites like those in the Focus on Genre section of this chapter (p. 56), use cell phones to text-message during tests, share files, hack into test databases, and so on. In other words, because it takes less and less effort to cheat, more and more students do it. Write a researched essay in which you explore emerging technologies and their influence on plagiarism.

The Changing Landscape of Family

Slava Veder, Burst of Joy, 1973

THE OPENING IMAGE FOR THIS CHAPTER IS A 1973 PULITZER Prize-winning photograph by Slava Veder, depicting the reunion of a prisoner of war with his family. This photo presents, in stark black and white, the ideal we have of family: the opened-arm welcome, the rush of emotion, the clear happiness and joy, the evocation of reunion and home. This family overcomes all adversity, weathers every storm, and stands strong. This family is traditional: married father and mother with children. This family does not exist.

Real families – including the one depicted in this photo – have always been much more complicated than a static two-dimensional image. And in the more than three decades since Veder took the photo, the family landscape has become even more complex and diverse. The nuclear family has exploded, leaving myriad permutations: single parents, same-sex parents, blended families, grandparents raising grandchildren, unmarried couples raising children. While the traditional family still persists and frequently thrives, it has been dramatically impacted by a host of social changes. What was nontraditional thirty years ago is fairly traditional today. Couples both marry and have children later. Mothers routinely work outside the home. Family members migrate apart for education, work, love, and adventure. If you were to survey your classmates, you would likely find as many images and expressions of family as there are students in the room.

This chapter asks you to consider the very definition of family from several vantage points. The very first selection in the chapter returns to and interprets the "ideal" family photo that opens this chapter. All the works that follow underscore the influence of our families from many perspectives. On the personal side, our language is full of aphorisms and clichés that capture this pull: The acorn never falls far from the tree. Chip off the old block. And more. Each hints at the shaping power of the family relationship. The metaphors associated with family, such as tie or bond, underscore its control. The authority vested in our families has even worked its way into political discourse, as when we speak of our "founding fathers." And as several of the pieces suggest, the shifting groundwork and ground rules of family have led to questions that are impacting not just personal decisions but also public policy. So, read on, and ask yourself, "What is a family, and why is it so important, anyway?"

Coming Home

By Carolyn Kleiner Butler

FROM: *Smithsonian*, January 2005

CONTEXT: This essay initially appeared in *Smithsonian* magazine, where it accompanied the photo that begins this chapter. It appeared as part of the magazine's "Indelible Images" feature, which focuses on an iconic historical photo, provides the background for the image, and updates readers on the events or individuals captured by the photo. *Smithsonian* describes itself as "a monthly magazine created for modern, well-rounded individuals with diverse interests," and all subscribers receive a complimentary membership to the Smithsonian Institution. Almost 80 percent of readers have attended college, 64 percent are between the ages of thirty-five and sixty-four, and they fall into the upper middle class in terms of income. Carolyn Kleiner Butler is a contributing editor to *U.S. News & World Report*, a magazine with a similar demographic. As you read this article, think about how the Vietnam War might have impacted the families of readers in the target demographic.

SITTING IN THE BACK SEAT OF A STATION WAGON ON THE tarmac at Travis Air Force Base, in California, clad in her favorite fuchsia miniskirt, fifteen-year-old Lorrie Stirm felt that she was in a dream. It was March 17, 1973, and it had been six long years since she had last seen her father, Lt. Col. Robert L. Stirm, an Air Force fighter pilot who was shot down over Hanoi in 1967 and had been missing or imprisoned ever since. She simply couldn't believe they were about to be reunited. The teenager waited while her father stood in front of a jubilant crowd and made a brief speech on behalf of himself and other POWs who had arrived from Vietnam as part of "Operation Homecoming."

The minutes crept by like hours, she recalls, and then, all at once, the car door opened. "I just wanted to get to Dad as fast as I could," Lorrie says. She tore down the runway toward him with open arms, her spirits — and feet — flying. Her mother, Loretta, and three younger siblings — Robert Jr., Roger, and Cindy — were only steps behind. "We didn't know if he would ever come home," Lorrie says. "That moment was all our prayers answered, all our wishes come true."

Associated Press photographer Slava "Sal" Veder, who'd been standing in a crowded bullpen with dozens of other journalists, noticed the sprinting family and started taking pictures. "You could feel the energy and the raw emotion in the air," says Veder, then forty-six, who had spent much of the Vietnam era covering antiwar demonstrations in San Francisco and Berkeley. The day was overcast, meaning no shadows and near-perfect light. He rushed to a makeshift darkroom in a ladies' bathroom on the base (United Press International had commandeered the men's). In less than half an hour, Veder and his AP colleague Walt Zeboski had developed six remarkable images of that singular moment. Veder's pick, which he instantly titled "Burst of Joy," was sent out over the news-service wires, published in newspapers around the nation and went on to win a Pulitzer Prize in 1974.

It remains the quintessential homecoming photograph of the time. Stirm, thirty-nine, who had endured gunshot wounds, torture, illness, starvation, and despair in North Vietnamese prison camps, including the infamous Hanoi Hilton, is pictured in a crisp new uniform. Because his back is to the camera, as Veder points out, the officer seems anonymous, an everyman who represented not only the hundreds of POWs released that spring but all the troops in Vietnam who would return home to the mothers, fathers, wives, daughters, and sons they'd left behind. "It's a hero's welcome for guys who weren't always seen or treated as heros," says Donald Goldstein, a retired Air Force lieutenant colonel and a coauthor of *The Vietnam War: The Stories and The Photographs*, of the Stirm family reunion picture. "After years of fighting a war we couldn't win, a war that tore us apart, it was finally over, and the country could start healing."

But there was more to the story than was captured on film. Three ₅ days before Stirm landed at Travis, a chaplain had handed him a Dear John letter from his wife. "I can't help but feel ambivalent about it," Stirm says today of the photograph. "I was very pleased to see my children — I loved them all and still do, and I know they had a difficult time — but there was a lot to deal with." Lorrie says, "So much had happened — there was so much that my dad missed out on — and it took a while to let him back into our lives and accept his authority." Her parents were divorced within a year of his return. Her mother remarried in 1974 and lives in Texas with her husband. Robert retired from the Air Force as a colonel in 1977 and worked as a corporate pilot and businessman. He married and was divorced again. Now seventy-two and retired, he lives in Foster City, California.

As for the rest of the family, Robert Jr. is a dentist in Walnut Creek, California; he and his wife have four children, the oldest of whom is a marine. Roger, a major in the Air Force, lives outside Seattle. Cindy Pierson, a waitress, resides in Walnut Creek with her husband and has a daughter in college. And Lorrie Stirm Kitching, now forty-seven, is an executive administrator and mother of two sons. She lives in Mountain View, California, with her husband. All four of Robert Stirm Sr.'s children have a copy of "Burst of Joy" hanging in a place of honor on their walls.

But he says he can't bring himself to display the picture. Three decades after the Stirm reunion, the scene, having appeared in countless books, anthologies, and exhibitions, remains part of the nation's collective consciousness, often serving as an uplifting postscript to Vietnam. That the moment was considerably more fraught than we first assumed makes it all the more poignant and reminds us that not all war casualties occur on the battlefield.

"We have this very nice picture of a very happy moment," Lorrie says, "but every time I look at it, I remember the families that weren't reunited, and the ones that aren't being reunited today — many, many families — and I think, I'm one of the lucky ones."

READING

1. Butler opens her piece with a portrait of Lorrie Stirm, who will play a significant role in the article. How does she position the reader to identify with Lorrie?

2. Butler mentions that the photographer, Slava Veder, spent most of his war career covering antiwar protests. Why is this information important? Consider the demographic of *Smithsonian* magazine. How might many of them have felt about the war?

3. Halfway through the essay, the tone changes significantly. Where does this occur? Who does the reader begin to hear from at this point? Who does the reader never hear from in the essay?

4. Butler lists the eventual paths that the lives of the Stirm family took. What does this catalog suggest about families today?

5. Lorrie Stirm says of the photo, "We have this very nice picture of a very happy moment." Today the photo is an iconic portrait of a family welcome, but what does Butler's piece suggest about any family photo? Think about your own family photos. What stories do these images reveal and conceal?

WRITING

1. Write a reflective essay or journal entry about the effects of absence on family relationships. Lorrie Stirm says of seeing her father after six years, "So much had happened — there was so much that my dad missed out on — and it took a while to let him back into our lives and accept his authority." Does absence make the heart grow fonder — or more forgetful?

2. According to Butler's research, only two of the Stirm family members still live in the same town, suggesting that — likely for many reasons — this once close family has fragmented over time. Is your family clustered closely together or has it moved apart? Write an essay that describes how distance impacts your family. Think about the network of relationships that connects family members; is it tight or loose? Is there a relationship between physical proximity and emotional connection?

3. Slava Veder says of the reunion that triggered this photo, "You could feel the energy and the raw emotion in the air." Write an essay in which you identify how Butler attempts to capture this energy and emotion in her short piece. Consider her diction, tone, and sources.

4. Find a family photo that seems to tell a story, one currently unknown to you. Interview those in the photo and the photographer, and record their versions of the story captured. From these interviews, construct an essay that relates the story behind the image. Integrate quotes from the interviews in your piece. As Butler does, provide your readers with an update on what the participants are doing today.

5. In the article "The American Family" (p. 94), Stephanie Coontz writes, "No particular family form guarantees success, and no particular form is doomed to fail. How a family functions on the inside is more important than how it looks from the outside." In the photo "Burst of Joy," the Stirms appeared to be the perfect family, but the inside story was quite different. Write a researched essay that tracks divorce rates among a population that would appear — from the outside — to have all it takes for marital success. You might select a specific religious group (for example, Mormons), anniversary date (for example, couples married twenty-five years or more), or other cohort (wealthy couples, celebrity couples). Your essay should explain your research methodology, document your results, and suggest some conclusions from your findings.

The American Family
By Stephanie Coontz

FROM: *Life*, November 1999

CONTEXT: This piece was originally published in *Life* magazine in November 1999. *Life* magazine was founded in 1936 and is known for its blend of traditional values and excellent photography. According to its media kit, the magazine "delivers over 27 million affluent, educated, action-oriented decision makers" to its advertisers. The median age of the readership is 48.4, the average household income is $67,908, and its readers are split almost equally between men and women. Stephanie Coontz is a professor at The Evergreen College in Washington State. She also has taught at universities in Hawaii and Japan and is a former Woodrow Wilson Fellow. She is the director of research and public education for the Council on Contemporary Families, which awarded her the first Visionary Leadership Award in 2004. Her book *Marriage, A History: From Obedience to Intimacy, or How Love Conquered Marriage* (2005) was selected as one of the best books of 2005 by the *Washington Post*. She has testified before the House Select Committee on Children, Youth, and Families; she speaks about family issues on national television – on CNN and on shows such as *Oprah* and the *Today* show. As you read this article, consider the data Coontz cites to argue that our contemporary families are in better shape than we think and how this is a particularly appropriate focus for *Life* magazine.

AS THE CENTURY COMES TO AN END, MANY OBSERVERS FEAR for the future of America's families. Our divorce rate is the highest in the world, and the percentage of unmarried women is significantly higher than in 1960. Educated women are having fewer babies, while immigrant children flood the schools, demanding to be taught in their native language. Harvard University reports that only 4 percent of its applicants can write a proper sentence. There's an epidemic of sexually transmitted diseases among men. Many streets in urban neighborhoods are littered with cocaine vials. Youths call heroin "happy dust." Even in small towns, people have easy access to addictive drugs, and drug abuse by middle-class wives is skyrocketing. Police see sixteen-year-old killers, twelve-year-old prostitutes, and gang members as young as eleven. America at the end of the 1990s? No, America at the end of the 1890s.

The litany of complaints may sound familiar, but the truth is that many things were worse at the start of this century than they are today. Then, thousands of children worked full-time in mines, mills, and sweatshops. Most workers labored ten hours a day, often six days a week, which left them little time or energy for family life. Race riots were more frequent and more deadly than those experienced by recent generations. Women couldn't vote, and their wages were so low that many turned to prostitution. In 1900 a white child had one chance in three of losing a brother or sister before age fifteen, and a black child had a fifty-fifty chance of seeing a sibling die. Children's-aid groups reported widespread abuse and neglect by parents. Men who deserted or divorced their wives rarely paid child support. And only 6 percent of the children graduated from high school, compared with 88 percent today.

Why do so many people think American families are facing worse problems now than in the past? Partly it's because we compare the complex and diverse families of the 1990s with the seemingly more standard-issue ones of the 1950s, a unique decade when every long-term trend of the twentieth century was temporarily reversed. In the 1950s, for the first time in 100 years, the divorce rate fell while marriage and fertility rates soared, creating a boom in nuclear-family living. The percentage of foreign-born individuals in the country decreased. And the debates over social and cultural issues that had divided Americans for 150 years were silenced, suggesting a national consensus on family values and norms.

Some nostalgia for the 1950s is understandable: Life looked pretty good in comparison with the hardships of the Great Depression and World War II. The GI Bill gave a generation of young fathers a college education and a subsidized mortgage on a new house. For the first time, a majority of men could support a family and buy a home without pooling their earnings with those of other family members. Many Americans built a stable family life on these foundations.

But much nostalgia for the 1950s is a result of selective amne- 5 sia — the same process that makes childhood memories of summer vacations grow sunnier with each passing year. The superficial sameness of 1950s family life was achieved through censorship, coercion, and discrimination. People with unconventional beliefs faced governmental investigation and arbitrary firings. African Americans and Mexican Americans were prevented from voting in some states by literacy tests that were not administered to whites. Individuals who didn't follow the rigid gender and sexual rules of the day were ostracized.

Leave It to Beaver did not reflect the real-life experience of most American families. While many moved into the middle class during the 1950s, poverty remained more widespread than in the worst of our last three recessions. More children went hungry, and poverty rates for the elderly were more than twice as high as today's. Even in the white middle class, not every woman was as serenely happy with her lot as June Cleaver was on TV. Housewives of the 1950s may have been less rushed than today's working mothers, but they were more likely to suffer anxiety and depression. In many states, women couldn't serve on juries or get loans or credit cards in their own names.

And not every kid was as wholesome as Beaver Cleaver, whose mischievous antics could be handled by Dad at the dinner table. In 1955 alone, Congress discussed 200 bills aimed at curbing juvenile delinquency. Three years later, *Life* reported that urban teachers were being terrorized by their students. The drugs that were so freely available in 1900 had been outlawed, but many children grew up in families ravaged by alcohol and barbiturate abuse.

Rates of unwed childbearing tripled between 1940 and 1958, but most Americans didn't notice because unwed mothers generally left town, gave their babies up for adoption, and returned home as if nothing had happened. Troubled youths were encouraged to drop out of high school. Mentally handicapped children were warehoused in institutions like the Home for Idiotic and Imbecilic Children in Kansas, where a woman whose sister had lived there for most of the 1950s once took me. Wives routinely told pollsters that being disparaged or ignored by their husbands was a normal part of a happier-than-average marriage. Denial extended to other areas of life as well. In the early 1900s doctors refused to believe that the cases of gonorrhea and syphilis they saw in young girls could have been caused by sexual abuse. Instead, they reasoned, girls could get these diseases from toilet seats, a myth that terrified generations of mothers and daughters. In the 1950s, psychiatrists dismissed incest reports as Oedipal fantasies on the part of children. Spousal rape was legal throughout the period, and wife beating was not taken seriously by authorities. Much of what we now label child abuse was accepted as a normal part of parental discipline. Physicians saw no reason to question parents who claimed that their child's broken bones had been caused by a fall from a tree. Things were worse at the turn of the last century than they are today. Most workers labored ten hours a day, six days a week, leaving little time for family life.

There are plenty of stresses in modern family life, but one reason they seem worse is that we no longer sweep them under the rug.

Another is that we have higher expectations of parenting and marriage. That's a good thing. We're right to be concerned about inattentive parents, conflicted marriages, antisocial values, teen violence, and child abuse. But we need to realize that many of our worries reflect how much better we want to be, not how much better we used to be.

Fathers in intact families are spending more time with their children than at any other point in the past 100 years. Although the number of hours the average woman spends at home with her children has declined since the early 1900s, there has been a decrease in the number of children per family and an increase in individual attention to each child. As a result, mothers today, including working moms, spend almost twice as much time with each child as mothers did in the 1920s. People who raised children in the 1940s and 1950s typically report that their own adult children and grandchildren communicate far better with their kids and spend more time helping with homework than they did — even as they complain that other parents today are doing a worse job than in the past.

Despite the rise in youth violence from the 1960s to the early 1900s, America's children are also safer now than they've ever been. An infant was four times more likely to die in the 1950s than today. A parent then was three times more likely than a modern one to preside at the funeral of a child under the age of fifteen, and 27 percent more likely to lose an older teen to death.

If we look back over the last millennium, we can see that families have always been diverse and in flux. In each period, families have solved one set of problems only to face a new array of challenges. What works for a family in one economic and cultural setting doesn't work for a family in another. What's helpful at one stage of a family's life may be destructive at the next stage. If there is one lesson to be drawn from the last millennium of family history, it's that families are always having to play catch-up with a changing world.

Many of our worries today reflect how much better we want to be, not how much better we used to be. Take the issue of working mothers. Families in which mothers spend as much time earning a living as they do raising children are nothing new. They were the norm throughout most of the last two millennia. In the nineteenth century, married women in the United States began a withdrawal from the workforce, but for most families this was made possible only by sending their children out to work instead. When child labor was abolished, married women began reentering the workforce in ever larger numbers.

For a few decades, the decline in child labor was greater than the growth of women's employment. The result was an aberration: the male breadwinner family. In the 1920s, for the first time a bare majority of American children grew up in families where the husband provided all the income, the wife stayed home full-time, and they and their siblings went to school instead of work. During the 1950s, almost two-thirds of children grew up in such families, an all-time high. Yet that same decade saw an acceleration of workforce participation by wives and mothers that soon made the dual-earner family the norm, a trend not likely to be reversed in the next century.

What's new is not that women make half their families' living, but 15 that for the first time they have substantial control over their own income, along with the social freedom to remain single or to leave an unsatisfactory marriage. Also new is the declining proportion of their lives that people devote to rearing children, both because they have fewer kids and because they are living longer. Until about 1940, the typical marriage was broken by the death of one partner within a few years after the last child left home.

Today, couples can look forward to spending more than two decades together after the children leave. The growing length of time partners spend with only each other for company has made many individuals less willing to put up with an unhappy marriage, while women's economic independence makes it less essential for them to do so. It is no wonder that divorce has risen steadily since 1900. Disregarding a spurt in 1946, a dip in the 1950s, and another peak around 1980, the divorce rate is just where you'd expect to find it, based on the rate of increase from 1900 to 1950. Today, 40 percent of all marriages will end in divorce before a couple's fortieth anniversary. Yet despite this high divorce rate, expanded life expectancies mean that more couples are reaching that anniversary than ever before. Families and individuals in contemporary America have more life choices than in the past. That makes it easier for some to consider dangerous or unpopular options. But it also makes success easier for many families that never would have had a chance before — interracial, gay or lesbian, and single-mother families, for example. And it expands horizons for most families.

Women's new options are good not just for themselves but for their children. While some people say that women who choose to work are selfish, it turns out that maternal self-sacrifice is not good for children. Kids do better when their mothers are happy with their lives, whether their satisfaction comes from being a full-time homemaker or from having a job.

Largely because of women's new roles at work, men are doing more at home. Although most men still do less housework than their wives, the gap has been halved since the 1960s. Today, 49 percent of couples say they share childcare equally, compared with 25 percent in 1985. The biggest problem is not that our families have changed too much but that our institutions have changed too little.

Men's greater involvement at home is good for their relationships with their partners and also good for their children. Hands-on fathers make better parents than men who let their wives do all the nurturing and childcare: They raise sons who are more expressive and daughters who are more likely to do well in school, especially in math and science.

In 1900, life expectancy was forty-seven years, and only 4 percent [20] of the population was sixty-five or older. Today, life expectancy is seventy-six years, and by 2025, about 20 percent of Americans will be sixty-five or older. For the first time, a generation of adults must plan for the needs of both their parents and their children. Most Americans are responding with remarkable grace. One in four households gives the equivalent of a full day a week or more in unpaid care to an aging relative, and more than half say they expect to do so in the next ten years. Older people are less likely to be impoverished or incapacitated by illness than in the past, and they have more opportunity to develop a relationship with their grandchildren.

Even some of the choices that worry us the most are turning out to be manageable. Divorce rates are likely to remain high, but more noncustodial parents are staying in touch with their children. Child-support receipts are up. And a lower proportion of kids from divorced families are exhibiting problems than in earlier decades. Stepfamilies are learning to maximize children's access to supportive adults rather than cutting them off from one side of the family. Out-of-wedlock births are also high, however, and this will probably continue because the age of first marriage for women has risen to an all-time high of twenty-five, almost five years above what it was in the 1900s. Women who marry at an older age are less likely to divorce, but they have more years when they are at risk — or at choice for a nonmarital birth.

Nevertheless, births to teenagers have fallen from 50 percent of all nonmarital births to just 30 percent today. A growing proportion of women who have a nonmarital birth are in their twenties and thirties and usually have more economic and educational resources than unwed mothers of the past. While two involved parents are generally better than one, a mother's personal maturity, along with her educational and economic status, is a better predictor of how well her child will turn out than her marital status. We should no longer assume that children raised by single parents face debilitating disadvantages.

As we begin to understand the range of sizes, shapes, and colors that today's families come in, we find that the differences within family types are more important than the differences between them. No particular family form guarantees success, and no particular form is doomed to fail. How a family functions on the inside is more important than how it looks from the outside.

The biggest problem facing most families as this century draws to a close is not that our families have changed too much but that our institutions have changed too little. America's work policies are fifty years out of date, designed for a time when most moms weren't in the workforce and most dads didn't understand the joys of being involved in childcare. Our school schedules are 150 years out of date, designed for a time when kids needed to be home to help with the milking and haying. And many political leaders feel they have to decide whether to help parents stay home longer with their kids or invest in better childcare, preschool, and afterschool programs, when most industrialized nations have long since learned it's possible to do both.

So America's social institutions have some Y2K bugs to iron out. 25 But for the most part, our families are ready for the next millennium.

READING

1. Coontz opens her article with a description of families that sounds alarming. How does this introduction hook the reader into reconsidering the data that follow about today's families?

2. What kind of historical detail does Coontz use to draw her negative picture of the family at the turn of the century? Are these examples effective? Which ones surprised you?

3. After the introduction, Coontz asks this question, which will provide the impetus for the rest of the essay: "Why do so many people think American families are facing worse problems now than in the past?" What are some of the answers that occurred to you before you read the rest of her essay? Do you agree that this is an important question to address?

4. Coontz states that much of the nostalgia for the idealized 1950s family "was achieved through censorship, coercion, and discrimination." Discuss the connotation of these words and the resulting shift in the tone of the essay.

5. In the end, Coontz supplies us with examples that demonstrate many positive aspects of family life today. What particular aspects of contemporary family life does she address? Are you convinced by her data concerning today's families? Why or why not?

WRITING

1. "The American Family" rests on the assumption that most of us believe modern families are in trouble and that we need to be convinced otherwise. Write a reflective essay or a journal piece in which you describe both the positive and negative aspects of your own family.

2. According to Coontz, the nuclear family is a recent invention. Write a short expository essay in which you compare and contrast the post-World War II idealized vision of the nuclear family and the negative underpinnings that Coontz catalogs.

3. Coontz states, "In 1955 alone, Congress discussed 200 bills aimed at curbing juvenile delinquency. Three years later, *Life* reported that urban teachers were being terrorized by their students." Write a researched essay in which you investigate these data. Define "juvenile delinquency." See if you can find any of the actual bills that were proposed. Investigate *Life*'s story on the terrorizing of urban

teachers. In your conclusions evaluate Coontz's argument in terms of the information you discovered.

4. Coontz refers to a television show that idealized the nuclear family: *Leave It to Beaver*, and two of the characters, June Cleaver and Beaver Cleaver. Go onto the Internet and see what information you can find out about this show and others of its kind. Write a report in which you summarize the characters and their personalities in *Leave It to Beaver* and at least one other television show depicting the family of that time.

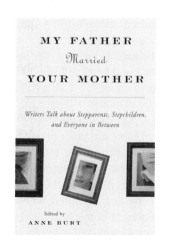

MY FATHER
Married
YOUR MOTHER

*Writers Talk about Stepparents, Stepchildren,
and Everyone in Between*

Edited by
ANNE BURT

Le Beau-Père

By Phyllis Rose

FROM: *My Father Married Your Mother: Writers
Talk about Stepparents, Stepchildren, and
Everyone in Between*, W. W. Norton, 2006

CONTEXT: This essay is from a collection of essays, *My Father Married Your Mother: Writers Talk about Stepparents, Stepchildren, and Everyone in Between*, published by W. W. Norton in 2006. An independent publisher since 1923, W. W. Norton is a company that prides itself on being "the oldest and largest publishing house owned wholly by its employees," according to its website. This New York-based company publishes college textbooks, general interest books, and professional books. Phyllis Rose is a well-known and respected biographer, essayist, memoirist, and literary critic who taught at Wesleyan University in Connecticut. Her degrees come from Harvard, Yale, and Radcliffe. In this piece, she describes her second marriage to Laurent de Brunhoff, the illustrator of the well-known *Babar* books. As you read the following essay about a stepfather, think about how important facets of both stepfathers and traditional fathers are revealed.

WHEN MY SON WAS THIRTEEN AND I HAD BEEN DIVORCED from his father for eleven years, I installed another man in our house. Laurent did not become Ted's official stepfather for another five years; he had to get divorced before we could marry. But for all practical purposes, he was the stepfather. He was always in the house with us. The three of us ate dinner together every night. We used the same bathroom, the only one in the house. Ted and Laurent shared a phone line and took messages for one another. Laurent and I cheered from the bleachers at all of Ted's high-school swim meets. We traveled to family weddings together, usually had Thanksgiving together, and took vacations together. We were — and have been since then — a family.

Laurent arrived at a good moment, just as Ted was about to enter adolescence. Ted had been a gallant little boy, with a strong sense of responsibility for my welfare. This was no doubt another burden that the breakup of our original family had imposed on him: He was the man in charge of Mom's well-being. Laurent's arrival let him off the hook. Someone else was there to take care of me. Not that I needed much taking care of. I wasn't an invalid or an alcoholic. I had a full-time job as a professor at a university, and we lived on the college campus, where things were pretty easy to manage. But I've always felt — and Ted confirms — that it was a relief to him to have me hook up with someone just then, so he could devote himself full-time to his teenage years. In the deep dark reaches of the psyche, he could stamp an upper case "Not My Problem" on Mom, which is as it should be.

Physical spaces within the house had to be redistributed when Laurent came to live with us. He is an artist, works at home, and needs a studio. Ted's bedroom and mine had been across the hall from each other, with my study and the bathroom on the same floor, the second floor of the house. Upstairs in the attic was another finished room, a guest room, largely unoccupied. This might have become Laurent's studio, but instead, Laurent moved into Ted's bedroom and Ted moved up to the attic. By leaving his childhood room behind, he gained privacy as well as the chance to play music as loud as he wanted. We both recall his move to the attic as a happy thing. Laurent made a sign to hang over the knob of the door to the attic stairs, saying TEDDY IS IN or TEDDY IS OUT, so when his friends called we would know his whereabouts without shouting up to the attic. This somehow made it seem all the more that Ted had a kingdom of his own up there under the eaves.

By the time I found Laurent, Ted and I knew pretty well what a bad stepfather was like. A bad stepfather would come into our household and want to change things. He would have strong feelings about everything and want to be obeyed. He would especially want Ted to conform to some image he had of what a child should be and do. He would weigh heavily. A bad stepfather would have some image of fatherhood in his mind that he was trying to fulfill, and to do so he would need Ted's cooperation. At his parodic worst, he would call Ted "young man" and slap him awkwardly on the back. He would try too hard to have a relationship with Ted, although Ted knew very well that the guy was not there for *his* sake, however much he might pretend to be. We both remember "the man with the chemistry set" as the epitome of the bad stepfather, the man bearing gifts that were really directives: "This is how you should be spending your time."

Tobias Wolff created a great portrait of the bad stepfather in 5 Dwight of *This Boy's Life*, a memoir of Wolff's years with his mother after she and his father split up. Dwight is always trying to shape Toby up. "Dwight made a study of me," Wolff wrote. "He shared his findings as they came to him." The list of Toby's deficiencies went on so unendingly that it lost its power to hurt and merely seemed like "bad weather" to get through. Dwight set Toby tasks, ostensibly because he needed discipline, really because Dwight himself was such a loser that bullying a kid was his only way to experience power. He made Toby take on a paper route, a low-paying, endlessly penitential paper route, whose proceeds he claimed to be saving for Toby but which he ended by confiscating. He made Toby — bizarre detail — shuck horse chestnuts every night after dinner and then let them rot in the attic.

Ted suffered nothing like that in the years before Laurent. The worst improvement he had to endure was the chemistry set, and what scorn the giver has since received for the gift. Pity the poor man who tries to insinuate himself between a woman and her son who understand each other and know which side their bread is buttered on — the side of their continued partnership. Pity the poor son who never knows what schlemiel his mother is going to fall for and bring into his life, adding to the wound of losing his father the wound of an impossible new person to deal with. Pity the woman trying to find a guy who suits both herself and her child.

Laurent proved to be an excellent stepfather, the very opposite of the man with the chemistry set or Tobias Wolff's Dwight. I don't believe in twenty years he's ever once told Ted what to do. He's never rebuked him in the slightest way. He's never suggested paths, implied direction, exerted pressure. He never imitates someone he thinks he should be, which makes him very cool. Children pick up on pretense and insincerity. In Laurent, there is none. He does exactly as he pleases and allows everyone around him to do the same. Perhaps because he is an artist, he is wholly self-contained. He doesn't need validation from anyone else. He has an inner life. He *is* someone. He never looked to Ted to complete him. This quality of his Ted calls "spaciousness."

If he is spacious, it must also be said he's a little spacey. He is a children's book illustrator, the world's leading expert on drawing elephants who stand up on their hind legs, wear clothes, and act French. He lives in never-never land. He's about as effective a manager as Snoopy. A moral dilemma for him is whether humanoid elephants can be depicted with animal pets on a leash or eating a hamburger. (The answer is no, after much inner debate.) Because he is French, many aspects of American life bewilder him. I once saw him hold a fast-food hotdog on a tray and try to figure out how to make the mustard in the plastic pump descend to it. What kind of authority figure could he be to an American lad who had worked with the mobile hotdog vendor across the street on football weekends and who had been taught the proper sequence of condiments in the most complicated order? The answer is, none. As an authority figure, Laurent was non-existent. He was Consort. He was Ornament. He was not a substitute father. And none of his Magoo-ishness made him any less splendid a member of our new family. In fact, it was largely responsible for making him the perfect stepfather. His haplessness — his instinctive belief that the world will take care of him — is part of his immense appeal. People flock to take care of him. People tend to see him as something rare and precious, which he is. His reluctance to impose himself on anyone else comes across as delicacy and grace, an ultimate tact. But I wonder if precisely the qualities that make him so appealing a human being and such a splendid stepfather aren't those that would have made him a frustrating and difficult father.

Laurent's children are grown and I didn't watch him fathering them, so my observations are based on his treatment of our dog. This is admittedly an undignified and perhaps meaningless sample population. Still. The aloof self-containment and reluctance to direct that were so wonderful in him as a stepfather were less useful as we tried to turn a puppy into a responsible, self-confident, and independent dog. Laurent's deeply egalitarian nature refused to accept that Vinny, our Yorkie, was really the ignorant and untrained animal I knew him to be. In Laurent's view, when Vinny misbehaved it was because he was justly angry at us and needed to punish us. Therefore, it was up to us to treat him better, for example, by giving him scraps from the table so he would be "happy" and stop whining for scraps as we ate. When Vinny interrupted our conversations with friends, demanding attention by placing a tennis ball in our laps, Laurent would offhandedly throw it to him, hoping to keep him amused for a while and then being surprised when Vinny himself didn't know it was "time to stop." When he takes Vinny for walks in the city, he returns home exhausted because the dog stops so often to sniff that the shortest walk seems to last forever. "Pull his leash," I say. "Say, 'heel.' Don't let him get away with it. You are supposed to take the lead, not the dog. Who's walking who?" What is a father if not an alpha male, whose strength and competence let children feel secure, whose directions provide children with structure and something to rebel against? But Laurent as father offers no directions, sets no standards, and demands nothing. Vinny loves him, of course. How could he not? But I can't help thinking Vinny would be a better Yorkie if Laurent had exerted more authority, in a way that would have been disastrous if he had tried it with his stepson.

The French word for "stepfather" is *beau-père* — literally, "beautiful father" — so much more appropriate for Laurent's relationship to Ted than the harsh-sounding English word, which emphasizes the marginality and sideway-ness of the relationship. In French there is no distinction between new family members acquired by one's own marriage, which we would call father-in-law and mother-in-law, for example, and those acquired by the remarriage of a parent, which we call stepfather or stepmother. In French, all these variations on the original nuclear family have the same name; *beau-père* means father-in-law as well as stepfather. Perhaps the language is onto something. Stepfamilies may be beautiful families, offering second chances, the possibility of improving on the originals. Those of us who were not so good the first time round have a chance to be successful the second time, in the beautiful version of our role, because of the very features, in some cases, that made us not so good the first time. Weak fathers can be effective stepfathers. The negligent can be enabling. The remote can weigh lightly. The cold can be cool. The other side of that coin, of course, is that we may be worse. The qualities that made us good parents, for example, firm control, loving supervision, may make us intrusive, unwelcome stepparents. To my mind that is a risk well taken in the interests of making the nuclear family a more flexible institution.

I'm with those who see the traditional western bourgeois family as potentially a breeding ground for neurosis (Freud went into this) and overwork for women (Margaret Mead and more recent feminists took this one on). Mead introduced twentieth-century Americans to the idea that "primitive" societies, with their extended families and cross-family living arrangements, had something to teach us. She pointed out the burden that the nuclear family and the traditional division of work placed on a mother, isolated from supportive women of another generation, with too intense a focus on her husband and children. The intensity, Mead felt, was not good for parents or for children. But the high-pressure, lifelong, isolated family she wrote about turns out to have occupied a rather fleeting moment in social history, created by the combination of improvements in health care and increased life expectancy with a lingering Victorian social rigidity. In the nineteenth century and before, death kept rearranging families. Even in the developed world, in the very seat of Empire, women died, especially in childbirth, much younger than now. Their husbands remarried, often widows with children of their own from a previous marriage. What mortality did then, divorce has been doing for decades. It works toward expanding the nuclear family and decreasing its inherent pressure. Families enlarge. Intensities dissipate. Responsibilities get spread. It's hard to tell a little boy who has lost his father in a divorce that his suffering is for the larger good of western civilization, but when he's grown, in retrospect, he may see the ways in which his life was enlarged and made beautiful by the precious possession of a *beau-père*.

READING

1. Rose opens her essay with a paragraph that suggests what makes a family. In her description, what makes her family a family? What kind of details and activities are key? What role does marriage have in this definition?

2. Rose presents the addition of Laurent to their household as a very positive event for her son. What are some of the concrete examples she cites that are benefits of having him "installed" in their house?

3. Rose suggests that what makes a good father does not necessarily make a good stepfather and vice versa. Discuss the qualities she and her son believe make a good stepfather. Why are these same qualities not good in a traditional father? Describe how the role of the "alpha male" can be both negative and positive in fathering.

4. Rose's tone is light, humorous, and anecdotal. Find examples in the text that establish and maintain this tone.

5. One of the key aspects of this essay, reflected in its title, is the difference in connotation between the French word for stepfather, *beau-père*, and the American word *stepfather*. That difference is central to the essay. Rose says, "In French there is no distinction between new family members acquired by one's own marriage, which we would call father-in-law and mother-in-law, for example, and those acquired by the remarriage of a parent, which we call stepfather or stepmother. In French, all these variations on the original nuclear family have the same name; *beau-père* means father-in-law as well as stepfather." What shift in connotation is suggested by these definitions? How does the meaning change?

WRITING

1. Write a reflective essay or a journal piece in which you describe the ideal qualities that you personally think are important for a father to have. Discuss in what particular ways your father has or doesn't have these qualities and how this affects your family.

2. Although most of her essay is informal, Rose does mention Margaret Mead and Sigmund Freud near the end of her essay as supporting her ideas about the traditional nuclear family. Research these two thinkers and find where Freud suggests (in Rose's words) "the traditional western bourgeois family is a breeding ground for neurosis" and where Mead suggests the traditional family results in "overwork

for women." Write a brief expository essay summarizing your findings and citing your sources.

3. Rose suggests that divorce and remarriage may actually be helping the institution of marriage, by "making the nuclear family a more flexible institution." Write a researched essay in which you examine this proposition. Can you find any evidence that supports Rose's claim? After investigating your data, what conclusions do you draw?

4. Create a set of interview questions about family naming and family relationships with which to interview your classmates. Find out, for example, what people's names for their fathers, mothers, grandmothers, grandfathers, stepparents, stepchildren, siblings, and so on are. Discuss your findings with your class in an oral presentation. Decide together what connotations you have found in your class's family naming practices. Write a brief essay describing your findings.

5. Rose in "Le Beau-Père" and Susan Dominus in "Growing Up with Mom and Mom" (p. 128) are each writing against the grain of our traditional expectations about family. Although one is writing about same-sex parents and the other is writing about stepfathers, they use similar strategies to make their essays friendly and convincing to their audiences. Write an essay in which you compare the styles of these two authors.

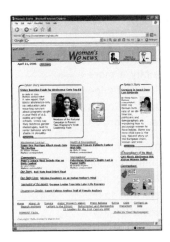

Rabenmutter: Germany in Angst over Low Birthrate

By Emma Pearse

FROM: Women's eNews, April 11, 2006
www.womensenews.org/article.cfm/
dyn/aid/2253/context/archive

CONTEXT: This piece comes from an online news service devoted to women's Issues, Women's eNews (WeNews). WeNews describes itself as "covering issues of particular concern to women and providing women's perspectives on public policy." It is one of many online journals devoted to a specific niche reading market. Like many of these journals, WeNews assigns stories to freelance journalists. Unlike many, it draws much of its funding from charitable foundations, including the John S. and James L. Knight Foundation, the Rockefeller Family Fund, and the Helena Rubinstein Foundation. Emma Pearse is an Australian journalist whose focus is pop culture and social issues. While writing this piece, she was living in Berlin. As you read the article, think about how Pearse's status as an outsider in the culture she is writing about impacts the piece.

IN GERMANY, THERE IS A WORD FOR A WOMAN WHO HAS BOTH a child and a full-time job. It's "rabenmutter" and it means uncaring mother. The term flourished in the 1930s through the heyday of the Nazi party and is now still used in "umgangssprache" or informal talk, especially in rural areas of Germany.

Then there's the word for housewife, "hausmutterchen," often used to slight women who choose to stay home with the kids. "It implies being a little bit stupid," says Kerstin Klopp-Koch, a working mother in Berlin. "Leaving all decisions to your husband."

While neither word is exactly on the tip of everyone's tongue in Germany, both words are common enough to bother young women who are making decisions about work and motherhood.

"I wish we didn't have this kind of moral judgment," says Maja Hampe, who lives in Gottingen, Niedersachsen, in northwest Germany.

Hampe, an English teacher, is staying home to raise her two-year- 5
old son. "I wish every woman could really decide on her own without
being seen as a 'rabenmutter' on the one hand or a 'hausmutterchen'
on the other."

Cultural, Political Debate

As women with children either work for pay or stay home with their
children, the choices they make are being closely studied amid growing national dismay over a declining birth rate.

At 1.3 babies per woman of child-bearing age, the birth rate is far
less than the 2.1 rate that researchers say is needed to maintain a
stable population. The not-so-funny joke among demographers here
is that unless women start having more babies, Germany could be extinct by 2020.

With federal elections approaching in 2006, the country's family
minister, Renate Schmidt, has made more child care — as a way of re-
versing the population decline — into a high-profile issue.

"When it comes to child care, compared with the rest of the European Union, Germany is a third-world country," Schmidt said at a
press conference last year where she announced the passage of a bill
to allocate $1.5 billion from 2005 to 2010 for full-day kindergartens
that would include children under the age of three.

Currently, child care is available for children between three and 10
six and operates only four hours a day, which is inadequate for parents who work full time.

Clinging to Traditions

Critics of the current child care system say it reflects a nation that has
been clinging to traditions that prescribe the man as breadwinner,
woman as procreator. The discomfort of being compelled to choose
between the two extremes apparently is influencing women to remain childless.

"The new Germany runs on a very old-fashioned model in which
the mainstream ideology dictates women as housewives," says Gisela
Erler, founder of a Berlin-based private company that acts as a go-
between consultant for women and their employers. "There is no way
out except to provide more child care."

The persistence of the "kindergeld" — a federal income tax break
that began in 1955 in West Germany — is another symptom of what
critics see as the country's adherence to traditional gender roles. The
break goes to married couples in which one of the couple — in practice it's usually the mother — earns no salary.

"The tradition is that the woman stays at home and the husband gets a tax break," says Kerstin Klopp-Koch, who organizes academic seminars for the German-American Fulbright Commission in Berlin.

Different Choices

Hampe and Klopp-Koch are women who have made different choices   15 about work and motherhood.

While Hampe has chosen to suspend her career to be at home with her children, Klopp-Koch is the married mother of an 18-month-old son who works for pay full time. The two women's choices echo differences that used to divide the country between a capitalist West and a communist East.

In Berlin, Klopp-Koch inhabits a pocket of diversity and opportunity in an otherwise highly traditional country. Women here have inherited some of the conditions of the former communist East, where all citizens — male and female — were required to work equal hours and child care was provided accordingly.

In Berlin today, women have more access to child care and undergo less social scrutiny than women such as Hampe, who lives in the rural, university town of Gottingen.

"Being a mother in Berlin is certainly different from being a mother in a town in West Germany," says Klopp-Koch.

One difference is that women in the more traditional areas of the   20 West — particularly those in the highly Catholic, southwestern regions where the stay-at-home mother is the norm — are having more babies.

The town of Cloppenburg in West Lower Saxony, for instance, boasts a birth rate of 1.92, higher than urban rates but still below what is needed to maintain a stable population, according to recent figures released by the Institute for Population and Development in Berlin.

"It is in the places where women accept these traditional rules that they are having more children," says Steffen Kroehnert, researcher for the institute.

By contrast, says Kroehnert, women outside of such traditional places appear even more reluctant about motherhood.

"In other areas, there is this contradiction between modern women and relatively traditional society," says Kroehnert. "Women who decide they want a modern life, with financial independence and their own professional career are very often deciding to have no children at all. The lack of child care makes women dependent on their husbands. And most women don't like this."

"We are a nation that is shrinking," says Erler, the Berlin business   25 consultant for family practices. "Perhaps some people will be happy about this, but it is true that the German people will become extinct if we don't deal with this problem of how a woman can have a child and continue working."

READING

1. In just the second paragraph of her article, Pearse mentions the Nazi party. How does this reference influence your perception of the issue from the beginning of the piece?

2. Pearse identifies two German terms that are applied to mothers. What are they? What do they mean? What impact does she suggest the ideas behind these words are having on families in Germany?

3. Pearse cites several sources in her article. Who are they? What authority on the topic do they seem to have? Do you feel she has conducted sufficient research in drawing her conclusions?

4. Germany's birth rate plays a significant role in the article. Why does Pearse suggest it differs from region to region? What is the birth rate in the United States? Does it differ from region to region as well?

5. Pearse points to several concrete steps that will encourage German women to have children. What are they? What evidence does she provide that these strategies will work?

WRITING

1. Write a reflective essay or journal entry about the two terms Pearse identifies. Did your mother work or stay home to raise children? How do you think she would feel about being labeled by either term?

2. Pearse writes, "The not-so-funny joke among demographers here is that unless women start having more babies, Germany could be extinct by 2020." This observation suggests that families sustain more than themselves: They provide the engine that sustains nations and cultures. Think about your own family. Write an essay in which you identify the ways in which it carries forward the values of a specific culture or ethnicity.

3. The article contrasts traditional and contemporary notions of motherhood in Germany. Does it seem to exhibit a bias toward one or the other? What evidence can you cite? Write an essay that analyzes Pearse's diction, tone, references, and examples and comes to a conclusion regarding her bias.

4. Germany is certainly not alone in having colloquial terms that refer to mothers . . . or to fathers. Make a list of terms that are commonly used in the United States to refer to parents of either sex (e.g., soccer mom, baby daddy). Survey at least a dozen people to see if they view these terms as being positive or negative, and research the

history of those seen as most positive and negative. Write an essay or give a presentation incorporating your research and summarizing your results.

5. Pearse quotes Germany's family minister as saying, " 'When it comes to child care, compared with the rest of the European Union, Germany is a third-world country.' " In "The Politics of Family," Robert Kuttner writes, "most Americans believe that married families would be stronger if government provided paid parental leave and high-quality child care" (p. 122), but he concludes that the United States is doing little or nothing on either front. Research the child care policies, practices and strategies in a European Union nation other than Germany. Using this research, write an essay that summarizes your findings and suggests policies that might be put in place in America to improve family life.

To Hell with All That

Loving and Loathing
Our Inner Housewife

Caitlin Flanagan

Executive Child
By Caitlin Flanagan

FROM: *To Hell with All That: Loving and Loathing Our Inner Housewife*, Little, Brown, 2006

CONTEXT: This essay is an excerpt from a collection of Caitlin Flanagan's work in her book titled *To Hell with All That: Loving and Loathing Our Inner Housewife*, published by Little, Brown, a division of Hatchett Book Group, USA, a conglomerate that also owns Warner Books. The essays in this book were first published, beginning in 2001, as a controversial series on modern domestic life in *The Atlantic*. These columns drew an outcry from feminists because Flanagan attacked professional women who hired others to raise their children. She asserted that stay-at-home motherhood is the best for the children and the husband of the family. Los Angeles-based Flanagan now writes for *The New Yorker* on the lives of modern women. She is also raising twins. Her work has been included in *The Best American Essays 2003* and *The Best American Magazine Writing 2003*. As you read the following piece on the overscheduled lives of children today, consider how you would describe Flanagan's attitude towards motherhood, and why her style and tone are considered so controversial — and how that may have resulted in Little, Brown publishing her first book.

I REMEMBER THE FIRST YEAR AND A HALF OF MY CHILDREN'S lives as being marked by a combination of elation and the low-level depression that dogs shut-ins the world over. My husband had taken a big corporate job to pay for the type of motherhood I had chosen to pursue, which involved round-the-clock worry about the babies and extremely infrequent separations from them. He was gone from seven in the morning until seven or eight at night, and I was lonely.

The babies and I were invited many places — to a gathering of mothers in the park, to a meeting of a twins-only playgroup at a friend's house — and I would mark these events on my calendar, sincerely intending to go to them. But when the appointed hour arrived, something always went wrong. One of the babies would suddenly demand an unscheduled feeding, or they would both suddenly knock off into a deep sleep, which only a fool would fail to recognize as a sign from God himself that it was time to make a cup of tea and chat on the telephone. It was my friends from work whom I longed for — full of gossip and talk of important matters — not the mothers in the park, who were either just as depressed as *I* was or spilling over with talk of diapers and breast milk and colic, topics with which I was similarly obsessed but which cheered me not at all to discuss ad infinitum.

Slowly the invitations dried up, and I became one of those out-of-sync, somewhat pitiable mothers, patrolling the streets with my enormous stroller during odd hours, spending far too much time in front of the television in my zip-front chenille bathrobe, getting in trouble at Starbucks for letting the babies pull bags of coffee off the rack while I was reading. My sister called from London and tactfully suggested I get a weekend babysitter and go out with my husband a little more often. My mother thought I should go back to work. People were starting to get a little worried about me.

And then one day I managed to get the three of us to the Westside Pavilion shopping mall for a desperately needed change of pace. We were performing a tour of inspection of the top floor, when I caught sight of several mothers purposefully pushing their strollers through the double doors of an establishment I'd never noticed before. I rolled my own stroller over and took a curious look at the yellow letters painted on the plate glass window: TUMBLE CAMP. It turned out to be a children's gym, with classes starting for babies as young as six months. I'd heard of such places, but I had thought they were for older children. Inside I was given a roster of classes, informed that tuition was nonrefundable, and shown the elaborate security procedures, whereby individual name tags would be printed by the computer every time we took a class. I joined immediately.

If motherhood abruptly wrested me from the world of adult en- 5 terprise, Tumble Camp put me back in business. It restored to me many of the things I had missed from work: an inflexible schedule, a sense of purpose, and colleagues engaged in a common pursuit. The classes were blessedly short and as focused as a board meeting: We sang a song, the mothers jollied the children through an obstacle course that changed every week, there was some free time, and then there was a good-bye song and hand stamps for the kids. The program was supposed to inculcate skills in the children — balance and coordination, and so on — but I knew that was a bunch of hooey. Every normally developing kid gains those skills naturally if he spends enough time in a playground or a backyard. But I wasn't there to improve the children; they were already perfect as far as I was concerned. What I liked was that I had a series of climate-controlled, time-limited, intensive little seminars to go to and a way of imposing structure on the endless, ungraspable days of early parenthood.

In due time I discovered that Tumble Camp was not the only game in town. There were also classes at outfits called Fit for Kids and Bright Child, and I enrolled in them, too. Our church nursery school offered a parent-toddler program once a week, which turned out to be a kind of pre-preschool, its core philosophy reminding me of the old Texas expression, "I'm fixin' to get ready to start." The zoo had classes for toddlers, as did the Natural History Museum and the YMCA. Before long we had something to do every day of the week; sometimes we had to eat lunch at McDonald's or the mall food court because we had two engagements. The boys, I'm sure, would have been just as happy with a daily trip to the park, but they took to the new routine willingly enough, and some of the classes we loved. We took Music and Motion from a beautiful young woman known to us as Miss Simona, and we all became quite taken with her. Patrick would murmur her name when he was falling asleep, and I would think of her brown eyes and complicated personal life (her husband had recently left her) whenever I played one of the two sing-along cassettes she had sold to us for forty dollars.

My life began to improve. The babies learned the one thing none of the classes taught — how to talk — and with that my loneliness began to abate. One day when I was loading the backpack for class, I sneezed, and from somewhere down near the floor a tiny voice said, "Bless you." In that moment I realized that what my shrink had been telling me every week was in fact true: The babies would get older; things would get easier. On a sunny October day the boys started nursery school five mornings a week. When I walked through my front door after dropping them off, my footsteps echoed on the hardwood floors of the empty house, and I realized that a chapter of my life had come to an end. I gave away the chenille robe and took the safety rails off the boys' beds. A few months later, when I was tidying up, I found one of Miss Simona's cassettes in a kitchen drawer, and I threw it in the trash. We had emerged.

The activities, however, stayed with us. The boys are first graders now, and they are a blur of motion. On Mondays Patrick takes an after-school class called Mad Science, on Tuesdays Conor plays T-Ball, and on Saturdays they both have basketball and an hour of semiprivate soccer coaching. Their school has an extended-day program — two hours of supervised play, art projects, and a snack — of which they are both exceedingly fond. They are yellow belts in karate; they take the occasional tennis lesson; they swim. In addition to these various lessons and classes, they have an intense and carefully structured playdate schedule, as well as a ceaseless round of birthday parties to attend. There is Sunday school, of course, and at school they are also quite busy, making action paintings in the style of Jackson Pollock, testing the pH balance of various liquids, working on computers, being introduced to and horrified by slavery, copying the complex patterns of Navajo blankets.

The boys are bullish on this schedule, but it is both a boon and a burden to me. I'm delighted to watch my sons happily engaged in one fun project or another, growing ever more accomplished at things I have never attempted, palling around with their numberless friends. These classes, of course, are expensive, and it is a point of pride to me that I am able to provide them to my children, just as (so long ago) it was a point of pride to my mother that she was able to provide her children with trips to Disneyland and a shining mountain of new toys every Christmas. Each generation hopes for more. But there is also a relentless, exhausting nature to this whirl of events, a sense that the children — barely seven years old — are engaged in the most impor-tant work of the household, that I must be ever vigilant about our schedule to ensure that we don't miss a lesson or a team photo or a trophy ceremony. In the long run, the extra hours that this program buys me are dwarfed by the amount of time and energy it takes to keep the thing up and running; it's a beast that must be thrown fresh meat daily. The roster of after-school activities offered at my sons' school includes not just Roving Reporters, Animal Invasion, and Lul-laby of Broadway, but also a class called Meditation and Yoga for Par-ents and Teachers. The image this conjures — of scores of tots furiously reporting the news and belting out "Second Hand Rose," while somewhere in their midst a cloistered cell of harassed adults tries desperately to unwind from it all — is mildly comical. Still, if I could find the time, I would take the class.

The old-fashioned, wholesome activities of the fifties and sixties — 10 scouting, for example — have become less popular because yuppie parents, obsessed with status and flush with the cash of the new pro-fessional class, believe that enterprises like the Boy Scouts suggest the exact kind of middle-middle-class earnestness that they eschew most powerfully. They are attracted to the pastimes of the American aristocracy, as they imagine it: tennis and soccer, art and advanced ac-ademics. What nobody seemed prepared for is the extent to which these activities would come to dominate family life.

READING

1. The title of this piece, "Executive Child" suggests a new kind of childhood. What kind of connotation does this title set up for the rest of the essay? What image of a child is suggested by the title?

2. Flanagan describes herself as "one of those out-of-sync, somewhat pitiable mothers, patrolling the streets with my enormous stroller during odd hours, spending far too much time in front of the television in my zip-front chenille bathrobe." Does this characterization of motherhood fit with your own experience or expectation? How does it make you feel about Flanagan?

3. Comb through the essay looking for word choices that shape the tone of the piece. Consider phrases such as, "I began losing my mind," "a sign from God himself that it was time to make a cup of tea," "I knew that was a bunch of hooey," or "both a boon and a burden to me." How would you describe Flanagan's voice in this piece?

4. Flanagan's husband takes a corporate job that entails being "gone from seven in the morning until seven or eight at night." She says his job pays "for the type of motherhood I had chosen to pursue." What is your reaction to this kind of fatherhood? What role, if any, did your father play in your life?

5. Break into small groups and discuss some of the issues about parenting brought up by this essay.

WRITING

1. Flanagan fills her essay with descriptions of the countless available programs, from sport activities to pre-preschool classes, for her children — almost all of which interest her. Write a journal entry or reflective essay describing the kinds of activities your mother provided for you. Were you an "Executive Child"? Why or why not?

2. This essay excerpt is divided into two sections. Write an essay summarizing the key points of each section. Pay special attention to the last lines of each segment and explain how these sentences lead into the next section of the essay.

3. Flanagan writes that as a mother with very young children she ended up "spending far too much time in front of the television" in a "zip-front chenille bathrobe." She is saved by Tumble Camp. She says, "What I liked was that I had a series of climate-controlled, time-limited, intensive little seminars to go to and a way of imposing

structure on the endless, ungraspable days of early parenthood." Write an essay in which you discuss the difficulties associated with being a stay-at-home mom for Flanagan throughout this piece.

4. Flanagan refers to her own mother's pride in being able to give her "trips to Disneyland" and "a shining mountain of new toys each Christmas." Research and write an essay on the spending patterns of parents today concerning their children. Consider things like allowance, clothing, trips, toys, as well as things like music lessons, athletics, and special courses. You may want to focus on a particular age group.

5. Stephanie Coontz, in "The American Family," says of the modern family, "Although the number of hours the average woman spends at home with her children has declined since the early 1900s, there has been a decrease in the number of children per family and an increase in individual attention to each child. As a result, mothers today, including working moms, spend almost twice as much time with each child as mothers did in the 1920s" (p. 97). Yet Flanagan, a self-described stay-at-home mom, seems to be going in another direction, intensively scheduling classes and activities for her children. With a small group explore the activities available in your community for pre-school, elementary-school, and middle-school children. Design a weekly program for your theoretical "executive child." Include time that you will spend exclusively with your child.

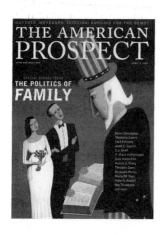

The Politics of Family
By Robert Kuttner

FROM: *The American Prospect*, April 8, 2002

CONTEXT: This piece is the introduction to a special double issue of *The American Prospect* devoted to "The Politics of Family," a public debate on the family by well-known journalists and sociologists. *The American Prospect* was founded in 1990 in order to advance "effective liberal politics" and "an enriched democracy." Its mission statement says, "*The American Prospect* does not back political candidates, nor does it attempt to achieve unanimity or even consistency among its writers. It seeks to provide a forum for working through the heated controversies and hard choices that vex its editors and writers as much as other Americans." It is a monthly magazine with 55,000 subscribers and has a companion website (www.prospect.org) that attracts over 3,000 visitors monthly. Robert Kuttner is a founder and co-editor of *The American Prospect* and a weekly columnist for *The Boston Globe*. He has taught at Harvard University's Institute of Politics, written for the *New England Journal of Medicine*, been a John F. Kennedy Fellow, a Woodrow Wilson Fellow, a Guggenheim Fellow, and a Radcliffe Public Policy Fellow. As you read his introduction, notice how he lays out the areas of agreement and disagreement between conservatives and liberals on family public policy.

Love in a hut, with water and a crust,
Is — Love, forgive us! — cinders, ashes, dust.
— JOHN KEATS, 1819

THE FEDERAL GOVERNMENT IS SUDDENLY VERY INTERESTED in marriage. The principal target of this matchmaking is the welfare population, though many traditionalists would turn the marriage movement into a generalized crusade. It adds up to something that most conservatives ordinarily abhor — social engineering, and in the most intimate of human realms.

Beneath the policy debates lies a much broader cultural clash, one that has caught liberals somewhat off guard and even opened some liberal schisms. For the fact is that most Americans (and most social scientists) believe children benefit from having two married parents. Many in the liberal camp, however, would qualify that proposition. Plenty of women justifiably leave abusive marriages. Single mothers often do heroic work as parents; society should not punish their children. Marriage would be more viable if employers paid living wages and did not punish mothers disproportionately for working, and if more men were committed to equal sharing. And if marriage is good for everyone else, why not open it to lesbians and gays? But as the right has advanced its marriage movement, many liberals find themselves seemingly on the minority side of a debate they basically won in the 1960s.

Most Americans, after all, believe women should not be consigned to the nursery and the kitchen. Most are tolerant of premarital sex and engage in it (though they are uneasy about the sexuality of early teens and about out-of-wedlock teen births). Most Americans support birth control over abstinence. And most Americans believe that married families would be stronger if government provided paid parental leave and high-quality child care. Even the idea that gays and lesbians should have the right to marry has become increasingly mainstream.

You need only read such conservatives as the gay arch-Tory Andrew Sullivan or David Brooks, the celebrant of "bourgeois bohemians," to appreciate that the left won the cultural war. Even most conservatives favor sex and rock and roll, if not drugs. However, this was one costly victory. It produced a backlash that energized the cultural right and perhaps helped install the economic right, even as libertarians were enjoying the new permissiveness in their own bedrooms. Somehow the right has papered over the schisms in its camp. Hence covenant marriage, abstinence education, shotgun welfare betrothals, and a lot of other foolishness that most Americans oppose but is now national policy. Ultimately, the prime object of this debate is children. Except where kids are concerned, few people care very much if you are married or single. It is bizarre that in the entire conservative campaign to promote marriage and force welfare mothers into paid employment, the right doesn't seem to care that children often get short shrift.

Keats, nearly two centuries ago, had it right: Love, like good values, will take you a long way. But it is no cure for poverty, and poverty is bad for kids. Moreover, as the charts on this spread show, child-poverty rates do not simply correlate with marriage, divorce, and single parenthood. They do reflect the quality of social policy: the proverbial village. 5

THE DECLINE IN MARRIAGE

	% OF ADULTS MARRIED	
	1970	1996
All U.S. adults	72%	60%
Whites	73	63
Blacks	64	42
Hispanics	72	58

Source: U.S. Census Bureau data, March 1998

THE RISE IN OUT-OF-WEDLOCK BIRTHS

% OF BIRTHS TO UNWED WOMEN (U.S.)

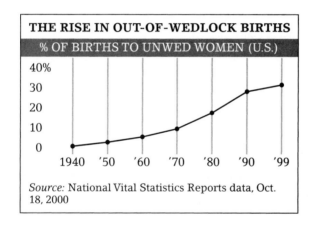

Source: National Vital Statistics Reports data, Oct. 18, 2000

THE RISE IN ONE-PARENT FAMILIES

	% OF CHILDREN LIVING WITH ONE PARENT	
	1970	1996
All U.S. adults	12%	28%
Whites	9	22
Blacks	32	57
Hispanics	—	33

Source: U.S. Census Bureau data, March 1998

CHILD POVERTY IN INDUSTRIALIZED NATIONS	
COUNTRY	% IN POVERTY
United States	22.4%
Italy	20.5
United Kingdom	19.8
Canada	15.5
Germany	10.7
France	7.9
Netherlands	7.7
Denmark	5.1
Sweden	2.6

Note: Poverty is defined as household income below 50 percent of the national median for households with children under 18.

Source: UNICEF data, 2000

CHILD POVERTY IN THE UNITED STATES		
	NO.*	% IN POVERTY
2000	11.6	16.1%
1990	13.4	20.5
1980	11.5	18.3
1970	10.4	15.1
1960	17.6	26.9

In millions

Source: Current Population Survey, 1959–2000 data for children under 18

The other liberal proposition that enjoys broad support is equal partnership within marriage and healthy (and private) sexuality. It is the religious right that has never quite come to terms with sexuality, much less sexual equality, and it's the right that battles repressed demons, often with violent or kinky results. As *Slate* memorably put it, commenting on the Catholic pedophilia scandal, "Does Abstinence Make the Church Grow Fondlers?"

So there are basically two contending narratives about family. In the first, modernity itself ruined the family and traditional values are the cure, helped along (as usual) by economic incentives. In the second, a lot of ugly realities were concealed by "traditional values"; the legal and economic emancipation of women was long overdue; and the task now is to reconcile gender equality with the healthy raising of the next generation.

The two narratives converge on the propositions that children need engaged and loving parents and that out-of-wedlock birth to teen parents is a bad idea — but on little else. In this special double issue of *The American Prospect*, we've invited distinguished journalists and social scientists to address the family debate. In a companion issue to be published in June, as Congress revisits welfare reform, we will focus on the debate about welfare policy.

Our liberal family may not agree on all the details. But at the end of the day, most Americans would not restore the traditional division of labor between the sexes nor revert to Victorian notions of sexuality. Most believe that social supports are good for families and children. If we can get the story out, this debate is ours to win.

READING

1. This essay begins with a quotation from a poem by John Keats. What do these lines of poetry tell us about Kuttner's audience? In what way do the images in the poem — hut, water, crust, cinders, ashes, dust — prepare us for the points he will argue?

2. At the end of his first paragraph Kuttner refers to "social engineering." What is social engineering and why would conservatives abhor it?

3. Kuttner mentions differences between liberals and conservatives concerning the politics of the family. What are these differences, according to Kuttner?

4. Discuss the graphs in this piece. What do these graphs tell you about child poverty? Are any of these data shocking to you? Why?

5. Since this is an introduction to a double issue of the magazine, Kuttner is writing in broad strokes. What are the key "narratives" he puts forth for us to observe in the articles that follow? Does he identify himself as a liberal or a conservative?

WRITING

1. Write a reflective essay or a journal entry in which you mull over the title of this piece, "The Politics of Family." How are families political anyway? What is your vision of the role of the family in national politics? Where does your family fit in with the various demographics Kuttner mentions? Do you think of your family as a political unit? Why or why not?

2. Go to the *Oxford English Dictionary* and look up the history of the term "social engineering." Then, write a short essay that explains the definition of this term. Discuss why, as Kuttner suggests, "it adds up to something conservatives ordinarily abhor." Provide at least three examples of social engineering that illustrate your assertions.

3. Kuttner states that "most Americans (and most social scientists) believe children benefit from having two married parents." He also states, "child-poverty rates do not simply correlate with marriage, divorce, and single parenthood." Go to this double issue of *The American Prospect* and read at least two essays that explore this idea, such as "Marriage Plus" by Theodora Ooms and "Is Lack of Marriage the Real Problem?" by Isabel V. Sawhill. Write a summary of each essay and compare and contrast their arguments.

4. Kuttner refers to a "cultural clash" concerning liberals' and conservatives' views of marriage. He cites problems with an either/or position on marriage such as abusive marriages (for example, domestic abuse or child abuse), "heroic single parents" (unmarried, widowed, or divorced parents), and lack of marriage options for same-sex parents (same-sex marriage). Choose one of these three topics and research the connection between your topic and the children of these parents. Write a researched essay in which you summarize your findings concerning the effect on the children of the particular kind of family you researched.

5. Kuttner writes of the prime importance of the standard of living when considering the definition of a successful family. However, even though Caitlin Flanagan, author of "Executive Child" (p. 115), is an upper-middle-class mother, she still expresses genuine concerns about her ability to help her children thrive and create a successful family. Research traditional families with a dad, mother, and children based on their income levels and see what conclusions you can draw about the effect of income on the children. Write a researched essay reporting your findings.

Growing Up with Mom and Mom

By Susan Dominus

FROM: *New York Times Magazine,*
October 24, 2004

CONTEXT: This article was included in the October 24, 2004, issue of the *New York Times Magazine.* The Sunday *New York Times* is read nationwide and has a circulation of almost 1.7 million copies. The company describes the readers of the Sunday magazine as "affluent, educated, inquisitive, and acquisitive." Research on the readers of the magazine reveals them to be almost three times as likely to hold a professional or managerial position, and more than two times as likely to have household incomes over $100,000. Susan Dominus is a writer for the *New York Times Magazine* and *Glamour.* She was a recipient of the Yale Fellowship in Law for Journalists in 1998 and an NIH (National Institutes of Health) 2002 Knight Medical Science Journalism Fellowship. She won the sixteenth Annual GLAAD (the Gay & Lesbian Alliance Against Defamation) Media Award for this article in 2005. ("Growing Up with Mom and Mom," and the cover of the *New York Times Magazine* copyright © 2004 The New York Times. Reprinted with permission. Photo © Robet Maxwell.)

RY RUSSO-YOUNG, A TWENTY-TWO-YEAR-OLD FILMMAKER and performer, has a lot to explain, starting with her name. It's Ry, just Ry, not short for Ryan, or a misspelling of Ray, or a nickname someone gave her as a child, or a pretension she took on in her teens. Ry is simply a name that her mothers liked the sound of when they named her, an act of creativity as novel and yet, to their minds, as natural as the conception of Ry herself, a feat that involved the sperm of a gay man, the egg of a lesbian in love, and one very clean glass syringe.

Earlier this year, over dinner at a small restaurant in the West Village, a few blocks from where she was raised, Ry was offering me a short lecture that she has been called on to deliver dozens of times, politely solving the puzzle that is her family for other people. She was explaining her name, explaining her mothers' relationship, explaining her older sister, whose name, Cade, also demands clarification. She was explaining how it is that she has no father, and when pressed further — after all, everyone has a father — she raised her eyebrows, dark and thick and finely shaped, just a little. "You mean who's my sperm donor?" she asked. I apologized — "father" can be a loaded word for children of lesbian mothers — but she shrugged it off with a small wave of her hand, her dark red nails flashing by. "It's O.K.," she said. "I'm not fussy about stuff like that."

Ry has long dark hair, a slightly breathy voice, and a hint of a tough-girl, New York accent. Tall enough that she has presence by default, she's a natural performer, inclined to stacked heels and deep red lipstick. On the subject of her parents, she is particularly confident in the quality of her material, and she unpacked the details at a leisurely pace. As for her own sexuality, she's straight, which she said she knows with increasing certainty with each passing year. "Yeah, you know, I made out with a girl in high school," she said. "I get an A for effort."

If she has volunteered to talk frankly to a stranger about her family life, not to mention her sex life, it's because Ry knows she's one of a relatively limited number of adults who were raised from birth by "out" gay parents (as opposed to a parent who revealed he or she was gay after marrying and having kids). As more and more gay men and lesbians feel comfortable coming out earlier in their lives and the possibility of legalized same-sex marriage appears to be gaining ground in select states, Ry's experience may represent the future of gay households. Already, the 2000 Census reported that some 150,000 same-sex couples had children in their homes. If the last three decades of the gay rights movement focused on sexual freedom and acceptance, the next three decades seem destined to continue the current battle for the right to marry and, by extension, the right to be a parent.

Of course, even without the benefit of legal protection, gay men 5 and women have been raising children for long enough and in large-enough numbers that they've become an acknowledged part of their communities. Schools in places like Los Angeles and Boston mount displays of famous gay figures and make sure the library includes books like "King and King," about a prince who marries a princess's brother. A well-worn anecdote circulates in Park Slope, Brooklyn, a progressive neighborhood, about two gay men who were concerned when a little boy teased their child for having no mommy — only to discover later that the little boy in question had two mommies. The story is funny precisely because it points to an antiquated anxiety, a fear from another era running up against the startling reality of this one.

Robert Maxwell, Family Photo

In some pockets of the country, the atmosphere is now sufficiently safe for the older kids of gay parents, kids like Ry, to start
speaking plainly about their childhoods, seeking each other out for
support or activism. But at the very moment when the cultural environment seems secure, the political environment has become hyper-
sensitive. A central argument advanced against gay marriage is that
gay relationships have a corrosive effect on the institution of the traditional family. In that context, the children of gay parents are not just
aspiring filmmakers, or dropouts, or Phi Beta Kappas, or cross-
dressers, or serial monogamists. They're also a form of evidence in the
political debate. How do the children of gay parents turn out, when
compared with the children of straight parents, in terms of eventual
marital status, income, psychological well-being? If gay couples give
birth, seek to adopt, or become foster parents, what kind of adult
members of society will they produce?

Although definitive studies of these families don't yet exist — the
sample size is still too small — that hasn't stopped states like Arkansas,

Mississippi, Utah, and Florida from passing laws to limit the rights of gays to adopt or to become foster parents. Policy makers on both sides of the culture wars are scrambling to find research to sway the debate: Conservative groups like the American College of Pediatricians argue that kids raised by gay parents grow up sexually promiscuous and confused; advocates like the American Civil Liberties Union point to studies that suggest that the kids are as well adjusted as their peers, if not more so — more resilient, more open-minded, more tolerant. As for Ry, who acknowledges that she is a living, breathing result of a new social endeavor, she says she's more than happy to discuss how having gay parents shaped her, to the extent that she has figured it out. Truth be told, she seems to enjoy being her family's self-appointed chronicler, often referring back to her experience in her films and performances. She may not be a statistically significant sample, and her stories may sound like ancient history to the kids born to today's gay parents, many of whom are assimilating seamlessly in their communities. But as she points out, in some ways she knows more about the subject than the conservative policy makers seeking to raise concerns about gay parents, or the mostly gay psychologists looking to validate the perfect normalcy of gay parents' kids.

Ry, the daughter of trailblazing lesbians, has spent so much time under a magnifying glass that it's almost as if her feelings about her family — and her own response to those feelings — have been permanently magnified. Any kid who grew up with gay parents has probably given some thought, at least in fleeting moments, to how her upbringing shaped her personality, her sexuality, her gender. As an artist, Ry scrutinizes those thoughts, performing them live, blowing them up on-screen so that every nuance is beautifully represented and crystal clear. "I'm an expert in this subject," Ry said as the meal drew to a close. "And I didn't even have to lift a finger."

Sitting behind a projector last April in the front row of a small theater in the East Village, Ry was looking apprehensive. Although her work has been shown at venues like the Turin Film Festival, she was now about to show a short film at a comparatively humble event called Avant-Garde-Arama. The festival's hosts, dressed in a look somewhere between bridal and bondage, were calling on audience members — straight, gay, strangers, whatever — to volunteer to be married onstage. It might have been great theater if anyone had, but no one did, and eventually the hosts introduced Ry, who started the projector rolling.

She had mounted three separate screens, and on each a different 10 variant of the shower scene from *Psycho*, recreated in stark black-and-white flatness, played itself out: on one, the stabbing of the doomed Janet Leigh figure happened on cue, while in another, a second actress playing Janet Leigh turned the knife on her attacker and left him bloody at her feet. That vengeful Janet Leigh figure then seemed to step, naked and dripping, into the third screen, where she took her knife to Janet Leigh figure No. 3. The film was visually interesting and unexpected, a slasher film with a brain, and the audience responded with enthusiastic applause.

After a few more acts — a nude dance, a rapper named Mint T — Ry's parents, Robin Young, forty-nine, and Sandy Russo, sixty-four, left their seats to meet Ry by the stage. Ry was dressed in vintage *femme fatale*, a black checked dress with fish nets and heels; her mothers wore jeans and glasses. Ry still looked uncomfortable, and Young and Russo (whom everyone calls by her surname) seemed less than enthusiastic, with shrugs passing for commentary. "I don't think they liked it," Ry reported later. "They're not into the violence-against-women thing, I guess." She'd been trying to comment on the hackneyed image of woman as victim, she said, but "Moms," as she and Cade sometimes call their parents, apparently saw only the same old thing. She sighed heavily: "Do you ever stop caring what they think?"

READING

1. The title of this piece immediately suggests a question: "How does a person get two moms?" The first paragraphs of the essay tell in very clear language what the essay will address – the children of lesbian mothers. What tone is established with this no-nonsense explanation? What does it suggest about the tone of the rest of the essay?

2. This article is developed through the character of Ry, a daughter of lesbian mothers. What kinds of questions does Ry find herself having to explain over and over again? What is her attitude about being "her family's self-appointed chronicler"?

3. Dominus cites two extreme groups engaged in "culture wars" concerning gay parents: "Conservative groups like the American College of Pediatricians argue that kids raised by gay parents grow up sexually promiscuous and confused; advocates like the American Civil Liberties Union point to studies that suggest that the kids are as well adjusted as their peers, if not more so – more resilient, more open-minded, more tolerant." Which side of this debate do you find yourself sympathizing more with? Why? Where would you place yourself on the continuum between these two extremes?

4. In the piece, Ry is described as "inclined to stacked heels and deep red lipstick" and "dressed in vintage *femme fatale*, a black checked dress with fish nets and heels." What effect does this have on your perception of Ry's sexuality?

5. At the end of this excerpt, Ry's parents, the moms, give her a lukewarm reception to her film at her show. She sighs, "Do you ever stop caring what they think?" Describe the relationship you imagine between Ry and her parents, based on this lament.

WRITING

1. According to this article, Ry is often asked to solve "the puzzle that is her family." Does your family have any puzzles that need to be explained? Write a reflective essay or a journal piece describing any puzzles in your family or the lack of them.

2. Dominus observes, "If the last three decades of the gay rights movement focused on sexual freedom and acceptance, the next three decades seem destined to continue the current battle for the right to marry and, by extension, the right to be a parent." Write a brief report in which you document the current number of states where

the right to marry and the right to be a parent are protected legally for gay people.

3. "Any kid who grew up with gay parents has probably given some thought, at least in fleeting moments, to how her upbringing shaped her personality, her sexuality, her gender," Dominus suggests. Write a researched essay in which you cite at least five online sources, such as the American Sociological Association (www.asanet.org), MentalHealth.about.com, or the American Psychological Association (www.apa.org), concerning the experience of children brought up by same-sex parents. Does your research support Dominus's point of view, or not?

4. The central argument against gay-parented families seems to be that this new kind of family will undermine the traditional nuclear family structure of heterosexual mom and dad, plus children. Investigate the claims on both sides of this debate and identify any key research that has been done on this subject. Provide an annotated bibliography of your findings.

5. Choose two of the sources above and analyze their arguments. See if you can drill down and find the studies that support the arguments. Which seems to be the most comprehensive? Which has the largest sample? Which is the most recent?

My Yiddishe Mama

By Henry Louis Gates Jr.

FROM: *Wall Street Journal,*
February 1, 2006

CONTEXT: This article was initially published in the *Wall Street Journal* around the time that Henry Louis Gates Jr.'s public television series on the same topic aired. Gates is the W. E. B. Du Bois Professor of the Humanities and director of the W. E. B. Du Bois Institute for Afro-American Research at Harvard. He has been awarded a MacArthur Foundation "Genius" grant and, in 1997, was named one of the twenty-five most influential Americans by *Time.* Gates is widely published in both the academic and popular press. The *Wall Street Journal* is a paper known primarily for a conservative approach to business journalism and is published by the Dow Jones Company. Nearly 60 percent of *WSJ* readers describe themselves as belonging to the top level of management in their companies, and the average household net worth of its readership is over $2 million. As you read this piece, think about how Gates specifically addresses the complications African Americans face in tracing their family trees.

SINCE 1977, WHEN I SAT RIVETED EVERY NIGHT FOR A WEEK in front of my TV, I have had *Roots* envy. Even if scholars remain deeply skeptical about his methodology, Alex Haley went to his grave believing that he had found the ethnic group from which his African ancestors originated before surviving the dreaded Middle Passage.

Two years before, I proudly told a fellow student at Cambridge, an Anglo-Ghanaian, that I could trace my slave ancestors back to 1819, the birth date of Jane Gates, my paternal great-great-grandmother. I wondered if he could do better?

He invited me to accompany him to the University Library, where, buried deep in the stacks, he found a copy of *Burke's Peerage*, then walked me through his mother's English ancestry with certainty back to one Richard Crispe, who died in 1575, and who, the book said "probably" descended from William Crispe, who had died in 1207. His father's side, members of the Asante people in Ghana, he could trace to the seventeenth century. The roots of my *Roots* envy?

After years of frustration, I determined to do something about it. So I decided to invite eight prominent African Americans to allow their DNA to be tested and their family histories to be researched for a documentary film. When the paper trail would end, inevitably, in the abyss of slavery, we would then try to find their African roots through science.

Having been involved in after-school programs, I was hoping to 5 get inner-city school kids engaged by the wonders of both genetics and archival research.

But I had ulterior motives, too. I wanted to find my white patriarch, the father of Jane Gates's children. Maybe genetics could verify the family legend that the father of Jane's children was an Irish man from Cresaptown, Maryland, a slaveholder named Samuel Brady. Perhaps I could give Jane her Thomas Jefferson–Sally Hemings moment!

I also had hopes for my African origins. Throughout my adult life, I've always been drawn to Nigeria's Yoruba culture — to its cuisine, its legends, its rhythms, and its songs. As a Fela Ransome-Kuti album played in my head, I wondered whether geneticists could determine that I had physical, not only spiritual, affinities to the Yoruba.

Our genealogists as well as our geneticists were given a tough assignment. Five generations ago, each of us has thirty-two ancestors, or two to the fifth power. If we go back ten generations, or 300 years, each of us has 1,024 theoretical ancestors, or two to the tenth power. Even with genetics, we can only trace two of our family lines. The first African slaves arrived in Virginia in 1619; the slaves were freed in 1865, and appeared with two legal names for the first time in the 1870 census. Penetrating the name barrier of 1870 required detailed and imaginative sleuthing through the records of slaveholders, praying that they somehow mentioned one of their slaves by first name, in wills, tax records, or estate division papers.

The stories that we found are not the sort found in textbooks, which tend either to recreate Black History through the narratives of great women and men, or else through broad social movements. We were able to find stirring stories of heretofore anonymous individuals who made heroic contributions against seemingly insurmountable odds. If the promise of America was the right to own land, very few blacks were able to do so before the middle of the twentieth century. But some did.

Oprah Winfrey's great-great-grandfather, Constantine Winfrey, a 10 farm worker in Mississippi, had the audacity to approach a white man, John Watson, in 1876, and make a wager: If he picked ten bales of cotton in one year, Watson would give Winfrey eighty acres of his land in return. (In 1870, a bale of cotton weighed 500 pounds.) On June 21, 1881, a property deed recorded the land exchange between the two. Constantine is listed in the 1870 census as illiterate; ten years later, he had learned to read and write. And when, in 1906, the local "colored school" was slated for destruction, Constantine arranged to save it by having it moved to his property.

Chris Tucker's great-great-grandfather, Theodore Arthur Bryant Sr., sold off parcels of his land to his black neighbors for below-market prices so that they would not join the Great Migration to the North, thereby saving the black community of Flat Rock, Georgia.

Whoopi Goldberg's great-great-grandparents, William and Elsa Washington, in 1878 received 104.5 acres in Alachua County, Florida, under the Southern Homestead Act of 1866. Less than 10 percent of black petitioners in Florida received land. "My country 'tis of thee," Whoopi exclaimed, when she received this news. "My country."

In the case of the astronaut Mae Jemison, we were able, incredibly, to trace three of her family lines deep into slavery, including discovering both a fourth great-grandmother and a fourth or fifth great-grandfather. Four of our subjects are descended from people who owned property in the 1800s, two well before the Civil War, and two more by 1881. The latter two, freed in 1865, in effect got their forty acres, if not the mule. Our genetic research also yielded a rich panoply of results, and a few surprises. My subjects share common ancestry with, among others, members of the Mbundu of Angola, the Kpelle of Liberia, the Tikar of Cameroon, the Igbo of Nigeria, the Mandinka and the Pepel of Guinea-Bissau, the Makua of Mozambique, and the Bamileke of Cameroon. I had expected the revelation of their African roots to form the dramatic climax of our research. But our subjects' reactions to their putative genetic identities remained somewhat abstract.

What really stirred them was the light shed on their American heritage, their known world, as Edward Jones put it. It was a world they could touch and imagine, through the branches of their family trees. Genealogy trumped genetics. It was as if Africa, as the poet Langston Hughes wrote, was "so long, so far away." Roots, like charity, start at home.

Contrary to conventional wisdom, and contrary to those who 15 worry about "the geneticization of identity," our sense of identity — in this case at least — seems to be more deeply rooted in the histories of family members we can name than in anonymous ancestors emerging out of the dense shadows of an African past, unveiled through a process admittedly still in its infancy. For my subjects, genealogy seems to have been a way of staking a claim on a richer American identity, an identity established through individual triumphs like the attainment of literacy and the purchasing of land.

What of my own case of *Roots* envy? We advertised for, and found, two male descendants of Samuel Brady, and compared their Y-DNA with mine. My haplotype, common in Western Ireland and the

Netherlands, has as much in common genetically with Samuel Brady as it does, I suppose, with half of the males in Galway and Amsterdam. So much for that bit of family lore.

On the other hand, our genealogical research uncovered, to my astonishment, one of my fifth great-grandfathers and two fourth great-grandfathers, two born in the middle of the eighteenth century. I learned that one, John Redman, a Free Negro, even fought in the American Revolution. Despite the fact that we didn't find Jane Gates's children's father, we believe that we have found her mother, a slave, born circa 1799.

As for my mitochondrial DNA, my mother's mother's mother's lineage? Would it be Yoruba, as I fervently hoped? My Fela Ransome-Kuti fantasy was not exactly borne out. A number of exact matches turned up, leading straight back to that African Kingdom called Northern Europe, to the genes of (among others) a female Ashkenazi Jew. Maybe it was time to start listening to "My Yiddishe Mama."

READING

1. Most *Wall Street Journal* readers would know that Gates is African American. What might they anticipate from the title of this piece? What does "yiddishe" mean?

2. Gates begins the essay by writing of his *Roots* envy. What does *Roots* refer to? Why might the ability to trace his ancestry be especially important to Gates or to his friend at Cambridge?

3. Gates describes the ancestry of several African American celebrities. Who are they? Given the general demographics of *WSJ* readers, would they recognize these names? Why might Gates pick these individuals to highlight?

4. The article makes use of vocabulary associated both with genetics and genealogy. How do these two areas of study differ? What are examples of the language associated with each?

5. Gates opens and closes his essay with his own ancestral search. What has he learned? Would the desire to trace and honor one's ancestry appeal to a *Wall Street Journal* reader? Why?

WRITING

1. Gates's self-portrait suggests that he is driven to learn about his ancestry. Write a reflective essay or journal entry describing your ancestry. How far back can you trace your lineage? Are you concerned with what you might find in your family tree?

2. Gates writes, "Throughout my adult life, I've always been drawn to Nigeria's Yoruba culture – to its cuisine, its legends, its rhythms, and its songs," though he has no proof that he has any connection to that country. Write an essay describing a culture to which you are drawn, regardless of any true familial connection. What attracts you to this culture?

3. The article includes a quick overview of African American history, especially as it relates to slavery. Write a short essay that expands on one of the topics that Gates touches on or references. Your essay should link the topic to the central theme of his piece: ancestry and family.

4. Gates observes of his research, "For my subjects, genealogy seems to have been a way of staking a claim on a richer American identity, an identity established through individual triumphs like the attainment of literacy and the purchasing of land." Interview a family

member (for example, your father or grandmother) about his or her parents to learn accomplishments that helped them "[stake] a claim on a richer American identity." Write an essay that describes these accomplishments and incorporates quotes from your interview subjects.

5. In "We're All Cousins and Other Web Revelations" (p. 141), Michael Schuyler — like Gates — traces his family history, but the two pieces have different approaches to the topic and are written for different audiences. Write an essay in which you compare the two, identifying how audience affects the style and tone of each.

We're All Cousins and Other Web Revelations

By Michael Schuyler

FROM: *Computers in Libraries,*
February 2000

CONTEXT: This article was published as part of a regular column, titled View from the Top Left Corner, by Michael Schuyler in the *Computers in Libraries* magazine. Schuyler is the deputy director of a regional public library. *Computers in Libraries* is an example of a special interest publication directed to a specific professional audience. It describes itself as a "monthly magazine that provides complete coverage of the news and issues in the rapidly evolving field of library information technology." Because of its narrow focus and target demographic, the magazine can assume much about its readership. As you read this piece, notice Schuyler's conversational tone and style as he writes to a group assumed to be his peers.

NOT LONG AGO MY FATHER PULLED OUT AN OLD BRIEFCASE with family photographs and a bunch of "old stuff." He gave me a yellow-aged cellophane envelope with something dark-brown inside it.

"Be careful when you open that," he said. "I got this as collateral when I went into the army in '42. I gave this guy $10 for it; he said it was worth $50. He never came back."

As I opened up the faded piece of paper, the words "Lincoln Assassination" appeared under the banner of the *New York Herald*. It was the front page of the paper from April 1865 with nothing on the obverse.

"It's a proof sheet," said my Dad. It had lain folded for sixty years, and perhaps fifty years before that, so it was cracked and flaking pieces of paper from the edge. I was impressed. I gingerly slid it back into the cellophane. It was almost to the point of falling into dust. It would need to be handled very carefully.

I hadn't thought much about preserving paper in a long time. I 5 had become increasingly concerned about computer files, though. I found some old disks, 5¼ inch for an Apple II that had old spread-sheets on them, but I really couldn't get at them. We no longer have computers that read Apple disks; indeed, we have no computers with other than a 3.5-inch drive in them anymore. Anything over ten years old and we copy back from paper, if it's available.

"So see how much it's worth," he said. "Get onto that Internet thing and see what you can do. It better be worth more than 10 bucks."

"OK," I said. And when I got back to "that Internet thing" I went out onto eBay.com to take a look. Typing "Lincoln newspaper" brought up an instant twenty hits, mostly for the *New York Herald*, 1865. They were going for $9.99 apiece. I called up my Dad.

"You lost a penny," I said, "if you don't count inflation."

"If I ever find that guy . . ." he said.

Our Best Customers

But it got me to thinking about all those people running through old microfilm of newspapers looking for obituaries. I've been working in public libraries for almost thirty years (I know, it's hard to believe, but I just counted it up), and I know many of us have just kind of cringed at these people when they came through the door. They always knew precisely what they wanted and that we didn't have it, so automatic interlibrary loan request. Then they'd sit for hours on end dominating the microfilm machines, running through reels and reels of tape. My colleagues would smile properly, though rolling their eyes in the background, and dutifully fulfill the requests.

They are, of course, the Genealogists. I always thought they were obsessive, at best. Today, however, the traditional genealogist, the one who spent years writing letters, visiting courthouses and cemeteries, and poring through thousands of reels of microfilm, is a little bit angry. Why?

Of Epidemic Proportions

The Internet. Genealogy is the second most popular subject on the Net. (You guess the first. When you think about it, they're related.) Look up anything vaguely genealogical on the Web, and you become instantly overwhelmed. There exist forums and mailing lists for most any surname.

Indexes of births, marriages, and deaths are everywhere. There are event-scanned images of the census available for certain years. There is a hard-core group of researchers dedicated to getting all the census information from 1790 to 1920 online as quickly as possible, along with ship passenger lists, county records, indeed, anything amounting to a historical record.

Further, all these amateur genealogists are placing all their material online on Web pages available to anyone. These are then indexed by various companies so that a Web search can yield instantaneous hits on your ancestors. Unfortunately, no one can vouch for the accuracy of this material, and that's what makes the traditional genealogists unhappy.

Suddenly a whole lot of misinformation is floating out there on the Net masquerading as fact. Documenting sources seems not to have occurred to most of the researchers now placing material online. Other than that small problem, there is a tremendous amount of material out there, and most of it is reasonably accurate.

More is showing up all the time. Just this year the Church of Jesus Christ of Latter-Day Saints (the Mormons) opened up much of its vast resources to the public for free. Just go to www.familysearch.com and type in a name. Not only does the church index its own site, but it also points to other Internet locations where there may be even more information. There are too many Internet resources to list, so just start with Cyndi's List at www.cyndislist.com and you'll see links everywhere.

The Mormons are the ones who developed the de facto database standard for genealogy files, called GEDCOM (Genealogical Data Communications), which are flat ASCII files. Any genealogy program can both export and import these files, so it's easy to trade trees with someone else.

Where to Get Started

Genealogy software abounds. Probably the most popular is Family Tree Maker, distributed by Broderbund (www.familytreemaker .com). This is a basic, easy program to use. Sierra Online (www .sierrahome.com) makes a program called Generations that is a bit more complex but provides beautiful charts. And the Master Genealogist (www.whollygenes.com) is widely considered to be the tool for the "professional." There's not enough room to list them all, but a good place to compare is genforum.genealogy.com/general/#computers.

It all started out when my cousin Randy called to ask a few questions about "our" ancestry. Problem was, I didn't know much. My mother had told me I was descended from Tennessee hillbillies who probably just started right there (snicker). I had one piece of information. My grandfather, Elum Mizell Russell, was born in Walnut Shade in 1872. He became a medical doctor and moved to Gunnison, Colorado, to work in the mining camps and to live in the dry climate. It didn't help his asthma, and my grandmother died at age forty of tuberculosis anyway. That's all I knew.

My father claims there was Cherokee Indian in his background 20 (Where have you heard this before? Everyone claims it), but with little to go on. So I always thought I was kind of a mutt and had no idea how far back any records went. I couldn't prove a thing. Out here in the Top Left Corner there's nothing much really old anyway. A house built in 1920 is ancient; we only became a state in 1889. (It was supposed to be named "Columbia," but politicians in Washington, D.C., decided that might be confused with the "District of Columbia" so they insisted it be changed to "Washington." Duh!) All the Native American stuff was made of wood, so except for what is in museums, not much has survived.

Well, It Worked for Me

My Uncle Bill, Randy's father, had been the family genealogist and had come to the conclusion that the family surname, Schuyler, had been changed from "Schyler" sometime in the past. This would make it German, not Dutch, and thus end the family feud on the pronunciation, as we're both wrong. So I went on the Web to www.genforum .com, typed in the forum for the surname, then searched on "Julius" as my ancestor's first name. Talk about instant feedback!

Julius Constantine William Schyler's father was a wealthy shipbuilder from Saxony, Prussia. His son was born on board ship about 1785. He was educated in Heidelberg and Oxford, but his father was upset that he had taken to religion and forced him aboard a ship, from which he jumped in America in 1810 or so, where he settled down and married Nancy Russell in 1818 in Guilford County, North Carolina. He earned a preacher's license by translating a sermon given in German to English on the fly.

This was just too easy. So I jumped on the Pack forum. Where Schuyler was a garden hose, this was a fire hose of information. There are Packs everywhere, even a book called *Countless Cousins* along with some controversy about a fellow named "Jeremiah Pack." I found the 1850 Cherokee County, North Carolina, census online at www .familytreemaker.com, looked up Jeremiah, listed as fifty-four years old in 1850, along with his seventeen-year-old son, Lafayette, my great-great-grandfather. There was a picture of the census right in front of me. No need to get microfilm rolls at all. He and Polly Gregory, his wife, are both listed as "illiterate." There's also a box for "idiotic." (It wasn't checked.)

In attempting to nail down who Jeremiah's parents were, another fellow was posting and responding to inquiries. I thought his e-mail address looked familiar so I wrote to him directly. Turns out he's my fourth cousin and lives ten miles from me in a place called Poulsbo. We worked on the issue together and found a probable link to Smith

Green Pack as Jeremiah's father. And where else do we find Smith Green? On the 1835 Indian rolls as a full-blood Cherokee, a descendent of Emperor Moytoy of the Cherokee Nation.

I'd not forgotten about Walnut Shade, Tennessee, so when things 25 started slowing down on the Packs, I flipped over to the Russell forum to ask a few questions. Meanwhile I went to www.ancestry.com where there are thousands of family trees submitted by users. I searched on Elum and the alternative spelling, Elam, and came up with a half dozen trees instantly. After downloading and peering at them in Family Tree Maker, it looked like a mess. I could see where the pros were having problems with information quality. One tree had my great-great-grandfather marrying his own granddaughter. Another had a fellow's mother born two years after he was.

Surnames kept popping up everywhere again and again. Families seemed to intermarry generation after generation. There were several first-cousin marriages. It's hard to keep track of that many people when the rule was to have ten kids and get married two or three times. Your first spouse died so you got another one in a hurry to take care of the kids.

In a response to a posting on Genforum, I found a second cousin in Illinois who invited me to the Smith County, Tennessee, listserv. I took a look and found "dozens of cousins" who had traced us back to 1619 in Jamestown, then back to England. Jesse James is a sixth cousin; Blackbeard the Pirate is rumored, but not proven. The Montagues, except for that accursed fifty-year "Montague Gap" making this just out of reach, go back to 1066. Captain Peter Montague, this one proven, made his money ferrying immigrants across the Atlantic.

Seeing a Portrait of the Past

With the benefit of a few months, now I look at this information and get a very different sense of life for our ancestors. During the Civil War, for example, you can see the havoc wrought upon families. Two Cornwell sisters married a Russell and a Parkhurst. Each family had half a dozen children. Then Parkhurst fought and died in the Civil War leaving a thirty-year-old widow with six kids. Her sister died in childbirth leaving Russell with six kids of his own. So he married the second Cornwell and had a few more kids with her.

I found the wills of several ancestors (it's all online on the Net) and discovered to my shock that some of these guys were slave owners who left slaves as property to their descendants. That 1619 fellow in Jamestown, John Woodson, bought some of the first slaves ever to come across. I had no idea, of course, and had always felt remote on that issue. But now it turns out these folks were willing participants.

Overwhelmed by this revelation, I have never felt so connected with the history of our country.

On the census tracts you see that the enumerators walked from 30 house to house, and relations lived next door to one another. Whole neighborhoods were composed of the same surnames over and over again. You look at an 1850 census, the first one with good information that enumerates people rather than gives numbers, then the 1860 or 1870 and see fathers living with daughters as they got old, or sisters-in-law living in a relation's household with a nephew after a father had died. You see tuberculosis ravaging through families like wildfire. If someone got to be seventy, that was very old, and hundreds of kids died before they were ten. From census to census, a ten-year span, you see names drop off, too.

Making Global Connections

It's almost guaranteed you'll meet some cousins you didn't know you had when you research these issues. Nearly everyone is helpful and willing to send information to you. After hearing about all the bad stuff on the Internet, here's a place that is good and helpful. It's a nice change.

Now at a certain point this gets absurd. A little math will tell you why. You have two parents, and if you accept that throughout history people got married a little earlier than they do now, there are at least four generations per century. In a thousand years you have a trillion ancestors when the population of the entire globe was several hundred million total.

Two points here: First, a lot of cousins married each other. They may have been second or third cousins, but there's no other way. There weren't enough nonrelated people to go around. Secondly, it doesn't take much to be related to everyone. We're talking 1,000 years here. Go back 2,000, still in recorded history. All it takes is one guy, a Marco Polo, perhaps, wandering around the world in exotic places. Just one to settle down and have kids and contribute to the gene pool. That means we are all related, regardless of race, a lot more closely than we might have thought.

That's why I think genealogy is a little more than people looking at rolls of microfilm. There ought to come a time, pretty soon in the future, where enough people have contributed their family trees so that someone could run a program and tie them all together. One place that encourages this is Rootsweb.com, which has a World Connect project that is seeking volunteers to index everything there is on genealogy. FamilyTreeMaker.com encourages input to World Family Trees as well, but once you contribute (for free) they include the tree on a CD-ROM and then sell it back to you.

It turns out that my father, who is eighty-four and lives in 35 Tacoma, has become pretty interested in this whole issue. He doesn't have Internet access, but this has perked him up a bit. I showed him a picture from the countless cousins book and he said, "My goodness, that looks just like Grandpa!"

"Well, they all have big ears," I said. Do you remember that Julius Constantine Schyler married Nancy Russell? Well, the Russells moved from Virginia and North Carolina to Tennessee about that time. On Genforum some people are trying to make a connection to a Nancy Russell born in the late 1700s in Guilford County, North Carolina. It seemed obvious to me, though I can't prove it yet.

"Dad," I said, "I think you married your cousin."

"Well, that explains how you turned out," he said.

READING

1. Schuyler opens the essay by relating an anecdote involving his father and his father's past. How does this set up the discussion that follows?

2. Schuyler uses headings throughout this piece to organize his ideas. How do these headings relate to the material they precede? Do you find them useful as a reader?

3. The essay references specific types of genealogy software and websites. Think about Schuyler's audience. How would they use this information?

4. Schuyler weaves his personal search throughout the piece and uses diction and style that might be characterized as fairly informal, especially given that he is writing in a professional journal. If you had to describe Schuyler as a person based upon what you have read, what would you say? Does his style appeal to you?

5. At one point in the column, Schuyler writes, "we are all related, regardless of race, a lot more closely than we might have thought." How do observations like this move the essay beyond being a simple "how to" piece about genealogy research? What seems to be his larger point?

WRITING

1. Schuyler's column reveals how much personal information is readily available on the web, making it quite easy for anyone to trace familial connections – and more difficult for anyone to conceal the same information. Write a reflective essay or journal entry describing your feelings about the lack of privacy created by the ease of information access he cites. How secret can family secrets remain in the Internet age?

2. Schuyler wryly observes, "My father claims there was Cherokee Indian in his background (Where have you heard this before? Everyone claims it). . . . " Every family has its own story of an exotic relative or momentous event. Write an essay recounting your family's favorite tall tale and discuss why this story is important to understanding your family.

3. The column suggests that there is conflict between traditional genealogists, who use archival source documents and classic research techniques, and amateur genealogists, who use the Internet almost

exclusively. Write an essay that defines the field of genealogy and explains why these two groups might be in conflict. Your essay should address how their research methodologies differ.

4. Writing in a publication targeted to librarians, Schuyler offers many websites that would assist librarian patrons in their research. Using one of these sites, research your own family and write an essay that discusses your findings. How confident are you in your research results?

5. We are often tempted to look nostalgically at the past, thinking of it as a simpler time that brought families closer together. But in his column, Schuyler provides a mini-history of life in the United States during the late 1800s that does not always seem pleasant or family friendly. Stephanie Coontz, in "The American Family" (p. 94), opens with a similar clear-eyed look at this era of our country's past. Select a decade between 1850 and 1900 and research family life during these years. Write a researched essay that summarizes your findings and compares the life of a typical family of that decade to your family's life today.

Roca Wear and Brooks Brothers Advertisements

FROM: *Cookie,* September 2006

CONTEXT: Both of the advertisements that follow come from *Cookie* magazine. *Cookie* is a relatively new Condé Nast publication with a mission to "provide all the best for your family." It espouses a belief that "being a good parent and maintaining your sense of style are not mutually exclusive." The majority of its subscribers are college-educated women with a median age of thirty-six, and almost 43 percent of its subscribing households have incomes over $100,000. One ad is for Roca Wear, a clothing company founded in the mid-1990s by rap impresarios Shawn "Jay-Z" Carter, Damon Dash, and Kareem "Biggs" Burke. Roca Wear is currently a $700 million dollar corporation that, according to its press kit, "defines the lifestyle for today's young hip consumer." The other is for Brooks Brothers, which is owned by Retail Brand Alliance (RBA), a holding company with almost $1.5 billion in revenue. After purchasing the Brooks Brothers brand from a British company, RBA has made a concerted effort to return it to its classic roots, and its image is now designed around the company's status as America's oldest clothing retailer. As you examine these ads, consider what market they seem to be targeting. (Tierney Gearon/Cookie. Copyright © 2006 Condé Nast Publications. Reprinted by permission. All rights reserved.)

Roca Wear

"Brooks Brothers®" and the Brooks Brothers' logos are registered trademarks of Retail Brand Alliance, Inc. and are used with permission.

RESPONDING

1. Each advertisement contains a tagline for its product. The line in the Roca Wear ad seems quite serious in tone, while that for Brooks Brothers plays off its blueblood heritage. Write a short essay that analyzes the text in each ad and describes the relationship of the text to the visuals. What does this relationship suggest about the target audience?

2. In its own way, each ad constitutes a commercialized family portrait. Pick one of the ads and write the biography of its family. In your biography, support your observations with visual and textual clues offered in the ad. Include references to design elements, such as spatial relationships, as well as the features, attire, and expressions of the models.

3. Roca Wear initially started as a purveyor of street wear for young men but branched into children's wear because it saw a market there. Research another hip brand that has moved into youth clothing (for example, Tommy Hilfiger, Sean John, Juicy Couture) and develop a presentation for your class that explains how this clothing is marketing to upscale parents. What message about family does this brand send?

4. In her essay "The American Family" (p. 94), Stephanie Coontz writes, "Women's new options are good not just for themselves but for their children. While some people say that women who choose to work are selfish, it turns out that maternal self-sacrifice is not good for children. Kids do better when their mothers are happy with their lives, whether their satisfaction comes from being a full-time homemaker or from having a job" (p. 98). Consider *Cookie*'s demographic and the image of family being depicted in these ads. Find at least two more ads from family-oriented magazines. Write an essay that discusses how all four ads appeal to a working mother who wants to believe that her choice has impacted both herself and her family in a positive way.

FOCUS ON GENRE

Memoirs

A Portfolio of Family Memoirs

YOU MAY REMEMBER A PARTICULAR MOMENT IN TIME THAT SEEMS to represent the essence of your family life. This memory might involve taking your children to Disney World, remembering how the cat used to sleep in the sink, attending baseball games with your uncle, sitting around the table at Thanksgiving, learning to drive, or the time you and your brother raced sleds down a steep hill.

We all have family stories, no matter who our family is – whether our family is created by blood, choice, or circumstance. In "Grandmothers," Ruth Reichl tells us about her favorite grandmother. "Aunt Birdie wasn't really related to me; she was my father's first wife's mother. But she desperately wanted to be a grandmother, so when I was born she went to the hospital, introduced herself to my mother, and applied for the job."

In the following memoirs, culled from essay collections, book-length memoirs, and regional journals, writers look back at their experiences of family – how a father-son relationship is nurtured through difficult adolescent years through a mutually intense appreciation of Nebraska Cornhuskers football – or how a granddaughter is cautioned against perfidious men by the elder women of her family telling stories about the community that she is allowed to overhear.

Through remembering family stories, we weave the strands of our lives together to form the new families that exist today. As you read the following memoirs, allow yourself to remember the family stories that are important to you.

The first selection is excerpted from Philip Weitl's "The Important Things," *Nebraska Life,* September/October 2005.

MY FATHER COULDN'T THROW A FOOT-ball overhanded like a real quarterback. The motion of raising the ball up and behind his ear and then swinging it forward like a snapping whip sent sharp pains through his shoulder joint, which had been broken down by years of heavy lifting and overuse that began when he was barely a teenager. Not to be prevented from playing catch with his son, he learned how to throw the ball underhanded, and in our backyard in York his spiral was as tight and true as a Joe Montana Super Bowl throw.

Football is important in Nebraska. Over the years, various observers have described fan support for the Nebraska Cornhuskers as a religious devotion. After living nearly twenty years in Nebraska and being married to a passionate Husker fan, my father had been converted from any allegiances he may have had to schools in his home state of Iowa. I took to this devotion quickly and easily. Like many Nebraska kids, my heroes wore scarlet and cream on fall Saturday afternoons. As a little boy, I ended every fantastical backyard game by throwing the game-winning touchdown pass to win Nebraska's first National Championship since 1971. If the large ash tree in the middle of the yard batted my pass down, my imaginary referee would always call a pass interference penalty and give me a second chance at glory. Sometimes, my father would play the role of quarterback. I would double as a famed Nebraska I-back and radio announcer.

"Okay, Dad, you ready?" I would ask him as we stood on one end of our rectangular backyard, as close as we could get to the chain-link fence without touching it.

"I'm ready," he would reply. "What's the score?"

"We're down by four," I'd say. "Ten seconds left on the clock. We need a touchdown. A field goal isn't enough."

Grandmothers
By Ruth Reichl

FROM: *Tender at the Bone: Growing Up at the Table,*
Broadway Books, 1999

I HAD THREE GRANDMOTHERS AND NONE OF THEM COULD cook.

My mother's mother didn't cook because she had better things to do. She was, as Mom proudly told everyone she happened to meet, an impresario.

My father's mother didn't cook because she was, until Hitler intervened, a very rich woman.

And Aunt Birdie didn't cook because she had Alice.

Aunt Birdie wasn't really related to me; she was my father's first wife's mother. But she desperately wanted to be a grandmother, so when I was born she went to the hospital, introduced herself to my mother, and applied for the job. She was well past eighty, and this looked like her last chance.

Mom was happy to take any help she could get, and Aunt Birdie threw herself into the job. About once a week I would come out of school to find her waiting on the sidewalk. My friends instantly surrounded her, enchanted by standing next to a grown-up who was just their size. At four foot eight, Aunt Birdie was the smallest grown-up any of us had ever seen and when she said, "Let's go to Schrafft's!" there was a general moan. Everybody envied me.

We always ordered the same thing. Then we ate our chocolate-marshmallow sundaes slowly, watching the women ascend the restaurant's wide, dramatic stairway and commenting on their clothes, their hair, the way they walked. Aunt Birdie always acted as if I were the world's most fascinating person. I wondered if she had been this way with her daughter, the one my father had once been married to, but each time I said the word "Hortense" she pretended not to hear me. Everybody did.

Afterward, Aunt Birdie always took me back to her house. After the long bus ride I'd run into the kitchen, throw my arms around Alice, and beg her to let me roll the dough for the apple dumplings she made every time I slept over. "Well now," she always said in the soft Barbados accent she had retained after sixty years in America, patting me with her floury hands. She was a handsome old woman with brown skin, short black hair, and a deeply wrinkled face. She smelled like starch, lemons, and if she was baking, cinnamon as well.

I loved helping her, loved feeling the fresh buttery pastry beneath my hands, loved the clean way the core came out of the apples. I loved carefully wrapping each apple in a square of pastry and pinching the top shut, just so. We'd arrange the dumplings on a baking sheet, Alice would put them in the oven, and we'd both go into the living room to watch *The Perry Como Show*. This was a big thrill too; my parents didn't own a television.

Alice always left as soon as the show was over. Then Aunt Birdie and I ate whatever she had left simmering on the stove for supper.

On Saturday mornings we ate the remaining apple dumplings. We brushed our teeth. We made our beds. And then we went into the kitchen to make potato salad for my father. It was the only thing Aunt Birdie ever cooked. "Alice is the cook in our family," she said.

My mother would have pointed out that Alice was not really in Aunt Birdie's family. She did not consider herself a particularly prejudiced person and she often pointed out that she and Dad were married by a black minister. "He was the husband of Dorothy Maynor, the singer," she'd go on, bragging about the beautiful music. But I had noticed that, with the exception of celebrities, Mom's world was entirely white and that she referred to whichever brown-skinned women happened to be cleaning our house as "the girl." Dad was different: he was totally without prejudice, a fact he attributed to having been brought up in Germany. He understood Alice's position perfectly.

And so each time Aunt Birdie handed him the jar of potato salad he would fold his tall frame until he could reach her cheek, kiss it, and say gently, "Alice is a fabulous cook. But *you* make the world's best potato salad."

Aunt Birdie's Potato Salad

3 pounds small potatoes	*⅓ cup vegetable oil*
Salt and pepper to taste	*½ cup white vinegar*
1 tablespoon sugar	*2 tablespoons water*
2 onions, sliced	

Boil potatoes for 15 to 20 minutes until just tender. Drain and let cool slightly. Peel and slice into even rounds.

Season with salt, pepper, and sugar. Add onions. Add oil and mix gently.

Dilute vinegar with water and bring to a boil. Add to potato mixture while hot and mix well.

Serves 6 to 8.

Alice's Apple Dumplings with Hard Sauce

2 cups flour	*5 apples, peeled and cored*
1 teaspoon salt	*¼ cup sugar*
¼ cups shortening	*1 teaspoon cinnamon*
¼ cup ice water	*1 tablespoon butter*

Mix flour with salt. Cut in shortening with two knives until the shortening is the size of peas. Add water slowly until you can gather the dough into a ball with a fork.

Roll out dough and cut into 5 squares. Put an apple in the center of each square.

Mix sugar and cinnamon. Fill the center of each apple with the sugar mixture. Put a dab of butter on top of each. Bring pastry up around the apple to make a package, dabbing edges with a bit of water if necessary to seal. Chill 30 minutes.

Preheat oven to 350°.

Bake for about 40 minutes, or until apples are tender.

Serve warm with hard sauce.

Serves 5.

Hard Sauce

¾ cup unsalted butter at	*Dash of salt*
room temperature	*2 teaspoons vanilla*
1½ cups sugar	

Cream the butter until soft. Gradually add sugar and salt until creamy and light. Add vanilla and chill.

Makes about 1 cup.

Where He Was: Memories of My Father

By Raymond Carver

FROM: *The Granta Book of the Family*, Granta Books/Penguin Books, 1997

MY DAD'S NAME WAS CLEVIE RAYMOND CARVER. HIS FAMILY called him Raymond, and friends called him C.R. I was named Raymond Clevie Carver, Jr. I hated the "Junior" part. When I was little, my dad called me "Frog," which was OK. But later, like everybody else in the family, he began calling me "Junior." He went on calling me this until I was thirteen or fourteen and announced that I wouldn't answer to that name any longer. So he began calling me "Doc." From then until his death on 17 June 1967, he called me "Doc" or else "Son."

When he died, my mother telephoned my wife with the news. I was away from my family at the time, between lives, trying to enroll in the School of Library Science at the University of Iowa. When my wife answered the phone, my mother blurted out, "Raymond's dead!" For a moment, my wife thought my mother was telling her that I was dead. Then my mother made it clear which Raymond she was talking about, and my wife said, "Thank God. I thought you meant *my* Raymond."

My dad walked, hitched rides, and rode in empty box cars when he went from Arkansas to Washington State in 1934, looking for work. I don't know whether or not he was pursuing a dream when he went out to Washington. I doubt it. I don't think he dreamed much. I believe he was simply looking for steady work at decent pay. Steady work was meaningful work. He picked apples for a time and then landed a construction laborer's job on the Grand Coulee Dam. After he'd put aside a little money, he bought a car and drove back to Arkansas to help his folks, my grandparents, pack up for the move west. He said later that they were about to starve down there; and this wasn't meant as a figure of speech. It was during that short while in Arkansas, in a town called Leola, that my mother met my dad on the sidewalk as he came out of a tavern.

"He was drunk," she said. "I don't know why I let him talk to me. His eyes were glittery. I wish I'd had a crystal ball." They'd met once, a year or so before, at a dance. He'd had girlfriends before her, my mother told me. "Your dad always had a girlfriend, even after we married. He was my first and last. I never had another man. But I didn't miss anything."

They were married by a justice of the peace on the day they left for Washington, this big, tall country girl and an ex-farmhand-turned-construction worker. My mother spent her wedding night with my dad and his folks, all of them camped beside the road in Arkansas.

In Omak, Washington, my dad and mother lived in a little place not much bigger than a cabin. My grandparents lived next door. My dad was still working on the dam and later, with the huge turbines producing electricity and the water backed up for a hundred miles into Canada, he stood in the crowd and heard Franklin D. Roosevelt dedicate the dam. "He never mentioned those guys who died building that dam," my dad said. Some of his friends had died there, men from Arkansas, Oklahoma, and Missouri.

He then took a job in a sawmill in Clatskanie, Oregon, a little town alongside the Columbia river. I was born there, and my mother has a picture of my dad standing in front of the gate to the mill, proudly holding me up to face the camera. My bonnet is on crooked and about to come untied. His hat is pushed back on his forehead, and he's wearing a big grin. Was he going in to work, or just finishing his shift? It doesn't matter. In either case, he had a job and a family. These were his salad days.

In 1941 we moved to Yakima, Washington, where my dad went to work as a saw-filer, a skilled trade he'd learned at the mill in Clatskanie. When war broke out, he was given a deferment because his work was considered necessary to the war effort. Finished lumber was in demand by the armed services, and he kept his saws so sharp they could shave the hair off your arm.

After my dad had moved us to Yakima, he moved his folks into the same neighborhood. By the mid-1940s, the rest of my dad's family — his brother, his sister and her husband, as well as uncles, cousins, nephews and most of their extended family and friends — had come out from Arkansas. All because my dad came out first. The men went to work at Boise Cascade, where my dad worked, and the women packed apples in the canneries. And in just a little while, it seemed — according to my mother — everybody was better off than my dad.

"Your dad couldn't keep money," my mother said. "Money burned a hole in his pocket. He was always doing for others."

The first house I clearly remember living in, at 1515 South Fifteenth Street, in Yakima, had an outdoor toilet. On Halloween night, or just any night for the hell of it, neighboring kids, kids in their early teens, would carry our toilet away and leave it next to the road. My dad would have to get somebody to help him bring it home. Or these kids would take the toilet and stand it in somebody else's backyard. Once they actually set it on fire. But ours wasn't the only house that had an outdoor toilet. When I was old enough to know what I was doing, I threw rocks at the other toilets when I'd see someone go inside. This was called bombing the toilets. After a while, though, everyone changed to indoor plumbing until, suddenly, our toilet was the last one in the neighborhood. I remember the shame I felt when my third-grade teacher, Mr Wise, drove me home from school one day. I asked him to stop at the house just before ours, claiming I lived there.

I had one bad spanking from my dad when I was little. He took off his belt and laid it on me when he caught me walking down a railroad trestle. As he was whipping me, he said, "This hurts me worse than it does you." Even at the time, as small and dumb as I was, I knew this wasn't true. It had the sound of something his father might have said to him under the same circumstances.

I can recall what happened one night when my dad came home late to find that my mother had locked all the doors on him. He was drunk, and we could feel the house shudder as he rattled the door. When he'd managed to force open a window, she hit him between the eyes with a colander and knocked him out. We could see him down there on the grass. For years afterwards, I used to pick up this colander — it was heavy as a rolling-pin — and imagine what it would feel like to be hit in the face with something like that.

It was during this period that I remember my dad taking me into the bedroom, sitting me down on the bed and telling me that I might have to go live with my Aunt LaVon for a while. I couldn't understand what I'd done that meant I'd have to go away from home to live. But this, too — whatever prompted it — must have blown over, more or less anyway, because we stayed together, and I didn't have to go live with her or anyone else.

For a time in the late forties we didn't have a car. We had to walk everywhere we wanted to go, or else take the bus that stopped near where they used to carry our toilet. I don't know why we didn't have a car, some sort of car, but we didn't. Still, it was all right with me that we didn't. I didn't miss it. I mean, we didn't have a car and that's all there was to it. Back then I didn't miss what I didn't have. "We couldn't afford a car," my mother said, when I asked her. "It was your dad. He drank it up."

If we wanted to fish, my dad and I would walk to some ponds that were only a couple of miles away, or to the Yakima river, only a little farther away than the ponds. With or without a car, we went fishing nearly every weekend. But once in a while my dad wouldn't want to get out of bed. "He feels bad," my mother would say. "No wonder. You better leave him alone."

I remember her pouring his whiskey down the sink. Sometimes she'd pour it all out and sometimes, if she was afraid of getting caught, she'd only pour half of it out and then add water to the rest. I tasted some of his whiskey once for myself. It was terrible stuff, and I didn't see how anybody could drink it.

When we finally did get a car, in 1949 or 1950, it was a 1938 Ford. But it threw a rod the first week we had it, and my dad had to have the motor rebuilt.

"We drove the oldest car in town," my mother said. "We could have had a Cadillac for all he spent on car repairs." One time she found someone else's lipstick on the floorboards, along with a lacy handkerchief. "See this?" she said to me. "Some floozie left this in the car."

Once I saw her take a pan of warm water into the bedroom where my dad was sleeping. She took his hand from under the covers and held it in the water. I stood in the doorway and watched. I wanted to know what was going on. This would make him talk in his sleep, she told me. There were things she needed to know, things she was sure he was keeping from her.

Every year or so, when I was little, we would take the North Coast Limited across the Cascade Mountains from Yakima to Seattle and stay in the Vance Hotel and eat, I remember, at a place called the Dinner Bell Café. Once we went to Ivar's Acres of Clams and drank glasses of warm clam broth.

Both my grandparents died in 1955. In 1956, the year I was to graduate from high school, my dad quit his job at the mill in Yakima and took a job in Chester, a little sawmill town in northern California. The reasons given at the time for his taking the job had to do with a higher hourly wage and the vague promise that he might, in a few years' time, succeed to the job of head filer in this new mill. But I think, in the main, that my dad had grown restless and simply wanted to try his luck elsewhere. Things had gotten a little too predictable for him in Yakima. Also, there were the deaths, within six months of each other, of my grandparents.

But just a few days after my graduation, when my mother and I were packed to move to Chester, my dad penciled a letter to say he'd been sick for a while. He didn't want us to worry, he said, but he'd cut himself on a saw. Maybe he'd got a tiny silver of steel in his blood. Anyway, something had happened and he'd had to miss work, he said. In the same mail was an unsigned postcard from somebody down there telling my mother that my dad was about to die and that he was drinking "raw whiskey."

When we arrived in Chester my dad was living in a trailer that belonged to the company. I didn't recognize him immediately. I guess for a moment I didn't want to recognize him. He was skinny and pale and looked bewildered. His pants wouldn't stay up. He didn't look like my dad. My mother began to cry. My dad put his arm around her and patted her shoulder vaguely like he didn't know what this was all about, either. The three of us took up life together in the trailer, and we looked after him as best we could. But my dad was sick, and he couldn't get any better. I worked with him in the mill that summer and part of the fall. We'd get up in the mornings and eat eggs and toast while we listened to the radio, and then go out the door with our lunch pails. We'd pass through the gates together at eight in the morning, and I wouldn't see him again until quitting time. In November I went back to Yakima to be closer to my girlfriend, the girl I'd made up my mind I was going to marry.

He worked at the mill in Chester until the following February, when he collapsed on the job and was taken to hospital. My mother asked me to come down there and help. I caught a bus from Yakima to Chester, intending to drive them back to Yakima. But now, in addition to being physically sick, my dad was in the midst of a nervous breakdown, though none of us knew to call it that at the time. During the entire trip back to Yakima, he didn't speak, not even when asked a direct question. ("How do you feel, Raymond?" "You OK, Dad?") He'd communicate, if he communicated at all, by moving his head or else turning his palms up as if to say he didn't know or care. The only time he said anything on the trip, and for nearly a month afterwards, was when I was speeding down a gravel road in Oregon and the car muffler came loose. "You were going too fast," he said.

Back in Yakima a doctor saw to it that my dad went to a psychiatrist. My mother and dad had to go on relief, as it was called, and the County paid for the psychiatrist. The psychiatrist asked my dad, "Who is the President?" He'd had a question put to him that he could answer. "Ike," my dad said. Nevertheless, they put him on the fifth floor of Valley Memorial Hospital and began giving him electric shock treatments. I was married by then and about to start my own family. My dad was still locked up when my wife went into the same hospital, just one floor down, to have our first baby.

After she had delivered, I went upstairs to give my dad the news. They let me in through a steel door and showed me where I could find him. He was sitting on a couch with a blanket over his lap. *Hey*, I thought. *What in hell is happening to my dad?* I sat down next to him and told him he was a grandfather. He waited a minute and said, "I feel like a grandfather." That's all he said. He didn't smile or move. He was in a big room with a lot of other people. Then I hugged him, and he began to cry.

Somehow he got out of there. But now came the years when he couldn't work and just sat around the house trying to figure what next and what he'd done wrong in his life that he'd wound up like this. My mother went from job to crummy job. Much later she referred to that time he was in the hospital, and those years just afterwards, as "when Raymond was sick." The word "sick" was never the same for me again.

In 1964, through the help of a friend, he was lucky enough to be hired at a mill in Klamath, California. He moved down there by himself to see if he could hack it. He lived not far from the mill in a one-room cabin, not much different from the place he and my mother had started living in when they went west. He scrawled letters to my mother, and if I called, she'd read them aloud to me over the phone. In the letters, he said it was touch and go. Every day he went to work he felt like it was the most important day of his life. But every day, he told her, made the next day that much easier. He said for her to tell me he said hello. If he couldn't sleep at night, he said, he thought about me and the good times we used to have. Finally, after a couple of months, he regained some of his confidence. He could do the work and didn't think he had to worry that he'd let anybody down ever again. When he was sure, he sent for my mother.

He'd been off work for six years and had lost everything in that time: home, car, furniture and appliances, including the big freezer that had been my mother's pride and joy. He'd lost his good name too — Raymond Carver was someone who couldn't pay his bills — and his self-respect was gone too. He'd even lost his virility. My mother told my wife, "All during that time Raymond was sick we slept together in the same bed, but we didn't have relations. He wanted to a few times, but nothing happened. I didn't miss it, but I think he wanted to, you know."

During those years I was trying to raise my own family and earn a living. But, with one thing and another, we found ourselves having to move a lot. I couldn't keep track of what was going on in my dad's life. But I did have a chance one Christmas to tell him I wanted to be a writer. I might as well have told him I wanted to become a plastic surgeon. "What are you going to write about?" he wanted to know. Then, as if to help me out, he said, "Write about the stuff you know about. Write about some of those fishing trips we took." I said I would, but I knew I wouldn't. "Send me what you write," he said. I said I'd do that, but then I didn't. I wasn't writing anything about fishing, and I didn't think he'd particularly care about, or even necessarily understand, what I was writing in those days. Besides, he wasn't a reader. Not the sort, anyway, I imagined I was writing for.

Then he died. I was a long way off, in Iowa City, with things still to say to him. I didn't have the chance to tell him goodbye, or that I thought he was doing great at his new job. That I was proud of him for making a comeback.

My mother said he came in from work that night and ate a big supper. Then he sat at the table by himself and finished what was left of a bottle of whiskey, a bottle she found hidden in the bottom of the garbage under some coffee grounds a day or so later. Then he got up and went to bed, where my mother joined him a little later. But in the night she had to get up and make a bed for herself on the couch. "He was snoring so loud I couldn't sleep," she said. The next morning when she looked in on him, he was on his back with his mouth open, his cheeks caved in. *Graylooking*, she said. She knew he was dead — she didn't need a doctor to tell her that. But she called one, anyway, and then she called my wife.

Among the pictures my mother kept of my dad and herself during those early days in Washington was a photograph of him standing in front of a car, holding a beer and a stringer of fish. In the photograph he is wearing his hat back on his forehead and has this awkward grin on his face. I asked her for it and she gave it to me, along with some others. I put it up on my wall, and each time we moved, I took the picture along and put it up on another wall. I looked at it carefully from time to time, trying to figure out some things about my dad, and maybe myself in the process. But I couldn't. My dad just kept moving farther and farther away from me and back into time. Finally, in the course of another move, I lost the photograph. It was then I tried to recall it, and at the same time make an attempt to say something about my dad, and how I thought that in some important ways we might be alike. I wrote the poem when I was living in an apartment house in an urban area south of San Francisco and at a time when I found myself, like dad, having trouble with alcohol. The poem was a way of trying to connect up with him.

Photograph of My Father in His Twenty-Second Year

October. Here in this dank, unfamiliar kitchen
I study my father's embarrassed young man's face.
Sheepish grin, he holds in one hand a string
of spiny yellow perch, in the other
a bottle of Carlsberg beer.

In jeans and flannel shirt, he leans
against the front fender of a 1934 Ford.
He would like to pose brave and hearty for his posterity,
wear his old hat cocked over his ear.
All his life my father wanted to be bold.

But the eyes give him away, and the hands
that limply offer the string of dead perch

> and the bottle of beer. Father, I love you,
> yet how can I say thank you,
> > I who can't hold my liquor either
> and don't even know the places to fish.

The poem is true in its particulars, except that my dad died in June and not October, as the first word of the poem says. I wanted a word with more than one syllable to it to make it linger a little. But more than that, I wanted a month appropriate to what I felt at the time I wrote the poem — a month of short days and failing light, smoke in the air, things perishing. June was summer nights and days, graduations, my wedding anniversary, the birthday of one of my children. June wasn't a month your father died in.

After the service at the funeral home, after we had moved outside, a woman I didn't know came over to me and said, "He's happier where he is now." I stared at this woman until she moved away. I still remember the little knob of a hat she was wearing. Then one of my dad's cousins — I didn't know the man's name — reached out and took my hand. "We all miss him," he said, and I knew he wasn't saying it to be polite.

I began to weep for the first time since receiving the news. I hadn't been able to before. I hadn't had the time, for one thing. Now, suddenly, I couldn't stop. I held my wife and wept while she said and did what she could to comfort me there in the middle of that summer afternoon.

I listened to people say consoling things to my mother, and I was glad that my dad's family had turned up, had come to where he was. I thought I'd remember everything that was said and done that day and maybe find a way to tell it sometime. But I didn't. I forgot it all, or nearly. What I do remember is that I heard our name used a lot that afternoon, my dad's name and mine. But I knew they were talking about my dad. *Raymond*, these people kept saying in their beautiful voices out of my childhood. *Raymond*.

Casa: A Partial Remembrance of a Puerto Rican Childhood
By Judith Ortiz Cofer

FROM: *Prairie Schooner*, Volume 63, Number 3, Fall 1989

AT THREE OR FOUR O'CLOCK IN THE AFTERNOON, THE HOUR of *café con leche*, the women of my family gathered in Mamá's living room to speak of important things and retell familiar stories meant to be overheard by us young girls, their daughters. In Mamá's house (everyone called my grandmother Mamá) was a large parlor built by my grandfather to his wife's exact specifications so that it was always cool, facing away from the sun. The doorway was on the side of the house so no one could walk directly into her living room. First they had to take a little stroll through and around her beautiful garden where prize-winning orchids grew in the trunk of an ancient tree she had hollowed out for that purpose. This room was furnished with several mahogany rocking chairs, acquired at the births of her children, and one intricately carved rocker that had passed down to Mamá at the death of her own mother.

It was on these rockers that my mother, her sisters, and my grandmother sat on these afternoons of my childhood to tell their stories, teaching each other, and my cousin and me, what it was like to be a woman, more specifically, a Puerto Rican woman. They talked about life on the island, and life in *Los Nueva Yores*, their way of referring to the United States from New York City to California: the other place, not home, all the same. They told real-life stories though, as I later learned, always embellishing them with a little or a lot of dramatic detail. And they told *cuentos*, the morality and cautionary tales told by the women in our family for generations: stories that became a part of my subconscious as I grew up in two worlds, the tropical island and the cold city, and that would later surface in my dreams and in my poetry.

One of these tales was about the woman who was left at the altar. Mamá liked to tell that one with histrionic intensity. I remember the rise and fall of her voice, the sighs, and her constantly gesturing hands, like two birds swooping through her words. This particular story usually would come up in a conversation as a result of someone mentioning a forthcoming engagement or wedding. The first time I remember hearing it, I was sitting on the floor at Mamá's feet, pretending to read a comic book. I may have been eleven or twelve years old, at that difficult age when a girl was no longer a child who could be ordered to leave the room if the women wanted freedom to take their talk into forbidden zones, nor really old enough to be considered a part of their conclave. I could only sit quietly, pretending to be in another world, while absorbing it all in a sort of unspoken agreement of my status as silent auditor. On this day, Mamá had taken my long, tangled mane of hair into her ever-busy hands. Without looking down at me and with no interruption of her flow of words, she began braiding my hair, working at it with the quickness and determination that characterized all her actions. My mother was watching us impassively from her rocker across the room. On her lips played a little ironic smile. I would never sit still for *her* ministrations, but even then, I instinctively knew that she did not possess Mamá's matriarchal power to command and keep everyone's attention. This was never more evident than in the spell she cast when telling a story.

"It is not like it used to be when I was a girl," Mamá announced. "Then, a man could leave a girl standing at the church altar with a bouquet of fresh flowers in her hands and disappear off the face of the earth. No way to track him down if he was from another town. He could be a married man, with maybe even two or three families all over the island. There was no way to know. And there were men who did this. Hombres with the devil in their flesh who would come to a pueblo, like this one, take a job at one of the haciendas, never meaning to stay, only to have a good time and to seduce the women."

The whole time she was speaking, Mamá would be weaving my hair into a flat plait that required pulling apart the two sections of hair with little jerks that made my eyes water; but knowing how grandmother detested whining and *boba* (sissy) tears, as she called them, I just sat up as straight and stiff as I did at La Escuela San Jose, where the nuns enforced good posture with a flexible plastic ruler they bounced off of slumped shoulders and heads. As Mamá's story progressed, I noticed how my young Aunt Laura lowered her eyes, refusing to meet Mamá's meaningful gaze. Laura was seventeen, in her last year of high school, and already engaged to a boy from another town who had staked his claim with a tiny diamond ring, then left for Los Nueva Yores to make his fortune. They were planning to get married in a year. Mamá had expressed serious doubts that the wedding would ever take place. In Mamá's eyes, a man set free without a legal contract was a man lost. She believed that marriage was not something men desired, but simply the price they had to pay for the privilege of children and, of course, for what no decent (synonymous with "smart") woman would give away for free.

"María La Loca was only seventeen when *it* happened to her." I listened closely at the mention of this name. María was a town character, a fat middle-aged woman who lived with her old mother on the outskirts of town. She was to be seen around the pueblo delivering the meat pies the two women made for a living. The most peculiar thing about María, in my eyes, was that she walked and moved like a little girl though she had the thick body and wrinkled face of an old woman. She would swing her hips in an exaggerated, clownish way, and sometimes even hop and skip up to someone's house. She spoke to no one. Even if you asked her a question, she would just look at you and smile, showing her yellow teeth. But I had heard that if you got close enough, you could hear her humming a tune without words. The kids yelled out nasty things at her, calling her *La Loca*, and the men who hung out at the bodega playing dominoes sometimes whistled mockingly as she passed by with her funny, outlandish walk. But María seemed impervious to it all, carrying her basket of *pasteles* like a grotesque Little Red Riding Hood through the forest.

María La Loca interested me, as did all the eccentrics and crazies of our pueblo. Their weirdness was a measuring stick I used in my serious quest for a definition of normal. As a Navy brat shuttling between New Jersey and the pueblo, I was constantly made to feel like an oddball by my peers, who made fun of my two-way accent: a Spanish accent when I spoke English, and when I spoke Spanish I was told that I sounded like a *Gringa*. Being the outsider had already turned my brother and me into cultural chameleons. We developed early on the ability to blend into a crowd, to sit and read quietly in a fifth story apartment building for days and days when it was too bitterly cold to play outside, or, set free, to run wild in Mamá's realm, where she took charge of our lives, releasing Mother for a while from the intense fear for our safety that our father's absences instilled in her. In order to keep us from harm when Father was away, Mother kept us under strict surveillance. She even walked us to and from Public School No. 11, which we attended during the months we lived in Paterson, New Jersey, our home base in the states. Mamá freed all three of us like pigeons from a cage. I saw her as my liberator and my model. Her stories were parables from which to glean the *Truth*.

"María La Loca was once a beautiful girl. Everyone thought she would marry the Méndez boy." As everyone knew, Rogelio Méndez was the richest man in town. "But," Mamá continued, knitting my hair with the same intensity she was putting into her story, "this *macho* made a fool out of her and ruined her life." She paused for the effect of her use of the word "macho," which at that time had not yet become a popular epithet for an unliberated man. This word had for us the crude and comical connotation of "male of the species," stud; a *macho* was what you put in a pen to increase your stock.

I peeked over my comic book at my mother. She too was under Mamá's spell, smiling conspiratorially at this little swipe at men. She was safe from Mamá's contempt in this area. Married at an early age, an unspotted lamb, she had been accepted by a good family of strict Spaniards whose name was old and respected, though their fortune had been lost long before my birth. In a rocker Papá had painted sky blue sat Mamá's oldest child, Aunt Nena. Mother of three children, stepmother of two more, she was a quiet woman who liked books but had married an ignorant and abusive widower whose main interest in life was accumulating wealth. He too was in the mainland working on his dream of returning home rich and triumphant to buy the *finca* of his dreams. She was waiting for him to send for her. She would leave her children with Mamá for several years while the two of them slaved away in factories. He would one day be a rich man, and she a sadder woman. Even now her life-light was dimming. She spoke little, an aberration in Mamá's house, and she read avidly, as if storing up spiritual food for the long winters that awaited her in Los Nueva Yores without her family. But even Aunt Nena came alive to Mamá's words, rocking gently, her hands over a thick book in her lap.

Her daughter, my cousin Sara, played jacks by herself on the tile porch outside the room where we sat. She was a year older than I. We shared a bed and all our family's secrets. Collaborators in search of answers, Sara and I discussed everything we heard the women say, trying to fit it all together like a puzzle that, once assembled, would reveal life's mysteries to us. Though she and I still enjoyed taking part in boys' games — chase, volleyball, and even *vaqueros*, the island version of cowboys and Indians involving cap-gun battles and violent shoot-outs under the mango tree in Mamá's backyard — we loved best the quiet hours in the afternoon when the men were still at work, and the boys had gone to play serious baseball at the park. Then Mamá's house belonged only to us women. The aroma of coffee perking in the kitchen, the mesmerizing creaks and groans of the rockers, and the women telling their lives in *cuentos* are forever woven into the fabric of my imagination, braided like my hair that day I felt my grandmother's hands teaching me about strength, her voice convincing me of the power of storytelling.

That day Mamá told how the beautiful María had fallen prey to a man whose name was never the same in subsequent versions of the story; it was Juan one time, José, Rafael, Diego, another. We understood that neither the name nor any of the *facts* were important, only that a woman had allowed love to defeat her. Mamá put each of us in

María's place by describing her wedding dress in loving detail: how she looked like a princess in her lace as she waited at the altar. Then, as Mamá approached the tragic denouement of her story, I was distracted by the sound of my Aunt Laura's violent rocking. She seemed on the verge of tears. She knew the fable was intended for her. That week she was going to have her wedding gown fitted, though no firm date had been set for the marriage. Mamá ignored Laura's obvious discomfort, digging out a ribbon from the sewing basket she kept by her rocker while describing María's long illness, "a fever that would not break for days." She spoke of a mother's despair: "that woman climbed the church steps on her knees every morning, wore only black as a *promesa* to the Holy Virgin in exchange for her daughter's health." By the time María returned from her honeymoon with death, she was ravished, no longer young or sane. "As you can see, she is almost as old as her mother already," Mamá lamented while tying the ribbon to the ends of my hair, pulling it back with such force that I just knew I would never be able to close my eyes completely again.

"That María's getting crazier every day." Mamá's voice would take a lighter tone now, expressing satisfaction, either for the perfection of my braid, or for a story well told — it was hard to tell. "You know that tune María is always humming?" Carried away by her enthusiasm, I tried to nod, but Mamá still had me pinned between her knees.

"Well that's the wedding march." Surprising us all, Mamá sang out, "Da, da, dara . . . da, da, dara." Then lifting me off the floor by my skinny shoulders, she would lead me around the room in an impromptu waltz — another session ending with the laughter of women, all of us caught up in the infectious joke of our lives.

RESPONDING

1. Each of these selections highlights a different way that family intimacy is established through certain rituals. Examine each family memoir and pick out the shared activities that emerge.

2. Some family rituals are recalled through significant rites of passage, such as birth, death, and marriage. At his father's funeral, Raymond Carver, who had been named after his dad and who had been called "Junior" for much of his life, says, "What I do remember is that I heard our name used a lot that afternoon, my dad's name and mine. But I knew that they were talking about my dad. *Raymond,* these people kept saying in their beautiful voices out of my childhood. *Raymond."* Consider the practice of naming the son for the father. Think about the practice of naming in families in general. What kinds of names does your family choose? Why are they important? What are some of your favorites?

3. Ruth Reichl, former food critic for the *New York Times* and editor-in-chief of *Gourmet* magazine since 1999, bases her entire book, *Tender at the Bone* (1998), on the role that food and gathering around the table played in the life of her family. Ironically, however, in this excerpt she says, "I had three grandmothers and none of them could cook." Some of her strong memories of food come instead from Alice, her adopted grandmother's Barbados cook. Consider the importance and influence that members of a family not connected by blood may have. Do you have important family members to whom you are not actually related by blood? What constitutes your definition of family?

4. Divorce rates in the United States are on the rise. As a result, we have in this culture many "blended" families – parents divorce and remarry and new families are created. The traditional terms for these relationships are stepmother, stepson, and so on. The new family may also have children born into the family resulting in half brothers and sisters. Design a research project in which you investigate this type of family in the United States. What are some of the common problems associated with these new combinations of family members? What are some of the advantages of belonging to a blended family? What insights can you offer from your own experience, or the experience of others you know?

READING DEEPLY

Complexity of Family Life among the Low-Income and Working Poor

By Patricia Hyjer Dyk

F R O M: *Family Relations: Interdisciplinary Journal of Applied Family Studies,* March 2004

THE FOLLOWING ARTICLE WAS WRITTEN AS THE INTRODUCTION TO A special issue of *Family Relations* that dealt with the intersection of poverty and family. *Family Relations: Interdisciplinary Journal of Applied Family Studies* is a publication of the National Council on Family Relations (NCFR), which describes its journal as "mandatory reading for family scholars and all professionals who work with families, including: family practitioners, educators, marriage and family therapists, researchers, and social policy specialists." The journal publishes empirical studies, literature reviews, and conceptual analyses with an eye to the public policy and intervention recommendations of this research. Patricia Hyjer Dyk is an associate professor in the Department of Community and Leadership Development at the University of Kentucky. In her academic work, she focuses on the social and economic influences on rural family life. She has written and presented extensively on many of the topics addressed in this literature review article.

To help you read more deeply and critically, we have provided annotations and boldfaced some terms or passages that call attention to the rhetorical choices Dyk has made in her article and to the hallmarks of a literature review which are present in this piece. As you read the essay and the annotations, consider how you are being led to think about the relationship between poverty and family – and to move from thinking to acting.

Notice that Dyk immediately includes us in her essay. We are in this investigation with her; she assumes we share her concerns and understanding.

How well **we all know that family life is complex, regardless of our income level**. Daily we juggle with meeting competing demands to care for our own physical, emotional, and psychological needs, as well as the needs of other family members. We rely upon our own sets of coping strategies and a history of either having successfully or not-so-successfully accomplished our goals. Often we turn to others for assistance. Besides maintaining these social relationships, we also dedicate energy to acquiring and allocating financial resources to sustain daily life. All of these activities are influenced by societal norms, values, policies, and institutions. If it is common that families experience these challenges and constraints, why focus on the complexity of family life among those who are low-income and working poor?

Those of you reading this article likely started the day by waking up in a warm, cozy bed (safe shelter). After taking a hot shower (utilities paid) and choosing among several outfits to wear (appropriate clothing), you headed for the refrigerator/ freezer/pantry to grab a nutritious breakfast for yourself and your children (food secure). Next, after checking for completed homework and lunch money in your children's backpacks (developmentally appropriate parenting skills), you probably headed for the car (reliable transportation). Once dropping the older children at school (instead of being bussed across town) and the preschooler at child care (a safe, nurturing, quality child care center), you headed to your job (with family medical

Dyk appeals to the everyday experience of readers who are not poor. In part, she can make this assumption because the audience for the journal *Family Relations* would be those with graduate degrees working in academic or professional settings. She asks them to consider all they take for granted on a day-to-day basis.

Dyk sources her article following the standards of the American Psychological Association (APA), which is generally used by the social sciences. Each parenthetical citation appears in full in the references section. The protocol of her research field requires that she refer to the current literature on a topic when making an assertion that needs to be backed up by research.

benefits). This would not be the beginning of a typical day for most low-income and working-poor families you will learn about in the following articles.Although they attempt to achieve the same basic conditions for their households, their ability to meet these objectives is affected greatly by their limited economic resources.

Low-income and working-poor families are different from middle- and upper-income families in part because of their exposure to and experience of substantial stressors. **These include high rates of parental unemployment, low-wage jobs, underdeveloped human capital (lower educational attainment), greater barriers to obtaining social services, unstable and unsafe living arrangements, family and community violence, and substance abuse (Seccombe, 2002).** Subsequently, these challenges affect their ability to care for their children. Parents may be piecing together a patchwork of two to three part-time jobs, with limited flexibility to schedule medical appointments, attend school conferences or programs, or participate in their children's activities. These parents also have more stress, because they are unable to give their children the lifestyle benefits associated with having a reliable income (Rubin, 1994).

Pervasiveness of Poverty

As defined by the Office of Management and Budget and updated for inflation using the Consumer Price Index, the average poverty threshold for a family of four in 2002 was

By providing the specific income levels – rather than a general statement about poverty – Dyk offers her readers a chance to compare their status to that of the groups she is discussing. Again, they can contrast their circumstances with those of the families studied.

$18,392 in annual income, compared with $14,348 for a family of three, $11,756 for a family of two, and $9,183 for unrelated individuals (U.S. Census Bureau, 2003). According to this most recent report released in September 2003, the poverty rate and number of families in poverty increased from 6.8 million in 2001 (or 9.2% of all families) to 7.2 million (or 9.6%) in 2002. Children under 18 had a poverty rate of 16.7% in 2002, unchanged from 2001. The number of people in severe poverty (those with incomes half or less of their thresholds) increased from 13.4 million in 2001 to 14.1 million in 2002, and the number of "near poor" (those with incomes between 100% and 125% of the poverty thresholds), 12.5 million, did not change (U.S. Census Bureau, 2003).

Poverty rates vary by region and residence. The South continues to have the highest poverty rate among regions. The official poverty rates ranged from about 5.6% in New Hampshire and Minnesota to about 18.0% in Arkansas, Mississippi, New Mexico, Louisiana, West Virginia, and the District of Columbia, according to a 3-year average. With regard to residence, inside central cities the poverty rate was 16.7%, compared to a rate of 14.2% among those living outside metropolitan areas (rural). Neither of these rates changed from the previous year (U.S. Census Bureau, 2003).

Keep in mind that many of the families categorized by these statistics, particularly those in the "near poor" designation, include at least one adult wage earner. Also consider that

It has likely been years since the readers of this journal have earned anything near minimum wage, so this reference again underscores the contrast and illuminates the difficulties encountered by the working poor.

APA in-text citations require the author(s)' last name and date of publication.

an employed parent with two children who earns minimum wage would not earn enough to be considered "near poor"; he or she would remain below the poverty threshold. For rural families with workers over the age of 25, 27% do not earn enough income to keep a family out of poverty **(Bauer, Braun, & Dyk, 2003).**

Understanding Family Challenges

Just knowing that poverty is pervasive in the United States is an insufficient basis from which to begin addressing the problem. We need to understand the who and why to better inform policy, design programs, or improve practice. **Hence, we turn to family scholars to provide sound research to guide our efforts.** In her decade review of family poverty scholarship, Seccombe (2000) summarized the many research articles that focused on the demographic, psychological, sociological, health, and developmental antecedents and consequences of poverty for families. Additionally, she identified eight themes that emerged from the literature: family diversity, the working poor, poverty's selection and mediating influences, the ecological approach, contributions of fathers, an integration of macro and micro explanations of poverty, an appreciation of qualitative rich description, and expanded concern with social policy. These themes served as the foundation for the development of projects emanating from the multidisciplinary study groups and for contributing to the scholarly research included in this special issue.

This statement signals to Dyk's readers that her essay takes the form of a review of the literature. In it, she will summarize studies most relevant to the topic at hand but will not discuss any original research of her own. The literature review is a standard genre in the social sciences.

Dyk's reader would expect a statement like this in a research review essay. It provides a snapshot of the specific studies that she will discuss in the remainder of her piece.

Dyk returns to direct address and suggests that this essay will not be a neutral literature review. Rather, the reader should emerge from the essay with sympathy, and perhaps empathy, for the families.

Building upon our understanding that factors contributing to the ability to transition from poverty to economic sufficiency can vary by race, gender, or ethnicity, the contributing authors to this issue have studied diverse populations. Their insights are informed by persistently poor rural Southern Black women, innercity families in the North, cohabiting couples, low-income rural women, Mexican American fathers, street-prostituted mothers, and families with young children. These families studied were engaged through program evaluations, ethnographic studies, and research projects specifically designed to understand the poverty experience from a particular perspective. **You will hear many of their voices as they describe their daily and sometimes lifelong struggles to make ends meet. You also will be encouraged by their strength and resiliency.**

Expanded Concern of Family Policy

Several years ago, Moen and Schorr (1987) defined family policy as "a widely agreed-on set of objectives for families, toward the realization of which the state (and other major social institutions) deliberately shapes programs and policies" (p. 795). Poverty has been one of the targets of well-intentioned programs and policies for many years.

Renewed interest in family policy was sparked when the 1996 welfare reform statute was enacted. The Personal Responsibility and

When the in-text citation includes a direct quote, the page number of the publication is given.

Welfare reform remains a controversial policy, and Dyk's comments here present her view on the topic clearly. They also situate them within a research context. These are not just her opinions; they are supported by data.

Work Opportunity Reconciliation Act (PRWORA) repealed the 60-year-old Aid to Families with Dependent Children (AFDC) entitlement program, replacing it with the Temporary Assistance for Needy Families (TANF) program featuring mandatory work requirements and a 5-year time limit on the receipt of cash benefits. The underlying goal of social welfare shifted from partially remedying income shortfalls to affecting behavioral change at the individual and family levels. The phrase "welfare-to-work" captured the intended course of action. **Behind the legislation were assumptions that jobs were available and would provide adequate income and benefits to replace the former safety net of entitlements. However, contrary to the widely agreed-on objective, securing employment does not ensure economic security or family stability. Working-poor families earning below 200% of federal poverty guidelines still live on the edge of poverty without the ability to save and build assets (Chun-Hoon, 2003).**

Bogenschneider (2002) suggested that the heightened interest in public policy is due in part to the devolution of program and policy authority to levels closer to where families are actually helped. Hence, changes, contradictions, redundancies, and gaps in existing programs are more apparent to practitioners and family advocates. There is renewed interest in developing policies that take a holistic approach to family well-being, particularly to members of one's own community. Low-income and working-poor families face competing

Following APA sourcing conventions for in-text citations, Dyk includes the author name "Bogenscheider" to introduce a summary of his findings with a date of publication in parentheses.

With this sentence, Dyk establishes the structure of the re-mainder of her essay. She will focus on the three topics iden-tified in the policy briefs—these become headings. She will break each down into component parts—these become the subheads. Writing in the social sciences is highly structured, and her readers would expect as much.

stressors and tensions, need support for their parenting roles, and will benefit greatly from enhanced economic stability.

To target these goals, study groups convened as part of a project funded by the Annie E. Casey Foundation to develop three policy briefs: Competing Stressors and Tensions (NCFR, 2003c), Promoting Effective Mothering (NCFR, 2003a), and Economic Stability and Financial Decision Making Processes (NCFR, 2003b). These fact sheets articulate the issues faced by low-income and working-poor families and offer policy and program rec-ommendations. We clustered the articles in this special issue to address the issues identified in these policy briefs.

Competing Stressors and Tensions

Low-income and working-poor families face competing stressors and tensions that decrease their ability to respond to their changing envi-ronments. This makes them vulnerable to family chaos, poor decision making, and the inability to plan beyond immediate needs. Compet-ing stressors may be internal to the family, such as poor health, domestic violence, or lack of education. They also may be external environmental factors, such as lack of employment opportunities, poor access to health care, poor schools, or community violence. **To achieve family stability, families need economic stability, safety, good health, and engagement in the larger commu-nity — needs that are interrelated.**

The reader now expects to see references and summaries of studies that address each of the identified needs.

Dyk's essay originally served as an introduction to a special volume of *Family Relations* that focused on low-income families. The studies that she highlights in this section of her piece are all included in the volume.

Persistent Deep Poverty

The competing tensions of low-income families prompted **Blalock, Tiller, and Monroe to examine their data for insights regarding persistently poor rural women's responsibilities for caring for kin, physical or mental work limitations, domestic violence, and the presence of an emotional or material support network**. Findings from their three waves of in-depth interviews with single Black women revealed vulnerability to numerous persistent barriers to self-sufficiency and the reality that their well-being rests largely within their support networks. They take each day as it comes and do what they can to meet the needs of their families. The authors recommended that policy makers expand the countable activities related to education allowed under the TANF program, giving women more time to improve their human capital through education. Once in the work force, safety net services need to be continued along with intensive "after-care" services aimed at job retention. However, they emphasized that training workers for jobs that do not provide a livable wage remains problematic in economically depressed rural areas, thus suggesting that limited success will result without renewed efforts at economic development and removal of structural impediments to obtaining stable employment.

Danger Management Strategies

Another component of family stability is safety. Jarrett and Jefferson focused on the danger management strategies of low-income African American mothers in a Chicago housing project. Through in-depth interviews, they revealed the community dangers, the nature of the violence experienced, and strategies used by mothers to effectively keep themselves and their children safe. Although these inner-city residents were unable to reduce the prevalence of violence, we learn that violence has specific physical locations, a particular set of actors, and a temporal rhythm. **They recommended that practitioners working with women living in dangerous environments be encouraged to provide positive acknowledgment and support of women's coping efforts that are critical for safety, being mindful (a) of barriers to collective action, (b) that fear of retaliation and lack of support from formal social control agents are their reality, and (c) that the roots of neighborhood violence are in limited economic, social, and institutional resources.** Aiding mothers in developing informal groups with common concerns and connecting those to larger agencies outside of their communities will empower women to build upon their already effective coping strategies.

Work-Family Tradeoffs

The voices of 46 low-income mothers in Cleveland and Philadelphia informed London, Scott, Edin, and Hunter about the effects on their children of competing stressors and tensions between work and fam-

The expectations of research publications in the social sciences is that they lead to recommendations. These might be for further research or for action. You will notice that Dyk routinely lists the study recommendations. Because this volume of *Family Relations* explicitly addresses policy concerns, almost all of the recommendations will be for action.

ily. Drawing upon ethnographic panel data, these authors examined the costs and benefits to women moving from welfare to work. The mothers reported benefits with regard to increased income, increased self-esteem, feelings of independence and social integration, and the ability to model work and self-sufficiency values for their children. These enhancements come with the cost of often working without increased income, overload, exhaustion and stress, and less time and energy to be with, supervise, and support their children. The findings made clear the importance of continuing to develop, expand, and fund work supports that not only "make work" but also enable single parents to continue to be engaged with their children. Among other things, they recommended that efforts be targeted at policy initiatives and programs designed to reconnect families to programs that ease the burden of low-wage work.

Resilience and Strengths

By examining a subsample of 373 low-income households participating in a North Carolina statewide telephone survey, Orthner, Jones-Sanpei, and Williamson provided valuable insights into the strengths and resiliency of this population. Despite health problems, poor living conditions, and other challenges, respondents reported that they function with a great deal of strength. The resilience of the families sprang from a sense of personal confidence in their problem-solving skills and abilities. Whether employed

Readers will want to know the methodology of each study in order to understand if it might be generalizable to other families or situations. Thus, you will notice that Dyk usually indicates the number of participants in the study and how they participated. Readers will know that a larger number of participants increases the validity of the results. The actual essay by Orthner et al. would go into great depth in discussing the methodology.

183

Notice that we learn more about the research sample here. This study dealt with only some of the aspects of a larger research project. And it addressed only families with preschool children. These results may not be applicable to families with teenagers, for example. Readers would likely keep any conclusions and recommendations within the context of families with preschoolers.

or not, they exhibited confidence in their ability to pull together and depended on each other when problems arose. However, the families were most vulnerable with respect to their economic stability, as only half have any savings, and paying their bills on time was difficult. The authors recommended more supportive services directed toward needs of families who were working, especially two-parent families.

Daily Rhythms

Roy, Tubbs, and Burton focused on how, on a daily basis, families negotiate access to services and programs offered under the broader national policy umbrella. **From 75 families with preschool children participating in the ethnographic component of the Three-City Study in Chicago, we learn how temporal rhythms of the typical workday define activities within these families.** They constantly improvised daily rhythms to obtain and sustain resources, including child care, transportation, and social services. Participants were proactive in identifying and coordinating resources to transition from welfare to work or to maintain paid employment. However, they must adapt to normative temporal expectations without access to reliable resources available to middle-class families (e.g., time-consuming dependency on other people's schedules; lack of vehicles meant longer commutes on public transportation; shift work meant restricted access to services). Expanding hours of accessibility of essential services such as child care and health care would enable the working-poor families in particular to better manage the competing stressors within their environments.

Effective Parenting

The topic of the policy brief focusing on effective mothering has been expanded to include fathers. Empowering all parents — including low-income and working-poor mothers — to achieve their full potential and raise their children in a healthy and nurturing environment enables parents to build strong families. The ecological model (Bronfenbrenner, 1989) stresses the interaction and interdependence of low-income and working parents within their family, community, and societal environments. Hence, policies supportive of providing access to education and training, making high-quality child care available, accessible, and affordable, and encouraging father involvement are integral in empowering low-income mothers to achieve economic stability.

Father Involvement

Coltrane, Parke, and Adams focused on fathers to understand predictors of higher levels of men's participation in family life. **Using longitudinal data from 167 Mexican American men in California, the authors investigated multiple components of father involvement: interaction with their school-age children, availability to the child, and responsibility for the care of the child.** Fathers' egalitarian gender attitudes and mothers' education

Here, Dyk describes the demographic of the study group: Mexican American men. This is a longitudinal study, meaning it was carried out over a longer time frame. However, as the summary continues, we learn there are aspects of Mexican American culture that directly impact the study. Thus, we would not necessarily want to generalize these results to other demographic groups.

were associated with higher levels of father involvement. In addition, fathers were more involved in monitoring and interacting with children when families placed more emphasis on family rituals. They suggested that fathering cannot be understood without paying attention to the social, economic, cultural, and family contexts in which it occurs. Given the pervasive emphasis on familism among Mexican Americans, programs that focus solely on fathers as the target audience are less likely to be successful than those that focus on both parenting partners and the family unit.

Barriers to Effective Mothering

Returning to effective mothering, Dalla focused on an often ignored and marginalized group: street-prostituted women. She asked how and to what extent effective mothering can be promoted among them. **From in-depth interviews with 38 mothers, we learn the extent to which they are indigent, suffer discrimination, lack political power, and have experienced lives dominated by exploitation and abuse (whether directly or indirectly) that convince them that they "deserve" what they get.** Thus, it is incumbent upon practitioners working with this population to address intergenerational familial patterns that have been impacted by abuse, exploitation, domestic violence, and emotional terrorism. Often without intention, those patterns are transmitted to children caught in the cycle of intergenerational dysfunction. Dalla advocates the necessity

> This is a classic example of a study with a very narrow focus. No researcher would want to draw conclusions from this study about "barriers to effective mothering" in low-income families in general. But, such a study can still generate recommendations for its narrow population of interest.

> One of the defining characteristics of much social science research is its qualitative—as opposed to quantitative—nature. In general, quantitative research involves numbers and statistics. Qualitative research involves narratives and interviews, which are then coded and studied. The study referenced here is qualitative.

of providing long-term, community-based intensive care aimed at addressing the physical and psychological needs of these mothers.

Private Safety Net

One of the formidable barriers to mothers' participation in the work force is the availability and accessibility of affordable, reliable, quality child care. **To understand rural low-income mothers' access to and reliance upon childcare resources, Katras, Zuiker, and Bauer used input from 52 women participating in the 14-state Rural Families Speak study. In-depth interviews reflected the struggles that rural women face in piecing together a reliable care network for their children (their private safety net).** Mothers were concerned about childcare availability in an environment that often had limited care options beyond those available in their own networks of family, friends, neighbors, and coworkers. Findings elucidated the strategies and challenges these mothers faced, many of whom expressed need for off-peak childcare. Because trust plays a major role in the decision-making process of finding child care, efforts to improve the quality and training of small-scale childcare providers is paramount, as is the need to develop subsidies that support both informal and formal care arrangements.

Caregiver Involvement

To investigate another dimension of the ability of low-income families

Another defining characteristic is the diction used in social science writing. As a science, it tends to use language that creates a formal distance—and adds to the word count. What does this whole section really say? Programs for lower-income mothers shouldn't disrespect them, otherwise the programs will fail.

to promote the well-being of their children, Unger, Tressell, Jones, and Park have engaged in a research–community partnership with program staff to understand how to enhance the provider–parent-child relationship. Low-income single caregivers (primarily African American mothers) of children with disabilities and developmental delays were engaged in a 3-year longitudinal study. **Results confirmed that caregivers who were more engaged with the programs were more likely to demonstrate more responsiveness in interactions with their children. When minority caregivers living in poverty view the programs as responsive to and respectful of their concerns, they are more likely to turn to them for help. To effectively inform practice, research investigating caregiver involvement must assess caregiver-program relationships and not merely the frequency of contacts or availability of involvement opportunities.** Hence, it is not sufficient to provide only programs or access; attention must be directed to how programs address the specific needs of families and children targeted by intervention.

Economic Stability and Financial Decision Making

If low-income and working-poor families are to gain economic stability, consistent income that provides for basic necessities is needed. When families have consistent access to resources, they are better able to prioritize, budget, set money aside, and plan for asset growth.

As a reader of *Family Relations*, you might be keen on learning more about this study. It has a large sample size (529) and does not have a restrictive ethnic or gender demographic. You still might use caution on generalizing any results outside of an urban setting, though.

Families are strengthened through increased access to education, training, work supports, childcare subsidies, affordable housing, and improved community development in low-income neighborhoods.

Childcare Subsidies

Danziger, Ananat, and Browning drew upon interview data from a three-wave panel study of 529 urban Michigan welfare recipients to examine how childcare subsidies help in the welfare-to-work transition relative to other factors. Findings indicated that subsidy receipt reduces childcare costs but not parenting stress or problems with care, and use of this safety net benefit predicted earnings and work duration net of other factors. All else being equal, subsidies have a strong effect on work outcomes. Hence, increased use of subsidies by eligible families and greater funding for childcare would help meet the demand for this important support for working poor families. Advocates and childcare policy analysts must monitor the trends in how many eligible families receive subsidies, how much of the cost of childcare is allayed by the subsidies, and the quality of care in the subsidized care facilities to assess reasons for low take-up rates in their communities.

Asset Building

Family economic success includes the presence of sufficient and predictable resources that allow families to participate in savings and

Dyk introduces each acronym with the full agency or policy name first. Then she uses the abbreviated acronym. The reader should expect this.

wealth accumulation plans. **One such approach is through Individual Development Accounts (IDA). Hogan, Solheim, Wolfgram, Nkosi, and Rodrigues engaged in an evaluation of one such program, the Minnesota Family Assets for Independence (FAIM) program,** to understand how low-income wage-earning families save money to reach their asset accumulation goals. Interviewing 25 participants over three waves of evaluation, they examined the financial vulnerability, personal attributes, social support, and resource management strategies of the families. Results indicated that a majority of these low-income wage-earning families were finding ways to save for asset building in spite of financial stressors. Some families focused on creative ways to reduce expenditures, whereas others found ways to increase their financial resources. These findings lend strong support for the continuation and enhancement of IDAs as a pathway out of poverty for low-income wage-earning families.

Resource Pooling

Last in the series is the Kenney paper, which focuses on the pattern of resource exchange and sharing that takes place within households. **Drawing upon data from 1,736 coresident couples participating in the Fragile Families and Child Wellbeing Study, she examined the household availability of cohabiting fathers' income.** Data from the mothers indicate that cohabiting parents do

Note that this study separates two ideas that the reader might immediately lump together: being married and living together. This distinction is key to understanding the results, and if you read through the summary too quickly, you might miss it. Sometimes research writing is a bit dense, and the temptation is to skim rather than read.

generally pool resources. However, it appears that the cohabiting couple's relationship with one another and/or coresident status are ultimately more important for resource sharing than either marital status or the biological ties between the cohabiting male and the children in the household. Couples' money management practices differ by marital status and the male's biological relationship to the child, as well as by race and ethnicity. Kenney notes that U.S. social policy is inconsistent in its treatment of cohabiting-parent households. Although welfare policy generally assumes that marital status should not affect the extent to which children benefit from each adult's income, tax policy and the poverty classification assume income pooling among married — but not cohabiting — parents. She provides an overview of some of the significant policy areas for which an understanding of household economic relations is important to evaluating the success of existing policies and to designing effective policies in the future.

Conclusions

As noted at the outset, families, regardless of their income levels, face the challenges of developing and maintaining safe and secure relationships, dealing with structural constraints, providing the necessities of food, shelter, and clothing, and caring for their children while juggling the demands of earning or securing financial resources to meet those needs. Research from studies reported here offer us

> Dyk is essentially setting up a framework to be used when reading the volume that follows her introductory essay. Notice that each question should trigger an action response (that is, develop a policy or program). The goal of her framework is to get the readers to understand that research in the family relations field should lead to practice. It should not be an end in itself.

encouragement that low-income and working-poor families are indeed resilient and resourceful. Yet, their voices tell us that they are in need of further education, services, and supportive policies to assist their quests for economic self-sufficiency. As educators, researchers, practitioners, and policy makers, we are left with critical challenges. **These researchers have raised some difficult but essential questions that must be addressed:**

1. What does it take for a parent/worker to participate in the world of work as a full-fledged member of the labor force while simultaneously maintaining and enhancing the economic, social, and psychological well-being of children?

2. How do we promote policies and design programs that encourage and enable economic self-sufficiency without ensuring persistent deep poverty among a subset of our citizens?

3. How do we develop programs and provide services sensitive to the physical, psychosocial, and resource needs of individual members in families who are embedded in their community contexts?

The contributors to this issue are hopeful that their research-based practice and policy suggestions will guide future efforts in partnering with families to strengthen them and the communities in which they are embedded for successful enhancement of children and families.

Following APA style, Dyk lists her works cited alphabetically, under the heading "References."

Entries are listed alphabetically by last name first, followed by initials, date of publication in parentheses, title of the work, page reference if any, and publisher information.

REFERENCES

Bauer, J. W., Braun, B., & Dyk, P. H. (2003, April). Health and the economic well-being of rural families (Fact Sheet). Minneapolis, MN: National Council on Family Relations.

Bogenschneider, K. (2002). *Family policy matters: How policymaking affects families and what professionals can do.* Mahwah, NJ: Erlbaum.

Bronfenbrenner, U. (1989). Ecological systems theory. In R. Vasta (Ed.), *Annals of child development* (Vol. 6, pp. 187–249). Greenwich, CT: JAI.

Chun-Hoon, W. L. (2003, February). In support of low-income working families: State policies and local program innovations in the era of welfare reform (Policy Brief). The Annie E. Casey Foundation. Retrieved October 6, 2003, from http://www.aecf.org/publications/data/support.pdf.

Moen, P., & Schorr, A. L. (1987). Families and social policy. In M. B. Sussman & S. K. Steinmetz (Eds.), *Handbook of marriage and the family* (pp. 796–813). New York: Plenum.

National Council on Family Relations. (2003a, January). Promoting effective mothering in low-income and working-poor families. Policy Brief, 1(1) Minneapolis, MN: Author.

National Council on Family Relations. (2003b, February). Economic stability and financial decision making processes in low-income and working-poor families. Policy Brief, 1(2) Minneapolis, MN: Author.

National Council on Family Relations. (2003c, April). Competing stressors and tensions in low-income and working-poor families. Policy Brief, 1(3) Minneapolis, MN: Author.

Rubin, L. B. (1994). *Families on the fault line: America's working class speaks about the family, the economy, race and ethnicity.* New York: HarperCollins.

Seccombe, K. (2000). Families in poverty in the 1990s: Trends, causes, consequences, and lessons learned. *Journal of Marriage and the Family, 62,* 1094–1113.

When a work has no author, the entry is alphabetized by its title.

Seccombe, K. (2002). Beating the odds versus changing the odds: Poverty, resilience, and family policy. *Journal of Marriage and the Family*, 64, 384–394.

U.S. Census Bureau. (2003, September). Poverty in the United States:
2002. Current Population Survey, 1–21. Retrieved September 27, 2003,
from http://www.census.gov/prod/2003pubs/p60–222.pdf.

For guidelines using APA style to document sources, you can
visit bedfordstmartins.com/rewriting and click on "Research
and Documentation."

MAKING CONNECTIONS ACROSS AND BEYOND THE DISCIPLINES

1. Like Dyk, Stephanie Coontz is a social scientist, and like Dyk, it is clear that Coontz has researched her piece on "The American Family" (p. 94). At times, they even hover near the same issues. However, in style, presentation, and tone, the two could not be more different. Write an essay that analyzes the effect that audience has on the style of each author. Does one seem more authoritative? Why?

2. In "The Politics of Family," Robert Kuttner writes, "Keats, nearly two centuries ago, had it right: Love, like good values, will take you a long way. But it is no cure for poverty, and poverty is bad for kids" (p. 122). The literature reviewed by Dyk seems to support this contention. Both authors reference several policies undertaken to move children out of poverty. Select one and research its effects — intended and unintended — and come to your own conclusion about the efficacy of the policy. Write up your research and conclusion in an essay and, following the lead set by Dyk's piece, recommend further action.

3. Dyk opens her essay with data from the U.S. Census Bureau regarding family poverty. Research this data for your home community or the community in which you are attending college. Data from the latest census is available via the Web, and most local governments can also provide poverty statistics for their communities. Working with several classmates, develop a presentation for your class that sets forth this information, suggests the impact it is having on the families in the community, and discusses some recommendations for addressing the needs of lower-income families (for example, for transportation, child care, etc.). As you develop your recommendations, you may wish to interview community leaders to get a sense of what they think is needed.

Defining Identity in a Virtual World

THE IMAGES THAT BEGIN THIS CHAPTER COME FROM A VIRTUAL community, Second Life, which is currently "home" to over 400,000 members from around the world. Look at these images. The skydive is perfect; the winter getaway ("Snow"), ideal. Even the disaffected youth in "Hanging" seem smooth, clean, and nicely styled. The slogan of Second Life is "Your World. Your Imagination." This chapter asks you to think about what happens when your world and your imagination move online into cyberspace. What type of world do you create? Who are you in this world? Is it a different self than you are in everyday face-to-face interactions? Much of our identity arises from the context of our community. You likely change your persona slightly with each interaction: your mom sees a different "you" than does your significant other or your chemistry professor. But what if you were in an environment in which you had almost complete autonomy to create a whole new "you"? The opportunities for new types of community in the online world offer equally new opportunities for discovery, disclosure, and deception.

When we ask ourselves why someone might create the worlds that are pictured or who would create these worlds, we are diving into a specific academic world: psychology. Questions about behavior are questions addressed by psychology, a word whose root is from the Greek term *psyche*, for mind or soul. The answers come from analysis of data: what was done, what was reported, what was written. More and more, communication forms and communities have arisen online – everything

Images from Second Life, a virtual community. From top: Hanging, Snow, Skydiving, and Overheard

from e-mail to blogs to wikis to social networks and everything in between; thus, the Internet offers a wealth of evidence on how people interrelate — especially how they relate when denied access to traditional cues (for example, physical appearance or tone of voice) and traditional social rules. As such, the Net becomes an ever-expanding laboratory for a discussion of how we form and reform our identities when given new freedoms.

When we participate in a chat room, post on a message board, upload a video to YouTube, or create a MySpace page, we are leaving traces of ourselves or who we wish to be. As movie hero Buckaroo Banzai once said, "Remember, no matter where *you* go, there *you* are." This chapter asks you to analyze how cyberspace has impacted the ways in which we create who we are — and how others perceive us. The readings address the intersection between the Internet and identity in ways serious and humorous, academic and social, emotional and financial. Taken together, they suggest that the Internet has changed our notions of self and community in ways that are still unfolding. As you read these works, think about your own engagement with the online world — where the personal becomes the digital.

Growing Up Online
By Bruce Bower

FROM: *Science News*, June 17, 2006

CONTEXT: This article initially appeared in *Science News*, a weekly magazine. While the publication is targeted at a general and scientific readership, the majority of subscribers are scientists and almost half hold at least one graduate degree. Most readers are older (over forty-six) and male. Articles in the magazine tend to be short and to target emerging issues and key research findings. *Science News* has been published for over eighty years by Science Service, an organization with a mission to "advance public understanding and appreciation of science among people of all ages through publications and educational programs." Bruce Bower, author of this piece, covers the behavioral sciences for the magazine. He has written on topics ranging from the influence of Sigmund Freud to Mexican archaeology. In reading this piece, think about how the audience for *Science News* influences how the information is presented, especially the characterization of "young people" as a field of study.

AS A CONVERSATION UNFOLDS AMONG TEENAGERS ON AN Internet message board, it rapidly becomes evident that this is not idle electronic chatter. One youngster poses a question that, to an outsider, seems shocking: "Does anyone know how to cut deep without having it sting and bleed too much?" An answer quickly appears: "I use box cutter blades. You have to pull the skin really tight and press the blade down really hard." Another response advises that a quick swipe of a blade against skin "doesn't hurt and there is blood galore." The questioner seems satisfied: "Okay, I'll get a Stanley blade 'cause I hear that it will cut right to the bone with no hassle. But . . . I won't cut that deep."

Welcome to the rapidly expanding online arena for teenagers who deliberately cut or otherwise injure themselves. It's a place where cutters, as they're known, can provide emotional support to one another, discuss events that trigger self-mutilation, encourage peers to seek medical or mental-health treatment, or offer tips on how best to hurt oneself without getting caught.

The conversation above, observed during a study of self-injury message boards, occupies a tiny corner of the virtual world that children and adolescents have aggressively colonized. Psychologist Janis L. Whitlock of Cornell University, the director of that study, and other researchers are beginning to explore how young people communicate on the Internet. The scientists are examining how various online contacts affect a youngster's schoolwork, social life, and budding sense of identity. Evidence also suggests that the Internet has expanded the reach of health-education efforts to teens in distant lands and provided unique leadership opportunities to a global crop of youngsters.

New findings, including six reports in the May *Developmental Psychology*, indicate that the Internet holds a special appeal for young people, says psychologist Patricia Greenfield of the University of California, Los Angeles (UCLA). That's because the Internet provides an unprecedented number and variety of meeting places, from message boards to instant messaging to so-called social networking sites such as myspace.com.

The one constant is that teens take to the Internet like ants to a summer picnic. Nearly nine in ten U.S. youngsters, ages twelve to seventeen, used the Internet in 2004, according to a national survey conducted by the Pew Internet & American Life Project in Washington, D.C. That amounted to 21 million teens, half of whom said that they go online every day. About three in four U.S. adults used the Internet at that time, Pew researchers found.

Teenagers, in particular, provide a moving target for Internet researchers, remarks psychologist Kaveri Subrahmanyam of California State University in Los Angeles. "By the time you publish research on one type of Internet use, such as blogging, teenagers have moved on to something new, such as MySpace," she says, with a resigned chuckle.

Express Yourself

Cyberspace offers a bevy of tempting opportunities to pretend to be who you're not. Yet teens don't typically go online to deceive others but to confront their own identities, according to recent studies. That's not surprising, Subrahmanyam notes, since adolescents typically seek answers to questions such as "Who am I?" and "Where do I belong?"

Consider the self-injury message boards studied by Whitlock's team. Five Internet search engines led the researchers to a whopping 406 such sites. Most of these attracted participants who identified themselves as girls between ages twelve and twenty.

On message boards, as in chat rooms, participants register as members and adopt screen names, such as "Emily the Strange." In many cases, both members and nonmembers can view messages, although only members can post them.

Whitlock and her coworkers studied the content of 3,219 messages at ten popular self-injury message boards over a two-month period in 2005. Many postings provided emotional support to other members. Participants also frequently discussed circumstances that triggered self-mutilation. These included depression and conflicts with key people in their lives. Some message senders detailed ways to seek aid for physical and emotional problems, but others described feeling addicted to self-injury. 10

More ominously, a substantial minority of messages either discouraged self-injurers from seeking formal medical or mental help or shared details about self-harm techniques and ways to keep the practice secret.

Online teen chat rooms generally don't have specific topics but, like message boards, attract a wide range of kids and present both helpful and hurtful communications. Subrahmanyam and her colleagues examined typical conversations at two online chat sites for teens. They monitored more than five hours of electronic exchanges selected at various times of the day during a two-month stretch in 2003.

On one site, an adult monitored conversations for unacceptable language. The other site was unmonitored.

More than half of the 583 participants at both sites gave personal information, usually including sex and age. Sexual themes constituted 5 percent of all messages, corresponding to about one sexual comment per minute. Obscene language characterized 5 percent of messages on the unmonitored site and 2 percent on the monitored site.

One-quarter of participants made sexual references, which was not unexpected given the amount of daily sex talk that has been reported among some teens. In the chat rooms, however, all members were confronted with the minority's sexual banter. 15

The protected environment of the monitored chat room resulted in markedly fewer explicit sexual messages and obscene words than the unmonitored chat room did, Subrahmanyam says. Moreover, the monitored site attracted more participants who identified themselves as young girls than did the unmonitored venue, which featured a larger number of correspondents who identified themselves as males in their late teens or early twenties.

Much of the explicit sexuality on the unmonitored site amounted to degrading and insulting comments, adding to concerns previously raised by other researchers that youths who visit such sites are likely to encounter sexual harassment from either peers or adults.

Subrahmanyam's team also conducted in-person interviews with teens who hadn't participated in the chat room study. The results suggest that only a small minority ever pretend to be other people on the Internet.

Intriguingly, teens who write online journals, known as blogs, often forgo sex talk for more mundane topics, such as daily experiences at home and school, Subrahmanyam adds. In 2004, she analyzed the content of 600 entries in 200 teen blogs.

Teen blogs offer an outlet for discussing romantic relationships 20 and, especially for boys, disclosing hidden sides of themselves, says psychologist Sandra L. Calvert of Georgetown University in Washington, D.C. In a 2005 online report with David A. Huffaker of Northwestern University in Evanston, Ill., Calvert described entries in 70 teen blogs, evenly split between bloggers who identified themselves as girls and as boys. The ages given ranged from thirteen to seventeen.

Bloggers routinely disclosed personal information, including e-mail addresses and other contact details, the researchers found. Half the blogs of both boys and girls discussed relationships with boyfriends or girlfriends. Ten boys, but only two girls, wrote that they were using the blogs to openly discuss their homosexuality for the first time.

"Teenagers stay closer to reality in their online expressions about themselves than has previously been suggested," Calvert asserts.

Net Gains

Give a middle school child from a low-income household a home computer with free Internet access and watch that child become a better reader. That's the conclusion of a new study that highlights potential academic consequences of the so-called digital divide separating poor kids from their better-off peers.

A team led by psychologist Linda A. Jackson of Michigan State University in East Lansing gave computers, Internet access, and in-home technical support to 140 children. The mostly twelve-to-fourteen-year-old African-American boys and girls lived in single-parent families with incomes no higher than $15,000 a year. The researchers recorded each child's Internet use from December 2000 through June 2002.

Before entering the study, these children generally did poorly in 25 school and on academic-achievement tests. However, overall grades and reading achievement scores — but not math-achievement scores — began to climb after six months of home Internet use. These measures had ascended farther by the end of the study, especially among the kids who spent the most time online.

Participants logged on to the Internet an average of thirty minutes a day, which isn't much in the grand scheme of teenage Internet use:

Teens in middle- and upper-class families average two or more Internet hours each day. Only 25 percent of the children in the study used instant messaging, and only 16 percent sent e-mails or contributed to online chat. These low numbers probably reflect a lack of home Internet access among the kids' families and friends. Also, their parents forbade most of the participating kids from contacting strangers in chat rooms.

Still, text-heavy online sites seem to have provided reading experience that translated into higher reading scores and grades, the researchers suggest. Although participants remained below-average readers at the end of the study, their improvement showed promise, according to Jackson and her colleagues.

These findings raise the unsettling possibility that "children most likely to benefit from home Internet access are the very children least likely to have [it]," Jackson's team concludes.

In stark contrast to their poor peers, wealthier middle school and high school students spend much of their time on the Internet trading instant messages with friends, an activity with tremendous allure for young people trying to fit into peer groups, says psychologist Robert Kraut of Carnegie Mellon University in Pittsburgh.

For teens, instant messaging extends opportunities to communi- 30 cate with friends and expands their social world, Kraut suggests. He and his colleagues probed instant messaging in interviews with twenty-six teens in 2002 and in surveys completed by forty-one teens in 2004.

Instant messaging simulates joining a clique, without the rigid acceptance rules of in-person peer groups, in Kraut's view. Each user creates his or her own buddy list.

Within these virtual circles, teens become part of what they regard as a cool Internet practice and, at the same time, intensify feelings of being connected to friends, even when sitting by themselves doing homework, Kraut says.

Still, Internet-savvy youngsters typically have much to learn about the social reach and potential perils of online communication, says education professor Zheng Yan of the State University of New York at Albany.

Yan interviewed 322 elementary and middle school students in a New England suburb. Participants also drew pictures to show what the Internet looks like and, when told to think of the Internet as a city, what types of people one would see there.

By ages ten to eleven, children demonstrated considerable 35 knowledge of the Internet's technical complexity, such as realizing that Internet sites act as data sources for many computers.

Not until ages twelve to thirteen, however, did youngsters begin to grasp the Internet's social complexity, such as the large numbers of strangers who can gain access to information that a person posts publicly. Even then, the kids' insight into the online social world's perils remained rudimentary compared with that previously observed in adults.

Children and teens plastering personal thoughts and images on websites such as myspace.com "often don't realize how many people have access to that information, including sexual predators," Yan asserts. He encourages parental monitoring of Internet activities and regular discussions of online dangers with children.

Worldwide Peers

Adolescents who form global Internet communities show signs of developing their own styles of leadership and social involvement, a trend that Northwestern University psychologist Justine Cassell and her coworkers view with optimism.

Cassell's team examined messages from an online community known as the Junior Summit, organized by the Massachusetts Institute of Technology. University officials sent out worldwide calls for youngsters to participate in a closed, online forum that would address how technology can aid young people. They chose 3,062 applicants, ages nine to sixteen, from 139 countries.

Those selected ranged from suburbanites in wealthy families to 40 child laborers working in factories. Computers and Internet access were provided to 200 schools and community centers in convenient locations for those participants who needed them.

During the last three months of 1998, children logged on to online homerooms, divided by geographic regions. Members of each homeroom generated and voted on twenty topics to be addressed by the overall forum. Topic groups then formed and participants elected a total of 100 delegates to an expenses-paid, one-week summit in Boston in 1999.

Cassell's group found that delegates, whom the researchers refer to as online leaders, didn't display previously established characteristics of adult leaders, such as contributing many ideas to a task and asserting dominance over others. While the delegates eventually sent more messages than their peers did, those who were later chosen as online leaders — regardless of age or sex — had referred to group goals rather than to themselves and synthesized others' posts rather than offering only their own ideas.

Without in-person leadership cues such as height or attractiveness, online congregants looked for signs of collaborative and persuasive proficiency, the researchers say.

Outside the controlled confines of the Junior Summit, teens even in places where few people own home computers find ways to obtain vital Internet information. Ghana, a western Africa nation in which adolescents represent almost half the population, provides one example.

Researchers led by Dina L.G. Borzekowski of Johns Hopkins   45
Bloomberg School of Public Health in Baltimore surveyed online experiences among 778 teens, ages fifteen to eighteen, in Ghana's capital, Accra.

Two-thirds of the 600 youngsters who attended high school said that they had previously gone online, as did about half of the 178 teens who didn't attend school. Among all Internet users, the largest proportion — 53 percent — had sought online health information on topics including AIDS and other sexually transmitted diseases, nutrition, exercise, drug use, and pregnancy.

Out-of-school teens — who faced considerable poverty — ranked the Internet as a more important source of sexual-health information than the students did, the investigators say.

In both groups, the majority of teens went online at Internet cafés, where patrons rent time on computers hooked up to the Internet.

Internet cafés have rapidly sprung up in unexpected areas, UCLA's Greenfield says. She conducts research in the southeastern Mexico state of Chiapas, which is inhabited mainly by poor farming families.

Small storefronts, each containing around ten Internet-equipped   50
computers, now dot this hard-pressed region, Greenfield notes. Primarily young people frequent these businesses, paying the equivalent of about $1 for an hour of Internet surfing.

"Even in Chiapas, adolescents are in the vanguard of Internet use," Greenfield remarks.

READING

1. The opening paragraph of Bower's article introduces a topic that would likely be unfamiliar to most readers – cutting. How do you think a middle-aged scientist would react to this opener? Why does Bower begin in this manner?

2. Throughout the piece, Bower refers to "youngsters," "teenagers," "adolescents," "teens," "kids," and so on. What sort of picture emerges of this age group? Does it ring true to you? How do you think the average *Science News* reader might respond?

3. At several points in his essay, Bower discusses the "digital divide" between wealthy to middle-class families and poorer ones. How does he suggest this divide impacts young people? Are there strategies that can address the divide?

4. One of the sources that Bower interviews, Zheng Yan, says that "Internet-savvy youngsters typically have much to learn about the social reach and potential perils of online communication." What evidence in the article supports this contention?

5. The chief purpose of the article is to summarize several studies of online usage by young people. What indications do you have as a reader that these studies have validity? What conclusions do they draw about how and why young people use the Internet for communications? Do you agree?

WRITING

1. Regardless of the study reviewed, Bower writes, "The one constant is that teens take to the Internet like ants to a summer picnic." Keep a log of the time you spend online for just two to three days (include any time text-messaging) and the activities you undertake while online. Write a reflective essay or journal entry that discusses this log. Did any aspect of it surprise you?

2. One study cited by Bower suggests that online communities allow leaders to emerge who otherwise might not emerge in face-to-face communities, where members are more likely to be judged by attractiveness. Think about the face-to-face groups to which you belong; these might include groups of friends or organized clubs/teams. Who seems to lead these groups? What qualities do they have? Write an essay about the qualities of a leader; include a discussion of how these qualities would manifest in a virtual environment – where all you have to go on is text.

3. The article runs quickly through many studies. Select one and research the original publication. Write a two- to three-page executive summary of the study's findings. The summary should be suitable for a general readership and should not rely on scientific jargon. Then, write a one-page reflection on this process. What was most difficult in the assignment?

4. Bower summarizes several studies that discuss the "digital divide" between the haves and the have-nots regarding technology. Research this issue in general and then localize your research to your community (either your hometown or your college location). Write a briefing for the administrative structure of this community (e.g., the mayor, the city council, the school board) identifying the critical issues impacting the digital divide in the area and suggesting some steps that could be taken to address these issues. Be certain to ground your suggestions in the research and make them specific to the community context.

5. In one study, researchers found that "bloggers routinely disclosed personal information, including e-mail addresses and other contact details." In part, the conclusion they draw is that blogs have become the personal diaries of the Internet generation – capturing the "more mundane topics" of everyday life. The Focus on Genre portfolio in this chapter provides several blogs (p. 265), and a quick Web search will lead to many others. Select an active blog that seems to follow the diary format. Follow the postings for several days. Then analyze them. Write a profile of the blogger from your research: What is the cyber identity of this individual? Who does the blogger want you to think he or she is? Are you convinced?

The MySpace Generation

By Jessi Hempel with Paula Lehman

FROM: *BusinessWeek*, December 12, 2005

CONTEXT: This selection was the cover story in *BusinessWeek Online*, the online companion site for *BusinessWeek*. It is "the world's most widely read business magazine, with more than 8 million readers each week." The audience for the magazine is affluent (the average reader has an income of over $200,000 per year) and technology literate (75 percent of readers are online every day). Jessi Hempel has been a staff editor at *BusinessWeekly* since she graduated from the University of California, Berkeley, in 2003. She writes frequently about cutting-edge technological issues. Paula Lehman is an ordained Mennonite minister, active in groups like the Advisory Board for Congregations Concerned for Children, where she sits on the board of directors. As you read this piece, ask yourself where your sense of community comes from, online or offline?

THE TOADIES BROKE UP. IT WAS FOUR YEARS AGO, WHEN Amanda Adams was sixteen. She drove into Dallas from suburban Plano, Texas, on a school night to hear the final two-hour set of the local rock band, which had gone national with a hit 1995 album. "Tears were streaming down my face," she recalls, a slight Texas lilt to her voice. During the long summer that followed, Adams turned to the Web in search of solace, plugging the lead singer's name into Google repeatedly until finally his new band popped up. She found it on Buzz-Oven.com, a social networking website for Dallas teens.

Adams jumped onto the Buzz-Oven network, posting an online self-portrait (dark hair tied back, tongue out, goofy eyes for the cam) and listing her favorite music so she could connect with other Toadies fans. Soon she was heading off to biweekly meetings at Buzz-Oven's airy loft in downtown Dallas and helping other "Buzzers" judge their favorite groups in marathon battle-of-the-bands sessions. (Buzz-Oven.com promotes the winners.) At her school, Frisco High —

and at malls and concerts — she passed out free Buzz-Oven sampler CDs plastered with a large logo from Coca-Cola Inc., which backs the site in the hope of reaching more teens on their home turf. Adams also brought dozens of friends to the concerts Buzz-Oven sponsored every few months. "It was cool, something I could brag about," says Adams, now twenty and still an active Buzzer.

Now that Adams is a junior at the University of North Texas at Denton, she's online more than ever. It's 7 p.m. on a recent Saturday, and she has just sweated her way through an online quiz for her advertising management class. (The quiz was "totally out of control," write classmates on a school message board minutes later.) She checks a friend's blog entry on MySpace.com to find out where a party will be that night. Then she starts an Instant Messenger (IM) conversation about the evening's plans with a few pals.

Kids, Bands, Coca-Cola

At the same time, her boyfriend IMs her a retail store link to see a new PC he just bought, and she starts chatting with him. She's also postering for the next Buzz-Oven concert by tacking the flier on various friends' MySpace profiles, and she's updating her own blog on Xanga.com, another social network she uses mostly to post photos. The TV is set to TBS, which plays a steady stream of reruns like *Friends* and *Seinfeld* — Adams has a TV in her bedroom as well as in the living room — but she keeps the volume turned down so she can listen to iTunes over her computer speakers. Simultaneously, she's chatting with dorm mate Carrie Clark, twenty, who's doing pretty much the same thing from a laptop on her bed.

You have just entered the world of what you might call Genera- 5 tion @. Being online, being a Buzzer, is a way of life for Adams and 3,000-odd Dallas-area youth, just as it is for millions of young Americans across the country. And increasingly, social networks are their medium. As the first cohort to grow up fully wired and technologically fluent, today's teens and twentysomethings are flocking to websites like Buzz-Oven as a way to establish their social identities. Here you can get a fast pass to the hip music scene, which carries a hefty amount of social currency offline. It's where you go when you need a friend to nurse you through a breakup, a mentor to tutor you on your calculus homework, an address for the party everyone is going to. For a giant brand like Coke, these networks also offer a direct pipeline to the thirsty but fickle youth market.

Preeminent among these virtual hangouts is MySpace.com, whose membership has nearly quadrupled since January alone, to 40 million members. Youngsters log on so obsessively that MySpace ranked No. 15 on the entire U.S. Internet in terms of page hits in

October, according to Nielsen//NetRatings. Millions also hang out at other up-and-coming networks such as Facebook.com, which connects college students, and Xanga.com, an agglomeration of shared blogs. A second tier of some 300 smaller sites, such as Buzz-Oven, Classface.com, and Photobucket.com, operate under — and often inside or next to — the larger ones.

Although networks are still in their infancy, experts think they're already creating new forms of social behavior that blur the distinctions between online and real-world interactions. In fact, today's young generation largely ignores the difference. Most adults see the Web as a supplement to their daily lives. They tap into information, buy books or send flowers, exchange apartments, or link up with others who share passions for dogs, say, or opera. But for the most part, their social lives remain rooted in the traditional phone call and face-to-face interaction.

The MySpace generation, by contrast, lives comfortably in both worlds at once. Increasingly, America's middle- and upper-class youth use social networks as virtual community centers, a place to go and sit for a while (sometimes hours). While older folks come and go for a task, Adams and her social circle are just as likely to socialize online as off. This is partly a function of how much more comfortable young people are on the Web: Fully 87 percent of twelve- to seventeen-year-olds use the Internet, vs. two-thirds of adults, according to the Pew Internet & American Life Project.

Teens also use many forms of media simultaneously. Fifteen- to eighteen-year-olds average nearly six and a half hours a day watching TV, playing video games, and surfing the Net, according to a recent Kaiser Family Foundation survey. A quarter of that time, they're multitasking. The biggest increase: computer use for activities such as social networking, which has soared nearly threefold since 2000, to one hour and twenty-two minutes a day on average.

Aside from annoying side effects like hyperdistractibility, there 10 are some real perils with underage teens and their open-book online lives. In a few recent cases, online predators have led kids into dangerous, real-life situations, and parents' eyes are being opened to their kids' new world.

One-hit Wonders

Meanwhile, the phenomenon of these exploding networks has companies clamoring to be a part of the new social landscape. News Corp. Chief Executive Rupert Murdoch has spent $1.3 billion on Web acquisitions so far to better reach this coveted demographic — $580 million alone for the July purchase of MySpace parent Intermix Media. And Silicon Valley venture capitalists such as Accel Partners and Redpoint Ventures are pouring millions into Facebook and other social networks. What's not yet clear is whether this is a dot-com era replay, with established companies and investors sinking huge sums into fast-growth startups with no viable business models. Facebook, barely a year old and run by a twenty-one-year-old student on leave from Harvard, has a staff of fifty and venture capital — but no profits.

Still, consumer companies such as Coke, Apple Computer, and Procter & Gamble are making a relatively low-cost bet by experimenting with networks to launch products and to embed their brands in the minds of hard-to-reach teens. So far, no solid format has emerged, partly because youth networks are difficult for companies to tap into. They're also easy to fall out of favor with: While Coke, Sony Pictures Digital, and Apple have succeeded with MySpace, Buzz-Oven, and other sites, P&G's attempt to create an independent network around a body spray, for one, has faltered so far.

Many youth networks are evanescent, in any case. Like one-hit wonder the Baha Men ("Who Let the Dogs Out") and last year's peasant skirts, they can evaporate as quickly as they appear. But young consumers may follow brands offline — if companies can figure out how to talk to youths in their online vernacular. Major companies should be exploring this new medium, since networks transmit marketing messages "person-to-person, which is more credible," says David Rich Bell, a marketing professor at the University of Pennsylvania's Wharton School.

So far, though, marketers have had little luck creating these networks from scratch. Instead, the connections have to bubble up from those who use them. To understand how such networks get started, share a blue-cheese burger at the Meridian Room, a dive bar in downtown Dallas, with Buzz-Oven founder Aden Holt. At 6 feet 9 inches, with one blue eye, one brown one, and a shock of shaggy red hair, Holt is a sort of public figure in the local music scene. He started a record label his senior year at college and soon turned his avocation into a career as a music promoter, putting out twenty-seven CDs in the decade that followed.

In 2000, as Internet access spread, Holt cooked up Buzz-Oven as 15 a new way to market concerts. His business plan was simple. First, he would produce sample CDs of local bands. Dedicated Buzzers like Adams would do the volunteer marketing, giving out the CDs for free, chatting up the concerts online, and slapping up posters and stickers in school bathrooms, local music stores, and on telephone poles. Then Holt would get the bands to put on a live concert, charging them $10 for every fan he turned out. But to make the idea work, Holt needed capital to produce the free CDs. One of his bands had recently done a show sponsored by Coke, and after asking around, he found the marketer's company's Dallas sales office. He called for an appointment. And then he called again. And again.

Coke's people didn't get back to him for weeks, and then he was offered only a brief appointment. With plenty of time to practice his sales pitch, Holt spit out his idea in one breath: Marketing through social networks was still an experiment, but it was worth a small investment to try reaching teens through virtual word of mouth. Coke rep Julie Bowyer thought the idea had promise. Besides, Holt's request was tiny compared with the millions Coke regularly sinks into campaigns. So she wrote him a check on the spot.

Deep Connections

By the time Ben Lawson became head of Coke's Dallas sales office in 2001, Buzz-Oven had mushroomed into a nexus that allowed hundreds of Dallas-area teens to talk to one another and socialize, online and off. A middle-aged father of two teens himself, Lawson spent a good deal of time poring over data about how best to reach youth like Adams. He knew what buzzer Mike Ziemer, twenty, so clearly articulates: "Kids don't buy stuff because they see a magazine ad. They buy stuff because other kids tell them to."

What Lawson really likes about Buzz-Oven is how deeply it weaves into teens' lives. Sure, the network reaches only a small niche. But Buzzers have created an authentic community, and Coke has been welcomed as part of the group. At a recent dinner, founder Holt asked a few Buzzers their opinions about the company. "I don't know if they care about the music or they just want their name on it, but knowing they're involved helps," says Michael Henry, nineteen. "I know they care; they think what we're doing is cool," says Michele Barr, twenty-one. Adds Adams: "They let us do our thing. They don't censor what we do."

Words to live by for a marketer, figures Lawson, particularly since Coke pays Buzz-Oven less than $70,000 a year. In late October, Holt signed a new contract with Coke to help him launch Buzz-Oven Austin in February. The amount is confidential, but he says it's enough for 10,000 CDs, three to four months of street promotions, and 50,000 fliers, plus some radio and print ads and a Web site promotion. Meanwhile, Buzz-Oven is building relations with other brands such as the *Dallas Observer* newspaper and McDonald's Chipotle restaurants, which kicks in free food for Buzzer volunteers who promote the shows. Profits from ticket sales are small but growing, says Holt.

Not so long ago, behemoth MySpace was this tiny. Tom Anderson, 20 a Santa Monica (California) musician with a film degree, partnered with former Xdrive Inc. marketer Chris DeWolfe to create a website where musicians could post their music and fans could chat about it.

Anderson knew music and film; De Wolfe knew the Internet business. Anderson cajoled Hollywood friends — musicians, models, actors — to join his online community, and soon the news spread. A year later, everyone from Hollywood teen queen Hilary Duff to Plano (Texas) teen queen Adams has an account.

It's becoming a phenomenon unto itself. With 20 million of its members logging on in October, MySpace now draws so much traffic that it accounted for 10 percent of all advertisements viewed online in the month. This is all the more amazing because MySpace doesn't allow those ubiquitous pop-up ads that block your view, much less spyware, which monitors what you watch and infuses it with popups. In fact, the advertising can be so subtle that kids don't distinguish it from content. "It's what our users want," says Anderson.

As MySpace has exploded, Anderson has struggled to maintain the intimate atmosphere that lends social networks their authenticity. When new users join, Tom becomes their first friend and invites them to send him a message. When they do, they hear right back, from him or from the one-quarter of MySpace's 165 staffers who handle customer service. Ask Adams what she thinks of MySpace's recent acquisition by News Corp., and she replies that she doesn't blame "Tom" for selling, she would have done the same thing. She's talking about Anderson, but it's hard to tell at first because she refers to him so casually, as if he were someone she has known for years.

That's why Murdoch has vowed not to wrest creative control from Anderson and DeWolfe. Instead News Corp.'s resources will help them nourish new MySpace dreams. Earlier this month they launched a record label. In the next few months, the duo says, they will launch a movie production unit and a satellite radio station. By March they hope to venture into wireless technology, perhaps even starting a wireless company to compete with Virgin Mobile or Sprint Nextel's Boost. Says DeWolfe: "We want to be a lifestyle brand."

It's proof that a network — and its advertising — can take off if it gives kids something they badly want. Last spring, Facebook founder Mark Zuckerberg noticed that the college students who make up most of his 9.5 million members were starting groups with names like Apple Students, where they swapped information about how to use their Macs. So he asked Apple if it wanted to form an official group. Now — for a fee neither company will disclose — Apple sponsors the group, giving away iPod Shuffles in weekly contests, making product announcements, and providing links to its student discount program.

The idea worked so well that Facebook began helping anyone 25 who wanted to start a group. Today there are more than a dozen, including several sponsored by advertisers such as Victoria's Secret and Electronic Arts. Zuckerberg soon realized that undergrads are more likely to respond to a peer group of Apple users than to the traditional banner ads, which he hopes to eventually phase out. Another of his innovations: ads targeted at students of a specific college. They're a way for a local restaurant or travel agency to advertise. Called Facebook Announcements, it's all automated, so anyone can go onto Facebook, pay $14 a day, and fill out an ad.

Sparkle and Fizzle

Still, social networks' relations with companies remain uneasy. Last year, for example, Buzz-Oven was nearly thrown off track when a band called Flickerstick wanted to post a song called "Teenage Dope Fiend" on the network. Holt told Buzzers: "Well, you can't use that song. I'd be encouraging teenagers to try drugs." They saw his point, and several Buzzers persuaded the band to offer up a different song. But such potential conflicts are one way, Holt concedes, that Buzz-Oven's corporate sponsorships could come to a halt.

Like Holt, other network founders have dealt with such conflicts by turning to their users for advice. Xanga co-founder John Hiler has resisted intrusive forms of advertising like spyware or pop-ups, selling only the conventional banner ads. When advertisers recently demanded more space for larger ads, Hiler turned the question over to Xanga bloggers, posting links to three examples of new ads. More than 3,000 users commented pro and con, and Hiler went with the model users liked best. By involving them, Hiler kept the personal connection that many say they feel with network founders — even though Xanga's membership has expanded to 21 million.

So far, corporate advertisers have had little luck creating such relationships on their own. In May, P&G set up what it hoped would become a social network around Sparkle Body Spray, aimed at tweens. The site features chatty messages from fake characters named for scents like Rose and Vanilla ("Friends call me Van"). Virtually no one joined, and no entries have comments from real users. "There wasn't a lot of interesting content to engage people," says Anastasia Goodstein, who documents the intersection between companies and the MySpace Generation at Ypulse.com. P&G concedes that the site is an experiment, and the company has found more success with a body-spray network embedded in MySpace.com.

The most basic threat to networks may be the whims of their users, who after all are mostly still kids. Take Friendster, the first networking website to gain national attention. It erupted in 2003, going from a few thousand users to nearly 20 million. But the company couldn't keep up, causing frustration among users when the site grew sluggish and prone to crash. It also started with no music, no message boards or classifieds, no blogging. Many jumped ship when MySpace came along, offering the ability to post song tracks and more elaborate profiles. Friendster has been hustling to get back into the game, adding in new options. But only 942,000 people clicked on the site in October, vs. 20.6 million who clicked on MySpace in the same time.

That's the elusive nature of trends and fads, and it poses a challenge for networks large and small. MySpace became a threat to tiny Buzz-Oven last year when Buzzers found they could do more cool things there, from blogs to more music and better profile options. Buzzer message board traffic slowed to a crawl. To stop the hemorrhaging, Holt joined MySpace himself and set up a profile for Buzz-Oven. His network now operates both independently and as a subsite on MySpace, but it still works. Most of Holt's Dallas crowd came back, and Buzz-Oven is up to 3,604 MySpace members now, slightly more than when it was a stand-alone network.

Even if the new approach works, Holt faces a succession issue that's likely to hit other networks at some point. At thirty-five, he's well past the age of his users. Even the friends who helped him launch Buzz-Oven.com are in their late twenties — ancient to members of his target demographic. So either he raises the age of the group — or replaces himself with someone younger. He's trying the latter, betting on Mike Ziemer, the twenty-year-old recent member, even giving him a small amount of cash.

Ziemer, it turns out, is an influencer. That means record labels and clothing brands pay him to talk up their products, for which he pulls down several hundred dollars a month. Ziemer has spiky brown hair and a round, expressive face. In his MySpace profile he lists his interests in this order: Girls. Music. Friends. Movies. He has 4,973 "friends" on MySpace. At all times, he carries a T-Mobile Sidekick, which he uses to text message, e-mail, and send photos to his friends. Sometimes he also talks on it, but not often. "I hate the phone," he says.

Think of Ziemer as Aden Holt 2.0. Like Amanda Adams, he's also a student at UT-Denton. When he moved to the area from Southern California last year, he started Third String PR, a miniature version of Buzz-Oven that brings bands to the 'burbs. He uses MySpace.com to promote bands and chats online with potential concertgoers. Ziemer can pack a church basement with tweens for a concert, even though they aren't old enough to drive. On the one hand, Ziemer idolizes Holt, who has a larger version of Ziemer's company and a ton of connections in the music industry. On the other hand, Ziemer thinks Holt is old. "Have you ever tried to talk with him over IM?" he says. "He's just not plugged in enough."

Exactly why Holt wants Ziemer on Buzz-Oven. He knows the younger entrepreneur can tap a new wave of kids — and keep the site's corporate sponsor on board. But he worries that Ziemer doesn't have the people skills. What's more, should Ziemer lose patience with Buzz-Oven, he could blacklist Holt by telling his 9,217 virtual friends that Buzz-Oven is no longer cool. In the online world, one powerfully networked person can have a devastatingly large impact on a small society like Buzz-Oven.

For now, the gamble is paying off. Attendance is up at Buzz-Oven 35 events, and if the Austin launch goes smoothly, Holt will be one step closer to his dream of going national. But given the fluid world of networks, he's taking nothing for granted.

READING

1. The subheading for this piece is, "They live online. They buy online. They play online. Their power is growing." Exactly what kind of power is the author suggesting "they" have? How does this sentence set up the focus of the piece?

2. The essay has an organizational strategy that uses bold subheadings between sections. The first is Kids, Bands, Coca-Cola. The last is Sparkle and Fizzle. Discuss these headings and how their connotations work with the structure of the piece.

3. Hempel makes the point that marketers are very interested in online social communities, but they have not been successful in creating their own networks associated with products. Holt, the founder of Buzz-Oven, has a new business strategy. Describe Holt's idea and discuss ways it differs from traditional marketing. Include a discussion of Coca-Cola's relationship to Buzz-Oven.

4. Hempel notes that "With 20 million of its members logging on in October, MySpace now draws so much traffic that it accounted for 10 percent of all advertisements viewed online in the month. This is all the more amazing because MySpace doesn't allow those ubiquitous pop-up ads that block your view, much less spyware, which monitors what you watch and infuses it with pop-ups. In fact, the advertising can be so subtle that kids don't distinguish it from content." Go to the MySpace network and observe the kind of online advertising that exists on the site now. Can you distinguish advertising from content?

5. One paradox of the new social networks is that the members feel a sense of intimacy with their "friends" on the network, even if they claim to have hundreds or thousands of friends. One of the network's problems is how to maintain the sense of intimacy and connection and still keep growing their membership. Auden Holt of Buzz-Oven is dealing with this problem by hiring a younger version of himself to become the "friend" of all new teen members of the site. He says, "Think of Ziemer as Aden Holt 2.0." How does this solution strike you? What is your definition of friendship? Of intimacy? Do you have online friends?

WRITING

1. Write a reflective essay or a journal entry describing your own online identity. Are you primarily a shopper? Do you belong to a social network? Do you take online courses? Do you read news online? Check stocks?

2. Hempel cites a Kaiser Family Foundation survey, which states, "Teens also use many forms of media simultaneously. Fifteen- to eighteen-year-olds average nearly six and a half hours a day watching TV, playing video games, and surfing the Net." Research current statistics regarding teens' use of media to see if these figures have changed since the publication of this article and write a report of your findings. You might see if the Kaiser Family Foundation has continued its research.

3. Write a narrative essay cataloging the sites you visit when you log on to your computer. What is your homepage? Have you personalized your homepage? What do you check first? Do you follow a pattern?

4. This article suggests that online marketing through social networks uses a new type of advertising. For example, "Xanga co-founder John Hiler has resisted intrusive forms of advertising like spyware or pop-ups, selling only the conventional banner ads. When advertisers recently demanded more space for larger ads, Hiler turned the question over to Xanga bloggers, posting links to three examples of new ads. More than 3,000 users commented pro and con, and Hiler went with the model users liked best." Clearly, having consumers choose their favorite ads is a new strategy. Go online and see how many types of advertising you can find on the sites you usually frequent. Write an essay classifying the type and number of ads you find. Discuss which you find the least intrusive and why.

5. "The MySpace Generation" discusses the target demographic of teens and opens with the example of sixteen-year-old Amanda Adams seeking peer approval and solidarity by buzzing local bands. Claudia Wallis, in "The Thing About Thongs" (p. 324), speaks of marketing's effect on her "tween" daughter and her choice of underwear. Wallis's article quotes Ron Taffel, author of *The Second Family: How Adolescent Power Is Challenging the American Family*, who argues that seeking peer approval is a "'statement to other kids that they are part of this very, very intense, powerful second family of peer group and pop culture that is shaping kids' wants, needs and feelings,'" a phenomenon, Wallis suggests, that is "gripping kids at ever earlier ages." Research a current fad or fashion for teens, or tweens, or younger, and write a short piece modeled on Wallis's essay.

R We D8ting?

By Sandra Barron

FROM: *New York Times*, July 24, 2005

CONTEXT: This article appeared in the column Modern Love in the *New York Times*. Each Sunday, the column features a different take on contemporary romantic and familial relationships; the work represented in the column comes from a wide range of authors. The writer of this piece is Sandra Barron, a freelance journalist living in Brooklyn. The *Times* is read nationwide and has a circulation of almost 1.7 million. The company describes the readers as "affluent, educated, inquisitive, and acquisitive." The weekday *Times* readers' annual median income is estimated at $140,000, and 76 percent of its readership have college degrees. As you read Barron's piece, think about how online communications have the potential to be understood and misunderstood outside the realm of face-to-face interactions. ("R We D8ting" by Sandra Barron. Text and front page, Copyright © 2005 The *New York Times*. Reprinted with permission.)

THE ORANGE MESSAGE LIGHT ON MY CELLPHONE STARTED blinking as I was getting ready for bed. Barely an hour had passed since our quick kiss goodnight at the subway, and I was surprised to see the screen light up with the initials I'd just entered into my phone. It wasn't voice mail; it was a text message, and it made me smile.

U miss me? ;-)

I'd met him a week before at my usual Wednesday night hangout. He was alone but gregarious, and he seemed to be pals with the female bartender — a tacit vote of confidence. He chatted with my friends and me and then left with a wave from the door, and when my friend Kate and I ordered our next drinks, the bartender said this round was on the guy we'd been talking to.

Surprised, we debated his motivations. I insisted that perfectly normal people sometimes buy strangers drinks just to be nice. Kate thought he was way too aggressive.

When I saw him at the bar the next Wednesday, I thanked him for 5 the drink. He asked if he could take me to dinner sometime; I said I'd think about it. He walked me to the subway and we exchanged numbers, but I thought it would be days before I heard from him, if ever, making this late-night text message all the more unexpected.

I like text messages. They fill an ever-narrowing gap in modern communication tools, combining the immediacy of a phone call with the convenience of an answering machine message and the premeditation of e-mail. And if they happen to be from a crush and pop up late at night, they have the giddy re-readability of a note left on a pillow.

So did I miss him? Certainly not yet. But I was flying from New York to West Virginia in the morning for work; maybe I'd miss him while I was away? I could already hear my friends citing his enthusiasm as evidence he was coming on too strong, but I'd had enough of aloof. I found his boldness refreshing.

Before I turned out the light and snapped the phone into its charger, I allowed myself one more grin at his message and a grimace at his middle-school style ("U"? A winking smiley face?). Then I deleted it.

He called the next afternoon while I was grounded in Pittsburgh between flights. He kept me company while I ambled down moving walkways and wandered through a loop of food courts. We talked about work for the first time; he said he worked intense hours as a freelancer so he could take months off at a time to travel, and he showed he had been paying attention by asking me about things we had discussed at the bar. He asked if we could have dinner when I got back to town, and I said sure.

A few hours later, as the prop plane taxied toward the gate in West Virginia, I turned on my phone and an animated lighthouse beacon indicated that it was searching for a signal. For three days, the light swept the dark cartoon sea in vain. Every time I saw "no signal" on the screen I felt unmoored and isolated. But as soon as the signal bars sprang to life on my trip home on Monday, that orange light flashed on and, sure enough, it was him. 10

Miss me now?

I'd missed having cellphone service, and my mind had indeed wandered at times to our airport conversation. But that degree of nuance was too much for the 12-button keypad, so I wrote, Hi! Sure. Talk when I get back.

This set off a volley of texts. Where did I live? What day is good? What about tonight? Tomorrow? We decided on dinner that Thursday and I finally signed off, thumb sore and eyes tired.

At the office on Tuesday, as the light blinked on again (Din in SoHo then drinks in the E Vil, and maybe a kiss), I wondered, Just who is this guy?

Google failed me. One time, armed with only a guy's first name 15 and the fact that he sold sneakers, I had found his full details and photos online. But all I had here was a cellphone number and initials, and Friendster, MySpace, and Technorati — the entire digital detective squad of the modern dater — were stumped.

I would actually have to learn about him the old-fashioned way, in person. Which is partly why, on a slushy, windy Wednesday after-noon, I liked his next message:

Dinner @ Raoul's 2morrow, I just made reservations 4 7:30.

I couldn't remember the last time I'd gone out with someone who'd made reservations.

Sounds good! I replied.

A message came back as I was leaving the office: Its better than 20 good — u r with me! Maybe I'll stop by the bar 2nite.

So he remembered I usually went on Wednesdays.

On the way over, feet soaked and fingers numb, I knew that I didn't want him to brave the sleet just to see me, especially since it would be awkward trying to get to know him better while hanging out with people he had never met. And after all, we had reservations for the next night.

Don't come out in this weather! I wrote. Can't really hang out anyway, see you tomorrow.

His reply was impossibly swift for its length: I live 45 seconds from there and I would be doing my own thing. I am not leachy. Very independent boy I am. I may or may not, depends where the wind takes me.

Was it just me, or had things just taken a hairpin turn for the hos- 25 tile? My message was meant to be friendly. Had it come out that way? Or was I reading him wrong? I needed to find a way to respond that was light, in case I was only imagining he was angry, but not flippant, in case he actually was.

I swallowed my distaste for cutesy abbreviations and tried: LOL! As you like, then. :-) I cringed slightly as I hit send; this suddenly seemed like a dangerously clumsy way of communicating.

Minutes later: Would u like me 2 stay away?

Oh, dear. At this point, yes. Wires were crossing that would prob-ably be best untangled in person, the next day.

Entering the bar, I waved to my friends in their booth and, before joining them, whipped off a quick response, attempting to be polite and clear: Yeah, I guess that'd be better; you'd distract me if you were here.

A minute later, after I'd settled in with my friends, the orange light 30 looked like a warning: 2 late, im here.

I looked up. Sure enough, there he was, talking to two girls at the bar. He drifted closer and hovered nearby but didn't make eye con-tact. By the time he came over and sat down, a full hour had passed.

He'd clearly had a few drinks, and our conversation went downhill as fast as it had on our phone screens. He said that I'd tried to "control" him by saying he shouldn't come to the bar and added that he hadn't come to see me but to see other people. After going on in this vein for a while, he suddenly softened and asked me to "promise one thing": a kiss before the night was over.

I stammered that I couldn't make any promises. He shook his head and stormed off, sloshing the beers on the table and sending a pool cue clattering to the floor.

Before I could process what had happened, he looked over from his perch on a nearby barstool and smiled, winked, and waved over his shoulder as if we'd never met. My friends, wide-eyed, asked what was going on. I wasn't sure, but I did know one thing: reservations or not, tomorrow's date was off.

Not so that evil blinking light. Only half an hour later, with both 35 of us still in the bar, no, was it possible? Another message?

What was that all about? he'd written. R we still on 4 2morrow?

I deleted the message and put my phone away, hoping to erase the whole encounter. Soon he seemed to have left, and as long as my phone stayed in the dark recesses of my purse, I believed that he was powerless to bother me.

But suddenly there he was again, standing a few feet from our booth, smiling and crooking his finger at me.

I shook my head.

"I need to talk to you," he said. 40

I told him we had nothing to talk about.

Turns out I wasn't the only person who found him menacing; within minutes the bartender took the stocky wine glass out of his hand and told him to leave.

I hoped he would be so embarrassed that he wouldn't dream of contacting me again. But the next morning the blinking orange light seemed louder than my bleating alarm clock. Three new messages. Mailbox full.

From 6:30 a.m.: I am done boozing for a while!! :-)

From 6:38 a.m.: What did I do 2 upset u? Do u not want to have 45 dinner?

At 6:45, as if he had waited long enough for a reply: Anyway, 2 bad, I would have liked 2 have gotten 2 know u.

I liked the finality of that one.

But had he really given up, or was there simply no more room in the inbox? I deleted those three and got on the subway. I emerged to find: Pls forgive me and join me 4 dinner. ;-[(

We are not going out, I wrote.

What did I do? 50

I'm at work and we're not discussing this.

Whatever, he wrote. U don't have 2 b ignorant. Peace.

I turned off the phone, dumbfounded. How had this happened? How had we managed to speed through all the stages of an actual relationship almost solely via text message? I'd gone from butterflies to doubt to anger at his name on the screen, before we even knew each other.

That was it, I decided: no more text-message flirtations for me. From now on I'd stick to more old-fashioned ways of getting to know a guy. Like e-mail.

READING

1. Barron's first-person opening to her column about dating establishes a conversational and friendly narrative. Given this tone, what might you imagine about the audience she is addressing?

2. Barron's paragraphs are short and her interactions with the man she meets in the bar are brief. Examine the text messages that they exchange. Then, examine their real-time interactions. Do these two ways of getting to "know" one another present different personas? If so, how?

3. On her business trip, before their first date, Barron feels "unmoored and isolated" when she has no signal on her cell phone. To what extent is this an indication of interest in her upcoming date and to what extent is it a sign that she is missing the constant contact and availability of her social network?

4. At what point in the piece does the tone of the messages change from friendliness to hostility? What are the word choices that alert you to this fact? In what ways was this shift foreshadowed in the piece?

5. Barron ends her essay on an ironic note: "That was it, I decided: no more text-message flirtations for me. From now on I'd stick to more old-fashioned ways of getting to know a guy. Like e-mail." Do you consider e-mail an "old-fashioned" way to get to know someone? In what ways might e-mail be a more old-fashioned way of getting to know someone? How are texting and e-mail similar? How are they different?

WRITING

1. Write a narrative or reflective piece on the way you got to know someone romantically. What were the specific ways of communicating that you used to get to know this person? Consider traditional social communities, online social networks, telephones, letters, conversation, e-mail, texting — as well as anything else that occurs to you (flowers?).

2. Divide into small groups in your class and choose a decade, beginning with 1900 and ending with the decade you live in now. Research courtship practices during those decades in the United States or in other countries. How did people meet? What was acceptable courting behavior? What were some of the rituals of dating? Take turns sharing your research with your class. Then, see what patterns you

can discern as technology became more commonplace as a social tool. What do you make of these changing traditions?

3. It is generally accepted that text-messaging is influencing our traditional patterns of writing. Research at least three articles from academic journals that have been written on this topic. Briefly summarize each article and comment on your findings. Do you find your own habits of writing changing?

4. Barron writes that when she began to wonder, "Just who is this guy?" she went online to Friendster, MySpace, and Technorati to find out more about him, with only a cell-phone number and his initials. What do you think someone could find out about you, using regular online channels? If you were researching someone today, where would you begin? Write an essay describing your search for information about yourself and what information you found in what venues.

5. To demonstrate the extent of online social networking, Jessi Hempel, in "The MySpace Generation" (p. 208), describes an online day for Amanda Adams, a college student:

> [H]er boyfriend IMs her a retail store link to see a new PC he just bought, and she starts chatting with him. She's also postering for the next Buzz-Oven concert by tacking the flier on various friends' MySpace profiles, and she's updating her own blog on Xanga.com, another social network she uses mostly to post photos. The TV is set to TBS, which plays a steady stream of reruns like *Friends* and *Seinfeld* — Adams has a TV in her bedroom as well as in the living room — but she keeps the volume turned down so she can listen to iTunes over her computer speakers. Simultaneously, she's chatting with dorm mate Carrie Clark, twenty, who's doing pretty much the same thing from a laptop on her bed.
>
> You have just entered the world of what you might call Generation @.

Barron in "R We D8ting?" is also looking at ways we use media in personal relationships, although she seems more uncomfortable with the ways she finds herself using media to connect with other people. How would you characterize yourself in terms of how you use media to connect with others? Are you a member of "Generation @"? If so, write an essay describing your generation and its habitual use of media in social situations. If not, what generation do you belong to and what characterizes your use of technology in your personal relationships?

The Sims: Suburban Rhapsody

By Clive Thompson

FROM: *Psychology Today*, December 2003

CONTEXT: The following article comes from *Psychology Today* magazine. The magazine defines its scope as "all aspects of human behavior, from the workings of the brain, to relationships and the larger cultural forces that influence our decisions." Although it is not an academic journal, the audience for *Psychology Today* is very well educated: 84 percent have college degrees. The magazine's primary readership is female (over two-thirds). This piece was written by Clive Thompson. Thompson is a contributing writer for the *New York Times Magazine* and has written for *New York* and *Wired* — most frequently about technology, science, culture, and politics. He also writes an active blog on technology issues: "collision detection." How do the links between the virtual Sims world and the real world expose some truths about human psychology?

LISA ANNE CRAIG KNEW SHE WAS IN TROUBLE WHEN THE social worker knocked on her door.

Halfway through her first pregnancy, Craig decided to take a high-tech approach to parenthood. She bought a copy of The Sims, the hugely popular computer game that lets you create and direct a household and a family — building a suburban home, finding jobs for the parents, and scrambling to keep everyone happy and healthy. She fired it up, selecting a young professional couple with a newborn. Hey, it was a game. How hard could it be?

Whoops. "You know what? The babies cry a lot in that game," she says. "So it's crying while I'm trying to juggle everything else, like getting the parents to work and making sure they clean the house." After a few hours of domestic chaos, her virtual baby was whisked away by a digital caseworker. "I was devastated! I was sure that I wouldn't be able to handle a real baby," Craig says with a laugh. She kept playing though, and by the time her actual baby arrived, she felt like a pro. "My family thought I was nuts, but I swear it got me through the pregnancy," she says.

At first glance, The Sims is an unlikely hit. It doesn't shred your dendrites with cutting-edge 3-D graphics. You don't blast aliens with plasma guns, drive high-speed race cars, or get to play basketball against the Knicks. Yet in 2003 it became the best-selling computer game in history, with more than 29 million fanatic players. It's popular not just with twitchy teenage boys but among people who typically never touch the stuff: women, professionals — even forty- and fifty-somethings.

Maybe that's because playing The Sims is almost exactly like coping with everyday suburban life. To begin, you build a home, choosing details down to the pattern of tiles on the kitchen floor and the shape of the backyard pool. Then you help your Sims along as they stumble along through existence. 5

Unlike nearly every other game, there's no winning or losing. You're just trying to keep your Sims happy and entertained. And as Lisa Anne Craig found out, although you may be the puppet master, the Sims play by their own rules. Leave a bunch of Sims teenagers unsupervised for a while as they try to make pizza? They just might burn the house down. Forget to send them to the bathroom? Eventually, they'll pee on the floor. Perhaps most eerily, your Sims have emotions: Their "happiness meter" will drop if they get hungry, or if you don't give them someone to fall in love with. Neglect them too much? They'll die.

These lifelike stakes give The Sims a genuinely existential edge, and therein lies the allure of the game. By toying with a virtual version of ordinary life, you can grapple with a very real question: What makes a person happy?

To understand the appeal of The Sims, it helps to understand a bit about Will Wright, the game's creator and co-founder of the game company Maxis. The forty-two-year-old is widely known as the philosopher king of the computer-game world, equally at home in the library as in the arcade. His games may be mass-market hits, but they're based on some very brainy theories about behavior, economics, and humanistic psychology.

Wright's intellectual path is about as eclectic as possible: He attended three different colleges but never graduated, sampling courses from computer science, architecture, and mechanical engineering to aviation.

One of the first games he designed, SimAnt, was inspired by evolutionary biologist Edward O. Wilson's famous studies of ant colonies. Wright became fascinated by Wilson's explorations of "emergent 10 complexity" — the idea that individual creatures operating with very simple goals can collectively produce incredibly complex behaviors. In the game, SimAnt players assemble an anthill and then marvel as it seems to grow a mind of its own. "Each ant is only doing a few simple things, but when you put tons of them together you suddenly have these really surprising results," he notes, including unusually complex ways of gathering and moving resources around.

When Wright began designing The Sims in the late '90s, though, he faced a more challenging task: How do you get virtual people to act the way real ones do? Ants are relatively easy to simulate, since their behavior isn't too complicated. But what are the fundamental building blocks of human behavior?

Wright boned up on psychologist Abraham Maslow's *Motivation and Personality*, including his famous theory of the hierarchy of needs. Maslow argued in the '40s and '50s that human behavior could best be explained as a quest to satisfy primal needs such as hunger and safety before addressing demands such as love or self-actualization. The Sims are programmed this way, which is why they seem so true to life. For example, your Sim won't enjoy a movie if she's hungry. Aesthetic appreciation of a movie is a higher-order pleasure — and she can't do it if her stomach is growling.

That means that you, the player, must learn and obey the rules that govern Sim life, many of which are hauntingly familiar. "You want to buy them a washer-dryer?" Wright asks. "OK, but you might not have enough money left over for a phone. So what's more important, communication with your friends, or saving time cleaning?" he laughs. "It lays bare all these ethics of everyday life. What you shop for implies these moral choices."

The game also incorporates the ideas of physicist-turned-economist David Friedman. In his book *Hidden Order*, Friedman argued that our everyday lives are a series of quasi-economic choices. In the grocery store, for example, we pick which line to stand in based on a calculus of anticipated time and hassle: "If we decide to move over to a line that seems to be moving faster," Wright notes, "we have to give up our spot in our current line. So it's a sacrifice hoping to get something out of it." To replicate these little mental trade-offs, Wright gave a Sim the ability to decide between, say, sleeping late (which will make him feel more rested) or cleaning up (which might make him feel happier about his house).

In Wright's hands, theories like Friedman's have fashioned a 15 game that allows you to play out your fantasies, relive your life, or rejigger your identity. Ever wonder what would happen if you had seven kids? Or if you were living in a huge frat house? Try it out — set up a Sim with that lifestyle and turn it loose. In one sense, The Sims is a private laboratory to experiment with the forbidden "what-ifs" of your existence. It may be the first form of high-tech self-gnosis: mass therapy disguised as a computer game.

The first thing most people do when playing the game is re-create themselves, says Wright, and they often learn something in the process. He once got a letter from the parents of an adopted Romanian boy, orphaned at age nine or ten. The child seemed depressed — even traumatized — and wouldn't talk about his background. "Then they got him The Sims," recalls Wright. "And he ended up replaying his childhood in the game for them. He created a version of his [biological] family and showed them what had happened. [The game] became a tool for self-expression."

"It gives you a model for a realistic environment," agrees Henry Jenkins, a professor of comparative media studies at the Massachusetts Institute of Technology and an expert in video gaming. "You can program your Sim to look and sound like your last girlfriend and figure out why your last relationship fell flat." Some psychologists say their patients actually discuss their Sims games on the couch, an updated version of the classic therapeutic technique of playing with dolls. "When The Sims works well, it's kind of like a projective test. You can really see a lot of their psyche spilling out into their games," says John Suler, a psychology professor at Rider University in Lawrenceville, New Jersey, who specializes in cyberculture. "I spoke to one teenager who created a version of herself and her boyfriend. Then she created another version of herself — an evil version — to try to steal her boyfriend. She wanted to see what it's like to be evil."

In fact, nefarious behavior may be the best part of the game. In real life, you wouldn't dream of doing nasty things to your friends and family. But in The Sims, the lid blows off your id. In hundreds of fan Web sites devoted to the game, players gleefully describe the wicked ways they've killed their Sims — such as putting them in the pool, then removing all the ladders, and waiting to see how long it takes them to drown. As in fiction and art, of course, tragedy can be powerfully cathartic. "People really love to explore 'failure states,'" Wright says. "In fact, the failure states are really much more interesting than the success states."

The strongest draw of The Sims, though, may be the way it allows you to indulge your acquisitive streak. Wright knew that buying stuff for your Sim household — designer clothes or wide-screen plasma TVs — would be a major part of self-expression, just as it is in real life. But possessions also suck up time, as documented by sociologist John Robinson, a scholar of "time studies" — how much time the average American spends on routine activities. Robinson discovered strange truths about our lives, like the fact that we might spend half an hour in total each day getting from place to place in the house; he also found that we spend 154 minutes watching television and twenty minutes on child care.

As players build increasingly lavish homes, they find that the high life can be more of a hassle than it's worth. "Your Sim winds up spending all his time just navigating the place," Wright says, laughing. "Sure, you've got the pool table in the west wing — but you've got to get there." Players buy their Sims more and more gadgets and toys, but reality bites back. "They want the dishwasher because they think it'll save them time. But if a player loads their house down too much, soon they find the stuff breaks and needs maintenance," Wright says. "Suddenly, these things you wanted so much all became time bombs, when you originally bought them as time-savers." 20

Nonetheless, most long-term players say designing Sim house-holds is the chief delight of the game. "I don't really even play with the families anymore. I just focus on the design. I spent a couple of days setting up a Moroccan-style house, complete with a courtyard and a market," says Andrea Grimison, a thirty-three-year-old woman in Germany who spends a few hours a day playing the game. "Now, this is a place I'd like to live!" She set up a Web site to share her work, and now thousands of fans download her concept every month.

By putting interior design at the heart of his game, Wright took a page from influential architect Christopher Alexander. The psycho-logically astute Alexander argues that ordinary people innately grasp how environments and urban planning affect us; it's why young couples often argue heatedly about what neighborhood or city to live in. "We intuitively understand the need for privacy or our affinity for light," Wright notes. "[Alexander] was always saying that you don't need a professional — you can do this yourself. He became kind of the anti-architect."

While reading Alexander, Wright discovered a curious fact: Home-design software sells millions of copies a year. Wright figured it was hardly likely that so many people were actually embarking on massive remodeling projects; in reality, they probably just wanted to play with architecture. The Sims, Wright deduced, could be a labora-tory for understanding not only our personalities but also our per-sonal spaces.

In the process of designing the ultimate split-level, players some-times learn a few things about their own lives. Grimison tried creat-ing a virtual replica of her own house. When she finished it, something weird happened: Her Sims didn't like it. "It was because my bathroom doesn't have windows since it's in the middle of the house. And my Sims always want light in all the rooms or they won't be happy." Lisa Anne Craig had a similar epiphany, but in reverse. "I actually used The Sims when I was painting the house. I couldn't decide what color to paint it, so I made a model of our house and I tried out various colors. Unfortunately, we picked a periwinkle. It's very Florida," she jokes, "but now I kind of hate it."

The Sims is still nothing like real life in some very important 25 ways: there are no taxes, children never grow into adults, and there aren't any tightly packed cities such as Chicago or New York. But the virtual citizens will soon be taking another great leap toward real life. Electronic Arts, Maxis' parent company, plans to launch The Sims 2. This sequel has the same basic plot but with a few intriguing refinements: In the new game, Sims will age and die. What's more, the events of their youth will leave them with psychological baggage as they get older. "If your Sims have particularly happy childhoods — or unhappy ones — you'll be able to see the way that's going to impact them later in life. You can see how they kind of ricochet on into the future," Wright says. He suspects it'll turn the game into an even more precise emulation of our existence — a spreadsheet for life." He's probably right. We'll play it, millions more of us, poking and prodding our virtual selves to see what happens.

READING

1. Thompson begins his piece with a sentence designed to capture reader attention. What is it? What is unusual about the situation it sets up?

2. According to Thompson, The Sims is just like suburban life. How?

3. Who is Will Wright? How do his background, interests, and experience shape this game? Who else seems to have influenced the world of The Sims?

4. Thompson argues that one of the biggest draws of The Sims is the ability to indulge your acquisitive streak. How does he support this claim? What does this aspect of the game reveal about our tendencies and desires?

5. Early in the essay, Thompson says that the game makes people "grapple with a very real question: What makes a person happy?" Based on the essay, how would you answer this question?

WRITING

1. Some aspects of The Sims are based on the concept that "our everyday lives are a series of quasi-economic choices." Write down the choices you make in one day, including both what you choose to do and what you choose *not* to do. What seems to be driving your choices? Write a reflective essay or journal entry that describes the "calculus of anticipated time and hassle" you use in your "quasi-economic" process.

2. Although The Sims allows the player the opportunity to live out any existence, Thompson writes that "the first thing most people do when playing the game is re-create themselves." Write an essay that discusses reasons why this might be true. What are people trying to learn about their identities and behavior in such a situation? Refer to some of the authorities cited by Thompson. Does The Sims serve a purpose much different from keeping a journal or a diary?

3. Thompson credits some of The Sims design emphasis to architect Christopher Alexander, who realized the importance of place and physical environment on our psyches. Consider one of your current physical environments (your home, your classroom, your workplace). Write an essay describing how you would change this space if you could move it into a virtual world. Why would you make the changes you describe? How would they change your psyche?

4. The piece notes that many video game players are teenage boys, which you might expect, but The Sims also appeals to a broad audience that usually avoids gaming. Research the video game market and write up a market analysis, including the revenue generated by games/gaming, the average age, income, and education of the customer, what the average customer spends on gaming each year, the most profitable sector of the market, and so on. Present your analysis as a briefing for a company thinking of entering into the video game market. Based on your analysis, what type of game would you suggest they design?

5. Thompson observes of The Sims, "nefarious behavior may be the best part of the game. . . . in The Sims, the lid blows off your id." By shifting undesirable behavior into an online sphere, users can "see what it's like to be evil." Similarly, in Second Life – discussed in other essays in this chapter – most of the property is designated "mature," and the site has been criticized for an abundance of virtual gambling houses and sex shops. Research the issue of violence and pornography in gaming. Then, write two short position papers based on your research. Each paper should be written from a different "virtual" self: the first by a parent concerned about her children who are active online gamers; the second by a game company owner concerned that the controversy will impact profits. Finally, write a short narrative explaining what evidence you left out of each position paper, and why.

Life or Something Like It

By Karen Moltenbrey

FROM: *Computer Graphics World*, July 2004

CONTEXT: This piece comes from *Computer Graphics World* magazine, a premiere publication for computer graphics, which focuses on the latest innovations and the people who create them. The target audience is professionals in high-end computer graphics work, from game technology to science and industry. The magazine boasts 318,729 subscribers. Fifty-eight percent of its readership are creative producers and 24 percent are corporate executives. Its appeal to both creators and CEOs is reflected in the following market research: "Over the next 12 months *CGW* subscribers plan to spend $690,000" on computers and related technology. Karen Moltenbrey is chief editor for *CGW*. She is an award-winning business and cutting-edge technology writer, a three-time national ASBP (American Society of Business Publication Editors) Gold winner and a Jesse H. Neal National Business Journalism Award finalist. As you read this piece, consider how she appeals to both enthusiasts and professionals with a blend of narrative details and technological information about Second Life.

IF YOU COULD REINVENT YOURSELF, WHAT CHOICES WOULD you make? Would you be tall or short, heavy or thin, outgoing or shy? Or would you become a different species, such as a dog or a cat? In Second Life, the massively multiplayer online role-playing game (MMORPG) from Linden Labs, players can be anyone, or anything, they ever wanted to be within this immersive, realistic 3D world.

"Second Life is a place where you can completely stretch your imagination and the boundaries of reality by exploring a personal fantasy that is outside the realm of possibility within real life," says Robin Harper, senior vice president of marketing and community development at Linden Labs, which was founded by the former CTO of RealNetworks, a streaming media company. "You can do anything you've dreamed about doing in your 'first' life but can't do or haven't done. In fact, our players often use the terms RL and SL — nomenclature for their real life and second life."

Allowing players to incarnate themselves is a novel concept, even in the fantasy realm of an MMORPG. That's because most MMO titles not only limit the activities and locations of the players, but they also restrict the avatars themselves, requiring subscribers to assume a persona that fits within the theme of a particular title, such as the medieval realm of Dark Age of Camelot. In contrast, the inhabitants of Second Life are free to be and do whatever they want inside. That's because the game is shaped entirely by its users — from the avatars and environments to the "events" hosted by the users. "People come to create, compete, explore, and socialize," notes Harper.

"Everything in the world is made by the users, or residents, in real time," says Cory Ondrejka, vice president of product development. "All the content is streamed in real time over a broadband connection, so it allows people to work collaboratively. For instance, two users can build a house together — one can construct the east wing and the other the west wing, and simultaneously see what each is doing. They can even place a blueprint on a billboard, and refer to it during construction."

A New Beginning

Linden Labs generated the game's initial terrain using procedural 5 textures and hand-drawn surfaces created with Alias's Maya and Adobe's Photoshop, respectively. The company also built the tropical island area, where newcomers learn game basics, and some objects in the start section. (Mac or PC users can log on to www.secondlife.com for a free seven-day trial. Residency requires a one-time fee of $9.95, plus a monthly or yearly subscription rate. No software purchase or install CD is required.)

Before visiting the island, however, players must create an avatar by choosing between a male or a female model, which also has been prebuilt by the developer in Maya. Then, players adjust their model by using approximately 200 available sliders, which alter everything from the avatar's girth and height to its facial detail. In fact, an avatar can be altered to a point where the character is no longer a human.

The remainder of the world content is built by players using a proprietary solids-based construction system consisting of a box, sphere, torus, and other primitives that can be scaled, hollowed, twisted, and distorted to make various shapes. Users also can combine the basic shapes to create far more complicated objects. "We haven't found a shape that can't be built fairly easily," Ondrejka says. Moreover, the primitives are easily compressed, making the data-streaming process faster for the user.

"Just like in real life, some people are good fashion designers and can make fabulous clothing," says Harper. "Someone made a wedding dress with layers and layers of delicate-looking cloth, which gave it an ethereal look." For those players possessing particular skills such as these, there is an in-world economy that allows them to set up shop and sell their wares to other players who may neither want to take the time nor possess the skills to make the clothing themselves. However, for those players who do, they can even upload textures into the game to make their own unique clothing.

Aside from augmenting their avatars, players also use the modeling system to build just about anything — houses, concert venues, bridges, retail outlets, helicopters, bridges, hot tubs, pet shops, cars, and motorcycles — all of which can be scripted through an embedded language similar to C code. "Some of our more prolific scripters never wrote code before," notes Ondrejka. "It looks imposing at first, but the world is full of sample scripts, and you can't break anything. You just tweak the code and see what happens, then continue."

One industrious player even made a spaceship that flies around the 10 world and occasionally hovers above an avatar before emitting a blue tracker beam that traps a character and beams it aboard. "The space avatars are dressed as aliens and use funny probes on the subjects before dropping off the victims in various parts of the world," says Harper. "Then they give the avatar a T-shirt that says 'I was abducted by aliens and all I got was this lousy T-shirt.' Now, the spaceship is legendary, and at one point avatars were standing around hoping to be abducted."

Recently, Linden Labs added support for complex character development and enhanced motion, enabling players to animate their avatars to do just about anything. Using an open .bvh file format supported by software such as Curious Labs' Poser, players can create and upload animation files, endowing the avatars with distinct moods and movement — creating, for instance, guitar-strumming rock stars to world-class swimmers. To date, users have staged realistic boxing matches, re-created action sequences from feature films, and choreographed elaborate dance routines.

To encourage creativity, Linden Labs now grants the ownership of in-world content to the subscribers who make it, revising its terms of service so users retain full intellectual property protection for the digital material they create, including the characters, clothing, scripts, textures, objects, and designs.

Building Fee

When the game launched last year, it contained a general store, a disco, and other attractions. Since then, ambitious residents have added a plethora of content, including an amusement park with more than thirty rides and "themed" towns (such as an Americana village and an anime area). These and other regions can be enhanced with streaming audio clips for ambient theme sounds. In a recent development, residents can now link to Internet audio sources broadcasting live sportscasts, talk shows, and DJ soundtracks directly from real-world clubs to Second Life clubs, for example.

One player even hosted the first known Virtual Book Club event, featuring science-fiction writer Cory Doctorow, that was attended by a number of avatars who lounged on couches and chairs as they discussed the writer's recent novel. "Since the game's introduction, residents have built businesses, designed wild vehicles, and introduced adventure games, all within the digital world," says founder Philip Rosendale.

Users are now free to build as many venues and objects as they 15 want in Second Life, as long as they stay within the object allocation limit for the land they own, whereas before, they were taxed on each object that remained in the world. "This discourages people from overbuilding," says Ondrejka. "Yet it encourages players to experiment and allows them to grow with the system by starting with something small, like a house, until they build up enough in game currency or real money to buy more land and attempt something larger." Recently, users were given the ability to purchase virtual private islands, which allows them to alter the terrain and even determine who can visit the area.

All residents earn weekly grants of in-world currency. In addition, they can earn bonuses, depending on several factors such as their rating on a leader board. So if others rate them positively because of their likability or the look of their avatar or home, then those players earn more in-world dollars — a system that encourages positive behavior. Residents also can earn virtual incomes by setting up shop and selling various wares. One person created a pet store where residents can purchase dogs and even buy "training" (scripted behavior) for them. Another built a nightclub and added a bouncer to take virtual dollars from people wanting to enter.

"Unfortunately, we never know what objects will be in the game at any given time," says Ondrejka. "An amazing building can disappear overnight. As a result, the world is constantly changing."

Indeed, content creation is a large part of the game, but some players forego that option and instead just walk around the virtual space and chat with other inhabitants or attend events, including scripting classes, quiz shows, sporting events, theatrical productions, and more.

"Because it is so different from the typical MMORPG," Harper notes, "some of our players won't even call it a game."

READING

1. The opening line of this piece asks, "If you could reinvent yourself, what choices would you make? Would you be tall or short, heavy or thin, outgoing or shy? Or would you become a different species, such as a dog or a cat? In Second Life . . . players can be anyone, or anything, they ever wanted to be. . . ." How did you find yourself answering these questions? What assumptions are made by the writer with this lead-in?

2. In the third paragraph, the word "incarnate" is used to refer to people creating new selves online. How does the definition of this word underscore the positive spin in the opening lines? What is the connotation of this word?

3. What are the aspects of Second Life which Moltenbrey foregrounds that make it a better MMORPG than others? From the information in this article, what qualities would you expect to discover in those who "play" it?

4. A portion of this piece is addressed to people knowledgeable about this kind of online gaming. Accordingly, some of the language is technical. After reading this description of Second Life — its creation and its workings — determine what parts of the article are most accessible to you as a college reader. What examples stand out to you as significant in illustrating how you could live an online "life"?

5. If you were hired to market Second Life, what quotations from the article would you pull for your approach? What authorities would you cite? What would you need to find out more about before you could proceed?

WRITING

1. Assume that you are going to visit Second Life and create an avatar. Write a reflective essay or journal entry that explores what possibilities you might choose. Male or female? (Note that in the article, that is the first choice you must make.) Human or not? Big or small? What qualities would you seek? Which would you avoid?

2. Linden Labs is mentioned several times in the article as the corporation responsible for the creation and maintenance of Second Life. Research Linden Labs and find out how they present themselves to the technological community in their media kit. Try to discover what other types of projects they run. See if you can discover the amount

of profit associated with Second Life. Write an essay reporting your findings.

3. In describing Second Life, Moltenbrey reports on aspects of virtual life that are present in actual life, such as attending book groups, making clothing, having pets, constructing buildings, earning money, and paying taxes. Visit Second Life online and report back to your class if you discover opportunities present in Second Life that are not present in actual life. Consider why much of online life is mapped similarly to actual life and how this might blur the line between the two.

4. After reading Moltenbrey's article, you might assume that these type of "games" are harmless, indeed are creative and enriching. However, even in less involved types of online social networking, such as MySpace, violence and other negative behaviors are reported. Research evidence of the not-so-positive side of simulated lives and online social networks, such as "Murder on MySpace" by Noah Shachtman (*Wired*, December 2006) and write an argument that foregrounds the negative possibilities, just as Moltenbrey has foregrounded the positive ones.

The Perils and Promise of Online Schmoozing

By Jane Black

FROM: *BusinessWeek*, February 20, 2004, www.businessweek.com

CONTEXT: This selection comes from the online companion site for *BusinessWeek*. The audience for the website is very technology literate. Almost 70 percent are online both at work and home, and over 75 percent are online each day. *BusinessWeek*'s target market is business decision makers and leaders and affluent consumers. The average reader has a household income of over $200,000. This story was written by Jane Black, who has covered topics for the magazine ranging from the wine region of Argentina to the Patriot Act, though the majority of her writing has concentrated on technology issues. As you read this piece, think about Black's informal tone and style and how this might relate to the context of the article and the intended audience.

THEY SAY EVERYONE IS CONNECTED TO EVERYONE ELSE IN the world by no more than six degrees of separation. Now a new set of dot-coms such as Friendster, Ryze, and Tribe.net are putting that notion to the test, allowing individuals to create an electronic Web of friends, families, and business contacts, who in turn, are connected to their other friends, families, and business contacts. The idea: By linking each of us into a broad but still relevant network, I can find whatever I'm looking for — a date, a new job, or a used TV.

The concept has certainly caught on. Social-networking sites have attracted more than $40 million in venture-capital money since last fall. In January, Web behemoth Google entered the fray with its own social-networking site, Orkut. But this is no dot-com bubble, with VCs and companies seeing promise where real people don't. Through my twelve friends on Friendster, I'm currently connected to a "personal network" of 130,834 people.

Social networks offer a way to create far more sophisticated and nuanced human interactions than those provided by a personal Web page or its more interactive cousin, the blog (see BW Online, 6/10/03, "The Wild World of 'Open Source' Media"). But they also raise plenty of privacy issues about how to protect these valuable connections from prying eyes or exploitation by crafty marketers and unethical associates.

Goldilocks's Dilemma

For example, as a journalist, I talk to a lot of high-placed executives. Will someone be able to use my name to contact a CEO when applying for a job just because he's a friend of a friend of a friend? If I connect to my book club through Google's Orkut, will it sell all of our names to Amazon.com (AMZN)?

Indeed, social-networking sites find themselves in a Goldilocks- 5 style dilemma: If they share too much information, the services become a spammers' paradise. Share too little, and they defeat the power of social networking, where you can discover and communicate with people you may not know but with whom you share something in common. The amount of information shared has to be just right.

Each startup has its own plan for how to deal with privacy concerns. Plaxo, a company that enables users to automatically update their Microsoft Outlook (MSFT) address books, aims to protect customers' information through one of the most stringent privacy policies I've seen: Contact information belongs to the individual. And if the company should ever be sold, its privacy policy — a contract with its paying customers — still stands.

Safe at Home?

At Tribe.net, a site that aims to revolutionize the classified-ads business by linking people with similar interests, users can only see detailed information on those within three degrees of separation. A yachting aficionado from half-way round the world may know that you also share his passion, but he will be unable to contact you or any of your friends at a personal e-mail address. His message is forwarded to a designated account within the Tribe.net system.

WiredReach, a Dallas startup, is trying a different approach. Its system uses peer-to-peer technology to keep users' data safe — right on their own hard drive. Founder and CEO Ash Maurya says the danger in social networking is uploading such personal information to a centralized server that's "just one hack away" from being exposed. Peer-to-peer technology has no central server. Two users who know each other can search each other's hard drives for, say, a recruiter at IBM or a senior writer at BusinessWeek. If they find a match, they request an introduction. Says Maurya: "We're trying to simulate real-world networking without losing any confidentiality."

Social-networking companies aren't just paying lip service to privacy. They know that striking a balance is the difference between success and failure. Witness Google's recent turnaround on Orkut's privacy policy. When the service launched on January 22, the policy warned visitors that "by submitting, posting or displaying any materials on or through the orkut.com service, you automatically grant to us a worldwide, non-exclusive, sublicenseable, transferable, royalty-free, perpetual, irrevocable right to copy, distribute, create derivative works of, publicly perform and display such Materials."

"An Intelligent Order"

Ouch! Privacy hawks sounded the alarm. Some even warned that the notice was eerily similar to that of Microsoft's computing platform. Was Google the new evil empire, they wondered? Within a week, Orkut's policy had been rewritten. It now states that Orkut "may share both personally identifiable information about you and aggregate usage information that we collect with Google Inc. . . . We will never rent, sell, or share your personal information with any third party for marketing purposes without your express permission."

Indeed, many social-networking firms are not only concerned about privacy but fired up to solve today's digital dilemmas. Tribe.net CEO Mark Pincus argues that social networking isn't the problem but the solution to privacy issues that have, until now, plagued the Internet age: "Social networking has the potential to create an intelligent order in the current chaos by letting you manage how public you make yourself and why and who can contact you."

Let's hope so. In the meantime, social-networking sites will continue to search for the most efficient way to make people more visible and more connected to people they know without exposing them to unwanted solicitations and information. The balance between sharing and protecting personal data will be key to their success. In the marketplace for social networking — at least for now — privacy rules.

READING

1. Black opens her piece with a short description of social networking sites. Look at this paragraph and those that follow. What might you discern about her audience from the brevity and directness of the paragraphs?

2. Black writes that through her twelve friends on Friendster, she has developed a "'personal network'" of over 130,000 people. What is the tone of this statement? Why is "personal network" in quotes?

3. What is "Goldilocks's Dilemma"? Why would such a dilemma be particularly troublesome for someone in business? What is the value of personal contacts in this context?

4. Black goes into privacy concerns in detail in the short piece, including a discussion of a change in privacy policy at Orkut. What changes were made in the company's policy? Why did they occur?

5. If you were a senior business executive who had never heard of Friendster before reading this article, what would you now understand? Would you be concerned or interested?

WRITING

1. Black opens her piece with a reference to an idea that has now become a social commonplace: that all of us are divided by just "six degrees of separation." Write a reflective essay or journal entry about this notion. How does social networking impact these six degrees? Are we really separated at all anymore?

2. This piece is specifically written for a business audience. Write an essay that identifies the elements within the article that help define its audience. Look at the examples, the tone, the format, and so on.

3. Black says of the "Goldilocks's Dilemma," that the "amount of information shared has to be just right." You likely have a social networking site, whether on Friendster or MySpace or another vendor; or you may have thought about putting one up. Write an essay that describes the process you go through (or would go through) in deciding the amount of information that is just right to share. If you have a site, consider a time when you might have shared too much or too little and what you learned from these situations.

4. Concerns have arisen about the use of MySpace and similar social-networking sites by business recruiters, who have used personal information disclosed on the sites to disqualify applicants. Some

colleges have even gone so far as to ban students or specific student groups (for example, athletes) from maintaining such pages. Research whether these concerns are valid based upon actual industry practice. Write an essay summarizing your findings. Based upon what you have learned, would you recommend that students limit the information they share through social-networking sites?

5. Black writes, "Social networks offer a way to create far more sophisticated and nuanced human interaction that those provided by a personal Web page or its more interactive cousin, the blog." In discussing the communities developed online, Adam N. Joinson and Beth Dietz-Uhler in the Reading Deeply section of this chapter (p. 272) argue that the Internet allows people "to elaborate and practice their hoped for possible selves or even to express a true self normally suppressed." Select the MySpace page of someone you do not know – even tangentially through your own personal network. Write an essay that describes who this individual presents him or herself to be, but follow the practice of Joinson and Dietz-Uhler in citing the primary text (in this case the page itself) in support of each of your assertions. At the end of your description, evaluate Black's opening statement. Based on your case study reading of this one page, is her claim valid?

The Business of Life: Making a Virtual Living Telecommuting to a Brave New World

By Peter Svensson

FROM: ABCNews.com, November 8, 2005, abcnews.go.com

CONTEXT: This piece comes from the online companion site for ABC News. The website divides the news into eleven categories, such as the United States, investigative, sports, and so on. The story that follows was covered in the business section of the site. Like many online news sites, ABC's site compiles information from its own and freelance or stringer reports. Peter Svensson, the author of this piece, is a technology writer for the Associated Press (AP). AP refers to itself as the "essential global news network." Svensson has written about a broad range of technology topics, from Internet-based phone services to online gaming to hacking Al Jazeera's website. As you read think about why this article would appear in the business section rather than in the technology one.

KASI NAFUS'S CLOTHING STORE SITS IN BUCOLIC SURROUNDings. There's a maple tree in fall colors outside, right across a brook. A little further away, a zebra munches on a bush.

If the customers arrive by foot, they have to wade through the brook. They don't really mind, though. The water is not, in fact, real. Nor is Nafus's clothing store. They only exist as three-dimensional representations in a virtual world called Second Life.

The clothes Nafus sells aren't physical either — they merely cover the virtual bodies people make for themselves in Second Life. But that doesn't mean the store, called Pixel Dolls, is not a real business. This is Nafus's full-time job.

"It's not something I'll get fabulously wealthy from, but it's a living wage," said the twenty-seven-year-old Seattle resident. She didn't specify her income.

An estimated 20 million people around the world are spending 5 time in so-called massively multiplayer online role-playing games, or MMORPGs. These online spaces are adding not only users but are also growing economies that interact with the real world.

Second Life, for instance, has its own currency that is convertible to U.S. dollars at a fluctuating exchange rate. Users can buy the virtual currency using their credit cards or sell it and get real dollars via checks or PayPal transfers.

Its 60,000 users trade $2 million a month, making its economy about the same size as that of the South Pacific island of Tuvalu. That's small, but large enough that it supports about 100 virtual jobs, according to Philip Rosedale, chief executive of Linden Research Inc., which created Second Life. Some design virtual buildings, others design schemes of movement that make virtual bodies dance or perform other complex actions. There's even a virtual journalist, though he's employed by Linden Research.

Edward Castronova, an economist at Indiana University, estimates that real-money trading surrounding virtual worlds is at least $100 million this year, and probably many times that.

Castronova also surveyed players of the online game Everquest four years ago, and found that 39 percent would like to quit their jobs or schools and make a living in the virtual world. Multiply that by 20 million gamers, and virtual jobs start looking like one of the more popular professions out there.

Nafus says part of the reason she started making a business of 10 Second Life was that she was practically spending a full work week on the game anyway. Designing the clothes is time-consuming: She spends a lot of time creating the "fabric" for the clothes in an image-editing program before uploading it to Second Life, where she shapes it into three-dimensional forms.

She sells her regular inventory (for instance, "Linen Tie Suit, Black") for about a dollar each and limited editions for around $5.

Selling digital clothes is quite different from selling real clothes. For instance, Nafus doesn't actually have to make each item, just design it. Also, the store runs itself — customers just click on images of the clothes and have copies of them transferred to their accounts.

Even so, some aspects of a virtual business are similar to the real world. Once, the Second Life computers didn't actually transfer goods to the buyers for three days. To Nafus, it was as if the post office had lost all her shipments.

Most virtual jobs are, however, quite different from Nafus's. Second Life is an unusual virtual world in that the residents have great freedom to shape the world and create objects in it, which creates an opening for skilled professionals.

The most popular virtual worlds, however, are centered on fight- 15 ing, and there's limited scope for creativity. There are plenty of jobs there, but some of these moved overseas pretty much as soon as they were created, in what is perhaps the fastest example ever of a new job category being outsourced internationally.

"I kill monsters and things to get their items," said Ilin Aurel, in the small town of Caracal, Romania. "It's very fun, we love it."

The nineteen-year-old, interviewed by phone, makes $200 a month, a good wage for Romania. He is employed by Gamersloot.net, which is based in Sunnyvale, California, to play online games like World of Warcraft and Guild Wars.

The Romanian office is staffed around the clock in three shifts with gamers (known as "gold farmers") who collect gold and other virtual riches, which are then sold on the Gamersloot Web site to people who don't mind spending real money to enrich their in-game characters.

"I think there's a future in this job," said Aurel.

The presence of gold farmers in a game is not necessarily popular among people who are playing for fun, and game publishers try to 20 limit it, with little success.

"It's almost impossible to design a game . . . that does not generate real-money trade, a secondary market," said Julian Dibbell, a freelance journalist who supported himself trading virtual gold, weapons and "real" estate for a year and has written a book about the phenomenon, to be published next year.

"I want to say that I don't think it could ever become a dominant sector of the economy. But look at the real economy itself . . . the huge, overwhelming proportion of economic transfers that take place in the world today are pure information transfers," Dibbell said.

READING

1. The first paragraph gives a few clues that the world being described is not real. What are they?

2. The article discusses a world called "Second Life." What is Second Life? What is an MMORPG? How does Second Life fit the definition of an MMORPG?

3. Although discussing a virtual world, Svensson consults some real-world sources. Who are they? What authority do they bring to the article?

4. Svensson identifies several individuals who are making money by playing MMORPGs. How are they earning a salary? How does money in the real world differ from money exchanged in Second Life?

5. One of the sources that Svensson cites discusses the need that each online game has for a "secondary market." What does this term mean in the context of the article?

WRITING

1. Svensson cites a study of online gamers that suggests a surprising number would like to quit their jobs and make a living through some virtual enterprise. Write a reflective essay or journal entry about a career you would like to have in the virtual universe. How does this career differ (if at all) from what you would do in the real world?

2. Kasi Nafus tells Svensson that she began selling clothes in her Second Life store because she was spending almost her whole work week on the site anyway. Her statement suggests that online gaming can become quite involving. Have you ever been involved in an online game? Do you have friends who game? Write an essay about your own experience or about your observations of your friends' experiences.

3. Svensson observes, "the most popular virtual worlds, however, are centered on fighting, and there's limited scope for creativity." Research this claim. Is it valid? Determine what the most popular virtual worlds are and classify them. Do they share characteristics? Write an essay that defines the characteristics of the most popular virtual worlds and discusses how each of the worlds adds slight variations to attract gamers.

4. According to Svensson, many of the secondary market jobs associated with online gaming have been outsourced internationally, even

if the company is based in the United States. Write a researched essay that might be a follow-up to Svensson's piece on the ABC News business site. It should examine the business aspects of the outsourcing of online gaming jobs. What type of work does someone like Ilin Aurel do? Why would such a job be outsourced? Be certain to maintain a neutral tone and focus on a business angle.

5. Writing about The Sims, Clive Thompson, in "The Sims: Suburban Rhapsody" (p. 226), says that the game "allows you to play out your fantasies, relive your life, or rejigger your identity," which accounts for a large portion of its popularity. Svensson reports that Second Life has attracted 60,000 users who live a "second life" online. Working with several other students, prepare a promotional presentation to attract a new citizen to the Second Life community. Target a specific market (for example, young professional, family, retiree). Consider how real-world communities attract new members by looking at the chamber of commerce or welcome site of your own communities. Your presentation should include images and data that would appeal to your target market.

COMMUNICATIONS of the ACM

October 2005 Volume 48, Number 10

THE DIGITAL SOCIETY

IT SKILLS IN
A TOUGH
JOB MARKET

DID MGM
REALLY WIN THE
GROKSTER CASE?

ACADEMIC
DISHONESTY
AND THE
INTERNET

SUMMARIZING ONLINE NEWS
UNDERSTANDING DATA QUALITY IN E-BUSINESS
A PROCESS PERSPECTIVE OF
PERSONALIZATION TECHNOLOGIES
WIRELESS WEB ADOPTION PATTERNS
IN THE U.S.

Community: From Neighborhood to Network

By Barry Wellman

FROM: *Communications of the ACM,*
October 2005

CONTEXT: This journal article comes from *Communications of the ACM* (Association for Computing Machinery), which has been publishing since 1957. The ACM comprises 80,000 computing professionals and students. Although its title sounds extremely hardware-oriented, the journal publishes pieces on a wide variety of subjects concerning the art and science of information technology. The ACM has a central goal of community, "the fundamental role that computing plays in shaping all scientific pursuits as well as our future." Barry Wellman is a professor of sociology at the University of Toronto and the director of NetLab. NetLab is a "scholarly network studying computer networks, communication networks, and social networks" based at the University of Toronto. Wellman is also the chair emeritus of both the Community and Information Technologies section and the Community and Urban Sociology section of the American Sociological Association. He is a member of the Ford Foundation's Program on Information Technology and has been a Fellow of IBM's Institute of Knowledge Management. As you read this piece, think about how his subheadings orient the reader to his argument.

COMMUNITIES ARE NETWORKS OF INTERPERSONAL TIES that provide sociability, support, information, a sense of belonging, and social identity. Well into the twentieth century, communities were equated with neighborhoods — bounded groups of people living near each other. This neighborhood-centered view of community made only partial sense because people have always had long-distance community ties either by traveling themselves or through connections with soldiers, artisans, peddlers, traders, marriage partners, shepherds, and the rich.

The neighborhood-centered definition of community still makes partial sense, even in these days of global Internet connectivity. Many communications — including online communications — are local, with concerns ranging from bringing home groceries to gossiping about current events to getting the job done right.

Yet, the proliferation of computer-supported social networks has afforded changes in the ways that people use community: "Community" is becoming defined socially and not spatially. By the 1970s (or earlier), neighborhoods rarely bounded communities in the developed world. Most community ties are with people who do not live within the same neighborhood. Many do not even live in the same metropolitan area. Interactions have moved inside private homes — where most entertaining, telephoning, and emailing takes place — and away from chatting in public spaces such as bars, street corners, and coffee shops. Physical places remain important, but auto, plane, Internet, and phone-based connectivity means there is less awareness of intervening spaces between homes.

From Door-to-Door to Place-to-Place

Once people stop seeing the same villagers every day, their communities are not groups but social networks. Most members of a person's community are not directly connected with each other, but are sparsely knit, specialized in role, varying in connectivity, and unbounded (like the Internet). Like the Internet, they are best characterized as a "network of networks" — a term I coined in 1973. 5

Operating as social networks has transformed community. Most community ties are now specialized, with different network members supplying emotional support, information, material aid, social identity, and a sense of belonging. Only a few ties are with neighbors, the rest are with friends, relatives, and work colleagues.

People move in multiple, partial social circles, with limited involvement in each. The ease of computer-mediated communication (CMC) with a large number of people facilitates ties that cut across group boundaries. Social circles tend to be sparsely knit (most participants are not directly linked), with limited control over participants' behavior and limited commitment to their well-being. Instead of isolated and tightly bounded groups, social circles are partial, permeable, and transitory, linked by cross-cutting ties. Maneuvering through networks provides opportunity, contingency, and uncertainty, with ties between different social circles being resources in themselves.

The Computerization of Community

CMC reinforces stay-at-home, place-to-place connectivity. "Glocalization" occurs: extensive global and local interaction. CMC makes it easy to contact many neighbors; and fixed, wired Internet connections root people at their home and office desks. CMC fights against face-to-face contact less than it complements it. CMC is the media by which people arrange things and fill in the gaps between meetings. For example, the broadband-using residents of a Toronto suburb neighbor more actively than their fellow unwired residents.

Are online relationships as good as face-to-face relationships where people can see, hear, and touch someone? Probably not, but the question may have a utopian assumption that if people were not online they would be engaged in stimulating community activities. Yet, CMC basically displaces TV watching. Indeed, most people communicate with their friends, relatives, neighbors and work colleagues by any means available, online and offline. The stronger the tie, the more media used. Online relationships are filling empty spots in people's lives now that they no longer wander to the local pub or café to take up with their neighbors.

What of fears that the move into CMC would kill community? Dystopians warned in the mid-1990s that anything other than face-to-face contact is substandard. The evidence does not support this warning. As the digital divide narrows in the developed world and people become more experienced and comfortable, CMC is no longer special and potentially alienating. CMC has increased the frequency and intensity of overall contact. Rather than replacing face-to-face contact, CMC adds to it, filling gaps between the fuller range of information and emotion in interpersonal encounters.

Yet, CMC is more than an inadequate simulacrum for face-to-face 10 communication. There already are unique online dynamics in community-building: the tendency for contact to be between two persons rather than within groups, folding-in of two disconnected friends into the same conversation, sending personal messages to participants in online discussion groups, typographical conventions of embedding interleaved responses inside original messages, using emoticons such as ";-)", and typing responses at the top of a series of messages rather than at the bottom.

From Place-to-Place to Person-to-Person Community

CMC is fostering changes in the unit of connectivity for community — from the place-to-place community of twentieth-century homes and offices to the person-to-person community of networked individuals. Internet accounts and mobile phone numbers are person-based and not place-based. The nature of community is changing: from being a social network of households to a social network of individuals.

Communities that interact extensively online often consist of like-minded people. Although this has the potential for engendering tunnel vision, in practice, the Internet has fostered diversity because of the multiplicity and overlap of most people's interests coupled with the ease of making new connections online. Friends forwarding messages to third parties provide indirect contact between unconnected people who can then make direct contact. In networked communities, weaker ties — online and offline — provide new information through their connections with other social circles. Thus, CMC extends the social range of networks: allowing people to maintain more ties and fostering more specialized relationships.

Mobile technologies reinforce person-to-person community because they foster contact without sociophysical context. Mobile phones, Net-connected PDAs, wireless computers, and personalized software foster liberation from place. Their use shifts community ties from linking people-in-places to linking people wherever they are. Wireless portability affords greater ease — and overload — of being available $24 \times 7 \times 52$. The person has become the portal, with each person operating a unique personal community network.

The result is a dynamic contradiction. In the short term, households remain important as the physical bases of computer-supported social networks. That is where most non-work computers are. Yet, the shift to person-to-person community is contributing to the de-emphasis of domestic and local relations. And the still-growing use of the Internet and lowering telephone costs affords greater involvement in far-flung communities of shared interest. Many people use multiple media to connect — face-to-face, telephone, and computer mediated — whatever medium is most convenient and appropriate at the time. It is a situation of networked individualism where individual autonomy and agency are heightened. In such a world, social networking literacy is as vital as computer networking literacy for creating, sustaining, and using relationships, including friends of friends.

READING

1. Wellman opens his piece with a review of the definition of the traditional neighborhood-centered community. How does this definition set the reader up for his new definition of community?

2. Although his essay opens informally, specialized terms like "glocalization" and "CMC" are used. Judging from his vocabulary, how would you describe the audience Wellman is addressing?

3. Wellman argues that, contrary to fears that CMC would lead to substandard human contact, it has actually improved it. How does he support this claim?

4. Wellman suggests that we are living in a time of "networked individualism." How does the role of community operate in this person-to-person dynamic he suggests?

5. Wellman asserts that fewer and fewer ties are with actual neighbors due to the proliferation of online social communities. Do you find this to be true in your own neighborhood? How would you describe your sense of community?

WRITING

1. Take the time to log how you connect with people throughout the day. How much of your contact is made through computers, cell phones, and so on? How much is based on place-to-place? How much is person-to-person? Write a reflective essay or journal entry that describes how you interact in your own community.

2. Look at your campus as a community and as a neighborhood. Wellman says, "Once people stop seeing the same villagers every day, their communities are not groups, but social networks." How do you view the classroom and the campus in terms of his description? To what extent is your educational community an online social network? To what extent is it a traditional door-to-door community? Write an essay describing how students form communities on your campus.

3. Wellman is the author of many articles concerning community and computer networks. Visit his site at NetLab www.chass.utoronto.ca/~wellman/main.html. Analyze it as an online social network. What sense do you get of the scholarly community he is creating at the University of Toronto? Write an essay reviewing the strengths and weaknesses of his site. You might discuss elements such as ease of

navigation, look and feel, graphics, availability of desired information, sense of community, and so on.

4. Wellman suggests that CMC does not act as a substitute for face-to-
   face relationships. Instead, "CMC basically displaces TV watching."
   Research this claim. Is it valid? Survey your classmates for data concerning how much time they spend watching TV and are engaged in
   CMC each day. Do they make a distinction between the two? Write a
   one-page summary classifying time spent interacting via technology
   (for example, computer, cell phone, telephone, BlackBerry) and
   watching TV. What conclusions can you draw, based on your findings? Do your findings support Wellman's claim? Where would you
   place iPods in these categories?

5. Wellman's essay focuses on how we form communities. Sherry
   Turkle, in "How Computers Change the Way We Think" (p. 256), focuses on how we think. She makes the point that when she "first
   began studying the computer culture, a small breed of highly trained
   technologists thought of themselves as 'computer people.' That is
   no longer the case. If we take the computer as . . . a way of seeing
   the world and our place in it, we are all computer people now." Write
   an essay comparing and contrasting the attitudes each of these
   writers has toward our burgeoning use of technology.

How Computers Change the Way We Think

By Sherry Turkle

FROM: *The Chronicle of Higher Education*,
January 30, 2004

CONTEXT: This piece appeared in the Information Technology section of *The Chronicle of Higher Education*, an academic news source and job marketplace publication aimed at people with advanced degrees in colleges and universities. "Website traffic is routinely more than 10 million pages a month, seen by more than 800,000 unique visitors." Sherry Turkle is the Abby Rockefeller Mauzé Professor of the Social Studies of Science and Technology at the Massachusetts Institute of Technology. She is the founder of the MIT Initiative on Technology and Self Program. Among her books are *The Second Self: Computers and the Human Spirit* (2005) and *Life on the Screen: Identity in the Age of the Internet* (1995). She is currently working on a book on robotics and the human spirit and editing the first volume of a three-volume collection titled *Evocative Objects: Things We Think With*. She is a media commentator for CNN, ABC, NPR, and NBC. As you read this article, consider how her conversational tone and jargon-free language appeal to a wide academic audience.

THE TOOLS WE USE TO THINK CHANGE THE WAYS IN WHICH we think. The invention of written language brought about a radical shift in how we process, organize, store, and transmit representations of the world. Although writing remains our primary information technology, today when we think about the impact of technology on our habits of mind, we think primarily of the computer.

My first encounters with how computers change the way we think came soon after I joined the faculty at the Massachusetts Institute of Technology in the late 1970s, at the end of the era of the slide rule and the beginning of the era of the personal computer. At a lunch for new faculty members, several senior professors in engineering complained that the transition from slide rules to calculators had affected their students' ability to deal with issues of scale. When students used slide rules, they had to insert decimal points themselves. The professors insisted that that required students to maintain a mental sense of scale, whereas those who relied on calculators made frequent errors in orders of magnitude. Additionally, the students with calculators had lost their ability to do "back of the envelope" calculations, and with that, an intuitive feel for the material.

That same semester, I taught a course in the history of psychology. There, I experienced the impact of computational objects on students' ideas about their emotional lives. My class had read Freud's essay on slips of the tongue, with its famous first example: The chairman of a parliamentary session opens a meeting by declaring it closed. The students discussed how Freud interpreted such errors as revealing a person's mixed emotions. A computer-science major disagreed with Freud's approach. The mind, she argued, is a computer. And in a computational dictionary — like we have in the human mind — "closed" and "open" are designated by the same symbol, separated by a sign for opposition. "Closed" equals "minus open." To substitute "closed" for "open" does not require the notion of ambivalence or conflict.

"When the chairman made that substitution," she declared, "a bit was dropped; a minus sign was lost. There was a power surge. No problem."

The young woman turned a Freudian slip into an information- 5 processing error. An explanation in terms of meaning had become an explanation in terms of mechanism.

Such encounters turned me to the study of both the instrumental and the subjective sides of the nascent computer culture. As an ethnographer and psychologist, I began to study not only what the computer was doing *for* us, but what it was doing *to* us, including how it was changing the way we see ourselves, our sense of human identity.

In the 1980s, I surveyed the psychological effects of computational objects in everyday life — largely the unintended side effects of people's tendency to project thoughts and feelings onto their machines. In the twenty years since, computational objects have become more explicitly designed to have emotional and cognitive effects. And those "effects by design" will become even stronger in the decade to come. Machines are being designed to serve explicitly as companions, pets, and tutors. And they are introduced in school settings for the youngest children.

Today, starting in elementary school, students use e-mail, word processing, computer simulations, virtual communities, and Power-Point software. In the process, they are absorbing more than the content of what appears on their screens. They are learning new ways to think about what it means to know and understand.

What follows is a short and certainly not comprehensive list of areas where I see information technology encouraging changes in thinking. There can be no simple way of cataloging whether any particular change is good or bad. That is contested terrain. At every step we have to ask, as educators and citizens, whether current technology is leading us in directions that serve our human purposes. Such questions are not technical; they are social, moral, and political. For me, addressing that subjective side of computation is one of the more significant challenges for the next decade of information technology in higher education. Technology does not determine change, but it encourages us to take certain directions. If we make those directions clear, we can more easily exert human choice.

Thinking about Privacy

Today's college students are habituated to a world of online blogging, 10 instant messaging, and Web browsing that leaves electronic traces. Yet they have had little experience with the right to privacy. Unlike past generations of Americans, who grew up with the notion that the privacy of their mail was sacrosanct, our children are accustomed to electronic surveillance as part of their daily lives.

I have colleagues who feel that the increased incursions on privacy have put the topic more in the news, and that this is a positive change. But middle-school and high-school students tend to be willing to provide personal information online with no safeguards, and college students seem uninterested in violations of privacy and in increased governmental and commercial surveillance. Professors find that students do not understand that in a democracy, privacy is a right, not merely a privilege. In ten years, ideas about the relationship of privacy and government will require even more active pedagogy. (One might also hope that increased education about the kinds of silent surveillance that technology makes possible may inspire more active political engagement with the issue.)

Avatars or a Self?

Chat rooms, role-playing games, and other technological venues offer us many different contexts for presenting ourselves online. Those possibilities are particularly important for adolescents because they offer what Erik Erikson described as a moratorium, a time-out or safe space for the personal experimentation that is so crucial for adolescent development. Our dangerous world — with crime, terrorism, drugs, and AIDS — offers little in the way of safe spaces. Online worlds can provide valuable spaces for identity play.

But some people who gain fluency in expressing multiple aspects of self may find it harder to develop authentic selves. Some children who write narratives for their screen avatars may grow up with too little experience of how to share their real feelings with other people.

For those who are lonely yet afraid of intimacy, information technology has made it possible to have the illusion of companionship without the demands of friendship.

From Powerful Ideas to PowerPoint

In the 1970s and early 1980s, some educators wanted to make programming part of the regular curriculum for K–12 education. They argued that because information technology carries ideas, it might as well carry the most powerful ideas that computer science has to offer. It is ironic that in most elementary schools today, the ideas being carried by information technology are not ideas from computer science like procedural thinking, but more likely to be those embedded in productivity tools like PowerPoint presentation software.

PowerPoint does more than provide a way of transmitting content. It carries its own way of thinking, its own aesthetic — which not surprisingly shows up in the aesthetic of college freshmen. In that aesthetic, presentation becomes its own powerful idea. 15

To be sure, the software cannot be blamed for lower intellectual standards. Misuse of the former is as much a symptom as a cause of the latter. Indeed, the culture in which our children are raised is increasingly a culture of presentation, a corporate culture in which appearance is often more important than reality. In contemporary political discourse, the bar has also been lowered. Use of rhetorical devices at the expense of cogent argument regularly goes without notice. But it is precisely because standards of intellectual rigor outside the educational sphere have fallen that educators must attend to how we use, and when we introduce, software that has been designed to simplify the organization and processing of information.

In *The Cognitive Style of PowerPoint* (Graphics Press, 2003), Edward R. Tufte suggests that PowerPoint equates bulleting with clear thinking. It does not teach students to begin a discussion or construct a narrative. It encourages presentation, not conversation. Of course, in the hands of a master teacher, a PowerPoint presentation with few words and powerful images can serve as the jumping-off point for a brilliant lecture. But in the hands of elementary-school students, often introduced to PowerPoint in the third grade, and often infatuated with its swooshing sounds, animated icons, and flashing text, a slide show is more likely to close down debate than open it up.

Developed to serve the needs of the corporate boardroom, the software is designed to convey absolute authority. Teachers used to tell students that clear exposition depended on clear outlining, but presentation software has fetishized the outline at the expense of the content.

Narrative, the exposition of content, takes time. PowerPoint, like so much in the computer culture, speeds up the pace.

Word Processing vs. Thinking

The catalog for the Vermont Country Store advertises a manual type-writer, which the advertising copy says "moves at a pace that allows time to compose your thoughts." As many of us know, it is possible to manipulate text on a computer screen and see how it looks faster than we can think about what the words mean. 20

Word processing has its own complex psychology. From a pedagogical point of view, it can make dedicated students into better writers because it allows them to revise text, rearrange paragraphs, and experiment with the tone and shape of an essay. Few professional writers would part with their computers; some claim that they simply cannot think without their hands on the keyboard. Yet the ability to quickly fill the page, to see it before you can think it, can make bad writers even worse.

A seventh grader once told me that the typewriter she found in her mother's attic is "cool because you have to type each letter by itself. You have to know what you are doing in advance or it comes out a mess." The idea of thinking ahead has become exotic.

Taking Things at Interface Value

We expect software to be easy to use, and we assume that we don't have to know how a computer works. In the early 1980s, most computer users who spoke of transparency meant that, as with any other machine, you could "open the hood" and poke around. But only a few years later, Macintosh users began to use the term when they talked about seeing their documents and programs represented by attractive and easy-to-interpret icons. They were referring to an ability to make things work without needing to go below the screen surface. Paradoxically, it was the screen's opacity that permitted that kind of transparency. Today, when people say that something is transparent, they mean that they can see how to make it work, not that they know how it works. In other words, transparency means epistemic opacity.

The people who built or bought the first generation of personal computers understood them down to the bits and bytes. The next generation of operating systems were more complex, but they still invited that old-time reductive understanding. Contemporary information technology encourages different habits of mind. Today's college students are already used to taking things at (inter) face value; their successors in 2014 will be even less accustomed to probing below the surface.

Simulation and Its Discontents

Some thinkers argue that the new opacity is empowering, enabling 25 anyone to use the most sophisticated technological tools and to experiment with simulation in complex and creative ways. But it is also true that our tools carry the message that they are beyond our understanding. It is possible that in daily life, epistemic opacity can lead to passivity.

I first became aware of that possibility in the early 1990s, when the first generation of complex simulation games were introduced and immediately became popular for home as well as school use. Sim-Life teaches the principles of evolution by getting children involved in the development of complex ecosystems; in that sense it is an extraordinary learning tool. During one session in which I played Sim-Life with Tim, a thirteen-year-old, the screen before us flashed a message: "Your orgot is being eaten up." "What's an orgot?" I asked. Tim didn't know. "I just ignore that," he said confidently. "You don't need to know that kind of stuff to play."

For me, that story serves as a cautionary tale. Computer simulations enable their users to think about complex phenomena as dynamic, evolving systems. But they also accustom us to manipulating systems whose core assumptions we may not understand and that may not be true.

We live in a culture of simulation. Our games, our economic and political systems, and the ways architects design buildings, chemists envisage molecules, and surgeons perform operations all use simulation technology. In ten years the degree to which simulations are embedded in every area of life will have increased exponentially. We need to develop a new form of media literacy: readership skills for the culture of simulation.

We come to written text with habits of readership based on centuries of civilization. At the very least, we have learned to begin with the journalist's traditional questions: who, what, when, where, why, and how. Who wrote these words, what is their message, why were they written, and how are they situated in time and place, politically and socially? A central project for higher education during the next ten years should be creating programs in information-technology literacy, with the goal of teaching students to interrogate simulations in much the same spirit, challenging their built-in assumptions.

Despite the ever-increasing complexity of software, most computer environments put users in worlds based on constrained choices. In other words, immersion in programmed worlds puts us in reassuring environments where the rules are clear. For example, when you play a video game, you often go through a series of frightening situations that you escape by mastering the rules — you experience life as a reassuring dichotomy of scary and safe. Children grow up in a culture of video games, action films, fantasy epics, and computer programs that all rely on that familiar scenario of almost losing but then regaining total mastery: There is danger. It is mastered. A still-more-powerful monster appears. It is subdued. Scary. Safe.

Yet in the real world, we have never had a greater need to work 30 our way out of binary assumptions. In the decade ahead, we need to rebuild the culture around information technology. In that new sociotechnical culture, assumptions about the nature of mastery would be less absolute. The new culture would make it easier, not more difficult, to consider life in shades of gray, to see moral dilemmas in terms other than a battle between Good and Evil. For never has our world been more complex, hybridized, and global. Never have we so needed to have many contradictory thoughts and feelings at the same time. Our tools must help us accomplish that, not fight against us.

Information technology is identity technology. Embedding it in a culture that supports democracy, freedom of expression, tolerance, diversity, and complexity of opinion is one of the next decade's greatest challenges. We cannot afford to fail.

When I first began studying the computer culture, a small breed of highly trained technologists thought of themselves as "computer people." That is no longer the case. If we take the computer as a carrier of a way of knowing, a way of seeing the world and our place in it, we are all computer people now.

READING

1. What do you infer about the tone of Turkle's piece from the first sentence? Does she maintain this tone throughout? Does it change at any point?

2. Turkle uses first person throughout her essay. Does this help you to identify with her subject? How does this impact the formality of her piece?

3. Turkle identifies six areas of concern she has of "information technology encouraging changes in thinking." In your view, which is the most pressing? Why?

4. Near the end of her introduction she mentions "'effects by design'" — how "computational objects have become more explicitly designed to have emotional and cognitive effects." What kinds of design features are important to you in terms of your "computational objects," emotionally and cognitively?

5. She says near the end of her essay, "We cannot afford to fail." What failure is she concerned about?

WRITING

1. Write a reflective essay or a journal entry describing the first time you remember using a computer. Tell the story of where you were, how old you were, who was there, how you felt, what the purpose for using the computer was.

2. Turkle's voice is authoritative, although she cites few authorities. One study she does cite is concerning use of PowerPoint software. Look up the study by Edward R. Tufte and read it in its entirety. Write an essay explaining how his piece supports the claims that Turkle is making about presentation software.

3. In a cautionary vein, Turkle states, "At every step we have to ask, as educators and citizens, whether current technology is leading us in directions that serve our human purposes." Find a faculty member on your campus who teaches online. Interview this professor about how the role of technology has changed his or her teaching practice. What are the specific differences in course design? In relationships with students? In creating a community within the class? Write an essay reporting your findings. In your conclusion, refer to Turkle's statement above, and assess whether, in this case study, technology is serving our educational purposes well.

4. Karen Moltenbrey, writing about Second Life in "Life or Something Like It" (p. 234), quotes Robin Harper of Linden Labs on the power of this simulated world: "'You can do anything you've dreamed about doing in your 'first' life but can't do or haven't done. If fact, our players often use the terms RL and SL — nomenclature for their real life and second life." Sherry Turkle also refers to the power of simulated worlds, but calls for a close examination of the values that the "culture of simulation" may encourage. If you are not already a player in a simulated world, visit Second Life at www.secondlife.com (there is a free seven-day trial period). Take notes on what steps it takes to enter this world and participate in it. What identity have you chosen? Who is in control of the environment? What options for activities do you see? What aspects do you find appealing? What aspects do you find threatening? Is there a binary "Scary/Safe" or "Good/Evil" aspect to the experience? Log in to other simulated worlds, if you wish. Write a narrative essay evaluating your experience of simulated life.

Blogs

A Portfolio of Personal Identity Blogs

A DECADE AGO, THE TERM "BLOG" DID NOT EXIST. TODAY, THERE ARE over 60 million Web logs (or blogs). Some are educational, some are commercial; they offer news, commentary, gossip, and humor. But the majority still adhere to the initial purpose of the blog: They serve as online diaries. A common thread is that bloggers share a part of themselves — or a part of who they wish to be — with the world in hopes of generating a response. Some are incredibly successful. According to Technorati, the most popular blog in the world is run by Chinese actress Xu Jinglei (blog.sina.com.cn/m/xujinglei), with over 50 million hits. Undoubtedly, in the global culture of celebrity, Ms. Xu is already the center of attention as fans clamor for more information about her every move. But, what about the author and subject of the blog "vanity run amok," who describes herself as "one yarn project short of becoming a spinster." Or the writer of the blog "me, my life + infrastructure," who offers simply that she is "originally from Kansas City, Missouri, . . . a grad student at an unspecified school on the East Coast." Or the medical student behind "My Life, My Pace," who diagnoses herself as "a 20-something-year-old woman with a 20+ year history of schooling . . . now presenting with frustration at her current lack of progress consistent with being stuck in a rut." None of these women are international superstars. Why are they sharing their lives with us? Why do we read?

Each blogger represented in this chapter and online has a historical writing cousin, Samuel Pepys. Pepys would likely have been lost to history as a seventeenth-century bureaucrat, an English naval administrator, were it not for one simple fact: He was absolutely obsessive about maintaining his diary. Pepys left a yellowed manuscript used to this day by historians as an original source document for information on events small (a winter cold, an extramarital fling) and large (the Great Fire of

London, the plague). From *The Diary of Samuel Pepys*, still widely available today, we gain a glimpse into a world otherwise lost to us. And, we get a sense of how one man wanted to be remembered by history and how history shaped him. It is too early to tell whether the blogs that follow — or any of the 60 million others — will survive four hundred years and provide future readers with a window into the early twenty-first century. It is not too early, however, to read each blog as an attempt by the writers to communicate who they are or who they wish to be. Unlike Pepys, who kept his diary under wraps until after his death, today's bloggers share their diaries with the world — literally. In the introduction to this chapter, we asked, "What if you were in an environment in which you had almost complete autonomy to create a whole new 'you'?" To this, we might add a second question: How much of this new "you" would you reveal, knowing that the whole world might be reading?

We have annotated one blog to demonstrate how it conveys the blogger's identity to the reader. When you log on to this site and the others listed, remember that they function as online diaries of people you do not know, making it difficult to determine what is actual and what is constructed reality. You might also consider how the blogs function as ads for the bloggers, so that you will start and keep reading. It is difficult to stand out in a crowd of 60 million, and as you look over these sites, think about which would draw an audience and why. Following the annotated blog, you will find an array of sites that represent the diversity of the blogosphere.

This is a '40s pinup image, which likely predates the birth date of the blog's author by 10 to 20 years. But its retro quality refers to the age of the writer (a woman in her forties). Its old-fashioned quality ironically undercuts the subtitle, letting the reader know what tone to expect in the posts.

Note the conversational tone of this post – you're immediately cast as her confidant and friend.

Brands give a sense of her size and style.

From the headlines you can guess her political leanings and attitudes; also see the "mom" come out in bullet #2.

Throughout this post she refers to her modest means in various ways, BUT she can't resist shopping and wish-list shopping.

More is for women forty and older.

References to her lack of money appear throughout the blog.

The order of her roles indicates this is a personal blog: first a mom and wife, then a writer.

Here's a glimpse into her emotional state.

Sponsors and recent posts suggest she's focused on fashion regardless of income (note: Herceptin® is a breast cancer drug, which fits with her age).

She reveals her location.

Categories reinforce her focus and her target readers: women over forty with families who like fashion and culture.

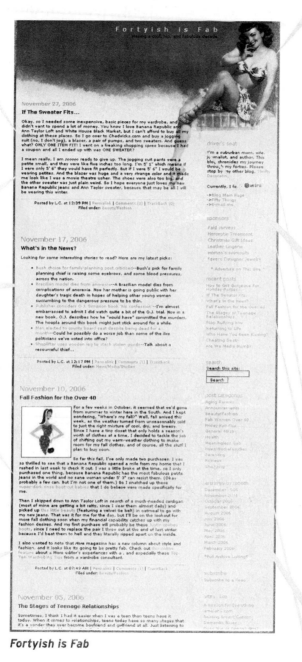

Fortyish is Fab

Vanity Run Amok

Me, My Life + Infrastructure

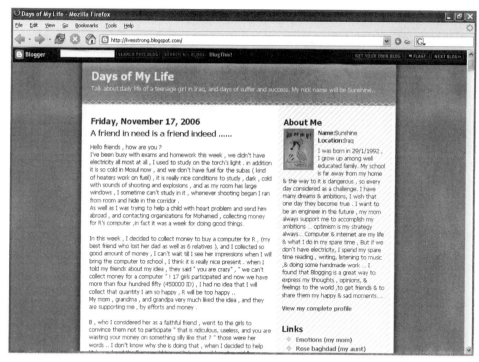

Live Strong

My Life Italian

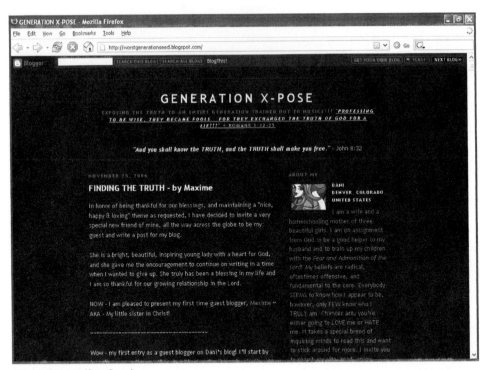

Worst Generation Seed

My Life, My Pace

RESPONDING

1. Like almost any printed reading material, a blog has standard conventions regarding what information goes where on the virtual page. From the example blogs provided, create a glossary that describes the various elements of a blog. It might be helpful to create a diagram of the component parts.

2. The blogs capture a diversity of writing voices. Which of these writers did you find most compelling? Least compelling? Why? Did your ability to identify with the writing persona play into your judgment?

3. In "Explanations for the Perpetration of and Reactions to Deception in a Virtual Community" (p. 272), Adam N. Joinson and Beth Dietz-Uhler write, "The visual anonymity inherent in most Internet-based communities provides ample opportunity to engage in deception and identity play. And yet there is a large body of empirical and anecdotal evidence to suggest that visual anonymity online encourages candid self-disclosure rather than falsehoods . . . and may even encourage the expression of a true self online." Select one of the blogs in this section and write an analysis of the blogger's persona and entries. What evidence would you use to support the position that the writer is either engaging "in deception and identity play" or revealing "a true self online"?

READING DEEPLY

Explanations for the Perpetration of and Reactions to Deception in a Virtual Community

By Adam N. Joinson and Beth Dietz-Uhler

FROM: *Social Science Computer Review,* August 2002

THE FOLLOWING ARTICLE WAS WRITTEN FOR THE *SOCIAL SCIENCE Computer Review,* an interdisciplinary, peer-reviewed academic journal. The journal has been published since 1982 in response to the growing influence of technology on social interactions. This article comes from an issue of the journal devoted to the intersection of psychology and the Internet. As with most scholarly publications, *Social Science Computer Review* is targeted primarily at academics (professors, deans, graduate students) doing research in the field. Adam N. Joinson is a lecturer in educational technology at the Open University in London; his research concentrates on Internet behavior. Beth Dietz-Huler is an associate professor of psychology at Miami University, Ohio; her research interests include intragroup and intergroup behavior, reactions to threats to social identity, and computer-mediated communication.

To help you read more deeply and critically, we have provided annotations and boldfaced some terms or passages that call attention to the rhetorical choices Joinson and Dietz-Uhler have made in their article and to the requirements of social science research that are present in this piece. As you read the essay and the annotations, consider how the authors present their argument about the behavior of virtual communities and support it with evidence drawn from the members' messages.

> The abstract provides a reader with an overview or summary of the research article that follows. It lets the reader know, in advance, whether the essay addresses topics germane to his or her research. It is a convention widely used in the social sciences.

Abstract

Cases of identity deception on the Internet are not uncommon. Several cases of a revealed identity deception have been reported in the media. In this article, the authors examine a case of deception in an online community composed primarily of information technology professionals. In this case, an established community member (DF) invented a character (Nowheremom) whom he fell in love with and who was eventually killed in a tragic accident. When other members of the community eventually began to question Nowheremom's actual identity, DF admitted that he invented her. The discussion board was flooded with reactions to DF's revelation. The authors propose several explanations for the perpetration of identity deception, including psychiatric illness, identity play, and expressions of true self. They also analyze the reactions of community members and propose three related explanations (social identity, deviance, and norm violation) to account for their reactions. It is argued that virtual communities' reactions to such threatening events provide invaluable clues for the study of group processes on the Internet.

Although initially envisaged as a network of computers, the development of e-mail soon after the implementation of ARPANET also allowed for connections between people **(Licklider & Taylor, 1968)**. By the early 1980s, dial-up systems like the WELL were providing a community-type experience for members of the public. Stone

> The authors follow APA (American Psychological Association) style in documenting their sources.

The authors argue that the responses of the online group they are studying reflect true community dynamics, so they acknowledge those who might disagree with their position.

(1991) argued that virtual communities are "incontrovertibly social spaces in which people still meet face-to-face, but under new definitions of both 'meet' and 'face-to-face'" (p. 85). **However, the idea that groups of people exchanging messages in cyberspace can form real (i.e., psychologically rewarding) relationships and communities has not been universally accepted.** An early complaint was that virtual communities, although looking to all extents and purposes like a real community, were actually pseudocommunities. The essence of a pseudocommunity is a lack of sincerity or genuineness (Jones, 1995)—a pattern of relating that, although looking like highly interpersonal interaction, is essentially impersonal (Beniger, 1987).

However, **as Rheingold (2000) noted, "It's hard to sympathize with the charge that all online relationships are unreal when you've stood in front of a person's friends and family at their funeral" (p. 327). In a similar vein, Haythornthwaite, Wellman, and Garton (1998) argued that "the question of whether or not one can find 'community' on-line is asked largely by those who do not experience it"** (p. 212). In more recent years, the discussion of virtual community has developed to consider the use of the Internet in social support (e.g., Constant, Sproull, & Kiesler, 1997; Preece, 1999) and the social-psychological impact of virtual interaction on the individual's psychological well-being (Kraut, Patterson, Lundmark, Kiesler, Mukopadhyay, & Scherlis, 1998).

To support their point of view, they then go on to cite authorities who do believe online groups form real communities.

The headings help the reader understand the organization of the article. The reader would know that what follows is a review of existing literature about deception on the Internet. Often a research paper will begin with a section like this, which puts the authors' paper in the context of previous research.

Deception on the Internet

Internet-based communities and social interaction represent the cusp of a paradox not yet well understood. The visual anonymity inherent in most Internet-based communities provides ample opportunity to engage in deception and identity play. And yet there is a large body of empirical and anecdotal evidence to suggest that visual anonymity online encourages candid self-disclosure rather than falsehoods (see Joinson, 1999, 2001), and may even encourage the expression of a true self online (McKenna, Green, & Gleason, in press).

A number of cases of deception in virtual communities have been reported in the press, and some gained almost a mythological status among early Internet users. For instance, one of the earliest cases was of the disabled "Joan" and "Alex," two popular figures in an online community in the early 1980s (Van Gelder, 1991). Joan was reluctant to meet people face-to-face because of her physical disability, but she did forge many friendships with other women in the community and was a confidant to several whom had real life affairs with Alex. **As it turned out, Joan was a persona developed by Alex, leading to a sense of shock, outrage, and betrayal within the community (O'Brien, 1999; Turkle, 1995).**

Feldman (2000) reported four cases of "Munchausen by Internet," where people in online support groups claim illnesses that they do not have. In one case, a woman called Barbara posted to a cystic

Note that each time the authors make a statement, they provide additional support for their claim. A reader can then go to these sources to verify the statement by Joinson and Dietz-Uhler.

> The authors provide a fairly detailed example in the case of Kaycee because it bears strong similarities to the incident they discuss later. Thus, it sets up the reader to better understand the remainder of their essay.

frombosis support group. Barbara claimed that she was waiting at home to die and was being cared for by an elder sister (Amy). The group sent many supportive messages to Barbara and were distressed to learn from Amy that she died a few days later. It was only when the group noticed that Amy shared Barbara's spelling errors that they questioned the story. Amy admitted to the hoax, and taunted the group for their gullibility. Feldman warned that a common reaction to such cases is for the online group to split into believers and doubters of the claims or for people to leave the group in disgust.

During 2001, **the case of Kaycee was the first large-scale deception to hit the weblog community**. Weblogging is the posting on websites of daily links to articles or events of interest on other websites. It is also the terminology for online diarists who often use the same software to post their daily diary. Like many similar stories, the deception seemingly began quite innocently when a group of school girls developed an imaginary friend (Kaycee) and developed some simple hoax Web pages sometime around 1997 or 1998. However, it would seem that when one of the girls' mothers (Debbie) found this out, she developed the imaginary teenager to be diagnosed with leukemia, and at around the same time Kaycee joined an online community called College Club. When the author of a weblog suggested that Kaycee and her mother begin a weblog on his own site, the tales of Kaycee's battles against cancer and her seeming recovery became popular among the weblog community, with many members sending

This heading sets up their original research. The term "case study" alerts the reader that what follows will be an explication of <u>one specific incident</u> that can be used to exemplify the reactions of an online community to an act of deception.

Kaycee cards and gifts. After a couple of years, when it was looking like Kaycee might be recovering fully, Debbie posted in early 2001 that she had died of an aneurysm. According to the Kaycee FAQ (rootnode.org/article.php?sid=26), "The community outpouring of support was remarkable and those who knew Kaycee well suffered serious bouts of grief." However, suspicions began when Debbie would provide no details about the funeral or address for condolence cards. Investigations by Internet users revealed no trace of Kaycee at any high schools or hospitals, or even an obituary. This and other evidence led to an admission by Debbie, who claimed that she had created Kaycee from a composite of three cancer sufferers she had personally known and that the picture of Kaycee was of one of these sufferers (as it turned out, this was not true either). According to the Kaycee FAQ, Debbie felt that she had done nothing wrong.

Case Study of Online Deception and Punishment:
The Death of Nowheremom
The Anandtech forums are asynchronous bulletin boards aimed at information technology professionals. There are 12 main forums covering issues such as hardware, CPUs, memory, and so forth. **The forum of interest in this case study is the "Off Topic" bulletin board.** In the Off Topic board, members of the forums can discuss issues not covered by the main forums. When people join the Anandtech forums they are able to select a username and icon to

The first paragraph simply explains the Anandtech forums so that the reader understands the context for the online discussion and who the participants usually are.

> Now, the authors move into the case of Nowheremom, setting up her role in the community.

visually represent themselves. They can also use .sigs and have profiles hosted of, for instance, their "rig" (the specification of their computer). The Anandtech forums also have a hierarchy of members based on activity, longevity, and, for promotion to the top level Elite member, some form of judgement from the community enforcers. Membership ranges from junior member through diamond and platinum to elite.

During October 1999 a new member, using the username Nowheremom (NWM), began posting to the Off Topic forum. Her postings were characterized by terrible spelling mistakes, something the community members seemed to find endearing. During the course of 1999, NWM was attracting the attention of a number of men on the forum, and a flirtation with fellow member DF began. Many other members of the community were seemingly enthralled by this developing relationship, some even describing it as a soap opera. However, on January 5, 2000, **DF posted the following message under the subject heading, "NOWHEREMOM's dead . . ."**

AUGGGGGGGGGGGGGGGGG!!! I just got a phone call from Mr. Anderson (her father) He said he tried to reach me all afternoon. I was at the university and just got back 15 minutes ago. He said that both Lili Marlene and Agnetha are dead . . . that they got killed just afternoon Newfie time. He said that it was very windy and there was some freezing rain along the coast and that they were walking back from Agnetha's school and that they

> The authors provide a primary text that forms part of their case study. The message is reproduced as originally written, so it contains all of the typos and unusual punctuation of the actual e-mail sent by DF. Part of their analysis will address the emotion conveyed through this message, so they need the reader to get a clear picture of what the community saw online.

were at the bottom of a hill in a curve walking on the roadside and that a car went too fast downhill and missed the curve and hit them. He said that Agnetha was killed istantly but that Lili Marlene survived for a little while and that she died on the way to the hospital. Too many internal injuries, she hemmoraged internally. He was called to identify them. The guy who killed them lives only 2 houses away and is in his focking late seventies. What the hell was he doing on the road driving in adverse conditions. Geriatric motherf. I'd strangle him with my bare hands

I am so focking sad. . . . What will I do? She was the light of my life. . . . She was so young so sweet so full of life and hope. were gonna mend our lives together Now she's been taken away from me. . . . She shone like a beacon and now theres only darkness. All we had was 9 days together. . . . I wanted a lifetime, not just 9 focking days. I never got a chance to meet Agnetha. I am so depressed. . . . I can't cry because I know when I start I will wail, but my eyes hurt so much. I can't keep all the tears in and it's dripping down my chin. I'm so angry I could kill a million people and even then she wouldn't come back. Why does life suck so much. Why us why us why us? We were so happy for crying out loud. . . . We had projects. We were so similar. We liked the same things knew many same things laughed at the same stuff We thought so alike that we could end each others sentence on the phone. We talked just last night I never got a chance to say goodbye.

Why o why o why o why is life so damn unfair???

Many members of the community expressed shock and grief, a

> These actions, honoring Nowheremom's loss, help support the authors' contention that the online users formed a community within expected norms of behavior.

reaction that continued for many months. The username and icon used by NWM were retired by the moderators of the community. During the next year, the loss of NWM was often referred to in discussions — and DF was given the role of protector of her memory. **Some members of the community also set up a memorial Web page to NWM (real name Lili Marlene Maltese).** However, a small number of members of the community began to investigate NWM's death further. They found no records of her death in local papers, and began to question her actual identity. On May 16, 2001, DF posted the following confession to the Off Topic forum:[1]

> **I, DF, come here today to reveal that I have deceived this community and deceived myself into believing that I was doing the right thing.**
>
> In October 1999, I created a cyberpersona called NOWHEREMOM partly out of elements from real people I had encountered, partly out of my imagination. I started this simply as a joke and to see what it would be like for a woman to post on the forums. Women were really scarce on the forums at that time and, as time went by, I deluded myself into thinking that this portrayal of a strong woman would help female lurkers be less afraid of overwhelming male presence and what I perceived as strong misogyny on the boards. NOWHEREMOM was hit on instantly by a couple of male posters in emails, so I decided to make her flirt with me to prevent this by having us be a declared couple. These male posters need not be afraid. Their identity is and will remain secret.

> Again, the authors reproduce a lengthy message from DF, which allows the reader to see how different this message is from the first. The tone, spelling, punctuation all differ dramatically, suggesting that DF's message following Nowheremom's "death" was crafted specifically to deceive the online community by using the writing style of someone distracted by grief.

DF's message reveals how seriously some in the online group took their communications. Here one member apparently suggested that DF and Nowheremom might marry. Again, this type of detail supports the authors' argument that online groups form communities with social expectations and norms.

Throughout November and December 1999, I engaged in a banter with this persona. At that time, I wanted mainly to bring some humour and entertainment to the forums. People were indeed entertained during those two months and some called it a soap opera. As time went by, NOWHEREMOM started to take an air of reality even to me. Once again, it never was my intention to hurt anyone. I simply had not realized how much people and even myself had become attached to her.

In early January 2000, after **Ornery mentioned the word "marriage"**, one day I simply panicked and in that instant, my mind was clouded enough that, instead of simply revealing that it was a hoax, I killed her.

I had never expected the grief that overcame this community. It even overcame me and I sobbed for three days as if she had been real. I came to the conclusion that to reveal the hoax would hurt too many innocent people and I was hoping that the whole thing would simply fade away. It was not meant to be.

In July 2000, a member named Vapor uncovered evidence of the hoax and revealed it to a few people. Instead of coming clean, still believing that the hurt to our community would be too great, I denied the whole thing. Vapor was villified and ostracized for this. To him, I can only offer my sincere apology for I am truly sorry for the way he was treated on this matter. I lied to some people closest and dearest to me because I thought that, in doing so, I was protecting them from becoming accomplices in my

> This fact supports the overall commitment of the members to the group: They posted over one message a minute on his confession.

cover-up. Unfortunately, many came to my defense in a spirited fashion and ended up unknowingly defending a lie.

The matter never rested and many of my friends and acquaintances ended up being divided into two clans. In particular, I know some outside individuals who would be pleased to no end watching the fabric of this community unravel over this. The well-being of this community is paramount in my book for I do consider you my Internet family.

It was simply a hoax which I thought was harmless and which got out of hand when I panicked 16 months ago. I sincerely apologize to everybody involved or hurt by this matter.

Before the thread was locked by the moderators of the conference, **458 messages had been posted in reply to the confession between the first (6:29 p.m. on May 17) and the last (2:03 a.m. on May 18) posting**.

Explanations of Online Deception

Explanations of deception on the Internet tend to focus on either category deception like gender switching (e.g., Bruckman, 1993; Donath, 1999) or misrepresentation (e.g., Cornwell & Lundgren, 2001), or the presentation of an idealized or true self (McKenna et al., in press; Turkle, 1995). The literature on category deception is based almost entirely on behavior in MUDs and Internet Relay Chat (IRC), where gender is often considered malleable and part of the game (Bechar-

> The authors now provide a framework of reasons why DF might have deceived the online group. Note that each reason that follows is supported by cited sources and by messages from the online forum that suggest the posters were assuming this reason was the cause for DF's post.

Israeli, 1998; Reid, 1995). Rarely are the reasons for category deception examined, except for pronouncements on various postmodern or fragmented aspects of the self online. Among the explanations for category deception considered here are psychiatric illness, identity play, and true self.

Psychiatric Illness

One possible explanation for category deception is that it is due to a preexisting (i.e., real life) psychiatric illness that is expressed online through attention seeking and deception. To be sure, the Internet would seem to provide an ideal playground for those with sociopathic tendencies, and cases of people claiming various illnesses in support groups have been termed *Munchausen by Internet* (Feldman, 2000). When a deception is seen as antinormative, there may be attempts to label the protagonist as mentally ill. For instance, in the ensuing discussion following DF's confession, a number of postings alluded to his mental state and need for help:

> dot you think Hess kind sick? why in the world would you start to impersonate a lover. i think its just plain weird. get some therapy and leave tot for a while, you need to get a grip.

> Really sick . . . You ought to seek some professional help. Many of us felt badly for days because of your little game.

Each writer wonders about DF's mental health, but notice how the postings provide a miniature portrait of the writer. Each has a different style, tone, voice. Joinson and Dietz-Uhler are encouraging the reader to "see" the members of the community as individuals with expectations about their fellow online participants.

> Loneliness does make people do some crazy stuff, and he prob-
> ably didn't mean to cause any harm when he created the persona.
> Probably a few people here have been depressed or lonely enough
> where they've contemplated suicide before so they can under-
> stand where he's coming from. In his case, he just created another
> persona instead

Although no doubt most Internet users who engage in multiple
persona generation are not mentally ill, the seeming willingness of
other users to label their behavior as such suggests that in general
such category deception is seen as unacceptable.

Category Deception, Game Playing, and MUDs

In the environment of **MUDs and IRC**, playfulness and, particularly,
playfulness with identity form a large part of the attraction for many
users (Bechar-Israeli, 1998; Curtis, 1997; Reid, 1995). The most hotly
debated form of identity play in MUDs is gender switching. Bruckman
(1993) noted that "without makeup, special clothing or risk of social
stigma, gender becomes malleable in MUDs" (p. 4). A number of educated guesses have posited that most IRC and MUD usernames are
gender neutral, thus allowing for gender-bending (Danet, 1998). Similarly, it is also estimated that more men gender bend than women.
For instance, Stone (1991) reported that the ratio of men to women on
a Japanese site was 4:1, but that on the actual site the number of male
presenters to female presenters was 3:1.

Notice that you are now assumed to know what this acronym
represents.

> Again, the authors are providing evidence that supports their contention that online communities have expectations for behavior and act just as face-to-face communities might.

Danet, Ruedenberg, and Rosenbaum-Tamari (1998) described five frames in IRC: real life, the IRC game, party, pretend play, and performance. Movement through the frames is in part determined by the design and assumptions of the specific environments (e.g., metamessages or room descriptions) and through the process of interaction (see also Postmes, Spears, & Lea, 2000). Danet et al. also noted that the type of play witnessed on the Internet is usually allowed only in children or in adults during masked balls or carnivals. **So, whereas category deception can be an accepted part of play in virtual interaction, its acceptability is socially constructed and controlled by the norms of the group and the environment itself.** In environments where the implicit assumption is for participants to be themselves, such play would, it is hypothesized, be unacceptable. Many of the posts in response to the NWM confession mentioned the word *hoax*. In general, the game of the hoax was (just about) acceptable, but the manipulation of other members' emotions was not:

> He had us (well, those of us who were here then) completely fooled. I'm torn between congratulating him on a hoax well done, & flaming him for playing with our emotions like that.

> Heh, whatever guys, it's the internet, stuff like this is to be expected. Congrats on a hoax well done, shame on you for toying with people's emotions, but either way, it shouldn't be a big deal.

This concept is important to the overall argument. The phrase, or something similar, is mentioned frequently (over a dozen times). As you read research writing, look for repeated terms or key phrases. They provide clues to the central ideas in the argument.

We would argue that responses like those above reflect the general acceptability of persona play on the Internet, but also that such play should be negotiated with other group members. We also note in the above quotes that the line is drawn at playing with emotions, not with deception per se. However, in communities where the local norm is for trust and candidness, persona development or identity deception might inevitably lead to an emotional reaction.

Expression of an Ideal or True Self

Turkle (1995) discussed a number of cases in which the development of an online persona seems to be an exercise in self-completion and attempts to achieve a desired identity rather than outright deception. For instance, Bruckman (1993) characterized MUDs as identity workshops. When discussing MUD devotee "Gordon," Turkle (1995) noted that "on MUDs, Gordon has experimented with many different characters, but they all have something in common. Each has qualities that Gordon is trying to develop in himself" (p. 190). In a similar case, Turkle discussed the high levels of Internet use by Stewart:

> In real life, Stewart felt constrained by his health problems, his shyness and social isolation, and his narrow economic straits. In the Gargoyle MUD, he was able to bypass these obstacles, at least temporarily. Faced with the notion that "you are what you pretend to be," Stewart can only hope it is true, for he is playing his ideal self. (p. 196)

The authors provide background for the participation in online forums: Why do people become this engaged in online communities? Who do they become when they "talk" to others online? Note that the authors' arguments are always supported and cited.

Perhaps, then, the use of online persona can serve a useful purpose for expressing and understanding our core selves unfettered by shyness, social anxiety, and physical states. Bargh, McKenna, and Fitzsimons (in press) argued that the Internet may allow people the freedom to express what Carl Rogers called the true self. According to Rogers (1951), a goal of therapy is to discover the true self to allow its more full expression in everyday life. In comparison, the self we express in everyday interaction is the actual self, the social persona we adopt that might not be what we truly are but is used to protect the self from vulnerability. In a series of experiments, Bargh et al. (in press) found that the salience of the true self was heightened (as measured by reaction time) following computer-mediated interaction compared to face-to-face interaction (where the actual self was most salient). McKenna et al. (in press) also reported that people are better able to present their true self online compared to face-to-face, and McKenna and Bargh (1998) found that participation in newsgroups can lead to the demarginization of stigmatized identities.

Curtis (1997) noted that a large number of personal descriptions in MUDs were of "mysterious but unmistakeably powerful" (p. 129) figures, suggesting that the development of personas in virtual worlds may well be an exercise in wish fulfillment. But at least for some users, the Internet also allows them to elaborate and practice their hoped-for possible selves or even to express a true self normally suppressed (McKenna et al., in press). In another sense, the Internet may provide an incentive for people to change in their real life existence — if one can act (and be perceived) as a certain type of person online, this may well serve as an incentive to achieve a similar state offline (McKenna & Bargh, 1998). There have been some claims that category deception involves the exploration of a true self (e.g., of a feminine side of the self or perhaps a chronically ill side). Reid (1995) quoted one MUD user saying,

> Um, I mud primarily to socialize. I also play female characters, despite being male. I don't think I'm the only person who's like this. I don't give my real gender to people very often . . . I'm exploring aspects of human interaction that are denied me in real life because I am male. (p. 180)

To be sure, the demarcation between an idealized or true self, identity exploration, and outright deception is fuzzy. **However, we would argue that in the vast majority of cases, category deception of the kind seen in the cases above is not representative of the exploration of a true or ideal self.** We would further argue that virtual communities, as opposed to MUDs, rely on a degree of honesty and trust. As the discussion of the Nowheremom deception continued, a number of postings referred to the integrity of the community and the presentation of self online:

> I have never, nor will ever, portray myself as anything more or less than

The authors want to argue that online communities offer participants a chance to reveal their "true selves," their inner identities that they might be constrained from showing outside of the virtual world. They want to distinguish this from deception, which is hiding one's true identity. Their position is that the reactions to DF's deception show an expectation of honesty in the online community — as would exist in a face-to-face community.

A message like this one helps to show the emotional reactions of the online community to the incident.

myself; online or otherwise. Come down to my pad and meet me. If I hate you, I will kick your @ss. If I like you, I will pull up my best chair and make a kick @ss dinner for you.

I happen to take these forums very seriously. I'm not one to deceive people, & I anticipate the same in return. I'm not a critical person, I take people at their word until I have reason not to. While some people may view this as "only" the internet, it's a community of real people.

But Internet forums are NOTHING if we can't have a degree of trust. What he did cannot be tolerated, not because any of us are perfect, but because it undermines EVERYTHING that an Internet community is supposed to be. We can't walk around saying "Anandtech is the best community on the net — we have over 50,000 members! But some of them are fake . . ."

Explanations for Community Members' Reactions to a Revealed Deception

Of particular interest are the reactions of other community members to the revealed identity deception. Community members' reactions were not quite as predictable as one would expect on the basis of previous cases (e.g., "Barbara/Amy" case, Jenny MUSH). There were clear indications that community members did not approve of DF's actions (e.g., "Wow, you're a sick dude. Get a life buddy"; "I can't believe you. I read all the stuff about you, and what happened to her and I truly felt

Note that the authors are portraying the messages as very much human. Their goal is for the reader to see the online community as composed of real people rather than virtual shells.

upset. You Denis, have lost all of my respect"). **But there were also a surprising number of messages showing support and forgiveness** (e.g., "I, for one, forgive you"; "I would like to take a minute to remind everyone that, while what he did was dreadfully wrong, do not forget what he has done to help people on the forums either. Weigh his character on his good and bad deeds"). As such, there is perhaps no single explanation which could account for the diversity of reactions to this revealed identity deception. Instead, the reactions can best be explained by examining them in the context of three related explanations: social identity, deviance, and norm violations.

Social Identity   When people are categorized into groups, their perceptions of and behavior toward their own group and other groups are often biased. People assign more rewards to members of their own group than other groups (e.g., Brewer, 1979), assume that actions taken by their group are correct (Abrams, Thomas, & Hogg, 1990; Turner & Oaks, 1989), and are more likely to help members of their own groups than other groups (Piliavin, Dovidio, Gaertner, & Clark, 1981), for example. Social identity theory suggests that group members are biased in favor of their own groups over other groups because group members derive esteem from the favorable comparisons that they can make between their in-group and relevant out-groups. In other words, people have a need to feel good about their groups so that they can feel good about themselves.

Joinson and Dietz-Uhler are establishing the authority of their observations by scaffolding them on established research on this topic. The level of their own research on this topic suggests that their analysis and conclusions have a firm grounding and can be accepted.

When an in-group member engages in behavior that is unfavorable or bad, group members' positive social identity is at risk. When one in-group member is bad, this reflects badly on the entire in-group. **Research suggests that group members can respond in several ways when their social identities are threatened (Dietz-Uhler, 1999). For example, group members can attempt to change their connections with the group (Doosje, Spears, & Koomen, 1995; Finch & Cialdini, 1989), derogate an out-group member (Cialdini & Richardson, 1980; Snyder, Lassegard, & Ford, 1986), make more group-serving attributions (Dietz-Uhler & Murrell, 1998; Wann & Dolan, 1994), and increase their commitment to the group (Ellemers, Spears, & Doosje, 1997). Related research (Biernat, Vescio, & Billings, 1999; DeCremer & Vanbeselaere, 1999; Marques, Abrams, Paez, & Hogg, 2001; Marques, Robalo, & Rocha, 1992; Marques & Yzerbyt, 1988; Marques, Yzerbyt, & Leyens, 1988; Matthews & Dietz-Uhler, 1998)** showed that when an in-group member engages in positive behavior or is described in positive terms, he or she is evaluated more favorably than an out-group member who engages in the same behavior or is described in the same positive terms. But when an in-group member engages in negative behavior or is described in unfavorable terms, he or she is evaluated more extremely unfavorably than an out-group member who engages in

> This distinction is important to their overall argument. The community members criticized DF for personal failings. Thus they saw him as a person and had expectations of his behavior within their community norms.

similar behavior or is described in unfavorable terms. This effect has been termed the *black-sheep effect* (Marques, 1990). Group members might derogate a "bad" in-group member so that they can distance themselves from him or her, thus restoring their sense of positive social identity.

In the current case of a revealed identity deception, there is ample evidence to suggest that community members attempted to "black sheep" DF. Interestingly, there are at least two ways in which DF and his actions could have been derogated: DF's character could be derogated or DF's actions could have been derogated. The majority of the community members who engaged in some form of derogation **chose to derogate DF's character more than his actions:**

I think you got a little wrapped up in this imaginary persona you created. I suggest you start thinking about taking a little bit more time away from the boards.

Dennis, I expected better of you, I am somewhat disappointed.

jesus man, this is intollerable. I to have lost all respect for you.

I think you will never have the same level of trust and respect from the general membership.

Man, I Fscking cried when you told that story. I'll never believe another word from you.

Notice the vocabulary of the discipline – psychology. This sentence essentially means: "some group members slammed DF because it helped them feel better about being such suckers." But, it certainly sounds more academic and authoritative as written by Joinson and Uhler-Dietz. As you read and write in a discipline, you need to become comfortable with the nomenclature and jargon.

Derogation of an in-group member's character is perhaps the most serious form of derogation. The seriousness of group members' responses likely parallels the seriousness of DF's infractions and allows group members to effectively rid the community of DF ("You are a weird, twisted, and demented person to run this, so . . . I just ignore you in the near, present and forever future"). **By derogating DF, community members can restore their sense of positive social identity.** Several members of the community did not derogate DF. Instead, they forgave him or excused his behavior:

Nowheremom was before my time, so I was unaware of the whole thing, but as the saying goes, to err is human.

I never hold grudges, it is bad Karma . . . and besides, Dennil has to live with this one on his conscience, that is enough punishment in my book.

Dennilfloss has repeatedly proven himself to be a benefit to these forums. So I have no reason to think of him as being anything but a benefit to these forums.

Social identity theory can also explain these reactions. When group members identify strongly with their group, they tend to derogate an errant in-group member (Branscombe, Wann, Noel, & Coleman, 1993). But when group members identify weakly with their group, they tend not to derogate an unfavorable in-group member because they have less to lose (Branscombe et al., 1993). Some of the

> Notice that the authors have already established DF as meeting both of these criteria in the previous discussion.

community members who forgave DF admitted to "not being around" when this happened, so they are likely to identify less strongly with the forum.

Rejection of Deviant Group Members   In effect, DF, who has become the black sheep of the online community, has also become a deviant group member. Briefly, deviance refers to something about an individual that sets him or her apart, thereby making him or her different. There are at least two bases on which a group member might be assigned the status of deviant (Pfuhl & Henry, 1993). **A person's behavior might be perceived to be objectionable. Another is that the person's character might be perceived to be objectionable.** The former refers to deviance that is achieved. In this case, the person could have avoided the label of deviant if he or she had not engaged in the objectionable behavior. Deviant status can also be ascribed. People might possess offensive traits or personality characteristics that are unavoidable.

Much has been written about ascribed deviance, most notably under the label of stigma. Stigma refers to an attribute or marking of a person that reduces him or her "in our minds from a whole and usual person to a tainted, discounted one" (Goffman, 1963, p. 3). Groups of people who have often been considered stigmatized include women, African Americans, the hearing impaired, homosexuals, cancer patients, people with AIDS, Christians, Jews, and the overweight (Crocker, Major, & Steele, 1998). It is important to recognize that the concept of stigma can be quite different from the concept of deviance. Deviance can either be valued or devalued, whereas stigmas are always devalued. For example, being extraordinarily rich and extraordinarily poor are deviant, but only one is valued (Crocker et al., 1998). In the current case, DF has been given the status of deviant, a clearly achieved status. Some members of the community perceived DF's deviance in a negative light:

> You have NO idea how real dennisd*ck made her seem! He told everyone he got a call from her father and made up this mile long story about how she was killed. Everyday after that, he would post about how much he missed her, looking for everyone's pity. If he just made her up and then came clean it wouldn't be a big deal, but he dragged it on for months, repeatedly bringing it back to the top, looking for more attention.

Other members of the community perceived DF's deviant actions in a more positive light ("I must say, i can understand exactly why you'd do such a thing. i was reading some of the old posts, and i also have to say congratulations on a hoax well done").

There is vast literature on how group members respond to a deviant group member (Levine & Moreland, 1994). **For example, Schachter (1961) had confederates play the role of a deviant, agreeable, or partially agreeable group member in a group discussion. Other group members reacted to the deviant member by refusing to communicate with him, evaluating him**

> The authors select two previous research studies that involved community reactions to face-to-face deception. The findings from these studies mirror the reaction of the online community to DF's deceit. Thus, Joinson and Dietz-Uhler further underscore that the online community differs little from traditional community.

less favorably, and appointing him to a low-status position in the group. In another study (Earle, 1986), a deviant confederate in a small-group discussion was rejected by the other group members. These investigations suggest, much like in the case of the black sheep, that group members derogate a fellow in-group member who does not go along with the group. In the NWM case, group members reacted to DF in much the same way as the participants in Schachter's (1961) and Earle's (1986) investigations:

> In the end you did the right thing, but I'm not even going to give you much credit for that because of the corner you backed yourself into.

> The killing off of the persona is a little bit tougher to take. I was really affected by that as were so many others here. It would have been less traumatic to just have had an imaginary argument with her then have her leave the forums.

> You, DF, is one crazy mofo.

Violation of Group Norms For a group to be able to reject a deviant group member, there must necessarily exist a group norm or norms that the deviant group member violated. Norms are sets of rules, guidelines, or procedures that prescribe the beliefs, attitudes, and behaviors of group members. The norms that form and exist in

> The authors again ground their assertions in the literature. But notice the dates on the cited research. There was no Internet in 1935 or the 1950s. By showing that the reactions of the virtual community map to those of traditional communities, Joinson and Dietz-Uhler again validate their argument that the two function similarly.

groups are functional; they help people to decide what they should think, feel, or do. When people are uncertain about how to respond, they tend to look to those around them for information. Informational social influence refers to the influence that others can have via the information they possess **(Deutsch & Gerard, 1955)**. In his classic study, Sherif (1935) found that in ambiguous situations, people look to the opinions of others for information. When people are motivated to gain approval or avoid disapproval by others, they might be influenced by normative social influence **(Deutsch & Gerard, 1955)**. **Asch (1951, 1956)** learned that in unambiguous situations, people will often conform to the group to avoid their disapproval.

There is evidence to suggest that the anonymity afforded in computer-mediated communication (CMC) groups increases the amount of influence that groups can exert on a group member because it enhances a group member's susceptibility to influence (Postmes, Spears, & Lea, 1999). For example, Spears, Lea, and Lee (1990) found that when participants discussed an issue in a CMC environment, they complied most strongly with group norms when they were isolated than when in the same room with other participants.

Clearly, group norms, whether constructed over time (e.g., Postmes et al., 2000) or evident from the outset, exert a powerful influence over group members' behavior. **As such, it is interesting to examine the consequences of a norm violation.** Norm violation by a member of the group leads to negative attributions, negative

> The authors are positioning DF's message about NWM as a norm violation.

Every assertion about the community reaction is supported with primary texts (e-mails, messages) from the community members. These messages provide compelling evidence in the members' own words.

intergroup behavior, and eventually mutual distrust (DeRidder & Tripathi, 1992). Of course, norm violations can be positive or negative. Imagine that someone is asked to do something for his or her supervisor. The person might decide not to do it at all (negative norm violation) or the person might do much more than he or she was asked (positive norm violation).

In the case of NWM, DF clearly engaged in a negative norm violation. **Community members were not expecting this type of behavior from one of their members ("He had us completely fooled"; "Denni has now compromised his credibility, so there is reason to take all his posts with a grain of salt").** DF clearly violated a norm of the online community and they responded by derogating him and his actions (as the previous samples have already shown). However, there was another norm that applied to this online community that DF's actions may not have violated. In online communities (and the Internet in general), it is sometimes normative for users to engage in identity play, whereby users pretend to be somebody they are really not. In NWM, DF made up a character and attempted to play the character's role. In effect, he intentionally deceived the members of the community. Many members of the community perceived DF's actions to be normative and in turn decided to forgive him:

This is the net and lots of people use it to escape from their jobs or life for a second and so something else or be someone else. I see how some people get carried away but this really isn't a harm towards anyone just someone who tried to do something and he didn't like the end result.

Denis, I don't blame you at all for the part about creating NOWHERE-MOM, it's so easy and tempting to do something of that sort especially in a forum like this one where so much kidding goes on.

i must say, i can understand exactly why you'd do such a thing.

I certainly won't hold it against you, at least not too much. Other than just a simple hoax to see what something was like that got out of hand. That's it.

I feel that ANYONE who holds ANY type of grudge against anyone over these forums is taking things too seriously here.

I applaud you DF for perfectly perpetuating such a hoax, but like all great hoaxes they come to an end.

This case is especially interesting because the members of the online community are also part of the larger Internet community. **From the perspective of the online community, important group norms were violated and DF was derogated as a consequence. But from the perspective of the Internet community, a group norm was confirmed and DF was not derogated or was congratulated for a "hoax well done."**

Notice how the authors account for primary evidence that doesn't seem to fit their argument. They appeal to a larger community and suggest that because hoaxing is a common act on the Internet as a whole, DF's behavior might be acceptable within these norms. Thus, what initially seems to violate their contention about community norms actually supports it.

299

> They are explaining why their research is different and new —
> how it has moved the discussion of this topic forward.

Conclusions

Most discussions of deception in online communities have, quite naturally, focused on either the reasons for the deception or the reaction of the community (e.g., MacKinnon, 1997; Reid, 1998). **We would argue that both aspects of the deceiver and the deceived, alongside the technology itself, need to be conceptualized as interdependent.** In the case of NWM, the deception was afforded by aspects of the technology, specifically visual anonymity and a lack of other controls. However, the varied reactions of the group suggest the existence and application of both local and wider group norms for the acceptability or otherwise of persona generation. Often, the condemnations of DF's actions were not based on the development of an alternative persona per se, but rather on its killing off and the subsequent effect of this on people's real life feelings. **Thus, the impact and reaction to the confession were seemingly grounded not only in the norms for the specific community but also in a consideration of the wider norms of Internet behavior and the real life implications of the deception.** Early theoretical discussions of psychology and the Internet tended to conceptually separate online and offline identities (e.g., Turkle, 1995). The case of NWM demonstrates that this approach is untenable, in that the reaction of the community was based on both local and Internet-wide norms and the effect of the deception on members' real-life emotions.

> Here they again establish two communities: the online group
> and the Internet as a whole.

In much research writing, conclusions are required to do at least two things: (1) recap why the approach and methodology taken in the study has merit and can be applied to other cases (i.e., the results are valid and generalizable to other similar situations); and . . .

(2) suggest directions for future research that can build upon the authors' findings and answer questions triggered by the current study.

The case of NWM also illustrates the potential strengths of studying virtual communities in their natural setting. It also highlights the value of identifying cases of virtual communities as they react to potentially community-threatening events. Perhaps only when faced with such threats does the true nature of a virtual community reveal itself.

Future research in this area could focus on several group process variables as they relate to a revealed deception in an online community. For example, the continued development of the group could be examined. In the face of the threat supplied by the revealed deception, does the community grow weaker or stronger? Cases of identity deception might also permit the investigation of norm development. When one community member deceived the community, do the norms surrounding identity deception change? Cases of a revealed identity deception in an online community provide unique opportunities to study these and other group process issues.

NOTE

[1]This confession has been abridged. Contact the authors for the full text.

REFERENCES

Abrams, D., Thomas, J., & Hogg, M. A. (1990). Numerical distinctiveness, social identity and gender salience. *British Journal of Social Psychology, 29,* 87–92.

Following APA style, a list of all the sources the authors cite appears at the end of the article. (See bedfordstmartins.com/nexttext for additional information on using and documenting sources.)

Asch, S. E. (1951). Effects of group pressure on the modification and distortion of judgements. In H. Guetzkow (Ed.), *Groups, leadership, and men* (pp. 117–190). Pittsburgh, PA: Carnegie.

Asch, S. E. (1956). Studies of independence and conformity: A minority of one against a unanimous majority. *Psychological Monographs, 70*(9).

Bargh, J. A., McKenna, K. Y. A., & Fitzsimons, G. M. (in press). Can you see the real me? Activation and expression of the "true self" on the Internet. *Journal of Social Issues*.

Bechar-Israeli, H. (1998). From <Bonehead> to <cLoNehEAd>: Nicknames, play, and identity on Internet relay chat. *Journal of Computer-Mediated Communication*, 1(2). Retrieved from http://www.ascusc.org/jcmc/voll/issue2/bechar.html.

Beniger, J. (1987). Personalization of mass media and the growth of pseudo-community. *Communication Research, 14*, 352–371.

Biernat, M., Vescio, T. K., & Billings, L. S. (1999). Black sheep and expectancy violation: Integrating two models of social judgment. *European Journal of Social Psychology, 29*, 523–542.

Branscombe, N. R., Wann, D., Noel, J. G., & Coleman, J. (1993). In-group and out-group extremity: Importance of the threatened social identity. *Personality and Social Psychology Bulletin, 19*, 381–388.

Brewer, M. B. (1979). In-group bias in the minimal intergroup situation: Acognitive-motivational analysis. *Psychological Bulletin, 86*, 307–324.

Bruckman, A. (1993). *Gender swapping on the Internet*. Retrieved from ftp://media.mit.edu/pub/asb/papers/gender-swapping.txt.

Cialdini, R. B., & Richardson, K. D. (1980). Two indirect tactics of impression management: Basking and blasting. *Journal of Personality and Social Psychology, 39*, 406–415.

Constant, D., Sproull, L., & Kiesler, S. (1997). The kindness of strangers: On the usefulness of electronic weak ties for technical advice. In S. Kiesler (Ed.), *Culture of the Internet* (pp. 303–322). Mahwah, NJ: Lawrence Erlbaum.

Cornwell, B., & Lundgren, D. C. (2001). Love on the Internet: Involvement and misrepresentation in romantic relationships in cyberspace vs. realspace. *Computers in Human Behavior, 17*, 197–211.

Crocker, J., Major, B., & Steele, C. (1998). Social stigma. In D. T. Gilbert, S. T. Fiske, & G. Lindzey (Eds.), *The handbook of social psychology* (4th ed., pp. 504–553). Boston: McGraw-Hill.

Curtis, P. (1997). Mudding: Social phenomena in text-based virtual realities. In S. Kiesler (Ed.), *Culture of the Internet* (pp. 121–142). Mahwah, NJ: Lawrence Erlbaum.

Danet, B. (1998). Text as mask: Gender, play, and performance on the Internet. In S. Jones (Ed.), *Cybersociety 2.0: Revisiting CMC and community* (pp. 129–158). London: Sage.

Danet, B., Ruedenberg, L., & Rosenbaum-Tamari, Y. (1998). "Hmmm . . . Where's that smoke coming from?" Writing, play and performance on Internet Relay Chat. In F. Sudweeks, M. McLaughlin, & S. Rafaeli (Eds.), *Network and Netplay: Virtual groups on the Internet* (pp. 41–76). Cambridge, MA: MIT Press.

DeCremer, D., & Vanbeselaere, N. (1999). I am deviant, because . . . : The impact of situational factors upon the black sheep effect. *Psychologica Belgica, 39*, 71–79.

DeRidder, R., & Tripathi, R. C. (1992). *Norm violation and intergroup relations*. Oxford, UK: Clarendon Press.

Deutsch, M., & Gerard, H. G. (1955). A study of normative and informational social influence upon social judgment. *Journal of Abnormal Social Psychology, 51*, 629–636.

Dietz-Uhler, B. (1999). Defensive reactions to group-relevant information. *Group Processes and Intergroup Relations, 2*, 17–29.

Dietz-Uhler, B., & Murrell, A. (1998). Effects of social identity and threat on self-esteem and attributions. *Group Dynamics: Theory, Research, and Practice, 2*, 1–12.

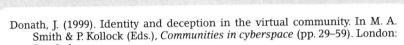
Donath, J. (1999). Identity and deception in the virtual community. In M. A. Smith & P. Kollock (Eds.), *Communities in cyberspace* (pp. 29–59). London: Routledge.

Doosje, B., Spears, R., & Koomen, W. (1995). When bad isn't all bad: Strategic use of sample information in generalization and stereotyping. *Journal of Personality and Social Psychology, 69,* 642–655.

Earle, W. B. (1986). The social context of social comparison: Reality versus reassurance. *Personality and Social Psychology Bulletin, 12,* 159–168.

Ellemers, N., Spears, R., & Doosje, B. (1997). Sticking together or falling apart: In-group identification as a psychological determinant of group commitment versus individual mobility. *Journal of Personality and Social Psychology, 72,* 617–626.

Feldman, M. D. (2000). Munchausen by Internet: Detecting factitious illness and crisis on the Internet. *Southern Medical Journal, 93,* 669–672.

Finch, J. F., & Cialdini, R. B. (1989). Another indirect tactic of (self-)image management. *Personality and Social Psychology Bulletin, 15,* 222–232.

Goffman, E. (1963). *Stigma: Notes on the management of spoiled identity.* Englewood Cliffs, NJ: Prentice Hall.

Haythornthwaite, C., Wellman, B., & Garton, L. (1998). Work and community via computer-mediated communication. In J. Gackenbach (Ed.), *Psychology and the Internet* (pp. 199–226). New York: Academic Press.

Joinson, A. N. (1999). Anonymity, disinhibition and social desirability on the Internet. *Behaviour Research Methods, Instruments and Computers, 31,* 433–438.

Joinson, A. N. (2001). Self-disclosure in CMC: The role of self-awareness and visual anonymity. *European Journal of Social Psychology, 31,* 177–192.

Jones, S. (1995). Community in the information age. In S. Jones (Ed.), *Cybersociety: Computer-mediated communication and community* (pp. 10–35). London: Sage.

Kraut R., Patterson M., Lundmark V., Kiesler S., Mukopadhyay, T., & Scherlis, W. (1998). Internet paradox: A social technology that reduces social involvement and psychological well-being? *American Psychologist, 53*(9): 1017–1031.

Levine, J. M., & Moreland, R. (1994). Group socialization: Theory and research. In W. Stroebe & M. Hewstone (Eds.), *European review of social psychology* (Vol. 5, pp. 305–336). Chichester, UK: Wiley.

Licklider, J. C. R., & Taylor, R. W. (1968). The computer as a communication device. *Science and Technology, 76,* 21–31.

MacKinnon, R. C. (1997). Punishing the persona: Correctional strategies for the virtual offender. In S. Jones (Ed.), *Virtual culture: Identity and communication in cybersociety* (pp. 206–235). London: Sage.

Marques, J. M. (1990). The black sheep effect: Outgroup homogeneity in social comparisons settings. In D. Abrams & M. A. Hogg (Eds.), *Social identity theory: Critical and constructive advances* (pp. 131–151). New York: Springer-Verlag.

Marques, J. M., Abrams, D., Paez, D., & Hogg, M. A. (2001). Social categorization, social identification, and rejection of deviant group members. In M. A. Hogg & S. Tindale (Eds.), *Blackwell handbook of social psychology* (pp. 400–424). Malden, MA: Blackwell.

Marques, J. M., Robalo, E. M., & Rocha, S. A. (1992). Ingroup bias and the "black sheep" effect: Assessing the impact of social identification and perceived variability on group judgments. *European Journal of Social Psychology, 22,* 331–352.

Marques, J. M., & Yzerbyt, V. Y. (1988). The black sheep effect: Judgmental extremity in inter- and intra-group situations. *European Journal of Social Psychology, 18,* 287–292.

Marques, J. M., Yzerbyt, V. Y., & Leyens, J. P. (1988). The "black sheep effect": Extremity of judgments toward ingroup members as a function of group identification. *European Journal of Social Psychology, 18,* 1–16.

Matthews, D., & Dietz-Uhler, B. (1998). The black sheep effect: How positive and negative advertisements affects voters' perceptions of the sponsor of the advertisement. *Journal of Applied Social Psychology, 28,* 1902–1914.

McKenna, K. Y. A., & Bargh, J. (1998). Coming out in the age of the Internet: Identity "demarginalization" through virtual group participation. *Journal of Personality and Social Psychology, 75,* 681–694.

McKenna, K. Y. A., Green, A. S., & Gleason, M. E. J. (in press). Relationship formation on the Internet: What's the big attraction. *Journal of Social Issues.*

O'Brien, J. (1999). Writing in the body: Gender (re)production in online interaction. In M. A. Smith & P. Kollock (Eds.), *Communities in cyberspace* (pp. 76–106). London: Routledge.

Pfuhl, E. H., & Henry, S. (1993). *The deviance process* (3rd ed.). New York: Aldine De Gruyter.

Pillavin, J. A., Dovidio, J. F., Gaertner, S. L., & Clark, R. D. (1981). *Emergency prevention.* New York: Academic.

Postmes, T., Spears, R., & Lea, M. (1999). Social identity, group norms, and "deindividuation": Lessons from computer-mediated communication for social influence in the group. In N. Ellemers, R. Spears, & B. Doosje (Eds.), *Social identity: Context, commitment, content* (pp. 164–183). Oxford, UK: Blackwell.

Postmes, T., Spears, R., & Lea, M. (2000). The formation of group norms in computer-mediated communication. *Human Communication Research, 26,* 341–371.

Preece, J. (1999). Empathic communities: Balancing emotional and factual communication. *Interacting With Computers, 12,* 63–77.

Reid, E. (1995). Virtual worlds: Culture and imagination. In S. Jones (Ed.), *Cybersociety: Computer-mediated communication and community* (pp. 164–183). London: Sage.

Reid, E. (1998). The self and the Internet: Variations on the illusion of one self. In J. Gackenbach (Ed.), *Psychology and the Internet* (pp. 29–42). New York: Academic Press.

Rheingold, H. (2000). The virtual community: Homesteading on the electronic frontier. Reading, MA: Addison-Wesley.

Rogers, C. (1951). *Client-centered therapy.* Boston: Houghton-Mifflin.

Schachter, S. (1961). Deviation, rejection and communication. *Journal of Abnormal and Social Psychology, 46,* 190–207.

Sherif, M. (1935). A study of some social factors in perception. *Archives of Psychology, 187,* 60.

Snyder, C. R., Lassegard, M., & Ford, C. E. (1986). Distancing after group success and failure: Basking in reflected glory and cutting off reflected failure. *Journal of Personality and Social Psychology, 51,* 382–388.

Spears, R., Lea, M., & Lee, S. (1990). De-individuation and group polarization in computer-mediated communication. *British Journal of Social Psychology, 29,* 121–134.

Stone, A. R. (1991). Will the real body please stand up? Boundary stories about virtual cultures. In M. Benedilt (Ed.), *Cyberspace* (pp. 81–118). Cambridge, MA: MIT Press.

Turkle, S. (1995). *Life on the screen.* New York: Simon & Schuster.

Turner, J. C., & Oakes, P. (1989). Self-categorization theory and social influence. In P. Paulus (Ed.), *Psychology of group influence* (2nd ed., pp. 233–275). Hillsdale, NJ: LEA.

Van Gelder, L. (1991). The strange case of the electronic lover. In C. Dunlop & R. Kling (Eds.), *Computerization and controversy: Value conflicts and social choice.* Boston: Academic Press.

Wann, D. L., & Dolan, T. J. (1994). Attributions of highly identified sports spectators. *Journal of Social Psychology, 134,* 783–792.

MAKING CONNECTIONS ACROSS AND BEYOND THE DISCIPLINES

1. Adam N. Joinson and Beth Dietz-Uhler have written this essay for an academic audience using the conventions of social science writing. Based on this essay — especially in comparison to the others in this chapter — create a catalog of these conventions along with annotations that explain how they fit the intended audience.

2. In "R We D8ting" (p. 219), Sandra Barron discusses a budding relationship that turned quickly sour because both parties had very different ideas of the norms of virtual communication. Joinson and Dietz-Uhler write, "Norms are sets of rules, guidelines, or procedures that prescribe the beliefs, attitudes, and behaviors of group members. The norms that form and exist in groups are functional; they help people to decide what they should think, feel, or do." Write an essay that defines the norms for social texting and online communication that you set for your friends or romantic relationships. Discuss how these norms are communicated and how you developed them.

3. Joinson and Dietz-Uhler discuss one specific case of Internet deception. As online discussions proliferate, so do such deceptions. Research the issue and identify another case. Analyze the reaction to this case using the framework established by Joinson and Dietz-Uhler involving group norms and reactions to their violations. Be certain to follow the authors' conventions and cite the sources of your grounding research and primary texts as evidence of the reaction.

Branding a Way of Life

AS BARBARA KRUGER'S PROVOCATIVE ART PIECE SUGGESTS, our role as consumers has come to be associated with our very sense of being. Her distinctive black and red and white photo text montage mimics the look of an advertisement, but actually engages us in a cultural critique of our desire to acquire material goods. Veronica Roberts of the Whitney Museum states that "Kruger criticizes the power of media in our culture not only by assimilating the style of advertisements (slogan over image) but also by co-opting the very space (billboards and newspapers) used by the media." This work ironically recasts the French philospher René Descartes' famous observation, "I think, therefore I am."

Like it or not, you are a part of a consumer culture. You are a market. Each day, you interact with hundreds, if not thousands, of messages that entice you to believe, to join, to commit, to buy. Some are obvious: a television ad for a car or a print ad for a local restaurant. Some are less obvious: a product placed in your favorite show or a T-shirt featuring a college logo. Each of these ads, regardless of its source, shares a rhetorical purpose: to sell a brand. Branding has become a commonplace of life: a tissue is a Kleenex, a soft drink is a Coke, a sticky note is a Post-It.

This chapter asks you to think about how consumer culture is constructed and how it delivers its messages through marketing – not only how we are sold products but ideas – ideas of better lives, better selves,

Barbara Kruger, Untitled (I shop, Therefore I am)

better futures, all of which can be achieved if we just buy the right stuff.

As consumers have been bombarded with ads, traditional advertisements have lost much of their ability to influence. For example, you can fast-forward through ads with TiVo® and even block pop-up ads on the Internet. On one level, marketing is simply a tool to inform potential customers about products they might be interested in purchasing. But financially, marketing is a complex and robust business that is taken very seriously. To those who work in the industry, marketing is a process that — if done well — means success.

So, companies have turned from traditional advertising that emphasizes a product and its brand to a new "softer" style of marketing which appeals to youth markets through street marketing, influence peddling, and product giveaways. Marketing lifestyles, not products, is the newest strategy to attract the disposable incomes of tweens, teens, Gen X, Gen Y, and even baby-boomer consumers. Branding, marketing, and popular culture have become inextricably mixed, as you will see in the following pieces.

Popular culture is the domain of the young, and many of the works in this chapter center on issues related to teen marketing. Having been a teen yourself, you know that these years can be fraught with issues about identity, esteem, belonging, and more. Some of the authors in this chapter are concerned about how marketing builds consumers by manipulation and exploitation of teens' emotions and needs.

In this chapter, we have included pieces by those who convince us to consume and those who critique our consumption. We ask you to engage with all of these works as a critical reader and a thoughtful writer. Expand your own knowledge base through further research and clarify your ideas in writing. Are you "boho chic," Anthroplogie, or all-American Abercrombie & Fitch? Are you sporting Timberlands or Birkenstocks? What is your identity — brand or antibrand?

Jane Hammerslough

What's Changed?
By Jane Hammerslough

FROM: *Dematerializing: Taming the Power of Possessions*, Da Capo Press, 2001

CONTEXT: This excerpt is from *Dematerializing: Taming the Power of Possessions*, originally published by Da Capo Press, an imprint of the Perseus Book Groups, which focuses on independent contemporary literature and serious nonfiction. Da Capo Press publishes widely in the fields of parenting, psychology, health, and education. Jane Hammerslough is an award-winning parenting columnist for the *New York Post* and has published articles in *Parenting* and *Child* magazines. She is known for her book *Everything You Need to Know About Teen Suicide* (1997). *Dematerializing* critiques our consumer-obsessed culture through research, personal experience, and real-world examples. Not just arguing against modern materialism, Hammerslough, with almost motherly concern, asks us to question our belief that possessions can actually fill our deepest human needs.

What's Changed?

THE SPIRITUAL, EMOTIONAL, AND SOCIAL SIGNIFICANCE OF objects is nothing new. For thousands of years, people have put their faith in objects, from amulets to icons, to control the unknown, offer protection from evil or misfortune, and bring good luck. Long before this vast amount of information on problems and material solutions existed, ownership and display of objects has been a way to communicate power, status, and wealth. What's different these days is how acutely we may feel the downside of placing faith in possessions — and the impact of the power of acquisition and ownership on the way we live, connect to others, and view ourselves. Where do we draw the line on that faith?

The fact that we are now inundated with messages linking objects and the limitless gratification of desires is just part of what's contributed to the current climate of materialism. But what other factors make possessions so powerful these days? Several things may contribute:

The Urgency of Technology

Basic needs such as food, shelter, and protection from dangerous elements haven't changed. However, as we have gained knowledge of and control over unknowns through technology, the concept of what we need to survive has grown. And not without reason: The accelerated pace of technological developments over the last three decades brings up new needs and different, possibly more efficient, solutions. Now, as in the past, survival may sometimes be a matter of possessing certain tools.

What's different now, however, is that today's frenetic pace involves an infinite, ever-changing variety of material solutions. This idea hit home one day in the early 1990s when I ran into a neighbor on my block in Brooklyn. A kind, gentle man who was once a well-known musician, he had gotten involved with drugs, was convicted for robbery, and had spent the better part of the last decade in prison. Now he was out, clean and sober, and quickly getting back on track with his music. That day he was hauling a Selectric typewriter home, a perfectly good find from a discard pile on the street. "Look!" he said, his eyes lighting up. "This is a great machine. I know," he said, grinning, "because I used to steal them!"

Admiring his haul, I didn't have the heart to tell him that Se- 5
lectrics were a dime a dozen on any given garbage day in our neighborhood at that time. Or that if he looked a bit more, he could probably even find an early, working PC and dot matrix printer. With my own mind occupied by whether I should have faster speed, laser printing, and other features that were then the latest in computer technology, my neighbor's delight in an old electric typewriter seemed a touching time warp.

To keep up with such speedy changes, we're forced to give material objects more thought. Solving problems we never knew about in the past has now become a pressing necessity.

Like the Luddites, the group of rebel British laborers in the early nineteenth century who destroyed textile-making machinery in hopes of preserving their jobs and way of life, we can rage against machines. But, as the Luddites soon discovered, the tide keeps coming in. Change occurs whether we want it or not; survival may depend on adapting to technology.

Just how much is uncertain. In recent years, rapid technological advances have resulted in more purchasable, problem-solving options than ever. Yet within the benefits of the new is a warning that works on a fear that's timeless: If you don't buy in now, you may be left behind, excluded, or even perish.

The Increasing Array of Problems and Products
In the 1950s, supermarkets displayed about 3,000 items; today, they may stock upwards of 30,000. Every day, around thirty-four new food products alone are introduced. The dizzying array of new items reflects a microsplitting of problems to create more "must-have" new solutions.

Take toothpaste, for example. The choice there is no longer a matter of simply picking up one brand over another. It now means considering an ocean of answers to a whole host of problems, such as a debate between "oral health" vs sex appeal, or gel vs paste. And then there are still the troubles of tartar, plaque, gingivitis, and halitosis that need attacking. The decision becomes still more complicated when you throw in factors like whiteness, brightness, tastiness, and cool appearance, like sparkles or stripes in the stuff. Yikes! 10

All those options demand attention. Okay, so maybe you don't have an existential dilemma every time you're in the pharmacy aisle. But the sheer number of choices requires engaging, if only for a few seconds, in order to make a decision. Sure, the bits of thought and effort you expend are small, but they can add up. And the process starts all over again when you move to, say, the snacks section.

In the early days of automobiles, Henry Ford announced that a customer could have a Model T in any color he wanted — so long as it was black. It made the choice of choosing a car simpler, for sure. But since we're not about to go back to such a "take it or leave it" approach to buying cars (or for that matter, anything else), we've now got to deal with nearly limitless options. Obviously, we want choices; we ask for them. But the growing number of choices of material things demands more of us.

More Products Connecting the "Spirit" of the Subject with Material Objects
The number of objects tied in to other subject — from characters in books, on television, or in movies, to real-life sports stars and other celebrities — has exploded in recent years. Consider the Davy Crockett coonskin cap of the past against today's billion-dollar licensing business, which includes everything from food to bedsheets to plastic figures, each imbued with the essence of a character's experience.

A truly massive number of these items are available today. And because many are available for a "limited time only," their shelf life is ever-shortening: What's hot among the under-ten set this season is likely to end up in a dump within a couple of years, since something new is constantly coming along to supplant it. However, the phenomenon linking the spirit of something to a material object is hardly limited to the "each sold separately" array of toys or trading cards ("collect them all!") that plague parents. The number of ways to tap into the intangible has grown for grown-ups as well.

In the early 1990s, Sotheby's held an auction of the estate of Andy   15
Warhol, the artist as much known for his prophesy that in the future, "everyone will be famous for fifteen minutes" as for his pop-art paintings. Like a giant tag sale, the auction of the artist's belongings included everything from furniture to paintings to his mammoth collection of old cookie jars — not rare ginger jars, but things he'd picked up at thrift shops. The surprise of the sale was how much the kitschy cookie jars commanded: People paid many hundreds of times what Warhol himself had spent, far more than what they might have paid had they found the same mass-produced product at a local church's tag sale. The fact that these were *Andy Warhol's* cookie jars, chosen and touched by an art superstar, made them intrinsically more valuable.

The Warhol auction — along with those of the late Jacqueline Kennedy Onassis, the Duchess of Windsor, Princess Diana, and lesser-known luminaries — demonstrates the current focus on how possessing a piece of private life, however remote, may provide a personal link to a public person. The fact that young John Kennedy was captured on film pulling on his mother's fake pearls when his father was in office pushed their sale price up to over $300,000. What sold the faux pearls and other items was not their inherent value (after all, for about fifty bucks, you could find a strand just like them almost anywhere) but the rare spirit of celebrity they contained: They were the *only ones* the First Lady actually wore in the photograph.

Even if you don't happen to be in the market for expensive stuff belonging to famous dead people, opportunities abound to buy things blessed by the essence of someone. Think of polo-playing Ralph's upscale items, cool Tommy's casual clothing, superstar Tiger's athletic wear, and tasteful Martha's home collections. With first-name familiarity, we can all have access to a bit of the magic, the success, the fame.

What comes first — the licensed product or the character or story which inspires it? What spawns what — the image of the creator or the object that's created? It's a chicken-and-egg issue these days. As opposed to, say, the twelfth century, when the bones of a saint or an alleged bit of the true cross became the object of pilgrimages, our current quests focus on that which is mass-produced. While reverence of relics is nothing new, the number of things linking ownership with the spirit of a person or an experience has grown dramatically.

Values: The New Consumable Good

The word "value" comes from the Latin *valere*, meaning to be strong or to be worth. Modern definitions can include the material or monetary worth of something, the relative rank, importance, or usefulness of something, or that which has intrinsic worth. As a verb, it can also mean "to estimate" or "appraise," or "to esteem" or "find worthy." A good value can be something that doesn't cost too much for what it delivers or provides to its purchaser; it can also be something that's a source of strength, purchasable or not.

The many different definitions of "value" have increasingly be- 20 come incorporated into consumption culture: A fairly low price and decent quality for an item are no longer the only standards of what makes for good "value." The other sense of value — a source of strength or esteem — creeps into material objects as well.

How? More than ever, we're asked to question our own values — the qualities we esteem most — in relation to purchasing something. Those questions may come from the ever-present external wisdom of advertisers. They may come from the judgments of our friends, coworkers, or even strangers. Or they may come from something inside ourselves. Whatever the source, the choice of a product may now imply a kind of moral decision that didn't exist in the distant past: Don't you care enough to send the very best flowers? Don't you want to protect your kids most effectively from germs? Shouldn't that anniversary bauble say "you'd marry her all over again"?

In response, the onus of ownership grows. The decision to buy something isn't simply just a way to get a little pleasure or to make life a bit easier or more convenient — it has become a crossroads. And the right choice may be equated with taking some sort of moral high road. After all, who *doesn't* want to do what's right for themselves, their friends, or their children?

If you can actually buy that kind of "righteousness," bully for you. Then again, anyone knows that objects of desire can't really embody the subtleties, challenges, and hard work of upholding what we believe is most important. We know it's simpler — and certainly smarter — to keep the two types of values separate, since rationally, we're aware that chance can toss a curveball at any moment: No matter what diamond ring you bestow, the relationship might fall apart. But sorting out various "values" isn't always so simple to do. And since there may be more fear than ever of those unpredictable curveballs, we hear about objects stepping up to the plate for us.

An advertisement for a brand of blue jeans brings this not-so-subtle point home. In the six-page spread, a series of captioned photographs chronicles the romances of several hip, young subjects, noting the length of each relationship: "Callie & Ty, three years," "Callie and Noah, one year, five months." Turn the page, and the luv do-si-do continues with other partners: Noah hooks up with Kim, then Kim moves on to Jeremy, and Jeremy winds up with Andrea. At least for now. The caption there tells us their bliss has lasted for a full week and a half.

In the final photo, Andrea's hugging a friend in a kitchen some-where. A poster that says "Mis Padres se Divorcian" appears in the background. Okay kids, put it together — your parents divorced and your own relationships begin and end like train wrecks? Never fear — jeans are here! With subtle nuances like that, we don't really need the caption that tells us, "At least some things last forever . . ." and identifies which brand to buy. 25

There's a strange, mixed-up cynicism here: You may want lasting love, but you'll have to settle for lasting jeans. The subtext is that if you buy the jeans, maybe love will endure, too.

Of course, it's only an advertisement. But it illustrates the current moral framework of materialism, which links intangible values with those you can buy. In this skewed framework, however, only some values are worth possessing; others, such as patience, forbearance, acceptance, compassion, modesty, thrift, and, uh, self-restraint, are notably absent.

READING

1. After reading this piece, do you feel Hammerslough thinks the emphasis on material goods is wrong? Explain your reasons.

2. Does Hammerslough feel that materialism is a product only of our modern culture? Why, or why not?

3. How does she introduce her discussion of the power of modern consumerism? Can you think of any objects that would be examples of her point in the first paragraph of her essay?

4. Hammerslough refers to "the increasing array of problems and products" as one of the factors that contribute to our fascination with material goods. She uses the example of many kinds of toothpaste. See what other examples you can come up with of objects that have a broad array of choices and list them with your classmates. Which have the biggest array? Which seem to be growing? Shrinking?

5. Hammerslough says that values are "the new consumable good." What kinds of definitions of value does she cite? Has the definition of value changed in our consumption culture? In what particular ways are values now a consumable good?

WRITING

1. "Ownership and display of objects has been a way to communicate power, status and wealth," says Hammerslough. Choose a possession that has a powerful resonance for you and examine it closely. Write a journal entry or a reflective essay on what this object communicates about you.

2. Look up the word "material" in the *Oxford English Dictionary*. Given the variety of definitions, which one is closest to the way this author is using the word? Write an essay in which you define the title of Hammerslough's book, *Dematerializing*. What might this mean to our consumer-driven culture? How does it reflect her overall argument?

3. Hammerslough refers to the Luddites, Henry Ford, Andy Warhol, and a blue jeans advertisement as examples for each of her four factors that make possessions powerful. Write an essay in which you explain the connection between each of these examples and the category in which it appears.

4. Hammerslough notes that some values are not worth possessing; these include "patience, forbearance, acceptance, compassion, modesty, thrift, and, uh, self-restraint." Look up the definitions of each

value she mentions. Then gather a series of three to five ads that re-flect the opposite of one of these values. Write an essay supporting Hammerslough's contention using the ads you've gathered.

5. Kalle Lasn in "The Cult You're In" (p. 376) suggests that we are all in some kind of cult:

> By consensus, cult members speak a kind of corporate Esperanto: words and ideas sucked up from TV and advertising. We wear uniforms – not white robes but, let's say, Tommy Hilfiger jackets or Airwalk sneakers (it depends on our particular subsect). We have been recruited into roles and behavior patterns *we did not consciously choose.*

Clearly, Hammerslough and Lasn are both concerned about the role that possessions play in our lives. Write an essay in which you ana-lyze the similarities of these two authors' arguments.

Elysia, Evan, and Alison
By Lauren Greenfield

FROM: **www.viiphoto.com/showstory .php?nID=191**

CONTEXT: This photo by Lauren Greenfield initially appeared as part of a photo essay on the teen brain. The text accompanying the essay notes: "Researchers now believe that teenagers' erratic and rebellious behavior may be a perfectly logical function of an immature brain. . . . different parts of the brain develop at different times – with the part of the brain that controls judgment and calms emotions maturing last." According to her online biography, Greenfield is recognized as "the preeminent chronicler of youth culture in the photography world. She has been named one of the twenty-five most influential photographers working today." Her work is in the collections of many museums, and in addition to her art photography, she continues to produce mainstream editorial and ad work, including spreads for the *New York Times Magazine, Time, The New Yorker, Harper's, ELLE,* and *Harper's Bazaar.* Looking at the photo on page 322, think about the aspects of youth culture and consumerism it captures.

Elysia, Evan, and Alison, all 14, and the self-titled "reject" group (self-named because they do not fit in with the "jocks" or "preps").

RESPONDING

1. Consider the photo in light of the quotation from Greenfield that "teenagers' erratic and rebellious behavior may be a perfectly logical function of an immature brain." How can you tell these young people are rebelling? What clues/codes are evident in the photo? What would you guess they are rebelling against?

2. On one level, these teens have created their own brand, the "reject" brand. It identifies them and their values. Based on this photo and your interactions with young people who seem similar in dress and appearance to Elysia, Evan, Alison, and their friends, discuss the "reject" brand. How might you market this brand and items connected to it?

3. In an interview on her website (laurengreenfield.com), Greenfield notes, "In my observations of teens, MTV and hip-hop culture had a visible influence . . . an over-the-top materialism with an emphasis on image, brands, clothing and cars was as strong with the kids of the ghetto as the kids of the rich." These teenagers do not seem to be as focused on materialism as their peers. Discuss their rejection of this materialism in light of Kalle Lasn's essay, "The Cult You're In" (p. 376).

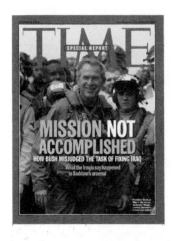

The Thing About Thongs
By Claudia Wallis

FROM: *Time*, October 6, 2003

CONTEXT: Claudia Wallis's "The Thing About Thongs" appeared in the October 6, 2003, *Time* magazine as the "Essay" feature, the last piece in each issue, which is reserved for a short personal piece on a topical issue. *Time* reaches more than 22 million readers each week, and about a third of these readers are college readers. The median age of its readers is forty-eight, which may be reflected in Wallis's comments. She is editor-at-large at *Time* and the founding editor of *Time for Kids*. In 1987, she was only the third woman to be named a senior editor at the magazine. Wallis typically addresses health and science, women's and children's issues, and education. Her work has won citations from the National Mental Health Association, the Newspaper Guild of New York, the Susan G. Komen Breast Cancer Foundation, and the Newswomen's Club of New York. Two of her cover stories have also been finalists for the National Magazine Awards. Here she takes a surprising topic and treats it both humorously and seriously – the amazing amount of money that girls spend on having just the right underwear. ("The Thing About Thongs" by Claudia Wallis. Text and *Time* Magazine cover © 2003 Time Inc. Reprinted by permission.)

ALL IN ALL, I HAD THOUGHT I WAS DOING PRETTY WELL IN bridging the "generation gap" — though my kids would say even this outmoded phrase betrays a certain cluelessness. In any case, my teenagers and I can readily agree on playing Radiohead and Coldplay during car trips. We laugh together at *Queer Eye* and Jon Stewart. Then there's Johnny Depp. My fourteen-year-old daughter and I are totally eye to eye on that one (as long as I don't remind her that he's closer to my age than hers). Luckily, we've been able to skirt such deal breakers as tattooing and body piercing. So far. But my self-image as a relatively cool mom unraveled like a cheap slip last month in the lingerie department of Lord & Taylor, where we were doing some back-to-school shopping. The bottom-line point of contention: underwear.

My daughter made it very clear that I just didn't get it. Why did I not grasp that one couldn't be seen in the girls' locker room sporting those packaged bikini underpants from Jockey or Hanes? Granny pants is what some kids call them. "Mom," my daughter wearily explained, "basically, every girl at school is wearing a thong." The only viable alternative, one that my daughter favored, was an item called boyshorts, a low-riding pair of short shorts loosely, or should I say tightly, based on Britney's stage-wear. Either way, it was going to be 8 to 20 bucks apiece, not three for $9. "But who sees them?" I sputtered. My daughter explained that besides the locker-room scene, girls liked to wear their overpriced thongs with a silky strap showing — not unlike the way they wear their bras.

She was right about my not getting it. How did a risqué item popularized as a tool of seduction by Monica Lewinsky become the de rigueur fashion for eighth- and ninth-graders? Yet the trend is undeniable. Sales of thongs to tweens (a market now defined ridiculously broadly as ages seven to twelve) have quadrupled since 2000, from a modest $400,000 to $1.6 million, according to NPD Fashionworld, a market-tracking firm. And there's nothing skimpy about what girls ages thirteen to seventeen spent on thongs last year: $152 million, or 40 percent of their overall spending on underpants. Do their mothers know?

Where this thing for thongs comes from is obvious: Britney, Beyoncé, *The Real World*, even PG movies like *Freaky Friday*. When a twelve-year-old wears a thong, "it's not about rebellion against adults," says child therapist Ron Taffel, author of *The Second Family: How Adolescent Power Is Challenging the American Family* (St. Martin's Press, 2001). In Taffel's view, the adult establishment has become too weak and weary to inspire rebellion. Getting thongs or tattoos or body piercings, he argues, is actually a "statement to other kids that they are part of this very, very intense, powerful second family of peer group and pop culture that is shaping kids' wants, needs, and feelings." This phenomenon is gripping kids at ever earlier ages. Peer pressure is at its most intense between fifth and eighth grade, says Taffel, "but it can begin in first and second grade."

Adult forces — parents, schools, churches — find it hard to compete with pop culture. Some schools have dress codes that outlaw visible underwear, but enforcing a ban on something as subtle as a thong isn't easy, as a vice principal at a San Diego high school learned to the detriment of her career last year. Her methodology left something to 5 be desired: She was demoted after she lifted skirts for an undies in-spection before allowing girls into a school dance.

Is the underwear battle worth picking? Those who think so are worried that the thong is a blatant sexual advertisement or, at least, a tempting tease for the opposite sex. This may not be so, according to developmental psychologist Deborah Tolman, author of *Dilemmas of Desire: Teenage Girls Talk About Sexuality* (Harvard University Press, 2002). "Kids are engaged with their sexuality at younger ages, but they're not necessarily sexually active," she says. The tween thong is, in a sense, the perfect symbol for the schizoid way that girls' sexual role has evolved. On the one hand, Tolman observes, girls are ex-pected, as always, to be the "gatekeepers" to sex. (God forbid that boys should be held responsible.) And, yet, she says, nowadays even young tweens feel social pressure to look sexy — without crossing over the murky line into seeming slutty. In short, says Tolman, "the good-girl, bad-girl thing has grown much more complicated."

Which is exactly what troubled me in the lingerie department. It wasn't until we got to the parking lot that I did what psychologists say a perplexed parent should do: I asked why the underwear mattered and listened hard to the answer. Tolman calls this the "authentic ask." My daughter's answer reflected her sense of style. But for many girls who want thongs, it may be pragmatism: What else works under tight low-rider jeans? I gave the O.K. to boyshorts at $8.50 a pair. She's de-lighted. "Mom," she said the other day, "you really ought to try them."

READING

1. In the essay's first paragraph, Wallis makes several pop cultural references. Why is she dropping these references? What type of authority do they help her establish?

2. Wallis includes marketing and sales data within her essay. Why does she include these figures? Did they surprise you as a reader? Why or why not?

3. As she makes her argument about the larger symbolic importance of her daughter's desire to purchase thongs, Wallis relies on several external authorities. Who are these authorities? What do they add to her argument?

4. Wallis and her daughter eventually reach a compromise. If you were the mother in this situation, what decision would you have reached? Do you feel "adult forces – parents, schools, churches – find it hard to compete with pop culture," as Wallis writes?

5. Consider the informal diction used by Wallis. How does it capture the tone of a parental conversation without losing the larger point about tween consumerism?

WRITING

1. Write a reflective essay or journal entry in which you describe a time when you differed with your parents on a purchase you wanted to make. Why did you want to make this purchase? Why did they disagree with your desire? How did you resolve the conflict?

2. Wallis writes, "Where this thing for thongs comes from is obvious: Britney, Beyoncé, *The Real World*, even PG movies like *Freaky Friday*." Do you feel that TV shows or movies can influence the behavior or dress of young people? Can you connect another specific trend to a star, movie, or television show? Write an essay in which you trace the relationship between a trend and a pop-culture phenomenon.

3. One of Wallis's sources, Ron Taffel, suggests that teens buy thongs or get tattoos to prove to their friends that they are part of the familial subculture of their peer group, to prove that they belong. Research the rituals involved with joining another group (for example, a fraternity, a sports team, even a clique at the high school you graduated from) and write an essay in which you describe the rituals. Assess the costs of participating in the rituals and the benefits that

accrue to those who become part of the group. Do you believe the benefit outweighs the cost?

4. The main reason Wallis's daughter wants to purchase thong under-wear is that all her friends have them and call traditional briefs "granny pants." Is the desire to fit in with one's peer group really a new phenomenon? Select a trend of the past (for example, rock and roll music in the 1950s, long hair for men in the late 1960s, Frank Sinatra bobby-soxers, Elvis fever, Beatlemania, or Madonna idolatry) and research it. Write an essay describing the trend, those who par-ticipated in it, and the contemporary commentary on the trend. After conducting your research, do you feel that wanting to fit in with a peer group has changed dramatically in the lives of teenagers over time?

5. Jane Hammerslough in "What's Changed?" (p. 313) observes that pur-chasing items has become a moral quandary, "Afterall, who doesn't want to do what's right for themselves, their friends, or their chil-dren." Consider, how, consciously or unconsciously, Claudia Wallis's daughter uses this moral quandary as a lever: Who doesn't want their daughter to fit in? Find several ads aimed at guilt-ridden par-ents and write an analysis of how the advertisers use this guilt to spur consumerism.

Tommy "Follow the Flock" Spoof Advertisement

FROM: *Adbusters,* adbusters.org/spoofads/fashion/tommy

CONTEXT: Adbusters is both an activist collective and a magazine dedicated to spreading the message of this group — "creative resistance" to our consumer culture through a variety of avenues, including "spoof ads." The magazine is published six times a year and has a total audience of 120,000. According to their website, "Our readers are professors and students; activists and politicians; environmentalists and media professionals; corporate watch dogs and industry insiders; kids who love our slick ad parodies and parents who worry about their children logging too many hours a day in the electronic environment." This spoof ad for Tommy Hilfiger suggests that buying Hilfiger clothes leads not to individuality but to assimilation into the social group.

Adbusters, Tommy "Follow the Flock" spoof advertisement

RESPONDING

1. This spoof ad features a flock of sheep. Why? What are the cultural associations with sheep that would lead Adbusters to select them as the featured "models"?

2. Locate an actual ad for Tommy Hilfiger clothing. How is the spoof ad similar to the real ad? What visual elements and grammar does it share? Select an ad for a product you are very familiar with – one whose "visual grammar" you could duplicate – and create a spoof ad.

3. Adbusters produces both a website and a glossy magazine. The group is not without its critics, some of whom critique the group for (in the words of one blogger) creating "a glossy, expensive, hip magazine for people to buy which encourages them not to buy glossy, expensive, hip things." Others are concerned that Adbusters itself is now a brand. Research the group and come to your own conclusion about Adbusters. As part of your research, think about accessing alternative media sources, such as blogs, to gather information and other voices.

The New York Times Magazine

8

What a Coach Can Do to a Kid
Was it abusive rage or tough love? By Michael Lewis

Sprite ReMix

By Rob Walker

FROM: *New York Times Magazine*, March 28, 2004

CONTEXT: This article was included in the March 28, 2004, *New York Times Magazine* as part of a regular column by Rob Walker, "Consumed." The column features essays on trendy products and is described by the *Times* as "part business report, part cultural anthropology." The Sunday *New York Times* is read nationwide and has a circulation of almost 1.7 million copies. The company describes the readers of the Sunday magazine as "affluent, educated, inquisitive, and acquisitive." Research on the readers of the magazine reveals them to be almost three times as likely to hold a professional or managerial position, and more than two times as likely to have household incomes over $100,000. Rob Walker is a contributing writer to the *New York Times* and *Inc.* – a business magazine targeted at small and growing companies. He has also written for *Slate, Fortune*, and the *New Republic*, among others. ("Sprite ReMix" by Rob Walker and *New York Times Magazine* cover. Copyright © 2004 by The New York Times Company. Reprinted by permission.)

ONE THING THAT CONSUMER BRANDS ARE SUPPOSED TO BE IS reliable. That's how you build loyalty. A Coke, a Pepsi, a Sprite — these are soda brands whose flavors are much as they have always been, because that's what you, the soda drinker, expect; it's what you're loyal to. Last year, a spinoff from Sprite called Sprite ReMix made its way into the market, offering drinkers a "tropical" take on Sprite's flavor. It seems to have got off to a good start, selling 55 million cases in 2003 — a very respectable debut, according to John Sicher, publisher of the *Beverage Digest* newsletter. But there will be no building of loyalty to the tropical flavor, because it's being done away with: Sprite ReMix, the name, will carry on, but it won't taste the same.

A complete flavor overhaul after just a year may sound like triage for a flat-lining product, but in fact, the short life of tropical ReMix was all part of the plan, which also calls for the new variation, Berryclear, to disappear about a year from now and be replaced by some other taste. "The strategy," said John Carroll, Sprite group director, "is to always change." And loyalty? Well, loyalty isn't what it used to be. If it were, there might never have been a ReMix.

The ReMix idea came out of Sprite's weekly talks with "teenagers and young people" about the drink and "society and popular culture," Carroll said. Sprite has for some years courted hip-hop artists and fans, seeing the music as a kind of lingua franca of youth culture. But last year, Sprite's share of the carbonated soft-drink market fell slightly, partly because of competition from newcomers like Sierra Mist. So Sprite tuned into its teen feedback crew's interest in musical remixing. Taking a familiar song and "adding a different and unique spin to it," as Carroll put it, sounded like a useful notion in a novelty-thirsty cultural moment. Sprite envisioned a soft drink that would riff off the familiar lemon-lime flavor and cultivate loyalty not to a consistent taste but to a consistent idea about taste.

Grabbing a trendy word like "remix" and slapping it onto an existing brand can backfire; so one way Sprite has tried to avoid alienating the subculture it has long cultivated has been to hire hip-hop professionals. Sprite retained Cornerstone Promotion, which was founded by two record-industry veterans to push music and entertainment properties, largely through a network of D.J.s and other taste-maker types called "the Cornerstone 1200 squad." Over time, the cofounders, Jon Cohen and Rob Stone, decided their contacts could be leveraged to promote other kinds of products.

Among other things, Cornerstone (which had worked with Sprite 5 before) distributed actual remixes — on clear vinyl, with a Sprite ReMix label — of new and classic hip-hop tracks to its D.J. contacts. They and other grass-roots "lifestyle influencers" also received early samples of the drink. The point was part buzz-making and part show of respect to the culture that invented remixing, on the theory that this trust-built network could help overcome skepticism about the product. "It's the same mind-set behind the launch of a great new fashion brand, a new pair of sneakers, a new record, a new film," Cornerstone's Cohen says. "A lot of these influencers, they live to turn people on to what's next."

The theory behind Sprite ReMix is that the widespread obsession with "what's next" causes problems not just for stalwart brands but also for new ones that open strong and fade quickly when the novelty wears off. Cornerstone's Rob Stone likens this to even the most ardent OutKast fan eventually wanting to hear the new thing after "Hey Ya!"

"With kids today, things change so quickly, it really does tie back to developing a brand that's about change," Stone said. "It almost doesn't matter if it's a berry flavor or a tropical flavor — it's the whole image of ReMix."

So here, perhaps, is a glimpse at how to balance a familiar brand name with an infinite loop of novelty. Besides, Carroll added, Sprite asked "people who are drinking a lot of ReMix" how they felt about the flavor changing, "and they liked the idea." It might seem startling — or damning — that people who are drinking a lot of a particular soda actually like the idea of its flavor being discontinued. But in this case, apparently, that answer is exactly what Sprite wanted to hear.

READING

1. Walker opens his essay by describing the foundations of brand loyalty: consumers value brands because they do not change. He writes, "A Coke, a Pepsi, a Sprite – these are soda brands . . . you're loyal to." Are you loyal to a specific soft drink brand? Why? What appeals to you in this drink?

2. Walker addresses the reader as "you" in the essay. How does this mode of address make the reader a part of the branding process? How does this relate to the topic of loyalty as brand concept and value?

3. Much of Walker's article addresses the connection between Sprite ReMix and hip-hop culture. How does he build this connection? What authorities does he include? After reading this piece, does it make sense to you to connect a soft drink to hip-hop?

4. Walker writes, "Grabbing a trendy word like 'remix' and slapping it onto an existing brand can backfire." Can you think of other examples in which a company has tried to add life to a stale brand by linking it to a trend? Were these successful? Have you ever been tempted to try a product simply because of its name? How important is a product's name in your decision to try it or buy it?

5. Sprite ReMix is being marketed as part of a specific lifestyle. Cornerstone's cofounder, Jon Cohen, compares this marketing strategy to that used in " 'the launch of a great new fashion brand, a new pair of sneakers, a new record, a new film.' " Can you think of specific examples to support Cohen's comment? What lifestyles are associated with these products? Are you receptive to lifestyle marketing?

WRITING

1. One driving force behind Sprite's decision to offer a "remixed" flavor is "the widespread obsession with 'what's next' " – in other words, the constant drive for novelty. Write a reflective essay or journal entry in which you consider this obsession. Do you share it? Can you see traces of the obsession in popular culture? How do you feel it shapes behavior?

2. Walker writes that the drink is about "cultivating loyalty not to a consistent taste but to a consistent idea about taste." What does he mean? Does "taste" have the same meaning in both instances? Write an essay in which you define "taste." How does one acquire a sense of taste? Can it be sold, as Walker suggests?

3. Sprite developed the idea for a ReMix by tuning into "its teen feedback crew's interest in musical remixing." What does the term "remix" mean in music? Why do artists remix songs? Write an essay in which you compare a remixed song to the original version. Answer the following questions in your comparison: How do the two cuts differ? Has the song been improved or weakened in the remix? Would the remix appeal to a different audience than the original? Why?

4. Conduct research to find others who have written about Sprite ReMix and its relationship to hip-hop culture. Does your research reveal that most feel Sprite is exploiting this culture or paying tribute to it? Write an essay in which you describe the various opinions on the topic and reach your own conclusion.

Urban Warfare

By Kate MacArthur and Hillary Chura

FROM: *Advertising Age*, September 4, 2000

CONTEXT: This article appeared in *Advertising Age* in September 2000. *Advertising Age* is a trade magazine that aims at advertising, marketing, and media professionals and is a part of Crain Communications, Inc. The Crain motto is "Where advertisers don't affect editorial principles . . ." and their website claims that their publication "has attracted readers who want independent and insightful analysis of their respective industries. It has helped build a readership unmatched in the industry including the most senior executives and decision-makers." The seventy-three-year-old publication claims an audience of over 235,000 and advertises itself as a "must read" for those in the industry. Kate MacArthur and Hillary Chura both write for *Advertising Age* on a variety of topics, frequently advertisement strategies about beverages. They are sometimes referred to in the field as beverage industry reporters. As you read their article, examine how they provide industry insiders with a snapshot of how brand marketing is enacted for soft drinks at the street level.

A PRE-TEEN GIRL, HER HAIR BRAIDED IN CORNROWS, STANDS in a Church's Chicken parking lot on Chicago's west side, holding a can of RC cola and staring at a storm drain. "I want to see you pour it out," Robert "Biz" Watson urges.

"What do you like to drink?" he asks, egging the girl on in front of a growing crowd as she emptied the can. "Coke," she replies sheepishly, before weaving her way through the group of 20 or so men and women waiting for a free can of the fizzy brown cola.

Just moments earlier, the parking lot had been empty. Within a quarter hour, two coolers of Coke have been emptied and Team Classic is packing up its van and moving on to a nearby housing project.

Welcome to the world of urban marketing, where guerrilla marketing groups take to the sweltering streets to engage in a block-by-block battle to win over the hearts and wallets of lower-income, mostly African American consumers.

Mr. Watson is the leader of Team Classic, an urban marketing 5 group deployed by Coca-Cola Bottling Co. of Chicago. Team Classic is far from alone; Pepsi-Cola Co. and Dr Pepper/Seven Up are also replaying summer street scenes such as the one above on a daily basis.

African Americans are seen as a crucial market for flavor-soda brands such as Coca-Cola's Sprite, PepsiCo's Mountain Dew, and Dr Pepper, which are growing faster than the carbonated soft-drink category as a whole.

Tapping into the hip-hop culture, in fact, has been a key driver in Sprite's growth, which shot up 128 percent to 671.5 million cases in 1999 from 295 million in 1990, according to *Beverage Digest*.

According to Target Market News, an urban research group, African Americans account for $1.26 billion in soft-drink sales annually, although other estimates have estimated the total as high as $8 billion or more. It's therefore clear why soft-drink marketers increasingly are turning to culture-savvy street marketers to attract their dollars — and those of Hispanics — as they focus on twelve-to-thirty-eight-year-old urban trendsetters.

Leery of Mainstream Media

Urban youth, leery of or unreachable by mainstream TV and radio, 10 view street marketing as more authentic, said Maze Jackson, director of urban marketing at Montgomery, Zukerman, Davis, Chicago, the ad agency that handles Coca-Cola Bottling Co. of Chicago's local urban initiative. "If they see something on the street, it lends credibility because it doesn't have a corporate feel," he says.

From April through October, Sunday through Thursday, the three to four person Team Classic and three to four person Team Sprite crisscross the country's third-largest city and surrounding area. They stop at parades, festivals, schools, and scheduled events, and make impromptu stops wherever there's a crowd, spending from fifteen minutes to four hours at each venue. Before the seven-month season is over, they may visit a single housing project, community center or local park thirty times.

With their red and green vinyl-wrapped vans, embellished with brand logos and murals of neighborhood landmarks, the two vans attract crowds — even before they park and start playing rearview mirror-shaking hip-hop music and dispensing icy sodas in Chicago's poorest neighborhoods. They distribute seventy cases each day — thirty of Sprite and fourty of Coke — promoting soft drinks as if they were a record label, with sampling, wild postings and image-making. The teams work ten- and twelve-hour days.

"We incorporate ourselves into the urban landscape, by being connected to the hip-hop lifestyle through music, sports, and fashion" Mr. Jackson says.

Most soft-drink companies conduct nationwide sampling programs, concentrating on low-volume areas or local markets as part of the larger effort. No. 3 marketer Dr Pepper/Seven Up, for example, teams with The Source for its Block Shaker Tour, blasting music, offering samples, and staging hip-hop performances from Philadelphia to Cleveland to San Francisco.

From spring through fall since 1997, No. 2 soft drink marketer Pep- 15 siCo has sent a fleet of six UPS-style step vans and six Ford F-150 trucks equipped with disc jockeys to black and Hispanic neighborhoods in twenty-two cities. As the DJs ask participants at schools, parks, and basketball courts to sing and rap for Mountain Dew items, workers distribute 20-ounce bottles with under-the-cap offers for another free bottle.

More Than Quenching Thirst

These programs have spurred high single-digit volume increases in black and Hispanic markets, says Stan Kaczmarek, marketing manager for the Greater Chicago Division of Pepsi-Cola General Bottlers. The effort is partially funded by local bottlers; Tracey-Locke Partnership, Dallas, and GMR Marketing, New Berlin, Wisconsin, provide marketing support. "We're getting a hand in the target market in a way that we really leave impressions with them that this is a cool product. There's more to it than quenching your thirst," a Pepsi spokesman says.

Nationally, Coca-Cola North America uses a variety of street marketing resources, including KBA, New York, for Manhattan and Los Angeles, and dRush, Union City, New Jersey, for New Jersey. A spokeswoman said additional local bottlers are looking to begin street marketing programs.

Locally, Coke's marketing efforts resemble a New Age beverage outfit rather than a 114-year-old company with billion-dollar brands.

"We want to be sure we're hopping around different neighborhoods," says Ron Nota, VP-marketing for Coca-Cola Bottling Co. of Chicago — which markets brands in Chicago, Wisconsin, Indiana, western Pennsylvania and upstate New York. "The street teams evolved like record-company promoters, going straight to consumers. That's how a lot of hip-hop artists got going."

The Chicago bottler started using sampling vehicles thirteen years 20 ago and staffed them with college students who worked part-time. The company aligned itself with the National Basketball Association just as the Chicago Bulls were building a basketball dynasty, and toured the city with a semi-trailer equipped with basketball hoops and music.

As the bottler began to refine its consumer target — inner-city residents — the idea of the NBA-oriented semi no longer made sense. "You're just not going to take this big vehicle into the neighborhoods," Mr. Nota says. So he converted one of his vans and souped it up with hip-hop imagery and musical equipment. Few workers, however, were willing to work the inner city.

Then came Mr. Jackson, a twenty-eight-year-old music promoter and son of a pastor and teacher, hired in 1997 by Montgomery, Zukerman, Davis to bring fresh ideas into the bottler's African American consumer marketing program. He devised a plan to use hip-hop marketing methods to make the Coca-Cola brands more relevant to urban consumers, including mobile promotions, wild postings musicians use to promote concerts, local rapper endorsements, and CD compilations. Record companies provide CDs, posters and other giveaways.

Strong Growth

Coca-Cola Bottling Co. of Chicago agreed to the plan, providing the ten-year-old van, cases of soda and a staff of two. Mr. Jackson would not give specifics but says that by the end of the first summer, sales grew at twice the national average. "Generally speaking, we've seen stronger sales growth in the inner city; it's outpaced the general growth rate," Mr. Nota says.

Within a year, Sprite leapfrogged over Pepsi-Cola to No. 2 in sales in Chicago's black neighborhoods, lagging only the discounted Royal Crown, Mr. Jackson says.

That's a claim Pepsi questions, a company spokesman says, not- 25 ing that brand Pepsi's share far outpaces Sprite's in Chicago.

The effort was considered successful enough, however, for Coca-Cola Bottling Co. of Chicago to step up its push. It outfitted shiny new vans with three Autotek amplifiers, four 15-inch subwoofers, four exterior-mounted speakers, and four 6 × 9 speakers powered by a Clarion stereo system. A costly effort, although neither Mr. Nota nor Mr. Jackson would discuss the budget for the marketing sweep.

With his background as an entertainment reporter and promotions coordinator for an adult urban contemporary radio station in Chicago, Mr. Jackson is a chameleon — sounding like his white visitors but shifting to street dialects when talking to potential Coke fans along the route.

"You can't just show up here and start marketing. You have to understand it, have to live it. If you don't live the lifestyle, you don't know, and it becomes very, very apparent very quickly," Mr. Jackson says. "It takes a special person to pull up to the Robert Taylor Homes," a notorious housing project on Chicago's south side.

Mr. Jackson assembled his team of top street promoters who were already working for music companies. They wear dreads, braids, red

Team Classic and green Team Sprite jerseys and loose — but not baggy — clothing. "We had to make sure they fit in the community but still fit with the Coke image," Mr. Watson says.

Team members are skilled street negotiators and navigators who 30 translate information gathered en route into marketing opportunities. Astute trendwatchers, they distribute ten-minute calling cards bearing the Coke logo in areas where many residents don't have telephones.

Logos Are Valued

Because name brands are popular among blacks, just about anything with a logo is a valued item. The team recently gave away 1-inch Coke stickers to kids who stuck them on their clothes in places populated by alligators and polo ponies in tonier neighborhoods.

"We try to look for things that are the most practical and have the most long-reaching effect in a community," Mr. Jackson says. "We look for things that will be valuable."

It wouldn't appear a marketer would have to work to give away seventy cases of soda on a hot Chicago day, but Mr. Watson says newcomers who don't show the proper deference will be shunned — or may not make it out of the projects with their persons or vans intact. He says a competing team ran into trouble last year and its vehicle was destroyed.

"You can't go in with the attitude like, 'We're trying to do you a favor' because if you do, they'll tell you, 'We don't need no charity,'" he says.

The teams must also learn to navigate gang-infested neighbor- 35 hoods. Mr. Jackson says one reason his plan has been successful in the canyons of housing projects is that his team understands the sway of the Folks, People, and other Chicago street gangs. In turn, the gangbangers — marked by their colors or the way they wear their hats — frequently help corral kids waiting for chilled soda cans. "We recognize everybody's authority," Mr. Jackson says. "Our street team has to know what will be offensive. It could be having a pants leg rolled up a certain way."

Even before the vans pulled into the west side's Rockwell Gardens projects and started playing their throbbing rap music (cleansed of profanity), kids dropped their basketballs and ran across the parking lot. As they lined up, team members reminded them to mind their manners.

Role Models

"We always make the kids say 'please' and 'thank you,'" Mr. Jackson says, while parked beside the United Center. "Some kids aren't the most well-trained."

They also urge the kids to pick up their cans, be polite, and stay in school, a tall order in a city where the dropout rate is 15.8 percent compared with 11.8 percent nationally. "We become role models by default," Mr. Jackson says.

The street teams don't open cans to parcel out the liquid — even when the crowd overwhelms supply. Instead they award cans to people who correctly answer impromptu quizzes — on sports ("What year did Michael Jordan enter the NBA?"), Chicago ("Who is your school named after?"), trivia ("What's the Sprite slogan?"), and black history.

Mr. Jackson says the bottler's urban initiative has gotten more ef- 40 fective at managing its marketing dollars, adding he has turned down $10,000 requests to put up a Coca-Cola or Sprite banner or sponsor an event because he can park outside for free. "This costs less than a billboard," he says. "When we pull up, everyone comes running to the vans anyway. How can you argue with mobile advertising?"

He says the outlay is less than TV or radio airtime and more effective than showing up at fund-raisers held by black civic groups. "Our target is twelve- to twenty-four-year-olds. How many of them go to $100-a-plate dinners?" Another reason for the teams' success is their agility, Mr. Jackson says. "It really takes a leap of faith. You have to be flexible. The problem with most corporations and marketers is that by the time something's hot or on their radar, the scene's already passed," Mr. Jackson says. He says the vans can shift from a dull location to a happening spot at the flick of an ignition.

Mr. Jackson is loyal to everything Coca-Cola. He drives a Coke-red Lincoln Navigator, says he's fired people for drinking Pepsi off the clock, and won't eat at restaurants that pour Pepsi, including PepsiCo spinoffs KFC, Pizza Hut, and Taco Bell.

"This is what feeds my family," says the father of an eight-month-old daughter and husband to his college sweetheart. "We work in teams. We walk, talk, eat, and sleep Coke and Sprite."

On the job, when breathless kids run up to the van and ask for a "pop," he tries to reinforce brand identity.

"You want a what?" Mr. Jackson chides one. 45

"A pop," the kid replies.

"A what?" he repeats.

"A POP," the child sputters, oblivious.

"You mean a Coke or a Sprite," Mr. Jackson says.

"Yeah," the kid smiles. 50

READING

1. Imagine the particular audience that would be attracted by this magazine and this article. In what context would a professional be reading this article?

2. Thinking as a writer, pay close attention to how MacArthur and Chura interweave narrative description and detail with data and marketing terminology. Pay special attention to the sources that they use to illustrate their points, both anecdotally and factually. What are a few examples of each type of source?

3. The title of this article is "Urban Warfare," and there are many other examples of military-influenced language throughout this essay. Make a list of all the military vocabulary you can find in this article. Why do the authors use this language? What do their language choices reveal about the business of marketing from the standpoint of the marketers?

4. As you read the article, think about the strategies being used to target urban youth and convince these teenagers of the importance of a soft-drink brand. Think about how these strategies are targeting this particular audience. How are these strategies similar to those identified in other pieces in this chapter?

5. This piece opens and closes with anecdotes about children engaging in interplay with marketers in order to get free sodas. Did these stories make you feel positively or negatively about the marketing tactics described in the article? Why do you think the authors included these anecdotes?

WRITING

1. This article describes the power of marketing strategies that target "twelve-to-thirty-eight-year-old-urban trendsetters" to influence their choice of soda. A Pepsi spokesperson in the article says, "We're getting a hand in the target market in a way that we really leave impressions with them that this is a cool product. There's more to it than quenching your thirst." Write a reflective essay or journal entry in which you recount the first time you decided a brand was "cool." How old were you? What was the brand? What events influenced you to feel this way?

2. Although the companies and their logos mentioned in this article are fierce competitors, they are using similar marketing strategies. Write a short expository essay in which you summarize three key

methods described in "Urban Warfare" to market soft drinks to lower income African Americans and Hispanics.

3. Examine the website for Team Jordan at www.nike.com/jumpman23/ team_jordan/index.jsp or a similar website. Identify the marketing strategies used by the site, and prepare a class presentation that compares and contrasts these strategies with those used by the companies in "Urban Warfare."

4. In this article Mr. Jackson of Coke says, "'You can't just show up here and start marketing. You have to understand it, have to live it. If you don't live the lifestyle, you don't know, and it becomes very, very apparent very quickly.'" Using specific examples from the article, write an essay that defines this lifestyle.

5. Collaborate with classmates to design an ad campaign for a common college object – a particular pen, a particular backpack, a particular snack food, for example. Use the strategies described in this article to make your campaign "street savvy." Then, present your product to the class as if you were actually marketing the product to them. In what context would you be selling this product? Design your market strategies to address the particular audience you are targeting.

The Age of Reason

By Kenneth Hein

FROM: *MediaWeek*, October 27, 2003

CONTEXT: This selection initially appeared in *MediaWeek*, a sister publication of *AdWeek* and *BrandWeek*. Together, all three cover complementary aspects of the marketing industry and are aimed at the business-sector reader. *MediaWeek* describes its target demographic as "Media decision-makers at the top 350 ad agencies in the United States, all top [media] buying services and client in-house media departments." Kenneth Hein, the author, was a senior editor at *BrandWeek* when the piece was published. In this position, he wrote often about marketing and advertising across a wide spectrum of products. Articles such as these are designed to provide industry people with an overview of developments in their field, and they assume the reader has a strong familiarity with the basic concepts of marketing, advertising, and branding. It is the content, rather than the author of the piece, that attracts the reader.

AS BRANDON, A FIFTEEN-YEAR-OLD HIGH SCHOOL SOPHO-more, leaves school, he text-messages his friend Gabe, who just bought the new Madden for Xbox, that he's heading home for a little online tournament. Then Brandon fires up his favorite MP3, "In Da Club" by 50 Cent, and he's on his way.

Brandon is a busy kid, with a lot of interests. When he's not in school, he's in front of some sort of screen: computer, videogame, cell phone. He's listening to music or researching the latest gadget he's saving his money for. He's playing videogames at a friend's house or hanging out at the mall. He's a moving target and, like most teens, he has been marketed to since the day he was born. He knows what advertising looks like. He knows what it smells like. He's seen it all before.

This is a fickle, seemingly sophisticated, fast-moving bunch, but marketers are undeterred. They can't ignore Brandon and his peers, who are expected to spend a significant $175 billion on themselves this year, a 3 percent increase over last year, according to Teenage Research Unlimited, Chicago.

And their disposable income keeps growing, says New York-based Youth Intelligence. A recent study found that 43 percent of males and 44 percent of females ages fourteen to eighteen spent more in the past six months than they did during the previous six months. A study conducted in June reports that males say they spend $71 in a week; females spend $61.50. "They are a recession-proof demographic. They're still getting allowance, mowing lawns, and babysitting," says Cynthia Engelke, manager of research and trends for Youth Intelligence.

The issue for advertisers is how to shake those dollars loose. The 5 problem often lies in the fact that marketers aren't that adept at the technologies teens use in their daily lives. SMS (short message service), photo-enabled phones, Instant Messenger, and even certain aspects of the Internet are beyond some marketers. And just how many hours have the people making the marketing decisions logged playing Grand Theft Auto?

"Teens are the most active target in the world," says Jarrod Moses, CEO and president of Alliance, an entertainment and strategic partnership, which is part of the New York-based Grey Worldwide. "If you think you'll reach them by just throwing an ad on the WB, you'll be wrong. You can't look at TV as a primary vehicle. You have to build a lifestyle campaign. The traditional way of advertising and marketing does not exist anymore."

Among teens thirteen to eighteen, 82 percent have computers, 62 percent have videogame consoles, 49 percent have cell phones, 32 percent have SMS, and 13 percent have PDAs, according to *Born to Be Wired*, a new study commissioned by Yahoo! with Carat Interactive. "Growing up with the Internet, cell phones, and other new information receptacles, teens today are multitaskers, able to easily assimilate multiple marketing communications simultaneously," says Richard Leonard, VP of New York's Zandl Group.

Realizing this, Coca-Cola, a company whose attempts to attract younger consumers have sometimes yielded less-than-stellar results, has tweaked its new fall under-the-cap promotion. The Cokemusic .com campaign has teens looking under the caps of specially marked bottles for a secret code. That code can then be keyed into the Web site for points (called Decibels) redeemable for prizes. For the first time, consumers can send a text message via SMS-enabled cell phones to Coke (653 is the short code) to have the points automatically entered into their accounts.

"The barrier we noticed, despite the success of our fall and summer programs, was that someone has to hang onto the cap and wait until they can get to a computer and enter the code," says Doug Rollins, associate brand manager for Coca-Cola. "Cell phones are an important accessory to teens. It's important to innovate against this [technology]. . . . It will be a learning experience [for us]."

Coke has the right idea, says Shawn Parr, CEO of Bulldog Drum- 10 mond, San Diego. "Technology is like a knife and a fork to them. They adapt technology into their everyday routines. They are not enamored with it like the generation before."

The companies that understand this are better able to put together seamless campaigns aimed at teens. For example, New Line Cinema will be the first to run fifteen- and thirty-second streaming-video ads on AOL Instant Messenger for its upcoming movie *Elf*, starring *Saturday Night Live* alumnus Will Ferrell. On November 7, regular users will see the ads running in the space atop the buddy list. New Line found earlier success running static banner ads for its hit horror movie *Texas Chainsaw Massacre*.

It almost goes without saying that the Internet is a vital part of the teen marketing mix. Music television network Fuse, renamed last May from MuchMusic, created the Interactive Music Exchange (interactivemusicexchange.com) as one way to get teens intimately involved with the artists that appear in its music videos. The online program has teens buy and sell hot artists on a virtual stock exchange to win prizes. "It's a program that young adults can feel ownership over," says Mary Corigliano, vp of marketing for the channel. "Teens don't have a credit card for an Xbox. If they are good at IMX, they can win one. Teens want free stuff."

Then again, music is an easy draw. One thing teens today share with teens of the past is the fact that they are influenced by their favorite artists. But forget about songs that talk about the hot boy or girl at the next locker. Hip-hop is a veritable laundry list of hot products. There have been 1,050 references of about sixty-six different brands in songs ranked in the Top 20 through the beginning of October, according to San Francisco-based brand consultancy LucJam. Burger King had sixteen mentions while Payless ShoeSource had twenty-five and Nike had twenty-one.

"Hip-hop is incredibly materialistic, making it a good place to talk about materialistic things," says Lucian James, president of LucJam. "It's about breaking news, culture, and the here and now. [And] it serves the eternal purpose of annoying parents."

Jameel Spencer, president of Blue Flame Marketing and Advertising and chief marketing officer of Bad Boy Worldwide, New York, says, "Hip-hop represents everything kids are into. It's cutting-edge, against the grain. It comes from [the] underclass and is highly aspirational. It can catapult a brand from obscurity to the mainstream in a minute's time, but it can make [it] go away just as quickly."

Tying in with hip-hop is a tricky business, for both brands and 15 artists. Artists aren't likely to rhyme about brands for cash — they would be viewed as sellouts. And old-school companies are fearful of forming partnerships due to sometimes-explicit lyrics. Pepsi, for example, ran into some trouble earlier this year: It had to pull ads featuring Ludacris because of objections to his profane lyrics.

A less controversial venue that is receiving more attention is video games. In-game advertising is not a new phenomenon, but it is becoming more accepted among advertisers. New Electronic Arts title SSX 3 has in-game product placement for the new 7 UP soda, dnL; *Need For Speed Underground* features McDonald's; and *James Bond 007 Everything or Nothing* features Porsche and Aston Martin.

"It's more about product interaction than product advertising," says Chip Lange, VP, marketing for Redwood City, California-based EA. "You have to figure out a way to permeate the teen lifestyle without being gratuitous." Lange says that as gaming moves online, ads will be able to be refreshed and altered within the games.

Buddying up with hot videogame properties in the real world has its advantages, as well. Microsoft Xbox and Mountain Dew combined to create "The Dew Den" at the Mall of America this past summer. The lounge allowed gamers to try the latest Xbox games and compete in Xbox Live tournaments for a chance to play on-air against a TV host from the cable channel G4, which is dedicated to videogames. The Dew Den was integrated into a national show that ran on the cable channel. "Like any good pop icon, you have to keep reinventing the brand," says Angelique Bellmer, brand director for Mountain Dew. "Gaming as a lifestyle is so relevant. It is about the same things Dew is: pushing the limits, being over-the-top, irreverence."

Bellmer says the brand, which is a teen staple, never takes a step without talking to its target market first. "They own it. They define it. They tell us what's cool. I feel like I've talked to every other teenager in America because of the amount of research we do," she says. Mountain Dew, which has the full backing of parent PespiCo's marketing heft, spent more than $62 million on media in 2002, according to TNS Media Intelligence/CMR.

Out of necessity, smaller brands have taken a less obvious and far 20 less expensive tack. Yoo-hoo, part of the Snapple Beverage Group, a division of Cadbury Schweppes, London, has a very small marketing budget relative to its competitors. Still, Yoo-hoo has managed to win teens over by hitting the alternative music festival Warped Tour since 1998 with free samples and off-the-wall contests. For example, teens can get free stuff if they chug the chocolate drink out of a boot. This is called a "shoe-hoo." Last summer, a radio contestant dove into a Porta-Potty filled with its new Double Fudge flavor in order to win free concert tickets.

"A little brand like Yoo-hoo has to make a big noise," says Kristin Krumpe, director of marketing for Yoo-hoo. "They have to get people scratching their heads like, 'I can't believe they're doing that.' Smaller brands are freer to take more risks. They are not as high-profile among stockholders or anyone else."

Adds John Bello, who built up SoBe teas and juices to such a height that Pepsi bought the company: "You need to be where they are. You need to be relevant. You need to be authentic. You need to blend. You need to give out swag and brand the event beyond the product. That's what sticks. Slick, polished, expensive does not work."

There are still a good number of brands trying to reach teens through their TV sets. This is not all for naught, says the Zandl Group's Leonard. "Good advertising is very effective in reaching teens," he says. "It alerts them to new products and helps keep mature brands relevant and top-of-mind. Two out of three teens on our consumer panel have a favorite commercial, so they are definitely paying attention. With the exception of the small, subversive, indie crowd, most teens are not anti-advertising. They are just anti-bad advertising — especially ads that appear to pander to them or try too hard to be cool."

Attempting to read the tea leaves about teen trends to see what will be cool in the coming months "is what leads marketers to the biggest mistakes," says Michael Wood, president of Teenage Research Unlimited. "They automatically assume they have to somehow associate themselves with cool. Then it ends up backfiring on them."

Whether it's Coca-Cola's recent "Life Tastes Good" effort, which 25 showed a handful of dorky surfers and kids leaving a concert on a miraculously empty train or any of a number of McDonald's' carousel of old creative, teens know what rings false. "Until recently, Coke tried everything so blatantly to reach this target audience," says Parr. "And McDonald's seemed to change every six to nine months. They lack a degree of consistency and authenticity. A lot of companies have spent millions to create an image of who they are. To then try and speak to teens in a different way — it doesn't work. Just be you. If you're McDonald's or Coke, just be McDonald's or Coke."

In fact, says the *Born to Be Wired* study, the basic tenets of marketing still apply. For instance, rather than worry about how to get mentioned in the next Jay-Z song, marketers should make certain they put a quality product on the market. According to the study, 86 percent of respondents said the most important aspect of a brand is that it's worth the money spent. And 83 percent said a company needs to make high-quality products. "There are brands you grow old with," says Blue Flame's Spencer. "People get on and off things quickly, but the brands that stay true to their core essence will stay around. Look at Timberland. They're good for the cold and the snow, and they maintain a fashion sensibility. They don't have to change their brand message.

"Once you go and change it and try and chase teens, you're trying to hit a moving target," continues Spencer. "No one does well with that."

Dead last on *Born to Be Wired*'s list of what influences a purchase: whether a product is endorsed by a celebrity they like. Only 7 percent said it's important. Case in point: Does anyone remember the "Life Tastes Good" ad starring the Wallflowers' Jakob Dylan? Neither do teens.

READING

1. Hein opens this article with a brief portrait of Brandon, the typical teen consumer. In contrast, the remainder of the piece is heavily data-driven. Why open with this short narrative? How does it help him grab the reader?

2. Hein observes about Brandon, "He's seen it all before." What has he seen before? How might this observation relate to the title of the article?

3. Hein interweaves numerous sources throughout this article and relies to a great extent on their observations and research to shore up his own points about teen consumers. Do you accept them as authorities on the topic? Why or why not?

4. Hein makes two observations that seem to conflict. At one point, he says, "One thing teens today share with teens of the past is the fact that they are influenced by their favorite artists." But, later in the article, he notes, "Dead last on *Born to Be Wired*'s list of what influences a purchase: whether a product is endorsed by a celebrity they like." How can both be valid positions?

5. Hein offers examples of effective and ineffective teen marketing campaigns. What distinguishes the two? Do you agree?

WRITING

1. In describing Brandon, Hein declares that "like most teens, he has been marketed to since the day he was born." Write a reflective essay or journal piece in which you describe your own childhood experiences with marketing. What is the first product you can remember begging your parents to buy you? Why did you want it? When was the first time you can remember realizing you were being "marketed to"?

2. Describing the relationship of young consumers to technology, Shawn Parr says, "'Technology is like a knife and a fork, to them.'" Write an essay in which you describe your interactions with technology over a single, twenty-four-hour period. Do your day's activities support Parr's comment?

3. Hein refers to hip-hop as a "veritable laundry list of hot products" and goes on to identify product placement in video games and on specialized cable networks. Select a song, game, or show and catalog all the brand-name products you can spot. Write an essay describing your experience. How do you feel about product placement

as a form of implicit advertisement? Has this exercise in brand-spotting made you more or less likely to purchase the products you have seen? Be certain to attach the product list to your essay.

4. One of Hein's sources is John Bello, whose success with SoBe teas is lauded by the author. Bello explains the secrets of marketing to teens: "'You need to be where they are. You need to be relevant. You need to be authentic.'" Later in the article, Shawn Parr also refers to the importance of a brand's "'authenticity.'" What does the word "authentic" mean in this context? How does this meaning relate to the standard denotative meaning of the term? Write an essay that defines "authentic" as Bello and Parr are using the word — as a marketable concept. Be certain to provide examples of "authenticity" as it is used to sell products in some high-profile ads.

5. Hein's fictitious "Brandon" could very well be the "you" that Kalle Lasn writes about in "The Cult You're In" (p. 376). However, the two authors have very different attitudes about the young consumer. Hein sees him as streetwise and savvy and supports his view with marketing data and statistics. Lasn sees him as co-opted and oblivious and offers a narrative dystopia. Write an essay in which you contrast the two portraits of the youth market. Which seems closer to your own experience?

The Buzz on Buzz

By Renee Dye

FROM: *Harvard Business Review*, November/ December 2000

CONTEXT: This article initially appeared in the *Harvard Business Review*. The magazine's website describes its readers as "achievers who embrace leadership in their jobs and in their lives." The magazine's media kit provides a clear portrait of its readership: most likely a middle-aged male who completed some graduate study, serves on a board of directors, has a median income of over $145,000, and has a net worth of over $1 million. The author, Renee Dye, is a strategic consultant with the firm McKinsey & Company. According to its website, "Since 1926, McKinsey has helped business leaders address their greatest challenges, from reorganizing for long-term growth to improving business performance and maximizing revenue." As a strategist, Dye provides a busy professional with an overview of a growing marketing avenue, "word-of-mouth promotion," using real-world examples to show how and why it works. After its initial publication in the *HBR*, the article was repackaged and sold as a short monograph, complete with talking points and a bibliography, suggesting that Dye's work hit its target audience fairly effectively. As you read this piece, think about how it addresses the practical needs of a corporate executive hunting for a new idea to increase his business.

WORD-OF-MOUTH PROMOTION HAS BECOME AN INCREASingly potent force, capable of catapulting products from obscurity into runaway commercial successes. But to harness the considerable power of buzz, companies must reject five common myths.

Buzz Is the Stuff of Marketing Legends

Dark and witty Harry Potter, the traffic stopping retro Beetle, the addictive Pokemon, cuddly Beanie Babies, the hair-raising *Blair Witch Project* — all are recent examples of blockbuster commercial successes driven by customer hype. For some reason, people like to share their experiences with one another — the restaurant where they ate lunch, the movie they saw over the weekend, the computer they just bought — and when those experiences are favorable, the recommendations can snowball, resulting in runaway success. But ask marketing managers about buzz, and many will simply shrug their shoulders. It's just serendipity, they say, or sheer luck.

My research suggests otherwise. Investigating the marketing practices at more than fifty companies, my colleagues and I at McKinsey have found that buzz — a phenomenon we've dubbed "explosive self-generating demand" — is hardly a random force of nature. Instead, it evolves according to some basic principles. My research shows that companies can predict the spread of buzz by analyzing how different groups of customers interact and influence one another.

Many executives have little idea how to orchestrate a marketing campaign that exploits the full power of customer word of mouth. Instead, they remain enslaved to five common misconceptions about the phenomenon. Before companies can reap the total benefits of buzz, they must understand the principles of how it works, and doing so requires a close examination of those five myths.

Myth 1: Only outrageous or edgy products are buzz-worthy.
Everyone can point to a buzz-driven consumer craze that was due in 5
part to the sheer inanity or fringe quality of a product — think of pet rocks or the movie *The Matrix*. Yet according to our analysis, a surprisingly large portion of the U.S. economy — a shade above two-thirds — has been at least partially affected by buzz. (See "What Buzz Affects" for an industry-by-industry breakdown.) Obviously, buzz greatly affects the entertainment and fashion industries, but it also influences agriculture, electronics, and finance. Indeed, few industries are immune these days, partially because of technological innovations like the Internet that enable customers to spread buzz quickly. Consider the pharmaceutical industry, which has recently witnessed a dramatic increase in the power of buzz. In the past, pharmaceutical companies marketed new prescription drugs primarily through a direct sales force that distributed educational materials and free samples to physicians. Consumers were rarely aware of new therapies except as prescribed by their doctors.

Today, thanks to extensive advertising and the Internet, consumers have access to health-care information on a scale undreamed of just ten years ago. Indeed, a revolution is under way, transforming people from passive to active participants. In choosing their treatments, such active consumers can — and do — generate and spread buzz. Case in point: Viagra, one of the most talked-about prescription drugs ever, even among those who don't need it.

Shrewd pharmaceutical companies are now taking a two-pronged approach to jump-start buzz among both doctors and consumers. For example, when Merck launched Fosamax, a therapy for osteoporosis, the company carefully chose scientists and physicians with high standing to conduct the clinical trials and to promote the new treatment. In addition, Merck increased the visibility of the new treatment by sponsoring symposia at international meetings. On the consumer side, the company launched a major marketing campaign in women's magazines to inform readers of the risks of osteoporosis and educate them about the value of screening and preventive treatment. Before long, the debilitating bone condition became a common topic of discussion among women and between women and their doctors. As a result of these efforts, Merck was able to generate significant buzz for a previously unnotable subject.

Medicine is one thing, but sometimes even the most ordinary products can benefit from buzz. Remember Hush Puppies? When the company discovered that hip New York City kids were snapping up vintage pairs of its shoes at secondhand stores, it rushed into action. It began making its shoes in shades like Day-Glo orange, red, green, and purple. Next, it sent free samples to celebrities, and not long after, David Bowie and Susan Sarandon were spotted wearing them. Then the company tightly controlled distribution, limiting the shoes to a handful of fashionable outlets. Soon high-end retailers like Saks, Bergdorf Goodman, and Barneys were begging for them. In just three years, from 1994 to 1996, Hush Puppies saw its annual sales of pups in North America sky-rocket from fewer than 100,000 pairs to an estimated 1.5 million.

Of course, not every product is a good candidate for buzz marketing. How, then, can managers assess buzz-worthiness? Two criteria make it possible.

First, products ripe for buzz are unique in some respect, be it in 10 look, functionality, ease of use, efficacy, or price. For Chrysler's PT Cruiser, the degree of difference from the competition clearly lies in its retro, gangster-era look. In the case of collapsible scooters, the key buzz-worthy factors are functionality and ease of use: what other product allows people to dash from place to place on a lightweight, folding device?

Second, products with great buzz potential are usually highly visible. For many products, that condition is a no-brainer. The popularity of fashion accessories, like Gucci's baguette bags, tends to spread like wildfire because they are easily seen by others. Every time someone in a meeting pulls out a Palm device to jot a note, the company gets another endorsement of its popular PDA.

But insightful companies have discovered that products can be made visible. One way is to create forums, such as Internet chat groups, where customers can exchange information about a product — such as a new medical treatment — that might otherwise have remained hidden. Often, creative approaches are needed to facilitate the discussion. Pfizer, the maker of Viagra, faced an uphill battle when trying to generate buzz for its breakthrough drug, because impotence was a taboo subject. But by popularizing the medical terms "erectile dysfunction" and "ED," the company transformed the undiscussable into fodder for the bedroom and backyard alike.

Myth 2: Buzz just happens.
Many people believe that buzz is largely serendipitous. Not so. We have found that buzz is increasingly the result of carefully managed marketing programs. Savvy managers have a portfolio of marketing tactics from which they assemble just the right sequence to generate and sustain buzz. Here are some of the most powerful tactics we've identified from our research.

Seed the vanguard.   All customers are not created equal. Some — the vanguard — have a disproportionate ability to shape public opinion. Increasingly, managers are recognizing that getting their products into the hands of the vanguard can pay off exponentially in how the mass market ultimately responds. Abercrombie & Fitch, for example, recruits college students from popular fraternities and sororities to work in its stores, knowing that they will then probably wear A&F clothes more frequently and, in doing so, implicitly endorse the fashions.

Ration supply.   People often want what they — or others — can't 15 have. The luxury-goods industry has long exploited this tendency, and today other companies are increasingly using it to their advantage.

Walt Disney has excelled at maintaining high demand and buzz for its animated films by carefully controlling their availability on video. The "Disappearing Classics" campaign of 1991 announced that the company would retire certain videos, allowing consumers just a limited time to purchase them. Films subsequently brought out of retirement were being re-released in theaters. Previous experience with this campaign led Disney to project in 1995 that video sales for some films could surge by as much as 400 percent.

Volkswagen took this tactic one step further in marketing its retro Beetle. A year after the car's introduction, the company offered Internet-only sales in two new colors, "vapor blue" and "reflex yellow," with exactly 2,000 cars available in each. This attention-grabbing maneuver triggered its own share of buzz and ignited an additional round of publicity for the already popular cars. Within two weeks, consumers had quickly snapped up half of the limited edition models.

Exploit icons to beget buzz.   Another tactic that companies use to trigger buzz is celebrity endorsement. Thanks to ad campaigns featuring icons like Michael Jordan and Tiger Woods, Nike has built its brand into a marketing juggernaut. Advertising, however, is merely one way to leverage the power of icons.

Tickle Me Elmo became the best-selling toy of the 1996 Christmas season in the United States after Rosie O'Donnell played with the doll on her daytime talk show. A public relations agency had cleverly engineered this runaway success by sending an Elmo to O'Donnell's son. Literary publicists eagerly lobby staffers at Harpo, knowing that many books Oprah Winfrey selects for her book club pole-vault onto the *New York Times* best-seller list.

Movies and television shows can also serve as powerful endorsers. During the funeral scene in the hit film *Four Weddings and a Funeral*, one of the characters reads "Stop All the Clocks," a poem by W. H. Auden. After the film opened, Vintage Books adroitly published a slender volume containing the poem and other Auden poems, which sold 50,000 copies in three years. (Most poetry books sell around 500 copies.) It's no wonder companies have been aggressively seeking, and sometimes paying huge sums for, key product placements. Luck had little to do with the appearance of a BMW Z3 Roadster in the James Bond flick *GoldenEye* or the prominence of an Apple laptop computer in *Mission Impossible*.

Tap the power of lists. Lists are potent tools for creating buzz because they're effective road signs for information besieged consumers who don't know where to focus their attention. Perhaps no one knows this better than movie executives, who hold their collective breath every Monday morning, waiting for the weekend box-office rankings that can either make or break new releases. Even in the world of ivory towers, the annual lists of colleges and universities by *U.S. News & World Report* can dramatically increase or decrease the number of applications to a given institution.

Some companies have begun to leverage lists in creative ways. In 1998, Modern Library, an imprint of Random House, surveyed its editorial board to compile a list of the top 100 novels of the twentieth century. The selections, which the company publicized on its website, became the focus of much animated discussion, in part because of a spat between the editorial board and the publisher over the process used to compile the list. Within five months, more than 1,000 articles and editorials had appeared about the controversial list. Even more remarkable, though, was that within weeks of the list's publication, four of the top five novels made their way on to Amazon.com's weekly list of paperback best-sellers, with James Joyce's *Ulysses* having pride of place at number two! Of course, Modern Library wasn't the only imprint to benefit from this buzz — any publisher with editions of the selected books experienced an upsurge in sales. But Modern Library

20

received a tremendous amount of free publicity, and traffic at its website surged by a jaw-dropping 7,000 percent.

Nurture the grass roots.   The final buzz tactic focuses on establishing and extending product loyalty throughout a community. At first, this tactic might sound similar to seeding the vanguard, but there is a critical difference. Members of the vanguard typically delight in being the first to know about a product; they revel in this exclusivity. When other people begin to adopt the product, the vanguard often moves on to the next big, exclusive thing. In contrast, a grassroots strategy relies on early adopters who try to convert other people — to turn them into users, too. With many new drug therapies, for instance, early patients who've been successfully treated wish for others to benefit. Users of network services like America Online try to recruit others because the usefulness of the service grows with the number of members. Or perhaps consumers identify so deeply with a brand that they want others to become a part of that community.

A powerful example of buzz nurtured at the grassroots level is the marketing campaign that Harley-Davidson used in its remarkable turnaround. In 1981, the motorcycle manufacturer was nearly bankrupt as Japanese competitors with superior quality and lower costs had demolished what was once a thriving U.S. industry. But the thirteen executives who bought Harley from parent AMF believed they could save the company by tapping into the fervent loyalty of its customers; for them, Harley-Davidson was not just a motorcycle but an identity. In 1983, the company established and sponsored the Harley Owners Group, or HOG, with numerous regional chapters around the United States. Strapped for cash, Harley used inexpensive buzz marketing techniques — newsletters and posters — to publicize HOG via the dealer network. More important, though, Harley relied on extensive word of mouth generated within these communities. HOG quickly grew in strength, sponsoring hundreds of rallies that drew Harley owners from across the country. Today, more than 350,000 owners belong to nearly 1,000 chapters around the world.

All of these tactics won't be relevant for every product. Depending on a product's characteristics, managers must decide which tactics to deploy and in what order. In general, seeding the vanguard and rationing the supply are used first to foster a sense of exclusivity, while using icons might come later in a mass-marketing campaign.

Consider the sequencing that Ty shrewdly used to touch off a national mania for its rather unremarkable bean-stuffed toys. Initially, Beanie Babies were available only through specialty toy retailers (supply rationing) that catered to upper-income families. Children from those households (the vanguard) took the first Beanie Babies to school, generating demand among other kids. Then Ty broadened the distribution by teaming with McDonald's (an icon) to give the toys away in Happy Meals. The craze intensified as the media ran stories of families buying dozens of meals and throwing out the food because they just wanted the toys. Meanwhile, Ty regularly retired some models from production (supply rationing), resulting in their selling for several thousand dollars on secondary markets. Eventually, adults, many without children, became fanatic purchasers, accumulating hundreds in their collections.

Myth 3: The best buzz-starters are your best customers.
In order to spark buzz, marketing managers often turn first to the opinion leaders from within the community that will eventually become the bulk of the market. But that can be a crucial mistake. The best vanguard for a product may not be immediately obvious. It may even come from a counterculture.

Take Tommy Hilfiger. The designer focused on young, urban African-Americans to imprint his brand with a street hipness. It worked. The popularity of Hilfiger clothes quickly spread from the inner city to the suburbs, reaching a broad audience of all ethnicities. Similarly, when the marketers of Absolut vodka wanted to spark buzz for its then lower-end no-name alcohol, they did not target married middle-aged males in the suburbs. Instead, they initially focused on the gay community in San Francisco. Buzz rapidly diffused outward and, combined with a funky, award-winning marketing campaign, helped catapult Absolut to the enviable position of topselling vodka in the United States.

Finding such unexpected vanguards is nearly impossible with marketing data that concentrate solely on what individual consumers think about a product — and not on how consumers influence one another about the product. Marketing researchers are thus developing new methodologies to account for customer-to-customer interactions. An obvious approach is to track the path of buzz for a similar product that was successful and then seek to replicate that pattern. More sophisticated techniques attempt to model how consumers interact with one another and how highly they value others as sources of information or as behavioral models. (For details of such an approach, see "Finding the Buzz-Starters.")

Myth 4: To profit from buzz, you must act first and fast.
Trendsetting companies may generate buzz, but copycat firms can 30 also reap tremendous benefits. The cosmetics industry provides insight into how trendsetting companies and their followers can create value for themselves.

Consider funky-colored nail polish, a buzz-created product if ever there was one. The rise to glory began when Dinah Mohajer, then a college student, wanted to paint her toenails to match her strappy blue sandals. So, she did what any budding entrepreneur would: she mixed some polish herself.

Mohajer's homemade concoction created such a stir on the University of Southern California campus that she and her boyfriend soon found themselves in business, mixing batches in her bathtub and wearing gas masks for protection from the noxious fumes. To distribute their product, dubbed Hard Candy, they selected exclusive clothing boutique Fred Segal in upscale Beverly Hills as their first outlet and then expanded to other trendy local salons. During this time, demand was solely driven by word-of-mouth hype among chic urban clientele (that is, the vanguard).

Hard Candy was gradually introduced into additional exclusive salons and stores, eventually becoming available in high-end chains such as Nordstrom and Neiman Marcus. Publicity for the product surged as the paparazzi photographed Hollywood icons like Quentin Tarantino and Drew Barrymore wearing Hard Candy. The buzz then reached near-excruciating decibel levels, when actress Alicia Silverstone gushed about her sky-blue polish to David Letterman on national television. In three years, Hard Candy sales hit an estimated $30 million.

The major cosmetics companies, such as Estée Lauder and Lancome, didn't just sit there. Many moved quickly to launch their own lines of funky-colored nail polish. But only after the craze became firmly entrenched did Revlon, the cosmetics mass-marketer, launch its StreetWear line.

Did Revlon miss the boat? In a word, no. Companies with established midmarket or downstream brands and large, loyal customer bases often have very good reasons for waiting until a trend is firmly established before building it into their product portfolios. Without having to invest time or money in product development, a copycat company can enjoy the rewards of buzz as a late participant — provided it knows when to enter the market and can do so quickly before the trend has faded. In its early days, the Limited could copy a fashion design from the runway, manufacture knockoff products, and distribute them to company stores in just thirty days.

Yet most companies don't have the right systems or processes in place to successfully follow trendsetters. By the time buzz works its way up a traditional marketing department, the trend may already be dead. To be successful, fast followers and mass-market adapters must develop an alternative set of practices for tuning in to buzz. *Teen People*, for instance, keeps a group of 4,000 "trend spotters" on call. The magazine encourages them to submit story ideas and respond to published articles. In addition, it invites them monthly into regional offices to discuss what's cool and, equally important, what's not.

35

Manufacturing and retailing companies commonly employ "cool hunters," individuals who specialize in knowing what's in vogue. The cool hunter for urban retailer Wet Seals routinely attends runway shows, scouts competitors' stores, reads popular magazines, watches hit television shows, listens to popular music, and interviews kids on the street in different international metropolises.

Another provocative and powerful buzz-spotting medium is the Internet. Many companies have discovered that by setting up chat sites like Gurl.com, they can establish an efficient and economical main line into what consumers are thinking. These websites can function as virtual focus groups operating in near continual session, enabling companies to track consumer buzz as it develops. With such methods, copycat firms can strike while the market is just heating up, not while a trend has already begun to cool.

Myth 5: The media and advertising are needed to create buzz.
While the media and advertising can help fan the flames of buzz, involving them too early can undermine buzz. Indeed, the vanguard will often reject a heavily promoted product that it otherwise would have embraced merely because of overexposure.

Buzz-hungry companies need to refocus their marketing lenses 40 on consumer-to-consumer communications be they verbal, visual, or digital. That's where buzz is born. In other words, to generate buzz, the objective is not to besiege consumers with advertising but to somehow encourage them to talk about a product or to use that product so that it's noticed by other people.

The founders of Hotmail, the free e-mail service, keenly understood this principle. The start-up company made its customers its most potent marketing force by appending a soft-sell line — "Get your free e-mail at Hotmail" — to every outgoing e-mail from one of its users. In its first eighteen months of business, Hotmail signed up 12 million people. (In comparison, AOL took more than six years to amass that many customers.) Yet the company spent a meager $500,000 on advertising during that period. By contrast, Hotmail advertisements with "Free e-mail" buttons on highly trafficked websites produced dwarfish response rates, suggesting that the company's remarkable success owed more to the marketing strategy of active messaging than to the free nature of the service itself. Today Hotmail, now owned by Microsoft, claims to have more than 80 million registered users.

But such programs, dubbed viral marketing, can also be dangerous, because consumers may feel that they are being exploited or are themselves taking advantage of others. Some companies have offered cash to people to provide the names and e-mail addresses of their friends and relatives, who would then have the same opportunity for financial gain in enlisting others. When such techniques smack of pyramid schemes, they are more likely to offend rather than entice.

The Future of Buzz

Globalization continues to expand the universe of trends and trend-setters and to make buzz ever more exportable across borders. Consider that the three hottest children's crazes in the United States today — Pokemon, Harry Potter, and Teletubbies — are imports from Japan or the United Kingdom. Advancements in mobile telephony, PC networking, and communications bandwidth will facilitate the creation of forums where buzz can flourish unconstrained by geography. And the continued proliferation of brands will encourage people's close associations with them, thus furthering buzz potential. Finally, rising disposable incomes worldwide will enable a wider participation in hype phenomena.

All these factors point toward a world in which buzz will dominate the shaping of markets. In fact, the phenomenon of buzz is already becoming an industry unto itself. Dot-com companies like Epinions.com have built their entire businesses and websites around customer word of mouth: consumers rate and review products, and the results are tallied for prospective shoppers to view. Such forums, as well as the past successes of buzz marketing, are themselves generating buzz about the growing power of customer hype. Indeed, companies that are unable to control buzz may soon find that the phenomenon is increasingly controlling them.

READING

1. Dye opens her article with a clear message to the reader about buzz marketing. What is this message? What does she promise to do with her piece?

2. Throughout the article, Dye uses active and vivid diction. For example, she chooses verbs like "orchestrate," "exploit," "enslaved." She also can be quite informal, as when she refers to Hush Puppies shoes as "pups." What is the effect of her language choice? Is it the type of writing you would expect to find in the *Harvard Business Review*? How might her style of writing relate to her topic: buzz marketing?

3. Dye's article follows a fairly straightforward classification/division mode of writing. She takes a broad topic and divides it into smaller subtopics or categories to make it more easily digestible and understandable to the reader. How does she divide up her broad topic? How does she use examples to help define her topic and the divisions?

4. As someone writing a piece for *Harvard Business Review*, Dye has a pro-business bias. Locate some examples of this bias in the text. Think about how an article on this same topic might be different if it were written by a consumer advocate or a financially strapped parent.

5. Dye cites the Internet as the driver of much buzz marketing, and many studies since her piece was written suggest that teens spend much more time surfing the Web than watching television or reading magazines – both of which have been the traditional mode of marketing to young people. How much does the Internet, in any of its forms, influence the purchases you make? Does your experience support Dye's contention?

WRITING

1. As described by Dye, the phenomenon, buzz marketing, relies heavily on the ability of a small group of consumers to influence many others. Write a reflective essay or journal entry in which you define yourself: are you an influencer or are you influenced? A trend-setter or a trend-follower?

2. Dye is writing from a clear, pro-business perspective for a corporate audience. She is lauding the practice of buzz marketing as an incredibly effective way of exploiting a consumer base and encouraging her readers to use the strategy to increase their sales. Assume

the persona of a sales executive and draft a memo to your staff that summarizes Dye's main points and charts a plan of action for integrating buzz marketing into their activities.

3. Dye's article provides five myths about buzz marketing, supporting her contention with many examples. Her article was written in 2000. Write an updated version in which you identify current examples that she might use if she were to write her piece today. Do her observations still hold true?

4. Dye cites Abercrombie and Fitch as a company that truly "[recognizes] that getting their products into the hands of the vanguard can pay off exponentially." As Benoit Denizet-Lewis writes about A&F in his piece "The Man behind Abercrombie & Fitch" (p. 364), this notion of the vanguard seems to play out in all aspects of the company. Write an essay that uses Dye's dictums for generating buzz to analyze the actions of A&F CEO Mike Jeffries, as described in Denizet-Lewis's piece.

The Man behind Abercrombie & Fitch
By Benoit Denizet-Lewis

FROM: Salon.com, www.salon.com/
mwt/feature/2006/01/24/jeffries/
index_np.html

CONTEXT: This essay initially appeared in the online magazine *Salon.com*, and its subject and style was intriguing enough to merit mention of the article in high-profile blogs like the Defamer and Gawker. Founded in 1995, *Salon* is one of the very few online journals to survive the dot-com bust, and it has gained a reputation for of-the-minute journalism. Google calls it "The web's best source and online magazine for smart, timely, lively, original reporting and commentary on news, politics, culture, and life." Its reader-ship includes 2.5–3.5 million distinct visitors, of whom 60 percent are male and 40 percent female. *Salon*'s readership is well educated: 74 percent have earned a college degree. The author of this piece, Benoit Denizet-Lewis, has been a contributing writer at the *New York Times Magazine* and has written pieces for youth-marketed magazines such as *Spin*, *Out*, *Jane*, and others. While writing this profile, he was working on a book on teen life and teen suicide in America. As you read the article, examine his attitude and interest in the influence of marketing strategies, particularly those directed at teens. ("The Man behind Abercrombie & Fitch" by Benoit Denizet-Lewis: This article first appeared in Salon.com at www.salon.com. An online version remains in the *Salon* archives. Reprinted with permission.)

MIKE JEFFRIES, THE SIXTY-ONE-YEAR-OLD CEO OF ABER-crombie & Fitch, says "dude" a lot. He'll say, "What a cool idea, dude," or, when the jeans on a store's mannequin are too thin in the calves, "Let's make this dude look more like a dude," or, when I ask him why he dyes his hair blond, "Dude, I'm not an old fart who wears his jeans up at his shoulders."

This fall, on my second day at Abercrombie & Fitch's 300-acre headquarters in the Ohio woods, Jeffries — sporting torn Abercrombie jeans, a blue Abercrombie muscle polo, and Abercrombie flip-flops — stood behind me in the cafeteria line and said, "You're looking really A&F today, dude." (An enormous steel-clad barn with laminated wood accents, the cafeteria feels like an Olympic Village dining hall in the Swiss Alps.) I didn't have the heart to tell Jeffries that I was actually wearing American Eagle jeans. To Jeffries, the "A&F guy" is the best of what America has to offer: He's cool, he's beautiful, he's funny, he's masculine, he's optimistic, and he's certainly not "cynical" or "moody," two traits he finds wholly unattractive.

Jeffries' endorsement of my look was a step up from the previous day, when I made the mistake of dressing my age (thirty). I arrived in a dress shirt, khakis, and dress shoes, prompting A&F spokesman Tom Lennox — at thirty-nine, he's a virtual senior citizen among Jeffries' youthful workforce — to look concerned and offer me a pair of flip-flops. Just about everyone at A&F headquarters wears flip-flops, torn Abercrombie jeans, and either a polo shirt or a sweater from Abercrombie or Hollister, Jeffries' brand aimed at high school students.

When I first arrived on "campus," as many A&F employees refer to it, I felt as if I had stepped into a pleasantly parallel universe. The idyllic compound took two years and $131 million to complete, and it was designed so nothing of the outside world can be seen or heard. Jeffries has banished the "cynicism" of the real world in favor of a cultlike immersion in his brand identity. The complex does feel like a kind of college campus, albeit one with a soundtrack you can't turn off. Dance music plays constantly in each of the airy, tin-roofed build-ings, and when I entered the spacious front lobby, where a wooden canoe hangs from the ceiling, two attractive young men in Abercrom-bie polo shirts and torn Abercrombie jeans sat at the welcome desk, one checking his Friendster.com messages while the other swayed subtly to the Pet Shop Boys song "If Looks Could Kill."

If looks could kill, everyone here would be dead. Jeffries' employ- 5 ees are young, painfully attractive, and exceedingly eager, and they travel around the campus on playground scooters, stopping occasion-ally to chill out by the bonfire that burns most days in a pit at the cen-ter of campus. The outdoorsy, summer-camp feel of the place is accentuated by a treehouse conference room, barnlike building and sheds with gridded windows, and a plethora of wooden decks and porches. But the campus also feels oddly urban — and, at times, stark and unwelcoming. The pallid, neo-industrial two-story buildings are built around a winding cement road, reminding employees that this is a workplace, after all.

Inside, the airy and modern workspaces are designed to encour-age communication and teamwork, and everywhere you look, smiley employees are brainstorming or eagerly recounting their weekends. "I'm not drinking again for a *year*," one young employee said to an-other as they passed me in the hall. There are few "offices" and even fewer doors at A&F central. Jeffries, for example, uses an airy confer-ence room as his office, and he spends much of his days huddling with designers who come armed with their newest ideas and designs.

The press-shy Jeffries rarely grants interviews, but he invited me to A&F's Ohio headquarters to promote the opening of his first flagship store, a four-story, 23,000-square-foot behemoth across the street from Trump Tower in Manhattan. To celebrate the opening, in November Jeffries threw a packed, ritzy, invitation-only party at the store, at which slightly soused women paid $10 apiece to have Polaroids of themselves taken with shirtless A&F model Matt Ratliff. And why not throw a party? Life is good for Jeffries, who in fourteen years has transformed Abercrombie & Fitch from a struggling retailer of "fuddy-duddy clothes" into the most dominant and imitated lifestyle-based brand for young men in America.

Valued at $5 billion, the company now has revenues approaching $2 billion a year rolling in from more than 800 stores and four successful brands. For the kids there's Abercrombie, aimed at middle schoolers who want to look like their cool older siblings. For high schoolers there's Hollister, a wildly popular surf-inspired look for "energetic and outgoing guys and girls" that has quickly become the brand of choice for Midwestern teens who wish they lived in Laguna Beach, California.

When the Hollister kids head off to college, Jeffries has a brand — the preppy and collegiate Abercrombie & Fitch — waiting for them there. And for the post-college professional who is still young at heart, Jeffries recently launched Ruehl, a casual sportswear line that targets twenty-two- to thirty-five-year-olds.

While Wall Street analysts and the companies' many critics glee- 10 fully predict A&F's impending demise every year or so, they have yet to be right. The company struggled some in the post-9/11 period, when, unlike other slumping retailers, it refused to offer discounts or promotions. But A&F's earnings have nonetheless increased for fifty-two straight quarters, excluding a one-time charge in 2004. "To me it's the most amazing record that exists in U.S. retailing, period," says A. G. Edwards analyst Robert Buchanan.

As his A&F brand has reached iconic status, Jeffries has raised prices, only to find that the brand's loyal fans will gladly pay whatever he asks. Total sales for November 2005 increased 34 percent over the year before, more than five times the gain made by A&F's main competitor, American Eagle. And while many retailers struggled during the Christmas season, Abercrombie thrived — it scored year-over-year gains of 29 percent in December, compared to 1.5 percent for other specialty retail stores.

Next, Jeffries plans to open his first store overseas, in London, and continue the transformation of A&F from American frat-bro wear to luxury lifestyle brand. I wouldn't bet against him. If history is any indication, Jeffries won't let anyone — "girlcotting" high school feminists, humorless Asians, angry shareholders, thong-hating parents, lawsuit-happy minorities, nosy journalists, copycat competitors, or uptight moralists — get in his way.

Mike Jeffries is the Willie Wonka of the fashion industry. A quirky perfectionist and control freak, he guards his aspirational brands and his utopian chocolate factory with a highly effective zeal. Those who have worked with him tend to use the same words to describe him: driven, demanding, smart, intense, obsessive-compulsive, eccentric, flamboyant and, depending on whom you talk to, either slightly or very odd. "He's weird and probably insane, but he's also unbelievably driven and brilliant," says a former employee at Paul Harris, a Midwestern women's chain for which Jeffries worked before becoming CEO of Abercrombie & Fitch in 1992.

Examples of his strange behavior abound. According to *Business Week*, at A&F headquarters Jeffries always goes through revolving doors twice, never passes employees on stairwells, parks his Porsche every day at the same angle in the parking lot (keys between the seats, doors unlocked), and has a pair of "lucky shoes" he wears when reading financial reports.

His biggest obsession, though, is realizing his singular vision of 15 idealized all-American youth. He wants desperately to look like his target customer (the casually flawless college kid), and in that pursuit he has aggressively transformed himself from a classically handsome man into a cartoonish physical specimen: dyed hair, perfectly white teeth, golden tan, bulging biceps, wrinkle-free face, and big, Angelina Jolie lips. But while he can't turn back the clock, he can — and has — done the next best thing, creating a parallel universe of beauty and exclusivity where his attractions and obsessions have made him millions, shaped modern culture's concepts of gender, masculinity and physical beauty, and made over himself and the world in his image, leaving them both just a little more bizarre than he found them.

Much more than just a brand, Abercrombie & Fitch successfully resuscitated a 1990s version of a 1950s ideal — the white, masculine "beefcake" — during a time of political correctness and rejection of '50s orthodoxy. But it did so with profound and significant differences. A&F aged the masculine ideal downward, celebrating young men in their teens and early twenties with smooth, gym-toned bodies and perfectly coifed hair. While feigning casualness (many of its clothes look like they've spent years in washing machine, then a hamper), Abercrombie actually celebrates the vain, highly constructed male. After all, there is nothing *casual* about an A&F sweatshirt worn over two A&F polos worn over an A&F T-shirt. (A&F has had less of a cultural impact on women's fashion. Its girls' line is preppy, sexy, and popular, but the company has mostly remained focused on pleasing the all-American college boy.)

For many young men, to wear Abercrombie is to broadcast masculinity, athleticism, and inclusion in the "cool boys club" without even having to open their mouths (that may be why the brand is so popular among some gay men who want desperately to announce their non-effeminacy). But because A&F's vision is so constructed and commodified (and because what A&F sells is not so much manhood but perennial *boyhood*), there is also something oddly emasculating about it. Compared to the 1950s ideal, A&F's version of maleness feels restrictive and claustrophobic. If becoming a man is about independence and growing up, then Abercrombie doesn't feel very masculine at all.

In that way, the brand is a lot like its creator. While Jeffries wears A&F clothes, the uniform doesn't succeed at making him seem boyish or particularly masculine. And for a man obsessed with creating a "sexy and emotional experience" for his customers, Jeffries comes off as oddly asexual. He is touchy-feely with some of his employees, both male and female, but the touch is decidedly paternal.

Remarkably little is known about Jeffries' personal life. There are few people who claim to know Jeffries well, and those who do wouldn't comment for this story. What is known is that Jeffries has a grown son, lives separately from his wife, and, according to *Business Week*, has a Herb Ritts photo of a toned male torso hanging over the fireplace in his bedroom.

Jeffries wouldn't discuss any of that with me, and he fidgeted nervously and grew visibly agitated when I asked about several of the many controversies and lawsuits he has weathered in his fourteen years at the helm of A&F. Our first bump came when I mentioned the 2002 uproar over the company's thongs for middle-school girls, which had "Eye Candy" and "Wink Wink" printed on their fronts. "That was a bunch of bullshit," he said, sweating profusely. "People said we were cynical, that we were sexualizing little girls. But you know what? I still think those are cute underwear for little girls. And I think anybody who gets on a bandwagon about thongs for little girls is crazy. Just crazy! There's so much craziness about sex in this country. It's nuts! I can see getting upset about letting your girl hang out with a bunch of old pervs, but why would you let your girl hang out with a bunch of old pervs?"

Later I brought up the brouhaha surrounding the A&F Quarterly, which, until it was discontinued in 2003, boasted articles about the history of orgies and pictures of chiseled, mostly white, all-American boys and girls (but mostly boys) cavorting naked on horses, beaches, pianos, surfboards, statues and phallically suggestive tree trunks. The magalog so outraged the American Decency Association that it called for a boycott and started selling anti-Abercrombie T-shirts: "Ditch Fitch: Abercrombie Peddles Porn and Exploits Children." Meanwhile, gay men across America were eagerly collecting the magazines, lured by photographer Bruce Weber's taste for beautiful, masculine boys playfully pulling off each other's boxers.

Jeffries nearly fell over in exasperation when I mentioned the magalog, although I'm not sure which charge — that he sells sex to kids or that his advertising is homoerotic — bothered him more. "That's just so wrong!" he said. "I think that what we represent sexually is healthy. It's playful. It's not dark. It's not degrading! And it's not gay, and it's not straight, and it's not black, and it's not white. It's not about any labels. That would be cynical, and we're not cynical! It's all depicting this wonderful camaraderie, friendship, and playfulness that exist in this generation and, candidly, does not exist in the older generation."

Jeffries alternates his grumpy defensiveness with moments of surprising candor, making him at times oddly endearing. He admitted things out loud that some youth-focused retailers wouldn't (which may be why he panicked and pulled his cooperation from this story two days after I left A&F headquarters, offering no explanation). For example, when I ask him how important sex and sexual attraction are in what he calls the "emotional experience" he creates for his customers, he says, "It's almost everything. That's why we hire good-looking people in our stores. Because good-looking people attract other good-looking people, and we want to market to cool, good-looking people. We don't market to anyone other than that."

As far as Jeffries is concerned, America's unattractive, over-weight, or otherwise undesirable teens can shop elsewhere. "In every school there are the cool and popular kids, and then there are the not-so-cool kids," he says. "Candidly, we go after the cool kids. We go after the attractive all-American kid with a great attitude and a lot of friends. A lot of people don't belong [in our clothes], and they can't belong. Are we exclusionary? Absolutely. Those companies that are in trouble are trying to target everybody: young, old, fat, skinny. But then you become totally vanilla. You don't alienate anybody, but you don't excite anybody, either."

Jeffries' obsession with building brands began when he was five. 25 He grew up in Los Angeles, where his father owned a chain of party supply stores for which a young Jeffries liked to organize and design the windows and counters. "I would always say to my parents, 'We need another store. We need another!'" Jeffries recalls. "I always wanted to expand and get bigger, and I would get off on saying, 'Why do we do the fixtures like this? Why don't we do it another way?' That totally turned me on."

Jeffries says he had a "very classic American youth," although he was not good at sports. "I broke my dad's heart because I wasn't good at basketball," he says. In high school in the late 1950s, Jeffries always wore Levi's jeans. "Actually, don't write that," he tells me, laughing. "But Levi's was definitely the uniform back then, kind of like what A&F has become. If you didn't wear 501s you were considered weird."

No one cool wore Abercrombie & Fitch when Jeffries went off to Claremont McKenna College and then to Columbia University, where he earned a master's degree in business administration. In fact, the company's best years were long behind it. Founded in 1892, in its heyday it served Presidents Hoover and Eisenhower (they bought their fishing equipment there), Ernest Hemingway (guns), and Cole Porter (evening clothes). During prohibition A&F was where the in crowd went for its hip flasks. But by the 1970s it had become a fashion backwater, holding on for dear life.

Leslee O'Neill, A&F's executive vice president of planning and allocation, remembers what the company was like before Jeffries got there. "We had old clothes that no one liked," she says. "It was a mess, a total disaster. We had this old library at our headquaters with all these really old books. There were croquet sets lying around. It was very English."

The company, which since 1988 had been owned by the Limited, was losing $25 million a year when Jeffries arrived and announced that A&F could survive and prosper as a "young, hip, spirited company." "We're all there thinking, Oh yeah, right. Abercrombie & Fitch?" recalls O'Neill. "But in the end we were like, Well, why not? It can't get any worse." Jeffries, then in his late 40s, dressed in oxford shirts and corduroy pants. "He was a lot more normal back then," O'Neill says. "Today he's much more eccentric, obviously."

Maybe, although former co-workers at Paul Harris recall that 30 Jeffries had an odd personal style even back then. "He wore the same outfit to work every day," recalls Thomas Yeo, a Paul Harris colleague. "Nearly worn-out suede loafers, a pair of gray flannel pants, and a double-breasted navy blazer. I don't think he ever changed his clothes. All that seemed to matter to him was the success of the brand."

Jan Woodruff, who also worked with Jeffries at Paul Harris, remembers him as a workaholic. "If he had a life outside work, it wasn't something people knew about," says Woodruff. But Woodruff and others say he has a superlative fashion mind. "It's so rare to find someone who is brilliant at both the creative and the business sides. But Jeffries is both. He's good at thinking in broad terms, but he's also obsessed with details. And I've never seen anyone as driven as Mike. I had no doubt he would be incredibly successful if he found the right venue. And he found it."

Soon after taking over A&F, Jeffries went looking early on for the right man to help him make A&F a sexy, aspirational brand. He settled on Bruce Weber, already a renowned photographer known for his male nudes. "But back then we couldn't afford him for an actual shoot," Jeffries told me, "so we bought one picture from him and hung it in a store window."

Fourteen years later, Jeffries' success is the envy of the fashion world. In a recent feature called "The Abercrombie Effect" in *DNR*, a newsmagazine about men's fashion and retail, the magazine noted that "not since Ralph Lauren's ascent in the 1980s has a single brand perfected a lifestyle-based look so often alluded to and imitated." Now Ralph Lauren's doing the imitating, opening a chain of collegiate, WASPy Polo knockoff stores called Rugby for young customers, featuring in-store grunge bands and beautiful salespeople.

"Imitation is the sincerest form of flattery," says Margaret Doerrer, national sales manager for young men at Union Bay, another youth-oriented label. "In the young men's market, for the longest time no one was creating a 'lifestyle.' Particularly in the department stores, everyone was focused on hip-hop and urban brands, and no one was creating that average, American Joe look. Jeffries never lost sight of who his customer is, and he created a quality brand that caters to the cool clique and has a sense of exclusivity, yet it still has a mass appeal, because people want to be a part of it. It's genius."

Maybe it's just the price of success, but it's not a normal day in 35 America if someone isn't suing (or boycotting, or "girlcotting") Abercrombie & Fitch, which has become a lightning rod for both the left and the right. In 2004 A&F paid $40 million to settle a class-action suit brought by minority employees who said they were either denied employment or forced to work in back rooms, where they wouldn't be seen by customers. While A&F denied any wrongdoing, Jeffries said the suit taught him a lesson: "I don't think we were in any sense guilty of racism, but I think we just didn't work hard enough as a company to create more balance and diversity. And we have, and I think that's made us a better company. We have minority recruiters. And if you go into our stores you see great-looking kids of all races."

In the latest episode, last fall a group of high school girls from Allegheny County, Pennsylvania, made the rounds of television talk shows to protest the company's "offensive" T-shirts. Of particular concern were shirts that read "Who Needs a Brain When You Have These?" "Gentlemen Prefer Tig Ol' Bitties" and "Do I Make You Look Fat?"

"Abercrombie has a history of insensitivity," the group's well-spoken Emma Blackman-Mathis, sixteen, told me, "and there is no company with as big an impact on the standards of beauty. There are kids starving themselves so they can be the 'Abercrombie girl,' and there are guys who think they aren't worthy if they don't look exactly like the guys on the wall."

The protest (which resulted in A&F pulling "Who Needs a Brain When You Have These?" and "Gentlemen Prefer Tig Ol' Bitties" but retaining "Do I Make You Look Fat?" and others) began after my visit, so I couldn't ask Jeffries about it. But I did ask him about other T-shirt dust-ups, including "It's All Relative in West Virginia" (which West Virginia's governor didn't find funny), "Bad Girls Chug. Good Girls Drink Quickly" (which angered anti-addiction groups), and "Wong Brothers Laundry Service — Two Wongs Can Make It White" (which triggered protests from Asian groups).

Remarkably, Jeffries says he has a "morals committee for T-shirts" whose job it is to make sure this sort of thing doesn't happen. "Sometimes they're on vacation," he admits with a smile. "Listen, do we go too far sometimes? Absolutely. But we push the envelope, and we try to be funny, and we try to stay authentic and relevant to our target customer. I really don't care what anyone other than our target customer thinks."

What about shareholders? Last year aggrieved Abercrombie   40
shareholders filed a suit against the company alleging that Jeffries' compensation was excessive. (The suit was settled; his $12 million "stay bonus" was reduced to $6 million, and he gave up some stock options. In 2004 he made approximately $25 million.) Other suits, still pending, accuse Jeffries of misleading stockholders about the company's profits. "You settle because it's a distraction," Jeffries told me. "I can't let anybody be distracted here. Me included. We are passionate about what we do here on a daily basis, and if any of us is tied up with this nonsense, it's counterproductive. We're a very popular company. We have a lot of money. And we're targets."

Jeffries dismisses the idea that he courts controversy deliberately to sell clothes, although the endless complaints about Abercrombie perverting the minds of America's youth undoubtedly makes the brand even more appealing to them. Meanwhile, the slogan-free items, which are for the most part as unthreatening as those of any other, less controversial label, fly under the parental radar. "Abercrombie remains a very acceptable look for Mom," says Union Bay's Doerrer. "I don't think many mothers of sixteen-year-old boys dressed in Abercrombie will make them go upstairs and change."

Jeffries says that A&F is a collaborative environment ("a diva-free zone," is how he put it to me), but in the end he makes every decision — from the hiring of the models to the placement of every item of clothing in every store. There are model stores for each of the four brands at A&F headquarters, and he spends much of his time making sure they're perfect. When they are, everything is photographed and sent to individual outlets to be replicated to the last detail. If there's an A&F diva, it's Jeffries.

I got a firsthand look at his perfectionism in action when he invited me along for the final walk-through for the Christmas setup of his stores.

"How does a store look? How does it feel? How does it smell? That's what I'm obsessed with," Jeffries said as we walked quickly toward the Hollister model store surrounded by a handful of his top deputies, including Tom Mendenhall, a senior vice president whom Jeffries recently lured away from Gucci.

Inside the dimly lit Hollister store, which is designed to look like 45 a cozy California beach house (there are surfboards, canoes, comfy chairs to lounge in, magazines to read, and two screens with live shots of Huntington Beach, courtesy of cameras permanently affixed to a pier), Jeffries paused in front of two mannequins and shook his head. "No, no, we're still not there, guys," he shouted over the No Doubt song "Spiderwebs," which blasted throughout the store. He stared at the jeans on the female mannequin. "The jeans are too high. I think she has to be lower."

A guy named Josh got down on his knees and started fidgeting with the jeans, trying to pull them down so they hung to the ground. "And we need to make the leg as skinny as we can," Jeffries said. "Should we clip the back of the leg in the knee?" Two employees scurried off to get clips. "We want it bigger at the top and skinnier at the legs. Yes, that's sexier. Much better. That's *less butch*." (Jeffries isn't a fan of the "butch" look, though when they were all the rage he grudgingly incorporated camouflage army pants into his Hollister line for girls.)

Jeffries then turned his attention to the male mannequin. "OK, how rugged and masculine can we make this guy?" he asked, prompting a couple of his assistants to fidget with the jeans, making them bigger in the leg. "Good, he looks cooler now. He's got more attitude. We love attitude."

There was more mannequin fixing at the A&F store, where a male one decked out in jeans wasn't looking very manly. "We have to fix this guy's package," Jeffries said. "We could stuff him," a girl suggested while a guy fiddled with the crotch, trying to make it poofier. With that fixed, Jeffries turned to a male mannequin in cargo pants. To make sure it looked realistic, he had a very attractive male employee put on a pair of the pants and stand next to the mannequin. "That looks great," he said as the young man did a 360, the pants sagging off his ass. Jeffries looked at the mannequin again. "Are the pants low enough? This guy's got it lower."

"They're right at the edge of falling off," said an assistant.

"OK, that's good," Jeffries said. "Let's get them as low as we can 50 without them falling off. We don't want him looking like an old guy."

READING

1. How would you describe the tone of this excerpt? Consider the use of words like "dude" and lines like "When I first arrived on 'campus,' as many A&F employees refer to it, I felt as if I had stepped into a pleasantly parallel universe." Choose passages in the piece that particularly reveal different aspects of the tone and read them aloud to the class.

2. Denizet-Lewis says of Mike Jeffries, the CEO of A&F, that "his biggest obsession . . . is realizing his singular vision of idealized all-American youth." What are some of the qualities pointed out in the article that define "all-American youth"? Do you agree or disagree with this vision? Why or why not?

3. Denizet-Lewis alludes to Jeffries as "the Willie Wonka of the fashion industry." What does this allusion mean? In what ways is the writer's visit to A&F headquarters like a trip to the chocolate factory?

4. How would you describe the audience of this piece? To whom is Denizet-Lewis addressing his satirical comments on the power of alienation and consumerism? Discuss the current image of the "cool boys club" and how it is being marketed today by A&F.

5. Keep a log of all the ads you see in just one day. Be sure to include logos on clothing, product placements in television shows and movies, as well as more straightforward ads. Note the number and types of ads that you logged and present your finding to the class.

WRITING

1. Write a reflective essay or journal entry about the sense of rebelliousness or belonging that owning a particular brand can bring. Think of your own material possessions and which ones are most important to you. Is the logo visible, or not? How does the brand advertise itself? As you select your brand are you excluding communities as much as building them?

2. Think back to your teen years and remember something that was very important for you to possess. Did you ever get it? If so, how? If not, why not? Write a narrative comparison/contrast essay in which you describe the value that this object had for you then and the value it has for you now. Do you still assign your object the same value? What has or has not changed?

3. The article states, "Much more than just a brand, Abercrombie & Fitch successfully resuscitated a 1990s version of a 1950s ideal – the white, masculine 'beefcake' – during a time of political correctness and rejection of '50s orthodoxy." Using the *Oxford English Dictionary* as a source, explore the history of the word "brand." Then write an essay in which you trace the evolution of the meaning and its shifts in connotation. Apply the most current definitions to the use of "brand" in this article.

4. Collaborate with a group of classmates to create a marketing strategy for a particular object that would target students on your campus, for example, a personal planning calendar put out by the school. Write a profile of the target audience you have in mind and how you would make your object appeal to them. How would you brand it? What values would your marketing strategies stress? Report your findings to the class in an oral presentation.

5. In the article "Urban Warfare" (p. 336) Kate MacArthur and Hillary Chura discuss how soda brands are targeting urban teen markets: "Hip-hop and street savvy are soda marketers' weapons in the battle for minority kids." Write a researched essay that compares and contrasts the marketing techniques of soda to urban minorities and fashion to "idealized all-American youth." Demonstrate how this targeting illustrates Scott Bedbury's contention in "The Value of Brand for the Commodity" (p. 392) that the "new," softer brand addresses "emotional needs [that] include . . . more complex motivations like yearning to belong, needing to feel connected, hoping to transcend, [and] desiring to experience joy and fulfillment."

The Cult You're In

By Kalle Lasn

FROM: *Culture Jam: How to Reverse America's Suicidal Consumer Binge – and Why We Must,* William Morrow, 1999

CONTEXT: This excerpt is from *Culture Jam: How to Reverse America's Consumer Binge – and Why We Must* and is a portion of a chapter called "The Cult You're In." *Culture Jam* originally appeared in hardback in 1999 and is published by William Morrow, a division of HarperCollins that focuses on hardcover mainstream literature for the "broadest possible audience." Currently, *Culture Jam* is published under the Quill imprint, HarperCollins's paperback nonfiction imprint, which specializes in self-help titles. Kalle Lasn, originally part of the traditional advertising world, founded a marketing research firm in the 1960s. He grew to have ethical doubts about marketing and shifted careers, first as a documentary filmmaker, then as the founder of *Adbusters* magazine and the Adbusters Media Foundation. Adbusters aims to "topple existing power structures and forge a major shift in the way we will live in the 21st century" (www.adbusters.com). *Culture Jam* presents Lasn's argument that individuals have lost their identity, becoming target markets whose purpose is to consume, and he urges readers to resist corporate influences. He claims that America itself has become a brand and has forsaken democracy for consumption.

A BEEPING TRUCK, BACKING UP IN THE ALLEY, JOLTS YOU OUT of a scary dream — a mad midnight chase through a supermarket, ending with a savage beating at the hands of the Keebler elves. You sit up in a cold sweat, heart slamming in your chest. It was only a nightmare. Slowly, you reintegrate, remembering who and where you are. In your bed, in your little apartment, in the very town you grew up in.

It's a "This Is Your Life" moment — a time for mulling and stock-taking. You are still here. Just a few miles from the place you had your first kiss, got your first job (drive-through window at Wendy's), bought your first car ('73 Ford Torino), went nuts with the Wild Turkey on prom night, and pulled that all-nighter at Kinko's, photocopying transcripts to send to the big schools back East.

Those big dreams of youth didn't quite pan out. You didn't get into Harvard, didn't get courted by the Bulls, didn't land a recording contract with EMI (or anyone else), didn't make a million by age twenty-five. And so you scaled down your hopes of embarrassing riches to reasonable expectations of adequate comfort — the modest condo downtown, the Visa card, the Braun shaver, the one good Armani suit.

Even this more modest star proved out of reach. The state college you graduated from left you with a $35,000 debt. The work you found hardly dented it: dreadful eight-to-six days in the circulation department of a bad lifestyle magazine. You learned to swallow hard and just do the job — until the cuts came and the junior people were cleared out with a week's severance pay and sober no-look nods from middle management. You began paying the rent with Visa advances. You got call-display to avoid the collection agency.

There remains only one thing no one has taken away, your only 5 real equity. And you intend to enjoy fully that Fiat rustmaster this weekend. You can't run from your problems, but you may as well drive. Road Trip. Three days to forget it all. Three days of living like an animal (in the best possible sense), alert to sights and sounds and smells: Howard Stern on the morning radio, Slumber Lodge pools along the I-14. "You may find yourself behind the wheel of a large automobile," sings David Byrne from a tape labeled "Road Tunes One." The Fiat is, of course, only large at heart. "You know what FIAT stands for?" Liv said when she first saw it. "Fix It Again, Tony." You knew then that this was a girl you could travel to the ends of the Earth with. Or at least to New York City.

The itinerary is set. You will order clam chowder from the Soup Nazi, line up for standby Letterman tickets, and wander around Times Square (Now cleaner! Safer!) with one eye on the Jumbotron. It's a place you've never been, though you live there in your mind. You will jog in Battery Park and sip Guinness at Michael's Pub on Monday night (Woody Allen's night), and you will dance with Liv in the Rainbow Room on her birthday. Ah Liv, who when you first saw her spraying Opium on her wrist at the cosmetics counter reminded you so much of Cindy Crawford — though of late she's put on a few pounds and now looks better when you close your eyes and imagine.

And so you'll drive. You'll fuel up with Ho Ho's and Pez and Evian and magazines and batteries for your Discman, and then you'll bury the pedal under your Converse All-Stars — like the ones Kurt Cobain died in. Wayfarers on, needle climbing, and the unspoken understanding that you and Liv will conduct the conversation entirely in movie catchphrases.

"Mrs. Nixon would like you to pass the Doritos."

"You just keep thinking, Butch. That's what you're good at."

"It's over, Rock. Nothing on Earth's gonna save you now."

It occurs to you that you can't remember the last time Liv was just Liv and you were just you. You light up a Metro, a designer cigarette so obviously targeted at your demographic . . . which is why you steered clear of them until one day you smoked one to be ironic, and now you can't stop.

You'll come back home in a week. Or maybe you won't. Why should you? What's there to come back *for*? On the other hand, why should you stay?

A long time ago, without even realizing it, just about all of us were re-   10 cruited into a cult. At some indeterminate moment, maybe when we were feeling particularly adrift or vulnerable, a cult member showed up and made a beautiful presentation. "I believe I have something to ease your pain." She made us feel welcome. We understood she was offering us something to give life meaning. She was wearing Nike sneakers and a Planet Hollywood cap.

Do you *feel* as if you're in a cult? Probably not. The atmosphere is quite un-Moonielike. We're free to roam and recreate. No one seems to be forcing us to do anything we don't want to do. In fact, we feel privileged to be here. The rules don't seem oppressive. But make no mistake: There are rules.

By consensus, cult members speak a kind of corporate Esperanto: words and ideas sucked up from TV and advertising. We wear uniforms — not white robes but, let's say, Tommy Hilfiger jackets or Airwalk sneakers (it depends on our particular subsect). We have been recruited into roles and behavior patterns *we did not consciously choose*.

Quite a few members ended up in the slacker camp. They're bunked in spartan huts on the periphery, well away from the others. There's no mistaking cult slackers for "downshifters" — those folks who have *voluntarily* cashed out of their high-paying jobs and simplified their lives. Slackers are downshifters by necessity. They live frugally because they are poor. (Underemployed and often overeducated, they may never get out of the rent-and-loan-repayment cycle.)

There's really not much for the slackers to *do* from day to day. They hang out, never asking, never telling, just offering intermittent wry observations. They are postpolitical, postreligious. They don't define themselves by who they vote for or pray to (these things are pretty much prescribed in the cult anyway). They set themselves apart in the only way cult members can: by what they choose to wear and drive and listen to. The only things to which they confidently ascribe value are things other people have already scouted, deemed worthy and embraced.

Cult members aren't really citizens. The notions of citizenship 15 and nationhood make little sense in this world. We're not fathers and mothers and brothers: We're consumers. We care about sneakers, music, and Jeeps. The only *Life, Freedom, Wonder*, and *Joy* in our lives are the brands on our supermarket shelves.

Are we happy? Not really. Cults promise a kind of boundless contentment — punctuated by moments of bliss — but never quite deliver on that promise. They fill the void, but only with a different kind of void. Disillusionment eventually sets in — or it would if we were allowed to think much about it. Hence the first commandment of a cult: *Thou shalt not think*. Free thinking will break the trance and introduce competing perspectives. Which leads to doubt. Which leads to contemplation of the nearest exit.

How did all this happen in the first place? Why have we no memory of it? When were we recruited?

The first solicitations began when we were very young. If you close your eyes and think back, you may remember some of them.

You are four years old, tugging on your mother's sleeve in the supermarket. There are products down here at eye level that she cannot see. Cool products with cartoon faces on them. Toys familiar from Saturday morning television. You want them. She keeps pushing her cart. You cry. She doesn't understand.

You are eight. You have allowance money. You savor the buying 20 experience. A Coke here, a Snickers bar there. Each little fix means not just getting what you want, but *power*. For a few moments *you* are the center of attention. *You* call the shots. People smile and scurry around serving you.

Michael Jordan goes up on your bedroom door. He is your first hero, throwing a glow around the first brand in your life — Nike. You wanna be like Mike.

Other heroes follow. Sometimes they contradict each other. Michael Jackson drinks Pepsi but Michael Jordan drinks Coke. Who is the false prophet? Your friends reinforce the brandhunting. Wearing the same stuff and hearing the same music makes you a fraternity, united in soul and form.

You watch TV. It's your sanctuary. You feel neither loneliness nor solitude here.

You enter the rebel years. You strut the malls, brandishing a Dr Pepper can full of Scotch, which you drink right under the noses of the surveillance guards. One day you act drunk and trick them into "arresting" you — only this time it actually *is* soda in the can. You are immensely pleased with yourself.

You go to college, invest in a Powerbook, ride a Vespa scooter, don 25
Doc Martens. In your town, a new sports complex and performing arts
center name themselves after a car manufacturer and a software
company. You have moved so far into the consumer maze that you can
smell the cheese.

After graduating you begin to make a little money, and it's quite
seductive. The more you have, the more you think about it.

You buy a house with three bathrooms. You park your BMW outside the double garage. When you grow depressed you go shopping.

The cult rituals spread themselves evenly over the calendar:
Christmas, Super Bowl, Easter, pay-per-view boxing match, summer
Olympics, Mother's Day, Father's Day, Thanksgiving, Halloween. Each
has its own imperatives — stuff you have to buy, things you have to do.

You're a lifer now. You're locked and loaded. On the go, trying to
generate more income to buy more things and then, feeling dissatisfied but not quite sure why, setting your sights on even greater income
and more acquisitions. When "consumer confidence is down," spending is "stagnant," the "retail sector" is "hurting," and "stingy consumers
are giving stores the blues," you do your bit for the economy. You are
a star.

Always, always you have been free to dream. The motivational 30
speakers you watched on late-night TV preached that even the most
sorry schleppers can achieve their goals if they visualize daily and
stay committed. *Think and grow rich.*

Dreams, by definition, are supposed to be unique and imaginative. Yet the bulk of the population is dreaming the same dream. It's a
dream of wealth, power, fame, plenty of sex, and exciting recreational
opportunities.

What does it mean when a whole culture dreams the same
dream?

READING

1. The title of this piece is "The Cult You're In," and Lasn writes, "A long time ago, without even realizing it, just about all of us were recruited into a cult." What is this cult? What are its shared rituals? Are you a member?

2. Early in the essay, Lasn chides the reader, saying "Those big dreams of youth didn't quite pan out." And he ends the essay with a question: "What does it mean when a whole culture dreams the same dream?" Describe the dream that is presented in the essay. Do you share this dream? Do you believe "the whole culture" does?

3. "The Cult You're In" includes the specific names of many brands and products. Take a few moments and list them. How many of them are immediately familiar to you? Why has Lasn referenced specific brands rather than generic product categories? How does your recognition of these brands support his claims?

4. Lasn adopts a judgmental tone in this piece, speaking as one outside the cult to you – a cult member. How does this tone strike you? Does it draw you into the piece or distance you?

5. Lasn chooses to write this piece in the second person ("you") so that he is directly addressing the reader. Does this personal emphasis add to the effect of the piece? If so, what does it add?

WRITING

1. Lasn writes, "The first solicitations [to the cult] began when we were very young. If you close your eyes and think back, you may remember some of them." Follow his suggestion and close your eyes. Think back to the first brand you remember, the first product you had to have. Write a journal entry or a reflective essay about this memory.

2. In "The Cult You're In," Lasn alternately blames and excuses the cult members, creating an interesting, edgy tone to the essay. Write a critical essay in which you draw a conclusion about his tone towards the cult members in the piece, supporting your observations with evidence. Do you feel his tone is effective at communicating his argument or is it too sharp to draw in the reader?

3. According to Lasn, one way the cult draws us in is through popular entertainment: our idolatry of movie and TV stars, our worship of sports and music figures, our reliance on video games, television shows, and movies for mind-numbing entertainment. For two or

three days, keep a log in which you enter the number of times your conversations with friends and family include some topic related to popular entertainment or sports and the amount of time you spend playing video games, watching TV, and so on. Review your log. Does it support Lasn's argument about our dependence on popular culture? Write an essay in which you use your log as evidence to support or refute Lasn's claim.

4. Lasn contrasts cult slackers with "downshifters – those folks who have *voluntarily* cashed out of their high paying jobs and simplified their lives." He is referring to a movement stressing frugality and simplicity that first gained wide-scale attention in the late 1990s. Research this movement and write a researched essay in which you compare the beliefs of this group with those of the cult described by Lasn.

P&G "Buzz Marketing"
Unit Hit with Complaint

By Bruce Horowitz

FROM: *USA Today*, October 19, 2005

CONTEXT: This article appeared originally in *USA Today*, America's best-selling newspaper. This newspaper appeals to a very broad audience and offers news on world, state, and regional issues. Its coverage is very wide, and its articles are known for their brevity. *USA Today* prides itself on "an economy of words [and] a wealth of information." When it was first launched in September of 1982, it was noted for its liberal use of color and its range of information. It set a new style in newspaper reporting by marketing to the entire country without affiliation with a specific locale. As you read this brief article, notice how it covers a lot of territory with few words and is directed toward a wide readership. ("P&G 'Buzz Marketing' Unit Hit with Complaint" by Bruce Horowitz and the front cover of *USA Today*, October 19, 2005. Reprinted with permission.)

IS PROCTER & GAMBLE — THE WORLD'S BIGGEST PACKAGED goods marketer — breaking the law by enlisting teens to coax friends to try teen-tailored products?

One consumer advocacy group thinks it is. Commercial Alert on Tuesday filed a complaint with the Federal Trade Commission that says P&G's word-of-mouth marketing unit, Tremor, targets teens with deceptive advertising.

If successful, the complaint would have broad impact on the ad business. So-called buzz marketing is the industry's hottest trend. More than 85 percent of the nation's top 1,000 marketers now use some form, estimates Marian Salzman, trend-spotter at JWT Worldwide.

383

Advertising Age estimates buzz marketing to be a $100 million to   5
$150 million industry. Though still relatively small in dollar volume,
the provocative practice ranks among marketing's highest growth
areas — and is causing genuine angst within the industry.

"This is a practice that may be illegal," says Jonah Bloom, executive editor of *Advertising Age.* "It's probably only a matter of time before someone jumps on it to stop it," he says.

Which is what Commercial Alert is trying to do. P&G, and several
smaller buzz marketing specialists named in its complaint, "are perpetuating large-scale deception upon consumers when people they
recruit to promote products by word of mouth don't disclose that fact,"
says Gary Ruskin, executive director of Commercial Alert. FTC officials declined to comment.

P&G's four-year-old Tremor division has a panel of 250,000 teens
ages thirteen to nineteen who are asked to talk with friends about
new products or concepts P&G sends them. About 75 percent of
members are female.

Steve Knox, CEO of Tremor, which works for outside clients as
well as parent P&G, had no comment on the complaint. But, he says,
"We're an incredibly ethical company." Panelists are not paid cash, he
says, but get product samples or other materials.

"To be a member is empowering for a teen," says Knox. "You have
a voice that will be heard, and you get cool information before your
friends receive it." Knox won't name any of Tremor's outside clients,
citing client confidentiality.

Tremor recently did a campaign for P&G's Clairol Herbal   10
Essences. The purpose was to help teens feel more comfortable about
coloring hair. It sent some members cardboard booklets that let them
push locks of their own hair through a hole and compare it with what
the hair would look like in a new color.

"If we've done our work correctly, they talk to their friends about
it," says Knox. Tremor doesn't tell members to say they are part of
Tremor, he says, "because you never tell a (panelist) what to say."

Ruskin says that's bogus. At a minimum, his complaint says, the
FTC should "issue subpoenas" to P&G executives at Tremor — and
other buzz marketers — to determine whether their endorsers are disclosing that they are paid marketers.

READING

1. Exactly what is "buzz marketing," according to this article? What re-lationship does Tremor have to P&G?

2. The original article subtitle was, "Group slams use of teens to coax friends to try items." Consider how the word choices in this phrase set up the conflict of the piece. Which words carry negative conno-tations? Which words are more neutral?

3. How would you describe the tone of this article? Quote several ex-amples that support your assertion.

4. What arguments does Steve Knox, CEO of Tremor, use to defend the use of "a panel of 250,000 teens ages thirteen to nineteen who are asked to talk with friends about new products or concepts P&G sends them"?

5. To your knowledge, have you ever been approached by a buzz mar-keter? What would your reaction be if a friend of yours told you about a cool new thing she liked and then you found out that she was working for that company?

WRITING

1. Write a journal entry or a reflective piece in which you describe what you would say to a friend who revealed that she was a buzz marketer.

2. This complaint, filed by the Federal Trade Commission, is brought by Commercial Alert, a consumer advocacy group. Go online and see what you can find out about Commercial Alert. See if you can find any other complaints that Commercial Alert has brought to the Fed-eral Trade Commission. See what information is available about Gary Ruskin, executive director of this consumer advocacy group. Write a descriptive essay in which you explain Commercial Alert's purpose and their range of activities.

3. Commercial Alert filed the complaint against Tremor, "and several smaller buzz marketing specialists," according to *USA Today*. Go on-line to Tremor's website and explore the kind of invitation it offers teens to encourage them to participate in marketing. Write an argu-mentative essay in which you defend/attack Tremor's use of teen marketers through their site.

4. Choose a brand not mentioned in this article that appeals to teens and investigate the marketing strategies and media it used in one of

its marketing campaigns. Write a researched essay on the marketing campaign and evaluate its use of influencers and the campaign's success or failure. Report your findings to your class.

5. Steve Knox, CEO of Tremor, is quoted in this article as saying, "To be a member is empowering for a teen. . . . You have a voice that will be heard, and you get cool information before your friends receive it." Set up a panel discussion in your class in which you discuss the pros and cons for these teens who sign up as panel members for buzz marketers. Write up a summary of your discussion.

Websites

A Portfolio of Buzz Marketing Websites

YOU MAY REMEMBER SOME "COOL" KID FROM HIGH SCHOOL, OR NO-
tice people in your classes who always seem to have the latest in clothing or electronic gadgets or knows the latest bands – people that others
identify as "cool" because of their style and knowledge of the the most
up-to-date trends. People like this have influence in their peer groups,
and because of this the following websites recruit and use their opinions
and influence as marketing tools.

Teens, especially, are recruited to join groups like Buzz-Oven or Universal Buzz Intelligence to promote their favorite bands or products,
both online and in real-life conversations. They are "paid," not with
salaries but with giveaways, chances to earn points for products, and
perhaps most ethically sticky of all, with a sense of belonging, and having their opinions heard, acknowledged, and sought. Buzz-Oven invites
"any teen or young adult willing to get involved in their local music scene
[to] join our collective." In this way, teens become "members," not employees. Yet, they are helping promote and sell their companies' products.

This method is decidedly different from the traditional image of
admen in grey business suits in tall buildings creating ads that seduce
the unsuspecting, naive public into purchasing certain products. As The
Intelligence Group states to its potential marketers, "We immerse ourselves in our consumers' environments to absorb their way of life, un-
cover their feelings and, ultimately, understand their preferences."

The following sites are vivid and attractive and all are using new advertising strategies, such as those described, to appeal to the youth
market and get their help spotting trends and capitalizing on them. Look
at how the sites are designed to be inviting to certain demographic
groups – tweens, teens, Gen X, Gen Y. Their clients range from The White
Stripes and Chanel to the ABC Television Network. "Street marketing,"
"buzz marketing," "lifestyle marketing," and perhaps most chillingly,
"viral marketing" have become big business.

Arrows signify movement forward of message/product.

The figure shows media and spread of buzz.

Juxtaposition turns buzz into value.

An androgynous figure = wide appeal.

The helmeted figure is looking at a single nonconforming star = our firm will make your product different, stand out.

Read as: Young, data oriented, one-stop shop.

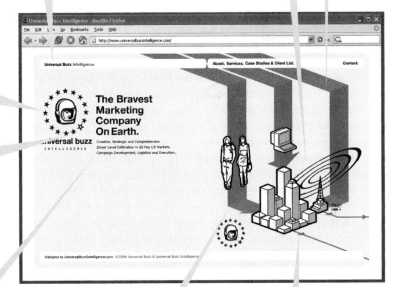

Universal Buzz Intelligence

Gen X and Y millennial figures are shown in a disaffected slouch.

Big city, big market, graphic echoes monopoly figures.

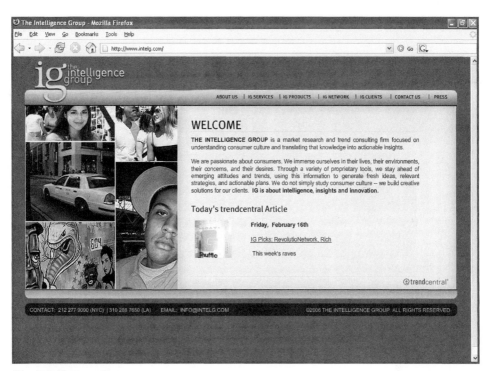

The Intelligence Group

Buzz-Oven

Street Attack

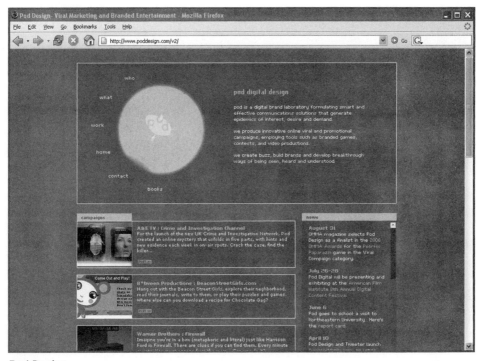

Pod Design

RESPONDING

1. A key selling point of buzz marketing is the ability to reach young consumers. What elements of the sites would suggest the firms can reach a youth market? Include images, text, colors, and music.

2. Each site functions as an ad, attempting to convince busy executives to buy the company's marketing services. Do the sites seem to offer the same types of services? What are they? What promises do they make to the companies that purchase their services?

3. The sites seem to share a common vocabulary of business buzz words. For example, the site Universal Buzz Intelligence advertises, "Creative, Strategic, and Comprehensive Street Level Infiltration in 60 Key US Markets. Campaign Development, Logistics, and Execution." Make a list of terms that seem to form the lingua franca of these sites and define each term. Do they seem to invoke certain metaphors or images? Why is it important for these businesses to develop their own language? How does this vocabulary assist in the efforts to promote buzz marketing as a valid field and a worthy investment?

4. Writing in 2000, Renee Dye, in "The Buzz on Buzz," predicts "a world in which buzz will dominate the shaping of markets. In fact, the phenomenon of buzz is already becoming an industry unto itself" (p. 361). And to her, such a shift is simply a new way of driving consumers. Kalle Lasn ("The Cult You're In" [p. 376]) would likely see the rise of firms like Street Attack and Pod in a very different light. Select one of the sites listed and discuss how Lasn would view it. Would he see buzz marketing as distinguishable from cult indoctrination?

5. Several of these sites include case studies from products that the companies have marketed. Do you recognize any of the campaigns? Using these case studies as templates, could you design a buzz marketing campaign for your college or university? What would be the key components?

The Value of Brand for the Commodity

By Scott Bedbury

FROM: *A New Brand World: Eight Principles for Achieving Brand Leadership in the 21st Century*, Viking Adult, 2002

THIS EXCERPT IS FROM A SECTION CALLED "DEFINING BRAND" IN Scott Bedbury's book *A New Brand World: Eight Principles for Achieving Brand Leadership in the 21st Century*. The book is published by Viking Adult, a division of Penquin Group, the second largest English-language trade books publisher in the world. Bedbury, who is perhaps America's most acclaimed marketing consultant, was the person behind the incredibly successful marketing campaigns for Nike and Starbucks. *A New Brand World* is representative of a new kind of business book – personal and anecdotal, not bland and fact-filled. Bedbury has now launched his own branding consultancy, Brandstream.

To help you read more deeply and critically, we have provided annotations and boldfaced some terms or passages that call attention to the rhetorical choices Bedbury has made in this piece. As you read the excerpt and annotations, consider the popular business audience Bedbury is writing for and the how it shapes his writing.

> Bedbury coins a new phrase that serves his topic by reordering the one we might have expected, "brand new world." The connotations of the first phrase then accrue to the second. This is not the old world, which will come in for criticism throughout his piece; this is the new, improved world.

So now we know that in the **New Brand World,** brand awareness and recognition, even when judiciously used, do not necessarily a viable or powerful brand make, though they are key aspects of the process. What then is the complete equation? What are all the forces that shape a brand? Is there one completely accurate definition?

For starters, let's examine what a brand is not. It is not, to cite just one example, best defined by an entry in a recent edition of the *Random House English Dictionary*.

1. A word, name, symbol etc. esp. one legally registered as a trademark, used by a manufacturer or merchant to identify its products distinctively from others of the same type and usually prominently displayed on its goods, in advertising etc. 2. A product, line of products or service bearing a widely known brand name. 3. informal. A person notable or famous, esp. in a particular field: The reception was replete with brand names from politics and the arts [1925].

This outmoded definition relies far too heavily on tangible quantities like products, services, and trademarks. Yes, brands are in part physical. They are often represented by products, places, and people. But we're now turning away from a half century best described by **Diane Coyle** in her excellent work *The Weightless World* as "the tyranny of the tangible." Since the advent of the Industrial Revolution, all that mattered in business were tangible assets: physical entities that either appeared on the corporate balance

> Bedbury begins a thread that will run through his piece: The ways in which we used to think about brands are no longer useful. He holds the key to the new definition and is offering it to us.

> Diane Coyle is a consultant whose firm is called "Enlightenment Economics." She has written several notable and award-winning books on global economics in the Internet age. By citing her, Bedbury adds an academic authority to his argument.

> Bedbury's definition of "brand" seeks to free it from direct product association so that the brand becomes more important than the product it represents. In doing so, he links it repeatedly to abstract concepts. For example, he writes of "today's knowledge-based, experience-driven society," implying that in the past society ignored knowledge and experience.

sheet as "hard assets" or, in the realm of abstraction, such easily quantifiable concepts as price-to-earnings ratios or quarterly earnings. The materials and power sources that drove the Industrial Revolution — steel, oil, electricity, lumber, heavy equipment, concrete, and automobiles — formed the tangible bedrock of the value equation. But in today's **knowledge-based, experience-driven society,** intangible and often weightless notions, intellectual properties, ideas, products, and services are driving more wealth creation than are materials.

Nowhere is this more evident than in the realm of brand development. It can safely be said that **Coca-Cola's** total market value is more an emotional quantity than a physical one. Hard assets like bottling plants, trucks, raw materials, and buildings are not as important to Coke — or Wall Street, for that matter — as the consumer goodwill that exists around the world toward the brand. Put another way, the loyalty that Coke has created is worth many billions, possibly hundreds of billions, of future dollars. Attempting to quantify this part of the balance sheet can drive even the best CFO nuts, but the value is there. In 2001 I was retained by Coke to help drive an important new brand-development process that would help reveal the dynamics that drive Coke's brand strength and help establish a **tracking system** that would **monitor** how the company's most important beverage brands were performing in key markets around the world.

> Bedbury plainly states his position by using Coca-Cola as an example. Brand value is an emotional value that rests in consumer loyalty and goodwill.

> However, despite his protestations about tangible qualities, Bedbury must resort to concrete measures to determine how much a brand is worth; otherwise he could not track its performance.

Bedbury introduces another authority, Plato, into his argument. As a philosopher, Plato is not usually quoted in a business essay. Bedbury is referencing Plato's "Allegory of the Cave." The most common reading of this piece suggests that Plato wishes to direct his students' attention to what is real and important (ideas), not what is transitory and physical. Using this ancient authority to define what is good about a brand is an interesting choice.

Defining the Softer Side of "Brand"

The more enlightened definition of branding that I'm going to propose here originated many centuries in the past. Well ahead of his time, **Plato** believed that behind and above and beneath everything concrete we experience in our daily lives is the *idea* of that thing, which gives the thing lasting, even everlasting, meaning. In a comparable way, every brand has a fundamental essence. This essence is not physical or defined exclusively or entirely by products or services.

Today, a brand is, if it is any *thing*, the result of a synaptic process in the brain. The great nineteenth-century Russian behavioral psychologist Ivan Petrovich **Pavlov** would understand this conception of branding. The pleasurable sensation that his dogs felt when he rang his famous bell — and their eager anticipation of the imminent arrival of food, which they demonstrated by salivating — is perhaps the best analogy I can think of to the psychological process that branding elicits in us when it works successfully. The concept of the brand — the Platonic idea, if you will — creates a response in its audience without the audience's seeing the product or directly experiencing the service. Think **Godiva** chocolates for a moment: the very name, perhaps even the logo, conjures up an image of sinful indulgence. Yes, it represents chocolate or ice cream, but it is the feeling and the anticipation of that feeling that the brand conveys most compellingly.

But for our purposes, even the Pavlovian model comes up a little short. I believe that the twentieth-century humanist psychologist

Bedbury now introduces Pavlov as another authority whose work can further illuminate modern branding concepts. Using Plato and Pavlov as examples is emblematic of Bedbury's tendency to support his ideas with diverse authorities.

Bedbury shifts to direct address to tempt the reader with the thought of Godiva chocolate. His example shows that money follows perception, underscoring his business principle that the brand is more (and more important) than the product.

Bedbury segues into the next section by introducing Abraham Maslow, the humanist psychologist. Bedbury also recharacterizes consumers, who are now "nuanced." These rhetorical moves again underscore his argument about the limitations of thinking under the industrial model, where all that mattered was "tangible assets."

Maslow's focus on human potential, something intangible, fits perfectly into Bedbury's schema.

Abraham Maslow offers us a model that may be more relevant for the more nuanced consumers of today.

Maslow's Hierarchy of Human Needs

The founder of what later became known as the "human potential" movement, the Brooklyn-born **Abraham (Maslow)** (1908–1970) completed his training in psychology when the field was dominated by the school known as behaviorism, led by B. F. Skinner. **Behaviorists** believed that the "human animal" was not fundamentally different from any other animal, and as such was primarily motivated by the basic physical and physiological needs for food, sex, warmth, shelter. Any "higher" emotions, goals, or ambitions were merely abstracted from these basic drives, and were thus not worthy of serious study.

But Maslow was not convinced that that was all there was to human psychology. By nature an independent spirit and thinker, he was no more impressed by the Freudian school (then gaining ground in America) than by the behaviorists. To illustrate his own theory of what motivates people, Maslow created a pyramid-shaped *hierarchy* of human needs. The primary, physiological needs for food and shelter are at the bottom, and progressively more complex needs — for safety, belonging, love, and esteem — are ranked progressively higher. At the top are our "highest" needs, for **self-actualization and spiritual fulfillment.**

Here Bedbury is actually rejecting behaviorism, which finds part of its foundation in Pavlov's work. Yet, earlier, he saw Pavlov's findings as crystallizing part of why brands work.

Maslow's hierarchy is topped with, as Bedbury notes, "self-actualization and spiritual fulfillment." Again, these are intangible qualities, which he wishes to associate with his new concept of branding.

Bedbury, in just a few sentences, moves from "spiritual fulfill-ment" to a "fiercely competitive and commoditized market-place" with little explicit connection between the two. Throughout his piece, Bedbury tends to place two ideas next to each other and to ask the reader to make the connection, even when there is a disconnect between them.

Old Brand World thinking concentrated on what marketers call "top-of-mind" awareness, which, ironically enough, is precisely the op-posite of what Maslow put at the top of his mental model. In traditional marketing lingo, "top of the mind" refers to unaided awareness of a brand, a product, or a product feature. This surface-level measure does not impart enough insight in today's **fiercely competitive and com-moditized marketplace**. And it does not begin to approach the notion of measuring brand loyalty. I am personally aware of a great number of brands I have no intention of ever buying because they are irrelevant to me, or they don't resonate deeply enough for me to trust them.

Today's brand positioning and behavior must reflect an under-standing of the deeper psychological issues that Maslow placed at the apex of his pyramid. Brands that respect the **"higher"** consumer needs and develop products, services, and marketing communications that intelligently leverage them will rise above the commodity fray, for they will become more meaningful. These emotional needs include more powerful, more subtle, more complex motivations like yearning to belong, needing to feel connected, hoping to transcend, desiring to experience joy and fulfillment. We will discuss these emotive drivers, particularly as they relate to Maslow's theories, in greater detail in chapter 4 [not reprinted here]. But for now, keep this "higher ground" concept in mind as we attempt to redefine the notion of a brand. Henry Ford did more than create the concept of mass production. The real power of the automobile in its early years was probably more

Bedbury's diction in this section stresses the higher level to which branding must move if it is to be successful. He draws authority from Maslow's work, with a goal to sell products by capitalizing on "'higher' consumer needs." Note that this sec-tion ends not with self-actualization, as does Maslow's hierar-chy, but with Henry Ford's creation of mass production.

Bedbury shifts dramatically from third person to second, directly addressing the reader and demonstrating how a "'higher ground'" concept of branding works. It sells not the Huffy brand but the idea of one's first bike and all the emotional, intangible memories that are wrapped up in this tangible product. The reader's memory makes Bedbury's point.

emotional than it was physical. It must have been much more than getting from one place to another. Imagine the emotional rewards that came with owning an automobile for the first time or just riding in one. If that's difficult, remember back to **your first bike**. Mine was a Huffy. Some of our greatest brand memories are primarily emotional.

This selection is an excerpt from a popular and widely available business book. Notice that it includes no endnotes, footnotes, or reference section. Its sources are casually introduced and not formally documented as is required in most academic writing. This is not uncommon in this context. (See bedfordstmartins.com/nexttext for complete information on using and documenting sources.)

MAKING CONNECTIONS ACROSS AND BEYOND THE DISCIPLINES

1. After reading Bedbury's definition of what constitutes a brand, visit one of your local Starbucks coffeehouses. Bring your laptop or your journal. Sit and have a beverage and notice the qualities of the experience that represent the Starbucks branding strategy. Notice the furniture and how it is grouped. Notice the music and how it is marketed. Notice the Starbucks-related things you can buy in the coffee shop. Analyze the menu and how the products are named. What kind of lifestyle do these things suggest to you? What particular lifestyle are you participating in when you go to your local Starbucks? If you have a chance, visit the same shop at the same time for a few days. Observe the people who come to Starbucks. Can you describe them as a community? Why or why not? Write a descriptive, narrative essay in which you associate the tangible experience of being at Starbucks with the intangible qualities that the brand evokes.

2. Kalle Lasn is the founder of Adbusters, which is both an activist collective, a website (www.adbusters.org), and a magazine dedicated to spreading the message of this group. According to their site, "Our readers are professors and students; activists and politicians; environmentalists and media professionals; corporate watch dogs and industry insiders; kids who love our slick ad parodies and parents who worry about their children logging too many hours a day in the electronic environment." The group recently began a new campaign to "unbrand America," complete with an alternate U.S. flag, where the stars are replaced with corporate logos. The Adbusters collective enacts "creative resistance" to our consumer culture through a variety of avenues, including "spoof ads." For example, the spoof ad for Tommy Hilfiger featuring the sheep (p. 329) suggests that buying Hilfiger clothes leads not to individuality but to assimilation into the social group. Go to the website and study some of the other spoof ads posted there. Think of Lasn's point of view in "The Cult You're In" (p. 376). Decide how a number of these spoof ads suggest a particular kind of "cult." Make a small group presentation to your class that compares and contrasts the original ads with the spoof ads and explain how each spoof works to expose a particular "cult."

3. Renee Dye in "The Buzz on Buzz" (p. 352) classifies some companies as possessing "established midmarket or downstream brands," citing Revlon as an example. These companies do not start trends but follow them – broadening the appeal of what would otherwise be purchased by just a few. With some of your classmates, research some possible trends by looking through issues of cutting-edge fashion and lifestyle magazines from a few months back. Then, visit

a local big-box retailer, like Wal-Mart or Target, or your local mall and note which of the ideas in these magazines have made their way into the wider market. Observe who seems to be buying or wearing the trendy items now. Write an essay or make a presentation that charts the trend from its beginnings to its end, including observations about the original and current consumers and how they differ. Include images to support your observations and be certain to map your observations back to Dye's ideas about the power of buzz marketing.

Making and Remaking History

THE IMAGES THAT BEGIN THIS CHAPTER RESULTED ALMOST AS an afterthought from a project undertaken by Human Rights Watch in Darfur, Sudan. In 2005, the organization was interviewing refugees to document the genocide occurring in the region – in effect, to create an oral history of the conflict. To keep refugee children busy, they gave them paper and pencils or crayons. Soon, agency workers realized that the children were capturing their own stories of the genocide in vivid detail in the language with which they felt most comfortable – pictures. These images convey a tragedy that has already rewritten the history of Sudan and has undeniably impacted the children's personal histories.

Drawings by refugee children in Darfur: Abdal-Rahman, 13

These drawings are, in historical terms, primary texts: items created contemporaneous to the event they document. In this manner, they are similar to the Declaration of Independence, the Civil War photos of Matthew Brady, or even a yellow LiveStrong bracelet. They are the material of history.

Yet, these drawings are not just sources for a historian; they also present the personal histories of their creators. Thus, the images suggest that there are many kinds of histories. Those with which you are most familiar come in the form of heavy textbooks thick with words and dense with footnotes – in which visual breaks come in the form of archival photos, presidential portraits, and demographic pie charts. But the field of history is wider and more complex; it includes biography, autobiography, graphic narrative, and texts written from competing theoretical perspectives (for example, feminist, conservative, libertarian, etc.). At base, all histories relate and interpret information about the past. Interpretation is critical because once historians move beyond simply providing a chronology of dates, they begin to shape our

Taha, 13 or 14

Leila, 9

understanding of events by creating a narrative, a causal chain. For example, the images drawn by the children of Darfur provide their subjective perceptions of the war. An academic historian could take them as primary sources and analyze the entire series to find consistent elements. These might support interviews she has conducted with survivors and military records she has found. As the historian begins to bring all these elements together, she crafts a single vision that synthesizes them into a coherent whole: a narrative. However, later, another historian might use the same sources and arrive at a different conclusion—one that revises the common view because of new information or a new perspective (for example, revisionist history). History, then, is not a static field; rather, it is an ongoing dialogue with the past that is always informed by the present.

In an oft-quoted turn of phrase, the Spanish American philosopher George Santayana once wrote, "Those who cannot remember the past are condemned to repeat it." This chapter asks you to consider *how* we remember the past: in what form, from what vantage point, to what end. The selections range from humorous to tragic, from traditional to alternative. Each suggests a way in which we keep pulling the past forward with us, personally and collectively. As you read these works, think about the strategies they use to engage you as a reader and as a member of a larger community. In the words of noted historical figure Abraham Lincoln (who awaits you in this chapter), "Fellow-citizens, we cannot escape history."

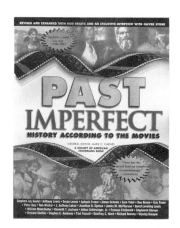

Malcolm X

By Clayborne Carson

FROM: *Past Imperfect: History According to the Movies*, Mark C. Carnes, ed., Henry Holt, 1996

CONTEXT: This essay by Clayborne Carson is a chapter in the book *Past Imperfect: History According to the Movies*, a collection of essays by prominent historians and academics who explore the connection – if any – between the films purporting to capture historical events and individuals and the actual historical record. It is published as a "Society of American Historians Book" and is marketed by its publisher, Henry Holt, as a trade paperback (for a general readership) and as a reference book. Carson is a professor of history at Stanford University, where he is also the director of the Martin Luther King Jr. Research and Education Institute. In this capacity, he recently collaborated with Roma Design Group of San Francisco on the winning proposal to design the King memorial in Washington, D.C. Carson has published on Malcolm X, specifically his surveillance by the FBI, and coedited the reader associated with the landmark PBS series on the civil rights movement, *Eyes on the Prize*. He has also served as a historical consultant on several films and documentaries. As you read this piece, think about the different audiences that a strictly historical narrative about Malcolm X and a popular film about him would have – and how this difference might guide the structure and the content of each.

NEAR THE BEGINNING OF SPIKE LEE'S CINEMA BIOGRAPHY, Malcolm X's father dies. As idealized in the film, Earl Little is a race leader, willing to brave white opposition to promote Marcus Garvey's Universal Negro Improvement Association. The film's flashbacks and narration by the Malcolm character leave no doubt that white racists murdered Little.

The Autobiography of Malcolm X, written with Alex Haley's assistance and published posthumously, paints a far less idealized portrait of Little. As remembered by his son, Little was an abusive husband and father who "savagely" beat his children, except for Malcolm. "I actually believe that as anti-white as my father was," Malcolm recalled, "he was subconsciously so afflicted with the white man's brainwashing of Negroes that he inclined to favor the light one." Only six at the time of his father's death in 1931, Malcolm remembered only "a vague commotion, the house filled up with people crying, saying bitterly that the white Black Legion had finally gotten him." Although the actual circumstances of Little's death remain ambiguous — contemporary police reports dismissed it as an accident, his insurance company suspected suicide — the *Autobiography* and the film have transformed an obscure event into a crucial part of a historical legend that blends personal memory with racial myth.

The film conveys neither the complexity nor the self-critical aspects of the *Autobiography*, which told Malcolm's story from the perspective of his final year. Throughout its more than three hours, Lee's film is resolutely respectful, glamorizing the truculence of Malcolm's Detroit Red period and the dogmatism of some of his speeches as a Muslim minister. As source documents, Lee used Malcolm's memoirs and public statements rather than the testimony of those who knew him. The resulting film is iconolatry rather than iconoclasm.

As a historian, I do not find it useful to quibble about inaccuracies, simplifications, invented characters, imagined dialogue, anachronisms, and various other improbabilities. To complain that Denzel Washington is not Malcolm X is to miss the point of the film and the book, which communicate a constructed image to a far larger audience than Malcolm ever reached during his lifetime. It is far more important to note the film's more serious limitations, particularly its failure to give adequate attention to Malcolm's evolving political ideas and activities during the last year of his life. Although these inadequacies derive from the *Autobiography*, which also focused on Malcolm's years as a petty criminal and then as a minister of the Nation of Islam, Lee further downplays those elements of Malcolm's narrative that indicated his capacity for rigorous self-criticism.

After his father's death in 1931, Malcolm watched his family fall apart. The strain of feeding and caring for seven children proved too much for Louise Little. Although she resisted as best she could pressure from social workers to place her children in foster homes, her psychological decline finally forced her admission to the Kalamazoo State Mental Hospital in December 1938.

At the time his mother was committed, Malcolm was living in a white juvenile home. When his half-sister Ella came to visit from Boston, where she lived, Malcolm thought she was "the first really proud black woman I had ever seen in my life." In 1940, when he was

5

fifteen, Malcolm made his first trip to Boston. On his return to Michigan, he noticed and became annoyed by treatment he had previously shrugged off: "Where 'nigger' had slipped off my back before, wherever I heard it now, I stopped and looked at whoever said it. And they looked surprised that I did."

The transformation of *The Autobiography of Malcolm X* into Spike Lee's film took almost a quarter of a century. Some admirers of Malcolm argued that only a black writer and director could do justice to his story. James Baldwin, the most prominent African American writer of the period, prepared the initial script, but his screenplay — later published as *One Day, When I Was Lost* (1972) — included a vast number of flashbacks and historical scenes that would have been prohibitively expensive to film. During the early 1970s, a white screenwriter, Arnold Perl, wrote another script, but the project lost favor in Hollywood as the nation's interest in black militancy waned. More than a decade later, Warner Brothers finally agreed to finance the film, and Lee was chosen to direct. (The announcement was made after Lee had publicly insisted that a black director should make *Malcolm X*.)

The film's most engaging scenes depict Malcolm's life as a hustler and later his speechmaking on behalf of the Nation of Islam. It largely ignores his activities outside the Nation. Instead of clarifying his mature political perspective, the film emphasizes his earlier cynicism, racial pessimism, and uncritical acceptance of Elijah Muhammad's teachings. The film treats Malcolm X's break with Muhammad as a son's disillusionment with a morally flawed surrogate father, but Malcolm left the Nation for political as well as personal reasons. The *Autobiography* makes it clear that before he learned of Muhammad's marital infidelities, Malcolm had already become dissatisfied with his leader's policy of nonengagement, which not only prevented members of the group from participating in civil rights protests but even forbade voting. Malcolm's sardonic verbal attacks on national black leaders — excerpts from which enliven the film — were harshly critical, but Malcolm's ties with militant civil rights activists actually became increasingly close late in his life.

As the southern black civil rights movement grew in scale during 1963, Malcolm recognized that the nonengagement policy was hurting his recruitment efforts in black communities. In the *Autobiography*, Malcolm admits his disappointment in the failure of the Nation of Islam to become involved in the expanding freedom struggle. "I felt that, wherever black people committed themselves, the Little Rocks and the Birminghams and other places, militantly disciplined Muslims should also be there — for all the world to see, and respect, and discuss. It could be heard increasingly in the Negro communities: 'Those Muslims *talk* tough, but they never *do* anything, unless somebody bothers Muslims.' "

This telling criticism of the Nation of Islam's stance regarding political action appears in the film, but Lee's misleading handling of it reflects his unwillingness to examine critically Malcolm's black nationalist rhetoric as a Muslim minister. In the film, the criticism precedes the only scene in which Malcolm and his fellow Muslims actually stand up to white authorities. Malcolm is shown demanding and getting hospital treatment for a member of the Nation, Brother Johnson (Johnson Hinton), who was beaten by New York City police in 1957. Although the incident confirms the notion that the Nation of Islam did not engage in militant action unless its members were threatened, Lee stages the event to suggest that the Nation was far more willing to challenge white authority than it was.

Malcolm initially defended Elijah Muhammad's nonengagement 10 policy and fiercely attacked Martin Luther King Jr.'s strategy of nonviolent resistance, but he later recognized that the Nation offered no real alternative to black activists who were facing vicious white racists in the South. It was easier to talk about armed self-defense in New York than to face Bull Connor's police dogs in Birmingham. Indeed, even though the film ignores this fact, Malcolm knew that the Nation of Islam was not above making deals with white people when such deals served its leaders' interests. Near the end of his life, Malcolm admitted that, even while criticizing civil rights activists for working with white liberals, he once, on Elijah Muhammad's orders, negotiated a mutual noninterference agreement with Ku Klux Klan leaders in Atlanta. Like Marcus Garvey's in the 1920s, Muhammad's insistence that all whites were devils made it possible for him to justify dealing with the worst of them.

Although the film depicts Malcolm's period of independence from the Nation mainly through scenes of foreboding, such as repeated threatening telephone calls, his final months consisted of much more than waiting for martyrdom. Among the many important episodes of Malcolm's last year that the film mentions only in passing, if at all, are:

- his brief meeting with Martin Luther King Jr. at the U.S. Capitol;

- his crucial "The Ballot or the Bullet" speech delivered at a symposium sponsored by the Congress of Racial Equality;

- his attendance at a meeting of the Organization of African Unity and subsequent talks with leaders of Egypt, Tanzania, Nigeria, Ghana, Guinea, Kenya, and Uganda;

- his day-long October 1964 meeting in Nairobi with leaders of the Student Nonviolent Coordinating Committee and the resulting cooperation between SNCC and Malcolm's newly formed Organization of Afro-American Unity;

- the December 1964 appearance of Fannie Lou Hamer and other Mississippi civil rights activists as Malcolm's honored guests at an OAAU meeting in Harlem.

The film shows Malcolm watching televised scenes of black protest activities (including some that occurred after his death!) but remarkably does not mention his February 1965 trip to Selma, Alabama, where he addressed young protesters and expressed support for the voting rights struggle. While in Selma, he met with Coretta Scott King, whose husband was then in jail. Malcolm affirmed his desire to assist King's voting rights efforts, explaining that if whites knew that Malcolm was the alternative, "It might be easier for them to accept Martin's proposals." Malcolm's increasing political involvement was further indicated in the weeks before his assassination by the telegram he sent to the head of the American Nazi party: "I am no longer held in check from fighting white supremacists by Elijah Muhammad's separationist Black Muslim Movement, and if your present racist agitation of our people there in Alabama causes physical harm to Reverend King or any other Black Americans . . . you and your KKK friends will be met with maximum physical retaliation."

Malcolm's political militancy led to increasing governmental repression and escalating threats from members of the Nation of Islam. Lee's handling of the assassination reflects his overall failure to indicate why Malcolm's independent political course caused him to attract such deadly enemies. The film shows various members of the Nation of Islam preparing to kill Malcolm, while also hinting that white operatives were involved. Malcolm is shown being followed, presumably by CIA agents, while on his trip to Mecca and Africa. We see a bug in Malcolm's New York City hotel room. When Malcolm and his wife, Betty, discuss the many threats they have received, Malcolm speculates, "The more I keep thinking about the things that have been happening lately, I'm not at all sure it's solely the Muslims. I trained them, I know what they can and cannot do, and they can't do some of the stuff that's recently been going on."

It is hardly revelatory for the film to suggest that the FBI and the CIA saw Malcolm as a threat, but speculation about government-sponsored conspiracy obscures the extent to which Malcolm's death resulted from a mentality that allowed some black people to define others as race traitors. Malcolm was a source as well as a victim of the

Nation of Islam's often vicious rhetorical militancy. His former pro-tégé, Louis X (later Farrakhan), declared in late 1964 that Malcolm was a Judas "worthy of death." Such self-righteous vilification created a climate that made Malcolm's death inevitable. Despite its reputation as an antiwhite group, the Nation of Islam directed nearly all of its vi-olence against black people, particularly defectors. Malcolm's death was a precursor of the kind of internecine warfare that weakened the Black Power movement and increased its vulnerability to outside at-tack. Although Malcolm ultimately struggled to find "a common solu-tion to a common problem," the film does not show him working in concert with other black political groups. In the film, Malcolm never completely leaves behind the smug self-righteousness of his years as a hustler and proselytizer. As a result, many young viewers may pre-fer to emulate the self-destructive rebelliousness of Malcolm's youth or the racist demagoguery of his years in the Nation of Islam rather than his mature statesmanship. Some may even mistake Farrakhan as Malcolm's modern-day counterpart.

Spike Lee frames Malcolm's life story with contemporary scenes: 15 opening footage of Los Angeles police beating Rodney King and an epilogue showing Nelson Mandela, in front of a classroom filled with South African children, affirming Malcolm's call for liberation "by any means necessary." This iconic mixture gives his film a greater sense of political importance than it would otherwise have had, but its politi-cal message is nevertheless ambiguous. Lee's strongest images sug-gest the immutability of white racism (King's beating) rather than possibility of overcoming it (Mandela). His film's Malcolm ends his life resigned to his fate rather than displaying confidence in his hard-won political understanding. The film's Malcolm becomes, like the filmmaker himself, a social critic rather than a political insurgent. Malcolm helped to create his own myth during a period when fundamental political change seemed feasible. Spike Lee has re-vised Malcolm's myth for a time when political cynicism prevails. *Malcolm X* thus reflects the current tendency in African American life to supplant politics with attitude — that is, to express diffuse racial re-sentment rather than to engage in collective action to achieve racial advancement.

READING

1. In the second sentence of this essay, Carson writes, "As idealized in the film, . . ." What do you immediately infer from Carson's use of the word "idealized"? What can you assume is his sense of the relationship between the real and film lives of Malcolm X?

2. Carson opposes two methods of treating a historical subject: creating an "iconolatry" or an "iconoclasm." What do these terms mean? How might they result in different types of history?

3. What bothers Carson most about the differences between the real Malcolm X and Spike Lee's Malcolm X? What essential aspects of Malcolm X does he feel Lee misses in the film?

4. Carson lists several events that played critical roles in Malcolm X's last year, events that suggest his political views were more complex than presented in the film. What limitations of film might cause these events to be left out?

5. Carson is a prominent historian who has previously written on Malcolm X. What about his writing would lead you to accept his critique of the film? His version of events? How does a writer gain an authoritative historical voice?

WRITING

1. Think about another biographical or historical film you have seen recently. Write a reflective essay or journal entry that examines the following questions: What drew you to this movie? When you were watching it, did you find the narrative factual or fictional? Did it change your attitude about the historical figure or event?

2. Following the release of Spike Lee's *Malcolm X*, clothing and products with Malcolm's image or the X logo became very popular among young African Americans. Similarly, after 9/11, clothing and even bumper stickers with the image of the fallen towers, with the last words of victims, and even with American flags became big sellers. Write an essay that examines why consumers would buy these products. What message are they sending?

3. Carson espouses strong opinions about Malcolm X, the Nation of Islam, the FBI, Spike Lee, and more. Write an essay that discusses Carson's use of language to characterize the players in this historical narrative. How does he use figurative language to create a narrative with a hero and more than a few villains?

4. At several points in his essay, Carson discusses Lee's unwillingness to treat his subject critically. He seems to be suggesting that Lee treats Malcolm X as an iconic symbol rather than as a complicated human being, which is not an unusual fate for a central historical figure. Write an essay that discusses this tendency to eliminate the complexities in the lives and personalities of important historical figures and reduce them to two-dimensional symbols. Draw on examples from American history (for example, the founding fathers).

5. Carson says of Malcolm X, he "helped to created his own myth," indicating that Malcolm participated in writing his own role in history — and in so doing, encouraged others to see themselves as able to shape the future. Consider how Marjane Satrapi creates her own myth in *Persepolis* (p. 478) by writing herself into major historical events and, in the process, helps us to understand the implications and impact of a complex conflict. Research another historical event with a focus on the personal narrative. Find at least three such narratives associated with the event; they can take any form (film, text, graphic narrative, etc.). Do these narratives align? Are they telling similar stories about the event? Write an essay that discusses your findings and the possibilities and limitations of personalized history.

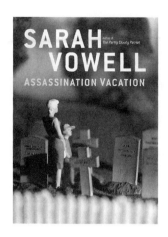

1776: A Musical about the Declaration of Independence

By Sarah Vowell

FROM: *Assassination Vacation*, Simon and Schuster, 2005

CONTEXT: This excerpt is from Sarah Vowell's book *Assassination Vacation*, which narrates a road trip through the assassinations of three presidents, including Abraham Lincoln – the subject of this piece. Vowell's career is an amalgam of academia and pop culture. She is both a fellow at the New York Institute for the Humanities at New York University and the voice of Violet Part in the animated movie *The Incredibles*. She is perhaps best known for her work with the radio anthology, *This American Life*, and her books, including *Take the Cannoli* and *The Partly Cloudy Patriot*. *Assassination Vacation* is published by Simon and Schuster, a mass market publisher that defines itself as "wholly focused on consumer publishing." The company is owned by Viacom, the same conglomerate that owns Paramount, CBS, and MTV. As you read Vowell's piece, think about how her background in pop culture helps her to appeal to an audience that might otherwise have little interest in this topic.

GOING TO FORD'S THEATRE TO WATCH THE PLAY IS LIKE GOING to Hooters for the food. So I had intended to spend the first act of *1776*, a musical about the Declaration of Independence, ignoring the stage and staring at Abraham Lincoln's box from my balcony seat. Then I was going to leave at intermission. Who wants to hear the founding fathers break into song? Me, it turns out. Between eloquent debates about the rights of man, these wiseacres in wigs traded surprisingly entertaining trash talk in which a deified future president like Thomas Jefferson is deplored as a "red-headed tombstone." George Washington's amusingly miserable letters from the front — New Jersey is full of whores giving his soldiers "the French disease" — are read aloud among the signers with eye-rolling contempt, followed by comments such as "That man would depress a hyena." Plus, Benjamin Franklin was played by the actor who played the Big Lebowski in *The Big Lebowski*. I was so sucked into *1776* that whole production numbers like "But, Mr. Adams" could go by and I wouldn't glance Lincolnward once, wrapped up in noticing that that second president could really sing.

Deciding to stay for act II, I spend intermission in the Lincoln Museum administered by the National Park Service in the theater's basement. There are the forlorn blood spots on the pillow thought to have cradled the dying Lincoln's head; the Lincoln mannequin wearing the clothes he was shot in; the key to the cell of conspirator Mary Surratt; the gloves worn by Major Henry Rathbone, who accompanied the Lincolns to the theater and was stabbed by Booth in the president's box; Booth's small, pretty derringer; and, because it's some kind of law for Lincoln-related sites to have them, sculptor Leonard Volk's cast of Lincoln's hands.

Intermission over, I found myself looking forward to the rest of the play, happily bounding back up to my seat. But I paused on the balcony stairs for a second, thinking about how these were the very stairs that Booth climbed to shoot at Lincoln and how sick is this? Then I remembered, oh no they're not. The interior of the Ford's Theatre in which Lincoln was shot collapsed in 1893, but then, in 1968, the National Park Service dedicated this restoration, duplicating the setting of one of the most repugnant moments in American history just so morbid looky-loos like me could sign up for April 14, 1865, as if it were some kind of assassination fantasy camp. So how sick is that?

Act II of *1776* isn't as funny as act I, and not just because Ben Franklin gets to crack fewer sex jokes. It's time for the slavery question. Jefferson and Adams want a document about liberty and equality to include a tangent denouncing kidnapping human beings and cramming them into floating jails only to be auctioned off and treated as animals. This is followed by the expected yelling of southerners who refuse to sign such hogwash, pointing out that slavery is in the Bible, their way of life, blah, blah. What's unexpected is the song. Edward Rutledge of South Carolina (his brother would go on to sign the Constitution) sings a strange but effective *j'accuse* called "Molasses to Rum," in which he implicates New England ships and merchants in the slave trade triangle, asking John Adams: Boston or Charleston, "Who stinketh most?"

This script as performed by these actors really does give the audience a feel for the anguish, embarrassment, and disappointment Adams and Jefferson went through yielding to the southerners' edit. "Posterity will never forgive us," Adams sighs, caving in.

Even though the scene couldn't be more gripping, my head snaps up away from the action to stare at Lincoln's box. The thing that makes seeing this play in Ford's Theatre more meaningful than anywhere else is that I can look from the stage to Lincoln's box and back

5

again, and I can see exactly where this compromise in 1776 is pointing: into the back of Lincoln's head in 1865.

"This country was formed for the white, not for the black man," John Wilkes Booth reportedly wrote on the day he pulled the trigger. (I say reportedly because the letter, to the editors of a Washington newspaper, was destroyed in 1865 but later "reconstructed" and reprinted in 1881.) Booth (again, reportedly, but it sounds like him) continued, "And, looking upon African slavery from the same standpoint as the noble framers of our constitution, I, for one, have ever considered it one of the greatest blessings, both for themselves and us, that God ever bestowed upon a favored nation." So this is whom we're dealing with— not the raving madman of assassination lore, but a calculating, philosophical racist. Then again, anyone who has convinced himself that slavery is a "blessing" for the slaves is a little cracked.

After the play I take a walk to the Lincoln Memorial. It's late. Downtown D.C. is vacant this time of night. Like that of the Lincoln administration, this is a time of war. Back then, Union soldiers camped out on the Mall. Nowadays, ever since the attack on the Pentagon in 2001, the capital has been clamped down. How is this manifested? Giant planters blocking government buildings, giant planters barricading every other street. Theoretically, the concrete flowerpots are solid enough to fend off a truck bomb. And yet the effect is ridiculous, as if we believe we can protect ourselves from suicide bombers by hiding behind blooming pots of marigolds, flowers whose main defensive property is repelling rabbits.

I walk down the darkened Mall past the white protruding phallus that is the Washington Monument. It looks goofy enough in the light of day but ugliest at night, when the red lights at its tippy top blink so as to keep airplanes from crashing into it, a good idea I know, but still, those beady blinking eyes make it come across as fake and sad, the way robots used to look in old movies before George Lucas came along.

I'm alone out here. Even though the Mall is a pretty safe place, 10 I've read way too many pulpy coroner novels with first sentences such as "I spent a long afternoon at the morgue," so I'm feeling a little mugable. Nervously, I shove my hands in my pockets. In the forensics novels the contents of a victim's pockets on the night of her death Say Something about her character. My Ford's Theatre ticket stub and Jimmy Carter key chain say that I am the corniest, goody-goody person in town. Luckily, I survived the evening unscathed so no one will ever find out about that losery Jimmy Carter key chain.

The Library of Congress has a whole display case of items in Lincoln's pockets when he died. His pocketknife, two pairs of spectacles, and a Confederate five-dollar bill are spread out on red velvet. They would probably display the lint too if someone had had the foresight to keep it. The items take on a strange significance. Those are the glasses he must have worn to read his beloved Shakespeare. He could have used the pocketknife to carve the apple he liked to eat for lunch.

The contents of John Wilkes Booth's pockets also get the glass case treatment. At Ford's Theatre, I looked at the five photographs of women in the womanizing Booth's pockets when he died, and I couldn't help but believe that I picked up new insight into his character, that he wasn't just a presidential killer, he was a lady-killer too. Four of the women were actresses he knew. The fifth picture captures Booth's secret fiancée, Lucy Hale, in profile. Lucy was spotted with Booth the morning of the assassination, probably around the same time her ex-senator father John P. Hale, Lincoln's newly appointed ambassador to Spain, was meeting with the president in the White House. Hale, a New Hampshire Republican, was the first abolitionist ever elected to the U.S. Senate. One reason he was so keen on absconding to Europe on a diplomatic appointment was to put an ocean between his pretty daughter and Booth, whom the senator knew to be a pro-slavery southern sympathizer and, worse, an actor. In fact, Hale would have preferred to marry Lucy off to another young man he had noticed admiring her — the president's twenty-one-year-old son, Robert Todd Lincoln.

The Lincoln Memorial is at its loveliest when the sun goes down. It glows. It's quiet. There are fewer people and the people who are here at this late hour are reverent and subdued, but happy. The lights bounce off the marble and onto their faces so that they glow too, their cheeks burned orange as if they've had a sip of that good bourbon with the pretty label brewed near the Kentucky creek where Lincoln was born.

I read the two Lincoln speeches that are chiseled in the wall in chronological order, Gettysburg first. Shuffling past the Lincoln statue, I pause under the white marble feet, swaying back and forth a little so it looks like his knees move. A moment of whimsy actually opens me up for the Second Inaugural, a speech that is all the things they say — prophetic, biblical, merciful, tough. The most famous phrase is the most presidential: with malice toward none. I revere those words. Reading them is a heartbreaker considering that a few weeks after Lincoln said them at the Capitol he was killed. But in my two favorite parts of the speech, Lincoln is sarcastic. He's a writer. And in his sarcasm and his writing, he is who he was. He starts off the speech reminding his audience of the circumstances of his First Inaugural at the eve of war. It's a (for him) long list, remarkably even-handed and restrained, pointing out that both the North and the South were praying to the same god, as if they were just a couple of football teams squaring off in the Super Bowl. Then things turn mischievous: "It may seem strange that any men should dare to ask a just God's assistance in wringing their bread from the sweat of other men's faces; but let us judge not that we be not judged." Know what that is? A zinger — a subtle, high-minded, morally superior zinger. I glance back at the Lincoln statue to see if his eyes have rolled. Then, at the end of this sneaky list of the way things were, he simply says, "And the war came." Kills me every time. Four little words to signify four long years. To call this an understatement is an understatement. To read this speech is to see how Lincoln's mind worked, to see how he governed, how he lived. There's the narrative buildup, the explanation, the lists of pros and cons; he came late to abolitionism, sought compromise, hoped to save the Union without war, etc., until all of a sudden the jig is up. The man who came up with that teensy but vast sentence, *And the war came*, a four-word sentence that summarizes how a couple of centuries of tiptoeing around evil finally stomped into war, a war he says is going to go on "until every drop of blood drawn with the lash, shall be paid by another drawn with the sword," is the same chief executive who in 1863 signed the Emancipation Proclamation. I've seen that paper. It's a couple of pages long. But after watching the slavery agony in *1776*, I like to think of it as a postcard to Jefferson and Adams, another four-word sentence: *Wish you were here*.

When I used to get to the end of the Second Inaugural, in which 15 Lincoln calls on himself and his countrymen "to do all which may achieve and cherish a just, and a lasting peace," I always wondered how anyone who heard those words could kill the person who wrote them. Because that day at the Capitol, Booth was there, attending the celebration as Lucy Hale's plus-one. In the famous Alexander Gardner photograph of Lincoln delivering the speech, you can spot Booth right above him, lurking. And what was Booth's reaction to hearing Lincoln's hopes for "binding up the nation's wounds"? Booth allegedly told a friend, "What an excellent chance I had to kill the president, if I had wished, on Inauguration Day!"

I used to march down the memorial's steps mourning the loss of the second term Lincoln would never serve. But I don't think that way anymore. Ever since I had to build those extra shelves in my apartment to accommodate all the books about presidential death — I like to call that corner of the hallway "the assassination nook" — I'm amazed Lincoln got to live as long as he did. In fact, I'm walking back to my room in the Willard Hotel, the same hotel where Lincoln had to sneak in through the ladies' entrance before his first inauguration because the Pinkerton detectives uncovered a plot to do him in in Baltimore before he even got off the train from Springfield. All through his presidency, according to his secretary John Hay, Lincoln kept a desk drawer full of death threats. Once, on horseback between the White House and his summer cottage on the outskirts of town, a bullet whizzed right by his head. So tonight, I leave the memorial knowing that the fact that Lincoln got to serve his whole first term is a kind of miracle.

READING

1. What do you infer about the tone of Vowell's piece from its first sentence? Does the remainder of the piece continue with this tone, or does it change at any point?

2. Vowell is at Ford's Theatre ostensibly to see *1776*. How does she use the musical to further some points in her narrative?

3. Vowell's account of her visit jumps rapidly from place to place, often following her thoughts rather than her physical location. Are you able to follow this movement? If so, what about her writing enables you to keep pace?

4. Near the end of her narrative, Vowell provides a critical reading of two of Lincoln's speeches. What are they? What message does she take from them?

5. In this excerpt (and throughout the book), Vowell consistently writes from the first person. How does this impact the formality of the piece? What do you learn about Vowell? Does this help you to identify with her and with the subject?

WRITING

1. In this piece, Vowell narrates her visit to the Lincoln Memorial, offering comments that are both irreverent and reverential. Write a reflective essay or journal entry describing your internal monologue on a visit to a historical site. The visit can be one you make specifically for this assignment or one you took long ago. What were you thinking when confronted with history?

2. Vowell says of the rather routine contents of Lincoln's pockets: "The items take on a strange significance." Write an essay about a common object you have kept through the years – something of little monetary value but significant emotional worth. Why has this object become so important? What does it capture about your own history?

3. Vowell lovingly describes the appearance of the Lincoln Memorial. Find several photographs of the memorial shot at different times of the day from different vantage points. Write an essay that describes the memorial and addresses its symbolic elements and the design elements meant to capture the spirit of the man it honors.

4. The Lincoln Memorial holds the text of two of his speeches, and Vowell describes the president as "a writer," saying "in his sarcasm and his writing, he is who he was." Select one and find the complete

text. Write an essay that analyzes the language of the speech. What is Lincoln saying? How does he use figurative language to convey this message? What portrait of the president emerges from the speech?

5. Vowell's narrative offers an informal and, certainly, a nontraditional history. Rick Geary's graphic history, *The Murder of Abraham Lincoln* (p. 486), also takes an alternative view of an academic subject. By presenting history outside of the standard academic, footnoted format, both Vowell and Geary may open the subject up to a younger and more diverse audience. Research the growing field of informal or alternative history writing. Discuss the controversy it sometimes engenders and whether you think these more pop culture-driven genres offer a valid way to present the past.

Frontlines: Dispatches from U.S. Soldiers in Iraq
Soldiers' Blogs

FROM: *New York Times*, April 15–May 3, 2006, www.frontlines.blogs.nytimes.com

CONTEXT: The following blog excerpts are from soldiers who have been, or are, stationed in Iraq. The *New York Times* invited these soldiers to share the experience of their everyday lives in a group blog in the *New York Times* website in TimesSelect. The *Times* boasts that it is the most read national newspaper; it also is the number one national newspaper among college students, readers whose median age is 20.4, an age where serving in the military is a real possibility. As you read the following blog posts, notice how history is being recorded by amateur participants in a nontraditional and electronic historical narrative of war. Consider how few of the posts are about actual battles, usually the focus of traditional historical narratives of war. ("Dispatches from U.S. Soldiers in Iraq" and the *New York Times* webpage copyright © 2006 the New York Times. Reprinted with permission.)

May 3 • 10:10 pm
The Milblog Phenomenon and My "15 Minutes"
Categories: Warrant Officer Michael D. Fay

In this life I've enjoyed a number of well-deserved titles — Father. Son. Brother. Uncle. Marine. Artist. Friend. Recovering Alcoholic. High School Senior Class Salutorian. I've also been the object of less desirable, but equally well-earned descriptors: Ex-Husband. College Dropout (thrice). Drunk. Defaulter. Lately a good former Marine buddy of mine has added a new one. He calls me a curmudgeon.

Recently I was invited to participate as a panelist at the first ever Milblog Conference hosted in Washington on April 22. The event was sponsored by the Veterans of Foreign Wars and Military.Com. In the past year it seems I've acquired another title — milblogger. Like curmudgeon, only time will tell if this will be worthy of mention in my obituary, or whispered about in embarrassed tones by friends and relatives at the wake. "What a shame, a curmudgeon AND a milblogger."

The conference was a combination tent revival and homecoming. Milbloggers are passionate about what they do, and our readers are equally passionate in seeking us out and reading our postings. A year ago I had no idea of what a blog was. Today, as witnessed this very moment by your reading, my thoughts and experiences as a Marine combat artist go out to the furthest reaches of the planet — what is affectionately tagged "the blogosphere."

To a person, every milblogger at the conference started out with one primary mission — to keep family and friends in the loop about our real-time experiences out in the war on terrorism. My nephew, First Lieutenant Richard "Joey" Fay, before he left for Iraq last July with his Marine battalion, started one with the help of his wife, Kris. His intent was simple, keep kith and kin informed while cutting down on e-mail traffic. *Want to know what I'm up to? Check the blog.* (His blog can be read at Fayboyo1.blogspot.com.) Setting the site up was both simple and free thanks to Blogger.com.

We milbloggers found a shared common philosophy in posting on 5 our sites. There was some debate over what to call the unwritten law we all found ourselves spontaneously adhering to, but the three-part guiding principle was universal — Don't post anything you didn't want your mom, your commanding officer, or Osama bin Laden to read.

Those of us chosen to be panelists at the conference had something else happen. Not only were acquaintances coming to our sites, but so were complete strangers . . . by the tens of thousands. "If you build it, they will come" took on new meaning for us. Me — the last analog guy in a digital world, the gent with sketchbook and pencil — found himself on the cutting edge of information technology and political influence. I was posting digital images of field drawings still reeking of cordite. I would sit hunched over my laptop at Camp Falluja, fresh in from the field, cathartically pecking out dispatches even as my superior and cubicle buddy, Marine Corps field historian Lieutenant Colonel Craig Covert, implored, "Fay, you're ripe! Please take a shower, NOW!" (Lt. Col. Covert's blog, here.) I would click the "publish post" button, and somewhere in Pittsburgh a technical writer's e-mail inbox would ping with a message alerting her. As Inspector Gadget loved to say, "Wowzers!"

May 1 • 10:15 pm
Through the Eyes of an Iraqi Man
Categories: First Lt. Lee Kelley

The following piece is a short work of fiction. I wrote it through the eyes of a local Iraqi man, who is a figment of my imagination. Much of the information and actual events I am privy to here are classified, but in this fashion I can share some of the realities about the Iraqi people that many Americans may not think much about or realize. Of course, it is not intended to represent a whole society or culture, but I know for a fact there are men like Abu, and I thought you might like to hear his "voice." Like all fiction, Abu's words and experiences are based, to some degree, in reality. — First Lt. Lee Kelley

My name is Abu Hassin. I am sitting right now outside of my small home on a chicken farm east of Ramadi, only miles from the fishing village where I grew up. I am smoking a cigarette and drinking my evening tea while I write these lines in a notebook.

I am very happy that the Americans helped to remove Saddam. Who else would help us? I remember the day when Saddam was captured. I have not cried and laughed so much in a very long time. In December I was so proud to see my wife go out and vote. She is a brave woman. Before my mosque came to be used by insurgents, my imam prayed for the Americans over the loudspeakers. Do they know we pray for them? Some say the Americans want to stay in Iraq, but I think they want to go to go home.

There is violence still, yes, but there has always been violence in 10 this land. Already life holds so much more promise for my people. I am old now, but for the children I am very happy. I am an elder in my village, so people listen to me. And I am sick and tired of these stupid men creating more violence. What will it solve? Don't they understand that if they stopped the violence, the Americans would leave? The Americans call them insurgents, but they call themselves "freedom fighters," as if the Americans want to take our freedom away. They are helping to free us!

I see these men acting so secretive and important, planning their attacks. I knew them when they were little boys playing barefoot in the dirt. I laugh at them. I am too old, so they leave me alone. They threaten me, but I know they will not harm me. I am not afraid of death anyway. My own father was dragged away in the night from my home by Saddam's men. We were never told why, and we never saw him again. All three of my uncles fled the country. Now these "freedom fighters" threaten their own people, hurting Iraq because they cannot truly hurt America. They are silly children who think they are all grown up.

April 28 • 10:06 pm

The Little Inconveniences of Army Life

Categories: Capt. Will Smith

When you are away from home for a year in a place like Iraq, there is a lot to miss. Of course you miss your family and friends and all the important parts of your life, but the little things can also add up and cause you to long for home even more.

For example, I have been wearing the same clothes every day for nearly a year. What am I wearing today? A funny looking green suit. What will I wear tomorrow? A funny looking green suit. It sure would be nice to wear some blue or red clothes! (Oh, yeah, but then I would stand out like a bull's eye. O.K., maybe green isn't too bad.)

Also, since arriving here, I have enjoyed my meals "picnic style" — with plastic forks, plastic plates, and paper cups. There just isn't anything like the excitement of steak night coupled with the challenge of cutting the meat with a dull plastic knife. At least my arms get a work-out from all the sawing back and forth. The spoons in the little packages are large enough to fill sandbags with in a pinch. When sampling the delicious Baskin Robbins ice cream as a dessert, the spoon size requires me to contort my mouth into odd positions to get the dang thing to fit — and every so often the spoon will have sharp edges that slice the inside of my cheek.

Of course we do not have indoor plumbing. You haven't lived until 15 you have sweated inside a porta-potty in 120 degree heat, smelling that awful odor. In the winter, it is nice that you can escape the gut-churning smells but somehow karma makes up for it with cold toilet seats and the toilet paper disappears twice as fast for some unknown reason.

April 26 • 10:06 pm

Revisiting Afghanistan

Categories: Warrant Officer Michael D. Fay

Things are finally settling down enough to allow me the time to do the actual thing I get paid to do: create art.

My first set of pieces will be based on a trip to Afghanistan last spring. I had previously gone to Afghanistan at the beginning of Operation Enduring Freedom during the winter of 2002, in the Kandahar region, Bagram, and Kabul. It was winter and the landscape was raw and desolate. I told folks back home, in all seriousness, that everything had a bullet hole in it and the national flower must be shrapnel. In fact, I keep a jagged and rusted shard of the stuff on display in my bedroom as a reminder. I also returned with intangibles: visions of the trees in Kabul festooned with kites, and the weary windburned faces of marines standing watch on the farthest unforgiving edge of the civilized world.

Last May I returned to Afghanistan and went out with the Third Battalion of the Third Marine Regiment, a Hawaii-based infantry unit. The three companies of this battalion had responsibility for three provinces smack dab in the foothills of the Tora Bora mountains on the Pakistani border; Nangarhar, Konar, and Laghman Provinces. The scenery was spectacular. The Afghanis themselves are a strikingly diverse nation. Many possess those penetrating otherworldly emerald green eyes made famous by Sharbat Gula, the Afghan girl on the *National Geographic* cover back in 1985. There are blondes, redheads, oriental features, Arabic faces, and distinctly European types; not surprising when you consider the conquering armies from both East and West that crisscrossed the wild valleys of the Pech and Kunar Rivers of these provinces.

The process of making art out of these experiences goes something like this: 1. Go through a couple thousand photographs and field sketches to identify themes. 2. Read personal journals; watch and listen to hours of digital audio and video recordings a couple of times. (I've got everything from personal interviews to firefights.) 3. Create a detailed work plan with projected pieces and the medium for each (I do oils, watercolor, and finished graphite drawings). 4. Stare at list and get overwhelmed. 5. Procrastinate. 6. Ruminate. 7. Drink too much coffee. 8. Begin. 9. Fantasize about a simple life flipping burgers or handing out happy face stickers at Wal-Mart. 10. Finish. 11. Repeat steps 1–10.

Most artists will tell you that starting is the easy part; you also 20 need to know when to end.

April 25 • 10:15 pm

Fighting with Honor

Categories: First Lt. Lee Kelley

It seems to me, in this chaotic enterprise we call Operation Iraqi Freedom, that we're providing a service to the entire planet. There's a simple formula to prove this. The fewer terrorists there are planning and carrying out attacks on civilians — and for that matter, the fewer terrorists left alive — the better our world must exponentially become. By that barometer alone, we are doing a wonderful service to all those opposed to terrorism.

As an army, we are trained to be merciful but relentless. We do not enter mosques unless we absolutely have to. We try to respect Muslim holy days (Friday) and other religious holidays. We provide security so the citizens of Iraq can vote. We do our best to keep noncombatants safe. We understand that it is better to let an insurgent get away than to harm an innocent civilian. We form up in lines and walk patrols, or we load up in vehicles and drive in. We know the rules of war, engagement, and the escalation of force. We understand the Geneva conventions. We try to live by Army values: loyalty, duty, respect, selfless service, honor, integrity, and personal courage. We provide medical care to enemy wounded just as we treat our own. Our actions are constantly being analyzed, modified, and improved to ensure we only kill those who would do us harm.

We don't run and hide. We are prepared for a fight and are not shy about it. We understand that war is a nasty business, but we are willing to fight the enemy face to face. These insurgents, on the other hand, set up explosive devices that can be remotely detonated, after which they run and hide like teenagers throwing eggs at a house. They fly airplanes into buildings full of civilians.

April 22 • 10:00 pm
The Conversation
Categories: First Lt. Jeffrey D. Barnett

Not long ago I was out with a patrol on a "knock-and-talk" operation, visiting Iraqis in their homes to give and get useful information. We happened upon a large house situated across from a small mosque. I knew it was a mosque because I read the Arabic sign above the door and recognized the loudspeakers rising above its roof.

Some children were standing in the entryway to the house's 25 courtyard, and they looked a little apprehensive as our Humvee pulled around the corner. As I exited the truck they moved away a bit and ducked back inside the courtyard, but still well within sight and hearing. I wanted to show them they had nothing to fear so I quickly shouted an Arabic greeting. That turned them around.

I approached them slowly and I began to speak with three of the boys, who turned out to be brothers. My conversation is transcribed below. Not everything is included, as there were lots of shrugs and hand signals used to make ourselves understood, but they seemed to understand most of what I was saying in modern standard Arabic, which is surprising given the Iraqi dialect. (A linguist later explained to me that children are usually taught modern standard Arabic in school, and, therefore, are probably the best at understanding me.) The older brother, Amar, led most of the conversation. I was thrilled to understand what he was saying and for him to understand me without the the help of a translator.

> Me: Welcome.
> Them: Welcome.
> Me: How are you today?
> Them: Praise be to Allah.
> Me: Good, praise be to Allah. Is that a mosque?
> Amar: Yes, a mosque.
> Me: It is a small mosque.
> Amar: Yes, small.
> Me: Do you play soccer?
> Them: Yes, we play soccer.
> Me: Good. Are these your brothers?
> Amar: Yes . . . sisters. (He used the English word "sisters," apparently excited he knew an English word.)
> Me: Oh, not sisters. Boys are brothers. Girls are sisters.
> Amar: Oh, brothers!

April 20 • 10:00 pm
Just Drop Me Off When This Is Over
Categories: First Lt. Lee Kelley

When this is over, take my weapon. I won't need it for a while. Take this body armor. I would look silly wearing it at the beach. Witness as I grow a goatee. And watch me indulge, at least for a while, in fast food, massive amounts of sleep, alcohol, channel-surfing, and many other things that I have lived without for long enough now that I remember liking them more than I actually do.

I have two wonderfully resilient children to whom I've dedicated my life and who will one day soon forget that their Dad was gone for so long. They are incredible, intelligent, and well-adjusted — and for that I thank my wife.

They won't notice if I'm gone another day or two.

So just drop me off when this is over.

30

I truly appreciate all the support, but I don't need parades or awards or speeches from the governor. I don't even need a ride. Just leave me on any interstate that has a friendly shoulder with nice loose gravel to kick at, or in a subway car full of morning New York commuters, or in a hotel room looking out at the arch in downtown St. Louis. Leave me in Atlanta, or Portland, Oregon; Gig Harbor, Washington, or in a lighthouse on the coast of Maine. I'll gladly be dropped off anywhere in North Dakota, Maryland, Alabama, or Florida. How about a rest area in Flagstaff, Arizona, or a four-way stop in Twin Falls,

Idaho? I'll be fine on my own, whether you leave me in a quiet forest, at a state fair, or in the middle of a mosh pit.

April 19 • 10:00 pm

Life Never Ends

Categories: Warrant Officer, Michael D. Fay

During my recent trip to New Orleans, I received a phone call from the father of Lance Cpl. Nicholas G. Ciccone, the subject of my April 3 posting. I had been expecting a call from Mr. Ciccone. The family wants to arrange a private viewing of his portrait.

Mr. Ciccone generously shared with me the circumstances around discovering the existence of his dead son's image. Matt, the stepbrother who contacted me, overwhelmed with thoughts of his beloved brother, couldn't sleep one night last week. So he did what many of us do during occasional dark nights of the soul — we Google. Matt Googled his brother's full name, and up popped a couple of sites with the drawing. Some light entered the dark night.

I can barely tell you how gratifying it was to hear this. A few days later I received an e-mail from his mother with effusive thanks. Several cousins of Lance Cpl. Ciccone have contacted me and the thread running through their messages is not simply their love for this young man, but that they have all been thinking of him intensely during the past few weeks. Whether parent, sibling, or friend, all have articulated in one form or another a common feeling — they've regained a piece of him, that he's returned, if only for just a short period of time. I am humbled.

April 17 • 10:00 pm

Listening to the Land

Categories: First Lt. Lee Kelley

War comes in waves and cycles. First, there's a little apprehension and a lot of excitement about the unknown future. There's bonding, adventure, hardship, and growth. After a while, even though the pace is still rapid and new occurrences are born daily, monotony sneaks up on you. You're always alert, sensitive to the sounds around you, but the nuances can become muted. You have to be a good listener.

Native Americans would put their ears to the ground to hear or feel vibrations of, say, a train coming, or a cavalry of soldiers on horseback. Out here we have intelligence analysts with their collective ears to the ground. They listen to the Americans fighting in Iraq and to the people of Iraq. They help us understand the sounds of the land. They spend their days poring over intelligence reports about things like the disposition of the Iraqis and enemy tactics. The intelligence flows from the battlefield, all the way up the chain of command. It is continuous, like a tide.

Some intelligence may be bad or from an unreliable source. But some can be very helpful. Here's an example: A few months back, a soldier noticed a hand print on the side of a house in the Al Anbar Province. For some reason, the soldier thought the hand print looked out of place amid all the dirt and cracks on the house, so he reported this small detail to his intelligence analyst. We finally realized that this symbol was being used in the area to let terrorists know that the house was "friendly" to them. If you were an insurgent who had just fired a mortar or a rocket-propelled grenade at an American base, this hand print designated the home as a place you could seek shelter.

We have many interpreters, or "terps" as we call them, who help us immensely. These are Iraqi men and women who appreciate what we're doing for their country and want to help us.

April 15 • 10:00 pm
A Lazy Sunday
Categories: First Lt. Jeffrey D. Barnett

It was another semirelaxed Sunday here at Camp Falluja.

A couple weeks ago the Marine Expeditionary Force Commanding General passed that all nonessential personnel shouldn't come into work until 11 A.M. on Sunday, or should generally get a few hours off. The 11 A.M. thing is kind of a farce because almost everyone is essential, but my team and I try to take the afternoon off if we don't have any operations going on. Such was the case a few Sundays back. It was the first one in a while I had spent totally inside the wire.

I spent the afternoon with my roommate organizing our room. We 40 had both received a plethora of care packages, and stacking and organizing all our new belongings (mostly food) was a challenge. Getting rid of the empty boxes requires a long walk to the dumpster, something we try to avoid by consolidating as much as possible. I turned off my chow supply from home after only a couple boxes because I quickly saw I would not be able to eat it all nor would I have a place to store it. My roommate did that a little later, about eight boxes into the game with more on the way. He's tried to give this stuff away any way he can, mostly by displaying it next to the coffee mess at our workplace.

I actually gave away some food as well. The marines at work hadn't taken to using my previously owned coffee pot, so since it had been sitting there for a couple of days, I bundled it up with some coffee and filters and gave it to the Ugandan gate guards outside our building. They said "Thank you," but didn't really seem enthused. Maybe they thought I was asking them to hold my I.E.D. Either way, they now are capable of making their own coffee, whether they choose to or not. (Update: I have seen the Ugandans using the coffee pot lately.)

I also got a haircut from one of the marines at work. He is what I call a "closet barber."

READING

1. These blogs come from individual soldiers' perspectives of the so-called war on terror, and so their voices are very different from the usual ones that report on this war — on television, for example. How would you describe the tone these soldiers establish in their comments? Do they all see the war from the same perspective?

2. Warrant Officer Michael D. Fay titles his post of May 3, 2006, "The Milblog Phenomenon and My '15 minutes.' " What is the allusion here and what is the milblog phenomenon? What reasons does he give for creating his blog?

3. As readers in America, we might question the security of having soldiers tell their experiences directly of this war. What does Warrant Officer Fay say is the "unwritten law" for all milbloggers?

4. First Lt. Lee Kelley, on May 1, 2006, posts a description of how an Iraqi man might view the American invasion of Iraq. What view of American soldiers comes through in his depiction of how local people view the American presence?

5. Compare the points of view of First Lt. Lee Kelley, "Fighting with Honor," on April 25 and First Lt. Jeffrey D. Barnett, "The Conversation," on April 22. How would you describe the purpose each sees in being a soldier in Iraq?

WRITING

1. Choose one of these posts or one of these soldiers that speaks to you and write a reply to the blog that explains your opinion of the war and your attitude toward what the soldier has reported.

2. These blogs sponsored by the *New York Times* all happen to be written by men. But of course women are serving in Iraq too. Do a search through Google or blogger.com and find any women soldiers posting their experiences of the war. Write a short descriptive essay detailing the kinds of events that the women report.

3. Reread First Lt. Lee Kelley's April 20 post "Just Drop Me Off When This Is Over." Then, write your own narrative essay cataloging the things in America that would be precious to you if you were overseas and at war and contemplating your return home. What would your attitude be?

4. Warrant Officer Michael D. Fay was hired to create art about the Marine Corps in combat in Iraq. He is also a combat Marine. One of the

portraits of a fellow soldier that he made and published on his blog was the last image the family of Lance Cpl. Nicholas G. Ciccone ever saw of their son and brother. They contacted Fay for copies of the portrait. You can see the portrait and read the posting at www.frontlines.blogs.nytimes.com/?p=33. Research the role of the combat artist and art that has been made during war by the participants, in this war and others, such as the Vietnam War. Write a researched essay in which you present the highlights of your findings, including images, to your class.

5. Ian Mortimer, in "Revisionism Revisited" (p. 450), writes about the controversy surrounding "revisionist" history and President Bush's attack on those who questioned his decision to "take military action against Iraq." Mortimer argues that the most trusted history has generally been written by professionals. In Frontlines, however, we read about the action in Iraq, written by amateurs. These men are not professional journalists, nor are they professional war correspondents or historians. Research the coverage of the war in Iraq by both professionals and amateurs and write an essay summarizing your conclusions and insights about which sources are the most trustworthy and why.

The States, Their Nicknames and Mottoes, and Other Facts Critical to Safe Travel
By John Hodgman

FROM: *The Areas of My Expertise*, Penguin, 2005

CONTEXT: This book was originally published in 2005 by Penguin Group, the second largest English language trade books publisher in the world. The company was formed in 1838 in New York by George Palmer Putman and John Riley, and today operates in the United States under numerous imprints, such as Berkley Books, Dutton, Grosset & Dunlap, New American Library, Penguin, Philomel, G. P. Putnam's Sons, Riverhead Books, and Viking. This widely known and prestigious publisher's list of authors is a "Who's Who of the industry," according to the Penguin USA website. John Hodgman is a contributing writer for publications including *McSweeney's*, the *Paris Review*, and the *New York Times Magazine*, where he is also the humor editor. He is perhaps most well known currently for his guest appearances as an "expert" on Jon Stewart's *The Daily Show* as well as his appearances in the "Get a Mac" ad campaign. As you read these entries from his fictional reference work, consider how his delivery mocks the encyclopedias and almanacs he is imitating.

AS MANY HAVE FORGOTTEN, OUR NATION IS DIVIDED INTO states, numbering fifty-one (of which only fifty are commonly known[1]). They are a remarkable natural occurrence of mysterious origin which when you fit them all together, perfectly cover the continental mass we call the U.S.A., leaving only the small hole or "district" of Columbia, where compasses spin wildly and magnets fail to function. In addition, the U.S. owns several territories and island protectorates, and twenty-five secret space colonies. That is all I can tell you about the space colonies. But if you are surprised to learn that there are secret space colonies, then you are more foolish than I thought.

When I was a child in Brookline, Massachusetts, everyone knew that "Massachusetts" was the "Bay State" due to its enormous bay-leaf-drying industry. And it was often on a eucalyptus-scented evening that I would dreamily ponder the exotic pictures conjured by the nick-names of other states: Rhode Island, or "Li'l Rhodie"; Connecticut, or "Normal-Size Rhodie"; Alaska, or the "Land of Mustaches." Perhaps I was just woozy from the bay leaves, but the nation seemed a magical place then, and I always had very clear nasal passages.

Few children are taught now to recite all the state nicknames and their mottoes, and so I provide this handy and most basic guide to the great jigsaw puzzle that is our nation and its many giant pieces, made of land.

Alabama

NICKNAME: State of the Golden Heads

MOTTO: "We Dare to Sculpt Our Own Heads."

NOTES: In this state, the governor is paid in gold ingots. It is customary at the end of his/her term to melt some number of them and return them to the state as a bust of his/her head. Traditionally, the gold sculpting was done by the governor himself. Anti–child labor Governor William D. Jelks was a particularly nimble sculptor, while George Wallace, for reasons unknown, gave himself a third eye in the middle of his forehead during his last term of office. Now the task is largely given over to professional sculptors and paid consultants, many from out of state, making this, for most Alabamans, a hollow exercise in professional politicking.

Alaska

NICKNAME: Land of Mustaches

SIZE: At 656,424 square miles, it is the largest state. If superimposed on the "Lower 49," it would stretch from Minnesota to Texas, destroying all beneath it.

NOTES: Also known as Seward's Folly or Seward's Icebox after William 5 Seward, who purchased the territory from the Russians in 1867 for the purpose of freezing American presidents. Seward, who was stabbed the same night as Lincoln was shot, believed that had Lincoln reached a massive, frozen tundra soon enough, he might not have died and instead might have been preserved until such time as future science could revive him. Alaska, thus, was designed as an icy safeguard against future assassinations, though it was never used. It is true that Gerald Ford was flown there after Squeaky Fromme's assassination attempt, but instead of being frozen, he visited a hospital and met Eskimos.

Arizona

NICKNAMES: The Complimentary Bolo Tie State, The Arrid Extra Dry State

STATE CAPITAL: Phoenix, which is ritually burned and rebuilt every fourteen years.

NOTES: The state mammal is the ringtail cat, a small, delicate member of the raccoon family known for its keen eyes, opposable thumbs, and consequent lockpicking skills. Since Arizona achieved statehood in 1912, a ringtail has always held an honorary position in state government, enjoying free passage anywhere within the state capitol building in Phoenix. By strange coincidence, the ringtail is always named John McCain. When the actual John McCain refused to be photographed eating chili with the ringtail McCain at Old Smoky's Restaurant in the town of Williams — a long tradition among Arizona politicians — he was accused of having a temper problem and a bad, anti-ringtail attitude.

Arkansas

NICKNAME: The Bauxite State

MOTTO: "In Bauxite, the Future."

NOTES: Arkansas was formed after the Louisiana Purchase by a scientific method using samples of the state of Kansas and the state of Ar^2 — the latter providing the seed of the state's bauxite veins, the magical ore that is transformed into aluminum, the metal of the future. Many Americans also flock to the continent's only public diamond field, and only a small number of the diamonds found are used to build city-destroying lasers.

California

CURRENT NICKNAME: The Golden State

OLD NICKNAME: Mexico

MOTTO: "Do Not Fear Our Giant Prehistoric Trees."

NOTES: Along with Texas, California was briefly an independent republic, declaring its independence from Mexico in 1846 as "The Bear Flag Republic." After a mere two weeks of self-rule, however, the Bears were defeated in battle and convinced to sign a treaty. They agreed to become citizens of the United States, to stop wearing clothes, and to cut back on the mauling. But the flag remains, still confusing schoolchildren today, who naturally associate California less with bears than with its fine organic produce, borax mining, and giant drive-thru trees.

Colorado

NICKNAME: The Dwarrodelf

STATE FLOWER: Formerly the Rocky Mountain Columbine, now renamed the Rocky Mountain Pretty, Pretty Flower.

NOTES: Organized as a territory in 1861 by hardscrabble settlers who had come west in search of good skiing and a place to hide their missile defense nerve center. They chose the Rocky Mountains because they were strong and largely Balrog-free, and there they delved deeply, hollowing the earth's heart of gold and building great halls and underground cities. The chief of these was NORAD, a sprawling dark metropolis that was ruled by a talking computer. Some say a few Coloradans still lurk there, in the hard hills, where they stare down from their empty vaults and echoing antechambers in a lonely vigil. But rumors that they will regularly sneak into your hot tub and drown there are largely inventions of the hot tub–grate industry.

Connecticut

CURRENT NICKNAME: The McCormick Brand Nutmeg State
OLD NICKNAME: The All Brands of Nutmeg State
MOTTO: *"Veritas"*

NOTES: The cradle of Yankee ingenuity in the eighteenth and nine- 10
teenth centuries, Connecticut gave the nation the cotton gin, the steel fishhook, the first American cigar, the mechanical nutmeg, and the collapsible hog as well as the first American submarine. The *Turtle* — a one-man, hand-powered submersible used in the Revolutionary War — was the creation of inventor David Bushnell, a citizen of Say-brook and graduate of Yale College, America's most prestigious school of literary theory and Secret World Government. While the *Turtle* failed in its mission to sink the HMS *Eagle*, Yale remains a naval power. From its secret harbor in the New Haven fjord, Yale still sends out one-man submarines to conduct surveillance and to convey secret messages to its branches in Paris, Beijing, and the Hague.

Delaware

NICKNAME: The Silverstone State, New Sweden
MOTTO: "First in the Union, First in Silverstone!"

NOTES: The fortunes of the "First State" have long been synonymous with DuPont, founded there as a gunpowder and dynamite company in the nineteenth century and now one of the world's largest corporations. Much of Delaware is parkland, an enormous estate owned by the rogue DuPont siblings: Cleve, Reynaud, Doc, Manfred, and Melissa. Long disassociated with the company that bears their name, their mutual loathing makes Delaware the playground of their rivalries. They fight one another endlessly, making frequent use of dynamite, assassins, and teams of lions. Melissa, the youngest, is now in her nineties. No one has seen the eldest, Cleve, since the 1970s, though an annual message is often sent from his lands to the local newspaper wishing health to Delawarians and death to his siblings. Reynaud is said to have extended his life via marvelous chemicals devised by his captive brother, Doc, and to travel the state in a suit of resilient, nonstick armor. Worst of all is Manfred, who lords over Dover, that sad port that accepts the country's military dead, whom, it is whispered, are reanimated by Manfred and employed as his footmen. This is why the press is no longer allowed to photograph the flag-draped coffins. While the DuPont corporation denies the existence of the terrible siblings, its board of directors, like the rest of the state, awaits the champion who will finally end their reign of terror.

Florida

NICKNAME: The Magic Kingdom, The Battleground State
MOTTO: "3,000 Theme Parks By the Year 3000."
NOTES: When they have neared the end of their productive life, here is where the honored elders of our nation are sent to tend to the magic orange groves. Younger visitors delight at the fascinating antics of the aged, especially after they have been rejuvenated by glowing alien pods. And thousands gather each year to watch the old ones sing and break dance at the Launching of the Harvest, when millions of pounds of citrus are loaded onto sea barges and then towed by manatees up the coast.

Georgia

NICKNAME: "Where Every Street Is Named Peachtree"
STATE COCKTAIL: The "Georgia-on-My-Mind": equal parts Coke, Peachtree schnapps, and dry sherry
NOTES: Georgia is a bounteous state marked by the near supernatural production of two remarkably versatile crops: peanuts and peaches. The former is commonly transformed into peanut butter, various roofing materials, and allergens; the latter are used to make Peaches 'n' Cream Lifesavers, accounting software, and glue. Both are made into schnapps. Martin Luther King Jr. was born in Atlanta, yet it would take a thousand clones of that great activist for peace and tolerance to erase Georgia's dark reputation as the birthplace of Stalin. Unfortunately, though, conservative anticloning ideologues within the U.S. government have conspired to keep MLK models #1–1000 in stasis in the basement of Georgia State University. Their fate is uncertain.

Hawaii

NICKNAME: The Lost Continent That Is Not Atlantis
MOTTO: *"Ua Mau Ke Ea O Ka Aina I Ka Pono"* ("The Land Mu Is Perpetuated in Righteousness.")
NOTES: The Kingdom of Hawai'i consists of only the tops of the highest mountaintops of what was once the ancient lost continent known as Mu. According to legend, Mu was an advanced, peaceful empire of hovercars and glowing pyramids in which all children were trained as both warriors and poets, largely using an early version of books-on-

tape. But their science could not hold back a vengeful sea, and so the empire was swallowed by the waves some fifteen thousand years ago or more. Chaos reigned among the various chieftains who ruled the remaining islands after the continent's demise. It was not until 1810 (A.D. 27,981, Year of Mu) that the islands would be unified under King Kamehameha the Great, who established a sophisticated constitutional monarchy guided by reason and modeled after the post–Enlightenment European states. Once again, hovercars traveled from island to island. The ukulele was invented, and the king initiated a massive project to raise the Lost Continent using giant balloons and crude nuclear explosives. This proved too threatening to the American-born plantation owners. Under the leadership of the attorney Sanford Dole, and with the backing of the U.S. Marines, they forced the last king to sign a new constitution at gunpoint, which would strip the native Hawaiians of their voting rights, effectively end the monarchy, and halt the ascent of Mu (at about the halfway mark). But: we got another state out of it.

Hohoq (also known as Ar)

NICKNAME: The Vanishing State, The Ford Thunderbird State

MOTTO: "Please Do Not Seek Us."

NOTES: A large, cloud-encircled plateau that moves mysteriously from place to place throughout America, and frequently goes completely unobserved for decades. Often forgotten on most maps and openly disdained by scientists who have not yet been able to explain it, it is supposedly home to the Thunderbirds — airplane-sized eagles capable of shooting lightning from their eyes, which were once considered a Native American legend. In 2001, when Ford Motor Company reintroduced its Thunderbird model, an attempt was made to capitalize on the legend of the 51st State. As a publicity stunt, 250 Thunderbird cars were sent out to find it and climb the cliffs to their airy heights. Most of the cars were never recovered (none of the drivers ever were). In 2005, one empty vehicle mysteriously washed ashore on Revere Beach in Boston, while another was found near Sacramento, appearing to have been dropped from a great height.

NOTES

[1]Please see "A Note on Ar," above.

[2]Common appellation. Officially known as "Hohoq" — please see individual state entry above.

READING

1. Examine the layout of this excerpt and identify the aspects that visually suggest that this is a valid or true account of "The States, Their Nicknames and Mottoes, and Other Facts Critical to Safe Travel," as his title suggests.

2. This piece of his book proceeds alphabetically, covering states from A to H. How does this alphabetic structure set up its readers for Hohoq?

3. Each entry begins with the state's nickname, but the second entry differs from state to state. Note and discuss these variations and how they play on the nickname or the state name.

4. One of the ways Hodgman's humor works is that he mixes "true" names and facts with total fabrications. For example, under Arizona, he mentions John McCain and a temper problem. In what ways is the situation he describes true? In what ways is it ridiculous? Find other examples of this method in the excerpt.

5. What kinds of authorities does he cite in his explanations to model the kind of references we would expect in an actual reference work, particularly what we would expect in a real history of the states?

WRITING

1. Ira Glass, the host of public radio's *This American Life,* says of Hodgman's book, "Sometimes I just stare at the paragraphs trying to figure out how he is doing it – like there is some hidden trick in his brave, deadpan sentences that makes them funnier than they have a right to be." Write a journal entry or reflective essay about what aspects of the descriptions of the states you found humorous. Then, try to describe how Hodgman's humor works from your point of view.

2. Pick a state that is not included in this excerpt from Hodgman's book. Research that state. Then, write your own entirely made-up entry for that state, as if it were to be included in this list of "The States, Their Nicknames and Mottoes, and Other Facts Critical to Safe Travel."

3. Find an actual brief history of each state in the United States – in an almanac, an encyclopedia, or textbook, for example. Then, write a critical analysis of the method used in the document to persuade its readers of its authenticity and truthfulness. In your conclusion, compare and contrast the "real" history with Hodgman's fake one.

4. Choose an official document from your school – perhaps the student handbook, for example, or even pages from the official school website. Divide the document among small groups in your class. Ask each group to rewrite their section together, using the John Hodgman method of being an "expert" that you have just studied. Be sure they mimic the original format and consider things like font, illustrations, and charts, as well as tone and language. They should mix complete fabrications with occasional kernels of truth. Then, assemble the entire document that has been created and present it to your class and instructor.

5. Hodgman appears regularly on Jon Stewart's *The Daily Show* as "Resident Expert." As such, he speaks on topics ranging from Iranian nuclear ambitions to *American Idol*. Stewart says of the show, "When we spot silliness, we say so out loud. We're not really Democrat or Republican. We're out to stop that political trend of repeating things again and again until people are forced to believe them. . . . That's the beauty of our show." How does a faux news show like Stewart's come to wield real political clout? How can a humorist like Hodgman make us question the nature of authority itself? Research the segments of *The Daily Show* Hodgman has appeared on and write a critical analysis of his persona as an expert.

Rewriting History

By Anne Scott MacLeod

FROM: *Teacher Magazine*, April 1998

CONTEXT: This essay appeared in *Teacher Magazine*, which is published by Education Week Press, a division of Editorial Projects in Education (EPE), a nonprofit, tax-exempt organization based in Washington, D.C. Education Week Press was formed to "further EPE's mission of elevating the level of discourse on K-12 education." The press focuses on school policy and reform. Anne Scott MacLeod is professor emerita at the University of Maryland College of Information Studies, a center for graduate education, research, and service. Her focus is the history and criticism of children's literature and the role of the library in social process. The MacLeod Literature Lecture Series is named after her. Its purpose is "to [expose] scholarly issues associated with children's literature to a broad audience." As you read this piece consider her argument for the ethics of representation in children's fiction.

EAGER TO PORTRAY WOMEN IN A MODERN LIGHT — STRONG, independent, and outspoken — writers have sometimes tested believability with their narratives, even going so far as to make a thirteen-year-old girl the captain of an eighteenth-century sailing ship.

By distorting the past to fit modern notions of right and wrong, authors of children's historical fiction do readers more harm than good.

I expect we can all agree that historical fiction should be good fiction and good history. If we leap over the first briar patch by calling good fiction an "interesting narrative with well-developed characters," we are still left with the question of what, exactly, good history is. Alas, there are nearly as many thorns here as there are among the briars. The German historian Leopold von Ranke said that writing history was saying "what really happened" — but according to whom? Writers of history select, describe, and explain historical evidence —

and thereby interpret. Not only will the loser's version of the war never match the winner's, but historical interpretations of what happened, and why, are also subject to endless revision over time. A transforming event of the past — say, the American Revolution — can be understood as a social, economic, or intellectual movement; as avoidable or inevitable; as a tragedy of misunderstanding or a triumph of liberty.

Historical revisionism makes its way into historical fiction, of course, including that written for children, usually in response to changing social climates. Esther Forbes wrote *Johnny Tremain*, her famous novel of the American Revolution, in the early 1940s, when the United States had recently entered the maelstrom of World War II. Forbes's story took the traditional Whig view that the Revolution was a struggle for political freedom, fought, as one of her characters said, so that "a man can stand up." The parallel Forbes saw with a contemporary war against political tyranny was implied but clear. A generation later, James and Christopher Collier's *My Brother Sam Is Dead* (1974) and Robert Newton Peck's *Hang for Treason* (1976) saw the same history through a different lens. Writing in a time of passionate division over a modern war, these authors looked back to the American Revolution and saw not idealism but the coercion, hypocrisy, cruelty, and betrayal that are part of any war in any country. In the Colliers' story, the success of the Revolution had to be weighed against the suffering it inflicted on ordinary people: "I keep thinking that there might have been another way, besides war, to achieve the same end." Peck looked behind the heroic legend of Ethan Allen and his band of Green Mountain Boys and found more greed for land than hunger for liberty and renegade tactics as barbarous as any tyrant's. In Peck's telling, Allen's brand of irregular warfare was terrorism, not a noble struggle for liberty.

Revisionist history is still history, subject to normal standards of 5 demonstrable historical evidence and sound reasoning. While the novels I've named approach the American Revolution from different points of view, they are firmly grounded in documented evidence. Different as they are in emphasis and attitude, all three stay within the bounds of eighteenth-century American social history. None ignores known historical realities to accommodate political ideology.

A good many recent historical novels for children do. Children's literature, historical as well as contemporary, has been politicized over the past thirty years; new social sensibilities have changed the way Americans view the past. Feminist rereadings of history and insistence by minorities on the importance — and the difference — of their experience have made authors and publishers sensitive to how their books portray people often overlooked or patronized in earlier literature. The traditional concentration on boys and men has been modified; more minorities are included, and the experience of ordinary people — as opposed to movers and shakers — gets more attention. American historical literature, including children's, takes a less chauvinistic approach to American history than it once did, revising the traditional chronicle of unbroken upward progress.

However, amid the cheers for this enlightenment are occasional murmurs of doubt — and there ought to be more. Too much historical fiction for children is stepping around large slabs of known reality to tell pleasant but historically doubtful stories. Even highly respected authors snip away the less attractive pieces of the past to make their narratives meet current social and political preferences. Many of these novels have been given high marks: "an authentic story," "fine historical fiction," say the reviews. Many are on recommended lists, and some have won awards. As fiction, the accolades may be earned; as history, they raise some questions.

Patricia MacLachlan's *Sarah, Plain and Tall* won the Newbery Medal in 1986. It is a simple, warmhearted tale, as popular with children as with adults, which cannot be said of every Newbery winner. The setting is a nineteenth-century farm on the American prairie, though exactly where and when is unspecified. As there is no mention of farm machinery, and because there is a reference to plowing a new field in the prairie, the period would seem to be the 1870s or 1880s. Sarah, an unmarried young woman, answers a newspaper ad and travels from Maine to the Midwest to stay with a widowed man and his two children for a month. The understanding is that if all goes well, she and the father will marry. If not, she will return to Maine. She comes alone and stays in the house with no other woman present.

The realities of nineteenth-century social mores are at odds with practically this entire scenario. It was unusual (though not impossible) for a woman to travel such distances alone, and much more than unusual for her to stay with a man not related to her without another woman in the house. Had she done so, it is unlikely that she could have returned home afterward with her reputation intact. MacLachlan has said that her story is based on a family experience a couple of generations ago, and I have no reason to question that. Even so, the story as told is highly uncharacteristic of its time and place.

Besides bypassing the usual social strictures of the time, the 10 novel also glides lightly over a basic reality of farm life in the last century: work. More than work, in fact — toil, a word that has all but disappeared from modern vocabularies. Hamlin Garland, who grew up on farms in Wisconsin and Iowa in the 1860s and 1870s, wrote about his experience in *A Son of the Middle Border*. Again and again, Garland describes the constant labor of a farm family's life. A farm

To see authors vaulting blithely over the barriers women lived with for so long brings to mind *Anna Karenina*. Anna's is the story these contemporary writers don't want to tell. When she left her husband and child for Vronsky, Anna suffered all the sanctions her society imposed on women who defied its rules. Whether the reader, or, for that matter, the author, believed that the rules were unfair or the sanctions too harsh is irrelevant. Tolstoy was telling the story of a woman who lived when and where she lived, who made the choices she made, and who was destroyed by the consequences.

It isn't that contemporary writers of historical fiction do not research the topics and the times they have chosen. They do, and they often include information about those facts and about the sources they have used. Yet many narratives play to modern sensibilities. Their protagonists experience their own societies as though they were time-travelers, noting racism, sexism, religious bigotry, and outmoded beliefs as outsiders, not as people of and in their cultures. So Birdy, though she approaches her first experience with Jews with all the outlandish prejudices of her society, overcomes them instantly. So Sarah insists on wearing overalls when it suits her, and her future husband accepts not only this, but all her nonconformities, without question, let alone objection. A ship crew's acquiescence to a thirteen-year-old girl's decision to join them as a working sailor — in 1832 — hardly needs comment.

And so, too, Ann Rinaldi's novel about the 1692 Salem witch hysteria, *A Break with Charity* (1992), in which all the significant characters are outsiders, one way or another, and all hold views closer to twentieth- rather than to seventeenth-century norms. No sympathetic character in this novel really believes in witches, though many seventeenth-century people did. Cotton Mather — who indeed took witchcraft seriously — appears once, wrapped in a black cloak, an onlooker at one of the hangings and the embodiment of evil. Puritanism was, and is, an ambiguous, complex, enduring influence on American culture; to picture it as simply evil or alien is to ignore the historical truth.

Didacticism dies hard in children's literature. Today's publishers, 20 authors, and reviewers often approach historical fiction for children as the early nineteenth century did — as an opportunity to deliver messages to the young. Bending historical narrative to modern models of social behavior, however, makes for bad history, and the more specific the model, the harder it is to avoid distorting historical reality. The current pressure to change old stereotypes into "positive images" for young readers is not only insistent but also highly specific about what the desirable image is, and often untenable. If the only way a female protagonist can be portrayed is as strong, independent, and outspoken, or, to take a different example, if slaves must always be shown as resistant to authority, and if these qualities have to be overt, distortion becomes inevitable. Betty Sue Cummings's novel about the American Civil War, *Hew Against the Grain* (1977), establishes her heroine's strength as a credible result of wartime conditions. Her picture of slavery, however, is less easily reconciled with history. How many slaves this Virginia family owns is not clear, but the four described in any detail are all free-thinking and outspoken — "Elijah neither looked nor acted like a slave" — and the two younger ones, at least, can read. The odds against such a situation in Virginia on the eve of the Civil War were considerable. More important, however politically acceptable it is, this kind of idealization glosses over the real price slaves paid for slavery.

What is at stake here is truth. It can't, of course, be true, and wasn't, that all or even most slaves and women rebelled openly, let alone successfully, against the legal and social limitations put upon them. Moreover, resistance takes a variety of forms, not all of them straightforward, some of them not even conscious. A literature about the past that makes overt rebellion seem nearly painless and nearly always successful indicts all those who didn't rebel: It implies, subtly but effectively, that they were responsible for their own oppression. Strength, too, has more than one face. As Louisa May Alcott judged it when she wrote *Little Women*, Mrs. March was a powerful figure, well in control of herself and what the nineteenth-century called the "woman's sphere." Today's feminism understandably disparages Marmee's kind of power, but that doesn't change the fact that it existed. Writers who impose twentieth-century formula feminism on narratives set in the 1860s only ensure that readers will not learn what readers of *Little Women* learn about the structures and strategies of nineteenth-century society.

Formulas deny the complexity of human experience and often the reality of it, as well. Most people in most societies are not rebels; in part because the cost of nonconformity is more than they want to pay, but also because as members of the society they share its convictions. Most people are, by definition, not exceptional. Historical fiction writers who want their protagonists to reflect twentieth-century ideologies, however, make them exceptions to their cultures, so that in many a historical novel the reader learns nearly nothing — or at least nothing sympathetic — of how the people of a past society saw their world. Characters are divided into right — those who believe as we do — and wrong; that is, those who believe something that we now disavow. Such stories suggest that people of another time either understood or should have understood the world as we do now, an outlook that quickly devolves into the belief that people are the same everywhere and in every time, draining human history of its nuance and variety.

But people of the past were not just us in odd clothing. They were people who saw the world differently; approached human relationships differently; people for whom night and day, heat and cold, seasons and work and play had meanings lost to an industrialized world. Even if human nature is much the same over time, human experience, perhaps especially everyday experience, is not. To wash these differences out of historical fictions is not only a denial of historical truth but also a failure of imagination and understanding that is as important to the present as to the past.

READING

1. MacLeod opens her essay with a clear example of historical inaccuracy. How does this particular example set up the tone and focus of the piece?

2. She sets up her argument by including us, the readers, by saying, "I expect we can all agree that historical fiction should be good fiction and good history." What is "good history," according to MacLeod, and what are some of the problems with writing good historical fiction? Are you sympathetic with her (our) point of view? Does she lose you as a reader at any point?

3. Because she is a scholar of children's literature, she focuses on influential children's books for her examples of "historical revisionism." Are the examples she chooses convincing to you? Do you agree with her objections?

4. When MacLeod objects to historical inaccuracy in the novels, such as the role of work on a farm, she states her objection and then supplies evidence from other sources to back her objections. What are the most convincing examples she uses, in your opinion? What kind of sources are they?

5. She says, "The current pressure to change old stereotypes into 'positive images' for young readers is not only insistent but also highly specific about what the desirable image is." What are some stereotypes of what young people should be like that you notice in today's culture (for example, "A" student, successful athlete)?

WRITING

1. MacLeod says, "By distorting the past to fit modern notions of right and wrong, authors of children's historical fiction do readers more harm than good." Think about your favorite children's books. Do you think they represent the characters in the books accurately for their time? Write a reflective essay or a journal piece describing some of your favorite characters or stories, discussing why or why not you feel they are good models for children.

2. MacLeod chooses historical fiction that has been awarded the Newbery Medal in many cases. Find out what the Newbery Medal is and what books have won the award lately. Read a novel that takes place in the past and evaluate it, using MacLeod's criteria for acceptable historical fiction. Would your book pass muster, according to MacLeod? Write an essay summarizing your findings.

3. MacLeod seems to be saying that in children's and adolescent literature, it is important to be realistic rather than idealistic. She says, "And therein lies the difficulty I find with these – any many other – historical novels of the past twenty years. They evade the common realities of the societies they write about." Develop a survey of two or three television shows of the past twenty years aimed at children and adolescents. Write an essay describing in what ways they are idealistic and in what ways they are realistic.

4. The difficulty with writing accurate historical fiction, MacLeod acknowledges, is that history can be interpreted in many different ways and from many viewpoints. She says, "Not only will the loser's version of the war never match the winner's, but historical interpretations of what happened, and why, are also subject to endless revisions over time." Take a historic event that happened in your lifetime (for example, 9/11, a presidential election, the invasion of Iraq) and write an essay describing your interpretation of the event and how you formed this interpretation. Then, research other versions of this event. Research sources outside the United States as well as sources within. Consider traditional news media, personal accounts, academic analyses, images, blogs, op-eds, and so on. Have you revised your interpretation of the event as a result of your research? Write an essay summarizing your findings.

5. Both Carson, in "Malcolm X" (p. 405), and MacLeod invite us to examine the ethics of representation. Is it unethical to portray only the positive aspects of our heroes – to omit or downplay their weaknesses or complexities? To allow them freedoms and strengths that they may not have had, historically? Choose a controversial historical figure and examine at least two conflicting portrayals of this figure in history, fiction, or entertainment (for example, Queen Elizabeth I, Malcolm X, Robin Hood, Susan B. Anthony, George W. Bush). Write an essay analyzing the differences in the portrayals.

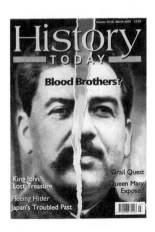

Revisionism Revisited

By Ian Mortimer

FROM: *History Today*, March 2004

CONTEXT: This article was initially published in *History Today*, which has been published monthly since 1951; the magazine is based in London. While it focuses on an academic subject and has an editorial board consisting chiefly of historians, *History Today* is not a university-based academic journal and instead aims at a wider, more popular readership. The author, Ian Mortimer, is the writer of a number of historical biographies and is a Fellow of the Royal Historical Society. He is an honorary university research fellow at Exeter University in Devon, England. As you read this piece, consider how Mortimer's own status as a writer and rewriter of history plays a role in his attitude about the topic.

ON JUNE 16, 2003, GEORGE BUSH GAVE A SPEECH IN WHICH HE defended his decision to take military action against Iraq. The description he gave of those who had suggested that there had never been a real threat from Saddam Hussein's regime was startling: "Now there are some who would like to rewrite history — revisionist historians is what I like to call them. . . ." While the phrase suggests that Mr. Bush is not particularly familiar with the nature or methods of revisionist history, his statement places in a very negative context anyone who might query whether assumptions about the past — including those assumptions made in the past — were actually correct.

This raises some important questions, not the least of which are: What is "revisionist history" and why has it come to have such negative connotations? Neither of these questions has a straightforward answer. Almost all original historical research is "revisionist" to some degree in that it revises something we previously thought. However, an article which seeks to "revise" our understanding of the origins of the Enlightenment would probably not be labeled "revisionist" as it deals with social history, largely the preserve of the professional. An article, however, which revises our understanding of the supposed murder of Edward V and Prince Richard in 1483 would definitely be considered "revisionist." Therefore, when Bush talks about "revisionist historians," he is mainly talking about those who challenge widely accepted and well-established historical narratives. So how come these people have succeeded in attracting such distrust that George Bush feels justified in placing his most implacable political enemies in their midst?

At this point, and before discussing why revisionists may have found themselves unpopular, I must confess to a personal interest in the debate. This is on account of the claim in my biography of Roger Mortimer (1287–1330), 1st Earl of March, that we can be sure that the traditional narrative of the death of Edward II in Berkeley Castle is based on false information, and that he was still alive in 1330, and possibly even in 1338–39. It could be said that this gives me an axe to grind; in fact, I could hardly claim otherwise. Yet it seems to me that this puts me in a better position than most to make some observations on the effects of this disparaging of revisionist history and the implications for broader historical enquiry.

There seem to be three fundamental reasons why revisionists have a low reputation. The first is simply that by no means all revisionist research and analysis is of the highest standard. We have all heard of remarkable theories — stone rows, circles, and pyramids leap to mind — based on evidence which, at best, might be described as "flimsy." Knowledge that such works are published, and sometimes sell in huge numbers, does nothing to confirm our faith in the intellectual quality control of commissioning editors. Furthermore, over the last 150 years the popular press has permitted (and, in some quarters, actively encouraged) new interpretations of events which may collectively be described as "conspiracy theories." When is a revisionist theory not a conspiracy theory? Historians may present several differences — including an author's credentials, knowledge, methods, judgment, and objectives — but it is not always easy for the public to be sure of the differences. Indeed, the perennial question of who shot President Kennedy (and why) has encouraged a welter of books, not all of which can be dismissed as ill-informed or simply sensationalist, although many are. It should thus not be considered surprising if public confidence in revisionist historical publications has been undermined by a culture which publishes theories of dubious merit far more often than works of revisionist scholarship.

This point only partly explains antirevisionism. While it would [5] explain why some works on, say, the identity of Jack the Ripper receive short shrift, it does not explain why a considerable number of books written by the well-informed and well-qualified are either overtly dismissed as "revisionist" or avoided by those whom one would expect to take an immediate interest. An example is Ann Wroe's recent book on Perkin Warbeck. A very well-known and respectable academic, interviewed on the *Today* program on BBC Radio Four, thought nothing of dismissing Dr. Wroe's observations on the inconsistencies in Perkin's forcibly obtained "confession" and on the support afforded Perkin afterwards, which cannot easily be explained within the framework of the traditional narrative. With regard to my own work on Roger Mortimer, I found it very interesting that the first two-thirds of the book received commendation from every single reviewer, and yet the much more thoroughly worked last third, dealing with the survival of Edward II, received a range of responses, from enthusiastic approbation to outright hostility. It seems that the same careful research process and individual's judgment may be praiseworthy in reaching uncontroversial conclusions but dismissed when those conclusions contradict a widely accepted narrative.

We need to look further, therefore, for the reasons why revisionism may be frowned upon. In particular, we need to consider public perceptions of professionalism. We live in an age in which the most trusted information is that derived from professional quarters, and experience tells us that, more often than not, the professional's advice is to treat extraordinary historical narratives with scepticism, if not a pinch of salt. Anyone who has spent much time reading medieval chronicles will be well aware that, time and again, one must discount contemporary "evidence" on the grounds that it can be shown to be nothing more than contemporary rumor and contrary to the facts as known from other, more reliable sources. The professional is thus perceived to be a "debunker" of myths. Therefore, if a writer propounds (as opposed to debunks) an extraordinary narrative, or proposes the acceptance of a previously rejected narrative, he may unwittingly associate himself with the popular conception of the amateur rather than the professional. This is not necessarily a perspective restricted to the nonspecialist: There are a number of fields in which some academics feel that it is professionally correct to dismiss an argument publicly regardless of the limits of their actual knowledge. The nature of Perkin Warbeck is a good example. Herein lies a danger, for just as it is wrong to accept romantic stories without question, so too it is wrong to dismiss them without evidence. Historical cynicism — as in unevidenced scepticism — is no more justifiable than historical naivety.

The third issue is much broader: that of the social acceptability of revisionism itself. This is a complicated matter, and in some respects it affects all historians. People at large, while willing to accept that it is good practice to question received wisdom, do not appreciate popular historical motifs being challenged or swept away in a cloud of analytical proof. Whether we are referring to Alfred burning cakes, the arrow in Harold II's eye, the red-hot poker in Edward II's rectum, or the murder of the princes in the Tower, there is a sense in which these stories have a cultural value over and above their historical importance: they are the stories from medieval history we all know, and to disprove any of them is to weaken the universality of our heritage. As has been said to me with respect to Edward II's murder, "If I am not allowed to believe that story, what else should I not believe? Nothing is beyond question." Nor does this problem of acceptability only relate to early modern and earlier periods. Although a case can be argued for claiming that heavier-than-air flight was first achieved in 1906 by Albert Santos-Dumont (see *History Today*, December 2003), the names of the Wright Brothers are probably forever enshrined in the cultural history of the twentieth century as the inventors of the first machine to "fly" under its own power in December 1903. Generally an individual, having been accepted as fulfilling a culturally significant role (whether as an inventor or murderer), is rarely — if ever — removed or supplanted in the popular imagination.

This last point forces us to confront the wider implications of antirevisionism, and this is a point which affects most, if not all, historians. If society is generally happy with its cultural heritage, why should revisionism of any sort be supported? Here we touch on the fundamental question of the role of history in modern society: Why do we study the past and encourage historical enquiry?

Some writers, academics included, have suggested that certain "revisionist" subjects are irrelevant to wider understandings of the past. On the face of it, they have a point. Why should we question our traditional heritage, especially when it acts as a culturally unifying force? Does it matter whether or not Alfred burnt the cakes, or that Edward II might have survived to 1339? Obviously the answer to this question has to be relative to the revision proposed. The cakes are merely emblematic; but Edward II's survival — widely believed in 1329–30 — had huge implications for the two dozen or so men who engineered the plot to reinstate him on the throne in that year (including the earl of Kent, the bishop of London, the archbishop of York, and the Pope). Likewise, the true identity of Perkin Warbeck was of great importance to those who had the power to help or hinder him, and relevance for understanding what may or may not have happened to the princes in the Tower.

Thus it is not hard to see why some "revisionist" ideas simply will 10 never go away. Some are merely poetic details, but others are fundamentally important to understanding fully the process by which a reign or a dynasty came to an end. It is the principle which is important. If the deaths of the princes in the Tower or Edward II are irrelevant historical questions, then what is relevant, and why? And who is to be the arbiter of which historical questions merit wider (and publicly funded) debate?

Revisionist historians thus face a number of problems. There is the risk of disparagement on a cultural level for challenging the veracity of widely accepted events, the risk of being classified along with lightweight conspiracy theorists for being controversial or being perceived to court public attention, and (in certain cases) the risk of being deemed unprofessional for urging a revisiting of a previously academically dismissed narrative.

Faced with such problems as these, George Bush is the least of our worries. Yet there are clear reasons to question some existing readings of controversial events, and there are important implications for the wider historical community. When it comes to a "revisionist" subject, committed historians are left with a stark choice. They can either seek to engage in a genuine and (hopefully) ultimately instructive debate, or they can restrict themselves to repeating the unambiguous evidence, eschewing the wider intellectual implications. Clearly history itself would be the loser if we all were to choose the latter.

READING

1. Mortimer starts his piece by placing an academic discussion in a real world context. How does this move provide relevancy to his article?

2. In large part, this article takes the form of a definition essay. What is Mortimer trying to define or redefine? Is he successful?

3. Mortimer provides a clear organizational strategy in writing, "There seem to be three fundamental reasons why revisionists have a low reputation." What are they? How does he flesh out this structure?

4. Because the *History Today* audience is largely British, Mortimer uses examples drawn from British history. Do you recognize the examples? If you were writing this essay for an American audience, which historical figures might you discuss?

5. Mortimer's broader point seems to be that we should be encouraged to question received historical wisdom. Do you agree with this point of view? Should all historical "fact" be open for question?

WRITING

1. As he delves deeper into the topic of revisionism, Mortimer asks what he calls a "fundamental question of the role of history in modern society: Why do we study the past and encourage historical enquiry?" Write a reflective essay or journal entry discussing why you think understanding the past is important to living in the present and planning for the future. Why do we care about history?

2. Mortimer writes, "People at large, while willing to accept that it is good practice to question received wisdom, do not appreciate popular historical motifs being challenged or swept away in a cloud of analytical proof." Most families have their own histories – stories shared from generation to generation. Sometimes these stories do not stand up well to questioning or scrutiny. Write an essay about one of your family's historical narratives that may or may not be true. Does the truth of this story matter to your family? Why?

3. Mortimer attempts to redefine revisionism as a positive activity. Write an essay in which you summarize his view on revisionism and contrast it with the negative definition that he is writing against. You may need to research the term "revisionist history" to help develop your essay.

4. In trying to delineate between revisionist theory and conspiracy theory, Mortimer writes that we should consider "an author's

credentials, knowledge, methods, judgment, and objectives." This is wise counsel in evaluating any research material. Find another article from a history journal and use Mortimer's framework to write an evaluation of the author. Would you view him or her as a valid source based on these criteria?

5. Mortimer writes that revisionist historians may be seen as simply "court[ing] public attention," and, indeed, much recent revisionist history has been presented through popular film. As Clayborne Carson's essay on Spike Lee's film, *Malcolm X* (p. 405), suggests, historians do not always look favorably upon films claiming to present history or historical figures. Identify a recent movie that has been accused of revising historical "fact." Research the controversy surrounding the historical accuracy of the movie you have selected. Write an essay that summarizes these issues and explains why they seem to be important. Discuss whether the film, in the words of Mortimer, opens up an avenue "to engage in a genuine and (hopefully) ultimately instructive debate" or simply offers a "'flimsy'" conspiracy theory.

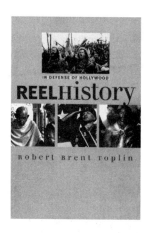

Judging Cinematic History
By Robert Brent Toplin

FROM: *Reel History: In Defense of Hollywood*, University Press of Kansas, 2002

CONTEXT: *Reel History* was published by the University Press of Kansas in 2002. The University Press of Kansas is a nonprofit scholarly press that represents the six state universities: Emporia State University, Fort Hays State University, Kansas State University, Pittsburg State University, the University of Kansas, and Wichita State University. The University Press of Kansas was founded in 1946 and has been most successful with its list of military and political books. Robert Brent Toplin is a history professor at the University of North Carolina at Wilmington. He is also editor of film reviews for the *Journal of American History* and contributes to the online *History News Network*. He has spoken on film for CNN, the History Channel, and C-Span, and he has created historical dramas for Disney and PBS. His books include *Michael Moore's "Fahrenheit 9/11": How One Film Divided a Nation* (2006), *Reel History: In Defense of Hollywood* (2002), *Oliver Stone's USA: Film, History, and Controversy* (2000), and *History By Hollywood: The Use and Abuse of the American Past* (1996), among others. As you read this piece, look at how carefully he argues for the necessity of filmmakers to use a blend of historical accuracy and artistic license when making films about history.

IN A SENSITIVE REVIEW OF THE 1993 MOVIE *SHADOWLANDS*, Carlos Villa Flor identifies several of the film's manipulations of historical facts but draws greater attention to its broader achievements. Flor notes that *Shadowlands* adjusts certain details in its portrayal of a late-life romance involving the distinguished British author, theologian, and professor C. S. Lewis (played by Anthony Hopkins). At various points in the drama, the filmmakers take artistic liberties in order to design a comprehensible and entertaining story, Flor notes. They show one son instead of the two belonging to Joy Davidman Gresham (Debra Winger), the woman who eventually becomes

Lewis's love interest. To give the story more action sequences, the filmmakers portray Lewis driving a car around Herefordshire (the real Lewis never mastered driving; he walked). Additionally, the movie associates Lewis with Oxford University (the most familiar symbol of English higher education, and a comfortable point of reference for moviegoers). In fact, Lewis worked at Cambridge during the years portrayed in the drama. Furthermore, *Shadowlands* places Mrs. Gresham in Lewis's home during the final days of her bout with cancer, even though she actually died in a hospital. Flor defends the artistic value of these manipulations and judges the production a success. *Shadowlands* views Lewis's life and the tragedy of Gresham's death intelligently. Its creators rearrange the historical record somewhat, yet the film holds together "as a balanced masterpiece."[1]

Flor's assessment of *Shadowlands* reveals an impressive sense of balance, a recognition that artists must shape evidence for dramatic effect and that these adjustments can sometimes serve a respectable purpose. The errors, omissions, simplifications, inventions, and manipulations in *Shadowlands* need to be identified, Flor demonstrates, but these matters do not destroy the movie's fundamental value. *Shadowlands* effectively studies the case of a talented and prominent individual who is confident of his intellectual sophistication and spiritual strength. His discovery of romance late in life and the eventual loss of his beloved wife present a stinging challenge to his Christian faith. Can Lewis maintain his confidence in the ultimate goodness of God after dealing with this tragedy? *Shadowlands*, based on an outstanding stage play, provides a thoughtful and ultimately uplifting view of Lewis's internal struggle. Despite its adjustments of the details in Lewis's life, the performance gives audiences plenty of attractive food for thought.

Flor's example is useful for a consideration of the challenges of assessing cinematic history. Much too often, reviewers are preoccupied with pointing out tiny factual mistakes. They focus on artistic liberties taken by filmmakers, comment cynically on Hollywood's cavalier relationship with historical evidence, and rail angrily at the cinematic artists who rearrange historical evidence in order to design compelling drama. These caustic critics can find an example of a more balanced and sophisticated analysis in Flor's insightful review.

One of the historians' favorite examples of a balanced and thoughtful approach to questions about artistic license is James M. McPherson's generous review of *Glory* (1989), which portrays the efforts of a group of African Americans fighting as Union soldiers during the Civil War. McPherson, a distinguished Civil War scholar, could easily have assumed a scolding attitude when dealing with the movie's treatment of history. As in all cinematic views of the past,

Glory's presentation includes manipulations of the evidence. McPherson points them out in his review but does not consider them outrageous. He observes, for example, that the real African American soldiers who participated in the battle of Fort Wagner attacked from south to north; *Glory* shows them making the assault from the opposite direction. Also, *Glory* focuses on an African American military unit made up of former slaves, when in fact, free blacks manned the real Massachusetts Fifty-fourth. A caption at the end of the picture claims that the bravery of the Fifty-fourth at Fort Wagner inspired Congress to authorize more black regiments for the Union army, but that actually occurred months before. The movie also leaves the impression that the Fifty-fourth concluded its activities with the bloody confrontation at Fort Wagner; in fact, the unit continued to serve through the war and participated in several more battles and skirmishes.[2]

Glory's misrepresentations do not, however, detract from its overall accomplishment, McPherson concludes. The adjustments can be defended. For example, the configuration of the Georgia beach where filmmakers shot the assault on Fort Wagner required a southward movement. Also, notes McPherson, most of the 188,000 black soldiers and sailors who served the Union in uniform *were slaves* until a short time before they enlisted. Furthermore, although the bravery of the Fifty-fourth at Fort Wagner was not the only factor in Congress's decision to authorize more black regiments, it at least helped to transform the experiment with black soldiers into a policy of black recruitment. *Glory*'s portrayal is not literally true in these and other depictions, but it certainly contains many *symbolic* truths. Movies can teach history, McPherson insists, as *Glory* nicely demonstrates.[3]

Our understanding of the conventions of dramatic development should also inspire a more balanced and tolerant view of cinematic history. As we have seen, these Hollywood traditions of storytelling often force manipulations of evidence. Moviemakers employ successful practices of their profession, attempting to create emotionally stimulating entertainment. For instance, they condense time and collapse several historic personalities into one or two figures. Filmmakers emphasize a biographical approach to history, treating the experiences of a few characters as suggestive of the troubles and progress experienced by many people. Moviemakers also establish a rather simple story structure, presenting history in the form of a three-act play that introduces situations, creates problems for the protagonists, and then resolves their difficulties or hints at a symbolic triumph in the final act. Cinematic history often delivers an uplifting conclusion, communicating a sanguine view of the potential for human progress. It also creates a tightly focused view of the past, giving specific attention to just a few people and events. Movies do not present the "big picture" very effectively. They leave out much — not only details but also analysis. Cinema is certainly not comprehensive in its approach to history. Frequently it privileges stories about war, personality conflict, romance, and tragedy. Its dramas characterize historic figures in white and black, as heroes and villains; portrayals in gray are much less evident. And of course, cinematic history often features fictional men and women, invented protagonists and antagonists whose actions and statements facilitate the filmmaker's efforts to create an entertaining tale. By employing invented characters, filmmakers can also take the action to diverse locales and give personality to specific individuals when, in fact, we know relatively little about the lives, thoughts, and emotions of these historic figures.[4]

The need for these forms of artistic license should be evident, yet critics of cinematic history continue to devote a good deal of energy to angry denunciations of Hollywood's playfulness with history. They fume against the collapsing of characters, the hero-villain depictions, the invented scenes, the simplification of plot, and other adjustments that filmmakers incorporate to produce dramatic effect. Critics also draw attention to specific factual errors, noting that *real* individuals did not speak or act in the ways depicted in the movies. They observe mistakes in presentation, too: the wrong uniform, erroneous chronology, or the placement of a leading figure where he or she could not possibly have been. By focusing on misrepresentation of details, they often miss the larger cinematic accomplishments. Preoccupied with small "lies," they fail to recognize larger "truths."

Of course, these lies can add up. They may accumulate to a disturbing level, destroying public confidence in a movie's relationship with history. Some films develop tainted reputations, and for good reason. Their manipulations of evidence take artistic license to excess. When media coverage of these problems in historical depiction becomes extensive, the negative publicity can harm a film financially and set critics against it. This condition may surprise some, because they assume that Hollywood filmmakers can distort history with impunity. But as I discuss later, some filmmakers have been called on the carpet in recent years for their failure to depict the past with integrity. They have paid a price for their manipulations in dollars and artistic reputation.

A serious and balanced look at cinematic history requires a more complex response to movies than the simplistic "thumbs up" or "thumbs down" approach of movie reviewers on television and in popular magazines. Even good cinematic history contains a great deal of fiction and manipulation of the facts, and even poor cinematic history that bends the facts to a troublesome degree can dramatize aspects of the past impressively. To state this case starkly, it is impossible to find an example of cinematic history that can be held up for unquestioned praise because it depicts the past without stretching the truth in any way. Conversely, it is difficult to find an example of cinematic history that distorts the record so thoroughly that it should be rejected for having no redeeming value. Even problematic films frequently offer insights. In sum, we need a sensitive effort to judge integrity and an informed view of film that balances the defense of artistic liberties with the recognition that some dramatic flourishes can be problematic.

A comparative view of four major Hollywood films of the 1980s 10 and 1990s is useful in this regard, because it helps distinguish between plausible distortions and more troublesome ones. James Cameron's *Titanic* (1997) is an example of defensible exercise of artistic license. Cameron's film manages to present an intelligent view of the past even though it contains significant manipulations of the historical record and a good deal of fictionalizing. Against the example of *Titanic*'s achievement we can consider three motion pictures that came under attack in the mass media for exceeding reasonable bounds of artistic license: *Mississippi Burning* (1988), *Amistad* (1997), and *The Hurricane* (1999). Each of these problematic films delivers some riveting drama, and each raises important questions about racial injustice. Yet all three stretch the truth in ways that undermine their interpretations of history. Some of the criticisms leveled against *Mississippi Burning, Amistad,* and *The Hurricane* were substantive, and justifiably, the public and the critics lost confidence in the movies' integrity.

NOTES

[1]Carlos Villa Flor, "Intertextuality in *Shadowlands:* From the Essay to the Love Story," *Literature Film Quarterly* 27, no. 3 (1999): 97.

[2]James M. McPherson, "The 'Glory' Story," *New Republic,* January 8 and 15, 1990, 22–27.

[3]Ibid. McPherson also discusses these issues in *"Glory,"* in Carnes, *Past Imperfect,* 128–131.

[4]Robert A. Rosenstone, *Visions of the Past: The Challenge of Film to Our Idea of History* (Cambridge: Harvard University Press, 1996), 55–60.

READING

1. Discuss how Toplin introduces his criteria for evaluating movies' historical accuracy by referring to other critics' evaluation of *Shadowlands* and *Glory* in his opening paragraphs. How does this help set up his credibility?

2. What kind of tone does he use in speaking about critics who evaluate movies' portrayals of historical events simply on the basis of historical accuracy?

3. Toplin says, "*Glory*'s portrayal is not literally true . . . but it certainly contains many *symbolic* truths. Movies can teach history." Consider this movie or other movies based on history you have seen. What kinds of "symbolic" truths are they able to deliver that "teach[es] history," as Toplin asserts? What kinds of truths does *Glory* itself offer?

4. Recall the audience Toplin is addressing. How might strict historians respond to his argument? How might literature scholars? Are you convinced by his argument? Why?

5. Toplin states that "errors, omissions, simplifications, inventions, and manipulations . . . need to be identified." In this excerpt, what kinds of inaccuracies does he identify as significant?

WRITING

1. We learn history in many different ways. We learn, of course, through our textbooks and history teachers in school. We also learn from our parents and friends as they teach us what they know or have experienced. Perhaps you learned about Operation Desert Storm or another war from a family member or friend who has served in the military, for example. Write a reflective essay or a journal entry recounting a piece of history you have learned from storytelling rather than textbooks.

2. Choose a historical figure or event that has been portrayed in a movie. Research an actual historical narrative of this person or event. Then, write an essay comparing the historical account of the individual's personality or the portrayal of events to the cinematic version. Identify what manipulations were made to round out the character or make the event more dramatic.

3. Toplin refers to the importance of the "conventions of dramatic development" in Hollywood's portrayal of history. Research and review

these conventions and write an essay defining each and illustrating each with an example of cinematic history.

4. Movies such as *Troy* and *Gladiator* are examples of a period of history that we cannot know about from any personal experience. With a small group, choose a movie that represents some period of ancient history. Be attentive to ways that the film manipulates historical accuracy to make it more palatable to a modern audience. Compare and contrast the actual historical events depicted and identify specific instances of artistic license. Then, choose clips that illustrate your points and show them to your class. Discuss how your group decided whether the movie falls into the category of a balanced and appropriate representation or a problematic and untruthful one.

5. At the end of this excerpt Toplin refers to three movies about racial injustice: *Mississippi Burning, Amistad,* and *The Hurricane.* He identifies these films as "three motion pictures that came under attack in the mass media for exceeding reasonable bounds of artistic license." Anne Scott MacLeod, in "Rewriting History" (p. 440) writes about historical inaccuracies in children's literature and what motivates it. She states, "Children's literature, historical as well as contemporary, has been politicized over the past thirty years; new social sensibilities have changed the way Americans view the past." Write an essay analyzing how "new social sensibilities" might motivate historical inaccuracies in the three films mentioned above.

The Mixed Reviews of the Museum of the American Indian

By Lynn Neary

FROM: *All Things Considered*, National Public Radio, August 17, 2005

CONTEXT: The following transcript originally aired on the National Public Radio (NPR) program *All Things Considered*, an evening news and events show described by NPR as having a "trademark mix of news, interviews, commentaries, reviews, and offbeat features." NPR is a not-for-profit organization that draws its support from individual memberships and corporate and foundation sponsorship. It reports a listening audience of 26 million Americans each week. Lynn Neary is the Arts Information Unit correspondent for NPR. During her almost three decades in radio, she has won many honors, including the Robert F. Kennedy Journalism Award, an Association of Women in Television and Radio Award, and the Corporation for Public Broadcasting Award. As you read this transcript, try to imagine how the background sounds described in the parenthetical notes might help set the scene for a listener.

ROBERT SIEGEL, host: From NPR News, this is *All Things Considered*. I'm Robert Siegel.

MICHELE NORRIS, host: And I'm Michele Norris. More than three million people have visited the National Museum of the American Indian since it opened last September. That opening was quite an event. Thousands of Native Americans from all over the country converged on the nation's capital for a celebration of Indian culture. But along with the celebration there was some harsh criticism of the museum's scholarship. NPR's Lynn Neary has a look at the institution as it approaches its first anniversary.

LYNN NEARY reporting: There's tobacco growing outside the National Museum of the American Indian, corn, too, and a number of other crops you don't expect to see in the shadow of the nation's Capitol. Most museums on the National Mall are landscaped with seasonal flowers and plants. These crops, representing some of the agricultural traditions of Native Americans, are just one indication of how this museum sets out to be and is different.

(Soundbite of museum activity)

UNIDENTIFIED WOMAN #1: Welcome.

NEARY: Inside a video greets visitors in English and tribal languages. 5
Nearby is a gift shop and, down the hall from it, a restaurant. To
view the exhibitions, visitors have to go up to the third and fourth
floors. There the first things they'll see are display cases that include arrowheads, dolls, and animals. Though beautifully arranged, the objects are presented in no obvious order. The very
old and the very new are mixed together. Visitors must consult a
nearby computer to get more information.

(Soundbite of computer recording)

UNIDENTIFIED WOMAN #2: This beautiful object is a wooden hunting hat
from the Aleutian Islands.

NEARY: Some early reviews of the museum objected to these displays
as frustrating and confusing, but the museum says the arrangements are meant to be aesthetically pleasing, and extensive information on each object is easily accessible on the computer.
Museum director Richard West says the museum wants to show
off as many of the 800,000 objects in its collection as possible, but,
he says, that is not its most important mission.

MR. RICHARD WEST (Director, National Museum of the American Indian):
This is not simply a palace of collectibles. This is about the associations between those magnificent collections and the peoples
who made them from a deep and distant past that goes back
thousands of years in this hemisphere right up to the present and
on into the future.

NEARY: This museum, says West, is meant to affirm what he calls the
"profound survivance" of Indian culture in spite of the destructive
effects of colonialism. According to West, this is a marked depar-
ture from the past, when museums portrayed Native Americans
as members of a vanishing race. Museums also routinely displayed objects that are considered sacred and even human remains. As a result, many Native Americans developed a profound
mistrust of these institutions.

MR. WEST: Native peoples, on the one hand, loved museums because 10
they held our stuff. And on the other hand, they could sometimes
hate museums because they held our stuff. It was this kind of
conflict that needed to be resolved. So what we did was to reach
out and include, on a collaborative basis, Native communities
themselves in the presentation of themselves in this institution.

NEARY: The museum consulted with members of 24 different tribes in
creating the three main exhibitions. Tribal curators chose which

objects from the museum's collection should be included in their tribe's displays and how they should be interpreted.

(*Soundbite of museum activity*)

UNIDENTIFIED WOMAN #3: This is 1800 and this is 1870.

UNIDENTIFIED MAN #1: This is the starting point so it's the winter of 1800 and 1801.

NEARY: In addition, the museum employs Native American interpreters to answer visitors' questions. In this case, a Crow interpreter explains what is known as the winter count using a replica of a buffalo hide on which time and events are recorded symbolically.

(*Soundbite of museum activity*)

UNIDENTIFIED MAN #1: Now I know this symbol because I am Crow.   15

UNIDENTIFIED WOMAN #3: Oh, OK. So, well, tell us . . . talk about this one.

UNIDENTIFIED MAN #1: All right. Well, there are different groups of different bands of Crow and Dakota and this is a symbol that represents that there was conflict with . . .

UNIDENTIFIED WOMAN #3: Between them.

UNIDENTIFIED MAN #1: . . . between the two tribes.

NEARY: But the exhibitions do not present history in a traditional way.   20 Dates and historical facts give way to stories and events important to individual tribes. Some obvious and painful aspects of Native American history, such as the Trail of Tears, are not even mentioned. *New York Times* critic-at-large Edward Rothstein says instead of substance and scholarship, there is self-celebration.

MR. EDWARD ROTHSTEIN (The *New York Times*): It does no good to respond to something that one feels is inadequate, which I imagine is the response to traditional museum exhibitions, with something that is pure pap.

NEARY: Rothstein is one of several critics who wrote scathing reviews of the National Museum of the American Indian when it opened a year ago. Rothstein says he likes the museum even less now. While curators intend to show the great diversity of tribes, Rothstein feels they present a homogenous view of tribal life tinged with New Age ideas.

MR. ROTHSTEIN: I would wager that there are any number of scholars of American Indian history who know far more about these tribes than the elders of the tribe. The point isn't that a museum should allow American Indian tribes to tell their own story. The point is that the museum should be able to give a complete portrait of the tribes and their history so that you actually know something of the truth.

NEARY: While not exactly inviting such criticism, the museum has left itself open to debate. In the section that deals with Native American history a video explicitly tells museum-goers to challenge what they see.

(*Soundbite of museum video*)

UNIDENTIFIED MAN #2: So view what's offered with respect but also 25 skepticism. Explore this gallery, encounter it, reflect on it, argue with it.

NEARY: But to do that, says Amy Lonetree, an assistant professor of Native American studies at Portland State University, visitors may need more information. Lonetree is editing an upcoming edition of the *American Indian Quarterly*, which is devoted to the museum. A variety of scholars including museum specialists, historians and anthropologists are among the contributors. Lonetree says while some scholars are critical, many applaud the museum's emphasis on the story of Native American survival.

PROFESSOR AMY LONETREE (Portland State University): Clearly that tackles head-on the vanishing race stereotype that many museums of the past had reinforced. However, they don't provide enough context on what native people were fighting to survive in the first place. And their failure to discuss the colonization process in a clear and coherent manner just, I think, makes those stories of survivance lose their power.

NEARY: The museum, says director Richard West, has heard the critics and as it looks toward the future it will look for ways to improve. But, he also says, some people may never fully accept the museum's underlying philosophy.

MR. WEST: Some people have a particular experience that is the basis 30 for their review and they're not departing at this point in their lives. And I don't begrudge them that, but let me be self-critical about the National Museum of the American Indian, too. I think that we have an obligation — and we have not done it absolutely correctly yet — of being more self-revealing about what it is we're doing as a matter of preparing our audiences for the different kind of experience they're going to get here.

NEARY: And, says Amy Lonetree, it is also crucial that the museum remains willing to listen to and engage the many people who have a stake in its future.

MS. LONETREE: Because there is no underestimating the importance of this site. It is on the National Mall. It's a site that indigenous people have fought for, and it is a tremendous accomplishment.

And its importance to being able to educate the public about who we are can't be emphasized enough.

NEARY: And for those who just don't get it, well, the invitation to encounter, reflect and argue still stands. Lynn Neary, NPR News, Washington.

SIEGEL: You're listening to *All Things Considered* from NPR News.

READING

1. *All Things Considered* host Michele Norris frames Neary's piece with a short summary. How does this summary help set up your expectations for what is to follow?

2. Neary opens the segment by describing the physical landscape of the museum — both exterior and interior. What does she gain by opening this way? Is her description objective or subjective?

3. Several different concerns seem to be expressed about the way in which the museum is presenting Native American history. What are these concerns?

4. Neary interviews several experts to establish the grounds for the controversies about the museum. Who are they? How do we know that we can give credence to their comments?

5. Throughout the piece, the reader/listener hears the comments of "unidentified" speakers. How do their remarks illustrate the issues that Neary is discussing concerning the museum's design and message?

WRITING

1. In one clip, Richard West tells Neary that the museum is "not simply a palace of collectibles." Rather, he believes the collections tell a specific narrative about Native American history. Write a reflective essay or journal entry describing a museum exhibit you have recently attended. What narrative did it tell? How did this narrative impact you?

2. Visit a museum or historical site and, using Neary's style of scene setting, write a short descriptive essay that would enable another to envision this place. Think about how you can get the reader to use all of her senses in responding to your writing. Then, write an analysis of the process you used in this exercise and consider this question: How important is a sense of place for capturing history?

3. Neary notes that Native Americans have developed "a profound mistrust" of museums because they frequently display sacred objects and even human remains. There is much discussion currently about how museums have obtained some of their antiquities and whether any museum has the right to appropriate the historical artifacts of another culture. Research this controversy and write an essay that identifies the issues at stake in this discussion.

4. Edward Rothstein complains to Neary that the method of exhibition in the museum offers "self-celebration" in lieu of "substance and scholarship," arguing that essential aspects of Native American history are missing from the museum. Select a historical event around which you would design a museum exhibit. Which elements of this event must appear in some fashion in the exhibit? How would you portray them? If possible, work with a group and design the promotional materials for your exhibit. How do these materials convey the narrative of the exhibit?

5. Neary describes a video on display at the museum that "explicitly tells museum-goers to challenge what they see." This request seems to mirror Ian Mortimer's statement in "Revisionism Revisited" (p. 450) that "there are clear reasons to question some existing readings of controversial events." Research a recent controversial museum exhibit or even a museum. What questions does this exhibit raise that seem to challenge accepted wisdom or history? What evidence does it provide for this alternate reading of events? Does it appear that this controversy will lead to any changes in the historical narrative? Write an essay summarizing your research.

Googling the Future

By John Leo

FROM: *U.S. News & World Report*, May 16, 2005

CONTEXT: This article was published in *U.S. News & World Report*, a weekly news magazine founded in 1933 and based in Washington, D.C. The magazine appeals to a broad, popular demographic rather than an academic one, and it has over 11 million readers. John Leo is a former columnist for *U.S. News & World Report* and a current columnist at Townhall.com. He has also written on social and political issues for *Time* magazine and the *New York Times*. As you read his comments on the mockumentary *EPIC 2014*, produced by journalists and online in the fictional Museum of Media History, consider the question he raises: Should news be tailored to each individual reader, according to his or her preferences? ("Googling the Future" by John Leo and cover of *U.S. News & World Report* © 2005 U.S. News & World Report, L.P. Reprinted with permission. JFK photo © CORBIS.)

THE YEAR IS 2014. THE PRESS AS WE KNOW IT NO LONGER exists. Traditional reporting has collapsed. News is churned out by the media giant Googlezon. (Google has taken over many companies and joined forces with Amazon.) The news consists of blogs, attitudes, discoveries, preferences, claims, and random thoughts, gathered and shaped by computers and a few human editors, then fed back to ordinary people who produce the continuing conversation. The *New York Times* is off the Internet. It still publishes, but the newspaper has become a newsletter read only by the elite and the elderly.

This is the finding of a clever, eight-minute mock documentary, *EPIC 2014*, produced by the fictional Museum of Media History (in reality, journalists Matt Thompson of the *Fresno Bee* and Robin Sloan of Current, a new cable news channel in San Francisco). Thompson and Sloan recently added a short section taking the history up to 2015. The mockumentary is starting to reach a mass audience at a time of unusually high anxiety for the news industry. The news business has been hobbled by a string of scandals and credibility problems. Skirmishes between reporters and bloggers seem like the beginning of a long war between old media and new. Newspaper publishers are nervous — some would say paralyzed with fright — over polls showing that young adults are not reading papers. Their audience is dying off. A lot of young people say they get their news from a brief look at headline news or from late-night comedians.

Rupert Murdoch, speaking at the recent convention of the American Society of Newspaper Editors, advised the members to encourage their readers to use the Internet more as a supplement to print coverage. Newspapers, he warned, risk being "relegated to the status of also-rans" if they don't make use of the Internet. Columnist Richard Brookhiser had a blunt comment in the *New York Observer*: Murdoch was just being polite — what he meant is that newspapers are dead. The older electronic media are nervous, too. According to *Advertising Age*, Google and Yahoo! will take in as much ad money this year as the prime-time revenues of the three major networks combined. Another sign of the times: Bloggers are now trying to set up a consortium to draw heavy advertising themselves.

In the mockumentary, the new electronic media basically blow away the old by paying attention to what people want, most of which would be called soft news or non-news today. In 2006, the mockumentary reports, Google combines its services — including Gmail, Blogger, and Google News — into the Google Grid, which provides limitless storage space and bandwidth for storing and sharing media. In 2010, Google defeats Microsoft in the news wars (no actual news organizations are involved in the conflict).

In March of 2014, Googlezon produces EPIC, the Evolving Personalized Information Construct. "Everyone contributes now — from blog entries to phone-cam images, to video reports, to full investigations," the video says. Everyone is a news producer as well as a news consumer. Computers strip and splice items, adjusting for each user's needs and preferences. News is prioritized according to the number of users who read each item. There are no gatekeepers who decide what we should see and which items are more important than others. 5

The video appears to be an unusually dry satire, but taken at face value, most of it is plausible — and scary. Without gatekeepers, no one stands ready to verify reports as accurate, so there's no difference between real news and agreed-upon gossip or low-level fluff. Issues debated today — Are bloggers real journalists? Is there a clear line between news and entertainment? — would be irrelevant. Everyone would be a journalist. And though some contributors would be paid, it isn't clear that the flow of money would be enough to fund complicated reports and investigations. Reporters would be paid according to how popular their stories were. Good luck if your job is to cover Rwanda or global warming.

In pointedly ponderous tones, the mockumentary breaks into one of those on-the-one-hand, on-the-other-hand analyses that we all love to hate. At best, we are told, EPIC is deeper, broader, and more nuanced than anything seen before. On the other hand, a lot of EPIC is shallow, trivial, and untrue. "But EPIC is what we wanted, it is what we chose, and its commercial success pre-empted any discussions of media and democracy or journalistic ethics." *EPIC 2014* is a very sharp bit of media analysis. Check it out at www.robinsloan.com/epic.

READING

1. Leo begins his critique with a summary of *EPIC 2014*'s premise. How did you react to this description of the future of media? Were you shocked, or did you think it sounded logical? Note his use of phrases like "a few human editors" in the first paragraph. How does his word choice indicate his attitude toward the subject?

2. Leo states, "The mockumentary is starting to reach a mass audience at a time of unusually high anxiety for the news industry." He mentions "skirmishes between reporters and bloggers." What is the basic conflict being examined here? What is your definition of news?

3. One thing that produces anxiety among the older media is that younger people are no longer turning to traditional formats to get their news. In your opinion, where do most of your peers go for news? Where do you go? Do you think Leo has a valid point here? Why, or why not?

4. The evolution of the media turned, in 2014, into the singular gigantic EPIC, the Evolving Personalized Information Construct. What method of organization does Leo use to bring us to this point in the essay?

5. Leo's point seems to be that the ordinary person is not capable of discerning what is important and what is not in political and social events. Do you agree with his worries about the lack of human "gatekeepers" and the predominance of computers making decisions about what news goes to which people? Explain your reasons.

WRITING

1. Write a reflective essay or a journal piece in which you reminisce about your earliest experience of news. What is the first piece of news you remember being aware of? How old were you? What was the context? What is the latest piece of news you are aware of having noticed? Where did it come from?

2. Go to the EPIC website epic.makingithappen.co.uk/new-masterfs1 .html and watch the eight-minute media critique. Write a short essay describing your reaction to the piece. Model your essay's organization on Leo's if you wish.

3. Leo writes, "According to *Advertising Age*, Google and Yahoo! will take in as much money this year as the prime-time revenues of the three major [TV] networks combined." Research the earnings of the

three major networks (ABC, CBS, NBC), Google, and Yahoo! over the last five years. Then, construct a graph that shows the relationship between the earnings of the "old" media (television, radio) and the Web earnings from advertising.

4. Choose a current political or social event reported in both traditional and new media. See how many instances you can find of the various media reporting your event. Then, write a critical analysis essay evaluating your findings concerning bias, attitude, method, focus, audience, and so on that you find in each example. Possibilities include focus on a local event, a national event, or an international event.

5. Both the EPIC video and John Hodgman's book (p. 432) offer satirical versions of social and political issues. Each uses an existing format with which to frame their piece. EPIC positions itself as a historical video that one might see at the Museum of Media History. Hodgman mimics the format of a social studies textbook to provide an overview of the states. Choose another instance of a social or political satire and analyze its format and method. You might use a movie, a television show, an article, a book, a cartoon, and so on.

FOCUS ON GENRE

Graphic Novels
A Portfolio of Historical Graphic Novels

HOW DO WE TELL HISTORY? MOST OF US WOULD PROVIDE A SINGLE answer to this question: through history textbooks, or popular history monographs, or history told in those multivolume, thousand-plus-page biographies of world leaders. Less likely, few of us would suggest that history can be told in the form of comic books. Yet, a whole subgenre of history has gained a foothold in graphic novels. The graphic history has gained popularity with readers more comfortable with comic books, anime, and even video games than with traditional texts. Because much of the narrative is told through visuals, these books appeal to those who have grown up in a world driven by the visual and the visceral. For this same reason, graphic histories are sometimes criticized for promoting illiteracy, but their potential to deliver a powerful historical message is undeniable. *Maus*, the seminal graphic history by Art Spiegelman excerpted here, was awarded a special Pulitzer Prize for Letters in recognition of its achievement in conveying the tragedy of the Holocaust on an extremely personal level. More recently, Marjane Satrapi's *Persepolis*, which captures her girlhood during the revolution in Iran, has been quickly adopted as a standard text on high school and college reading lists, and noted political and cultural figures such as Bill Clinton, Edward Said, and Christopher Hitchens have written the forwards to graphic histories. And, as the children's drawings of the Darfur tragedy that open this chapter suggest, sometimes words can fail to fully express what happens when the individual collides with the catastrophic. In such cases, the cliché may be true: A picture may actually be worth a thousand words.

We have annotated an excerpt from *Maus*. As you read this graphic history and those that follow, think about how each contains at least three levels of communication: the text, the images, and the messages conveyed as text and image interact. Realize that graphic narratives are subjective creations. Each attempts to take history and make it a story that captures the reader by providing an opening for understanding a possibly vague and opaque event. In your reading, try to discern the style and grammar of the graphic novel as well as the messages they are conveying.

Spiegelman's father is recounting his experience to his son, so the narrative moves from present to past.

Spiegelman portrays Jews as rodents. Why? In World War II propaganda, they were called vermin. Also, mice are small, helpless in a world of cats, the Nazis.

This is a dark world, full of shadows, which captures the dread felt by the Jewish people.

As readers, we know now that these stories are true, which adds drama to this conversation. We know the fate that awaits them.

This is not a formal history full of academic prose. People talk like people. We can hear our voices, our parents' and grandparents' voices, when they speak.

The frame is packed with people – including children – helping to convey the magnitude of the issue.

Even in these relatively undetailed drawings, Spiegelman conveys the stress on the Jewish people. Note the bags under their eyes.

Note his father's voice and use of dialect break into the narrative to express outrage.

Art Spiegelman, "Maus: A Survivor's Tale"

477

THE TRIP

Marjane Satrapi, "The Trip" from "Persepolis: The Story of a Childhood"

AND THEN SOME DAYS LATER...

THE MINISTERY OF EDUCATION HAS DECREED THAT UNIVERSITIES WILL CLOSE AT THE END OF THE MONTH.

OH NO!

THE EDUCATIONAL SYSTEM AND WHAT IS WRITTEN IN SCHOOL BOOKS, AT ALL LEVELS, ARE DECADENT. EVERYTHING NEEDS TO BE REVISED TO ENSURE THAT OUR CHILDREN ARE NOT LED ASTRAY FROM THE TRUE PATH OF ISLAM.

OF COURSE, OF COURSE!

THAT'S WHY WE'RE CLOSING ALL THE UNIVERSITIES FOR A WHILE. BETTER TO HAVE NO STUDENTS AT ALL THAN TO EDUCATE FUTURE IMPERIALISTS.

THUS, THE UNIVERSITIES WERE CLOSED FOR TWO YEARS.

YOU'LL SEE. SOON THEY'RE ACTUALLY GOING TO FORCE US TO WEAR THE VEIL AND YOU, YOU'LL HAVE TO TRADE YOUR CAR FOR A CAMEL. GOD, WHAT A BACKWARD POLICY!

A CAMEL?

NO MORE UNIVERSITY, AND I WANTED TO STUDY CHEMISTRY. I WANTED TO BE LIKE MARIE CURIE.

I WANTED TO BE AN EDUCATED, LIBERATED WOMAN. AND IF THE PURSUIT OF KNOWLEDGE MEANT GETTING CANCER, SO BE IT.

IT'S I WHO DISCOVERED THE NEWEST RADIOACTIVE ELEMENT.

AND SO ANOTHER DREAM WENT UP IN SMOKE.

MISERY! AT THE AGE THAT MARIE CURIE FIRST WENT TO FRANCE TO STUDY, I'LL PROBABLY HAVE TEN CHILDREN ...

IN NO TIME, THE WAY PEOPLE DRESSED BECAME AN IDEOLOGICAL SIGN. THERE WERE TWO KINDS OF WOMEN.

THE FUNDAMENTALIST WOMAN

THE MODERN WOMAN

YOU SHOWED YOUR OPPOSITION TO THE REGIME BY LETTING A FEW STRANDS OF HAIR SHOW,

THERE WERE ALSO TWO SORTS OF MEN.

THE FUNDAMENTALIST MAN

BEARD

SHIRT HANGING OUT

THE PROGRESSIVE MAN

SHAVED, WITH OR WITHOUT MUSTACHE

SHIRT TUCKED IN

ISLAM IS MORE OR LESS AGAINST SHAVING.

BUT LET'S BE FAIR. IF WOMEN FACED PRISON WHEN THEY REFUSED TO WEAR THE VEIL, IT WAS ALSO FORBIDDEN FOR MEN TO WEAR NECKTIES (THAT DREADED SYMBOL OF THE WEST), AND IF WOMEN'S HAIR GOT MEN EXCITED, THE SAME THING COULD BE SAID OF MEN'S BARE ARMS. AND SO, WEARING SHORT-SLEEVED SHIRTS WAS ALSO FORBIDDEN.

THERE WAS A KIND OF JUSTICE, AFTER ALL.

IT WASN'T ONLY THE GOVERNMENT THAT CHANGED. ORDINARY PEOPLE CHANGED TOO.

LOOK AT HER! LAST YEAR SHE WAS WEARING A MINISKIRT, SHOWING OFF HER BEEFY THIGHS TO THE WHOLE NEIGHBORHOOD. AND NOW MADAME IS WEARING A CHADOR. IT SUITS HER BETTER, I GUESS.

AS FOR HER FUNDAMENTALIST HUSBAND WHO DRANK HIMSELF INTO A STUPOR EVERY NIGHT, NOW HE USES MOUTHWASH EVERY TIME HE UTTERS THE WORD "ALCOHOL."

AND THEIR SON SAYS HE PRAYS EVERY DAY!

IF ANYONE EVER ASKS YOU WHAT YOU DO DURING THE DAY, SAY YOU PRAY, YOU UNDERSTAND??

OK...

AT FIRST, IT WAS A LITTLE HARD, BUT I LEARNED TO LIE QUICKLY.

I PRAY FIVE TIMES A DAY.

ME? TEN OR ELEVEN TIMES... SOMETIMES TWELVE.

IN SPITE OF EVERYTHING, THE SPIRIT OF REVOLUTION WAS STILL IN THE AIR. THERE WERE SOME OPPOSITION DEMONSTRATIONS.

TOMORROW THERE'S GOING TO BE A MEETING AGAINST FUNDAMENTALISM.

I'M COMING TOO!

NO! IT'S TOO DANGEROUS.

SHE'S COMING TOO.

SHE SHOULD START LEARNING TO DEFEND HER RIGHTS AS A WOMAN RIGHT NOW!

SINCE THE 1979 REVOLUTION, I'D GROWN OLDER (WELL, A YEAR OLDER) AND MOM HAD CHANGED.

SO I WENT WITH THEM. I PASSED OUT FLYERS...

GUNS MAY SHOOT AND KNIVES MAY CARVE, BUT WE WON'T WEAR YOUR SILLY SCARVES!

...WHEN SUDDENLY THINGS GOT NASTY.

THE SCARF OR A BEATING!

FOR THE FIRST TIME IN MY LIFE, I SAW VIOLENCE WITH MY OWN EYES.

DAD!

THAT WAS OUR LAST DEMONSTRATION.

EVERY MAN FOR HIMSELF!

THINGS GOT WORSE FROM ONE DAY TO THE NEXT. IN SEPTEMBER 1980, MY PARENTS ABRUPTLY PLANNED A VACATION. I THINK THEY REALIZED THAT SOON SUCH THINGS WOULD NO LONGER BE POSSIBLE. AS IT HAPPENED, THEY WERE RIGHT. AND SO WE WENT TO ITALY AND SPAIN FOR THREE WEEKS...

...IT WAS WONDERFUL.

RIGHT BEFORE GOING BACK, IN THE HOTEL ROOM IN MADRID.

LOOK AT THIS.

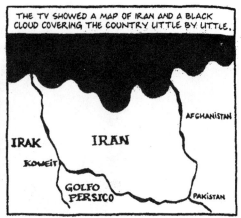

THE TV SHOWED A MAP OF IRAN AND A BLACK CLOUD COVERING THE COUNTRY LITTLE BY LITTLE.

IRAK

IRAN

AFGHANISTAN

KOWEIT

GOLFO PERSICO

PAKISTAN

WHAT IN THE WORLD IS THIS?

TOO BAD WE DON'T KNOW SPANISH.

MAYBE THEY'RE TALKING ABOUT POLLUTION. YOU KNOW, TEHRAN IS THE FOURTH MOST POLLUTED CITY IN THE WORLD.

IT LOOKS LIKE THEY'RE TALKING ABOUT THE WHOLE COUNTRY, NOT JUST THE CAPITAL.

THE NEXT DAY MY GRANDMOTHER CAME TO PICK US UP AT THE AIRPORT.

GRANDMA! I GOT YOU A BLACK DRESS!

SHE LOOKED WORRIED.

EVERYTHING OK, MOM?

YES...

485

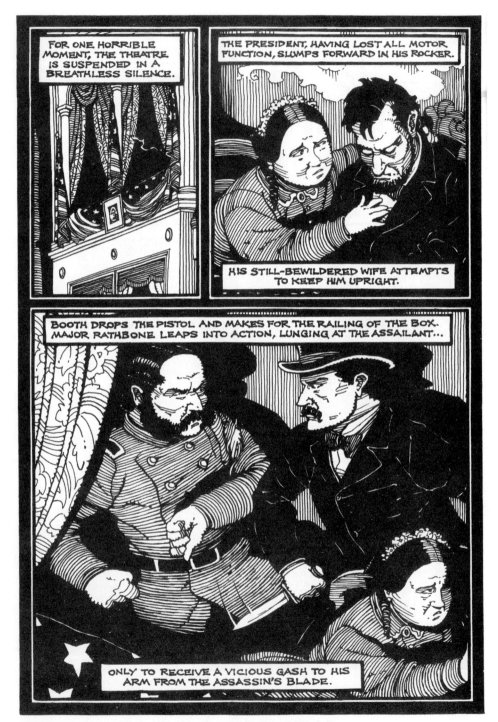

Rick Geary, excerpt from "The Murder of Abraham Lincoln"

AT THE SAME MOMENT THAT BOOTH ENTERS THE PRESIDENT'S BOX, ANOTHER DRAMA UNFOLDS ON LAFAYETTE SQUARE.

LEWIS POWELL AND DAVID HEROLD ARRIVE AT THE HOME OF WILLIAM H. SEWARD.

HEROLD WAITS IN THE STREET WHILE POWELL KNOCKS ON THE DOOR, POSING AS A MESSENGER FROM SEWARD'S PHYSICIAN.

ONCE INSIDE, POWELL LEAPS UP THE STAIRS . . .

ONLY TO BE CONFRONTED BY FREDERICK SEWARD.

THE INTRUDER AIMS HIS REVOLVER . . .

BUT IT FAILS TO FIRE.

HE THEN USES IT TO BELABOR THE POOR MAN ABOUT THE HEAD.

HE MAKES HIS WAY TO SEWARD'S BEDROOM, WHERE THE SECRETARY HAS LAIN IMMOBILE SINCE HIS ACCIDENT . . .

ATTENDED BY HIS DAUGHTER, FANNY, AND A SOLDIER-NURSE, GEORGE ROBINSON.

BEFORE LONG, IT IS DECIDED THAT THE VICTIM MUST BE MOVED TO A MORE COMFORTABLE LOCATION.

SIX MEN VOLUNTEER TO CARRY HIM DOWN THE STAIRS AND OUT OF THE THEATRE.

THE WHITE HOUSE BEING TOO DISTANT, ONE OF THE RESIDENCES ACROSS 10TH ST. SEEMS THE LIKELIEST DESTINATION.

THE STREET IS A SEA OF CURIOUS, UNBELIEVING FACES, AND THE PARTY MAKES ITS WAY BUT SLOWLY.

OUT OF THE WAY!

FROM THE BOARDING HOUSE OWNED BY WILLIAM PETERSEN, A YOUNG TENANT, HENRY STAFFORD, OFFERS A ROOM.

BRING HIM IN HERE!

Aaron Renier, "Just Answer the Phone" from "9-11 Artists Respond"

Joe Sacco, "Brotherhood and Unity" from "Safe Area Gorazde: The War in Eastern Bosnia 1992-95"

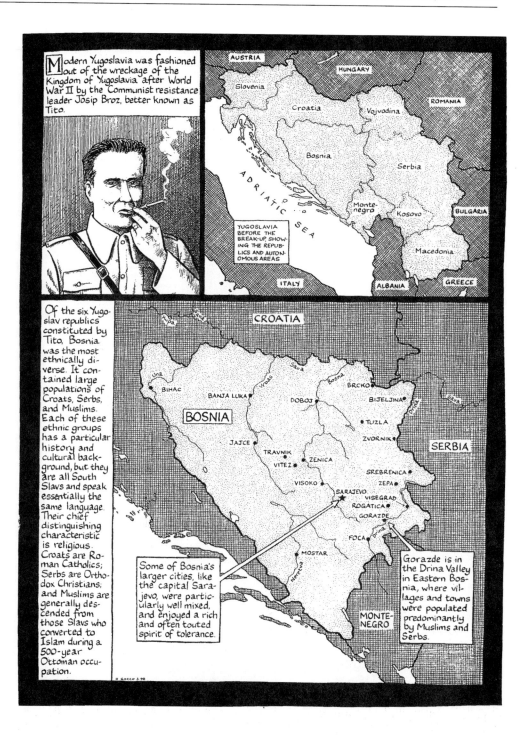

Modern Yugoslavia was fashioned out of the wreckage of the Kingdom of Yugoslavia after World War II by the Communist resistance leader Josip Broz, better known as Tito.

YUGOSLAVIA BEFORE THE BREAK-UP, SHOWING THE REPUBLICS AND AUTONOMOUS AREAS

Of the six Yugoslav republics constituted by Tito, Bosnia was the most ethnically diverse. It contained large populations of Croats, Serbs, and Muslims. Each of these ethnic groups has a particular history and cultural background, but they are all South Slavs and speak essentially the same language. Their chief distinguishing characteristic is religious. Croats are Roman Catholics; Serbs are Orthodox Christians; and Muslims are generally descended from those Slavs who converted to Islam during a 500-year Ottoman occupation.

Some of Bosnia's larger cities, like the capital Sarajevo, were particularly well mixed, and enjoyed a rich and often touted spirit of tolerance.

Gorazde is in the Drina Valley in Eastern Bosnia, where villages and towns were populated predominantly by Muslims and Serbs.

497

More than a million Yugoslavs died in the war, mostly at the hands of other Yugoslavs.

When the Axis powers occupied and dismembered the Kingdom of Yugoslavia in 1941, they installed Croatian fascists, the Ustasha, in their own state, which was expanded to include Bosnia. The fury with which the Ustasha carried out their genocidal program of wholesale slaughter, forced religious conversion, and expulsion of the Serb population left even the Nazis aghast. Ustasha victims fed the ranks of two competing resistance groups, the Chetniks and the Partisans.

The Chetniks were a somewhat loose alliance of groups of Serb nationalists and royalists who typically sought the establishment of a Greater Serbia cleansed of non-Serbs. The Chetniks waged a ruthless war against Bosnia's Croat and Muslim citizenry, whom they viewed as Ustasha collaborators, and against the Partisans, whom they saw as likely post-war rivals.

The Partisans, the Communist resistance force led by Tito, also were a predominantly Serb group (Tito himself was half-Croatian, half-Slovenian), but they welcomed a growing number of Muslim and Croatian recruits as disillusionment with the Ustasha regime increased and Chetnik outrages continued. The Partisans fought a generally defensive war against Axis forces and waged an aggressive campaign against the Chetniks, whom they eventually crushed.

Bosnia's Muslims could be found on all sides of the conflict. A few even allied themselves with the Chetniks. Others joined in the Ustasha persecution of the Serbs. Several thousand volunteered with the Germans for a Muslim S.S. division which carried out anti-Serb atrocities.

As chaos spread, some Muslims formed autonomous defense units for protection against any and all threats, and in greater and greater numbers Muslims joined the multi-ethnic Partisans, which led to more Chetnik reprisals.

Hundreds of thousands of Serbs were killed in the war, mostly by the Ustasha, but the Muslims lost a greater percentage of their population, mostly in Chetnik attacks and massacres, many of which took place in Eastern Bosnia.

THERE WAS PLENTY OF KILLING IN THE WAR, MUSLIMS BY CHETNIKS.

"They were coming and going whenever they liked, in small groups, burning houses, killing people, raping women... Muslims in this area did not have anything to defend themselves with.

"The Chetniks raped and slaughtered... so many of my cousins and Muslims in this area. The worst things happened in Foca. The village of my family, Bucije ...over the River Drina, the Chetniks completely blew up, and whomever they found they killed. We're talking about the men...

"When people heard that these groups were coming, as fast as possible they were hiding themselves or escaping somewhere. My grandfather hid himself with the help of his wife for nearly one year under the cows' shed in the ground...

"In that time, Muslims...escaped from Gorazde... They organized themselves in groups and ran from one place to the other because of the traitors, the Chetniks and the Ustasha. My grandparents were able to go to Brcko and Visoko.

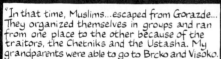

"My grandfather and grandmother sometimes tried to explain to me what happened during World War II, but I did not listen, or listened with one ear."

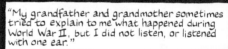

RESPONDING

1. In his forward to *Safe Area Gorazde*, Christopher Hitchens writes, "The first thing that one must praise is the combination of eye and ear." How do "eye and ear" relate in these excerpts? As you think about this question, it might be helpful to analyze how each frame achieves its own feeling/tone about its subject and then identify how the look of each differs in everything from drawing style to textual font.

2. Most of these excerpts have a definite first-person narrator, and this voice shapes the subjective history that is recounted. Who narrates the excerpts? What do you know about this speaker? How does his or her involvement in the story shape the history that is being told? You might want to use Rick Geary's piece as a contrast to the others; it takes on a third-person voice in the narration, though the visuals convey a clear point of view.

3. Aaron Renier's short work is one of many written in response to the tragedy of 9/11, and it comes from a collected volume of such pieces. Art Spiegelman (*Maus: A Survivor's Tale*, p. 477) also authored a graphic novel about these events. These graphic narratives were among the first artistic responses to the attacks; some were written and published within days after the Twin Towers fell. Research the comics and graphic narratives written about 9/11 – and the analyses of these works. Write an essay that discusses why the graphic narrative served to capture this particular event in such a compelling manner. Include the themes and symbols that quickly became associated with 9/11 and how these might lend themselves to the grammar of the graphic novel.

4. Select a historical event with which you have great familiarity, something you may have studied in another course or on your own. Working with another student who has a similar interest, create a mock-up of two pages of a prospective graphic narrative that captures this event. Present your work to the class, providing an explanation of the choices you made in text, image, tone, and so on.

From the Profane to the Sacred: Ritual and Mourning at Sites of Terror and Violence

By Janet Jacobs

FROM: *Journal for the Scientific Study of Religion*, **September 2004**

THE FOLLOWING ARTICLE WAS WRITTEN FOR THE *JOURNAL FOR THE Scientific Study of Religion*, an interdisciplinary, not-for-profit, academic journal. The journal has been published quarterly for forty years and explores the relationship of religion to sociology, psychology, political science, anthropology, and history, providing a scholarly analysis of topics such as the relationship between religion and social attitudes, and the growth of fundamentalism, sacralization, and secularization. Part of its mission is "to help the scholarly community take advantage of advances in information technologies." To this end, they maintain an extensive online archive of scholarly articles and journals. As with most scholarly publications, *Journal for the Scientific Study of Religion* is targeted primarily at academics (professors, deans, graduate students) doing research in the field. Janet Jacobs is a professor of sociology at the University of Colorado at Boulder. Her focus is on religion and women's studies. She was awarded the Hazel Barnes Prize for outstanding teaching and research in 2005.

To help you read more deeply and critically, we have provided annotations and boldfaced some terms or passages that call attention to the rhetorical choices Jacobs has made in her article and to the requirements of social research that are present in this piece. As you read the essay and the annotations, consider how the author presents her observations about sacralization on sites of violence, terror, and genocide.

Jacobs opens her essay with a discovery at a site of terror Americans recognize immediately — Ground Zero. She demonstrates the impulse to create sacred ground at once when the "cross" is discovered. This is an anecdotal and personal way into her argument.

Three days after the attacks on the World Trade Center, **Frank Sileccha, a construction worker at Ground Zero, reportedly found two metal beams in the shape of a cross standing upright amid the debris of the twin towers. The media coverage surrounding the "accidental discovery" of the cross was extensive, with almost every newspaper in the region, including the *New York Times* and the *New York Post*, disseminating images of what had quickly become a sacred icon at Ground Zero.** Within days, rescue workers began to pray and meditate at the 20-foot cross while religious services were held there on a regular basis. The importance of the cross as a perceived presence of God at Ground Zero contributed to the almost immediate sanctification of the site, **a turning toward the sacred that was evident not only in the worship at the cross but in the creation of the many other popular shrines and ritual spaces that spontaneously appeared in and around the wreckage**.

This ritual response to September 11, in what is without question one of the most sophisticated and cosmopolitan urban centers in the world, signifies the significant role that the sacred assumes in memorializing violence and mass trauma. Just as the "iron" cross at Ground Zero became a religious shrine to the fallen and the victimized, the placement of other sacred objects at the site — rosary beads, religious medals, and memorial candles — helped transform the landscape of carnage and death into sacred ground. **The tendency toward the**

The impulse was not limited to the symbol of the cross alone — people began spontaneously to create "shrines and ritual spaces" in response to the tragedy. Americans can remember the media coverage of the photographs, placards, notes, and objects that were placed to create sacred space.

Notice here how she makes the transition from Ground Zero to Holocaust sites in Europe, which we may not be as familiar with as we are with Ground Zero.

sanctification of sites of violence is perhaps one of the more interesting and poignant aspects of religious life today, especially in those cultures that are seeking ways to publicly remember and memorialize acts of terrorism. In this regard, Holocaust sites throughout eastern and western Europe offer some of the most startling examples of this trend toward sacred memorialization. Particularly in the last decade, former death camps and massacre sites have increasingly become sacred ground where the performance of rituals and death rites mark and reclaim these surviving landscapes of violence and genocide.

I first became aware of this phenomenon while doing fieldwork on the role of gender in the representation of Holocaust trauma. Early on in the research process, I began to observe the role that Jewish mourning played in the preservation of Holocaust memory in postwar European culture. As the research progressed from Austria to the Czech Republic and finally to Poland, I witnessed firsthand how sacred spaces had been carved out of landscapes of horror and atrocity, even as the memory of genocide was pervasive and overwhelming. These observations led me to consider the ways memorial spaces are sanctified and reconsecrated in the aftermath of terror and violence. It is this aspect of memorial culture to which this essay on religion and violence is addressed — the transformation of the profane into the sacred at monuments and memorial spaces that recall and remember the history of human

At this point Jacobs uses first person, and as readers, we see that she has observed these Holocaust sites in postwar Europe firsthand.

As she states her thesis, notice the more formal language she uses to address her fellow scholars and researchers.

Subheadings help organize the essay into distinct sections.

atrocities and the trauma of ethnic extermination. In this discussion, **I will explore the complex ways the sacred becomes embedded in cultural remembrance, and the conflicts and tensions that arise out of the sacralization of monuments and museums that commemorate the horrors of the past.**

The Death Camp at Mauthausen and the Reconsecration of Technologies of Genocide

My research into cultural memory and the Holocaust began with my visit to the memorials and museum that are housed at the former death/labor camp in Mauthausen, Austria. Although the site is situated above the village of Mauthausen, there is little in the way of direction to the museum or evidence of its existence in the tourist literature that the village provides. **The negligible role that the museum/memorial plays in the tourist culture of the surrounding area is perhaps, as James Young suggests, a reflection of the "painfully self-conscious memorial culture" that has for the most part been defined by an Austrian ambivalence toward remembering the past (Young 1993:91).** Despite its relative geographic obscurity, however, the memorial site at Mauthausen is nonetheless a powerful and dramatic landscape where monuments to the dead have been erected in a beautiful sculpture garden that borders the buildings that house the original gas chamber and crematorium.

Her citation of another scholar's work shows that she is familiar with the literature on the subject.

Her images are concrete and visual. We can "see" the camps and the memorial objects with her.

Beginning in the 1950s, the sculpture garden, which is located on a rolling hillside outside the gates of the original death camp, was designated as an official memorial park, the place where at least 20 countries were invited to construct monuments to the Nazi victims of World War II. More recently, another kind of memorial space has been created within the walls of the museum/camp grounds. Here "outsider groups," including Roma (Gypsies) and gays and lesbians, are memorialized with handmade plaques, makeshift alters, and flower-strewn courtyards that call special attention to both the racialized and sexualized context of Nazi persecution. In comparison with the state-sponsored memorials, the countermemorials inside the camp walls offer a somewhat different perspective on the nature of genocidal history. **Marked by handwritten notes and prewar photographs, the individually created memorials** remind the visitors both of the political nature of collective memory and the personal tragedies and loss of World War II.

It was also at Mauthausen that I first became aware of the transformation of the profane into the sacred in those areas of the museum where the crematorium and gas chamber have been preserved. In the open ovens of the immaculately maintained crematorium, I witnessed Jewish memorial candles burning alongside frayed and yellowed pictures of women, men, and children. In an adjacent room, the shower stalls that once served as gas chambers were similarly covered with pictures of the dead. At the entrance to both the

> The images gain in intensity as she witnesses the "technologies of genocide."

crematorium and the gas chambers, I watched as visitors prayed and meditated, leaving behind scraps of paper on which the words for God and spirit had been written in Hebrew, Spanish, English, and a myriad of other languages.

Particularly at Mauthausen, these acts of remembrance have helped to reframe their context. **Technologies of genocide** are transformed and redefined as religious spaces, and the sacred and profane are brought together in a spiritual reconsecration of the death campsite. Accordingly, Mauthausen is perhaps unique among memorials to the Holocaust, a place where national memory and religious culture converge in the commemoration of death and suffering. The countermemorials inside the museum together with the national monuments that frame the surrounding campgrounds make visible the enormity of loss that affected a wide range of individuals and cultures from diverse national, ethnoreligious, and sexual backgrounds. **The sense of inclusivity that Mauthausen conveyed, however, was not typical of other sites I visited. Especially in Poland, where the tensions and conflicts over national as well as sacred memory remain strong, the potentially divisive aspects of memorialization were more clearly in evidence.**

Memorializing Genocide at Majdanek and Treblinka

The memorialization of the Holocaust in Poland has a contentious history. Beginning with the Sovietization of Poland immediately fol-

> Jacobs calls attention to the next strand of her argument—that memorials may not always be inclusive. Her further observations lead her to see how they caused divisiveness as well.

Again, she refers to the scholarly literature to locate her thinking within the framework of research, not just personal observation. Jacobs uses the standard American Psychological Association reference form throughout her essay. Each parenthetical citation appears in full in the references section.

lowing the war, the preservation of death campsites as national monuments focused on the memory of German atrocities as these were promulgated against the Polish and Russian people. **As many scholars have since pointed out (Irwin-Zarecka 1990; Young 1994), this construction of atrocity memory helped obscure the history of genocidal policies that were aimed specifically at the Jews and Roma. It has only been in the last decade, with the political and social changes brought on by the dismantling of the Soviet Union, that Polish death camp memorials now include narratives that identify the three million Polish Jews and the hundreds of thousands of Roma who were systematically targeted by the Nazis (Lentin 1997).** The recent inclusion of these narratives of Jewish and Roma persecution are emerging at a time when the sites themselves have in some ways become contested terrains of national memory. The developing tensions over Holocaust memorials in Poland today can in part be explained by two social factors: the close proximity of sites of genocide to residential areas and the reemergence of Catholicism as the Polish state religion in the wake of Poland's transition from a communist culture.

The memorials at Majdanek and Treblinka in particular emanate a certain cultural tension that has become manifest in the sometimes strained or uncomfortable relations between visitors to these sites and the nearby Polish residents. The area around Majdanek, for example, is surrounded by Soviet-era apartment complexes that were

> Notice her use of "the visitor." We become visitors with her, witnessing the aftermath of the Holocaust.

developed on the land adjacent to the former death camp. Residential buildings and shops are therefore scattered along the borders of the original barbed-wire fences that today enclose the former barracks, gas chambers, and crematoria. At the entrance to the park, a huge stone sculpture marks the site as a national monument, creating an impression of a modern and abstract memorial space. Once inside the camp, however, it is the memory of genocide that becomes most enduring and pervasive.

In entering Majdanek, perhaps more so than any other Holocaust site, the visitor is returned to an almost unaltered geography of horror and death that has remained unchanged since the Nazis fled the camp in the final days of the war. In one apparent concession to postwar tourist culture, the state-run museum has provided road signs that point the way to the death camp's many sites. At the main crossroads where the campgrounds begin, painted wooden arrows direct the visitors to the prisoner's barracks, the crematorium, and the gas chambers. A separate arrow points the way to the "mausoleum," a site within the camp that is undoubtedly Majdanek's most distinguishing feature. **The mausoleum, which is located at the far end of the camp, is an immense dome-shaped structure that contains the ashes of the 350,000 people, most of whom were Jews, who were murdered there.** Because the remains of the victims are both visible and accessible to the visitor, no other memorial space in eastern Europe

> We may have heard generally about the atrocities, but this particularly horrific example makes her point vividly.

conveys the reality of the Holocaust in quite the same way as does Majdanek. Further, because the mausoleum is an actual gravesite, it is here that visitors, survivors, and family members come to say Kaddish (the Jewish prayer for mourning), lining the edges of the mountain-size urn with stones and pebbles in the custom of Jewish tradition. Yet, because of the death camp's proximity to the residential areas, the visitor/mourner culture has also created a sense of uneasiness with the neighboring communities.

While doing fieldwork at Majdanek, I observed visitors in prayer at the mausoleum while neighboring families walked to and from the houses and shops that border both sides of the camp. As I observed the ritual life taking place within the memorial park, Polish mothers and daughters, shopping bags in hand, routinely passed the Jewish mourners, careful to avoid eye contact with the visitors as they moved up and down the steps that circled the mausoleum. Scenes such as these have in recent years become more commonplace in Poland as survivors, as well as other Jewish groups, recite prayers of mourning on the streets of former ghettos, at forested massacre sites, and in the death memorials. Thus, in Poland in particular, where the genocide of the Jews was most pronounced, the boundaries between the sacralization of the horrors of the past and the day-to-day lives of those living in the present have become uncomfortably blurred.

This aspect of Holocaust memorialization was painfully evident on a recent visit I made to Treblinka. Just as I was

Again, she uses a very concrete observed example to illustrate the assertion she made earlier about divisiveness.

leaving the park, a small group of mourners from Israel were preparing to pray when a Polish father and his two sons entered the memorial grounds on bicycles, laughing and joking as they rode past the survivor families. The hostile glances that were exchanged between the two groups of visitors to the park were indicative of the stresses that currently exist in this region of Poland, where much of the surrounding area is covered with the remains of Holocaust atrocities. As a memorial site, Treblinka has been artfully reconstructed over the ruins of the original death camp. In place of the gas chambers and crematoria, which were destroyed by the Germans before evacuating the camp, thousands of gravestones have been erected on acres of charred land, each stone representing a village, town, or city in Poland and the murdered Jewish residents from these areas. Thus, in its memorial restructuring, Treblinka, more so than most other Holocaust sites in Poland, has been reconstituted as a Jewish graveyard.

And yet, because Treblinka is situated at the edge of a well-maintained forested area, it has also become a recreational space. It is therefore not unusual to see Polish families playing among the ruins of the former death camp. The tensions that exist between neighboring Polish residents who use the park for recreational purposes and Holocaust survivors who view Treblinka as sacred illuminate the difficulties that societies face in preserving landscapes that have multiple meanings for past and present generations.

Now she asserts her claim again, this time in formal, academic language.

This controversial aspect of genocide memorialization has been most problematic at Auschwitz-Birkenau where conflagrations over religious dominance and spiritual appropriation continue to inform the sociopolitical dimensions of Holocaust commemoration in European culture.

Auschwitz-Birkenau and the Contested Arena of Religious Remembrance

Perhaps more than any other Holocaust site, the death camp at Auschwitz has become the most renowned symbol of ethnic genocide and Nazi atrocities. Since its designation as a Polish national memorial following the end of World War II, the death camp has been refurbished and reconstructed numerous times, with the present museum currently designed to accommodate the large number of visitors who tour the site each year. **The original entrance to the camp is now a massive parking lot, while a partial reconstruction of the original crematorium lies outside the borders of the main gates (Dwork and van Pelt 1994:232). Up until very recently, the official guidebooks and camp narratives failed to acknowledge the extent to which Jews in particular were the target of genocidal policies, emphasizing instead the martyrdom of Polish nationals (Irwin-Zarecka 1990).** This representation of national memory was in part made possible by the fact that most of the actual killing at Auschwitz took place a few miles away at

As she has done near the beginning of each new section, she cites authorities on her subject, thus placing her argument in a scholarly context.

the adjoining camp of Birkenau, a notorious extermination center where up to 60,000 people were killed each day. Because the tour guides and the tourist literature primarily focus on Auschwitz, Birkenau receives far fewer visitors, an aspect of concentration camp tourism that tends to obscure the reality of Jewish genocide at the Auschwitz-Birkenau site.

Nevertheless, Auschwitz-Birkenau, as a museum/camp memorial, remains one of the most important sites of Jewish loss in post-Holocaust Jewish culture, and therefore is a particularly hallowed ground where Jews from all over the world come to pray, say Kaddish, and light candles for the hundreds of thousands of Jews who died there. Since the 1980s, however, Auschwitz-Birkenau has become the focus of numerous controversies surrounding issues of religious memory and cultural and national histories. The religious tensions surrounding Auschwitz first came to international attention with the construction of a Carmelite convent in a warehouse that had once been used to store the lethal Zyklon B gas. **The establishment of a Catholic-based religious organization at a site that was so identified with the atrocities of Auschwitz led to protestations on the part of Jewish groups, some of whom maintained that the convent represented the religious and spiritual appropriation of a Jewish burial ground and cemetery.** After years of tense dialogue and negotiation in which the Vatican and the Polish government intervened, the convent has moved to an area further

> Here, the intrusion of other religions into spaces initially dedicated to Jewish mourning causes conflict as the space expands to serve others.

from the walls of the camp and has subsequently reopened as an information bureau as well as a religious center (Irwin-Zarecka 1990, 1994). Further down the road, the railroad tracks that wind through the remains of the buildings and crematoria at Birkenau have also become the locus of religious activity. On any given day, Catholic clergy as well as other religious devotees can be found meditating and praying on the train tracks that, like the gas chambers and the crematoria, have become designated areas of ritual practice where acts of mourning and repentance are performed. Because of Birkenau's significant role in the murder of so many Nazi victims, the camp has become one of the most important arenas of spiritual healing in post-Holocaust society. Nonetheless, controversies and tensions over religious hegemony and moral responsibility still prevail, as contestations over the form and content of the sacred remain central to the ritual life of eastern European memorial culture.

Conclusion: Violence, Terrorism, and the Return to the Sacred

The proliferation of religious rites at sites of death and genocide both in the United States and Europe highlights the need for ritual in contemporary society, particularly as the dangers of violence and terrorism continue to inform the geopolitical dimensions of national and international conflict. **As communities and nations struggle to cope with the fear, loss, and tragedy of terrorism and massive**

In her conclusion, she restates her argument and suggests further direction for thought and research.

death, the damaged landscapes caused by these acts of violence are fast becoming hallowed ground where the presence of God is sought and revitalized. In light of this significant phenomenon, the question as to why the sites themselves are so essential to commemoration is important to consider. For some endangered societies, the trend toward sanctification is related to the characterization of these sites as cemeteries and graveyards, while for others, notions of the sacred are tied to beliefs and ideologies that imbue the land with the spirit of the dead (Baer 2000). My own view is that the sacralization of these sites also serves to connect survivors to the victims, creating a shared terrain of suffering, grief, and mourning. Thus, particularly in Western culture where theories of secularization tend to prevail, it is significant to note how collective trauma and social devastation have led to a return to the sacred — especially in those places where the actual violence occurred. At the same time, however, the tensions surrounding the creation of sacred space point to the complex ways religious ritual functions in traumatized societies. **Although, in the aftermath of terrorism and atrocity, public rites of mourning may provide a source of cultural cohesion and a shared experience of loss, the difficulties between Polish Catholics and Jews at Auschwitz-Birkenau also illustrate how bringing in the sacred can form obstacles to social bonding. This phenomenon has been all too evident in the United States as well. No sooner had the steel-beamed**

> She summarizes the main points of her essay, a common strategy in longer, academic articles.

Jacobs ends with a strong statement about the paradox of religion leading both to social bonding and cultural cohesion and to providing the reason for religious terrorism. (See bedfordstmartins.com/nexttext for additional information on using and documenting sources.)

cross been discovered at Ground Zero, than did the culture wars erupt over the appropriateness of Christian symbolism at the World Trade Center disaster site. A contentious debate immediately arose among atheists, Christians, and non-Christians alike: Should the cross be allowed to stay and, if so, where should it be placed? Culture conflicts such as these reflect the social and religious meanings that societies attribute to catastrophic events, especially those that call into question the security and safety of a nation and a people under attack. The reemergence of the conflicts over the sacred at the death campsites in Europe and more recently at Ground Zero in the United States confirms that, **contrary to predictions of the death of God, the spiritual and religious aspects of social life continue to have value in a world marked by political destruction and crimes against humanity, even as the persistence of such values may contribute to the furthering of violence and the promulgation of religious intolerance.**

Following APA style, a list of all the research Jacobs cites appears at the end of her article.

REFERENCES

Baer, U. 2000. To give memory a place: Holocaust photography and the landscape tradition. *Representations* 69:38–62.

Dwork, D., and R. van Pelt. 1994. Reclaiming Auschwitz. In *Holocaust remembrance: The shapes of memory*, edited by G. H. Hartman, pp. 232–51. Cambridge, MA: Blackwell.

Irwin-Zarecka, I. 1990. *Neutralizing memory: The Jew in contemporary Poland.* New Brunswick, NJ: Transaction Publishers.

_____. 1994. *Frames of remembrance: The dynamics of collective memory.* New Brunswick, NJ: Transaction Publishers.

Lentin, R., editor. 1997. *Gender and catastrophe.* London: Zed Books.

Young, J. E. 1993. *The texture of memory: Holocaust memorials and meaning.* New Haven, CT: Yale University Press.

MAKING CONNECTIONS ACROSS AND BEYOND THE DISCIPLINES

1. Jacobs states, "The proliferation of religious rites at sites of death and genocide both in the United States and Europe highlights the need for ritual in contemporary society, particularly as the dangers of violence and terrorism continue to inform the geopolitical dimensions of national and international conflict." Choose an event that has been memorialized that was a site of terror or violence and is now a sacred space – for example, a Civil War battleground, an airplane crash site, or a roadside shrine for a traffic fatality – and research its history. Write an essay giving the background of the site and telling how it calls attention to the sacredness of its space. Be descriptive and detailed, as Jacobs is in her description of the shrines at Ground Zero and the European Holocaust sites.

2. Another way to memorialize is to create art, as the children did in their drawings of the atrocities at Darfur at the beginning of the chapter, or the combat artist in his photographs of the Iraq War. Research other sites of conflict and the art that is created that memorializes it. You might look at photographs, movies, or poetry, for example.

3. Clayborne Carson, in his essay on the movie *Malcolm X* (p. 405), says, "The film conveys neither the complexity nor the self-critical aspects of the *Autobiography*, which told Malcolm's story from the perspective of his final year. Throughout its more than three hours, Lee's film is resolutely respectful, glamorizing the truculence of Malcolm's Detroit Red period and the dogmatism of some of this speeches as a Muslim minister." Choose a movie about another historical figure or event – for example, *Gandhi, JFK, The Alamo, Apollo 13* – and contrast the movie version with the more accurate historical version. Write an essay on your findings, calling attention to what has been left out or glamorized in order to make the history appeal more strongly to its intended audience.

Mapping the Human Genome

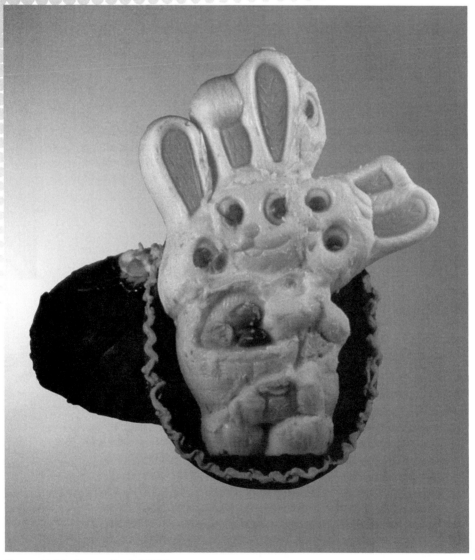

Susan Robb, Bunny Test, 2000

T HE OPENING IMAGE OF THIS CHAPTER CAPTURES ONE
sculpture in a series by Susan Robb called *Bunny Test*. In her
work, Robb uses art to convey her concerns about the path of science.
Bunny Test – in manner both humorous and horrifying – explores one
potential outcome of genetic engineering in a series of grafted Easter
bunnies. On first glance, *Bunny Test* seems like an odd joke, an
ironic commentary on science wrought in chocolate. Oh, those wacky
artists! But, on second glance, the image starts to become more disturbing than funny. The grafting has mangled the chocolate as though
it had been melted and left to decay in the effort. The eyes seem to be
pleading, especially those of the split-eyed bunny on the left. The extra
paws of the grafted figures thrust their way through the middle of the
sculpture, as if seeking some role in this new creation. What was at
first a candy-coated joke, a piece of fanciful art, has begun to leave a
very bad taste and to trigger real concerns about the scientific activities that are being parodied in chocolate.

In describing Robb's work, Anna Fehey writes, "She forces recognition of the fine line between scientist as mad artist and artist as mad
scientist, inciting a dialogue about our relationship to science and to nature and to the utterly arbitrary – indeed nonexistent – division between
the two." This "fine line" is the focus of the readings that follow. The advent of genomic research and biotechnology has brought with it a new
kind of science, one that has the potential to change what it means to
be human in fundamental, biological, and technological ways. One of the
writers in this chapter, Carol Becker (p. 559), goes so far as to label our
current era "posthuman." What it means to be human is the essential
subject of art – hence the descriptive term "the humanities." With the
tools available through genetic engineering, scientists can take on the
role of creator – a role more typically associated with art. And, as you

will find, when science pushes into the realm of art, art pushes back, with intriguing and not always especially supportive results.

This chapter asks you to consider *how* science and art interact to shape our view of the world: How they convey information that can either garner support or encourage suspicion of complex new paths and knowledge. The creators of these pieces are scientists, artists, or sometimes both. Some view the potential of genetic engineering as a remarkable opportunity for human growth and enrichment; some see it as a threat to humanity. As you analyze these works, think about the approach each takes to the topic: Are you being reassured about rightness of purpose or being encouraged to engage in deep personal reflection? Does one approach map more closely to art or to science? Or have the distinctions become too blurred in the "posthuman" era? In 2000, in recognition of the significance of the advances in genetic engineering, the American Museum of Natural History launched a large-scale multimedia exhibit on what it called "The Genomic Revolution." The introductory comments to attendees ended with a single question: "The genomic revolution is here – are you ready?" The texts that follow ask you – almost a decade later – to ponder the same question. Ready or not, here it comes.

A Tale of Two Loves

By Alan Lightman

FROM: *Nature*, March 17, 2005

CONTEXT: This article comes from the magazine *Nature*, an international weekly journal that has been publishing since 1869. Its website claims, "In 2005 *Nature* generated nearly 10,000 more citations than in 2004, and 26,000 more citations than its closest competitor, making it the world's most highly cited multidisciplinary science journal." *Nature*'s mission is twofold: "First, to serve scientists through prompt publication of significant advances in any branch of science and to provide a forum for the reporting and discussion of news and issues concerning science. Second, to ensure that the results of science are rapidly disseminated to the public throughout the world, in a fashion that conveys their significance for knowledge, culture, and daily life." Alan Lightman, the author of this piece, is a novelist, physicist, and teacher. He is adjunct professor of humanities at the Massachusetts Institute of Technology (MIT), where he also teaches creative writing and physics. His webpage tells us that he "received his A.B. degree in physics from Princeton University in 1970, Phi Beta Kappa and Magna Cum Laude, and his Ph.D. in theoretical physics from the California Institute of Technology in 1974." As you read this piece, think about why it would appear in a science journal rather than a humanities journal.

IN CHILDHOOD, I WROTE DOZENS OF POEMS. I EXPRESSED IN verse my questions about death, my loneliness, my admiration for a plum-colored sky, and my unrequited love for fourteen-year-old girls. Reading, listening, even thinking, I was mesmerized by the sounds and the movement of words. Words could be sharp or smooth, cool, silvery, prickly to touch, blaring like a trumpet call, fluid, pitter-pattered in rhythm. And, by magic, words could create emotions and scenes. When my grandfather died, I buried my grief in writing a poem, which I showed to my grandmother a month later. She cradled my face with her veined hands and said, "It's beautiful," and then began weeping all over again. How could marks on a white sheet of paper contain such power and force?

Between poems, I did scientific experiments. These I conducted in the cramped little laboratory I had built out of a storage closet in my house. In my homemade alchemist's den, I horded resistors and capacitors, coils of wire of various thicknesses and grades, batteries, switches, photoelectric cells, magnets, dangerous chemicals, test tubes and Petri dishes, Bunsen burners. I loved to find out how things worked.

When my experiments went awry, I could always find certain fulfillment in mathematics. When my math teachers assigned homework, I relished the job. I would save my maths problems for last, right before bedtime — like bites of chocolate cake awaiting me after a long and dutiful meal of history and Latin. Then I would devour my cake. In algebra, I loved the abstractions, letting x's and y's stand for the number of nickels in a jar or the height of a building in the distance. I loved solving a set of connected equations, one logical step after another. I loved the shining purity of mathematics, the logic, the precision. I loved the certainty. With mathematics, you were guaranteed an answer, as clean and crisp as a new $20 bill. And when you had found that answer, you were right, unquestionably right. The area of a circle is πr^2. Period.

Mathematics and science contrasted strongly with the ambiguities and contradictions of people. The world of people had no certainty or logic. People confused me. My Aunt Jean continued to drive recklessly and at great speed, even though everyone told her she would kill herself. My Uncle Edwin asked me to do a mathematical calculation that would help him run the family business with more efficiency, but when I showed him the result he brushed it aside with disdain. Blanche, the dear woman who worked for our family, deserted her husband after he abused her and then talked about him with affection for years. How does one make sense out of such actions and words'?

A long time later, after I became a novelist, I realized that the am- 5 biguities and complexities of the human psyche are what give fiction, and perhaps all art, its power. A good novel gets under our skin, provokes us, and haunts us long after the first reading, precisely because we never fully understand the characters. We sweep through the narrative over and over again, searching for meaning. Compelling characters must retain a certain mystery and unfathomable depth, even for the author. Once we have seen to the bottom of their hearts, the novel is dead for us.

There are questions with answers and questions without. Scientists work on questions with answers. Although science is constantly revising itself in response to new ideas and data, at any moment each scientist is working on what is called a "well-posed problem" — that is, a problem of such a kind and stated with such clarity that it is certain to have a definite answer. That answer may take ten years to find, or a hundred, but an answer exists. By contrast, for artists the question is often more interesting than the answer, and often an answer doesn't exist. How does one answer a question such as "What is love?" or "Would we be happier if we lived to be 1,000 years old?" One of my favorite passages from Rilke's *Letters to a Young Poet* is this: "We should try to love the questions themselves, like locked rooms and like books that are written in a very foreign tongue."

Science has much to offer the arts. When Salman Rushdie spoke to an audience at the Massachusetts Institute of Technology in late 1993, he said: "Many of us writers of my generation have felt that in many ways the cutting edge of the new is to be found in the sciences." Science has always been a source of new ideas, and artists thrive on ideas. Nicolaus Copernicus, Darwin, Einstein, James Watson, and Francis Crick have all changed our view of the world and our place in it.

Then, there is the portrayal of the scientist. By now, it is well known that the picture of the scientist as the eccentric personality without human feeling, pursuing truth by the numbers, wearing sterile gloves at all times, is false. But the particular way that a person trained in logical thinking must negotiate his or her way through the illogical world of human passions — that is a subject worthy of art.

The arts and humanities, in turn, offer the sciences an essential store of other ideas, images, metaphors and language. These connections are often subtle. For his highly nonintuitive postulates of relativity, Einstein partly credited the philosopher David Hume's notion that the truths of nature cannot always be arrived at by experiment but sometimes must originate in the mind. The great atomic physicist Niels Bohr compared the invisible nucleus of an atom to an oscillating drop of liquid. Modern string theorists describe the hypothesized smallest constituents of matter and energy, which will probably never be seen by the most powerful instruments, as "vibrating strings" that "stretch" and "break" and "merge." Such images, metaphors, and vocabulary arise both from direct sensual experience and from the language of artists and humanists who portray that experience. Scientists, in turn, must use the same language to describe their extreme worlds, far beyond sensual experience, because no alternative exists except for mathematical equations.

It seems to me that the most important gift the sciences and the arts have to offer each other is a recognition and synthesis of their different approaches to thinking, their different ways of being in the world. When these differences come together, often uneasily, we witness the full complexity and the mystery, and ultimately the grandeur, of being human. What makes Michael Frayn's *Copenhagen* so powerful, in part, is the unspoken contrast between the neat world of atomic physics, where one can solve mathematical equations for wavefunctions and the neutron mean free paths, versus the world of politics, war, and ethical dilemmas. And in the film *A Beautiful Mind*, the precision of John Nash's mathematical mind forms a disturbing counterpoint to the confusion in his hallucinatory illusions. When I was writing *Einstein's Dreams*, I resisted the urge to make each dream world, with its own theory of time, logically consistent. My Einstein, the most celebrated envoy of rational thought, was also a dreamer, a person of deep loneliness, struck with the frailties and urgencies of the human heart — indeed a scientist who might have failed to achieve what he did without his sometimes irrational personal commitments and passions.

Somehow, we human beings have a wondrous capacity for being 10 both rational and irrational, detached and passionate, deliberate and spontaneous, craving of certainty and uncertainty, seeking questions with answers and questions without. We are a splattering of contradictions. In my own case, I have always felt these juxtapositions as a creative tension necessary for my work, a continual rumbling in my gut, an unsettled joy.

READING

1. Lightman begins his piece with a personal history designed to capture the reader's attention. What is it? What is unusual about the situation it sets up?

2. According to Lightman, one of the beauties of science is that scientists work on "'a well-posed problem.'" Discuss the ways he suggests that art's questions and answers are different than science's in this passage.

3. Who is the poet Rilke? How does the poem Lightman quotes shape Lightman's discussion of the relationship between science and art? Who else seems to have influenced Lightman?

4. Lightman argues that one of the biggest challenges of science is to describe events that cannot be physically perceived. How does artistic language help solve this problem?

5. Late in the essay, Lightman says the mix of rationality and irrationality, of certainty and ambiguity in his profession offers him a "creative tension" necessary for his work. Discuss the way his introduction and his conclusion echo the thesis of his piece.

WRITING

1. Lightman says, "Scientists work on questions with answers." What kinds of questions do you find yourself grappling with as you go through your academic day? Write a reflective essay or journal entry that describes the types of questions your education asks.

2. Lightman writes, "The arts and humanities, in turn, offer the sciences an essential store of other ideas, images, metaphors, and language." Make a list of the metaphors and images used by Lightman. Write an essay analyzing at least two of the figures of speech from your list. Be certain to discuss what they add to his essay.

3. Lightman mentions Copernicus, Darwin, Einstein, Watson, and Crick and says that they "have all changed our view of the world and our place in it." Look up each of these famous scientists and write an essay documenting and defining how each of their discoveries changed our view of the world.

4. Lightman believes that "the most important gift the sciences and the arts have to offer each other is a recognition and synthesis of their different approaches to thinking, their different ways of being in the world." Johannes Borgstein in his essay "The Poetry of Genetics," in this chapter (p. 537), uses a literary model to explain a genetic sequence. Write a critical analysis of both of these essays, contrasting and comparing the way they use both literary and scientific ways of looking at the world to make their points.

Humbled by the Genome's Mysteries
By Stephen Jay Gould

FROM: *New York Times*, February 19, 2001

TWO GROUPS OF RESEARCHERS RELEASED THE FORMAL report of data for the human genome last Monday — on the birthday of Charles Darwin, who jump-started our biological understanding of life's nature and evolution when he published *The Origin of Species* in 1859. On Tuesday, and for only the second time in thirty-five years of teaching, I dropped my intended schedule — to discuss the importance of this work with my undergraduate course on the history of life. (The only other case, in a distant age of the late '60s, fell a half-hour after radical students had seized University Hall and physically ejected the deans; this time at least, I told my students, the reason for the change lay squarely within the subject matter of the course!)

I am no lover, or master, of sound bites or epitomes, but I began by telling my students that we were sharing a great day in the history of science and of human understanding in general.

The fruit fly Drosophila, the staple of laboratory genetics, possesses between 13,000 and 14,000 genes. The roundworm C. elegans, the staple of laboratory studies in development, contains only 959 cells, looks like a tiny formless squib with virtually no complex anatomy beyond its genitalia, and possesses just over 19,000 genes.

The general estimate for Homo sapiens — sufficiently large to account for the vastly greater complexity of humans under conventional views — had stood at well over 100,000, with a more precise figure of 142,634 widely advertised and considered well within the range of reasonable expectation. Homo sapiens possesses between 30,000 and 40,000 genes, with the final tally almost sure to lie nearer the lower figure. In other words, our bodies develop under the directing influence of only half again as many genes as the tiny roundworm needs to manufacture its utter, if elegant, outward simplicity.

Human complexity cannot be generated by 30,000 genes under 5 the old view of life embodied in what geneticists literally called (admittedly with a sense of whimsy) their "central dogma": DNA makes RNA makes protein — in other words, one direction of causal flow from code to message to assembly of substance, with one item of code (a gene) ultimately making one item of substance (a protein), and the congeries of proteins making a body. Those 142,000 messages no doubt exist, as they must to build our bodies' complexity, with our previous error now exposed as the assumption that each message came from a distinct gene.

We may envision several kinds of solutions for generating many times more messages (and proteins) than genes, and future research will target this issue. In the most reasonable and widely discussed mechanism, a single gene can make several messages because genes of multicellular organisms are not discrete strings, but composed of coding segments (exons) separated by noncoding regions (introns). The resulting signal that eventually assembles the protein consists only of exons spliced together after elimination of introns. If some exons are omitted, or if the order of splicing changes, then several distinct messages can be generated by each gene.

The implications of this finding cascade across several realms. The commercial effects will be obvious, as so much biotechnology, including the rush to patent genes, has assumed the old view that "fixing" an aberrant gene would cure a specific human ailment. The social meaning may finally liberate us from the simplistic and harmful idea, false for many other reasons as well, that each aspect of our being, either physical or behavioral, may be ascribed to the action of a particular gene "for" the trait in question.

But the deepest ramifications will be scientific or philosophical in the largest sense. From its late seventeenth century inception in modern form, science has strongly privileged the reductionist mode of thought that breaks overt complexity into constituent parts and then tries to explain the totality by the properties of these parts and simple interactions fully predictable from the parts. ("Analysis" literally means to dissolve into basic parts.) The reductionist method works triumphantly for simple systems — predicting eclipses or the motion of planets (but not the histories of their complex surfaces), for example. But once again — and when will we ever learn? — we fell victim to hubris, as we imagined that, in discovering how to unlock some systems, we had found the key for the conquest of all natural phenomena. Will Parsifal ever learn that only humility (and a plurality of strategies for explanation) can locate the Holy Grail?

The collapse of the doctrine of one gene for one protein, and one direction of causal flow from basic codes to elaborate totality, marks the failure of reductionism for the complex system that we call biology — and for two major reasons.

First, the key to complexity is not more genes, but more combi- 10 nations and interactions generated by fewer units of code — and many of these interactions (as emergent properties, to use the technical jargon) must be explained at the level of their appearance, for they cannot be predicted from the separate underlying parts alone. So organisms must be explained as organisms, and not as a summation of genes.

Second, the unique contingencies of history, not the laws of physics, set many properties of complex biological systems. Our 30,000 genes make up only 1 percent or so of our total genome. The rest — including bacterial immigrants and other pieces that can replicate and move — originate more as accidents of history than as predictable necessities of physical laws. Moreover, these noncoding regions, disrespectfully called "junk DNA," also build a pool of potential for future use that, more than any other factor, may establish any lineage's capacity for further evolutionary increase in complexity.

The deflation of hubris is blessedly positive, not cynically disabling. The failure of reductionism doesn't mark the failure of science, but only the replacement of an ultimately unworkable set of assumptions by more appropriate styles of explanation that study complexity at its own level and respect the influences of unique histories. Yes, the task will be much harder than reductionistic science imagined. But our 30,000 genes — in the glorious ramifications of their irreducible interactions — have made us sufficiently complex and at least potentially adequate for the task ahead.

We may best succeed in this effort if we can heed some memorable words spoken by that other great historical figure born on February 12 — on the very same day as Darwin, in 1809. Abraham Lincoln, in his first Inaugural Address, urged us to heal division and seek unity by marshaling the "better angels of our nature" — yet another irreducible and emergent property of our historically unique mentality, but inherent and invokable all the same, even though not resident within, say, gene 26 on chromosome number 12.

READING

1. Gould begins his essay in the *New York Times* with a personal anecdote about the day the formal news about the number of genes on
   human DNA was released – Darwin's birthday – and ends the essay
   with a quotation by Abraham Lincoln. Discuss how these references
   to famous men and their contributions frame this announcement for
   Gould himself and the scientific community at large.

2. What is the "central dogma" of gene research, according to Gould,
   and how does the discovery that humans have only 30,000 genes
   affect it?

3. The average reader of the *New York Times* is affluent and college-
   educated. How is this readership reflected in the content, style, and
   even language found in this piece?

4. Although the scientific community at large was taken aback at the
   discovery of how few genes humans have, Gould was not. He sees an
   opportunity for a new kind of thinking. Discuss how he describes this
   new kind of thinking in his article.

WRITING

1. Investigate the vocabulary of Gould's piece. Pull out the key scientific terminology necessary for a clear understanding, such as
   "exon" and "intron." In a reflective essay or a journal entry, define
   these terms for yourself from what you learned in the article itself. Then, consult a glossary of genetic terms, such as genome.gov/
   glossary.com, to enrich your comprehension and check your accuracy.

2. In this article Gould alludes not only to Charles Darwin and Abraham
   Linclon but also to Parsifal and the Holy Grail. Write an essay in
   which you discuss how these allusions frame the sweeping significance of the relative simplicity of the human genome.

3. Gould ends paragraph 8 with the question, "Will Parsifal ever learn
   that only humility (and a plurality of strategies for explanation) can
   locate the Holy Grail?" To what mythic event is Gould referring? How
   does this allusion resonate given the essay's topic?

4. Gould asserts that the belief that humans would be found to have
   over 100,000 genes – not a mere 30,000 – is indicative of "the old
   view of life." In an essay compare the "old" view with the "new" view

of life that Gould suggests. What does he mean by "organisms must be explained as organisms, and not as a summation of genes?"

5. Although wildly different in style, Gould's "Humbled by the Genome's Mysteries" and Dave Barry's "Genes Cleaned and Starched, While You Wait" (p. 554) have much in common. For one thing, the authors would probably agree that human beings, and perhaps especially scientists, should not laud themselves too soon for discovering the secret of life. Write a critical analysis in which you compare the styles of these two writers. Pay particular attention to how they each argue for humility in scientific thinking.

Creative Time DNA Deli Coffee Cups (2000)

By Roz Chast and Tom Tomorrow

FROM: www.creativetime.org

CONTEXT: The following cartoons by Roz Chast and Tom Tomorrow appeared in a series of artist-designed deli coffee cups commissioned by the group Creative Time as one of its DNAid public art projects. According to its website, the groups seeks to "address the implications of today's genetic research on our global futures." The cups were distributed in 2000 throughout New York City at participating delis. Customers who purchased coffee were given the art project cups in lieu of their everyday paper cups in hopes that they would "consider what they are ingesting into their bodies, thus inspiring multiple associations that range from genetically modified food to new DNA specific drugs." Roz Chast is a staff cartoonist for *The New Yorker*, where her work frequently addresses domestic and family life. She has also published in the *Harvard Business Review* and *Scientific American*. Tom Tomorrow is the pseudonym of Dan Perkins. He draws a syndicated cartoon, which has spawned a blog, both named "This Modern World." His work is known for its liberal political perspective. In reading these cartoons, think about how your feelings about and understanding of them might change were they to grace your morning cup of coffee.

Roz Chaz, Genetic Engineering Hits a Snag

MOST HISTORIANS AGREE THAT THE GOLDEN AGE OF MANKIND BEGAN IN THE 29TH CENTURY, WHEN POPULATION GROWTH WAS STABILIZED THROUGH THE **OFFICIAL CLONING ACT**...NOW, NOT ONLY DID EVERYONE WEAR THE SAME BRANDS AND EAT AT THE SAME FRANCHISES--BUT THEY ALL **LOOKED** EXACTLY THE SAME AS WELL!

LIFE IS MUCH SIMPLER THIS WAY-- DON'T YOU AGREE, DAVID 40928423?

ABSOLUTELY, DAVID 320329!

Tom Tomorrow, The Official Cloning Act

RESPONDING

1. Both cartoons draw their humor from our belief that we can some-how genetically engineer a more perfect future. What does each suggest about this dream? What elements of the cartoons (verbal and visual) lead you to this conclusion? Which of these cartoons would be more effective in making you think about genetic re-search? What appeals to you about the cartoons?

2. In discussing the deli coffee cup project, Creative Time writes on its website, "That 'first cup of the day' ritual offers a direct line into the waking minds of the public. What better way to inspire thoughts on how genetic research is impacting so many different areas of human endeavor?" Imagine you were recruited by Creative Time to partici-pate in the next phase of this project. What everyday object would you suggest tagging with a cartoon? Why did you select this item? Try your hand at designing a cartoon for this purpose that would "in-spire thoughts" on genomics.

3. Both Chast and Tomorrow use humor to address a significant social issue that does not, at first glance, seem to provoke much laughter: genetic engineering. This approach is similar to that used by Dave Barry in "Genes Cleaned and Starched, While You Wait" (p. 554). In each case, humor offers a point of entry into a complicated topic for the general public. Still, while these writers and artists share a hu-morous perspective, the tone and direction of each piece differs. Discuss how, in these cases, humor can lead readers to the contra-dictory emotions of both relief and concern.

THE LANCET

Volume 351, Number 9112 • Founded 1823 • Published weekly • Saturday 2 May 1998

EDITORIAL
Defensible leprosy, a very rare bird

COMMENTARY
Antibiotic resistance
P W Hunter

Teaching heart failure patients how to breathe
A J N Fialho

Dimensions of asthma
S J Holgate

All fat is not alike
P Astrup

ARTICLES
Use of selective serotonin-reuptake inhibitors in thrombo-
antihypercoasis and risk of hip fractures in elderly people
B Liu and others

Effect of breathing rate on oxygen saturation and exercise
performance in chronic heart failure
L Bernardi and others

Is current opsonin-poiicy failure almost exclusively on retained
salvipude in deaf with blindness in India?
L Dandona and others

EARLY REPORTS
Nevochubiior Entamoebid deficiency in asthmatic respiratory
failure
B Dacher and others

Cellular cytokinin response induced by DNA vaccination in
HIV-1-infected patients
S Calmia and others

CASE REPORT
A woman who trembled, then had chorea
F Kageyama and others

RESEARCH LETTERS
No evidence for remote, energy, and
totally neutrosomctrical achievements
bowel disease in sullen in a 20-year
prospective study
A Pollock and others

Tetanus prevention survey, sheep
disease with profuse maltose
M Harris and others

Mucinm oxygen stress of tetani
related in Pupus from Rebus
M Mirralles and others

Presence of Intra-specific pltec in
plasma of kidney and liver transplant
recipients
P W Lo and others

A urinary marker for multiple sclerosis
C Mantua-Dei and others

5-HT: in brain and risk of Alzheimer's
disease
G Bortbert and others

NEWS
Science & medicine

US drug doses hospital for Earth's
orbital care

US tools wrinkle for Safety ban

CFRF hiking latest control in Spy with
support

Homeopathic disease attention strains

Turk navigational begin many of time

Kenia child arrest against centre

Turning investigative hour blot

Feature

Framing the pending progression of
medicine

Dispatches

Labour's final vote in UK health

Dengue and hanatits in Brazil

Policy & people

Congress splints Hubo dismal

Effects of Iran environment disbanse

Demand trouble NHS wait

International noncurishness in China

Account of Europe on child abuse

Children ragging in south near

Nobel winners in fish

Osteoporosis in military seduction

FDA learn heart town

SEMINAR

Orrheumatoids
K Svensson

DEPARTMENT OF ETHICS

Critical ethical issues in
clinical trials with
complicated patients
R T Meinhard

VIEWPOINT

Early genetic disease: disease
or possible illness?
A W Eureka, T M Jost

ESSAY

The poetry of genetics
J Borgstein

Contents list continues inside

The Poetry of Genetics
By Johannes Borgstein

FROM: *The Lancet*, May 2, 1998

CONTEXT: This article initially appeared in *The Lancet*, a British peer-reviewed medical journal. It is the world's oldest general medical journal, founded in 1823, and is ranked third in influence worldwide. While the publication is targeted at general and scientific readership, the majority of subscribers are physicians. *The Lancet* has been published since 1823 by Elsevier, "the world's leading publisher of science and health information [which] serves more than 30 million scientists, students, and health and information professionals worldwide," according to its website. *The Lancet* "is an independent and authoritative voice in global medicine. [It seeks] to publish high-quality clinical trials that will alter medical practice; [its] commitment to international health ensures that research and analysis from all regions of the world is widely covered." Johannes Borgstein, of the University Hospital Rotterdam, writes frequently on medical and philosophical issues. In reading this piece, consider how his metaphor of language clearly reveals the complexity needed to think about the human genome.

THE HUMAN-GENOME PROJECT MAKES THE SUBTLE PROMISE that once all the human chromosomes are mapped we will be in a position to determine the genetic makeup of each individual, and, as a natural consequence, be able to "correct" many of the genetic errors encountered (while carefully avoiding any allusion to the possibilities of misuse).

However, the human genome, as the infinite variety and expression of characteristics demonstrates, is vastly more complex than the sequence of codons would imply, for they can be read in different sequences depending on where the reading starts, which sequences are read, and which ones are suppressed — as a book that has several stories intermingled. To follow only one story, words or passages must be skipped in different places, whereas in other parts, continuous sequences are read.

We may conveniently make an analogy with a sequence of letters, rather than of words, which are followed in variable order, with variable starting sequence. A complex code is thus required to interpret it.

Most classic literary works, furthermore, may be read at multiple levels; generally speaking, the better the book, the more levels may be read in it. A Shakespeare play, for example, may be interpreted as a simple story, suitable for children; a complex story, interpreted by adults; a collection of aphorisms and sayings; or a source of life's wisdom. Similarly, by analogy, there are multiple levels to the human genome, whose expression varies in response to environmental factors, so as to weave a complex fabric of life at a number of levels and layers which make it extremely complex to interpret.

How the Genetic Sequences May be Read

Through a simple model or analogy, we can explore how a series of genetic sequences may be read in the cell. It is likely that, in reality, it is far more complex at all levels, with a larger number of intertwined "messages," and that further higher levels of complexity exist in the expression within the cell, leaving aside for now all the possible extracellular effects of the proteins formed. Nevertheless, the analogy gives us some idea of what we are dealing with, and how difficult an interference or "correction" would be at *any* of these levels.

Let us take the following sequence of letters:

Ikeeptoseeaworldsixhonestservingmen(theytaughtmeallIknew)in agrainofsandtheirnamesarewhatandHeaveninawildflowerwhyandhold infinitywheninthepalmofyourhandandhowandwhereandwhoeternity inanhour (level 1)

Summary

Level 1 — letter sequence in Latin script (genetic sequence)

Level 2 — language (English)

Level 3 — separate words

Level 4 — indication of sequence in which mixed messages should be read

Level 5 — separate poems (or proteins?)

Level 6 — meaning: elementary

Level 7 — complex, abstract concepts

With the knowledge that the sequence is written in the English language (level 2), I may begin, with some difficulty, to make out the words:

> I keep to see a world six honest serving men (they taught me all I knew)
> in a grain of sand their names are what and a Heaven in a wild flower why
> and hold infinity when in the palm of your hand and how and where and
> who eternity in an hour (level 3)

I then need some knowledge of literature and poetry to be able to separate the phrases, which belong together and are to be read sequentially:

> I keep *to see a world* six honest serving men (they taught me all I knew)
> *in a grain of sand* their names are what **and** *a Heaven in a wild flower* why
> and *hold infinity* when *in the palm of your hand* and how **and** where and
> who *eternity in an hour* (level 4)

Until, finally, the two quatrains are set down separately:

> To see a world in a grain of sand
> and a Heaven in a wild flower
> hold infinity in the palm of your hand
> and eternity in an hour. (William Blake)[1]

> I keep six honest serving men
> (they taught me all I knew)
> their names are What and Why and When
> and How and Where and Who. (Rudyard Kipling)[2]

It is then largely a matter of maturity, education, and environment that determines what these poems mean to me, and how I capture the different levels and use or transmit the implied concepts.

Thus, at least seven levels (panel) may be distinguished in this very simple model of a DNA sequence. The first level is the interpretation of the individual sequence of Latin letters or bases. (One could conceive, perhaps, of one lower level in which the signs need to be interpreted as letters.) The second level requires us to be conversant with the language in which the letters are written, so that the third level permits identification of whole words out of the continuous sequence of letters; from this sequence, in the fourth level, we attempt to make out the phrases that under certain circumstances belong together, but which have been intermingled (some knowledge of the authors involved is probably necessary, and the genetic code must carry instructions as to which sequences should be read and which ones are suppressed). The fifth level of interpretation is to select the separate poems or protein instructions, which then go through a number of subsequent steps, just as a poem may be read on various levels. The purely visual imagery that a child might capture of sand and flowers and the rhythm of the language, and the adult interpretation of the complex abstract ideas, sensations, and emotions that the poem induces, makes them different for everybody — though with adequate emotional similarities for us to identify with the poet and with our fellow reader.

The actual DNA contains a large number of intermingled messages that not only control protein synthesis but also the expression or suppression of other messages.

With our present knowledge, we are only just beginning to interpret the letter sequence. To extrapolate from our model to human genetic engineering (as is too readily assumed and, at times, probably even practiced) has further implications.

To insert a viral-linked sequence of genetic material into the correct section of the right chromosome — as has been suggested and attempted for "correction" of genetic defects encountered — is tantamount to throwing a dart at a small distant target, blindfolded. Moreover, it raises questions such as: How can we be sure the sequence will be accommodated into the right place? How do we know it will be expressed correctly? How can we be certain it will not have undesirable side effects? And how can we be sure the viral "carrier" does not affect the sequence or have other side effects?

A virus will merge into the genetic sequence at a predestined site 15 (for the virus), which is unlikely to coincide with our chosen site. It will be a matter of chance that it is expressed at all, and even if not expressed, it may interfere with the expression or suppression of other sequences with unpredictable results. Then, we should enquire what the function of the virus is in the first place, and what its other sequences are able to affect.

In theory, astonishing results may be obtained, but there are too many uncertainties, too many unanswered questions and variables, and probably hazardous consequences that are inadequately considered. To trust to chance is perhaps too simplistic, and even then it may work against us with unforeseen complications (and how can we foresee all the possible complications of a process so little understood?).

The expression of the genetic code may thus be viewed as a language with almost limitless possibilities of expression within the framework of a fixed alphabet (four base pairs and a zero making five possible symbols?) and a structured grammar. Were it otherwise, physical expression would repeat and duplicate itself rather than giving rise to circumstances in which, despite overpopulation, there are not two people alike in the world; or two leaves of a tree for that matter.

Genetic expression is modulated, as a language, by the environment (a language only developed in a social context). The surrounding cells somehow determine the expression and differentiation

initally, followed by the addition of neural and more centralised hu-
moural mechanisms as the organism grows in complexity, and, finally,
by external environmental factors (think only of the calusses on the
hands of a gymnast, where a purely mechanical stimulus induces
thickened skin layers). Some environmental stimuli induce a whole
series of "programmed" changes, as occurs in the developing embryo,
whereas others may induce only minor modulations. All these factors
contribute to a unique physical expression — even among identical
twins, despite a variable resemblance at some levels. Although the
leaves are all different, they are similar enough for us to identify the
tree they came from. One of the striking conditions of living systems
is that nothing is ever exactly the same; nothing can be static or in
equilibrium. To state that evolution is the result of random mutations
is akin to assuming that random typing by a monkey will produce the
complete works of Shakespeare if we wait long enough — an overly
simplistic concept that takes no account of grammar and language, let
alone of meaning at its different levels. The poetry of genetics runs a
lot deeper than we suspect; perhaps deeper than we *can* suspect.

REFERENCES

[1]Blake W. *Auguries of Innocence*. London: Penguin, 1968.

[2]Kipling R. *Just So Stories (The Elephant's Child)*. London: Penguin, 1987.

READING

1. The opening paragraph of Borgstein's article presents a topic that by now would likely be familiar to most readers – the Human Genome Project. How does this opening statement position the reader for the argument that follows? Why does Borgstein begin in this manner?

2. Throughout the piece, Borgstein refers to the ways literary language can help explain science. How do you think the average *Lancet* reader might respond?

3. At several points in his essay, Borgstein discusses the levels needed for understanding why we cannot merely substitute a faulty gene for a perfect one. Discuss each level he explains, both in the literary model and the genetic model. Does this use of analogy help you understand the complexity of a genetic sequence? Are there other strategies that could help you address this complexity?

4. One of the sources that Borgstein uses is the poetry of Blake. Another is Kipling. What do these allusions suggest about his audience?

5. The chief purpose of the article is to emphasize and deflate simple explanations for genetic research. What indications do you have as a reader that his contentions have validity? Do you agree?

WRITING

1. Borgstein writes that "there are multiple levels to the human genome, whose expression varies in response to environmental factors, so as to weave a complex fabric of life at a number of levels and layers which make it extremely complex to interpret" (para. 4). Write a reflective essay or journal entry in which you describe the many layers of meaning associated with another code sequence: your name. How is this too complex to interpret? What fabric of life does it weave?

2. Borgstein sets up an analogy that compares poems to protein instructions. Write an essay exploring this analogy. Does it help a non-scientist understand this complex topic?

3. Borgstein attempts to redefine genetic research as a much more complex process than both the general public and fellow scientists might allow. Write an essay in which you summarize his view on genetic manipulation and contrast it with the positive view that he is writing against.

4. Borgstein states, "To extrapolate from our model to human genetic engineering (as is too readily assumed and, at times, probably even practiced) has further implications. . . . In theory, astonishing results may be obtained, but there are too many uncertainties, too many unanswered questions and variables, and probably hazardous con-sequences that are inadequately considered." Taking his words into account, research current corporate advertising on this topic. In-clude corporations that have been involved with this research from the beginning, such as Celera – and also other more recent arrivals to the scene, such as Open Biosystems. Make a presentation to your class, demonstrating the results of your findings.

5. Borgstein writes, "The poetry of genetics runs a lot deeper than we suspect; perhaps deeper than we *can* suspect." He cautions us against accepting simple solutions based on gene manipulation. Stephen Jay Gould, in "Humbled by the Genome's Mysteries" (p. 528), sounds the same alarm. Indeed, much thinking about the con-sequences of genetic research has been presented through popular film and fiction. Identify a recent movie or novel that has addressed the consequences of genetic manipulation or cloning, such as *Gat-taca* or *The Island* (movies), or *Oryx and Crake* or *Never Let Me Go* (novels). Research the controversy surrounding the movie or novel you have selected. Write an essay that summarizes these issues and explains why they seem to be important. Discuss whether the film or novel opens up new ways of imagining our future, based on current theory, that are beneficial or harmful.

Ban All Human Cloning
By Art Lentini

FROM: *USA Today*, August 11, 2005

CONTEXT: This piece originally appeared in *USA Today*, a popular nationwide news-paper read by over 5 million people daily. It has a readership of about 66 percent men and 34 percent women, and the average age of the reader is forty-six. The median household income is $74,000 a year, and 72 percent have attended college or beyond. *USA Today* prides itself on "an economy of words [and a] wealth of information." Most readers spend about thirty-three minutes a day reading three issues a week, accord-ing to its media kit. It is known for its use of color in its format and its national, not local, focus. The author of this editorial, Arthur J. "Art" Lentini, was a Republican state senator in Louisiana from 1996 to 2006 and twice sponsored bills to ban human cloning. As you read, think about how strongly and clearly he states his opinion, how quickly a reader can understand his point of view, and how this brevity is appropriate for this publication. ("Ban All Human Cloning" reprinted with permission of the author, Sen. Art Lentini. Cover of *USA Today* © 2005 USA Today. Reprinted with permission.)

THOSE OF US WHO SUPPORT A BAN ON ALL TYPES OF HUMAN cloning do so because we believe that ultimately no good can come from the procedure.

There are only two uses for a cloned human embryo: To create a cloned human being, or to create human life in the lab in order to de-stroy it so cells can be harvested for other purposes.

Creating human life for the purpose of sacrificing it — even for beneficial research — is morally and ethically wrong.

That is why it's not permissible to harvest the organs of a dying human being to save the life of another. The involuntary harvesting of organs from a convicted murderer prior to execution? It will never happen. The taking of vital organs from a consenting terminally ill patient? No doctor will touch it.

Some say that a human embryo is not entitled to the same protections as a human baby. Then why does the federal law that imposes criminal and civil penalties for killing a bald eagle provide the same punishment for the destruction of its eggs? Because both acts result 5 in the death of a bird the government believes is important to protect.

Must human life be endangered to be afforded the same protection as animal life?

There's also no good reason for cloning embryos to produce "stem cells" for study. In fact, such research siphons off precious funding from more promising and fruitful research into the therapeutic uses of adult stem cells, which already exist.

Both sides of the debate on cloning agree on one point: Cloning for the purpose of producing a viable cloned human being should be prohibited. So why not pass legislation to ban, at least, that form of human cloning?

Because it's impractical. There is no way to monitor the thousands of embryos that will be created if any form of cloning is permitted. And what if prohibited reproductive cloning occurs? The only way to stop it, once discovered, would be to destroy the embryo.

That's precisely the problem with human cloning. Inevitably, it 10 leads to taking an innocent human life.

READING

1. Lentini opens his op-ed piece in first-person plural (we), thus imply-
   ing there is a group of supporters for whom he speaks. How does
   this inclusive opening sentence set up the subtext for this piece?

2. Notice how many paragraphs are only one sentence long. What is the
   effect of this brevity in the overall tone of the piece? What characterizes these one-sentence paragraphs?

3. Lentini uses dramatic diction in his editorial – "destroy," "execution,"
   "sacrificing," etc. How does such language impact the reader? How
   might the urgency of his diction be linked to the meaning of his piece?

4. What kind of support does Lentini provide for his argument against
   human cloning? What examples does he cite? Are you convinced of
   his point of view?

5. Lentini's title reflects his idea clearly: "Ban All Human Cloning."
   What are some of the reasons he puts forward that those in favor of
   human cloning might use as acceptable scenarios. Do you accept
   any of these as valid reasons for human cloning? Why? Why not?

WRITING

1. Write a reflective essay or a journal entry where you argue either for
   or against cloning human organs to replace people's damaged organs. Take the point of view of a parent with a sick child.

2. Lentini's opinion, so forcefully stated, is very simple. Research the
   current state of thinking on human cloning.

3. With a small group in your class, collaborate on a study that examines
   current legislation concerning stem-cell research. What are the main
   issues being argued? Who is arguing them? What is the position of corporate interests? Do your findings support Lentini's argument or not?

4. With your class, devise a questionnaire to administer on your campus concerning human cloning. Create at least five scenarios where
   an argument could be made for cloning. Before you interview students on your campus, prepare with your class a position paper that
   represents the class's thinking. After you have interviewed your subjects and discussed the scenarios with them, revisit your position
   paper and see if you have changed your thinking.

5. Both Art Lentini and Tom Tomorrow (in "The Official Cloning Act,"
   p. 535) address the possible ramifications of human cloning. However, they take different approaches and achieve different tones.
   Write an essay comparing the two pieces, which are both quite brief.
   Which seems more effective at conveying its message? Why?

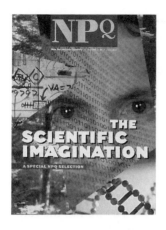

Genome Ethics

By James Watson

FROM: *New Perspectives Quarterly*, Fall 2000

CONTEXT: Watson's book, *A Passion for DNA* (from which this excerpt was taken), concerning his Nobel Prize-winning work, was published by the prestigious Oxford University Press (2000). The press is housed at Oxford University in Great Britain and traces its history as far back as 1478 – soon after the invention of movable type. Oxford University Press is the largest university press in the world and its missions is "to further the University's objective of excellence in research, scholarship, and education by publishing worldwide." This excerpt first appeared in *New Perspectives Quarterly*, a journal specializing in "cutting-edge debate for current affairs." James Watson is the well-known discoverer, along with Francis Crick, of the double helix, which revealed the structure of DNA. He received the Nobel Prize in Physiology or Medicine in 1962 and was the first head of the National Center for Genome Research from 1985 to 1992. As you read his essay, consider how his initial discovery of the double helix has colored his attitude toward current gene research and its implications.

I SEE THE GENOME MAP AS HAVING TWO MAJOR PURPOSES. Clearly, the first is the ability it offers to medicine to vastly speed up the rate at which important disease-causing genes can be found. Most genetically predisposed diseases are not rare conditions limited to small numbers of families; they encompass a wide spectrum of common diseases like diabetes, arteriosclerosis, Alzheimer's disease, and many cancers. In the past, they have not been included among genetic diseases since the time of onset and severity have strong environmental components. For example, whether an individual comes down with late-onset diabetes is a function not only of his or her genetic constitution but also of dietary history. Likewise, a combination of genes and diet determines an individual's probability of having a heart attack. And whether a woman comes down with breast cancer depends not only on the genes she inherits from her parents, but also upon her later exposure to cancer-causing agents that may be present in her food and in her environment.

Equally important, the human genome is our ultimate blueprint providing the instructions for the normal development and functioning of the human body.

That we are human beings and not chimpanzees is not due in any sense to our nurturing but to our natures; that is, our genes. This does not mean that we have highly different sets of genes. In fact, both sets of some 100,000 genes carry out roughly the same biochemical tasks. But the 5 million years of evolution that has separated us from the chimps have led to significant divergencies from chimps as to the exact times at which some human genes function as well as the rates at which they produce their respective protein products.

Successive changes in certain key genes have led to the retention of many juvenile chimp features into adult human life. For example, the shape of our adult brain is that of the baby chimp brain with our general lack of body hair resembling the situation of baby ape. With the completion of the Human Genome Project we have the power to understand the essential genetic features that make us human. A key, though obviously not immediately ascertainable, objective is the set of instructions that led to the development of those human brain features which give us the capacity for our written and spoken languages.

Opposition to mapping the genome has arisen out of fears concerning the ethical, legal, and social consequences of precise human genetic information. In particular, worries have been expressed that we would be generating new forms of discrimination in which individuals genetically predisposed to serious diseases would be unable to obtain or hold jobs as well as obtain life and health insurance.

The question of how to protect genetic privacy is clearly central to these concerns.

Moreover, there are anxieties as to whether we as human beings will be able to cope psychologically with the ever-increasing knowledge about our genes. And how soon will it be before we are able to give our citizens the genetic education needed for them to make informed choices as to what information they want and even the consequences of using or not using these facts?

To try to begin to address these problems, when the Human Genome Project was initiated within the United States, we made the decision to create a specific new program to consider the ethical, legal, and social issues (ELSI) of the Genome Project. At its start in 1989, we devoted 3 percent of our genome monies to such issues, with now 5 percent of such funds going to these ELSI programs.

Complicating the ELSI agenda has been the increasingly obvious fact that different genetic diseases present quite different spectra of ethical, legal, and social dilemmas. Handling the complexities arising from cystic fibrosis, whose victims now can live into their 30s if not longer, is bound to be different from our approaches to diseases like Tay-Sachs, whose victims live in almost perpetual agony during their brief one to two years of life. Only the state of California has passed any law aiming to ban genetic-based discrimination by health and life insurance companies. And nobody has specifically come up with regulations or laws protecting the privacy of individual genetic records.

Even when appropriate satisfactory laws and regulations are in place, there will still be many dilemmas that cannot easily be handled by these means. What responsibility, for example, do individuals have to learn about their genetic makeups prior to their parenting of children? In the future will we be regarded as morally neglectful when we knowingly permit the birth of children with severe genetic defects? And do such victims later have legal recourse against their parents who have taken no action to help prevent their coming into the world with few opportunities of living a life without pain and emotional suffering?

Genetic Destiny

Those who think this way have to have the counterarguments that if we try to control the genetic destiny of our children, we are in effect eugenicists following in the dreadful footsteps of the Nazis, who used genetic arguments when they used gas chambers to kill some 250,000 already sterilized inhabitants of their pre-World War II mental institutions. While early in the twentieth century eugenics had almost the ring of a prospective movement attracting the support of many prominent Americans, the horrors of these later Nazi aspects have to make us fear that eugenic arguments might again in the future be used to promote the elimination of supposed genetically unfit political philosophies or ethnic groups.

Such worries come not only from minority groups who fear for their futures, but also, in particular, from many Germans whose revulsion of their own history leads them to oppose any aspect of genetic engineering, believing the technologies so developed provide a slippery slope for rekindling of Nazi-type eugenics actions.

Equally strong opposition to programs aimed at preventing the birth of severely genetically impaired children comes from individuals who believe that all human life is a reflection of God's existence and should be cherished and supported with all the resources at human disposal.

Such individuals believe that genetically impaired fetuses have as much right to exist as those destined for healthy, productive lives. But

549

such arguments present no validity to those of us who see no evidence for the sanctity of life, believing instead that human as well as all other forms of life are the products not of God's hand but of an evolutionary process operating under the Darwinian principles of natural selection.

This is not to say that humans do not have rights. They do, but 15 they have not come from God but instead from social contracts among humans who realize that human societies must operate under rules that allow for stability and predictability in day-to-day existence.

Foremost among these rules is the strict prohibition in virtually all societies against the killing of a fellow human being unless necessary self-defense is involved. Without this rule, our lives as functioning humans would be greatly diminished with no one able to count on the continued availability of those we love and depend upon.

In contrast, the termination of a genetically damaged fetus should not diminish the future lives of those individuals into whose world it would otherwise enter. In fact, the prevailing emotion must largely be one of relief of not being called to give love and support to an infant who never can have an existence whose eventual successes you can anticipate and share.

Agony and Religion

Thus, I can see only unnecessary agony from laws that use the force of arbitrary religious revelations to impose the birth of genetically sick infants upon parents who would much prefer to terminate such pregnancies, hoping that their next conception leads to a healthy infant.

Using the name of God to let unnecessary personal tragedies occur is bound to upset not only those who follow less dogmatic guidelines for life but also many members of those religious groups whose leaders proclaim the absolute sanctity of all human life. These latter people are bound to ask themselves whether the words of God, as then interpreted, are more important than the health of their children or those of their friends.

In the long term, it is inevitable that those authorities who ask 20 their followers to harm themselves in the name of God will increasingly find themselves isolated with their moral pronouncements regarded as hollow and to be ignored.

Nonetheless we would not be surprised by increasing opposition to the Human Genome Project, which is seen as the most visible symbol of the evolutionary biology/genetics-based approach to human existence. But because the medical objectives of the Genome Project cannot easily be faulted, those who fear its implications will emphasize that its reductionist approach to human existence fails to acknowledge the overriding importance of the spiritual aspect of human existence, which they will argue is much more important than our genes in determining whether we are successes or failures in our lives.

Under that argument, we would be making better use of our monies in trying to improve the economic and moral environments of humans as opposed to the finding of genes that opponents believe will only marginally affect our health and social behavior.

The Unhealthy Fetus

With time, however, the truth must emerge that monies so spent have effectively no chance of rolling back the fundamental tragedies that come from genetic disease. So, over the next several decades we shall witness an ever-growing consensus that humans have the right to terminate the lives of genetically unhealthy fetuses.

But there remains the question as to who should make the decisions that lead to the termination of a pregnancy. Under no circumstances should these choices be assigned to the state, because even in our more homogeneous cultures, there exists wide divergency as to what form of future human life we have to encourage. Instead such decisions are best left solely in the hands of the prospective mother and father (if he effectively plays this parental role).

Such unregulated freedom clearly opens up possibilities for irre- 25 sponsible genetic choices that only can harm all concerned. But we should not expect perfect results in handling genetic dilemmas any more than we can expect them from other aspects of human life. And we will have reason to hope that our genetic choices will improve as general knowledge of the consequences of bad throws of the genetic dice become better appreciated.

Clearly we must see that genetics assumes a much more prominent place in our educational curricula. Equally important, the appropriate genetic-screening procedures must become widely available to all our citizens regardless of their economic and social status.

At the same time, we must always be aware that the human society will only come to the genetics way of thinking haltingly. Even many of the firmest supporters of genetic science will worry at times that we may be moving too fast in assuming the roles that in the past we have assigned to the gods. Only they could predict the future as well as have the power to change our future fates from bad to good or from good to bad. Thus today we have some of those same powers.

Clearly this is a situation that is bound to make many people apprehensive, fearing we will misuse our powers by helping create immobile, genetically stratified societies that do not offer the prospect of hope and dignity for all their citizens.

In so moving through genetics to what we hope will be better times for human life, we must proceed with caution and much humility.

READING

1. Watson opens his essay with a question about the ethical choices presented by the mapping of the human genome. What is the assumption underlying his own answer to his question, as he begins the second paragraph of the essay?

2. Watson is a famous scientist writing for a prestigious publishing house. What kind of vocabulary is he using? Do you, as a lay reader, have trouble understanding the points he is making? For what audience is he writing?

3. Near the beginning of the article he calls the human genome "our ultimate blueprint." How does this metaphor illustrate the value he places on the Human Genome Project?

4. How do the subheadings Genetic Destiny, Agony and Religion, and The Unhealthy Fetus map out the structure of his argument?

5. Near the end of this piece, in para. 27, Watson calls for two things we must do in order to address the concerns of those who oppose his overwhelmingly positive opinion of the value of what he calls "genetic destiny." Having read his essay and his suggestions for addressing genetic ethics, what concerns are you left with?

WRITING

1. In the first half of his essay, Watson focuses on how we might avoid the suffering certain kinds of diseases cause by manipulating the human genome and suggests the choices we might make to prevent the birth of children with genetic defects. Write a reflective essay or a journal entry, imagining yourself faced with the choice he suggests you might have. How does this strike you? What action, if any, would you as a potential parent take?

2. This essay was originally published in 2000. At that time it was still believed that the human genome might contain at least 100,000 genes. Now we know that the human genome contains approximately 30,000 genes. Other discoveries have been made since this article was written that represent changes in significant aspects of genetic research. Research three articles about current work in disease prevention connected to the human genome. Write a brief, informative report summarizing what you found about current thinking in this area, citing your sources, and briefly abstracting your findings.

3. We now understand that there is still much work to be done before we have truly decoded the entire human genome. There are areas of mystery, such as the role of what is commonly called "junk DNA." Investigate this term and write an essay defining and explaining the speculation about this aspect of the DNA sequence.

4. The Human Genome Project echoes other scientific projects, such as the Manhattan Project, which have had tremendous consequences in terms of what it is possible for humans to do for and to each other. Research the history of the Manhattan Project and the history of the Human Genome Project. Write an essay comparing and contrasting the history and the consequences of these two massive scientific undertakings. Also discuss the roles of public opinion and scientific pride in your conclusion.

5. Stephen Jay Gould, in "Humbled by the Genome's Mysteries" (p. 528), speaks of the "old view that 'fixing' an aberrant gene would cure a specific human ailment." He calls this a "simplistic and harmful idea." How would Gould respond to Watson's piece? How would he explain the "new" scientific thinking to the grand old man of DNA? Write an essay in which you assume the perspective of Gould talking to Watson.

Genes Cleaned and Starched, While You Wait
By Dave Barry

FROM: *Miami Herald*, July 23, 2000
www.miamiherald.com

CONTEXT: Dave Barry's column appeared in the *Miami Herald*, a large, prize-winning South Florida newspaper with a daily readership of a million. According to its website, its readership is split about evenly between women and men from twenty-five to fifty-four years old; 20 percent are college graduates and 33 percent have a partial college education. Barry has been a nationally syndicated columnist for the *Herald* since 1983, and he won the Pulitzer Prize for commentary in 1988. He is a prolific and wide-ranging writer; his most recent book is *The Shepherd, the Angel, and Walter the Christmas Miracle Dog* (2006), a humorous Christmas fable, which was recognized by *Kirkus Reviews* as a book of unusual merit. Here Barry comments on the fanfare engendered by the announcement that the Human Genome Project (HGP) had successfully deciphered the human genetic code. Barry's exaggerations and irreverence suggest that we may have inflated ideas about what the mapping of the human genome actually means. As you read, consider how Barry humorously questions the discovery's significance to "those who still secretly believe that radio works by magic."

RECENTLY, AN ORGANIZATION CALLED "THE HUMAN GENOME Project" — which, incredibly, turns out NOT to be a rock band — announced that it had deciphered the human genetic code. Scientists reacted by holding a celebration so joyous that many of them woke up the next day with undershort stains that they believe could take years to fully analyze.

Clearly, then, cracking the genetic code is a big deal for the scientific community. But what does it mean to you, the nonscientist who still secretly believes that radio works by magic? To answer that question, we need to review basic biology.

I studied biology under Mrs. Wright at Pleasantville (New York) High School in 1963. It was an intensive course, including a laboratory segment in which each student was issued a jar containing a dead worm, a dead frog, a dead grasshopper, and a dead perch. From these specimens we learned a key scientific principle that unites all living creatures: If you put them in a jar, they die. We also learned that if you

cut them open, you found that all of them (except the worm) contained internal organs, without which certain pranks would not have
been possible.

But the question is: What makes these creatures different? When
frogs reproduce, how come they produce another frog, instead of, say,
a perch? For that matter, how DO frogs reproduce? Because they do
not have sexual organs (if they did, we definitely would have noticed
in biology lab). Perhaps they reproduce by adoption.

We do not yet have the answers to these questions, but we know 5
that the key lies in the science of genetics. According to Mrs. Wright,
genetics was discovered in the nineteenth century by an Austrian
monk named Mendel, who spent many years in his garden observing
the reproduction of pea plants (in those days there was no HBO).
Mendel noticed that the baby pea plants would often inherit certain
characteristics of the mommy and daddy pea plants, such as height,
eye color, and personality. Mendel found that by mating a certain pea
plant with a certain other pea plant, he could cause a third pea plant
to go into a violent jealous rage, resulting in injuries to vegetables as
far away as the zucchini section.

What can we learn from these experiments? I have no idea, and
Mendel refuses to return my phone calls. What we do know is that scientists eventually discovered that every living organism except Jesse
Helms contains genes, which are tiny things that scientists call "the
blueprints of life" because they are found inside tiny filing cabinets in
tiny architects' offices. Inside these genes are molecules made out of
a substance called "DNA." From the start, scientists suspected that
"DNA" was actually an acronym that stood for longer words, but they
couldn't figure out what, because it was in some kind of genetic code.

And that is where the "Human Genome Project" came into the
picture. For decades, researchers with a powerful magnifying glass
and a background in crossword puzzles worked on decoding a DNA
molecule. It was not easy. There were many disappointments, such as
the time, after six years of intensive work, when they discovered that
the molecule was in fact a nose hair.

But finally they finished their historic task and were able to announce to the world the message contained in the human genetic
code (it begins: "To Whom It May Concern"). And although much work
remains to be done, we have — in the stirring words of Al Gore, who
revealed that he did most of the work — "found the combination to the
padlock of understanding on the gym locker of human life."

But what does this mean, in practical terms? It means that someday, doctors will be able to isolate, and then yank out with tiny scientific tweezers, the genes that cause certain humans to have certain
genetic defects that until now have been incurable, such as rooting for

the Yankees; or continuing to say "Whasssssup!" long after it stopped being funny; or failing to turn left immediately when the green left-turn arrow lights up; or buying movie tickets with a credit card when there are ninety-four people in line behind you; or putting a huge pile of groceries on the supermarket checkout counter, then informing the people behind you that you have to go back and get "just a few more things"; or never being able to order ANYTHING at a restaurant without giving the waiter special instructions about how it must be prepared (". . . and to drink I'd like water, no ice, chilled to thirty-eight degrees, with a lemon on the side, sliced thin, but not too thin . . .").

Yes, we are heading toward a day when, thanks to genetics, the 10 entire human race will be completely free of defects — a day when everybody, and not just the fortunate few, will be a professional humor columnist.

READING

1. Recall the metaphor that Barry's title sets up for his audience. What is the metaphor? In what way does it prepare the nonscientist for the main idea of the piece?

2. What are the key points in the review of biology that Barry lays out in order to prepare for his definition of the HGP?

3. List some of the quips that establish the humorous tone of the article. How do these remarks influence your understanding of what Barry is presenting? Do they undercut it? Enhance it? Is Barry actually making fun of the fanfare surrounding this event? How does this humorous tone shape your understanding of the discovery?

4. Barry's main purpose, of course, is to be funny. He is a popular columnist, not a scientist, so his explanation does not have to be scientific, or even rational. In your opinion, in spite of the levity of his piece, does he communicate a serious concern? If so, what is his concern?

5. Barry's article is a newpaper column. Because his column is syndicated and therefore a regular feature of many newpapers, readers come to it with certain expectations about structure – the length of the column, its placement in the newspaper, and the tone of the writing. Discuss the audience for which this piece is framed.

WRITING

1. Examine Barry's explanation of basic biology and genetics beginning with Mrs. Wright's biology class. In a reflective essay or a journal essay, discuss the roots of your education in biology and your current understanding of human genetics.

2. Comb through the article, sorting the "real" scientific facts from the humorous anecdotes and commentary. Within each short paragraph, for example, there is at least one fact, surrounded by nonsense. Write an essay in which you discuss the key facts buried in this humorous column.

3. Barry juxtaposes two wildly different subjects when he uses the metaphor of dry cleaning as a title for his column. Write an essay in which you analyze how this metaphor puts this event in an ordinary framework for a nonscientific reader.

4. Barry captures his audience through his humorous voice and irreverent tone. Write an essay analyzing his voice and tone — his diction and use of exaggeration, surprise, and lack of logic, for example.

5. Barry's column suggests that the importance of decoding the human genome may have some unintended consequences when he says, "Yes, we are heading toward a day when, thanks to genetics, the entire human race will be completely free of defects — a day when everybody . . . will be a professional humor columnist." Write an essay contrasting the styles of Barry's column with James Watson's serious, academic article, "Genome Ethics" (p. 547). Do these pieces have anything in common?

GFP Bunny

By Carol Becker

FROM: *Art Journal*, Fall 2000

CONTEXT: This essay originally appeared in *Art Journal*, a peer-reviewed publication of the College Art Association. The journal describes its mission as providing "a forum for scholarship and visual exploration in the visual arts; . . . to be responsive to issues of the moment in the arts, both nationally and globally; to focus on topics related to twentieth- and twenty-first-century concerns; to promote dialogue and debate." The editorial board of *Art Journal* consists of both academics and artists, and according to the journal's media kit, "among [its] estimated 35,000 readers are art historians (30 percent), artists (35 percent), institutions (20 percent), and curators, conservators, and administrators (15 percent)." The writer of this essay, Carol Beck, is an artist, art historian, and dean of faculty and senior executive vice president for academic affairs at the School of the Art Institute of Chicago. She is the author of numerous articles and several books; her writings cluster around the intersection of art and politics, with a special focus on gender. In reading this piece, think about how the assumed audience for *Art Journal* influences the language and vocabulary Becker uses throughout.

WHEN IT WAS FIRST PROVEN THAT DOLLY, THE CLONED sheep, had a genetic makeup the age of her host, it threatened to end the fascination with cloning as a viable method of reproduction. (Why would a member of any species want to start out old?) But in April 2000, when scientists at Advanced Cell Technologies in Worcester, Massachusetts, announced that their cloned cows "possessed cells with clocks that are set like newborns," this was a revelation.[1] It would seem that finally humans had found the fountain of youth. Now able to replicate other species (and someday ourselves) ad infinitum, they (we) could always remain young.

At the core of the Human Genome Project, cloning, and biotechnology, there appears to be a desperate desire to find "the secret of life," a search intended to foil the most fearsome elements of our genetic programming — the inevitability of imperfection, deterioration, disease, and death. Perhaps the conversation about the "posthuman" is fundamentally about our desire to flee from human vulnerability, mortality, and our subjective awareness of these conditions. And if such experimentation and theorizing is a personal, ontogenetic attempt to defy death, it is also a phylogenetic effort to continue to evolve as a species when it would appear that all dramatic "natural" evolutions of the physical body have come to completion. Simultaneous with this interest in immortalizing the physical body is an attempt to create a new, virtual body, unencumbered by gravity. One day we might decant our old "self" or core into a cybernetic shell stored on some version of a floppy disk from which our singular and collective identities could be eternally retrieved (but hopefully not erased). These complex motivations are often couched in the discourses of transcendence and liberation.

If, in the art world, the theorizing of the 1980s and 1990s were about issues of identity — the mining of the nuance of one's historical self, conceptualized in society, or what one is, then perhaps this new era will be characterized by what one is not, and focus on the incorporation of otherness; the recombination of the natural and the fabricated; the physical and the virtual; the breakdown of distinctions between art and science; the site of visual experimentation now become the actual, material body, no longer merely its representation; the interrogation of the permeable parameters of species differentiation — new hybridities — as well as the cyborgization and robotization of the human body, and the humanization of the machine. Perhaps we are now enamored with the notion of the posthuman precisely because we perceive humanity as an outdated Enlightenment construct impossible to obtain. Dystopian — unable to imagine the transformation of society and social structures, we have become fascinated with something pre-social: the source of life and all its differentiations as manifested in the Human Genome Project. Is our focus now shifted to the origins of being to deflect us from the question of being in society? Or is this actually the issue of identity taken to an even more basic level: What is human? What is animal? Where do the two come together? How can we truly gain mastery of the code that makes us human and differentiates us from the 98 percent of our makeup that is genetically similar to that of apes? Are we nostalgic for our placement in the world of animals (the 98 percent) or committed to leaving such categorizations behind once and for all (the 2 percent), through our ability to control how all animals, including ourselves, evolve? Or are we simply bored, fearful that our apparently intransigent relationships between mind and body, sentient and nonsentient will remain unchanged for eternity? Into this wildly unpredictable, potentially dangerous, philosophically rich field of experimentation, one marked by a lack of examination of motivation and potential consequence, enter artists, many of whom love to create in such spaces of metaphor, ambiguity, virtuality, multiplicity, artificiality, utopianism, risk, and chaos.

Eduardo Kac is such an artist who has navigated these new geographies for some time. Kac believes, "If we leave technology behind in art, if we don't question how technology affects our lives, if we don't use these media to raise questions about contemporary life, who is going to do that?"[2] He has used each of his art pieces and spectacles to attract media attention and thereby encourage public dialogue about the social issues his interactions and interventions address. Among other projects, Kac has grown a single seed in a gallery in New Orleans through light sent by individuals around the world via the Internet (Teleporting an Unknown State). He has implanted a chip in his own leg registering himself as both animal and owner on a Web-based animal identification database (Time Capsule). And he has created a performance where a robotic device designed to aerate his own extracted blood was then able to use it to ignite a flame (A-Positive).

In his most recent piece, Kac has collaborated with geneticist [5] Louis-Marie Houdebine to create a "GFP rabbit" — a transgenic albino bunny whose genetic makeup is altered with a gene obtained from a Pacific Northwest jellyfish that contains GFP, green fluorescent protein. Scientists have previously used this substance to track genetic changes in frogs and mice. Kac had originally wanted to create a "GFP K-9" — a dog that would turn fluorescent under a blue light or glow green in the dark, like the rabbit. But the technology was not yet advanced enough to permit bringing the fluorescence into the coat of a dog. Hence Alba, the albino bunny. But Kac insists that Alba alone is not the art project. Rather, according to Kac, "It is one gesture — the creation, social integration, and response" that comprises the actual piece.[3]

Eduardo Kac hopes to live with Alba (now several months old) in a gallery context in Avignon, France (as part of the art festival AvignoNumerique), where he will attempt to "normalize" his relationship with her, constructing a domestic space where he and Alba will cohabitate over the course of two weeks. There, visitors will be able to see the rabbit and to observe her glow under a blue light. As a result of the weeks in Avignon and the conference framed around the multifarious issues this piece will generate, Kac hopes to "displace the discourse of a transgenic animal from a scientific model into that of a social subject." Kac then intends to return to Chicago with Alba, where she will become a "member of his family."[4] He is interested in finding the place of public dialogue beyond the obvious polarizations — the utopianism that can surround bioengineering as well as the fear that often accompanies its potential outcomes. He is also interested in how the issues around such "transgenic" (cross-species genetic transplanting) art are discussed in the public arena and how Alba's existence, and his response to it, might, in his words, "introduce much-needed subtlety and ambiguity" into the debate.

Here the artist has assumed the role of educator, researcher, scientist, social critic, inventor, and co-creator of life. His struggle as an artist is no longer to interrogate his own "hybridity" to register his own "agency," but rather to actually be part of creating a visually and genetically new, transgenic creature, and then focus on her integration into society, her agency, individuality, and potential designation as "other."

In the universe of the posthuman it would appear that the human species will now not only fuse with machines to determine their destiny and how human they will become, but also, no longer the victim of nature ourselves, will become even more the choreographers, curators, and programmers of all other existent, and yet-to-be-imagined species. As Kac says, "I'm interested in science and technology because they allow me to intervene in reality in a way that has a sense of immediacy."

Had we done better as humans in relationship to each other and the "natural world," perhaps we could be more optimistic about what to expect from such posthuman interventions in the realm of the "real." But there is no turning back. Such work to expand the notion of self/other, sentient/nonsentient — visually and conceptually — will inevitably continue. Many scientists and artists will be seduced by the challenges and also imagined good that certain types of research might achieve. Some will also be taken with the glamour, power, and money connected with creating "the first of its kind." All that can be done is as Kac has proposed: create forums where conversations about "consensual domain"[5] between ourselves and other creatures can take place; interrogate the motivations behind such projects; develop ethical discourses to help honestly evaluate the effects of such experiments and art endeavors on those other humans, part-humans, posthumans, and nonhumans with whom we cohabitate and whom we will increasingly seek to perfect and control.

NOTES

[1]Taken from a report in *USA Today*, April 28–30, 2000.

[2]Eduardo Kac: Teleporting an Unknown State, October 1998.

[3]All quotes by Eduardo Kac are taken from an interview with the author, May 2000, in Chicago.

[4]Ibid.

[5]This term of "consensual domain" is very important to Kac and came up repeatedly in our conversation. This raises serious questions about how to achieve consensual domain with an animal.

READING

1. Becker begins her essay by evoking Dolly, the world-famous cloned sheep. Why? What does Dolly symbolize?

2. Becker employs a high-level vocabulary drawn from the worlds of both art and science. Make a list of the terms you do not immediately understand in her essay and find their definitions. What does this list suggest about the intended audience for "GFP Bunny"?

3. Throughout the first half of her essay, Becker defines the world of the "posthuman." What does this term mean? How does it relate to the Human Genome Project, cloning, and biotechnology?

4. The essay shifts from a general discussion of the intersection of art and technology to a specific discussion of the works of Eduardo Kac. Where does this shift take place? How does the first section prepare the reader for the second? Why does Becker seem to have chosen Kac as her exemplar of "an artist who has navigated these new geographies for some time"?

5. Now that you have read the entire piece, return to its title, "GFP Bunny." Does the title represent the entirety of Becker's essay? What seems to be her thesis? Can you think of an alternate title that might be more representative?

WRITING

1. Becker's first few paragraphs discuss the human desire to "always remain young." She sees our interest in cloning and biotechnology as largely situated in this constant search for the fountain of youth. Write a reflective essay or journal entry about this desire. If you could stop time at any age, would you? Why or why not? What age would you choose?

2. According to Becker, the new era of art is defined by "what one is not" because we now "perceive humanity as an outdated Enlightenment construct." This is the "posthuman" era. Consider how Becker defines "posthuman." Write an essay that defines the term, using examples from your life in the "posthuman" era that explicate Becker's concept.

3. In the third paragraph, Becker introduces a series of questions meant to illuminate the complexity of the issues raised by the scientific "transformation of society and social structures." In one sense, the point of these questions is that none has a single answer;

rather, they trigger many answers that lead to further questions. Given that, take one of the questions and write a response that represents your personal philosophy on the topic. Include in your essay the context for this philosophy. That is, do not just articulate what you believe, also state why and how you came to this belief.

4. This essay was initially published in 2000, and it outlines Kac's artistic motive for creating Alba, the GFP Bunny, whose photo appears in the chapter as well (p. 567). As might be expected, Kac's work generated incredible controversy. Taking on the role as a publicist for an artist thinking about creating a new transgenic species, research Alba's reception in the artistic and animal-rights communities. Prepare a two- to three-page brief that summarizes your findings for your artist client. Include a recommendation based on your new understanding of the situation: Should your client go forward with this project?

5. Becker writes of Kac's work that "the artist has assumed the role of educator, researcher, scientist, social critic, inventor, and co-creator of life." Her description of Kac seems to mirror – in part – Tamar Schlick's description of the ideal relationship between art and science as expressed in "The Critical Collaboration" (Reading Deeply, p. 573). However, Becker herself seems less optimistic about the future that science will bring than does Schlick. Write an essay that compares these two pieces: one written from the point of view of an artist, the other by a scientist. In your essay, identify the differences in voice, tone, and perspective. Discuss how these differences may be emblematic of the philosophical gap between the two fields.

FOCUS ON GENRE

Genomic Art

A Portfolio of Art about the Human Genome Project

WHAT DOES THE INTERSECTION OF SCIENCE AND ART LOOK LIKE? How has technology – in all its forms – influenced the ways in which art is created and artists represent their world? These questions hover over this chapter, and the works that follow represent the responses of several artists to what Carol Becker refers to as the "posthuman" age. In writing of his own exploration of the realm where science and art collide, in his paper "Genomic Art and Culture" (www.mi.sanu.ac.yu./vismath/proceedings/brodyk.htm), artist Andre Brodyk writes, "Genetic Art is a creative, metaphoric, fictional equivalent of genetic engineering processes, a transformative and shaping medium." Suzanne Anker and Dorothy Nelkin, in their book, *The Molecular Gaze: Art in the Genetic Age* (2003), observe that genomic art is focused on five recurring themes: "human reductionism to a molecular text, manipulation of the human form, blurring of boundaries between humans and animals, eugenics, and commercialization of cells and genes." Each of these themes cuts to the core of what it means to be human in an age when what is imperfect can be perfected and what was once deemed perfect can be refined and modified to be ever more efficient and effective. The works that follow represent both traditional art forms (for example, photography, installations) and new forms that have emerged both to address the concerns and take advantage of the opportunities offered by this new age: from transgenic species (Green Alba) to interactive multimedia (Genochoice).

We have annotated one work to demonstrate how it both poses and responds to questions and dilemmas triggered by the genomic revolution. Following this annotated piece, you will find a series of genomic art works for your analysis and discussion. As you examine this art, think about how its impact might be different if you encountered it in a gallery or museum, where you could experience the works not on a flat page but immediately in the "real" world – a world that engages your senses and emotions more directly. Does the context of these pieces change their ability to influence your thinking? Would it clarify the point of these works to have them situated in a defined space?

In 2000, Kac's artwork was revolutionary, and it stirred great ethical and artistic debate about whether a transgenic creature could be "art." In the years since, many cells and animals have been altered by inserting GFP into their structure, often for commercial reasons. (See *Glowing Genes: A Revolution in Biotechnology* [2005], by Marc Zimmer, for more information.)

Kac initially planned, as part of his art project, to take Alba home to live with him. However, he was denied custody of Alba by the lab that helped in her creation, which faced great controversy over its involvement in the project. He turned this denial into its own work of art by flying a flag with Alba's image in front of his home to signify her loss. Speculate about how this emotional display might become part of the comment on the blurring between humanity and technology.

The meaning of the name "Alba" is "white." Think about how the rabbit's name becomes a part of Kac's artistic message. Also, how might Alba's color change lead the viewer to ponder what other fundamental changes can be achieved through genetic engineering (i.e., race, gender, etc.)?

Kac worked with a French geneticist to splice a gene from a jellyfish containing green fluorescent protein (GFP) into a real rabbit, thus creating an albino rabbit that glows green in blue light. Kac describes the project as "a complex social event that starts with the creation of a chimerical animal that does not exist in nature." What is the "social event" that Alba's creation might trigger?

Kac writes, "As a transgenic artist, I am not interested in the creation of genetic objects, but in the invention of transgenic social subjects" (www.ekac .orgtgfpbonny .html/# gfpbunnyanchor). Think about how and why, as an artist, his creation of Alba differs from the creation of other GFP transgenic species by scientists.

Eduardo Kac calls this piece *GFP Bunny*. Identify the connotative differences between "bunny" and "rabbit" and how these differences encourage the viewer to engage with Alba.

Eduardo Kac, GFP Bunny, 2000. Alba the Fluorescent Rabbit.

Virgil Wong, Genochoice Homepage

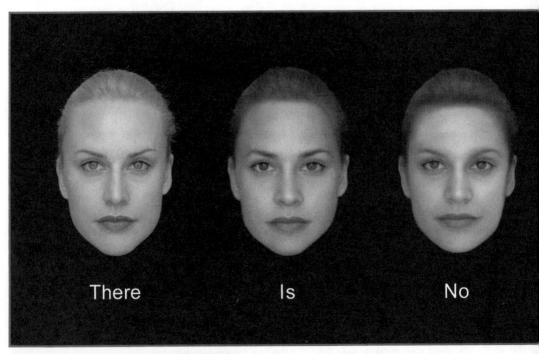

Nancy Burson, There Is No Gene For Race

Carrie Mae Weems, Gibbon and Child at Play, 1999

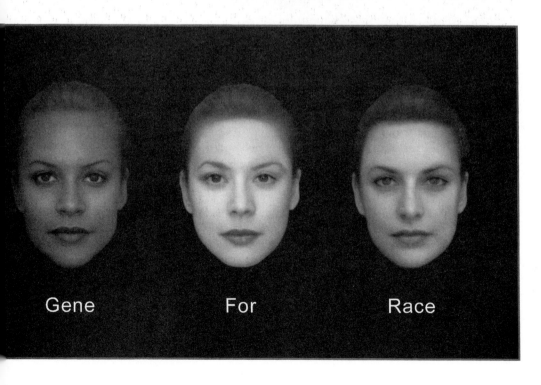

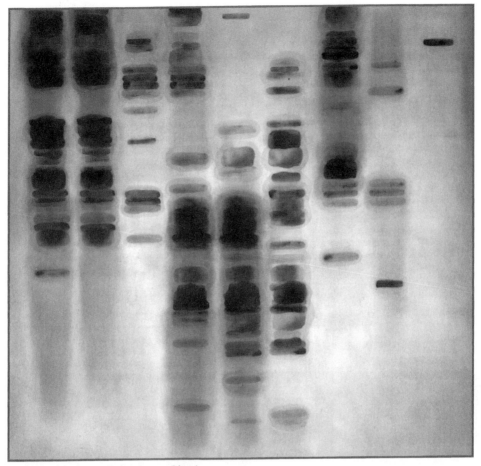

Dennis Ashbaugh, Jolly Green Giant

Christy Rupp, Tell Us What We Are Eating

RESPONDING

1. These artworks represent a gamut of forms and approaches to visual texts. In each case, the form chosen by the artist should assist in conveying the message of the work. Which work did you find most interesting? How was your interest (or lack of interest) shaped by the art's form and media? If you were commissioned to create a work of genomic art, what form would it take?

2. The introduction to the portfolio identifies five key themes in genomic art. Classify the artworks according to these themes (some may address more than one). Now, take one of the works and describe how it fits this subject. What questions central to the topic is it posing or addressing? What is its view of the genomic world? What elements within the art work lead you to this conclusion?

3. In "The Critical Collaboration" (Reading Deeply, p. 573), Tamar Schlick, a scientist, argues for exhibits of genomic art that would "encourage the general public to become more engaged in the applications of the biological sciences and to appreciate the complex scientific and societal implications of genomic research." Select one of the pieces represented in this portfolio and research more about the artist behind the work. With your new knowledge about the artist, think about Schlick's desire for art that would support the path of science. Is this the goal of the artist you selected? Why do you draw this conclusion?

LEONARDO

Journal of the International Society for the Arts, Sciences and Technology

Volume 38 Number 4 2005

The MIT Press
$15.00

The Critical Collaboration between Art and Science: *An Experiment on a Bird in the Air Pump* and the Ramifications of Genomics for Society

By Tamar Schlick

FROM: *Leonardo, August* 2005

THIS ARTICLE INITIALLY APPEARED IN THE ACADEMIC JOURNAL *Leonardo,* a publication of the Leonardo/International Society for the Arts, Sciences, and Technology. This nonprofit group sees its mission as serving "the international arts community by promoting and document-ing work at the intersection of the arts, sciences, and technology, and by encouraging and stimulating collaboration between artists, scientists, and technologists." The editorial board for the journal includes interna-tional scientists and media artists, among them Eduardo Kac, whose *GFP Bunny* can be found elsewhere in the chapter (p. 567). Pieces published in *Leonardo* are subject to internal and external editorial review, a prac-tice common in a journal with an academic focus. The author of this article, Tamar Schlick, is professor of chemistry, mathematics, and com-puter science at New York University. There, she heads a research group that, according to her website, studies "how the structures and motions of complex biological systems regulate fundamental functions like DNA transcription, replication, and recombination and the initiation of dis-ease." Schlick is widely published in her field and is the author of the foundational textbook *Molecular Modeling in a Simulation* (2002).

To help you read more deeply and critically, we have provided anno-tations and boldfaced some terms or passages that call attention to the rhetorical choices Schlick has made in her article and to the conventions of an academic piece. As you read the essay and the annotations, con-sider how she positions art as a vehicle for increased popular under-standing and accepting science – and uses examples drawn from art and media to convey difficult scientific concepts to her readers.

The abstract is common in academic journals; it provides a very brief synopsis of the article that follows, essentially to let readers know if it is on a topic of interest or applicability to their research.

These quotations are called "epigraphs." They are used to set the tone for the piece that follows and should reflect its content or point of view.

Abstract

Inspired by a famous eighteenth-century painting by Joseph Wright, the author discerns similarities between issues relevant then and the public's current reception of scientific ideas from modern biology in the wake of the Human Genome Project. She proposes educational and scientific initiatives and advocates more positive and balanced portrayals of scientific themes in the arts to help engage the public in a discourse about the ramifications of genomics science and technology for our lives.

> *We especially need imagination in science. It is not all*
> *mathematics, nor all logic, but is somewhat beauty and poetry.*
> — MARIA MITCHELL

> *Science is emphatically an important part of culture today, as scientific*
> *knowledge and its applications continue to transform the world, and*
> *condition every aspect of the relations between men and nations.*
> — VANNEVAR BUSH

The Need for a Modern Lunar Society

In the 50 years since the description of DNA's double helix structure, we have witnessed a revolution made possible by the marriage of science and technology. Variously referred to as the DNA, Genomics, or Modern Biology Revolution, its discoveries and advances over the

An engineer often seen as the great-grandfather of the World Wide Web.

America's first professional female astronomer.

This first-person approach would be unheard of in a scientific journal, but in a humanities journal, like *Leonardo*, it is acceptable. As a rhetorical device, it helps draw the reader into a difficult topic.

As Schlick describes the eighteenth-century Lunar Society, she introduces the idea behind the header for this section — what type of Lunar Society is needed today.

past 50 years have changed virtually every aspect of our lives, from health to law to society. As we embark on the twenty-first century, the challenges that have emerged from this technology cover political, medical, ethical, and legal territories.

I pondered this state of affairs recently while immersed in a dusty, oversized library book about the life and work of the eighteenth-century British artist Joseph Wright of Derby (1734–1797). Wright was part of an elite scholarly clique called the Lunar Society (so named for their monthly Monday meetings near times of the full moon), passionately devoted to learning and discussing the latest developments in science, engineering, and industry. The group, which included industrial ceramics pioneer Josiah Wedgwood and Erasmus Darwin, a scientist, poet, and grandfather of the evolution pioneer Charles Darwin, sought to dispel notions remaining from the Dark Ages, such as religious superstition and political and social intolerance, by promulgating a liberal worldview based on rational thought and advocating an open, intelligent society. Wright's meticulously executed works include many paintings and sketches that convey the depths of human emotions and the beauty of landscapes. Notable also are his complex interdisciplinary works that demonstrate the impact of the new scientific movement on society.

Wright's dramatic 1768 painting *An Experiment on a Bird in the Air Pump* strikingly anticipates our current pre-

This painting (see p. 577) is Schlick's foundation for the link between art and science, wherein art can illuminate scientific concerns.

dicament involving applications of the biological sciences as perceived by the general public. In the painting, a long-haired scientist demonstrates to an audience of men, women, and children that air is vital to life; inside an instrument devoid of air a delicate cockatoo hovers between life and death; the bird's fate will be determined by the demonstrator, who can open the air passage. The curious observers offer a window on society. They experience this scientific demonstration with various emotions: awe, fright, and anxiety, but also admiration and hope. The recent quantum advances made possible by the revolution in modern biology can similarly help us to advance as a society, but the consequences of many applications are also associated with sacrifice, fear, and the need for change.

We are challenged similarly today to define new rules and limits for the usage and application of our newly conceived science and technology. Because today's general public is arguably less knowledgeable about contemporary science and technology than were the educated sectors of 250 years ago, general confusion, denial, or dread about scientific developments must be alleviated so that we do not err on the side of unnecessary caution. Scientists and artists can help spread a balanced, informed view of scientific and societal dilemmas to address current manifestations of the modern biology revolution. A modern incarnation of the eighteenth-century Lunar Society is needed, in which our efforts should promote a positive global mission with a vision that transcends world factions, just as the Apollo space program

At base, this section uses two standard methods of organization: description and comparison/contrast. Our position in relation to science today is very much like that in the eighteenth century. We are at the dawn of a new age.

(1961–1969), which dawned as the world grappled with the Cold War, culminated in the triumphant expedition to the moon.

Joseph Wright of Derby, An Experiment on a Bird in the Air Pump, 1768.

The Modern Biology Revolution: No Longer Science Fiction

There is a pleasing symmetry in the key biological developments of the twentieth century, which began in 1900 with the discovery (in fact a rediscovery) of Gregor Mendel's pioneer-

Part of Schlick's rhetorical strategy is to situate the unfamiliar in the familiar, again through comparison. She assumes *Leonardo* readers have a sense of science as history.

Notice the format of the references. It is dictated by the standards set by the journal. While you might be most familiar with MLA or APA style sheets, some journals use other style manuals.

ing laws of genetics [1] and ended with publication of the first draft of the human genome. An opportunity for reflecting on the current state of affairs came in April 2003 with the fiftieth anniversary of Watson and Crick's report of DNA's **structure [2].** This birthday was celebrated worldwide through meetings; dedicated journal issues (from *Science* to *Nature* to *Seed*); library, art, and photography exhibits; theater performances; and much more. "Like a genetically manipulated virus," wrote S. Mawer, "DNA has now escaped the laboratory and infected the whole world. We are in the midst of a pandemic" [3].

Indeed, the DNA code describes in 3 billion letters important instructions for human life through its specification of gene products (such as proteins and RNA regulators) that ultimately determine human traits. United States President Bill Clinton described DNA in a 2000 speech as "the language in which God created life." Of course, we now also appreciate **the wealth of other processes aside from our genotype that influence our phenotype, such as environmental factors and RNA editing, and examples of "epigenetic" factors (those not encoded in our DNA) that determine gene products, such as proteins and RNA, and human behavior [4].**

This biological goldmine, coupled with computer technology now in use, suggests new opportunities for society in many areas. Thus, among the "ten hottest jobs" predicted by *Time* magazine on 22 May

Because she is writing in a humanities-focused journal, Schlick assumes her audience will need some complex scientific terms defined (for example, epigenetic). Note her use of the parenthetical definition in the next paragraph.

Schlick now shifts a bit. She has established the importance of genetic research, so she moves on to its infusion into art and popular culture.

2000, five involved such products of computers and biology: *tissue engineers* (designers of organs on petri dishes), *gene programmers* (creators of customized genes), *pharmers* (developers of genetically engineered crops that produce therapeutic proteins such as vaccine-laden potatoes), *Frankenfood monitors* (watchdogs of dangerous engineered creations), and *data miners* (developers of tools for extracting knowledge from biological information).

This range of jobs indicates the breadth of the public's response to modern biology research. It also suggests why DNA and scientific subjects have become attractive for artists. DNA has stimulated designers such as Eric Harshbarger to build Lego models of it (see p. 586) and artists to portray it as the *Mona Lisa* of Science [5]. Artists whose work revolves around genetics include, for example, Brandon Ballengee [6], Bryan Crockett [7], and George Gessert [8].

DNA is a regular presence in Hollywood film — the movies *Spider-Man* and *Gattaca* have mentioned and featured it. In related contexts, DNA figures prominently in science-fiction literature, such as in the works of Robin Cook (*Outbreak, Chromosome 6, Vector*), Michael Crichton (*Jurassic Park, Timeline*), and John Darnton (*The Experiment*).

In the theater, "DNA is God!" is the declaration of one of the exonerated death-row inmates in a recent New York off-Broadway play, *The Exonerated* [9]. DNA also appears as a harbinger of ethical or social dilemmas, as in Jonathan Tolins's play *The Twilight of the Golds*.

Although this is a researched, academic piece, note how Schlick makes use of common rhetorical forms. This passage of the essay is essentially exemplification. Her catalog of examples supports her point about the pervasiveness of DNA/genetic concerns and influence in art, culture, and life.

Even in the hit Broadway musical *Avenue Q*, a puppet refers to another's sexual orientation by saying, "It's in his DNA" [10].

Moving beyond these expected venues, DNA has been used to coin business or product names because its association with the "core" of a person is exploited to imply a core brand (an original source). Examples include a San Francisco disco (DNA Lounge) [11], a skateboard brand developed by Syndrome Distributors in California [12], the name of a web design company in the United Kingdom (DNA) [13], a specialty nursery in Alberta, Canada (DNA Gardens) [14], a Greek magazine (*DNa*) [15], a vitamin supplier in England (DNA Vitamins) [16], and a gay men's magazine in Australia (*DNA*) [17].

Indeed DNA's information is central to numerous everyday procedures. The practical applications of DNA and modern biology techniques in medicine, archaeology, crime, and forensics are well known. For example, DNA analysis is used in medical diagnoses to identify gene origins for cancer, schizophrenia, and Parkinson's disease. For historical analysis, archaeologists and scientists can team up to identify gene signals in human populations to discern human origins, evolutionary changes in whales, or even the lineage of modern wines [18].

Examples of DNA profiling in crime conviction and forensics are abundant today in the press; the requisite analysis has provided important work for mathematicians and statisticians who must translate the results of DNA sequence comparison to probabilistic terms. Since the first prisoner in the United States was exonerated in 1993

> Schlick's examples are easily understood by the layperson. They also provide a foundation for her contentions about the overall importance of current biological discoveries.

because of DNA evidence, dozens of death-row inmates have also been exonerated. DNA profiling has also implicated individuals in murders or trysts based on DNA extracted from clothing (for example, O. J. Simpson's black glove and Monica Lewinsky's dress). **Studies of DNA have been important in identification of remains following tragedies like the September 11 attacks on the World Trade Center and the Pentagon. The same science is useful in paternity suits.**

How far, however, can and should this technology be carried? Scott Adams's comic strip *Dilbert*, 9 July 2000 [19], shows the pointy-haired bête noire boss being briefed on a new software that can "create human simulations from DNA samples." **This cartoon underscores the urgent need for the general public to receive more education in science so as to be able to separate science from fiction.** Indeed, the announcement in spring 2003 by Clonaid, part of the peculiar Raëlian movement [20], that humans had been cloned caused confusion and controversy, soon to be replaced — for some — by disappointment.

Interestingly, biologist Lewis Thomas suggested over two decades ago that we should strive in the direction opposite to cloning:

> Set cloning aside, and don't try it. Instead, go in the other direction. Look for ways to get mutations more quickly, new variety, different songs. Fiddle around, if you must fiddle, but never with ways to keep things the same, no matter who, not even yourself. Heaven, somewhere ahead, has got to be a change [21].

> This is a central point in Schlick's paper. As a scientist, she is struggling with how to translate incredibly complex scientific discoveries into information that can be absorbed by the general public. In a way, her article represents an attempt to do just that.

> The catalog of questions that begins with this one are meant to underscore the essential role that genetic research and discoveries play in society. Each of these questions is designed to trigger a personal response in the reader. In rhetorical terms, such questions comprise the trope of anacoenosis. These are not abstract issues; they are concrete concerns.

Societal Ramifications of the Modern Biology Revolution

Clearly, many societal, ethical, economic, legal, and political issues must also be addressed as this colossal research, made possible by the Human Genome Project, goes forward (see p. 594). **For example, what, if any, restrictions should there be on stem-cell research, which can potentially lead to many medical advances but utilizes precious tissue from discarded embryos?** What rules should be imposed on cloning of animals, including humans, and the cross-breeding of species? Should genomics-based knowledge of human health be released to the individual, to employers, to insurers, or to family members who may be directly affected? How available should our DNA imprint be to law enforcement agencies? What aspects of scientific discoveries should be privatized or patented? What restrictions should be placed on applying this scientific technology? Undoubtedly, as our scientific and technological sophistication increases, the possibilities of the practical applications increase steeply. Will our future progeny reflect a society of designer babies? Will our endless search for beauty, health, intelligence, and perpetuity produce "a nursing home for sluggish Methuselahs" [22], with new possible problems and dangers?

From Copernicus's astronomy to the Human Genome Project, scientific advances are inevitable, as it is human nature to push possibilities to their limit. Accordingly, fear and anxiety are better replaced by prudent preparedness. **First and foremost, this readiness requires more people to be knowledgeable about the sciences.**

> Here, Schlick restates more directly the same point she made above in relation to the Dilbert cartoon. This statement is the core of her essay – the rationale for her piece.

Schlick has just provided the structure for the next part of her article. Note that this section is essentially about a very basic writing concern: audience. How can scientists communicate with each other and the general public to assure an appropriate level of understanding?

A molecular model of the classic DNA double helix.

Multidisciplinary Science Education and Training

Two broad educational areas require substantial revision and expansion to deal with the new scientific challenges of the twenty-first century: within the scientific community on one hand, and between scientists and the general public on the other.

Training the Scientists First, innovative multidisciplinary educational and research paradigms are required in the biological sciences. **Phil Bourne, former president of the International Society for Computational Biology (ISCB),** has written that computational biology, which combines biology at different scales with computer science, has recently come to earn the status of a scientific discipline. The high demand for qualified computational biologists has given rise to ISCB, which

To establish authority with scientists, Schlick (herself a scientist) cites a recognized authority in the field.

Schlick identifies an issue of audience within the science community: there is little communication across disciplines. The increased specialization has created gaps in discourse. Notice that she provides concrete examples of these communication barriers.

is dedicated to the advancement of scientific understanding of living systems through computations.

Unfortunately, the field's growing recognition has not translated automatically into training innovations. Although programs in computational biology and bioinformatics (certificates and graduate degrees) have been appearing, they vary widely because of the field's unique challenges.

While the interest in computational biology is growing rapidly, the transition to productive research in the field is difficult for non-biologists. **There is a growing need for professionals who can translate scientific problems in biology into mathematics and computations;** for such productive work, familiarity with modern scientific computing approaches, as well as key biological challenges, is essential. It is not only a matter of in-depth knowledge of biological subjects (which is itself a challenge), but also one of the ability to acquire a very different scientific perspective and approach, which may deviate from the accuracy and order that mathematicians and physicists are trained to seek. At the same time, biological scientists may lack sufficient training in mathematics, computer science, and physics to perform many analyses, modeling, simulation, and database systematics of biological systems. Yet a multidisciplinary approach is critically needed to merge descriptions of the functional and cellular picture (from biology) with atomic and molecular details (in chemistry), the electronic level with underlying forces (in physics),

Again, she supports her position with an authority within the field. Note that she clearly identifies this as an international concern. This magnifies the severity of the problem. Also, remember that *Leonardo* has an international focus and audience.

appropriate numerical models and algorithms (in mathematics), and practical implementation on high-speed and extended-communication platforms (computer science and engineering). This synergy is critical because the best computational approach is often closely tailored to the biological problem. In the same spirit, close connections between theory and experiment are essential: Computational models evolve as experimental data become available, and biological theories and new experiments are performed as a result of computational insights.

A recent report spearheaded by the Human Frontier Science Program (HFSP), with panelists from Europe, North America, and Japan, presents a bold new paradigm for education and training in the natural sciences [23]. It argues that the traditional model of "pipelining" — unidirectional disciplinary tracks that produce research professors in narrow specialties — is inadequate to deal with the complex scientific, social, and economic problems of our times. It also states educational and social challenges that we must address. **Among them are these needs: to develop a new scientific culture that cultivates and rewards interdisciplinary expertise; to train and reward teachers and other educational leaders; to train our science students for a wider range of career outcomes (academe, government, industry, health care, education, business, journalism, politics, and law); to encourage the participation of women and ethnic minorities in the sciences; to provide ethical and career guidance, including writ-**

When you include long lists, the items need to have parallel structure (to develop . . . to train . . . to encourage, etc.)

585

Schlick now proposes a solution to the problem she raised earlier. As in other parts of the essay, she is using a very familiar rhetorical form, problem/solution, to structure this subsection of her article.

ing and management skills; and to integrate science with society.

To achieve this transformation in scientific training, new educational programs for master's and doctoral degrees are essential to train researchers to be competent in computational methods as well as knowledgeable in biological systems. Such innovative degree programs have already been the focus of the Burroughs Wellcome Interface Program, the Sloan/ Department of Energy initiative in computational biology, and the (U.S.) National Science Foundation's Integrative Graduate Education and Research Traineeship Program (IGERT) institutional awards. Programs like these can prepare our future generations for successful careers in bioinformatics, biotechnology, and allied fields. A blend of academic, industrial, and

Eric Harshbarger's 2003 LEGO creation of a DNA helix.

Within the article, this artistic interpretation is juxtaposed with Schlick's model on page (583). The reader begins to see how scientific ideas are filtered through art. Here, there is a nice irony in Harshbarger's use of child's building blocks to create a human building block.

This heading identifies a change in subject. She is moving on to the second audience, which is more likely to comprise the readership of this journal.

government experience, as well as computational and experimental work, is also important to familiarize students with the multifaceted nature of biological research.

Besides this training of scholars in the requisite life-science, computational, and interdisciplinary skills, the training of health professionals in hospitals and medical schools should include training in genomics, bioinformatics, and allied fields. These modern fields have radically evolved since current professionals were in school, and this gap in knowledge should be addressed by devoting concerted workshop training efforts to practicing doctors on a regular basis. These programs would enable physicians and other health providers to better understand modern scientific tools, such as bioinformatics, for utilizing genomic and other available scientific data in medical diagnosis and treatment.

Training the General Public   On the second front, to prepare future generations to deal with the ramifications of science and technology, children should be introduced at an early age to the increasingly important disciplines of science, mathematics, and computing. **Although the level and quality of education in science, mathematics, and computing varies widely across the world, many Western countries such as the United States still suffer from the lack of strong programs at the elementary and high-school levels in these disciplines, although this requirement is widely recognized.** Perhaps one problem is that we emphasize rote scientific

The problem/solution set-up should now be familiar to the reader; this section parallels in form the one immediately preceding it.

learning instead of team problem-solving — a central feature of today's interdisciplinary scientific efforts. Graduate schools are just beginning to put more emphasis on this additional level of learning, and these methods can be adapted for younger students. In higher institutions, subjects such as mathematics are so feared that professors find they need to inflate grades to retain students. As science's image improves, it should be possible to boost classroom training both by increasing the level of minimum required mathematical and computer skills and by introducing specialized workshops to familiarize young students with current scientific research in computational biology. Greater commitment of resources and effort to education, as well as enhancement of the reward system for teachers, will be required to make these tall orders a reality.

In addition to such formal programs, efforts to bring science to the public's everyday life are also crucial. The Public Broadcasting Service (PBS) has recently introduced a regular science feature during the nightly *News Hour with Jim Lehrer*, and the Discovery Channel deserves credit for bringing science to all. Terry Sejnowski recently suggested that a cable science network (CSN) could also serve that purpose [24]. By providing science education — lectures by scientists, or presentations and discussion from international meetings and public conferences — we can hope to bring to everyone's living rooms pertinent information on topics ranging from global warming to biological warfare to epidemics/crises such as

Schlick moves from education to popular culture – and returns to her central point from earlier in the article: how to increase understanding of science in the general public.

Again, Schlick's international examples would appeal to an international readership.

SARS, anthrax attacks, and environmental hazards. More town hall-like meetings to discuss scientific issues in public forums, such as presidential debates, or sessions in scientific meetings that are open to the public, could also help spread good solid science and a better image for science to every city in the world.

An elevated level of scientific information in our governmental and legal sectors would make the crucial difference in closely advising the people and groups responsible for making far-reaching decisions regarding the application of scientific and technological advances. **For example, the International Science and Technology Reference Forum, with the support of the United Nations, is establishing a permanent team of legal experts and scientists to mediate between science and the legal sector [25]. Another network centered at the University of Pavia, Italy, entitled European Network for Life Sciences, Health, and the Courts, has similar goals [26].** Such opportunities for marrying expertise — in this case, that of life scientists and law professionals — could be realized between other groups, for example between agriculturalists and biologists; between environmentalists or oil producers and scientists knowledgeable about pollution, ecology, and the chemical industry; **between military personnel and research scientists who specialize in chemical and biological warfare; or between health professionals and basic-science researchers in biomedicine.** Funding for these programs could come from all

As she did earlier, Schlick carefully maintains parallelism in these stacked examples.

> Headings provide assistance for readers in long pieces. They should be short and function as titles for the section that immediately follows. Schlick also uses this title to restate her central contention, which reinforces its impact.

levels of government and national/international public and private funds, starting from a small scale.

Art and Science Collaboration — a Necessity

Another way to help guide the application of our scientific developments and the public's understanding of science and technology is to draw the sciences and the arts closer to one another, and to do so positively. **C. P. Snow argued for such connections and collaborations 45 years ago [27]. The ancient Greeks did not make clear distinctions between literature and science, and the schism that Snow refers to is a modern phenomenon.** Part of the gap in knowledge is simply inevitable: The body of scientific knowledge grows so rapidly that most scientists have become so specialized that they cannot comprehend most other scientists' works.

Scientists seek the truth, just as artists do, in sometimes unusual ways. To inspire my students of mathematical biology to develop computational models that incorporate details where necessary but approximations where appropriate, I recall for them **Pablo Picasso's saying: "Art is the lie that helps us tell the truth." Similarly, artists such as Leonardo da Vinci, Albrecht Durer, Victor Vasarely, and M. C. Escher have borrowed from or been inspired by scientific ideas**.

A synergy between the sciences and the arts can be achieved by

> Academic writing should be situated in the historical and ongoing discussion on the topic at hand. Schlick links her position to C. P. Snow's views. In the mid-twentieth century, Snow argued (quite vehemently) that education was in decline in part because of the growing rift between art and science. Snow himself was both a novelist and a scientist.

> Readers of the journal *Leonardo* would be very familiar with all of the artists cited.

However, these same readers may not know about the plays listed by Schlick, all of which had their runs either shortly before or concurrently with the publication of this article. Thus, she returns to the parenthetical definition to help the reader follow the logic of her examples (in other words, exemplification).

featuring science in artistic narratives in supportive ways — as in films such as *Good Will Hunting* and *A Beautiful Mind,* or in stage productions such as Michael Frayn's *Copenhagen* (on Bohr and Heisenberg), David Auburn's *Proof* (on the authenticity of a mathematical proof by a young woman), Peter Parnell's *QED* (on physicist Richard Feynman's life and work), Jacquelyn Reingold's *String Fever* (on string theory), Tom Stoppard's *Arcadia* (on a young mathematical genius), Gabriel Emanuel's *Einstein: A Play in Two Acts* (on the eccentric and brilliant physicist), or John D. Barrow's *Infinities* (about the great paradox of mathematical infinity, presented with aspects of philosophy, science, and theater). A list of approximately 100 plays written on scientific topics was assembled by Brian Schwartz and Marvin Carlson of the Graduate Center of the City University of New York [28].

Notable from the nineteenth century is the British clergyman Edwin A. Abbott's book *Flatland* (1884), a whimsical tour of basic geometry. In the 1990s, physicist George Gamow introduced readers to an amateur science enthusiast, C. G. H. Tompkins, whose initials were chosen after fundamental physical constants (the speed of light, the gravitational constant, and Planck's constant). Since the 1960s, prominent scientists such as Carl Djerassi, Stephen Jay Gould, Roald Hoffman, Alan P. Lightman, Dan Lloyd, Christos H. Papadimitriou, Carl Sagan, Lewis Thomas, James D.

Schlick again places her position firmly in a long-standing history of the popularization of science. This contextualization lends support to her ideas.

Schlick returns to her concerns about public understanding. Notice that she immediately deems the fears expressed in the exhibit as "unfounded," but does not immediately support this contention with evidence.

Watson, and Steven Weinberg have helped public audiences appreciate, and become more excited about, science.

However, not all portrayals of science by artists are positive, and **some skeptical or antagonistic views may spread unfounded fears about scientific technological practices.** The works of art featured in the exhibition Paradise Now: Picturing the Genetic Revolution, curated by Carole Kismaric and Marvin Heiferman [29], include some positive renderings of products associated with genetic research, but pieces such as *The Farm* by Alexis Rockman depict potential horrors of bioengineering by portraying in an imaginary soybean field, plants and animals altered to suit commercial interests, such as flat tomatoes and featherless chickens. Other works by Bryan Crockett, Mark Dion, Laura Stein, and Eva Sutton also depict the horrors of transgenic cross-breeds and genetically modified organisms.

The Human Genome Project is apparently stimulating more and more artists to address issues of social responsibility and the profound implications of our newly found discoveries in biology for many aspects of our lives. At the time of this writing, a traveling museum exhibit entitled Gene(sis): Contemporary Art Explores Human Genomics, curated by Robin Held, is on view at Northwestern University [30]. **The exhibit's 60 works by 24 artists contain disturbing representations of transgenic species, such as Eduardo Kac's fluorescent albino rabbit (created by splicing a jellyfish's bioluminescence gene into a rabbit), which challenges us to**

Although she does not offer an explanation of the difference, Schlick clearly sees something positive in the Gene(sis) exhibition that she did not see in the Paradise Now exhibition described above. While one challenges the public, the other encourages unfounded fears.

After using 2 examples of negative portrayals of science by artists, Schlick returns to the main point in this section of her piece.

ponder the limits of our technology, the influence of science on art, and the ethics of biotechnology. Still, such exhibits encourage the general public to become more engaged in the applications of the biological sciences and to appreciate the complex scientific and societal implications of genomic research. Caryl Churchill's provocative play *A Number* prods us to consider the nature-versus-nurture debate and the advantages versus the dangers of genetic engineering through a thriller about three sons, the original and two clones, of a man who suffered loss as a young father; the ending is a stunner that shatters our expectations and our view of the playwright's stance.

Indeed, we must encourage artistic expressions that depict science and scientists positively. In addition to the theater and film examples above, Lynda Williams aims to popularize physics in her stage persona, the Physics Chanteuse, through songs with pro-science lyrics (for example, an adaptation of Madonna's "Material Girl" titled "Hi-Tech Girl" [31]). Organizations such as ASCI (of New York) and Ylem (in the San Francisco Bay Area) have long brought scientists and artists together, and organizations such as the Sloan Foundation and the Wellcome Trust have funded initiatives to encourage artists to tackle scientific topics.

A successful Science and the Arts series was recently developed by the Graduate Center of the City University of New York [32]. The program presents dance, theater, music, and art

The programs and events presented in this paragraph seem to take the form of proposed models that readers could emulate if they wished to help in solving the problem.

In her table there is an inverse relation between the actual complexity of the entity and the complexity of the drawing. But, the detail reflects where Schlick's expertise falls.

with science as the theme and spreads their products to other locations such as Brookhaven National Laboratory and the New York Academy of Sciences, and to an audience of nonscientists of all ages. Among the program's notable events was an exhibition titled Genomic Issue(s): Art & Science. Other events include a rock opera in tribute to

The outgrowth of numerous scientific disciplines stemming from The Human Genome and other sequencing projects. In the progression from DNA constituents (the nucleotides) to cells to organisms, many scientific disciplines are traversed, and so are the possible applications.

Biological Scales	Biological Entities	Research Disciplines
10^9	Organisms	Evolutionary and Developmental Biology, Comparative Genomics, Origin of Life
10^8 (1 cm) Milli	Organs	
10^7 (1 mm)		Physiology, Neuroscience, Immunology
10^6	Cells	
10^5 Micro		Cellomics, Metabolomics – Cellular and Signaling Networks, Metabolic Pathways, Regulation of Gene Expression
10,000 (1 µm)	Biomolecules	
1000		Structural and Functional Genomics – Characterization of Gene Products (Instrumentation and simulation), Proteomics, Ribonomics
100 Nano		
10 (1 nm)	RNA HIV2-Protease Chromatin	
1 Ang.	Nucleotides	Genomics – Genome Sequencing Projects

Biological Size and Complexity

> Although Schlick offers specific examples throughout her essay, she does not explain what she means by "modern and prudent compromises." The reader is left to wonder.

the planned termination of the Jupiter-circling spacecraft *Galileo*; plays about Feynman and the Curies; and a discussion with author Israel Horovitz on his new play on bioethics revolving around one biologist's struggle between altruism and financial rewards. Also, on the first Sunday evening of the month, at the Cornelia Street Café in New York's West Village, chemist and Nobel laureate Roald Hoffman hosts an innovative science-and-art evening program [33]. These positive presentations of science and exposure to scientific dilemmas achieve the crucial goal of making the audience curious about and engaged with science and technology. **This engagement is a prerequisite to our mutual development of modern and prudent compromises to address problems at the frontiers of the revolution in modern biology.**

Conclusion

A scientifically literate and appreciative society could make the crucial difference between the abuse of science and scientific breakthroughs for the betterment of society. A revamped scientific training and educational infrastructure that emphasizes interdisciplinary approaches to complex problem solving rather than rote learning is also essential to addressing the multidisciplinary and global challenges of our twenty-first century. Indeed, the recent multidisciplinary Euroscience Open Forum 2004 in Stockholm, Sweden, made clear that science has become truly global in nature. However, it

> As a scientist, Schlick might be presumed to have a pro-science bias. Here, this bias is made clearly manifest.

> As a writer, you have likely been told to restate your main point in the conclusion. Notice that Schlick follows this advice (several times) but never makes the mistake of repeating herself. Essentially, she is saying the same thing at the end of the paragraph as she did at the very beginning. She also expands on her ideas to emphasize the magnitude of her concerns.

also revealed that the U.S. climate for science following the attacks of September 11 has led to a major shift of priorities in the support of science favoring defense and homeland security at the expense of many other domains. These dilemmas underscore the complex relations between science and national politics and ideology, **requiring highly informed, open-minded, and forward-looking leadership to exploit scientific talent and technology**.

With attention to urgent scientific fronts such as the quality of our environment, alternative energy sources, genomics-based health care systems, and exploration of life beyond Earth, **we could become the admirers and beneficiaries of our labors, like the scholars in Wright's painting and the Lunar Society. Prudence and devoted embrace of our science and technology will give us the wisdom needed to manage our wondrous possibilities. Whether we choose to live until the age of 600 — if ever possible — or compromise between what science offers and the lives we want to live — as Odysseus did in choosing to be with his wife Penelope for a short period rather than being immortal without her [34] — we can make well-informed and openminded decisions if artists and scientists collaborate on scientific themes in a supportive manner**.

> Schlick brings us back to her initial image and closes the loop nicely on her essay. Also, notice the conditional rhetorical flattery she offers: if we listen to her, we can benefit, can be wise, can have "wondrous possibilities," can be "well-informed," can be "open-minded." If we do not, more's the pity. She is also clear in identifying the parties responsible for helping the general public see the light: the readership of *Leonardo*.

> Coleridge was a British Romantic poet (nineteenth century). This quotation essentially functions as a postscript on Schlick's essay: a summation of her thoughts. That it is drawn from the world of arts and letters rather than science supports her thinking on the role of the arts.

The proper and immediate object of science is the acquirement, or communication, of truth.
— SAMUEL TAYLOR COLERIDGE

ACKNOWLEDGMENTS

I thank Carse Ramos and Jennifer Isbell for technical assistance with this article and Richard Solway and Adrienne Klein for critical reading and valuable suggestions. I also thank my genomics and computational biology students, who have inspired me.

REFERENCES AND NOTES

1. R. M. Henig, *The Monk in the Garden: The Lost and Found Genius of Gregor Mendel, the Father of Genetics* (New York: Houghton Mifflin, 2001).
2. J. D. Watson and F. H. C. Crick, "A Structure for Deoxyribose Nucleic Acid," *Nature* 171, No. 4356, 737–738 (1953).
3. S. Mawer, "DNA and the Meaning of Life," *Nature Genetics* 33, No. 4, 453–454 (2003).
4. J. S. Mattick, "The Hidden Genetic Program of Complex Organisms," *Scientific American* 291, No. 4, 60–67 (2004).
5. M. Kemp, "The *Mona Lisa* of Modern Science," *Nature* 421, No. 6921, 416–420 (2003).
6. <http://www.artincontext.org/artist/b/brandon_ballengee/index.htm>.
7. <http://www.lehmannmaupin.com/home.html>.
8. <http://www.viewingspace.com/genetics_culture/pages_genetics_culture/gc_w02/gc_w02_gessert.htm>.

> The format of these notes is dictated by the source journal. Frequently, publications will set their own style sheet that should be followed by the authors, as is the case here. (See bedfordstmartins.com/nexttext for additional information on using and documenting sources.).

9. <http://www.45bleecker.com/exonerated.html>.

10. <http://www.avenueq.com>. The genetic basis of homosexuality remains an open area of scientific research, but emerging data suggest that genetic characteristics may play a role. See a recent summary of this research in Q. Rahman and G. D. Wilson, "Born Gay? The Psychobiology of Human Sexual Orientation," *Personality and Individual Differences* 34, No. 8, 1337–1382 (2003).

11. <http://www.dnalounge.com>.

12. <http://www.syndromedist.com>.

13. <http://www.dna.co.uk>.

14. <http://www.dnagardens.com>.

15. <http://www.dnamag.gr>.

16. <http://www.dnavitamins.co.uk>.

17. <http://www.dnamagazine.com.au>.

18. R. Lewis, "Of Sheep and Grapes: DNA Fingerprinting Tracks Ancestry," *The Scientist* 13, No. 19 (1999) p. 6.

19. <http://www.dilbert.com>.

20. <http://www.clonaid.com>.

21. L. Thomas, *The Medusa and the Snail: More Notes of a Biology Watcher* (New York: Bantam Books, 1980) p. 45.

22. N. D. Kristof, "Where Is Thy Sting?" *New York Times*, Tuesday, 12 August 2003, Op-Ed Columns.

23. Human Frontier Science Program, "The Pipeline and the Tree: Towards a New Paradigm for Education, Training, and Career Pathways in the Natural Sciences," *Technical Report* (2001) <www.hfsp.org/pubs/PositionPapers/funders.htm>.

24. T. J. Sejnowski, "Tap into Science 24-7," *Science* 301, No. 5633 (2003) p. 601.

25. <http://www.einshac.org/istref/index.html>.

26. <http://www.unipv.it/BIOL/ENLSC.html>.

27. C. P. Snow, *The Two Cultures and the Scientific Revolution* (New York: Cambridge Univ. Press, 1959).

28. <http://web.gc.cuny.edu/sciart/StatgingScience/staging_science.htm#list>.

29. <http://www.genomicart.org/pnhome.htm>.

30. <http://www.genesis.net>.
31. <http://www.scientainment.com>.
32. <http://web.gc.cuny.edu/sciart>.
33. <http://www.corneliastreetcafe.com>.
34. Kristof [22].

MAKING CONNECTIONS ACROSS AND BEYOND THE DISCIPLINES

1. Schlick's position on the nature of any collaboration between the arts and science is quite clear: "Indeed, we must encourage artistic expressions that depict science and scientists positively." In this chapter, you have studied several works of art that address the genomic revolution. Write an essay that assesses these works from Schlick's position. Which works would she find acceptable? Which would trouble her? Why? You might find it helpful to first create a clear framework of her viewpoint by culling concrete examples of positive artistic expressions from her essay.

2. In "A Tale of Two Loves" (p. 523) Alan Lightman writes, "Somehow, we human beings have a wondrous capacity for being both rational and irrational, detached and passionate, deliberate and spontaneous, craving of certainty and uncertainty, seeking questions with answers and questions without. We are a splattering of contradictions." Although he is also a scientist and is also writing about the connection between art and science, his piece takes a very different path than Schlick's and seems to arrive at a different destination. Write an essay that compares their views on the relationship between art and science. Which seems more "artistic," which more "scientific"? Why?

3. One of Schlick's central concerns is that the general public is poorly equipped to develop opinions or draw conclusions about complicated scientific questions. Investigate the validity of Schlick's claim. Spend some time researching the basics of DNA: What is it? Why is it important to human life? What are some current concerns arising from DNA research? From the information you have gathered, create a short set of quiz questions on DNA 101. Working with a team of your peers, quiz a representative set of students at your college and record their responses. Write an essay on your findings. How much does the average student know about DNA? What is the ratio of information to misinformation? Structure your essay using the exemplification and problem/solution frameworks used by Schlick. Draw a conclusion regarding her concern: Is it valid?

Acknowledgments *(continued from page iv)*

David Callahan, excerpt from *The Cheating Culture: Why More Americans Are Doing Wrong to Get Ahead.* Copyright © 2004 by David Callahan. Reprinted by permission of Harcourt, Inc.

Rebekah Nathan, *My Freshman Year: What a Professor Learned by Becoming a Student.* Copyright © 2005 by Rebekah Nathan. Used by permission of the publisher, Cornell University Press.

J. D. Heyman et al., "Psssst . . . What's the Answer?" J. D. Heyman/*People* © 2005 Time, Inc. All rights reserved. The cover of *People* Weekly © 2005 Time Inc. All rights reserved.

Jason Stephens, "Justice or Just Us? What to Do about Cheating?" Reprinted with permission of the Carnegie Foundation. www.carnegiefoundation.org.

William Gibson, "God's Little Toys: Confessions of a Cut and Paste Artist." Reprinted courtesy of the author. *Wired* © 2005 Condé Nast Publications, Inc.

Ed Tenner, "Rise of the Plagiosphere: How New Tools to Detect Plagiarism Could Induce Mass Writer's Block." © 2005 MIT *Technology Review.* Reproduced with permission via Copyright Clearance Center.

Pages 56–58: Photos © Randy Faris/CORBIS.

©samedayresearch.com. Reprinted by permission.

©fastpapers.com. Reprinted with permission of the Paper Store Enterprises, Inc.

Malcolm Gladwell, "Something Borrowed." © Malcolm Gladwell. Reprinted with permission. *The New Yorker* © 2004 Condé Nast Publications, Inc.

Chapter 2

Opening Image: © Slava Veder/Associated Press.

Carolyn Kleiner Butler, "Coming Home." © Carolyn Kleiner Butler. Originally appeared in *Smithsonian* (January 2005). Reprinted with permission. *Smithsonian* cover photo © Mark Newman/MStock/Stock Connection.

Stephanie Coontz, "The American Family." *Life* ® Used by permission of Life, Inc. Cover photograph © James Rexroad. Used by permission.

Phyllis Rose, "Le Beau-Père." © 2006 by Phyllis Rose, with permission of the Wylie Agency. From *My Father Married Your Mother: Writers Talk about Stepparents, Stepchildren, and Everyone In Between,* edited by Anne Burt. Used by permission of W. W. Norton & Co.

Emma Pearse, "Rabenmutter: Germany in Angst over Low Birthrate." © 2006 Fund for the City of New York from Women's eNews, April 11, 2006. Reprinted with permission conveyed through Copyright Clearance Center.

Caitlin Flanagan. *To Hell with All That: Loving and Loathing Our Inner Housewife.* Copyright © 2006 by Caitlin Flanagan. By permission of Little, Brown and Co., Inc.

Robert Kuttner, "The Politics of Family (Introduction)," *The American Prospect,* Vol. 13, No. 7, April 8, 2002. Reprinted with permission from the author. *The American Prospect,* 11 Beacon St., Boston, MA 02108. All rights reserved. Cover art © Kathy Osborn.

Susan Dominus, "Growing Up with Mom and Mom," and cover of the *New York Times Magazine.* Copyright © 2004, The New York Times Company. Reprinted with permission. Photo © Robert Maxwell.

Henry Louis Gates Jr., "My Yiddishe Mama." Copyright © 2006 Henry Louis Gates Jr. Originally published in the *Wall Street Journal.* Front page: the *Wall Street Journal* © 2006 Dow Jones & Company. All rights reserved.

vanityrunamok.com. Reprinted by permission of the author.

memyi.us. Reprinted with permission of the author.

livesstrong.blogspot.com. Reprinted by permission of the author.

mylifeitalian.blogspot.com. Reprinted by permission of the author.

Dani Kekoa, worstgenerationseed.blogspot.com. Reprinted by permission of the author.

mylifemypace.com. Reprinted by permission of the author.

Adam N. Joinson and Beth Dietz-Uhler, "Explanations for the Perpetration of and Reactions to Deception in a Virtual Community," from *Social Science Computer Review*. Fall 2002. © Adam N. Joinson and Beth Dietz-Uhler. Reprinted by permission of Sage Publications, Inc.

Chapter 4

Opening Image: Barbara Kruger, "Untitled" (I shop, Therefore I am), 111" x 113" photographic silkscreen/vinyl, 1987. Courtesy of the Mary Boone Gallery, New York.

Jane Hammerslough, "What's Changed." From *Dematerializing: Taming the Power of Possessions* © 2001 Jane Hammerslough. Reprinted by permission of DaCapo Press, a member of Perseus Books, LLC.

Lauren Greenfield, "Elysia, Evan, and Alison, all 14, and the Self-Titled 'Reject' Group." © Lauren Greenfield/VII.

Tommy, "Follow the Flock." Courtesy www.adbusters.org.

Rob Walker, "Sprite Remix," and the *New York Times Magazine* cover. Copyright © 2004 by the New York Times Company. Reprinted by permission.

Kate MacArthur and Hillary Chura, "Urban Warfare." Reprinted with permission from *Advertising Age*. Copyright © 2000 Crain Communications, Inc. Firestone tire photo © Bob Riha Jr.

Kenneth Hein, "The Age of Reason." Reprinted with permission from *MediaWeek*. Copyright © 2003 VNU Business Media, Inc.

Renee Dye, "The Buzz on Buzz." Reprinted by permission of the *Harvard Business Review*. Copyright © 2000 by the Harvard Business School Publishing Corporation. All rights reserved. Illustrations © Daniel Vasconcellos.

Benoit Denizet-Lewis, "The Man behind Abercrombie & Fitch." This article first appeared in Salon.com at www.Salon.com. An online version remains in the Salon archives. Reprinted with permission.

Kalle Lasn, "The Cult You're In." Thumbnail reproduction of book cover and text of pp. 51-57 from *Culture Jam: How to Reverse America's Suicidal Consumer Binge* by Kalle Lasn. Reprinted by permission of HarperCollins Publishers/William Morrow.

Bruce Horowitz, "P&G 'Buzz Marketing' Unit Hit with Complaint," and the front cover of *USA Today*, October 19, 2005. Reprinted with Permission.

Pages 387-90: Marketing Websites

www.universalbuzz.com. Reprinted with permission of Universal Buzz Intelligence.

www.intelg.com. Reprinted with permission of The Intelligence Group.

www.buzz-oven.com. Reprinted with permission of buzzoven.com.

www.streetattack.com. Reprinted with permission of Street Attack Marketing.

www.poddesign.com/v2/. Reprinted with permission of poddesign.com.

Scott Bedbury, "The Value of Brand for the Commodity," from "All Aboard the Brandwagon," from *A New Brand World: Eight Principles for Achieving Brand Leadership in the 21st Century*. Copyright © 2000 by Scott Bedbury. Used by permission of Viking Penguin, a division of Penguin Group (USA) Inc.

Chapter 5

Opening Images: Human Rights Watch. Photos and captions from "Darfur Drawn: the Conflict in Darfur Through Children's Eyes." "Taha" located at www.hrw.org/photos/2005/darfur/drawings/2/htm. © 2004 Human Rights Watch. "Leila," located at www.hrw.org/photos/2005/darfur/drawings/5/htm. © 2004 Human Rights Watch. "Abdal-Rahman," located at www.hrw.org/photos/2005/darfur/drawings/1/htm. © 2004 Human Rights Watch.

Clayborne Carson, "Malcolm X" in *Past Imperfect: History According to the Movies,* edited by Mark C. Carnes. Copyright 1996 Agincourt Press. Reprinted by permission of Henry Holt and Company, LLC.

Sarah Vowell, *Assassination Vacation.* Reprinted with the permission of Simon & Schuster Adult Publishing Group. Copyright © 2005 by Sarah Vowell. All rights reserved.

Soldiers' Blogs, "Dispatches from U.S. Soldiers in Iraq," and the *New York Times* web page copyright © 2006, The New York Times Company. Reprinted with permission.

John Hodgman, "Our 51 United States," from *The Areas of My Expertise.* Copyright © by John Hodgman. Used by permission of Dutton, a division of Penguin Group (USA) Inc.

Anne MacLeod, "Rewriting History." Reprinted with permission of the author and *The Horn Book Magazine. Teacher Magazine* cover reprinted with permission, © 1998 Editorial Projects in Education.

Ian Mortimer, "Revisionism Revisited." Text and periodical cover © 2004 *History Today.* Reprinted with permission.

Robert Brent Toplin, "Judging Cinematic History," from *Reel History: In Defense of Hollywood.* Text and cover © 2002 University Press of Kansas. Reprinted by permission.

Lynn Neary, "The Mixed Reviews of the Museum of the American Indian" broadcast August 17, 2005 on NPR. © 2006 National Public Radio, Inc.

John Leo, "Goggling the Future," and cover of *U.S. News & World Report* © 2005 U.S. News & World Report, L.P. Reprinted with permission. JFK photo © CORBIS.

Pages 477-50: Graphic Novels

Art Spiegelman, from *Maus I: A Survivor's Tale: My Father Bleeds History.* Copyright © 1973, 1980, 1981, 1982, 1984, 1985, 1986 by Art Spiegelman. Used by permission of Pantheon Books, a division of Random House, Inc.

Marjane Satrapi, *Persepolis: The Story of a Childhood,* translated by Mattias Ripa and Blake Ferris. Copyright © 2003 by L'Association, Paris, France. Used by permission of Pantheon Books, a division of Random House, Inc.

Rick Geary, *The Murder of Abraham Lincoln.* © 2005 NBM Publishing. Used by permission.

Aaron Renier, "Just Answer the Phone." From *Pen and Ink* © 2002. Reprinted by permission of the artist.

Joe Sacco, *Safe Area Gorazde: The War in Eastern Bosnia, 1992-95.* © 2000 Fantagraphics Books. All rights reserved. Used by permission.

Janet Jacobs, "From the Profane to the Sacred: Ritual and Mourning at Sites of Terror and Violence." © 2004 *Journal for the Scientific Study of Religion.* Reprinted by permission of Blackwell Publishing.

Chapter 6

Opening Image: Susan Robb, "Bunny Test." © 2000 Susan Robb. Used by permission of the artist.

Index of Authors and Titles